CHINESE LITERATURE

William McNaughton is the author of *The Taoist Vision* (1971), and *The Book of Songs* (1971), and co-author (with Lenore Mayhew) of *A Gold Orchid* (1972). His articles have appeared in *Hudson Review, Texas Quarterly, Delos,* and *Journal of the American Oriental Society*. He holds a Ph.D. in Chinese language and literature from Yale University. As assistant professor of Chinese at Oberlin College, Oberlin, Ohio, he founded one of the better-known undergraduate Chinese programs in the United States. In 1967 he prepared the first videotaped Chinese language course to be used in the United States.

Mr. McNaughton, who has traveled and lived extensively in the Far East, is currently devoting all his time to research and translation, under the auspices of the Asia Society.

McNAUGHTON, William, ed. Chinese literature; an anthology from the earliest times to the present day. C. E. Tuttle, 1974. 836p bibl 73-75284. 15.00. ISBN 0-8048-0882-1

Formerly assistant professor of Chinese at Oberlin College, McNaughton is currently devoting himself to research and translation. He is author of *The book of songs* (1971); editor of *The Taoist vision* (CHOICE, Sept. 1971); and co-translator, with Lenore Mayhew, of poems in *A gold orchid* (1972). The present anthology brings together samples of China's greatest literary works from the earliest period to the present century. Translations, all eminently readable, show a large variety of hands, from the free interpretations of Ezra Pound to the more faithful renditions of Burton Watson, with a number of contributions by the editor himself, who makes a valiant attempt to capture the virtues of both Pound and Watson in his own style. Each of the six parts of the collection covers a period of several centuries (excepting modern, of course), emphasizing major literary genres; the six parts are subdivided into 24 chapters, each chapter illustrating the genres with selected authors and works, prefaced with a brief introduction by the editor, and followed by a bibliography. The chapter on modern fiction and modern verse gives virtually no information about literature in post-liberation China and would have been more aptly entitled "the beginnings of modern literature." Suitable for a general audience, but should be read in conjunction with, and certainly not instead of, C. Birch, ed., *An anthology of Chinese literature* (2v.; CHOICE, June 1966, Mar. 1973).

CHINESE

LITERATURE

AN ANTHOLOGY

FROM THE EARLIEST TIMES
TO THE PRESENT DAY

edited by WILLIAM McNAUGHTON

CHARLES E. TUTTLE COMPANY
Rutland, Vermont & Tokyo, Japan

REPRESENTATIVES

For Continental Europe:
BOXERBOOKS, INC., *Zurich*

For the British Isles:
PRENTICE-HALL INTERNATIONAL, INC., *London*

For Australasia
PAUL FLESCH & CO., PTY. LTD., *Melbourne*

For Canada:
HURTIG, PUBLISHERS, *Edmonton*

This book was assisted by the Asian Literature Program of the Asia Society, New York, under a grant from the National Endowment for the Humanities.

Published by the Charles E. Tuttle Company, Inc.
of Rutland, Vermont & Tokyo, Japan
with editorial offices at
Suido 1-chome, 2-6, Bunkyo-ku, Tokyo

Copyright in Japan, 1974
by Charles E. Tuttle Co., Inc.

Library of Congress Catalog Card No. 73-75284
International Standard Book No. 0-8048 0882-1

First printing, 1974

PRINTED IN JAPAN

TABLE OF CONTENTS

ACKNOWLEDGMENTS   9

1 : INTRODUCTION   13

    Historical Chart of Chinese Literature   28

PART ONE: THE FOUNDATIONS

2 : The Book of Songs   41

3 : Not Giving Up on It: The Philosophy of
    Confucius   88

4 : Lao-tzu and Chuang-tzu: Taoism   109

5 : Ecstasy Cults and Elegies   129

6 : Mr. Left's History and Policies of War   144

PART TWO: HAN AND THE SIX DYNASTIES

7 : Prose-Songs   163

5

8 : Country Music 196

9 : The Poetry of Exile 210

10 : Nature Poetry 218

   Farm and Garden Poetry 218

   Mountains and Rivers Poetry 226

11 : Erotic Poetry 232

   Jade Terrace Poems 233

   The Seraglio Poets 252

PART THREE: T'ANG, FIVE DYNASTIES, AND SUNG

12 : Strange Legends of T'ang 261

13 : The Golden Poets: Wang Wei, Li Po, and
   Tu Fu 307

14 : The Broken Sentence: *Chüeh-chü* 342

15 : Short Stories of Sung 359

16 : Brothel Songs and Art Songs 444

PART FOUR: PLAY, AND SHORT STORIES:
YUAN AND MING

17 : Yüan Drama 469

   The Butterfly Dream 472

   Romance of the West Chamber 498

18 : Ming Short Stories   525

PART FIVE: THE NOVELS OF MING AND CH'ING

19 : A Tale of Three Kingdoms   569

20 : A Saga of the Marshes (The Bridge-Mountain
       Gang)   607

21 : The Way West   653

22 : The Golden Lotus   673

23 : Dream of the Red Chamber   729

PART SIX: THE LITERATURE OF MODERN CHINA

24 : Modern Fiction and Modern Verse   759

     INDEX   829

ACKNOWLEDGMENTS

The new translations in this anthology were assisted by the Asian Literature Program of The Asia Society, New York, which acknowledges the support of the National Endowment for the Humanities.

The editor wishes to acknowledge a special debt, for encouragement and advice, to Ms. Bonnie R. Crown, director of the Asian Literature Program of the Asia Society, and to Ms. Junnko Tozaki and Ms. Zelda Bradburd of the Asian Literature Program. He also wishes to express his gratitude to the staff of the Charles E. Tuttle Co. for their contribution to the publication of this book.

The editor wishes to acknowledge use of previously published material from the following sources:

Ezra Pound, trans., *The Classic Anthology Defined by Confucius* (Cambridge, Mass.: Harvard University Press), copyright 1954 by the President and Fellows of Harvard College. Selections from *The Book of Songs* reprinted by permission of the publisher.

Ezra Pound, trans., *The Great Digest and the Unwobbling Pivot* (New York: New Directions, 1947), copyright 1928 by Glenn Hughes, copyright 1947 by Ezra Pound. Selections reprinted by permission of New Directions and of Peter Owen, London.

Ezra Pound, trans., *The Analects* (New York: New Directions, n.d.), copyright 1950 by Ezra Pound. Selections reprinted by permission of New Directions Publishing Corporation and of Peter Owen, London.

E. E. Cummings, *Eimi* (New York: Grove Press, n.d.), copyright 1933 by E. E. Cummings.

Burton Watson, trans., *Early Chinese Literature* (New York: Columbia University Press, 1962), copyright 1962 by Columbia University Press. Material from *Mr. Left's History, Policies of War,* and selected prose-songs reprinted by permission of the publisher.

James I. Crump, Jr., trans., *Intrigues* (Ann Arbor: University of Michigan Press, 1964), copyright 1964 by the University of Michigan. Material from *Policies of War* reprinted by permission of the publisher.

Arthur Waley, trans., *The Temple and Other Poems.* "The Kao T'ang Fu" and "Poverty" reprinted by permission of George Allen & Unwin, Ltd.

Ezra Pound, *Personae,* copyright 1926 by Ezra Pound. Poems from "Country Music," "The Poetry of Exile," "Nature Poetry," and "The Golden Poets" reprinted by permission of New Directions Publishing Corporation.

Ezra Pound, *Collected Shorter Poems of Ezra Pound.* Material in "Country Music," "The Poetry of Exile," "Nature Poetry," and "The Golden Poets" reprinted by permission of Faber & Faber, Ltd.

Arthur Waley, *Translations from the Chinese.* Poems in "Nature Poetry" section reprinted by permission of Alfred A. Knopf, Inc.

Arthur Waley, trans., *170 Chinese Poems*. Poems in "Nature Poetry" section reprinted by permission of Constable and Company, Ltd.

Lenore Mayhew and William McNaughton, trans., *A Gold Orchid* (Rutland, Vt. & Tokyo: Charles E. Tuttle Co., 1972).

Ch'en Shou-yi, *Chinese Literature: A Historical Introduction*, copyright 1961 by the Ronald Press Co., New York. "Song of the Langya King" and translations in "Brothel Songs and Art Songs" by Ch'en and by John C. H. Wu reprinted by permission of the publisher.

Jerome Ch'en and Michael Bullock, trans., *Poems of Solitude* (London: Abelard-Schuman, 1960), copyright 1960 by Jerome Ch'en and Michael Bullock. Poems in "The Poetry of Exile" section reprinted by permission of the publisher.

Cyril Birch, trans., "Peach-Blossom Spring," copyright by Cyril Birch. Reprinted by permission of the translator.

Wang Chi-chen, trans., *Traditional Chinese Tales*, copyright 1944 by Wang Chi-chen. Material in "Strange Legends of T'ang" and "Short Stories of Sung" sections reprinted by permission of the translator.

Wang Chi-chen, trans., *Contemporary Chinese Stories*, copyright 1944 by Wang Chi-chen. Modern stories reprinted by permission of the translator.

Chang Yin-nan and Lewis C. Walmsley, trans., *Poems by Wang Wei*, copyright 1958 by the Charles E. Tuttle Co. Selections in "The Golden Poets" chapter reprinted by permission of Charles E. Tuttle Co.

C. H. Kwock and Vincent McHugh, trans., *Why I Live On the Mountain*, copyright 1958 by C. H. Kwock and Vincent McHugh. Material in "The Golden Poets" and "Brothel Songs and Art Songs" sections reprinted by permission of the translators, C. H. Kwock and Vincent McHugh.

Henry H. Hart, trans., *The West Chamber: A Medieval Drama,* copyright 1936 by the Board of Trustees of Leland Stanford University; copyright renewed 1964 by Henry H. Hart. Material from "Yuan Drama" section reprinted by permission of Stanford University Press.

Pearl S. Buck, trans., *All Men Are Brothers,* copyright 1933, 1937 by Pearl S. Buck. Sections reprinted by permission of Harold S. Ober Associates, Inc.

Arthur Waley, trans., *Monkey,* copyright 1943 by the John Day Company, Inc. Sections reprinted by permission of the John Day Co., Inc., publishers for the U.S., and George Allen & Unwin, Ltd., publishers for the rest of the world.

Clement Egerton, trans., *The Golden Lotus.* Sections reprinted by permission of Routledge & Kegan Paul, Ltd.

Florence and Isabel McHugh, trans., *The Dream of the Red Chamber,* copyright 1958 by Pantheon Books, Inc. Sections reprinted by permission of Random House, Inc.

Hsu Kai-yu, trans., *Twentieth Century Chinese Poetry,* copyright 1963 by Hsu Kai-yu. Selections reprinted by permission of Doubleday and Co., Inc.

1

INTRODUCTION

Almost three thousand years of Chinese literature have been gathered together in *Chinese Literature: An Anthology from the Earliest Times to the Present Day*. The earliest preserved folk songs of the peasantry; the major works of the "Golden Age" of Chinese philosophy; the "prose-songs" and the later skillful poems of the T'ang dynasty; the short stories and plays; the novels; and the poems and stories of men who have made modern China—all these are represented in this anthology, in complete works or in excerpts.

Aristotle said that literature "does not tell what has actually happened, but what might happen—the kinds of thing a certain kind of person will say or do (probably or necessarily) in a given situation." The literature of a nation may tell us about the same probabilities and necessities of the people that has produced it. It will tell us in large part by leading us, cleverly and gently, to "feel our way into" the other man's, or people's, life. That is what I hope *Chinese Literature: An Anthology* will do: help its reader feel what it was like to be inside a Chinese skin in 500 B.C. . . . A.D. 300 . . . 1890 . . . 1949 . . . and beyond.

The Chinese are not a restless people: energetic, but not restless. In their language, China is "the Middle Kingdom," and they understand the attribute in a sense of moderation, balance, and order, as well as in the more obvious sense of the center of world civilization and culture. They have struggled to hold onto that order—what we might call the Chinese way of life—against three great enemies: flood, famine, and "the barbarians." In their literature we can find an exact idea of what that order was, and we can follow the story as they struggled to defend it.

For the Chinese, life was determined by wind and water: even today eighty percent of all Chinese farm for a living, and in the old days the percentage was even higher. In drought years as late as the 1930s, more than sixty percent of the population starved to death in certain Chinese counties. Perhaps the earliest Chinese literary work we have is a peasant song (23rd or 24th century B.C.):

> Sun up; work
> sundown; to rest
> dig well and drink of the water
> dig field; eat of the grain
> Imperial power is? and to us what is it?
>
> (EZRA POUND)*

* "Canto XLIX," *The Cantos* (New York: New Directions, 1948; London: Faber & Faber), p. 5.

In the traditional social order, there were three other classes besides farmers: scholar-administrators (that is, administrators of the affairs of state, from the local through the imperial levels), artisans, and merchants. The hierarchy put the scholar-administrator at the top, farmers next, then artisans, and finally merchants. This was the theoretical hierarchy and was based on suppositions about *te,* or moral worth. In actual fact the wealth of a man had some effect on his social reception, and merchants were often not at the bottom.

In China there have been three ways to organize one's thoughts about things. The Chinese call them the Three Teachings: Confucianism, Taoism, and Buddhism. Since one's thoughts produce actions, each of these three ways implies a different way of life. In actual fact, however, many individual Chinese see things one day one way, the next day another way—or simultaneously see things all three ways. But it is convenient, as we proceed, to consider these three visions separately. The first two of them, Confucianism and Taoism, are "native Chinese." The Buddhist outlook came to China from India.

CONFUCIANISM

Confucianism is named after the man generally taken to be its founder—Confucius (551–479 B.C). But one reason the Chinese people have respected Confucius for millenia is that he respected popular values. "I'm a transmitter," he said, "not an inventor." He transmitted the values which the Chinese people had cherished for ages. So it is not so much that China is Confucian, as that Confucius is Chinese. It is the written record which Confucius and Confucians left, however, that preserved for later generations the coherent form and subtle interrelationships of these "popular values," and taught imperial administration after administration the techniques of social organization to realize them. The imperial administration thought it was so important to realize them that it required the scholar-administrator to pass rigorous examinations in the Confucian literature before he was employed by the state.

As Confucians see it, the social order is held together by "five relations" and rests on "four foundations." The five relations are those between prince and minister, father and son, elder brother and younger brother, husband and wife, and friend and friend. The four foundations are:

jen: natural human feeling for others, graded according to one's relationship to them;
i: a commitment to the common good;
li: respect for social and religious forms;
chih: a liberal education.

The Confucian philosopher Mencius (372–289 B.C.) said that if enough people have these four things, it will be enough to create and preserve world order; but if too few have them, a man will have trouble taking care of his mother and father.

It is significant, of course, that three of the five relations are familial. In traditional China the individual's devotion to his family is practically unlimited, and the relationship to the father is truly one of reverence. This devotion takes on religious forms after the parents have died. In every home is a family altar, on which the parents' small ancestral tablets are placed; here incense is burned, offerings are made, and prayers are addressed to the deceased parents. In China the family relationship is felt to extend each way to the fifth generation—back to the great-great-grandparents and forward to the great-great-grandchildren. Of course this puts a person's third cousins (descendants of the great-great-grandparents) in the family group. The ideal was to have all this group living in a great compound; but in actual fact, economics usually dictated that only parents, their unmarried children, the eldest son and his wife, and the latter's children could live together.

The Chinese nation was envisioned as a family on a grand scale. *The Book of Documents* (dealing with the remotest antiquity and compiled by Confucius) says:

> Heaven and Earth are the father and mother of the ten thousand things. . . . The principal ruler is the father and mother of the common people.

The Great Learning (fifth century B.C.) begins:

> What is "the Way" of *The Great Learning?* To bring to light men of illustrious virtue; to treat the common people like relatives.

It was the ruler's job to coordinate the three great forces in the ancient cosmology: the heavenly, the earthly, and the human. He did it by self-discipline and proper performance of the rituals. Early texts, like *The Record of Rituals*, give an interesting picture of those rituals. They included a mixture of practical conservation with religious ceremony. There were instructions for prayers to the spirits of hills, streams, and lakes, as well as rules about such things as the fineness of fishing nets and hunting and fishing seasons. Definite times were specified to repair dikes and dams and to build flood-walls.

Chinese officials through history continued to honor these instructions and to try to protect the common people against famine and flood. Here is a poem to prove it, written by Po Chü-i (A.D. 772–864) at the end of his tour as a government official in Hangchow:

—GOODBYE TO HANGCHOW—

The old and the very old
                line the road.
Wine jars cover the festive mats.

But here are no pear trees
like the pear tree of Officer Shao.
So why do they weep?

Heavy taxes, widespread poverty,
the sun without water
                bringing famine

And all I managed was a dam
one dam we built together
against new bitter years.

                                    (LENORE MAYHEW)

An important part of Confucianism was the doctrine called *T'ien ming.* or "Heaven's Mandate": Heaven appoints certain men to rule, and these men may enjoy this appointment until they begin to misrule; misrule, however, confers on common people the right, and even the duty, to rebel and to replace the rulers with other men. Historians recognize now that by the fourth century B.C. the doctrine of Heaven's Mandate had become "a general justification of revolution."

The personal ethic in Confucianism was defined by the idea of the *chün-tzu* or "superior man." Among the necessary virtues of this ideal man are *chih* (being straight, not twisty or devious: not the same *chih* we saw above); *i* (a commitment to the common good); *chung* (loyalty); *jen* (natural human feeling for others); *hsin* (credibility); *wen* (knowledge of the culture); and *li* (respect for social and religious forms). Confucius himself once identified *shu*, "reciprocity," as the core of his teaching and said it meant, "What you don't want done to you, don't do to the other man."

Confucianism not only shaped Chinese life for two and one-half millennia; it also affected people's attitudes and actions throughout East Asia and into Southeast Asia. In Japan, for example, Confucianism was adopted as the state creed in the sixth or seventh century A.D. The Japanese studied it in the imperial Japanese university and were examined on it before they could enter the civil service. The Japanse emperor appointed scholars to produce definitive versions of the Confucian classics. In the fifteenth century A.D. in Korea, Confucianism, the Chinese examination, and formal education in the Confucian literature were taken up on a grand scale. In Vietnam, as in Confucian China, the basis of social organization was (and is) the family, and the patriarchal Confucian ethic prevailed. The Vietnamese keep the same family altar in their homes, and they explain political upheavals by "Heaven's Mandate." The Vietnamese emperor used to go up into a "Spirit Tower to examine the clouds," in imitation of Confucian rulers.

TAOISM

Taoism is usually taken to stem from Lao-tzu (b. 570 B.C.). It is quite different from Confucianism. The Taoist vision is characterized by the belief that "everything flows," by a heightened attentiveness to the natural directions of that flow in any particular moment or situation, by great respect for these "natural directions," and by a patience which is born of that respect. The flow is called by Taoists *wu hua*, or "transformation." The respect and patience just mentioned are combined in the idea of *wu wei*.

The emperor Liang Chien-wen-ti (A.D. 503–551) gave in a poem one of the clearest expositions of *wu hua*, insofar as it can be made clear, and of its consequences:

—IN THE MIRROR—

We make a disc of gold
          essence of gold
And hang this disc as mirror in the hall.
It hangs before the Seven-Dragons Net
Emits four rays of pearl

And there it turns
              and seems to be the moon
Or turns and seems to be
              a pendant from a belt,
              an ear-ring of jade.

Humanity and long life
              gather up the ten thousand things.
Prince An explains the four regions;
In the end, existence and non-existence are one thing:
Do they matter? These roads to the Tao?

(MAYHEW)

This led to a theory of action in which natural process is pretty much left alone—in which such action as taken should "go with" natural process. Prince An (d. 122 B.C.) explains the theory as follows:

> Now this "Tao" covers Heaven and carries Earth. It spreads to the four regions and strikes the eight uttermost points. . . . A man should be calm: "anti-act and never fail to affect." A man should go easy: anti-govern and nothing will remain ungoverned. Now this "anti-act" [*wu wei*] we're talking about, it means not to get ahead of things when you act. This "never fail to affect," it's based on what things do of themselves. This "anti-govern" means don't change nature or natural process. This "nothing will remain ungoverned" is based on the fact that things adjust each other.

The Taoism that we have been discussing is "philosophical Taoism." There is another attitude toward the world, quite different from this, that also goes by the name Taoism. To distinguish it from philosophical Taoism, we can call it "cultistic Taoism." In cultistic Taoism there are a number of points of view, about four in all, which differ also from one another. Cultistic Taoists, however, all have one thing in common: they are looking for a secret of physical immortality.

The earliest cultistic Taoists may have been men who believed you could preserve the body if you breathed right and exercised (some scholars call them "hygienists"). The Taoist philospher Chuang-tzu (365–290 B.C.) wrote, without much respect, of men who "pant, puff, hoot and sip and practice bear-hangings and bird-stretchings." Then there were men who looked for "the Isles of the Blest"—a fairyland supposed to be off the northeast coast of China. The blest ate a magic mushroom and lived forever. Many maritime expeditions, some of them under imperial auspices, sailed out to find these isles. The third group of cultistic Taoists were the "magicians." They tried to concoct, perhaps from herbs, a medicine of immortality. A group similar to them, usually called "alchemists," tried to produce a "pill of immortality" in primitive laboratories. Finally there were various other groups, interested also perhaps in the techniques of immortality already enumerated, who believed that sex could be used "to nourish the vital principle" and so to achieve long life.

Beginning in the middle of the second century A.D., Taoist healers and magicians began to organize "churches."

It is impossible to inventory their practices, but most of these practices derived from the various cultistic points of view we have just looked at. The Taoist churches, of course, had a political hierarchy, and some of them became so popular and powerful that they threatened the imperial sway. The "Yellow Turbans" rebellion, for example, that lasted from A.D. 184 to 215, grew out of a Taoist church movement. The Taoist churches did a great deal to elaborate, or at least to transmit, a Chinese "pantheon." The sources of this pantheon were numerous and varied: Chinese popular legends; personification of natural forces and of metaphysical concepts; gods of places, of mountains, of rivers, of springs. Eventually many Chinese came to believe that a deity called the Jade Emperor presided over all these, and that the metaphysical world was organized like the Chinese imperial system.

BUDDHISM

According to the tradition, the emperor Ming-ti had a dream in A.D. 64 as a result of which Buddhism was introduced into China from India. In the second century, a Parthian prince, named in Chinese An Shih-kao, was busy in the Chinese capital at Loyang translating Buddhist scriptures. Late in the fourth century, the Indian Kumarajiva, captured by a Chinese military force, translated ninety-eight scriptures for the Chinese. But the most famous event in the transmission of Buddhism to China was the trip to India and back by the Buddhist monk Hsuan-tsang between A.D. 629 and 645. He returned to China with a large number of scriptures. The record of his journey, brilliantly fictionalized, became one of the masterpieces of Chinese literature (see Chapter 21).

The basic teaching of Buddhism begins with the Four Noble Truths:

> Life is inevitably sorrow.
> The cause of sorrow is desire.
> The elimination of sorrow lies in the elimination of desire.
> Desire can only be eliminated by following the Eightfold Path.

The Eightfold Path enjoins rightness in (1) knowledge, (2) intention, (3) speech, (4) conduct, (5) means of livelihood, (6) effort, (7) mindfulness, and (8) meditation. The folds of right speech and right conduct have been elaborated in the Five Precepts: (1) Do not take life (including animal and insect life); (2) Do not take what isn't given; (3) Do not take illegal sexual pleasure; (4) Do not lie; (5) Do not take intoxicants.

In the Buddhist vision, everything in the physical universe is an aggregation; since aggregates come apart with time, each thing and creature is transient and will pass away, and none of them has any lasting individuality—no self or eternal soul. The things of the physical universe come apart and join together again to form new aggregates according to the Chain of Causation. The Chain operates by the processes of birth, of death, and of rebirth. Birth, death, and rebirth occur because of illusion—the illusion that individuality and permanence exist.

It is only by achieving Nirvana that one can escape from this Chain. *Nirvana* literally means "a blowing-out," as of a candle. It is supposed to be possible to achieve Nirvana by seeing correctly into the nature of things and then by following the Buddhist path of moral conduct, concentration, and meditation. The individual personality ceases to exist, and there is nothing to be reborn.

The early Buddhist doctrine taught that there are three kinds of perfected beings. There are Buddhas who see the truth and teach it to others; there are Pratyeka-Buddhas ("private-Buddhas") who see the truth and do not teach it; and there are Arhats ("worthies") who learn the truth from others, rather than seeing it at first for themselves, and who then teach it. In time the ideal of the Arhat gave way to another ideal called the Bodhisattva. The Bodhisattva had stepped up to the threshhold of Nirvana but did not step across, because he wanted to stay and help other men achieve Nirvana. The Bodhisattva, then, was a sort of "god of mercy." The Buddhist scriptures describe the Bodhisattva's self-sacrifice in some of the world's most moving religious literature.

When the ideal of the Bodhisattva replaced the ideal of the Arhat, a significant change had taken place in Buddhist doctrine. This difference of ideal is the main difference between the older sect (sometimes called Hinayana Buddhism) and the newer sect (Mahayana Buddhism). This Mahayana Buddhism, with its ideal of the Bodhisattva, spread throughout China.

THE HISTORY OF CHINESE LITERATURE

Chinese literature is probably the oldest and richest tradition in world literature. It is, after all, the literary tradition of one-fourth of mankind. An image of that tradition is presented by the excerpts that appear in *Chinese Literature: An Anthology*. I have tried to arrange the material to show Chinese literature as an organic development. In this attempt I have been much aided by recent work published in Chinese by native scholars and critics, which had not been available before outside China. I have written introductions to each of the twenty-three chapters, which I hope will make it easier for the general reader to use the book as a "history of Chinese literature." At the end of this chapter is an outline, very much simplified and in chart form, of the literature and its history.

Chinese literature, after its earliest period, flows in two simultaneous currents: "folk literature" and "mandarin literature." But these two currents cut and shift, flow into one another and out again in new directions. From time to time the mandarin literature has been renewed—has derived new forms and new energy—from the folk literature. The mandarin literature did not have such an effect on popular literature: in subject matter and vocabulary, and eventually in the language itself, mandarin literature was remote from, and inaccessible to, the common people.

The popular literature, however, was usually not inaccessible or remote to the mandarins. There were two reasons for this. First was the remarkable system of Chinese civil service: in order to become a scholar-administrator, a man had to pass a series of rigorous examinations. This greatly reduced the importance of wealth and family; in fact, the system worked so well that the

lists of successful candidates in 1148 and 1256, for example, showed that more than half of the new "mandarins" came from families with no record of civil service
status in the paternal line during the three preceding
generations. This "social mobility," and the "new blood"
it brought in, kept the mandarinate closer to the people.

In the second place, the government employed scholars
in a special bureau to collect and edit the songs of the people (see Chapter 8). Even the mandarin poets throughout
Chinese history continued to write some of their poems
in the forms and style of these folk songs. Chinese drama
and the Chinese novel owe even more, perhaps, to
popular literature, to the work of people whose names
we don't even know any more.

In choosing translations, I have tried to use only such
work as can appeal to the modern Western reader on
literary grounds alone. No translation has been included
merely because it has historical or archaeological interest.
Among the translators represented are Pearl Buck,
Arthur Waley, Ezra Pound, Vincent McHugh, C. H.
Kwock, Lenore Mayhew, Lewis Walmsley, Chang Yin-
nan, Wang Chi-chen, Hsu Kai-yu, and Burton Watson.
Much of the material has not been published before in the
United States, and many of the inclusions represent new
material prepared especially for this anthology.

The translations have been reprinted here as they were
originally published. Discrepancies in spelling, punctuation, and style between one translator's ·work and
another's have not been edited; each work remains as the
translator rendered it. The translator's name can be
found at the end of each selection.

Historical Chart of Chinese Literature

Date	Dynasties	Leading Figures
B.C. 1766	Shang-Yin dynasty founded	
1122	Chou dynasty founded	
		Lao-tzu (b. *ca.* 570)
		Confucius (551–479)
		The Buddha in India (*ca.* 500)
		Mencius (372–289)
		Chuang-tzu (*ca.* 365– *ca.* 290)
		Ch'ü Yuan (4th-3rd centuries)
		Sung Yü (3rd century)
221	Ch'in dynasty founded	
206	Han dynasty founded	Mei Sheng (before 200– 140)
		Ssu-ma Hsiang-ju (179– *ca.* 118)

B.C

A.D. 25	Later Han dynasty restores Han power after a 17-year break	Ts'ao Chih (192–232)

Literary Works	Miscellanea
Book of Changes	
Book of Documents	
Book of Songs	
Tao Te Ching	
The Analects	
Mr. Left's History	"Warring States Period"
The Mencius	(403–221)
The Chuang Tzu	
Policies of War	
The Elegies of Ch'u	
	Books burned by Ch'in Shih
	Huang Ti (213)
	Great Wall built (Ch'in
	dynasty)
Prose-songs (*fu*) flourish	
Poems in five-syllable meter	
(*wu-yen-shih*) begin to be	"Music Bureau" (*yueh-fu*)
popular (200); begin to	restored (125)
dominate shih poetry (*ca.*	Imperial university founded
200 A.D.)	(124)
	Imperial examination system
	begins (2nd century B.C.)
	Buddhism comes to China
"Nineteen Old Poems"	(1st century A.D.)
(popular *ca.* 200)	

Date	Dynasties	Leading Figures
222	"Six Dynasties" begin	Juan Chi (210–263)
		T'ao Ch'ien (365–427)
		Hsieh Ling-yun (385–433)
		Shen Yueh (441–513)
		Emperor Liang Chien-wen-ti (503–551)
589	Sui dynasty founded	
618	T'ang dynasty founded	
		Wang Wei (701–761)
		Li Po (701–*ca.* 762)
		Tu Fu (712–770)
		Po Chü-i (772–846)
		Wei Chuang (fl. late 9th century)
907	"Five Dynasties" begin	
		Li Yü (937–978)

Literary Works	Miscellanea
	The wars of the "Three Kingdoms Period" (220–265) 'Ch'ing-t'an'' movement (third century)
	Kumarajiva translates Bhuddist scriptures (after 382)
Wen hsuan (ca. 530) *Jade Terrace Anthology (ca.* 550)	
"Strange Legends" flourish	Hsuan-tsang travels to India and back (629–645) Ch'an (Zen) Buddhism appears (achieves prominence in 9th century)
Poems in seven-syllable meter (*ch'i-yen-shih*) flourish Regulated verse (*lü-shih*) and *chüeh-chü* flourish	An Lu-shan rebellion (753–763)
	The "commercial revolution" begins (lasts 8th-13th centuries): guilds proliferate; foreign trade multiplies; an advanced money economy develops Woodblock printing in use in China (9th century)
Collection Among the Flowers (940); *tz'u* become popular	

Date	Dynasties	Leading Figures
960	Sung dynasty founded	
		Su Tung-p'o (1035–1105)
		Li Ch'ing-chao (*ca.* 1083–after 1141)
		Lu Yu (1125–1210)
		Hsin Ch'i-chi (1140–1207)
		Kuan Han-ching (*ca.* 1220–*ca.* 1307)
		Wang Shih-fu (b. *ca.* 1250)
1279	Yuan (Mongol) dynasty founded	
1368	Ming dynasty founded	Lo Kuan-chung (fl. *ca.* 1364)
		Wu Ch'eng-en (1500–1582)
		Wang Shih-cheng (1526–1590)
1644	Ch'ing (Manchu) dynasty founded	Nara Singde (1655–1685)
		Ts'ao Hsueh-chin (1719–1763)
		Lu Hsun (1881–1936)

Literary Works	Miscellanea
"Prompt book" (*hua-pen*) fiction flourishes	Moveable-type printing done in China (*ca.* 1030)
	Jürcheds invade; Sung capital moved south (1127)
Chu-kung-tiao (narrative "medleys") flourish	
	Exam system ceases to function in North (1237); in South (1274)
Yüan drama flourishes	First direct contacts with West (1240–1340)
Ch'ü poems continue the *tz'u* tradition, and develop it	Marco Polo in China (1275–1292)
	Exam system revived (1315)
A Tale of Three Kingdoms	
A Saga of the Marshes	
The Way West	
Golden Lotus	
	First Anglo-Chinese "Opium War" (1839–1842)
Dream of the Red Chamber	Second "Opium War"; summer palace sacked by British and French troops (1856)

Date	Dynasties	Leading Figures
		Hu Shih (1891–1962)
1912	Republic established	
1949	People's Republic established	

Literary Works	Miscellanea
	First Sino-Japanese War (1894–1895)
	Boxer Rebellion; Peking occupied by European and American troops (1898–1900)
Fiction and poetry in modern Chinese begin to flourish	Hu Shih proclaims *pai-hua* (colloquial literature) movement (1917; 1918)
Western literary influences become important	"May Fourth Movement" (1919)
	Second Sino-Japanese War (1931–1945)

Some Further Readings

Birch, Cyril, ed. *An Anthology of Chinese Literature,* 2 vols. New York: Grove Press, 1965, 1972.

Bodde, Derk, trans. *A History of Chinese Philosophy,* by Fung Yu-lan. 2 vols. Princeton: Princeton University Press, 1952.

Ch'en Shou-yi. *Chinese Literature: A Historical Introduction.* New York: Ronald Press, 1961.

Davis, Albert Richard, ed. *The Penguin Book of Chinese Verse.* Translated by Robert Kotewall and Norman L. Smith. Baltimore: Penguin Books, Ltd., 1962.

de Bary, William Theodore; Chan Wing-tsit; and Watson, Burton, comps. *Sources of the Chinese Tradition.* New York: Columbia University Press, 1960.

Demiéville, Paul, ed. *Anthologie de la poésie Chinoise classique.* Paris: Gallimard, 1962.

Hightower, James Robert. *Topics in Chinese Literature.* Cambridge, Mass.: Harvard University Press, 1962.

Lin Yutang. *The Importance of Living.* New York: John Day, 1937.

———. *The Importance of Understanding.* Cleveland and New York: World, 1960.

———. *The Wisdom of China.* London: Michael Joseph, 1949.

Liu, James J. Y. *The Art of Chinese Poetry.* Chicago: University of Chicago Press, 1962.

Liu Wu-chi. *An Introduction to Chinese Literature.* Bloomington: Indiana University Press, 1966.

Payne, Robert, ed. *The White Pony: An Anthology of Chinese Poetry from the Earliest Times to the Present Day, Newly Translated.* New York: John Day, 1947.

Waley, Arthur. *Chinese Poems.* London: Allen & Unwin, Ltd., 1946.

———. *More Translations from the Chinese.* New York: Alfred A. Knopf, 1919.

———. *170 Chinese Poems.* New York: Alfred A. Knopf, 1919.

———. *Translations from the Chinese.* New York: Alfred A. Knopf, 1919.

Watson, Burton. *Chinese Lyricism: Shih Poetry from the Second to the Twelfth Century, with Translations.* New York: Columbia University Press, 1971.

———. *Early Chinese Literature.* New York: Columbia University Press, 1962.

PART ONE:

THE FOUNDATIONS

2
THE BOOK OF SONGS

Confucius was a teacher—the head, as it were, of a private school. His students were either careermen who wanted to advise princes, or sons themselves of the nobility who wanted to polish their manners and conversation. Confucius collected an anthology of poems to teach his school style and manners (teachers are always making anthologies), and today the Chinese read his anthology as *The Book of Songs*.

Suppose someone wished to make an anthology of American poetry and decided to collect three hundred of the best folk songs, popular contemporary songs, art songs, and hymns. Suppose further that he wished the folk songs to represent each area of the nation: he might organize his songs according to such sections as New England, Middle Atlantic states, Southern states, Appalachia, the Deep South, the Middle West, Great Lakes region, the Southwest, the West, the Rocky Mountain states, the Far West, the Pacific Northwest, Hawaii, the Yukon, and New York City. He would then have, as it were, an American *Book of Songs*. This is precisely what Confucius did for China, and his anthology for more than two millennia has been a major element in the cultural and ethnic solidarity of China.

Apart from the folk songs, the anthology has a section of "Courtly Songs" and a section of "Odes." The Courtly Songs include seventy-four "Minor Courtly Songs" and thirty-one "Major Courtly Songs." Chu Hsi says that the Minor Courtly Songs were sung at court entertainments and the Major Courtly Songs were sung when the feudal princes got together. The Odes are religious songs and are sometimes called "Odes of the Temple and Altar." The Great Preface to *The Book of Songs* says: "The 'Odes' describe perfect virtue in its beauty, so as to announce its attainment to the Spiritual and Radiant Beings."

The songs that make up the anthology give us a broad and clear picture of China and Chinese life in Confucius's time, and they also tell us much about the customs and the history of his time and of earlier times. We can say that *The Book of Songs* truly is China's epic. I would say that no book (including the Homeric poems and the Judaeo-Christian Bible) ever has influenced its civilization or the literature that came after it more than *The Book of Songs*. We do not know who wrote more than two or three of the songs that make up the ancient Chinese anthology.

THE COMPOSITE IMAGE

If the reader really is to follow and to respond to *The Book of Songs* poems, he must have some understanding of the "composite image." Unlike most of the other expressive devices of Chinese poetry, the composite image does not occur, at least as consciously or as frequently, in Western poetry as it does in Chinese poetry, so it would seem wise briefly to consider it here. The device is remarkably like the cinematographic technique called by Sergei Eisenstein "montage." We may, in fact, find that *The Book of Songs* contains the earliest known use of montage for artistic purposes.

Let's look at a few examples. The poem "Over the Hills" presents a young conscript's state of mind. The following composite image occurs as the first line in each of the three stanzas:

> (St. 1) On and on, over tree-covered hills
> (St. 2) On and on, over tree-less hills
> (St. 3) On and on, over rocky spurs

The poet thus effects a "time-shift." The landscape changes each time, into wilder and more barren terrain, as the army moves farther and farther from civilization and home.

Sometimes the composite image suggests rather than presents. A suggestive composite image also occurs in "Over the Hills." The young draftee thinks back to his home. He imagines in successive stanzas the anxiety that his situation causes to his father, mother, brother: (1) I hope he will come, and won't be kept on; (2) I hope he will come, and won't get cut off; (3) I hope he will come, and won't get killed. The sequence tensely keeps in the potential the story that it suggests: (1) the boy fails to get leave or discharge; (2) he becomes separated from his unit; (3) he gets killed in action.

Let us take one more example of this device, and then you should be ready to find composite images yourself as you read and to relate them to the poet's "total message." The poet protests that taxes or *corvée* have left the populace on the verge of starvation. He uses an image of carrion birds:

(1) They settle on the bushy oaks
(2) They settle on the thorn-trees
(3) They settle on the mulberry trees

Since mulberry trees in China were planted closest to the house, to make it easier to feed the silkworms; since the thorn-trees probably were used as hedges or wind-breaks; and since the oaks would be largest and farthest away of all, the poet has used his composite image to show that human energy diminishes, and that the carrion birds grow bolder and move in.

THE LITTLE STARS

The institution of concubinage, practiced in China until recent times, is quite unfamiliar to Westerners. Since "the little stars" is a term used to refer to a ruler's lesser concubines, the poem "The Little Stars" that appears below may be incomprehensible to the Western reader unless he gets some information about the institution before he reads the poem.

Joseph Needham, in *Science and Civilisation in China*

(vol. 4, part 2 [Cambridge: Cambridge University Press, 1965], pp. 477–78), presents us with the following interesting and relevant information about the institution:

> It will be recalled that the Chinese emperor was a cosmic figure, the analogue here below of the pole star on high. All hierarchies, all officialdom, all works and days, revolved around his solitary eminence. It was therefore entirely natural that from time immemorial the large number of women attending upon him should have been regulated according to the principles of the numinous cosmism which pervaded Chinese court life. Ancient texts give us remarkable insight into the ranks of his consorts and concubines. Though their titles differed considerably during the two millennia which followed the first unification of the empire, the general order comprised one empress, three consorts, nine spouses (etymologically protegées or client ladies), twenty-seven beauties (concubines), and eighty-one attendant nymphs (assistant concubines). The *Chou Li* (Record of the Rites of the Chou Dynasty) even gives us what might be called a pernoctation rota.
>
> "The lower-ranking (women)," it says, "come first, the higher-ranking come last. The assistant concubines, eighty-one in number, share the imperial couch nine nights in groups of nine. The concubines, twenty-seven in number, are allotted three nights in groups of nine. The nine spouses and three consorts are allotted one night to each group, and the empress also alone one night. On the fifteenth

day of every month the sequence is complete, after which it repeats in the reverse order.''

Thus it is clear that the women of highest rank approached the emperor at times nearest to the full moon, when the Yin influence would be at its height, and matching the powerful Yang force of the Son of Heaven, would give the highest virtues to children so conceived. . . . In the +9th century Pai Hsing-Chien complained that all these rules had fallen into disorder, saying:

"Nine ordinary companions every night, and the empress for two nights at the time of the full moon—that was the ancient rule, and the Duennas-Secretarial kept a careful record of everything with their vermilion brushes. . . . But alas, nowadays all the three thousand (palace women) compete in confusion. . . .''

What was at stake was the imperial succession. Chinese ruling houses did not always follow the primogeniture principle, and the eldest son of the empress was not necessarily the heir apparent. Towards the end of a long reign an emperor would have quite a number of princes from which to choose, and in view of the importance of State astrology in China from very ancient times it may be taken as certain that one of the factors in this choice was the nature of the asterisms which had been culminating at the time of the candidate's conception. Hence the importance of the records which had been kept by the Duennas-Secretarial.

I have arranged the poems below by subject matter rather than by position in *The Book of Songs*, although within any one subject I keep the anthology's order.

Where no translator is identified, the translation is by the editor.

§ LOVE

From "The Songs of Cheng"

Confucius says: "Banish the Songs of Cheng."

—PLEASE, CHUNG—

Please, Chung. 'Ware my town,
don't break my willows down.
The trees don't matter
but father's tongue, mother's tongue
       Have a heart, Chung,
           it's awful.

Please, Chung. Don't jump my wall
nor strip my mulberry boughs,
The boughs don't matter
But my brothers' clatter!
       Have a heart, Chung,
           it's awful.

Please, Chung. That is *my* garden wall.
Don't break my sandalwood tree.
The tree don't matter
But the subsequent chatter!
                    Have a heart, Chung,
                              it's awful.

                                   (EZRA POUND)*

—SO HE WON'T—

So he won't talk to me when we meet?
Terrible!
              I still can eat.

So clever he won't even come to dinner;
Well, beds are soft,
                    and I'm no thinner.

                                   (POUND)

—THE EASTERN GATE—

At the Eastern Gate of the City
Are girls like the clouds of Spring.
But I disdain their charms
For in her white blouse and under her thick veil
My friend is far more beautiful.

*A minor change has been made in Pound's version.

At the tower and covering wall
Are girls like the flowers of Spring.
But I disdain their charms
For in her white blouse and under her yellow skirt
My friend is sweeter still.

From "The Songs of Ch'en"

—NOTHING TO DO—

On that marsh, on its slopes
Are sedges now, and lotus leaves.
There was a beautiful guy I loved
—It hurts me now, how shall I say?
Sleeping-waking, nothing to do:
I cry and complain, and dry my eyes.

On that marsh, on its slopes
Are sedges now, and lotus fruit.
There was a beautiful guy I loved.
He was a tall, tender man.
Sleeping-waking, nothing to do;
In my heart, I'm sick of 'sick.'

On that marsh, on its slopes
Are sedges now, and lotus flowers.
There was a beautiful guy I loved.
He was a tall, a graceful man.
Sleeping-waking, nothing to do.
I twist my pillow, and toss, and turn.

From "Shao and the South"

—THE LITTLE STARS—

Trembling indeed
        are the little stars.
Now three, now five
        are in the east.
Hurry up, hurry up
        Tonight they go,
Some early, some late,
        to see the duke.
Their lot
        is not the same

Trembling indeed
        are the little stars.
There's Orion.
        There's the Pleiades.
Hurry up, hurry up!
        Tonight they go,
Catch their covers
        and clutch their sheets.
Their lot
        does not
            match hers.

§ POEMS OF SEPARATION: LOVER OR HUSBAND

From "The Songs of Pei"

—PHEASANT-COCK—

Pheasant-cock flies on easy wing,
absent lord, to my sorrowing.

As the bright pheasant flies
wind lowers and lifts the tone;
sorrow: my lord gone out,
I am alone.

Look up to the sun and moon
in my thought the long pain,
the road is so long, how
shall he come again.

Ye hundred gentlemen, conscienceless
in your acts, say true:
He neither hates nor covets,
What wrong shall he do?

(POUND)

From "The Songs of Wang"

—RAPIDS FLOAT NO FAGOT HERE—

Rapids float no fagot here
nor can she guard Shen frontier.
        Heart, O heart, when shall I home?

Ripples float no thorn-pack thru
nor will she fight by us in Fu.
        Heart, O heart, when shall I home?

Freshets float no osier here
nor can she guard Hsu frontier.
        Heart, O heart, when shall I home?
                (POUND)*

—SPRING WATER—

Ware spring water that flows to the K'i,
flowing thought is jeopardy.
Every day my thought's in Wei,
where pretty cousins would talk to me
we would devise right pleasantly.

*The last line of Pound's translation is omitted as having no equivalent in the original.

To Tsy for the night, and farewell cup at Ni:
When a girl marries she goes out
far from her parents and close male kin;
there's a feast and she
asks her aunts and sisters all in.

Now I would night by Kan and Yen.
"Grease the axle and fit the lynch-pin"
anything to get quickly to Wei
without roadside calamity.

"By Fei-Ts'üan's winding stream"
of Hsu and Ts'ao is all my dream,
and all I can get is a p.m. drive
to keep my inner life alive.

(POUND)

—PLUCKING THE VINE LEAVES—

Plucking the vine leaves, hear my song:
"A day without him is three months long."

Stripping the southernwoods, hear my song:
"A day without him is three autumns long."

Reaping the tall grass hear my song:
"A day without him's three years long."

(POUND)

§ POEMS OF SEPARATION: FAMILY, KIN, AND FRIENDS

From "The Songs of Pei"

—SWALLOWS, SWALLOWS—

Swallows on swallows fly, fly.
Zig, zag go their wings.
She shall go to her new home.
I go along into the waste
And gaze till she fades from sight
And tears fall like the rain.

Swallows on swallows fly, fly.
They straighten their necks, they stretch their necks.
She shall go to her new home
Into the distance I follow her
And gaze till she fades from sight
And stop and stand and weep for it.

Swallows on swallows fly, fly.
Rising, falling, are their voices.
She shall go to her new home.
I go along far to the South
And gaze till she fades from sight
And this thing works on my heart.

. . .

From "The Minor Courtly Songs: The Minister of War Decade"

—YALLER BIRD—

"Yaller bird, let my corn alone,
Yaller bird, let my crawps alone."
These folks here won't let me eat,
I wanna go back whaar I can meet
the folks I used to know at home,
            I got a home an' I wanna' git goin'.

"Yalla' bird, let my trees alone,
Let them berries stay whaar they'z growin."
These folks here ain't got no sense,
can't tell 'em nawthin' without offence,
Lemme, lemme, le'mme go home
           I got a home an' I wanna git goin'.

"Yalla' bird, you stay outa dem oaks,
Yalla' bird, let them crawps alone."
I just can't live with these here folks,
           I gotta home and I want to git goin'
           To whaar my dad's folks still is a-growin."
                    (POUND)*

*Some changes in wording and punctuation have been made from the Pound version.

§ PASSING TIME

From "The Songs of Wei"

—PROWLS FOX—

K'i dam, prowls fox,
a heart's to hurt
and someone's there has got no skirt.

By the Ki's deep on the prowl;
got no belt on, bless my soul.

Tangle-fox by K'i bank tall:
who says: got no clothes at all?

(POUND)

From "The Songs of Ts'i"

—SUN'S IN THE EAST—

Sun's in the East,
her loveliness
Comes here
To undress.

Twixt door and screen
at moon-rise
I hear
Her departing sighs.

(POUND)

—IN THE EAST, IT IS STILL NOT LIGHT—

In the East, it is still not light.
He twists and turns his kilt and coat
Twisting them, turning them,
To the court they summon him.

In the East, there is still no sun
He twists and turns his coat and kilt,
Turning them, twisting them,
To the court they order him.

He breaks the willows and the fenced-in flowers
A mad man with a bird's eyes,
He doesn't make it morning or night:
Comes too early and goes too late.

From "The Songs of Ch'en"

—NEATH EAST GATE WILLOWS—

Neath East Gate willows
'tis good to lie.
She said:
      "this evening."
      Dawn's in the sky.

Neath thick willow boughs
      —'twas for last night.
Thick the close shade there.
      The dawn is axe-bright.

(POUND)

From "The Minor Courtly Songs: The Red Bows Decade"

—THE COURTYARD TORCHES—

What of the night?
It is not yet midnight
The courtyard torches blaze
His Excellency is coming.
The bit-bells sound ts'iang! ts'iang!

What of the night?
The night is not yet done
The courtyard torches fade.
His Excellency is coming.
The bit-bells sound ching! ching!

What of the night?
The night is almost gone.
The courtyard torches smoke.
His Excellency is coming
There you can see the flags.

§ SPECIAL OCCASIONS: WEDDINGS

From "Chou and the South"

—"KUAN!" CRIES THE HAWK—

"Kuan! Kuan!" The fish-hawk
Keeps to the river-strait.
Nilling-willing noble daughter,
Royal son's perfect mate.

Ragged, jagged *hsing* plants
Leftward, rightward drifting:
Nilling-willing noble daughter—
Waking-sleeping sought her
Sought her yet not got her
And waking-sleeping thought of her.
                    Iu-tsai! Iu-tsai!
Turning, churning, still distraughter

Ragged, jagged *hsing* plants
Leftward, rightward lifting:
Nilling-willing noble daughter,
Lute and zither brought her!

Ragged, jagged *hsing* plants
Leftward, rightward sifting:
Nilling-willing noble daughter,
Bells and drums, applaud her!

—PEACH-TREE FAIR—

O peach-tree thou art fair
to shine with flaming flower
that goest to wed
and order thy house and bower.

O peach-tree thou art fair
to promise solid fruit
that goest to wed
and order thy bower and house.

O peach-tree thou art fair
as leaf on leaf in bough
that goest to wed
and order thy people and house.

From "Shao and the South"

—JAY'S NEST—

Dove in jay's nest
to rest,
she brides
with an hundred cars.

Dove in jay's nest
to bide,
a bride
with an hundred cars.

Dove in jay's nest
at last
and the hundred cars
stand fast.

(POUND)

From "The Songs of Yung"

—THE OX-TAIL FLAG—

Flapping, flapping are the ox-tail flags.
They are in the suburbs of Sun.
With white silk they have braided them.
Fine horses—he has four of them
And he himself's a goodlooking man
What shall I give as a present to him?

Flapping, flapping are the falcon flags
They are past the outer wall.
With white silk they have corded them.
Fine horses—he has five of them.
And he himself's a goodlooking man
What shall I offer as a gift to him?

Flapping, flapping are the feather flags
They are past the inner wall.
With white silk they have tied things on.
Fine horses—he has six of them!
And he himself's a goodlooking man
What shall I have to say to him?

§ SPECIAL OCCASIONS: PARTIES

From "The Minor Courtly Songs: The Deer Sing Decade"

—DEER SING—

"Salt
lick!" deer on waste sing:
grass for the tasting, guests to feasting;
strike lute and blow
pipes to show how
feasts were in Chou,
                    drum up that basket-lid now.

"Salt
lick!" deer on waste sing:
sharp grass for tasting, guests to feasting.
In clear sincerity,
here is no snobbery.
This is to show how
good wine should flow
                    in banquet mid true
                    gentlemen.

"Salt
lick!" deer on waste sing,
k'in plants for tasting, guests to feasting;
beat drum and strumm
lute and guitar,
lute and guitar to get
deep joy where wine is set

mid merry din
let the guest in, in, in, let the guest in.

(POUND)

From "The Minor Courtly Songs: The White Flower Decade"

—FISH TO NET—

Fine fish to net,
ray, skate;
Milord's wine is
heavy and wet.

Fish to trap,
bream, tench,
Milord has wine
to drink and quench.

Fine fish to trap
carp and mud-fish,
Milor' has wine
in quantities'h.

Food in plenty
say good food
Plenty of food
all of it good,

This the song each guest agrees on:
Milor's good food all fits the season.

(POUND)

§ NOW IS THE TIME

From "Shao and the South"

—PLUM TIME NOW—

"Oh soldier, or captain,

Seven plums on the high bough,
plum time now,
seven left here, 'Ripe,' I cry.

Plums, three plums,
On the bough, 'Plum time!' I cry.

'No plums now,' I cry, I die.
On this bough
Be no plums now."

(POUND)

From "The Songs of T'ang"

—THORN-ELM ON MOUNTAIN—

Thorn-elm on mountain, white elm on slope,
the clothes you never wear,
carriages idle there
be another's fact or hope
        when you are dead, who now but mope.

Kao tree on crest, shrub in low-land,
dust in your courtly dancing place,

bells on rock and drums unlaced
shall be others' jollity
    when you've proved your mortality.

Terebinth stands high on the crest, chestnut in vale,
wine thou hast and lutes in array,
undrunk, unstruck today
who makest not carouse:
    another shall have thy house.

                    (POUND)

From "The Songs of Ts'in"

—CHARIOTS, RANK ON RANK—

Chariots, rank on rank
With white-fronted horses;
You'd see Milord?
        Eunuchs are bosses.

Terebinth on the hill, chestnuts in valley;
Once you're inside, there are lutes in each alley.
    Delight, delight
    and the long night
        coming.

Mulberries on the crest,
willows in marsh-land valley,
        drum-beat and shamisan,
            dally, dally
    Death's up the alley.

                    (POUND)

§TAO

From "The Songs of Wei"

—HUT IN THE VALE—

Made his hut in the vale, a tall man stretched out
sleeps, wakes and says: no room for doubt.

Lean-to on torrent's brink, laughter in idleness,
sleeps, wakes and sings: I will move less.

In a hut on a butte, himself his pivot, sleeps,
wakes, sleep again,
swearing he will not communicate
with othe · men.

(POUND)

From "The Minor Courtly Songs: The Haw Finch Decade"

—'NEATH THICK WILLOW—

'Neath the thick willow 'tis good to lie,
Let the Imperial foot pass by
If he gi' me a low job it would lift me too high.

Better stay 'neath the willow bough
than crush a toe beneath the Imperial car,
if he gave me a lift, it would take me too far.

A bird can circle high over cloud,
a man's mind will lift above the crowd
reaching employ on high above us all
to dwell in deeper misery when he fall.

(POUND)

§ SOCIETY: WAR

From "The Songs of Pei"

—MAO MOUNT—

Mao Mount's vine-joints show their age,
Uncles and nobles, how many days?

Why delay here with no allies;
Why delay here in lack of supplies?

Fox furs worn thru, without transport,
Uncles and nobles, sorry sport!

We be the rump of Li with tattered tails,
a lost horde amid fears,
and your embroidered collars
cover your ears.

(POUND)

From "The Songs of Wang"

—HE'S TO THE WAR—

He's to the war
for the duration;
Hens to wall-hole,
beasts to tall,
shall I not emember
him at night-fall?

He's to the war
fo the duration,
fowl to their perches,
cattle to byre;
is there food enough
drink enough
by their camp-fire?

(POUND)

From "The Songs of Ngwei"

—OVER THE HILLS—

On and on, over tree-covered hills
Look away and think of your father.
Your father will say, "Aiya!
"My own son has marched off to war
"And early and late, he will not rest.
"God, I hope he will keep his head
"And will come home and won't stay on."

On and on, over treeless hills.
Look away and think of your mother.
Your mother will say, "Aiya!
"My own baby has marched to war
"And early and late, he'll never sleep.
"God, I hope he will keep his head,
"Will come home, and won't get cut off."

On and on, over rocky spurs
Look away and think of your brothers.
Your brothers will say, "Aiya!
"Our kid brother has marched off to war
"And early and late, he'll hang in there.
"God, I hope he will keep his head
"And will come home, and won't get killed."

From "The Songs of T'ang"

—THE BUZZARDS FLY—

Flapping, flapping the buzzards fly.
They settle on the bushy oaks.
Working for the King, there's no rest
Now we cannot tend our grain;
How shall the parents be sustained?
Grief, grief. O blue Sky
When will these things, too, pass by?

Flapping, flapping the buzzards sail.
They settle on the bushy thorn-trees
Working for the King there's no rest.

Now we cannot tend our grain
How shall the parents be maintained?
Grief, grief. O blue Sky
When will these things, too, go by?

Flapping, flapping the buzzards line up.
They settle on the bushy mulberries.
Working for the King, there's no rest.
We cannot plant millet or rice
What shall the parents have to eat?
Grief, grief. O blue Sky,
When will these things be set right?

From "The Minor Courtly Songs: The Deer Sing Decade"

—PICK A FERN—

Pick a fern, pick a fern, fern sprouts rise,
"Home," I'll say: home, the year's gone by,
no house, no roof, these huns on the hoof.
Work, work, work, that's how it runs,
We are here because of these huns.

Pick a fern, pick a fern, soft as they come,
I'll say "Home."
Hungry all of us, thirsty here,
no home news for nearly a year.

Pick a fern, pick a fern, if they scratch,
I'll say "Home," what's the catch?
I'll say "Go home," now October's come.
King wants us to give it all,
no rest, spring, summer, winter, fall,
Sorrow to us, sorrow to you.
We won't get out of here till we're through.

When it's cherry-time with you,
we'll see the captain's car go thru,
four big horses to pull that load.
That's what comes along our road,
What do you call three fights a month,
and won 'em all?

Four car-horses strong and tall
and the boss who can drive 'em all
as we slog along beside his car,
ivory bow-tips and shagreen case
to say nothing of what we face
sloggin' along in the Hien-yun war.

Willows were green when we set out,
it's blowin' and snowin' as we go
down this road, muddy and slow,
hungry and thirsty and blue as doubt
(no one feels half of what we know).

(POUND)*

*The first line of Pound's version is slightly altered here.

From "The Old Capital Decade"

—LILY BUD—

Lily bud floating, yellow as sorrow,
grief today, what of tomorrow?

Gone the bud, green the leaf,
better unborn that know my grief.

Scrawny ewes with swollen heads,
the fish traps catch but stars.

What man has food now
after these many wars?

(FOUND)

—CRANES AND GEESE—

Cranes and geese are flying,
And each wing tilts and lifts.
Your sons are on the march,
We fight and sweat in the wilds.
Weep for them, even these men,
And cry for the children and wives.

Cranes and geese are flying,
And flock in the heart of the marsh.
Your sons are at the sides,
The fifty-foot walls are raised.
Though we have sweated and fought,
Shall we live, in the end, in peace?

Cranes and geese, still flying,
Cry, grieving Knaw! knaw!
There are those, intelligent men,
That speak of us sweating and beat.
There are those, ignorant men,
That speak of our "glory" and "aims."

§ POEMS OF PROTEST AND BLAME

From "Shao and the South"

—FLEECY COATS—

In fleecy coats with five white tassels,
affable snakes, the great duke's vassals glide
from his hall
to tuck their court rations inside.

In lambskin coats with five wider tassels,
affable snakes, the duke's vassals all
glide out to dinner
on leaving the hall.

With quadruple tassels or seams to their coats,
lambskin and all, with that elegant look,
noble vassals, affable snakes
glide out to consume what they get from the Duke.

(POUND)

From "The Songs of Ts'i"

—THE WICKER IS BROKE—

The wicker of the weir is broke,
loose fish are out again
as the Lady of Ts'i comes home
with a cloud in her train.

The wicker of the weir is broke
as ex-Miss Ts'i comes home again,
luce and perch be broken out
as many as drops of ra n.

The wicker of the weir is broke
and these fish make a very great clatter.
The Lady of Ts'i comes home with a train,
all of them loose as water.

(POUND)

From "The Songs of Ngwei"

—RATS—

RATS,
stone-hea rats lay off our grain,
three years pain,
enough, enough, plus enough again.
More than enough from you, deaf you,
we're about thru and ready to go
where something will grow
untaxed.
Good earth, good sown,
and come into our own.

RATS,
big rats, lay off our wheat,
three years deceit,
and now we're about ready to go
to Lo Kuo, happy, happy land, Lo Kuo, good earth
where we can earn our worth.

RATS,
stone-head rats, spare our new shoots,
three years, no pay.
We're about ready to move away
to some decent border town.
Good earth, good sown,
and make an end to this endless moan.

(POUND)

From "The Minor Courtly Songs: The Lesser Compleynts"

—CASTRATO—

Such elegant streaky lines in brocade
till the solid shell is made;
liars by littles ply their trade.

Stitch-a-sky, dot, the South Sieve's made.
Who loves to aid
these smearers in the smearing trade?

Wingin',
gad about,
tittling, tattling
to be found out.

The quickness of the hand deceives the eye
and repetition suaves mendacity,
unopposed,* you'll be ousted bye and bye.

Proud men ride high to watch the workers sweat,
O'er-hanging heaven look down upon their pride
and pity those on whom the yoke is set.

Take therefore, I say, these smearers
and fellow travellers, chuck 'em
to wolves and tigers, and if the striped cats spew 'em forth,
offer 'em to the Furthest North.
If the old pole decline to spare 'em place,
kick 'em clean off it into stellar space.

And here's my address, I am still
at Willow Hollow Road by Acre Hill,
Meng Tsy has lost his balls but makes this verse,
let the administration heed it, or hear worse.

(POUND)

From "The Minor Courtly Songs: The Haw Finch Decade"

—BLUE FLIES—

Flies, blue flies on a fence rail,
should a prince swallow lies wholesale?

Flies, blue flies on a jujube tree,
slander brings states to misery.

*"Non obstat" in Pound's version.

Flies, blue flies on a hazel bough
even we two in slanderers' row

        B'zz, b'zz, hear them now.

                (POUND)

§ GOOD MEN AND TRUE

From "Shao and the South"

—SWEET PEAR TREE—

Don't chop that pear tree,
Don't spoil that shade;

Thaar's where ole Marse Shao used to sit,
Lord, how I wish he was judgin' yet.

                (POUND)

From "The Songs of Pin"

—AXES BROKEN—

Axes broken, hatchets lacking,
Eastward packing, the Duke of Chou gained
four states, and the Emperor reigned
over them all. He pitied our men,
Yet they were trained.

We have blunted our axes,
We lack work-tools,
Chou's Duke invades and rules as is fit
the four states of the East to their benefit;
Pity our men's condition,
his praise carries them on.

Axes broken, work-tools lacking,
Chou's Duke corrected
four states and connected
them all under one rule and test;
By his pity of fighting men
they now find rest.

(POUND)

—NINE MESHES—

Nine meshes of the net enclose
two sorts of fishes, bream, these, rudd, those:
Behold our Prince in his bright-broidered clothes.

Wild geese a-wing circle the isle;
The Duke's coming's so short a while;

Wild geese seek land as but a pause in flight;
Return, and not to be here but a night;

The Dragon-Robe in so brief a stay,
Who'd neither cause us grief, nor stay away.

(POUND)

From "The Minor Courtly Songs: The Haw Finch Decade"

—FISH IN TSAO—

Fine fish in weed, that is their place.
And the king's good wine in his palace.

Fish in pond-weed wagging a tail
And the king in high Hao at his wassail.

While fish in pond-weed lie at ease
the kings of Hao may live as they please.

(POUND)

§ LI

From "The Songs of Pei"

—GREEN ROBE—

Green robe, green robe, lined with yellow,
Who shall come to the end of sorrow

Green silk coat and yellow skirt,
How forget all my heart-hurt?

Green the silk is, you who dyed it;
Antient measure, now divide it?

Nor fine nor coarse cloth keep the wind
from the melancholy mind;
Only antient wisdom is
solace to man's miseries.

(POUND)

From "The Songs of Yung"

—THE TRIBULUS GROWS ON THE WALL—

The tribulus grows on the wall.
Pull not this vine away.
The things they do in the harem—
Give not the tale away.

The things they do in the harem—
There is no shame to the things.

The tribulus grows on the wall.
Pull not the vine away.
The things they do in the harem—
Give not the truth away.
The things they do in the harem—
There is no end to the things.

The tribulus grows on the wall.
Pull not the vine away.
The things they do in the harem—
Give not the tale away.
The things they do in the harem—
There is no grace to the things.

—A RAT TOO—

A rat too has a skin (to tan)
A rat has a skin at least
But a man who is a mere beast
might as well die,
his death being end of no decency.

A rat also has teeth
but this fellow, for all his size, is beneath
the rat's level,
why delay his demise?

The rat also has feet
but a man without courtesy need not wait
to clutter hell's gate.

Why should a man of no moral worth
clutter the earth?
This fellow's beneath the rat's modus,
why delay his exodus?

A man without courtesy
might quite as well cease to be.

(POUND)

From "The Songs of Pin"

—HOW CUT HAFT?—

How cut haft for an axe?

Who hacks
holds a haft.
To take a wife
properly
one gets a notary.

To hack an axe-haft
an axe
hacks;
the pattern's near.

I have found her at last:
food stands
in the ritual dish.

(POUND)*

---

*Pound's version except for the last stanza.

From "The Major Courtly Songs: The Decade of Sheng Min"

—DIP THE FLOOD WATER UP—

Cleared by its flowing, dip the flood water up
and it will steam thy rice or other
grain; a deferent prince is
to his people both father and mother.

Rain-water cleared by its overflood
if thou ladle it out will wash thy altar jar;
To a fraternal prince will his folk
return, as to home from afar.

In a fraternal prince his folk have rest,
as from rain water
cleared by its flowing thou hast
a pure house, or thy garden is blest.

(POUND)

From "Odes of the Temple and Altar: The Temple Odes of Chou"

—THINK TO THINE ART—

Think to thine art, Lord Grain.
By thy power to drink down
cup for cup of heaven's own
stablish thou us by damp and heat.
Without thee is naught complete,
barley and wheat from thee we cull,

Over-sky gave thee the rule
how to feed us. Lead us,
not by this field bourne held in,
that the fruitage ever run
in season's of the Hia's sun.

(POUND)

§ HISTORY

From "The Songs of Ts'in"

—YELLOW WINGS—

Ever unstill, cross, cross,
yellow wings come to the thorn.

Who? with Duke Mu?
Shay Yen-si. Who?
Shay Yen-Si, pick of ᵢn hundred men,
Shook at the grave's edge then.

Dark heaven, you take our best men,
An hundred; to have him again.

Ever unstill, cross, the yellow birds
come to mulberry boughs.

Who? with Duke Mu?
Shay Chung-Hang. Who?
Shay Chung-hang who'd block an hundred men
Moaned at the grave's brink then.

Dark heaven you take our best men,
An hundred to have him again.

Ever unstill, cross, cross,
The yellow wings come to the thorn,

Who? with Duke Mu?
Shay K'ien-Hu, who could hold an hundred men,
Shook at the grave's brink then.

Dark heaven, you wipe out our best men.
We'd give an hundred
To have him again.

(POUND)

From "The Major Courtly Songs: The King Wen Decade"

—SPREAD—

As gourd-vines spread, man began
leaf after leaf and no plan
overgrowing the Tsü and Ts'i,
living in caves and in stone hives
ere ever they knew a house with eaves.

Old Duke T'an Fu galloped his horses
along the western water courses
along their banks to the slopes of K'i
and took Lady Kiang for his company
to set up the House of Dynasty.

Dark violets filled the Chou plain
and thistles sweet as an artichoke
where T'an 'gan plan
and to invoke
the scorched divining shell.
"Time: now; place: here; all's well,"
said the shell, "Build wall *ad hoc*."

Gave men comfort and quietness;
settled, right, left, with boundaries;
with laws, drainage and harvesting,
from West to East all was to his ordering.

He called assistants for all this
called a proctor of prentices
to build him a house, to build them a home;
with plummet, tightened frame boards, and line,
raised a temple to his forebears
with wings wide to the moving airs.

Earth in baskets for the wall, lime at call;
whacked it with paddles, scraped and beat,
scrape and repeat,
each day 5,000 feet,
moving faster than the drum beat.

Reared they a great draw-bridge and gate
and a gate of state with a portcullis;
built also the great chthonian altar
for hecatomb ere they went to war
or did any other large business,

Some trash T'an could not annihilate
but held to his honour at any rate;
cleared out the bushy thorn and oak
to make road for travelling men
and so discouraged the hunting hun.

Then King Wen brought to civility
the lords of Yü and Ju-i;
taught 'em to bow and stand aside,
say: after you, and: if you please,
and: this is no place for barbarities.

(POUND)

—THE SPIRIT-TOWER—

When he planned to begin a spirit tower
folk rushed to the work camp and overran
all the leisure of King Wen's plan;
old and young with never a call
had it up in no time at all,

The king stood in his "Park Divine,"
deer and doe lay there so fine,
so fine so sleek; birds of the air
flashed a white wing while fishes splashed
on wing-like fin in the haunted pool.

Great drums and gongs
hung on spiked frames
sounding to perfect rule and rote
about the king's calm crescent moat,

Tone unto tone, of drum and gong.

About the king's calm crescent moat
the blind musicians beat lizard skin
as the tune weaves out and in.

POUND)

Some Further Readings

McNaughton, William. *The Book of Songs.* New York: Twayne, 1971.

Pound, Ezra, trans. *The Classic Anthology Defined by Confucius.* Cambridge, Mass.: Harvard University Press, 1954. (Also available as a New Directions paperback under the title *The Confucian Odes.*)

Waley, Arthur, trans. and ed. *The Book of Songs.* London: Allen & Unwin, Ltd., 1937. (Also available as a Grove Press paperback.)

3

NOT GIVING UP ON IT:
the Philosophy of Confucius

How could one deny that Confucius influenced his culture and his people as much as any man who ever lived? He must be the most oft-quoted individual in human history. Yet it was not because of his (what the West would call) "original thought" that Confucius had this impact. Voltaire said of him, "I admire Confucius. He was the first teacher not to receive divine illumination." Confucius had a great impact on China's history because he transmitted the ideals and the values which the Chinese had held and had cherished for generations. We associate his name with these ideals and values because he made an anthology of poems in which they receive literary expression, and because in the record of his conversations (called the *Analects*) we find the most succinct and summary exposition of these values and ideals.

China was an empire, not a nation. Sectional differences and prejudices are as easy to find in China as in Europe or America. But the Chinese people have been united, spiritually, by one great thing: what the West thinks of as "ancestor worship," the artistic—if you like, ritualistic or even religious—expression of an exalted sense of family and clan. We find in Confucius the expression of this familial loyalty and familial solidarity.

Chinese literature cannot make much sense without Confucian thought—or, better, Confucian feeling. So although the "lecture notes" of students—which is what the *Analects* are—may not seem to be authentic literary form, the ideas which we find in this section, and in the following section on Taoism, invite our attention. We find in the *Analects* both a charming and laconic style and an affectionate insight into other individuals, so we can read the *Analects* as very good literature indeed.

Confucius lived from 551–479 B.C. I have already said something, in Chapter 2, of his native vocation. He belonged to a family which enjoyed aristocratic privilege in the Shang-Yin Dynasty, and he came from the Boston of ancient China—a little state called Lu. But the Shang-Yin Dynasty was done for long before Confucius ever lived, and although Confucius got a polite education in books and "culture," he also got the hard-boiled education a man gets when he has to work for a living from an early age, even at menial tasks. Or so at least is the story. He taught, of course, in his maturity, and he traveled a lot. I have called this section "Not Giving Up On It: the Philosophy of Confucius," because of the following passages from "canonic" Confucian writings:

> Tze-lu was passing the night at Stone Gate. The gate guard struck up a conversation. "Where are you from?" he asked.

Tze-lu said, "The clan of Confucius."

The gate guard said, "Isn't he the one that knows there's nothing can be done, but he keeps on trying?" (*Analects* XIV, 51)

*

If there is something he have not studied, or having studied be unable to do, he does not file it away in the archives; if there be a question he have not asked, or to which, after research, he have not found an answer, he does not consider the matter at an end; if he have not thought of a problem, or, having thought, have not resolved it, he does not think the matter is settled; if he have tried to make a distinction but have not made it clear [as between things or categories] he does not sink into contentment; if there be a principle which he has been unable to put into practice, or if practicing, he have not managed to practice with energy or vigor, he does not let up on it. If another man gets there with one heave, he heaves ten times; if another succeed with a hundred efforts, he makes a thousand.

Proceeding in this manner even a fellow who is a bit stupid will find the light, even a weak man will find energy.*

Among Westerners, who tend to exalt "the indivi-

*Confucius, *The Great Digest* and *The Unwobbling Pivot*, trans. Ezra Pound (New York: New Directions, 1951), pp. 169–71.

dual," and especially among the young Westerners who are "trying to get my parents out of my life," there is a lack of feeling for the Confucian viewpoint. The Chinese feel this way about it, and most Westerners don't, and that's that. But the reader who cannot "sympathize" should also consider that the individual in Chinese society, from whatever causes, was virtually impotent. From the economic standpoint, an individual without family was sufficiently without resources or power that he might starve.

The following readings on the philosophy of Confucius, unless otherwise noted, all come from Confucius's conversations—the so-called *Analects*. The translations are by Pound, unless another translator has been identified after the item. Note that Pound sometimes uses the Chinese style "Kung-tze" for Confucius's name.

After each item a reference is given to its source in the *Analects*: the Roman numeral indicates the book, and the Arabic numeral the chapter.

1. WHAT WAS CONFUCIUS LIKE AS A PERSON?

He said: The Shao (songs) are completely beautiful and wholly good. The Wu are beautiful, completely, but not completely good. (III, 25)

*

Chi Wan thought three times before he took action. Confucius heard it and said: Twice might be enough. (V, 19) (WM. McNAUGHTON)

*

The wise delight in water, the humane delight in mountains. The wise are active, the humane are tranquil. The wise enjoy, the humane endure. (VI, 21) (McNAUGHTON)

*

Confucius went to see Miss South. Tse-lu didn't like it. Confucius said: If I did something wrong, Heaven will strike me down. Heaven will strike me down. (VI, 26) (McNAUGHTON)

*

The Minister of Crimes in Ch'an asked Confucius if the Duke Chao knew the correct procedure. Confucius said: He knew the procedure.

Confucius went out, and (the Minister) beckoned to Wu-ma Ch'i saying: I hear the gentleman is not prejudiced (partisan) yet he is partisan. The prince married a Wu, of the same surname as (himself) and called her Wu-elder. If that's knowing proper procedure, who don't know procedure?

Wu-ma Ch'i reported this. Confucius said: I am lucky. If I make a mistake it's bound to be known. (VII, 30)

*

If Confucius was with a man who sang true, he would make the man repeat and would sing in harmony with him. (VII, 31) (McNAUGHTON)

*

Standing on a river-bank, Confucius said: "It indeed is what passes like that, not stopping day, night." (IX, 16) (MCNAUGHTON)

*

He said: Never inert in conversation, that was Hui. (IX, 19)

*

There are sprouts that do not flower, flowers that do not come to fruit, that's right. (IX, 21) (MCNAUGHTON)

*

(On Friendship)
When the weather gets cold, then we know pine and fir. (IX, 27) (MCNAUGHTON)

*

Confucius was away at court, and the stable burned. He asked, Any of the men hurt? He did not ask about the horses. (X, 12) (MCNAUGHTON)

*

Tze-Lu, Tsang Hsi, Zan Yu, and Kung-hsi Hwa were sitting with Confucius.

He said: I am a day older than you, but pay no attention to that.

You sit round saying: We are unknown, if somebody should recognize you, what would you do?

Tze-Lu replied straight off the bat: Thousand chariots' state. Shut in between large states, and armies of invasion, grain and provision famine, I could give the people courage if I had three years' run, and teach 'em the rules, put 'em on the square. The big man smiled.

Ch'iu, how about you?

Replied: Give me the job of a sixty, seventy or fifty *li* square district. I could give 'em abundant crops in three years. It would need a superior man to teach 'em the rites and music.

What about you, Ch'ih?

Replied: I don't say I could do that sort of thing, should like to study, serve in the ancestral temple, at audience of the princes, ceremonial chapter style to be lesser assistant.

Chieh (clever-boy), what about? Struck his *se* [25-string lute] with curious jingling, laid down the lute and got up, answering: Differ from the three of 'em in what they grasp at.

Confucius said: What harm, let each say what he wants.

(Chieh) said: Toward the end of spring, in nice spring clothes, with five or six fellows who have been capped, and six or seven kids, go bathe in I river (Shantung), [take the air at the rain altars, and then go home singing].

The big man heaved a sigh of assent: I am with Chieh.

The three went out, Tsang Hsi delaying, and said: What about these three men's words? Confucius said: Each one expressed his preference, that's all. (XI, 25)

*

He was drumming on the musical stone in Wei, a man with a straw hamper on his back passed the door of the Kung family house, and said: What a mind he's got beating that stone, *n'est ce pas?*

That was that, then he said: How vulgar! Persistent, water on stone, water on stone. When one is not recognized that's the end of it, end of it. "Over deep with your clothes on, pick 'em up when the water is shallow." (*Odes* I. iii. 9)

He said: Certainly, no difficulty about that. (XIV, 42)

*

He said: I hate the way purple spoils vermilion. (XVII, 18)

*

Confucius said, There are two things I do not understand: women, and the common people. And I fail for the same reason to understand them: If you are stand-offish with them, they resent it; and if you are familiar with them, they take advantage of it. (XVII, 25) (MCNAUGHTON)

2. HOW DID CONFUCIUS FEEL ABOUT LEARNING?

He said: Those who know aren't up to those who love; nor those who love, to those who delight in. (VI, 18)

*

He said: Transmitting not composing, standing by the word and loving the antient. I might get by in old P'ang's class. (VII, 1)

*

He said: Three of us walking along, perforce one to teach me, if he gets it right, I follow, if he errs, I do different. (VII, 21)

*

He said: In the old days men studied to make themselves, now they study to impress others. (XIV, 25)

*

He said: I've gone a whole day without eating, and a whole night without sleep, meditating without profit, it's not as useful as studying particular data. (XV, 30)

3. WHAT WAS CONFUCIUS LIKE AS A TEACHER?

He said: Young men should be filial in the home, and brotherly outside it; careful of what they say, but once said, stick to it; be agreeable to everyone, but develop friendship (further) with the real men; if they have any further energy left over, let them devote it to culture. (I, 6)

*

If you study and don't think, you fall into a net. If you think and don't study, you are running along the edge of a cliff. (II, 15) (MCNAUGHTON)

*

He said: Yu, want a definition of knowledge? To know is to act knowledge, and, when you do not know, not to try to appear as if you did, that's knowing. (II, 17)

*

He frequently spoke of (and kept refining his expression about) the Odes, the Historic Documents, the observance of rites (ceremonial, correct procedure) all frequently (or polished) in his talk. (VII, 17)

*

He took four subjects for his teaching: culture, conduct of affairs, loyalty, standing by one's word. (VII, 24) (MCNAUGHTON)

*

He said: Aroused by the Odes.
Stablished by the rites.
Brought into perfect focus by music. (VIII, 8)

He said: Hui's no help, he's pleased with everything I say. (XI, 3)

*

The intelligentsia, said Confucius, goes to extremes, and the monkey-minds don't get started.

Hearing this, the disciple Tze-ching asked: So the intelligentsia is better

Confucius said: No. (XI, 15) (MCNAUGHTON)

*

Tze-lu asked if he should act [LEGGE: immediately] on what he heard.

He said: Your father and elder brother are alive, why should you act on what you hear?

Zan Yu asked if he should act on what he heard. He said: When you hear it, do it.

Kung-hsi Hwa said: (Tze-Lu) Yu asked if he should act when he heard a thing, and you said: Your father and brother are alive. Ch'iu asked if he should act on what he heard, you said: Go to it. I am perplexed and venture.
. . . Confucius said: Ch'iu is slow, therefore I prodded him; "the Sprout" too active, so I tried to slow him down. (XI, 21)

*

Fan Ch'ih asked to be taught agriculture. He said: I am not as good as any old peasant. Asked to study gardening. He said: I am not as good as any old gardener.

Fan Ch'ih went out. He said: What a nit-wit, that Fan. (XIII, 4)

*

Tze-kung asked about this business of manhood. He said: The craftsman wanting to perfect his craft must first put an edge on his tools.   (XV, 9)

*

He said: See that education has no snob divisions. (XV, 38).

*

Kung-tze said: Those who know instinctively (as at birth) are the highest; those who study and find out, come next; those who are hampered and study come next. Those who are boxed in [LEGGE: stupid] and do not study constitute the lowest people.   (XVI, 9)

*

He said: Men are born pretty much alike, it's practicing something that puts the distance between them.   (XVII, 2)

4. AROUND WHAT ONE PRINCIPLE DID CONFUCIUS "POLARIZE" ALL HIS TEACHING?

Confucius said: "Tz'u, do you suppose that I learned a great deal and tried to remember it all?" The disciple replied: "Yes, it is not so?" Confucius said: "No, I have one principle that runs through it all." (XV, 2; *Sources of Chinese Tradition* [N.Y.: Columbia Univ. Press])

*

Tze-kung asked if there were a single verb that you could practice through life up to the end.

He said: Sympathy [LEGGE: reciprocity], what you don't want (done to) yourself, don't inflict on another.   (XV, 23)

5. WHAT DID CONFUCIUS HAVE TO SAY ABOUT "HU-
MANITAS" (JEN)?

He said: Only the fully humane man can love another
person, or can really hate him. (IV, 3) (MCNAUGHTON)

*

Someone said: What about "requiting injury with
kindness?" Confucius said: Then how will you requite
kindness? Requite injury with justice, and requite kindness
with kindness.   (XIV, 34) (MCNAUGHTON)

6. DID CONFUCIUS ALK MUCH ABOUT FILIAL PIETY?

Tze-Yu asked about filiality. He said: Present day filial
piety consists in feeding the parents, as one would a dog
or a horse; unless there is reverence, what difference is
there? (II, 7,

*

The Duke of Sheh said to Kung-tze: There are honest
characters in my village, if a man steals a sheep his son will
bear witness to it.
Kung-tze said: There are honest men in my village with
this difference; a father will conceal his son's doing, and
a son his father's. There's honesty (straight seeing) in that,
too.   (XIII, 18)

*

He said: He is not fully humane, a child does not leave
its parental arms till it is three; three years' mourning is
observed everywhere under heaven, did (Tsai Wo) Yu
have three years' parental affection? (XVII, 21

7. WHY DID CONFUCIUS ATTACH SUCH IMPORTANCE
   TO RITES AND MUSIC?

Confucius said: Govern by laws, keep order by punishments, the people will flee from you or lose all self-respect. Govern by *te*, keep order by rites, the people will keep their self-respect and will come to you of their own accord.   (II, 3)   (MCNAUGHTON)

*

Tze-Hsia asked the meaning of:
   "The dimpled smile, the eye's clear white and black,
    Clear ground whereon hues lie."
He said: The broidery is done after the simple weaving.
(Hsia) said: You mean the ceremonial follows. . . ?
He said: Shang's on, I can start discussing poetry with him.   (III, 8)

*

He said: When the Emperor has poured the libation in the acrifice to the Source of the dynasty, I have no wish t wa ch the rest of the servic .
Someone said: What does the sacrifice mean? He said: I do not know. If one knew enough to tell that, one could govern the empire as easily as seeing the palm of one's hand.   (III, 10–11)

*

—Stove Versus Altar—
Wang-sun Chia asked the meaning of: It is better to pay court to the hearth [present lexicons: stove] than to the mysterious [the household gods].
He said: It simply isn't. Who sins against heaven has nothing to pray to.   (III, 13)

Tze-Kung wanted to eliminate the sheep from the sacrifice to the new moon.

He said: You, Ts'ze, love the sheep, I love the rite. (III, 17)

*

At Battle-Wall he heard the sound of stringed ins u-ments and singing.

The big man smiled with pleasure saying: Why use an ox knife to kill a fowl?

Tze-yu replied, I'm the man, sir, who once heard you say: If the gentleman studies the process and loves men, the lower people will study the process and be easy to rule.

He said: You fellows, Yen's words are on the line, I was just joking round it.   (XVII, 4)

*

He said: Rites, they say, Rites! How do we place the jewels and the silk robes? Music, they say, Music! Where do the gongs and drums stand?   (XVII, 11)

8. What about religion?

He did not expatiate on marvels, feats of strength, disorder or the spirits of the air.   (VII, 20)

*

Chi Lu asked about the service for ghosts and spirits. Confucius said: You cannot be useful to the living, how can you be useful to ghosts?

"Venture to ask about death."

He said: Not understanding life, how can you understand death?   (XI, 11)

9. WAS THERE A CONFUCIAN "IDEAL GENTLEMAN" OR "PROPER MAN"?

The proper man is not a dish.   (II, 12)

*

Tze-Kung said: What is a proper man? He said: He acts first and then his talk fits what he has done.   (II, 13)

*

He said: A proper man is inclusive, not sectary; the small man is sectarian and not inclusive.   (II, 14)

*

He said: The proper man understands equity, the small man, profits.   (IV, 16)

*

Tze-Kung said: What about me, Ts'ze? Confucius said: You're a dish. What kind? Confucius said: Oh, a jewelled one for the altar.   (V, 3)

*

Tsai Yu was sleeping in day-time. Confucius said: Rotten wood cannot be carved; a wall of dung won't hold plaster, what's the use of reproving him?

He said: When I started, I used to hear words, and believe they would be acted on; now I listen to what men say and watch what they do. Yu has caused that adjustment. (V, 9)

*

He said: Ning Wu when the country was well governed behaved as a savant; when the country was in chaos he acted as a simple rustic; one can attain this wisdom but not this simplicity. (V, 20)

*

He said: Mang Chi-fan doesn't brag. He was in the rear of a retreat, but when nearing the (city) gate, whipped up his horse and said: not courage keeping me back, horse wouldn't go. (VI, 13)

*

He said: More solidity than finish, you have the rustic; more finish than solid worth, the clerk; accomplishment and solidity as two trees growing side by side and together with leafage and the consequence is the proper man. (VI, 16)

*

Tze-lu asked about serving a prince. He said: Don't cheat him, stand up to him [withstand him to his face]. (XIV, 23)

*

Duke Ling of Wei asked Kung-tze about tactics. Kung-tze replied: I have heard a bit about sacrificial stands and dishes, I have not studied the matter of army arrangements. He left next morning.

In Chan, provisions cut off, those following him sickened so no one could get up.

Tze-Lu showing his irritation said: Does a gentleman have to put up with this sort of thing? He said: A gentleman gets obstinate when he has to; a small man dissolves [when he's up against it]. (XV, 1)

*

The proper man seeks everything in himself, the small man tries to get everything from somebody else. (XV, 20)

*

Kung-tze said: The proper man has three awes; he stands in awe of the decrees of destiny [heaven's mouth and seal], he stands in awe of great men, and of the words of the sages.

The piker does not recognize the decrees of heaven, he is cheeky with great men, and sneers at the words of the sages. (XVI, 8)

10. DID CONFUCIUS REALLY BELIEVE THAT THE PRIN-
CIPLE OF GOVERNMENT WAS PERSONAL VIRTUE
(TE)?

Tze-Kung asked about government. He said: Enough food, enough weapons, and that the people stand by their word [have confidence in their ruler].

Tze-Kung said: If you can't manage this, which do you omit first? He said: The armaments.

Tze-Kung: If you can't manage the other two, which do you omit first? He said: The food. All must die, but if the people be without faith [fail of their word] nothing stands. (XII, 7)

*

Duke Ching of Ch'i asked Kung-tze about government. Kung-tze replied: Prince to be prince; minister, minister; father, father; son, son.

The Duke said: Good. I stand by that, if the prince be not prince; minister not minister; father not father; son not son, although there is grain, can I manage to eat it all? (XII, 11)

*

Chi K'ang asked Confucius about government: What about killing the wayward for the benefit of the well behaved?

Kung-tze answered: Why kill to govern? If you want the good, the people will be good; the proper man acting according to his conscience is wind, the lesser folk acting on conscience, grass; grass with wind above it must bend. (XII, 19)

*

He said: When a prince's character is properly formed, he governs without giving orders [without orders, things go on]. If his character is twisty he can give orders, but they won't be carried out. (XIII, 6)

*

When he went to Wei, Zan Yu drove.

He said: What's the population?

Zan Yu said: Well populated, what next? Said: Enrich them.

Said: They are rich, what next? Said: Educate. (XIII, 9)

*

He said: Honest men govern a country a hundred years, they could vanquish the malevolent and get rid of the death penalty. I mean these precise words. (XII, 11)

*

He said: Shun governed without working. How did he

do it? He soberly corrected himself and sat looking to the south [the sovereign sat on a throne looking south], that's all. (XV, 4)

*

He said: When the mob hate a man, it must be examined. When everybody likes a man, it must be examined, and how! (XV, 27)

*

Ther᠎ are five activities of high importance under heaven, and they are practiced with three virtues. I mean there are the obligations between prince and minister; between father and son; between husband and wife; between elder and younger brothers; and between friends. Those are the five obligations that have great effects under heaven. The three efficient virtues are: knowledge, humanity and energy; and they are to be united in practice, do not attempt to split them apart one from the other. (from *The Doctrine of the Mean*; Pound's title: *The Unwobbling Pivot*)

*

—On the "Mandate of Heaven"—
(1)
The K'ang proclamation has said: "The Mandate of Heaven" is not given in perpetuity. Proceeding with rightness, you attain it. Proceeding with unrightness, ou let it get away. (MCNAUGHTON)
(2)
To love what the people hate, to hate what the people love, is called doing violence to man's inborn nature. Calamities will come to him who does this, definite physi-

cal calamities. The wild grass will grow over his dead body. (from *The Great Learning*; Pound's title: *The Great Digest*)

11. OR WAS HE MORE INTERESTED IN CYBERNETICS?

He said: A cornered dish without corners; what sort of a cornered dish is that? (VI, 23)

*

Tzu-lu said: The Prince of Wei wants you to help him form a government. What will you do first?

Confucius said: "Will" do? *Must* do: name things right.

Tzu-lu said: I guess that's a joke. It's irrelevant. Why name things right?

Confucius said: Yu, you are a yokel. If a superior man hears about something he doesn't understand, he shows some reserve.

If you don't name things right, you cannot communicate accurately about them with language. If you cannot communicate accurately about them, what has to be done cannot be done properly. If what has to be done doesn't get done properly, ritual and music will not spring up. If ritual and music do not spring up, the law will not punish the guilty or protect the innocent. If the law doesn't punish the guilty or protect the innocent, the common people will not know how to move hand or foot.

Therefore, when a superior man names a thing, you can talk about it; and when he talks about a thing, you can act on it. You don't have to look through a superior man's words for his meaning like something lost in the grass, and the meaning won't change on you from one time to the next. (XIII, 3) (MCNAUGHTON)

He said: Problem of style? Get the meaning across and then STOP. (XV, 40)

*

You can neither stroke
  the precise word with your hand
Nor shut it down under a box-lid.
         (from *The Doctrine of the Mean*)

Some Further Readings

Hughes, E. R., ed. and trans. *Chinese Philosophy in Classical Times.* London: Dent, Everyman's Library, 1954. (Also contains material relevant to Chapter 4.)

Legge, James, trans. *The Chinese Classics.* Five vols. New York and London: Oxford University Press, 1960.

Lin Yutang, ed. and trans. *The Wisdom of Confucius.* New York: Modern Library, 1943.

Waley, Arthur, trans. *The Analects of Confucius.* New York: Vintage, n.d

———. *Three Ways of Thought in Ancient China.* New York: Doubleday, 1956. (Also contains material relevant to Chapter 4.)

Watson, Burton, trans. *Han Fei Tzu: Basic Writings.* New York: Columbia University Press, 1964.

———. *Hsun Tzu: Basic Writings.* New York: Columbia University Press, 1963.

———. *Mo Tzu: Basic Writings.* New York: Columbia University Press, 1963. (Mo Tzu and Han Fei Tzu are not Confucian philosophers. Professor Watson's translations of their work are listed here as interesting collateral reading.)

Wilhelm, Richard, trans. *The I Ching or Book of Changes.* Rendered into English by Cary F. Baynes. 3rd ed. Princeton, N.J.: Princeton University Press, 1970.

4

LAO-TZU AND CHUANG-TZU:

Taoism

Some Westerners think that there are two kinds of Chinese: Confucians and Taoists. The way the Chinese look at it, every Chinese soul has in it a Taoist half and a Confucian half. Nevertheless, the distinction between a Taoist attitude and a Confucian attitude is probably useful, and Ssu-ma Ch'ien himself (145–86 B.C.), the father of Chinese historiography, says:

> Nowadays those who study Lao-tzu put down Confucianism, and the Confucians put down Lao-tzu. The doctrines are not the same, there will never be a consensus. Who is to say, "This is correct," and "This is in error"? (*Historical Records,* "Biography of Lao-tzu")

We have taken a look at Confucian doctrine in Chapter 3. What then is Taoism? The Chinese often call Taoism "Lao-Chuang philosophy," because the two men Lao-tzu and Chuang-tzu wrote it up for us. We shall find out about Lao-tzu and Chuang-tzu by reading from each man's book.

According to Chinese tradition, Lao-tzu was born about 570 B.C. (The Chinese words *Lao-tzu* are not really a name but mean "the Old Guy." His real name is thought to have been Li Erh.) We do not know when he died. He kept the Royal Archives for the Eastern Chou Dynasty rulers for a long time. There is a story that Confucius visited him between 518 and 511. Why someone with Lao-tzu's attitudes—someone who says, "Knowers don't speak, speakers don't know"—should write a book is a question that often perplexes students. The story is, Lao-tzu wanted to leave China, and the passport officer at the Western Pass would not let him through unless he wrote a book to instruct the officer. The book is called *Tao Te Ching,* which means "Classic on Tao and Te." One wonders what the passport officer made of it after it was written.

Chuang-tzu is supposed to have lived from 365–290 B.C. His personal name is Chou (pronounced like Joe), and he is often also called Chuang Chou. His family name, Chuang, as a word in Chinese means "serene" or "calm." He may have worked for a while as a minor clerk in Sung, his home state.

The basic Taoist subjects are *Tao,* "Self-like," *Te* (effect), *Wu-wei* (anti-action), *Hsu* (emptiness), and epistemology. As far as epistemology (questions like "How do we know, and how do we communicate?") is concerned, the Taoist attitudes led to the Zen view that you don't get enlightened by studying sacred writings—the view behind Zen paintings like "The Sixth Patriarch

Tearing up a Sutra"—and have led to the development of special Zen teaching methods like the *koan*.

Of all the basic Taoist subjects, the most troublesome for Westerners seems to be *wu-wei*. Since *wei* means "action," the Westerner takes *wu-wei* to be "non-action." But to the Taoist, action and non-action are the same thing. Like speech and silence:

> The Tao is out there at the end of things, you can't load it into words, and you can't load it into silence, either. (Chuang-tzu)

Like "mind" and "no-mind":

> You can't get it with mind. You can't get it with no-mind, either. (from Eicho [d. 1574])

I prefer to translate *wu-wei* as "anti-action."

I used to visit Ezra Pound at St. Elizabeth's. I knew from my reading that it had been his habit, from an early age, to compose verse with a metronome running. One day, guests arrived at the hospital and stood outside his room for a while; inside the room you could hear a metronome beating rapidly. Suddenly the door flew open and Pound stepped out, saying, "Gar damn it, I've wasted forty years listening to the clicks that thing makes, instead of to the pauses between the clicks!" Does that help any on *wu-wei*?

Another basic Taoist subject is "emptiness." Chinese paintings in which there are great empty spaces perhaps give the best artistic expression to the Taoist view on this subject. The director of one of America's great museums once tried to get his trustees to buy a perfect example of such a painting. In the painting a little man sat in the lower left corner and watched a wisp or two of cloud rise in the upper right corner. The rest of the painting was empty, and the trustees couldn't see why the museum should pay so much for a painting that was "mostly empty space." Finally the director said, "Look at it this way, you're paying for what you don't get." They bought it.

From the Impressionists (who learned from Zen painters how to "cut it down") to John Cage, Taoism and its principles in Zen Buddhism have changed the very premises of the modern Western arts. Cage says, "Zen . . . invigorates action. . . . What I do, I do not wish to be blamed on Zen, though without my engagement with Zen . . . I doubt whether I could have done what I have done" (*Silence* [Middletown, Conn.: Wesleyan University Press, 1961], p. 11). Cage writes a book about music and calls it silence. Cage writes music that is "indetermined," that musicalizes (as he puts it) "the purpose of purposelessness." That's Chuang-tzu's:

> Everybody knows that useful is useful, but nobody knows that useless is useful, too.

E. E. Cummings says to a Supermachine (the locomotive on his train):

> Through you I greet all itgods. And I tell them of a singular He, indivisible or individual, one Being natural and unafraid, for whom exists no sign no

path no distance and no time. . . . I prophecy to faultless them a moving within feelfully Himself Artist, Whose will is dream, only Whose language is silence . . . "he who knoweth the eternal is comprehensive; comprehensive, therefore just; just, therefore a king; a king, therefore celestial; celestial, therefore in Tao; in Tao, therefore enduring"*

Well, do what you can with it.

§ THE OLD GUY

Tao. There is a thing vast and perfect that existed before Heaven and Earth were born. Vast! Waste! It stands alone and does not change. It gets into everything and encroaches on nothing. We can see it as the mother of everything under Heaven. I don't know what its name is, so I call it by the nickname *Tao*. (25)†

*

Self-like. Man's rule is Earth. Earth's rule is Heaven. Heaven's rule is Tao. Tao's rule is Self-like. (25)

*

*E.E. Cummings, *Eimi* (New York: Grove Press, 1933), pp. 418–19.
 †The material in this section is all translated from Lao-tzu's *Tao Te Ching* by the editor. The numbers in parentheses indicate chapters in the original text.

Te ("Effect"). The higher effect doesn't affect. That's why it effects. The lower effect forever affects. That's why it never effects. The higher effect anti-works, and that's why it always works. The lower effect always works, that's why it never works. (38)

*

Hsuan ("Dark"). Heaven and Earth begin from what isn't. The ten thousand things are born from what is. What is, what isn't came out together but got different names. Together we call them "Dark." This is darkness redarkened, the gate of all craft. (1)

*

Anti–action. If you want to stretch a thing, you must shrink it first. If you want to weaken a thing, you must strengthen it first. If you want to abolish a thing, you must exalt it first. If you want to get a thing, you must give it away first. . . . The ten thousand things interact, and so I watch for the rebound. (36. . .16)

*

Hsu ("Emptiness"). The thirty spokes join on one hub, and just where they aren't is where they are useful to the carriage. The clay lump is used to make a dish, and just where it isn't is where it's useful as a dish. You cut out doors and windows to make a room, and just where they aren't is where they are useful to the room. (11)

*

The Age of Perfect 'Te'. If there were a small country without overpopulation, you could see to it that though there were utensils and tools ten-to-a-man, a hundred-to-a-man, they wouldn't use them. You could see to it that the people paid attention to their lives and that their eyes weren't in the ends of the earth. Then though they had boats and carriages, they wouldn't be climbing into them all the time. And though they had arms and armor, they wouldn't be marching off in them all the time. You could have them knot cords to keep records again. Let them learn to cook, beautify their clothes, find rest in their homes, and enjoy their local customs. They could see the neighboring states and hear their dogs bark and their roosters crow, but all their lives they wouldn't come and go. (80)

§ CHUANG-TZU

The morning's mushroom doesn't know the moon wanes and waxes; the mole-cricket doesn't know that Spring changes to Fall. (1)*

*

The complete man has no self, the man with soul has no glory, the wise man has no name. (1)

*

Among the men of Sung, there were some who had a special medicine that kept hands from getting chapped. These men generation after generation worked as silk-bleachers. A traveler heard about their medicine and offered them one hundred ounces of gold for the formula. They called the clan together, these silk-bleachers, and discussing the offer they said, "We've bleached silk for generations, and we've never accumulated more than a few ounces of gold. Now in a single morning we

*The material in this section is all from *Chuang-tzu's Book,* translated by the editor. Numbers in parentheses indicate chapters in the original text.

can sell our secret for a hundred ounces of gold. Let's do it."

The traveler eventually showed up at the court of Wu. Wu at the time was having trouble with Yueh. So the king of Wu commissioned this traveler as general of Wu's forces. In dead winter he engaged Yueh's men in a sea-battle and won a great victory over Yueh. The king of Wu divided up the land and enfeoffed the man who'd bought the medicine. Now the virtue of the medicine was always the same—it kept hands from getting chapped. One man used it and was enfeoffed; other men used it and bleached silk generation after generation. The difference was in the use to which the virtue was put. (1)

*

The Ailanthus-tree. Hui-tzu said, "I have this big tree, what people call an 'Ailanthus.' The big roots crowd up and gnarl. You can't mark it off with compass and square. Put it beside a highway, no carpenter would take a second look. Now, your doctrine is great, but what use is it? It's a thing most people turn their back on."

Chuang-tzu said, "Haven't you ever seen a weasel or bobcat? They flatten down their bodies so they can't be seen, waiting for what may come by; and they can leap back and forth from roof-beam to beam, but whether they leap high or crouch low, they run slam into the springe and die in a hunter's net. Then there's the yak. The yak is big like the clouds that hang on Heaven's face, and we can call that big all right, but this yak can't even catch mice.

"So you've got this big tree, and you're bitter it can't be used for something. Why didn't you plant it out somewhere all by itself, like in some wide and empty field? You could walk back and forth beside it and practice anti-action. You could fall out under it and sleep in peace. To it the broadaxe is no threat, there's nothing in the universe that's going to hurt it.

There's no use it can be put to. So what's there to cry about?"
(1)

*

> But I tell you this,
> And to die is different from what any one supposed,
> and luckier.
> —WALT WHITMAN, "Song of Myself," 6

How do I know it's not a mistake to think we're lucky to be alive? How do I know that to hate death is not to be a child was lost and doesn't know when he's home? The beautiful girl of Lu, whose father was border guard at Ai—when the King of Chin first got her—she soaked her dress with tears. Then when she got to the King's place, got into that big square bed with the King, or ate the meals of grass-and-grain-fed meat, she wondered what she'd cried about. How do I know the dead don't wonder why they once hung on to life? (2)

*

Some guy dreams he's drinking wine, and in the morning he may weep. Some guy dreams he weeps, and in the morning he may hunt. When they dream, they don't know they're dreaming. And another may dream he can understand his dream, and after he wakes up he knows he was dreaming.

Well, there's a great waking-up, too, and after it we'll know that this is a great dream, too. The dummies think they're awake already, oh, they *know* it fact for fact. Kings! Cowboys! Hard-headed, you said it. Your authorities, and you too, are dreaming. And I that say you dream am dreaming too. (2)

*

The Butterfly Dream. One day Chuang-tzu dreamed he

was a butterfly, fluttering by enjoying what butterflies enjoy. The butterfly did not know that it was Chuang-tzu. Then Chuang-tzu started, and woke up, and he was Chuang-tzu again. And then he began to wonder whether he was Chuang-tzu who had dreamed he was a butterfly, or was a butterfly dreaming it was Chuang-tzu. (2)

*

The Cook. The cook was cutting up a beef for Prince Wen-hui. Where the cook set his hand, or leaned in with his shoulder, where he pushed with his foot, or pressed with his knee, (kweck! kiang!), the singing knife (kwak!) never missed a beat; you could have done the dance "Mulberry Grove" to it, you could have played the melody "Ching Shou."

Prince Wen-hui whistled and said, "Fine! Your craft has developed to this point, has it!?"

The cook put down his knife and said, "What gives your servant his skill is the *Tao*. The *Tao* transcends all craft. Way back when I was just starting to cut beef, what I saw was always just that—a beef. After three years, I no longer saw it as a whole cow. Until now, going through it with my spirit, I don't even look at it with my eyes. As the faculties fall away, the spirit will proceed, will flow according to the natural patterns, zip through the main joints, travel along main gaps, lay off the solid parts, and with craft it will weave through the space between tendon and bone, how much more won't it miss the big knots of cartilage and bone!

"A first-rate cook, he'll change his knife once a year because he nicks it. An ordinary cook, he'll change his knife every month because he breaks it. I've had this knife for nineteen years, and I've cut up several thousand cows with it. The blade on this knife is as new as if it'd just come off the whetstone. Now there are spaces at the animal's joints, and the knife blade is thin: being thin it moves through the spaces. There's plenty of room for the moving blade, got to be! So that nineteen years, and the blade's still new like it'd come straight off the whetstone. But whenever I come to a bundle or knot, when I see it's going to be difficult, I go slow as if there were warnings up, my gaze is fixed, my progress is slow, I move the knife gently, gently, laying it open, and suddenly it comes apart like a clod dropping to the ground. Then I take the knife up and stand straight, look this way and that way, I stroll around like a man waiting for no one, like a man who has everything he wants, and then I clean the knife and put it away."

Prince Wen-hui said, "Great! I listen to what the cook says, and learn from it about nourishing life." (3)

*

The Big Oak Tree. A carpenter named Rock was going to Ch'i. When he got to Crooked Shaft, he saw a big oak tree inside an altar compound. The tree was so big it could give shade to several thousand cows; it was ten thousand feet around; in height it was like a mountain; the first branches that grew from t were eighty feet up. If you used it to make boats you'd get ten craft and more. People crowded around, like at the market, to stare. The master-carpenter didn't even turn around, he went on down the road and never stopped. The carpenter's apprentice started and stared. Then he moved on and caught up to Rock, the carpenter. The apprentice said, "From the day I picked up an axe to study carpentry with you, I've never seen a beautiful lot of material like in that tree! Maestro, you didn't even look at it, you just walked by without stopping, How come?"

Rock said, "That's enough, don't talk about it, the tree was trash. Make boats with it, the boats would sink. Make coffins with it, the coffins would soon rot; make dishes with it, the dishes would soon break; make doors with it, the doors would be sticky with sap; make pillars and beams with it, the bugs would eat them full of holes. There's no *material* in that tree at all, nothing you can use, that's how come it's lived to such an age.''

When Rock the carpenter was home again, he dreamed about the oak tree at the altar. The tree said, ''What are you going to compare me to? Are you going to compare me to crop trees? Compare me to the sour plum, pear, orange, pumelo? To gourd and low fruit-bearing shrubs and the like? When the fruit's ripe, then rip! rip! they get stripped off, the limbs get broken, the branches yanked off—this is how because of their special virtue, their vital energy is impaired. So they don't live up their natural lives, but halfway through, zap! They *asked for* rough and vulgar hands to rip them off! It's like this for every thing. So I've tried to have no useful quality, put it off, put it off, death's approach, until now I've done it, it's been very useful to me. Suppose I had been useful, would I still have reached this size, do you think? You're like me, you're a thing, too. So? Both being things, getting near death, does a man that's trash know a tree that's trash?''

Rock woke up and told about his dream. The apprentice said, ''If it really wanted to be useless, how come it grew there by the altar?

Rock said, ''Shhh! You should keep quiet. It grew there on purpose; it supposed that people who didn't understand would talk against it. And if it wasn't there by the altar, maybe it would've gotten pruned, unh? Now the means it has used to preserve itself are different from everybody else's; when you start explaining it in the usual terms, aren't you missing the point?'' (4)

*

. . . The trees on the mountainside steal from themselves, the fat in the fire burns itself. The cinnamon tree can be eaten, so it gets cut down. The varnish-tree can be used, so it gets hacked up. Everybody knows that useful is useful, but nobody knows that useless is useful, too. (4)

*

Now a person who wants to protect himself against thieves that cut cases, get into bags, and open boxes, he's going to tie his stuff up with ropes and lock it with heavy locks. And everybody is going to say he's smart. Well, when expert thieves come along, they'll shoulder the boxes, pick up the cases, and carry the bags on a pole, and get away. They hope the cords *are* strong, they hope the locks *are* tight. So this, what most people call "smart," isn't it just getting things ready for the big thieves? (10)

*

One guy steals a belt buckle, and they execute him. Another guy steals a country, and they make him a prince. A prince's door, that's where kindness and fair dealing are preserved, right? But is it the case, or isn't it, that they *steal* kindness, fair dealing, wisdom and knowledge? You tell me. So they just belong there with the big thieves. They've been made princes, the guys that steal kindness, fair dealing, and the profit of pecks, bushels, weights, measures, accounting practices and records, and although they have the rewards of carriages and crowns, it doesn't make them better men, and fear of the axe doesn't inhibit their conduct. (10)

*

Now, emptiness, stillness, calm, insipidity, peace, quiet and anti-action are the balance of Heaven and Earth, and the maximum point of *Tao* and of power. . . . Emptiness, stillness, calm, insipidity, peace, quiet, and anti-action are the root of the ten thousand things. (13)

The Wheelwright P'ien. Duke Hwan was up in his hall reading a book, and a wheelwright named P'ien was down in the yard making wheels. The wheelwright put down his hammer and chisel and went up. He asked Duke Hwan, "May I ask what the book is you are reading?"

The duke said, "It's the words of the sages."

"Are the sages still alive?"

"No," said the duke. "They are dead."

"Well then, what your majesty is reading—it's just left-overs and remnants from the men of antiquity."

Duke Hwan said, "The Chief Executive reads a book, and his wheelwright criticizes it! If you can explain yourself, do it. If you can't explain yourself, you die!"

The wheelwright P'ien said, "Your servant looks at it from the point of view of his craft. When I make wheels, if I hold back then it's not firm; if I attack it, then it's rough and won't fit. If I neither hold back nor attack it, I can take it in my hand and shape it to my idea. But this is a thing I can't pass on with words from my mouth; there's a skill lies in it, in there somewhere, I can't teach it to my son, my son can't learn it from me. So though I'm seventy years old I go on making wheels.

"The men of antiquity likewise died with things they knew but couldn't communicate, and so what your excellency reads, it's only the left-overs and remnants of the ancients, that's all!" (13)

*

The Autumn Flood. The season of autumn floods had come. A hundred rivers poured their waters into the Ho. The waters flowed so far over the two banks, looking over the waters between the new shores, you couldn't tell a horse from a cow. Well, with this the Spirit of the Ho felt real good. He was pleased with himself. He felt that all the beauty of the universe was concentrated in himself. Going with the current, he moved on toward the east. And suddenly he found himself in the ocean, and he looked to the east, and he could see no end to the water. Well, with that he began to turn his head and eyes, and looked across the ocean toward the ocean god Jo, and sighed and said, "In the countryside, folks say, 'He's heard a hundred things and thinks nobody can compare to him.' They could say it about me!"

. . . Jo, Spirit of the Ocean, said, "The frog in a well, you can't talk to him about the ocean, he's stuck in his hole. The summer bug, you can't talk to him about ice, he's confined to his season. The specialized scholar, you can't talk to him about the *Tao,* he's wrapped up in his education. Just now when you came out from between your banks, you began to know your limitations. You'll be somebody one can talk about the great principles with.

"Of all bodies of water under the sky, none's as big as the ocean—ten thousand rivers empty into it, no one can say when they stop, and yet the ocean is never filled. It all flows out at Wei Liu, no one can say when it ceases, and yet the ocean is never emptied. In Spring, in Fall it does not change. It pays no attention to floods and droughts. In it flow rivers greater than the Yangtze or the Yellow River. How much bigger? You can't measure or count. And yet I've never thought I was big because of this; I compare my physical size to the earth and sky, and think how I get my vital breath from Yin and Yang. Look, in the space between earth and sky, I'm like a pebble or a bush on a big mountain. . . ."

The spirit of the Ho said, "Well then, shall I take Earth and Sky to be the Big, and shall I take a hair's end to be the Small? Is this possible?"

Jo of the ocean said, "No, it's not. In the physical universe, all measure is relative. You can never stop time, never regulate destiny, never fix beginnings and ends. So that a man who really *knows* looks into the far and the near, what's small is not small to him, what's big is not big. He knows that all measure is relative. . . .

"The Tao doesn't end or begin, things die and are born, they do not stay in their prime, sometimes they empty, sometimes they fill up, they never stay put in a particular form. You can't bring back the years, you can't stop the seasons. Decay, growth, fullness, emptiness—something ends, then there's a beginning. That's why we say there's a frame of great laws, and talk about the principles in the ten thousand things. . . .

"So some say, 'What's natural's inside, what's artificial is outside, and virtue is in the natural.' Know the progress of natural and artificial, set your roots in the natural, take your place in its virtue, and you can step up or step back, consolidate or expand, return to essences, and talk about 'ultimates.'

". . . So they say, 'Don't wipe out the natural with the artificial. Don't wipe out destiny with effort. Don't sacrifice your delight for fame's sake. Keep at it like this, not letting go, and you may get back to origins and to innocence.' " (17)

*

Chuang-tzu's wife died. Hui-tzu came to say how sorry he was, and when he arrived Chuang-tzu was squatting on his heels, beating a tinpan and singing. Hui-tzu said, "The woman lived with you and raised your kids, now she's gotten old and her body has died; well, if you don't cry, all right. But to sing and beat a tin pan, isn't this too much?"

Chuang-tzu said, "I don't think so. My wife, when she died— at first I . . . well do you think that I'm so weird I wasn't moved? But then I thought about it. In the first place, she once had no life, and not only she had no life, but once she had no form. Not only she had no form, but once she had no vital breath. She was mixed with the elements unborn—a change, and she had vital breath; the vital breath changed, and she had a form; the form changed, and she had life. Now she's changed again and come to death. These things lead each to each like Spring, Fall, Winter, and Summer move on. She lies asleep now in the Great Room—if I sobbed and then cried for her, it would seem to me to show I didn't understand our appointed destiny, so I stopped." (18)

*

You soldier best when you're not soldiering,
you wage war best when you're not waging war.

—LAO-TZU

The Fighting Cock. Chi Hsing-tzu was getting a fighting cock ready for the king. After ten days, the king asked Hsing-tzu, "Is the cock ready yet?"

Hsing-tzu said, "Not yet. Right now he's vain and cocky, and he depends on his adrenalin."

Another ten days went by. The king asked about the cock. Hsing-tzu replied, "He's not ready yet. He still responds to sound or sight of another cock."

After another ten days, the king asked again. Hsing-tzu said, "He's not ready yet. He's still got a mean stare, he still gets all psyched up."

Ten more days went by. The king asked again. Hsing-tzu said, "He's ready now. Let another cock crow, your fighter doesn't react at all. To look at him, you'd think he was a cock made of wood. His powers are complete, no other cock will stand against him. They will all turn and flee." (19)

*

Chuang-tzu had an audience with Duke Ai of Lu. Duke Ai said, "There's a lot of scholars in the country, but few of them can compare to you."

Chuang-tzu said, "There's not a lot of scholars in the country."

The Duke said, "Why, everywhere you look in Lu you see scholars. How can you say there's not a lot?"

Chuang-tzu said, "I've heard that these scholars, if they wear round hats they're meteorologists, if they wear square shoes they're geologists, and if they wear those little insignia hanging from their belts, they adjudicate various matters that come up. A superior man that has the *Tao* doesn't necessarily wear the clothes, the guy that wears the clothes doesn't necessarily know the *Tao*. If you think I'm wrong about this, why don't you just proclaim it in the country, like this: 'Anybody who doesn't know his stuff and still wears the clothes will be condemned to death.' "

So the duke proclaimed it, and five days later there was nobody in Lu wore the scholars' clothes.

Only one old man wore them, and he stood in the street at the duke's gate. The duke called him in and asked him about statecraft. The old man knew a thousand turns and ten thousand twists.

Chuang-tzu said, "So there's only one man in Lu knows anything; I wouldn't call one 'a lot,' would you?" (21)

*

Mr. "East Kuo" asked Chuang-tzu, "This so-called *Tao*, where is it?"

Chuang-tzu said, "There's nowhere where it's not."

Mr. East Kuo said, "Be specific. That's no answer."

Chuang-tzu said, "It's in the ant there."

"Where else is it?"

"It's in the grass."

"Where else?"

"In that crock."

"Where else?"
"In the shit and piss."
Mr. East Kuo did not ask again. (22)

*

What's named, what's embodied, exists where things reside. What's unnamed, what's unbodied, exists where things are not. We can talk about it, we can think about it, the more we talk the more off we get. There was a time before I was born, what can I do about it? There will be a time after I die, what can I do about it? Death and life are not far apart, but the principle— who can see into it? Did someone cause it? Did nobody make it? Worry about this, you'll never get your head on straight.

I look at its root, it goes on forever; I reach for its branches, they come on without end. "Forever, without end"—that's the end of talk, or you subsume it to the principles of the physical universe. "Someone caused it, nobody made it"— that's the root of talk, it begins and ends with things. The *Tao* cannot be what is, what is can't be what isn't. Give the *Tao* a name, that's a pretense allows you to proceed. "Some One caused it, nobody made it," that's to twist it up with things, what do such speculations have to do with the Great Frame?

If words could do it, we would talk till sundown and explain the *Tao* in full. Words can't do it, so we talk till sundown and only explain things. The *Tao* is out there at the end of things, you can't load it into words, and you can't load it into silence, either. What's not words and not silence, that's what's out there at the end of talk about. (25)

*

Chuang-tzu was about to die. His students wanted sumptuously to bury him. Chuang-tzu said, "I have the sky and the earth for my coffin and case, the sun and moon are my jade symbol, the stars and constellations are my pearls, the ten thousand things will go with me like mourners. So what can you possibly add to my funeral service?"

The students said then, "We are afraid the kites and crows will eat you, sir."

Chuang-tzu said, "Above ground, kites and crows eat you. Below ground, bugs and worms eat you. Can you give me a reason to pick one over the other?" (32)

Some Further Readings

Lin Yutang, ed. and trans. *The Wisdom of Lao-tse*. New York: Modern Library, 1948.

McNaughton, William. *The Taoist Vision*. Ann Arbor: University of Michigan Press, 1971.

Waley, Arthur. *The Way and Its Power*. London: Allen & Unwin, Ltd., 1934.

Watson, Burton, trans. *Chuang Tzu: Basic Writings*. New York: Columbia University Press, 1964.

———. *Complete Works of Chuang Tzu*. New York: Columbia University Press, 1968.

Welch, Holmes. *Taoism: The Parting of the Way*. Boston: Beacon Press, 1957.

5

ECSTASY CULTS AND ELEGIES

Central and northern China nurtured the Confucian clarity, and the people living in these areas created the ideals and wrote the poems which are preserved for us in *The Book of Songs*. The ideal attitude toward "the gods"—which Confucius enunciated but did not invent—was: "Give honor to the spirits, and keep them at their distance." The state of Ch'u, in southern China, encouraged an altogether different religious sensibility, and the people of Ch'u had a totally different attitude toward "the gods."

According to the records, the Ch'u attitude was "Play music and perform dances in order to delight the gods and call them in on us." China's second great anthology, the *Ch'u Tz'u*, contains poems from this alien and exotic region, and it expresses or reveals the different attitudes and the different sensibilities of these wild Southerners. Accordingly, Chinese literary historians have come to say that "China's classical, or realistic, genius flourishes

129

in *The Book of Songs,* and China's romantic, or imaginative, genius flourishes in the *Ch'u Tz'u.*"

Of *Ch'u Tz'u,* the two most important parts are the "Nine Songs" and the "Li Sao." The "Li Sao" is a rather long poem by the man who generally is recognized as China's first poet, because he left the first name to be attached to any very large body of poetry: Ch'ü Yuan. Ch'ü Yuan also is said variously to have written the "Nine Songs," to have rewritten them, and to have revised them. He lost his official post because of court intrigue and wrote the "Li Sao," so the critics say, to express his sorrow about it. Eventually he drowned himself in the Milo River, and the Chinese even today honor his spirit with something called "The Dragon Boat Festival."

We shall read only selections from the "Nine Songs" below. Although they are traditionally called the "Nine Songs," there are in fact eleven songs—an inconsistency for which there is no explanation. Most of the songs deal with various southern divinities, and more than one has ecstatic overtones. One of them, the last, is a song in praise of heroic war dead.

It doesn't take much imagination to see that the poems "T'ai I" and "Lord of the Clouds" describe sexual experiences, although sensuality had gotten so mixed up with mythology that the anthology remained respectable. It may help the non-Chinese reader to know that "the dragon" is a Chinese term for the woman's sexual equipment, but in context it would be difficult to miss that "the Room of Life" means vagina. Likewise the phallic suggestion of "long sword" is obvious and is not peculiarly Chinese, but the "jade clasp" might mean nothing to a western reader unless he had read *The Golden Lotus* or knew that Chinese men sometimes wore jade rings to stimulate and to increase the woman's pleasure in love. By the time he comes to "the orchids," the reader's mind should be set, and he should be prepared to make his own inferences.

The "River God" in the poem "Ho Po" is the god of the Yellow River. No other god, among those praised in the "Nine Songs," had so long-lasting a legend or so enduring a cult as Ho Po. The Historical Records tell us that the Honanese every year gave a "wife" to the river god. Shamans went from house to house until they found a beautiful girl. Then they washed her off and set her for ten days or so in a special house on the river bank. Eventually she was garbed and made up as a bride and set adrift on the river on a "bridal bed." The river god got her pretty soon. People of the area with beautiful daughters often emigrated.

Mountain spirits, like those of which the poet sings in "Shan Kuei," also received young Chinese as spouses. Governor Sung Chün in A.D. 56 discovered that shamans near Lüchow regularly dedicated local boys and girls as husbands and wives to two nearby hills. Naturally—save for what might happen between the hill spirits and the "spouses"—the boys and girls so dedicated were supposed to remain celibate. The governor sent down an order that, from then on, only the offspring of shamans could marry the hill spirits. The custom disappeared.

"The Great Fate-Master" presents the god who determines whether men shall live or die—who decides how long any living thing shall continue to live. In some places people offered him dried meat in spring and autumn, and he was given other things like goblets and tripods.

Even the attitude shown in the song for heroic war dead ("Pro Patria Mori") differs from the northern Chinese, or Confucian, attitude. The southern poet seems out-and-out to sing their praise and their glory—and this contrasts with the "war songs" in *The Book of Songs.* For in *The Book of Songs,* the soldiers are usually hungry, wet, lonesome, homesick, and miserable, and the tone— often even the very words themselves—almost always is anti-war.

The translations in this chapter are by the editor.

§ THE ELEGIES OF CH'U

—T'AI I, LORD OF THE EAST—

This is the day of delight:
>"the dragon is lucky."

Bow then: we shall take joy
>in the god above.

Stroke the long sword
>and its jade clasp;

The lin-liang stones
>sound as silver and jade.

The mat is of jewels,
    The weights are of jade.
We shall gather now
    the clouds of sweet smoke.
Mix basil and flesh.
    The orchids are spread.
Set wine and cinnamon
    spices and brew.
He raises the stick
    strikes the drum.
The beat is distant and slow
    the singing is hushed.
Reed-organ and zither
    respond and resound.

The god goes down, goes up
    in bright-woven robes
Smoke trembles and tumbles
    from high wall to wall,
The five notes inweave
    redouble, reweave
Lord! delight, delight
    pleasure, and peace.

—LORD OF THE CLOUDS—

I bathe in orchid water,
    I wash in perfume.
My clothes are inworked with blosssoms,
    an artifice of flowers.

The god, curving, curling,
                is caught now and held:
Fires burning burn
                unceasing still.

He goes down and soon shall move
                in the Room of Life.
He joins sun to moon,
                he sets the light in lines.
The dragon is yoked
                the god is ensheathed.
Now drifting leftward, now rightward,
                he twists, he turns.
The god, as light upon light,
                comes down all the way
Now, now, now we lift up
                and enter the clouds:
We can see Chi-chou,
                can see beyond
Cross the four seas,
                carry on without end.
Think of him tender and bold.
                Sigh, breath on breath.
The heart, in the end, worries on,
                wears off, wearies out.

—HO PO (THE RIVER GOD)—

I shall go with you
                down the nine rivers.
A tumult of winds arises
                and cuts across the waves.

We take the water-chariot
                its awning is lotus-leaves.
We yoke the pair of dragons,
                we harness the griffins.
We go up K'un-lun and gaze
                north, south, east, west
The heart flies and leaps up.
                Marvel and terror!
The sun touches earth's edge
                and I have forgotten "Return."
Only the farthest-out shore,
                unsleeping, do I desire.

The rooms are scales of fish,
                the hall, of dragons.
The entrance is purple shell,
                the walls, vermilion.
Why does the god go down
                and live in the waters?

He goes on a white turtle's back,
                before him go patterned fish.
He shall go with you
                on the islands of the river.
The eddying water is high,
                the water soon shall fall.

You shall cross your hands
                and go to the East.
We take you, beautiful one,
                as far as the southern shore.

The waves, surge on surge,
                    come to welcome you;
The fishes, shoal on shoal,
                    take us on our way.

—SHAN KUEI (THE MOUNTAIN SPIRIT)—

It's as if there were a man
                    there, in the mountain's fold.
He's dressed in the winding vine,
                    he wears a wisteria belt.
He holds on his mouth, gazing
                    —and forms again—a smile.
So you desire me
                    and admire, willing-nilling?

He rides a crimson panther
                    before him go patterned leopards.
His chariot is made of magnolia,
                    his banners are tied with cassia
He carries an orchid of stone,
                    he wears red-pear at his belt.
Go gather the scented herb
                    and give to the one that is loved.
I live in the dark bamboo groves.
                    You never see through to the sky.
The road is twisted and steep;
                    one comes alone in the end.

You stand there all alone
                    on the mountain's utter height
The clouds, drift on drift,
                    fall away below.

Gathering gloom on gloom
               makes the light go dark.
In the East, the wind whines
               the spirits and god bring rain.
You wait a long time for the god;
               untroubled, forget to return.
The season already darkens.
               Who is going to flower me?

I gather the triple flowers
               on the cliffs and clefts.

Rocks,   rocks   rocks
               rocksrocks   rocksrocks

               the creepers curve and crawl
Lust for this prince of princes,
               grieve, and forget to return.
He, He even, thinks of us;
               there shall be no break.
The person amid the mountains
               is scented as though with red-pear.
He drinks from the rocky springs
               and curls in cypress and pine
He, He even, thinks of us.
               How should he fail to push it?
Thunders roar and reroar;
               Rain darkens the dark.
The apes grieving grieve;
               again, in the night, they cry.
The wind sways and swings,
               the trees sough and sigh
Think of him, prince of princes.
               Vanity, bitterness, apathy.

—THE GREAT FATE-MASTER—

They open wide
        the gates of the sky
I ride on a turmoil
        of darkening clouds
The cool winds, the whining winds
        ride on before me.
They push the heated rains,
        and beat on the dust.

The Lord recircles his flight
        and drops toward the earth.
He steps over K'ung-sang
        and comes on after you.
In turmoil, the masses mass
        in all the nine provinces.
How shall living or dying
        rest in us?

Upward he flies
        and wings straight on
He rides the green air
        and gathers the light, the darkness.
We shall join this Lord:
        bow down and be humble.
He guides us to Ultimate God
        across the Nine Peaks.

The robes of the god
        fold, ply over ply.
The jade belt-stones
        quiver and quaver.

Here darkness,
        here light
Of them all, none knows
        the work I shall do.

I pick the shattered hemp
        and the shaken flower.
Shall take them and send them on
        to separate homes.
Old age sneaks in, sneaks out
        having reached its end:
It will neither proceed
        nor further recede.

I ride the dragon
        He roars and roars.
He leaps to the heights
        and cuts through the sky
I tie the cinnamon branch
        and pause for a time.
Grief! Think on and on,
        unhappy man.

Unhappy man,
        what is the good?
You wish that the present hour
        went on and on without end.
So: the fates of men
        already are set
The joining, disjoining
        —who can master its action?

—EASTERN LORD—

He shall come out any instant
        in the eastern sky.
I light up the balconies
        from the mulberry *Fu-sang*.
I stroke my horses now
        and drive slowly on.
The night divides and departs
        and suddenly: Light.

He harnesses the dragon-shaft,
        he rides the thunder.
He carries the banners of cloud
        that swirl and swarm.
He sighes, long and loud
        ready to rise.
His heart pauses and pulses;
        he looks back and remembers.
Grief! Sounds and colors
        give delight to people
Who looks ahead shall forget
        and shall not return.

They stop the zither strings
        and counterweave the drums.
They touch the bells,
        they rock the stands
They blow on flutes,
        they wail on pipes.
Think: the protective gods
        are beautiful and wise.

They fly now here, now there
>> like kingfishers, sinking, soaring.
They sing these songs
>> to match the dance.
They balance the meters
>> and catch the beats.
The gods, going, coming,
>> cover the sun.

The bluish clouds are clothes,
>> the brilliant rainbow is robes.
He gathers his slender arrows
>> and shoots the Heavenly Wolf.
I catch up my reins,
>> turn my wheels and go up;
Draw out the Northern Dipper
>> and pour the cinnamon wine.
I rein out
>> and gallop and fly above
The gloom lowers and glowers
>> onward, onward I ride the East.

—PRO PATRIA MORI—

They shake their clamorous spears,
>> they have hide jackets and shields.
They drive the chariots together,
>> they cross the short swords.
Their banners cover the sun,
>> their enemies move like clouds.
Arrows—criss, cross—fall,
>> the soldiers move on and on.

They overrun our patrols,
          they break across our lines.
Leftward, the horses fall
          rightward, the blades draw blood.
The chariot-wheels are blocked
          and hang on the coupled horses.
Draw out the sticks of jade,
          strike the strident drum.
Heaven times the fall;
          the dangerous gods are mad.
They are bitterly slain to the last
          and strewn on the open fields.

They joined and shall not rejoin,
          turned out and do not return.
The flats stretch on without end,
          the road leaps over the earth.
They wore, at the belt, long swords,
          and under each arm, thick bows.
Their bodies and heads are disjoined,
          their hearts shall never defer.
Yea, they were bold in extreme;
          again and again they armed.
To the end, they were haughty and hard;
          none could bring them down.
Their bodies indeed are gone;
          the gods will gather their souls,
Drive the unbodied ghosts,
          make heroes among the dead.

Some Further Readings

Hawkes, David, trans. *Ch'u Tz'u: The Songs of the South*. London and New York: Oxford University Press, 1959. (Also available in a Beacon Press paperback.)

Waley, Arthur, trans. *The Nine Songs*. London: Allen & Unwin, Ltd., 1935.

6

MR. LEFT'S HISTORY AND
POLICIES OF WAR

Although the Chinese have highly prized historical writing and have devoted to it much talent and much genius, it probably still would fall outside the scope of "literature" were it not for the narrative and novelistic skills with which the earliest histories are written, and were it not for the influence—stylistic as well as substantial—which this early history had on later fiction.

Mr. Left's History (in Chinese *Tso Chuan*) covers the period 722–468 B.C. It gives us this history in the conversations, the conspiracies, the plans, the undertakings, the *amours,* even the dreams of the rulers and the ministers who made history. The author gives local habitation and name to every event, and to the antecedents and the consequences of every event, which might be recorded in a historical outline of the period.

Mr. Left created a work which could serve, in its intent "to encourage good and to censure evil," as a model for all later Chinese historical writing. *Mr. Left's History* has a definite and very clear desire to show that

Confucian principles explain the prosperity and decline of men and of kingdoms. Of the Confucian principles, the most important is the principle of *li*. *Mr. Left's History* itself says, *"Li* is the constant principle of Heaven, the Righteousness of Earth, and the proper action of mankind. . . . *Li* determines the relations of high and low; it is the warp and woof of Heaven and Earth and that by which the people live."

The personages in *Mr. Left's History* talk a lot. They talk in two different ways: sometimes they chat or converse, and sometimes they orate. It is mostly in the formal, oratorical passages that the moral, or ethical, doctrine is presented. When we think about our Western civilization, and even when we get to the *Policies of War,* we shall find it of interest that there was an art of oratorical speaking in China at this period.

We finally should note of *Mr. Left's History* that the supernatural and the prophetic play a large role in it. Sometimes later Confucians, wishing to maintain the Confucian precept "Give honor to the gods, and keep them at their distance," grieve that the gods and spirits in *Tso Chuan* mix so much in human lives. We can only assume that Mr. Left wrote down the history as he saw it or heard about it, and we can enjoy the drama and tension which he introduced to his tale with prophecies and with spirits.

Policies of War covers the period of early Chinese history called the Warring States Period, which runs from 403–221 B.C. In no way is it comprehensive, or even a coherent history like *Mr. Left's History*. *Policies of War* is a collection of anecdotes focused on persuasive or effective speeches, and the incidents and people mentioned all belong to the Warring States Period. So important, in fact, are the speeches—and so studiously and elaborately are they worded—that scholars now believe *Policies of War* was a handbook for orators and would-be advisers to princes. It worked as a rhetorical model for generation on generation of later Chinese speakers. No ethical purpose is to be found running through the book, and the author seems even to deprecate the earlier, and simpler, moral values—the values to which Mr. Left gave so much attention. For the author of *Policies of War,* the main point is that the speaker should be engaging, convincing, witty, and effective.

Unless otherwise noted, material in this chapter is translated by Burton Watson.

§ MR. LEFT'S HISTORY

(1)

In the winter [628 B.C.] Duke Wen of Chin died. On the day *keng-ch'en* preparations were made to inter the body at Ch'ü-wo, but as it was being carried out of the capital at Chiang, a sound issued from the coffin like the lowing of an ox. The diviner Yen urged the high officials to bow down, saying, "Our lord is speaking to us of a grave affair. He says that an army will come from the west to invade our land and that if we attack, we will win a great victory!"

Ch'i Tzu [the commander of a garrison of Ch'in troops

stationed in the state of Cheng] sent a report from Cheng back to his sovereign in Ch'in saying, "The men of Cheng have given me custody of the keys to their north gate. If you send an army in secret, you can capture the city!"

Duke Mu of Ch'in questioned his minister Chien Shu about this, and he replied, "I have never heard of wearing out the army attempting to make a surprise attack on a distant state! If our army is worn out and its strength exhausted, while the ruler of the distant state has meanwhile been preparing for our attack, will not the outcome be disaster? If our army knows what it is doing, then Cheng will certainly find out as well, and if in spite of all our precautions we fail to win success, we will surely be faced with discontent. Anyway, if we have to march a thousand *li*, who could fail to guess what we were up to?"

But the duke declined to listen to his advice and, summoning Po-li Meng-ming, Hsi Ch'i, and Po I, he ordered them to lead the army out of the eastern gate.

Chien Shu wept and said, "Lord Meng-ming, I see the army going forth, but I shall not see it return!"

The duke sent someone to reproach him, saying, "What do you know about this, old man? If you had died at a decent age, the trees on your grave mound would be a span around by now!"

Chien Shu's son was with the army. Chien Shu wept and, taking leave of him, said, "If the men of Chin move to block your advance, it will surely be at Yao. There are two ridges at Yao. That on the south bears the grave of Emperor Kao of the Hsia dynasty. That on the north is where King Wen of the Chou dynasty retired to escape the wind and rain. You will die between these two and I will go to gather up your bones there!"

The Ch'in army then proceeded east.

Thirty-third year [627 B.C.], spring. The Ch'in army passed by the northern gate of the king's capital at Chou. The archers on the left and the lancers on the right of the carriage drivers doffed their armor and dismounted out of respect for the king, but when they came to mount again, the men of some three hundred carriages leaped up into their vehicles without waiting for them to stop. The royal prince Man, though still a young lad, watched them and then said to the king, "The army of Ch'in is overconfident and has no sense of propriety. It will surely be defeated. He who is overconfident lays few plans and he who has no sense of propriety easily slips up. If one enters a dangerous situation and slips up, and if on top of that he does not know how to plan, can he escape defeat?"

The army had reached the city of Hua [on the Cheng border] when Hsien Kao, a merchant of Cheng who was on his way to market in Chou, chanced to meet it. Quickly grasping the situation, he presented four tanned hides, followed by twelve oxen, as a gift to the army, saying, "My sovereign, the ruler of Cheng, hearing that you were about to lead your army through his humble territory, takes the liberty of presenting these gifts to your followers. Poor as are the resources of his humble territory, he has made preparations to provide your troops, who have been so long away from home, with a full day's supply of grain and fodder if you should decide to make camp, and an escort throughout the night if you should decide to march straight through without halting."

He then sent a fast rider to report the advance of the Ch'in army to the ruler of Cheng.

Having received the news, Duke Mu of Cheng sent men to keep a watch on the guest lodge where the Ch'in envoys Ch'i Tzu, P'eng Sun, and Yang Sun were staying. They found the envoys busy getting their baggage together, sharpening their weapons and feeding their horses. The duke then sent Huang Wu-tzu to say to the envoys, "Gentlemen, you have resided for a long time in my humble territory, and I fear that the supplies of dried meat, grain, fresh meat, and animals which were provided you are all used up. That is the reason, I suppose, that you are preparing to leave. However, Cheng has its Yüan Gardens, much like the Chü Park of your native state of Ch'in. How would it be if you gentlemen were to help yourselves to the deer from the Yüan Gardens and remain at leisure here a while longer?"

Their plot discovered, Ch'i Tzu fled to the state of Ch'i and P'eng Sun and Yang Sun fled to Sung.

Po-li Meng-ming said to the other commanders of the Ch'in army, "Cheng has already made preparations for our attack. We can hope for nothing! Now, even though we attack we cannot win, and though we surround the city we cannot maintain a siege. We had better go home!" With this they destroyed the city of Hua and began the march back. . . .

At the Chin court, Hsien Chen said, "Ch'in ignored Chien Shu's advice and has worn out its people on a mission of greed. Heaven presents us with this opportunity, and an opportunity thus presented must not be lost! One must not allow an enemy to escape, for to do so means trouble in the future, while to reject the offer of Heaven is unlucky. We must attack the Ch'in army!"

Luan Chih objected, saying, "We have not yet repaid the kindness which our late sovereign, Duke Wen, received from Ch'in in the past. Now if we were to attack its army, this would be to treat him as dead indeed!"

But Hsien Chen replied, "Ch'in without showing any pity for the fact that we are in mourning for our sovereign, has attacked Hua, a city of our own clansmen. It is obvious that Ch'in has no sense of propriety. Why worry about obligations to such a state? I have always heard that he who acts leniently towards his enemy for a single day brings on himself generations of trouble. If we plan now for the future safety of the sons and grandsons of the ruling family, how can we be said to be treating our late sovereign as dead?"

So the order was finally issued to attack the Ch'in army and a fast rider was dispatched to enlist aid from the Chiang barbarians. The late duke's heir dyed his mourning garments black and put on a white hemp sash. Liang Hung drove his chariot for him and Lai Chü stood by his right side in the chariot. In the summer, the fourth month, the day *hsin-ssu*, he defeated the Ch'in army at Yao and took Po-li Meng-ming, Hsi Ch'i, and Po I prisoner. Then he returned to Chin and, still wearing his black garments, buried his father, Duke Wen. This was the beginning of the Chin custom of wearing black mourning garments.

Wen-ying [a princess of Ch'in who became the wife of Duke Wen but was not the mother of Duke Wen's heir] asked her stepson, the new ruler of Chin, about the fate of the three Ch'in commanders. "It was they who actually brought about the trouble between the rulers of the two states!" she declared. "If my former lord, the ruler of Ch'in, could only lay his hands on them, his wrath would scarcely be appeased even by eating their flesh! Therefore, my lord, why demean yourself by executing them here? Send them back to Ch'in to be punished and you will make it possible for the ruler of Ch'in to accomplish his desire for vengeance!"

The new duke consented to this proposal.

When Hsien Chen appeared at court, he asked what had happened to the Ch'in captives.

"At the urging of my father's widow, I set them free," replied the duke.

Hsien Chen was furious. "Prizes won by the warriors at great labor on the field of battle—and at a word from a woman they are allowed to leave the state! He who deliberately discards the fruits of battle and nourishes the strength of his enemy need not wait long for the day of his destruction!" he exclaimed and, without turning his head, he spat.

The duke dispatched Yang Ch'u-fu to pursue the Ch'in commanders, but when he reached the banks of the Yellow River he found that they had already embarked in a boat. He immediately unharnessed the left horse from his team of four and shouted to Po-li Meng-ming that the duke wished to present the horse to him. But Po-li Meng-ming was not taken in and only bowed his head from the boat and replied, "Through the kindness of your lord I have been spared the usual fate of prisoners—having my blood smeared on the war drums. Instead I have been sent back to be punished by Ch'in. Even though I should be executed by my sovereign in Ch'in, I shall never forget the gratitude I owe your lord. And if my sovereign out of pity should pardon my offense, I will assuredly be back within the next three years to accept your lord's gift!"

The ruler of Ch'in, wearing white mourning garments, camped in the suburbs of his capital to await the return of the army. He greeted the commanders with tears, saying, "I failed to heed the advice of Chien Shu and brought this shame upon you. The fault is mine!"

He did not deprive Po-li Meng-ming of his command, but said, "I was in error. What fault have you committed? How could I, because of one failure, forget the great deeds you have done?" —DUKE HSI 32–33 (628–627 B.C.)

(2)

The people of Cheng were in the habit of discussing the administration of the state when they gathered at leisure in the village schools. Jan Ming said to Tzu-ch'an, the head of the government, "How would it do to abolish the village schools?"

"Why do that?" said Tzu-ch'an. "In the morning and evening when the people have finished their work and are at leisure, they gather to discuss the good and bad points of my administration. The points they approve of I encourage, and those they criticize I correct. They are my teachers. Why should I do away with them? I have heard of wiping out resentment through goodness and royal service, but I have never heard of stopping it by force. True, one can cut it off for a time. But it is like damming a river. When there is a major break in the dikes many men are bound to suffer. If the people's resentment were to break out in the same way, I would never be able to save the situation. It is better to leave a little break in the dikes for the water to drain off. It is better that I hear the people's complaints and make them my medicine!" . . . When Confucius later heard of this incident, he remarked, "People say that Tzu-ch'an was not a good man, but judging from this I find it impossible to believe." —DUKE HSIANG 31 (542 B.C.).

(3)

Duke Ching dreamt that he saw a huge ogre with disheveled hair that hung to the ground, beating his chest and leaping about, saying, "You killed my grandsons [Chao Tung and Chao K'uo], an evil deed! God has promised me revenge!" The ogre broke down the main gate of the palace, and then the door to the inner apartments, and came in. The duke fled in terror to his chamber, but the ogre broke down that door as well. At that moment the duke awoke and sent for the sorcerer of Mulberry Field. The sorcerer, without asking what had happened, described the duke's dream just as it had been.

"What will become of me?" asked the duke.

"You will not live to eat the new grain!" replied the sorcerer.

The duke fell gravely ill and sent for a doctor from the state of Ch'in. The ruler of Ch'in dispatched a physician named Huan to treat the duke. Before the physician arrived, the duke dreamt that his illness appeared to him in the form of two little boys. One boy said, "He is a skilled physician and I am afraid he will do us injury. Where can we flee?" The other replied, "If we go to the region above the diaphragm and below the heart, what can he do to us?"

When the physician arrived, he told the duke, "I can do nothing for your illness. It is situated above the diaphragm and below the heart, where treatment cannot affect it, acupuncture will not penetrate, and medicine will not reach. There is nothing I can do."

"You are a good doctor," said the duke and, entertaining him with all courtesy, he sent him back home.

On the day *ping-wu* of the sixth month the duke decided he wanted to taste the new grain and ordered the steward of his private domain to present some. When his butler had prepared it, he summoned the sorcerer of Mulberry Field and, pointing out the error of his prophecy, had him executed. Then he started to eat the grain, but his stomach swelled up and, hurrying to the privy, he fell down the hole and died.

One of the duke's servants had dreamt in the early morning hours that he was carrying the duke on his back up to Heaven, and consequently he was delegated that day to bear the duke's body on his back out of the privy, after which he was executed so that his spirit might accompany the duke in death.—DUKE CH'ENG 10 (581 B.C.)

(4)

The duke of Chu was on the terrace at the top of the palace gate, looking down into his courtyard. The gatekeeper at the time was dousing the courtyard with water from a pitcher. The duke, spying him from afar, was greatly annoyed. When he questioned the gatekeeper, the latter explained, "Lord I Yeh-ku pissed in the court there!"

The duke ordered I Yeh-ku arrested. When I Yeh-ku could not be found, the duke, more furious than ever, flung himself down on his bed with such violence that he fell off into the ashes of the brazier and burned to death. . . . Duke Chuang was a very impetuous and fastidious man, and therefore he came to such an end.—DUKE TING 3 (507 B.C.)

§ POLICIES OF WAR

(1)

When the queen was ill and at the point of death, she admonished her son Chien, saying, "Among the various court officials, those who can be of use to you are So-and-so—"

"May I write that down?" asked the king.

"Fine!" replied the queen, but when the king had fetched a brush and writing tablet and was prepared to take down her words, she said, "I have already forgotten what I said."— CH'I TS'E 6

(2)

The queen dowager Hsüan of Ch'in loved a man named Wei Ch'ou-fu. When she fell ill and was at the point of death, she issued an order saying, "At my burial, see to it that Master Wei is put to death and buried with me!"

Master Wei, deeply distressed, got Yung Jui to speak to the queen dowager on his behalf. "Do you believe that the dead have consciousness?" Yung Jui asked the queen.

"No, they have no consciousness."

"If Your Majesty is wise enough to understand that the dead have no consciousness, then why would you cause one whom you loved while you were alive to be buried in vain with an unconscious corpse? And should the dead perhaps have consciousness after all, then your husband, the late king, will have been piling up a store of jealous anger for a long time. Your Majesty will have all you can do trying to excuse your faults. What leisure could you expect to have for dalliance with Wei Ch'ou-fu?"

"You are right," said the queen dowager, and abandoned the idea.—CH'IN TS'E 2

(3)

The king of Wei sent the king of Ch'u [King Huai] a beautiful girl. The king was delighted with her, and his consort, Cheng Hsiu, aware of the king's infatuation, treated the girl with special affection. . . . When she was sure that the king would not suspect her of jealousy, she said to the new girl, "The king is much taken with your beauty, but he does not seem to care for your nose. When you go to see him, I suggest you always keep your nose covered." Accordingly, whenever the new girl visited the king, she would cover her nose.

"I notice," said the king to Cheng Hsiu, "that when the new girl is with me she covers her nose. Why is that, I wonder?"

"I could tell you why," said Cheng Hsiu.

"If you know, then tell me, no matter how bad it is," the king insisted.

"It would seem," said Cheng Hsiu, "that she does not like the way you smell."

"What insolence!" exclaimed the king. "Let her nose be cut off at once!" he ordered. "See that there is no delay in carrying out the command!"—CH'U TS'E 4

(4)

Tsou Chi, the prime minister of Ch'i, was over eight feet tall and had a very handsome face and figure. One day as he was putting on his court robes and cap and looking at himself in the mirror, he said to his wife, "Who do you think is better looking, I or Lord Hsü of Ch'eng-pei?" His wife replied, "You are much better looking! How could Lord Hsü compare to you?" Lord Hsü of Ch'eng-pei was one of the handsomest men in the state of Ch'i.

Tsou Chi was not entirely confident, however, and so he put the same question to his concubine. "Who is better looking, I or Lord Hsü?" "Lord Hsü could never compare to you!" she replied.

The next morning a guest came to call and while Tsou Chi was sitting and chatting with him, he asked, "Who is better looking, Lord Hsü or I?" "Lord Hsü is nowhere near as good looking as you!" said the guest.

The following day Lord Hsü himself came to visit. Tsou Chi stared very hard at Lord Hsü and realized that his own looks could not compare, and when he went and looked in the mirror it was obvious that the difference between them was great indeed.

That night when he went to bed he thought over the incident. "My wife says I am better looking because she is partial to me, my concubine says I am better looking because she is afraid of me, and my guest says I am better looking because he hopes to get something out of me!" he declared.

The next time he went to court and had an audience with King Wei, he said, "I am certainly not as good looking as Lord Hsü. And yet my wife, who is partial to me, my concubine, who is afraid of me, and a guest of mine, who wants something from me, all have told me that I am better looking than Lord Hsü. Now the state of Ch'i is a thousand *li* square and contains a hundred and twenty cities. In this vast realm, there are none of the palace ladies and attendants who are not partial to Your Majesty, none of the court ministers who do not fear you, and no one within the four borders who does not hope to get something from you. If that is so, think how great must be the deception you face!"

"You are right," said the king, and issued a notice saying that, to any one of the officials or people of the state who would attack his faults to his face, he would give first prize; to anyone who would submit a letter of reprimand, he would give second prize; and to anyone who would spread critical rumors in the market so that they reached his ears, he would give third prize. When the notice was first issued, the officials who came forward with criticisms packed the gate of the palace until it

looked like a market place. After several months, there were still people who came forward with criticisms from time to time. But by the end of a year, though the king might beg for reprimand, no one could any longer find anything to criticize.
—CH'I TS'E 1

*   *   *

(1)

"I hear that the north fear Chao Hsi-hsü," said the king. "What say you to this?"

None of the ministers replied, except Chiang Yi, who said, "The tiger hunts all the animals of the forest and devours them, but once when he caught a fox, the fox said, 'You dare not eat me. The Lord of Heaven ordained me chief among beasts; if now you kill me you will be disobeying the will of Heaven. If you doubt it, follow behind me through the forest and watch the animals flee when they see me.' The tiger did indeed doubt the fox and therefore followed him. Animals saw them and fled, but the tiger did not know the animals ran because they feared him—he thought they were afraid of the fox.

"Now your majesty's country is five thousand miles square and in it are a million first-class troops, all of whom are under Chao Hsi-hsü. Therefore when the north fears Hsi-hsü, in reality it fears your majesty's arms, just as the animals of the forest feared the tiger." (*Intrigues* 32, 3)

(J. I. CRUMP. JR.)

(2)

The queen of Chao had just assumed authority when Ch'in suddenly attacked. Chao sought succor of Ch'i, which country sent word that the queen's son, Prince Ch'ang-an, must be sent as hostage before the soldiers of Ch'i would come forth. The queen was unwilling, but her ministers so strongly importuned that she cried out to the courtiers: "Whosoever again urges Prince Ch'ang-an be a hostage, I will spit upon his face!"

The elderly commander, Ch'u Che, asked audience of the queen. She contained her anger enough to greet him. When he entered he walked very slowly and having reached her he apologized for himself.

"It is because your minister's feet pain him that he cannot walk quickly," he said, "and because of this it has been long since I have had audience with your majesty. But while I was excusing my absence for this reason it occurred to me that perhaps your majesty's own comfort might be similarly impaired; which is why I asked audience."

"I go about only in the palanquin," she replied.

"The quality of your majesty's meals has not diminished?"

"I eat only to live."

"Your minister lately had a similar disinclination for food, so he forced himself to walk a short distance each day. This slightly increased the appetite, and—it is good for one's health."

"I am not able to do it," said the queen whose color had somewhat subsided.

"Your Majesty," said the commander after a moment, "I grow old and though my son Shu-ch'i is worthless and quite young I love him greatly and beseech your majesty to grant him the black uniform of the palace guards that he may win fame by risking his life for her."

"It is granted, of course," replied the queen. "How old is the boy?"

"Fifteen. But young as he is I want to put him in your majesty's service before I fill my grave."

"Does a brave man love and cherish a young son then?" asked the queen.

"More than a woman!"

The queen laughed. "Ah, a woman is a different thing entirely!"

"Your majesty," said the commander, "in my ignorance I assumed you favored your daughter, the queen of Yen, over Prince Ch'ang-an."

"My minister is completely mistaken! Prince Ch'ang-an is dearer to me."

"But when a parent loves his offspring he is ever mindful of planning far in advance for the child," replied the commander. "When your majesty parted from her daughter she clasped her daughter's feet and wept—wept for the distance that would separate them, and it saddened us. Nor did your majesty forget her when she had left, you thought of her at the time of sacrifice and prayed for her. Yet, this prayer was always, 'let her not return!' Was this not because your majesty was thinking far in the future for her child?—praying that her sons and grandsons would succeed each other as kings?"

"It was."

"But your majesty," continued the commander, "before the present three generations, and back as far as the beginnings of the kingdom of Chao have there been many sons and grandsons succeeding a king to his throne?"

"No, there have not," replied the queen.

"Has it been only Chao? Have any of the other lords been succeeded by their sons and grandsons?"

"I have not heard so."

"This is why it is said, 'an error of the present strikes the living, an error for the future strikes sons and grandsons,'" said the commander. "Surely it is not that among rulers of men sons and grandsons *must* be bad! Is it not rather that high position is given where no merit exists, that favored treatment is gotten with no effort, and much wealth has come too easily to hand?

"Your Majesty has raised Prince Ch'ang-an to high position, favored him with the richest lands and given him much wealth, but she does not order him in this present instance to show mettle for his country. When a new royal tomb is raised, what reasons will Prince Ch'ang-an have had to devote himself to Chao? This, your Majesty, is why your minister assumed you favored your daughter, the queen of Yen, since your hopes for her were of longer range."

"Let it be done as my minister wishes," said the queen.

Ch'ang-an was given a retinue of one hundred carts and went into Ch'i as hostage. And the troops of Ch'i were sent forth. (*Intrigues* 48,18)

(CRUMP)

Some Further Readings

Crump, James I., Jr. *Intrigues: Studies of the Chan-kuo Ts'e*. Ann Arbor: University of Michigan Press, 1964.

Watson, Burton. *Records of the Grand Historian of China*. 2 vols. New York: Columbia University Press, 1961.

———. *Ssu-ma Ch'ien, Grand Historian of China*. New York: Columbia University Press, 1958.

PART TWO:

HAN AND THE SIX DYNASTIES

7

PROSE-SONGS

The longest of all Chinese poetic forms is the *fu* or "prose-song." A *fu* has two stylistic features which differentiate it strikingly from other Chinese verse: (1) the *fu*-meters are freer than other meters, so free in fact that the *fu* sometimes has been called "metrical prose," "rhyme-prose," or "prose-song"; (2) the *fu* achieves its effects by an upheaping of details (the technical rhetorical term is "hypotyposis").

The word *fu* in its earlier occurrences (*viz.*, two occurrences in the *Shih Ching*) means definitely "to orate." If you put this together with the *fu*'s length, with its metrical fluidity, and with its rhetorical repetitiveness, you may be led to conclude that the *fu* is a kind of showcase speech. The *fu* that we have, in fact, in genius and in inspiration, are very like the orations of Gorgias and the "Second Sophistic." We even can find in the classically perfect *fu*, like Lu Chi's *Fu on Literature,* a structure like that of the classical oration: (1) introduction (exordium), (2) statement of facts (narration), (3) the question (proposition), (4) proof (confirmation), (5) attack on other viewpoints (refutation), and (6) summary (peroration). I am convinced by these things that the poets in China worked up the art of forensic, as did their cospirits in Greece, until it became a distinct literary form—called in China the *fu*.

Ezra Pound wrote of the "great free-verse poems of the Han poets." He was referring without doubt to the *fu*, which flourished as a poetic form in the Han Dynasty. The verse moves with much greater freedom in *fu* than in other Chinese poetic forms, but it very often fluctuates in *fu* within a rather limited range: a four-syllable or six-syllable line. The *fu* may be considered, in fact, an earlier form of the rhetorical prose called "four/six prose." The *fu*-poets used rhyme occasionally, where they felt like it or where the subject matter seemed to demand it of the form. The *fu* usually begins with an introduction in out-and-out prose, and the poet describes the circumstances under which, or the reasons for which, the *fu* was composed.

The *fu* achieves its effects by an upheaping of details. Some of the writers of the most famous *fu* were lexicographers, and they seem to have used their *fu* as word-bags into which they dumped all the words they knew or had uncovered in their research. The poet may heap up the names of a dozen or more different birds to present the bird life in some place, or he may heap together verb after verb to present a river as it falls down a cliffside. When the *fu*-poet heaps up noun on noun, he may sound to the modern reader like Whitman in his "catalogues";

Whitman was another poet who was consciously influenced by the orator's art.

Whether we delight in this upheaping, or feel that it is "too much, too much," we should know about the *fu* as one of China's most important literary forms and as a literary form which "reigned supreme" during the Han Dynasty. One tale has it that the people so loved Ssu-ma Hsiang-ju's *fu* that the demand for editions of it caused the price of paper to go up in that province. But this story may be a joke about the poem's length.

In Chinese literary criticism, *fu* usually are sorted into four categories: (1) narrative *fu,* (2) "chant things" *fu,* (3) "speak patterns" *fu,* and (4) "imitate *Sao*" *fu.* In the "chant things" *fu,* the poet takes as his subject some real object (or collection of objects, like a place) and tries to tell us all there is to know about it, which sometimes is more than we want to know. The "thing" about which the poet chants may be a lute, the wind, a famous park, or even (Lu Chi wrote one) literature. The "speak patterns" *fu* is philosophical in drift: the word "patterns" (*li*) refers to the abstractions and generalities in which philosophical discussions deal. In "imitate *Sao*" *fu,* the poet imitates Ch'ü Yuan's *Li Sao* (see page 130).

Of the *fu* which you will read, most are "chant things" *fu;* this type was the most popular. *The Owl Fu* most obviously is a "speak patterns" or philosophical *fu.* The general outline of a hunt in *The Kao T'ang Fu* might, or might not, qualify it as a narrative *fu.*

The Kao T'ang Fu

by Sung Yü (third century B.C.)

Once when Hsiang, King of Ch'u, was walking with Sung Yü on the Cloud Dream Terrace, he looked up at the Kao T'ang Shrine. Above it was a coil of mist, now pointing steadily skywards like a pinnacle of rock, now suddenly dissolving and in a single moment diffused into a thousand diverse shapes. Then the King questioned Sung Yü, saying, "What Cloud-spirit is this?" And Yü answered: "It is called Morning Cloud." The King said: "Why has it this name?" and Yü answered: "Long ago a former king was wandering upon this mountain of Kao T'ang. When night came he was tired and slept beyond the dawn. And early in the morning he dreamt that a lady stood before him saying, 'I am a girl from the Witches' Hill. I have come as a stranger to Kao T'ang, and hearing that my lord the King was travelling on this same mountain, I desired to offer him the service of pillow and mat.' So the King lay with her, and when they parted, she said to him: 'My home is on the southern side of the Witches' Hill, where from its rounded summit a sudden chasm falls. At dawn I am the Morning Cloud; at dusk, the Driving Rain. So dawn by dawn and dusk by dusk I dwell beneath the southern crest.'

"Next day at sunrise he looked towards the hill, and it was even as she had said. Therefore he built her a shrine in the place where she had come to him and called it the Temple of the Morning Cloud."

Then King Hsiang questioned Sung Yü, saying, "Tell me of this Morning Cloud, in what guise does she first appear?" And Yü answered: "Still is she and sombre as a forest of tall pines, where tree stands close to tree; but soon she kindles with a shimmering light; as when a beautiful lady, looking for her

lover, raises lawn sleeves to shade her eyes from the sun.
Suddenly her being is transformed; swiftly now she races as a
chariot whirled onward by galloping steeds, with feathery flags
outspread. From the rain a dankness she borrows, and from the
wind an icy breath. But soon the wind has dropped, the rain
has cleared, and Morning Cloud has vanished from the sky."

The King said: "May I too visit the mountain whereon she
was met?" Sung Yü answered: "Your Majesty may do so."
The King said: "What manner of place is it?" Yü answered:
"It is a high, conspicuous hill, from whose summit immeasur-
able prospects may be scanned. Broad is it and vast; parent
and home of ten thousand creatures. Its summit is in the realms
of Heaven; its base is founded in the deep. Its marvels cannot
be told, nor its giant prodigies rehearsed." The King said:
"Nevertheless I beg you to sing of it for me," and Sung Yü
did not refuse.

To what shall I liken this high and desolate hill?
In all the world it has no kin.
The Witches' Mountain
Knows no such terraces, such causeways of coiling stone.
Climb the treeless rocks, look down into the deep.
Where under their tall banks the gathered waters lie.
After long rain the sky has cleared afresh.
A hundred valleys hold concourse! In silent wrath
Mad waters tussle, the high floods
Brim abreast and tumble to their home.
The shallows spread and spread, the restless pools
Mount their steep shores.
Ever the wind blows; great waves are piled
Like barrows on a lonely field;
Now on a widening bed
They jostle savagely or beat upon their shores;

Now cramped, they draw together and are at peace.
Now in precipitous creeks, with violence renewed,
High they bound as breakers that an ocean-ship
Sees on the Stony Foreland flung.
The pebbles grind their flinty sides, grate and churn
With a din that shakes the sky.
The great rocks drown; rise up, and sink again,
Or suddenly above the waves stand high and bare.
The turbulent eddies reel and swirl;
Great waves go floundering;
They run, they leap into the air, they dance;
Scrimmage like clouds, could clouds echo
With cataractine roar.

Wild beasts dance in terror, fly headlong from the flood,
Quaking tiger, panther, wolf and buffalo dismayed—
Panting they skelter; eagle and osprey, falcon and kite
Take wing and hide themselves away;
Haunch quaking, breath bated—
No heart to pounce or snatch.

And now the creatures of the water, scaly kind
And serpent, chased by panic from their dens,
Mount to safe sunshine one and all upon an island-bank;
Scorpion and alligator, turtle and giant crab
In scrambling shoals criss-crossed,
Fins floundering, scales flourished—
Now slithering, now twining,
They gain the middle bank and stare afar.

They see dark trees whose winter-flowers
Dazzle the eye; white shine those woods
As a full heaven, where star is blent with star.

And over many woods of chestnut-trees
Thick leaf and blossom brood;
Here twin catalpas trail their cups
From branches subtly twined.
Through the dark leafage ripples roam.
Tides run; to east and west
The forest spreads her wings
In delicate wafting of innumerable thrills;
Green leaves, purple fruit-skins,
Red buds, white stems
And slender branches wailing
Reed-music to the wind.
Climb higher, look afar.
Tall cliffs by their dizzy winding
Confound the eye. Yonder in rank are propped
Stupendous spires; here are great boulders split
In hideous escarpment, leaning crags,
And cliffs from whose disrupted crest
Rock slithers after rock
Into a chaos of disastered stone.
Horned pinnacles rear back at the chasm's brink,
Dismayed and staggering.

So in huge conglomeration
Bulk is strewn on bulk, pile heaped on pile;
Till, topping all, the pillared summit soars
Like a great mowers'-stone
Erect beneath the towering of the inland hills.

Above, a rainbow glistens on the hill's grave crest;
Below, a void whose chasms seem
Bottomless, save for the voice
Of pine-trees carried upward on the wind.

Steep tilts the sodden bank, noisy with filtering waters;
Bear-wise clambers the traveller, slinging from tree to
    tree.
Will the climbing never be ended?
Sweat pours from his limbs;
He stops, he is bewildered, dares not move.
Loneliness besets him, disappointment and weak irresolute
    grief.
Often in such case
The soul is changed, fears causeless come,
Hearts fabled stout, of Meng Fen or Hsia Yü,
Forget their boldness. For suddenly (whence came they?)
Flock bestial legions, hairy multitudes.
Creatures magically spawned, children of ghost or god,
Some winged, some footed; all terrible, huge and strange,
Beyond the power of tale to tell.

Around the shrine
Flat spreads the mountain-roof and wide,
A mighty flail, on whose broad palm
Thick grow the scented herbs, orchis and river-broom,
Crow's-fan, clustering thyme, grey lavender.
Delicately the grasses dip and myriad bushes blend
The scent of tender boughs, wherein,
Each seeking his lost mate,
Small birds lament; from neighbouring twig
Trill answers trill—the royal-coot,
The yellow witwall, herald-of-dusk, warbler of Ch'u,
Desolate-bride, sister-come-home again
And trailing pheasant housed in his high nest
In the fresh season carol at their play
Lusty and heedless; or in sudden choir declaim
Skilled music matched to the stream's pause and flow.

Here dwell masters of magic, wizards of the North;
On high they roam in happy throngs, to gather in
The sacrificial grain. See, now they dedicate
The stainless victim, hymn the Lord
Of the Revolving Chamber, to the many Gods
Libations pour; with worship venerate
The Unity Supreme.
The prayers are over, the liturgies incanted.
Then shall my lord the King
Ride in a magic chariot of jade
By tawny dragons drawn.
Banners and tall gonfalons shall he trail
Whose pennons intertwine. Harpers shall pluck
Their giant chords, and courtly music flow,
Tinged by the eager winds that pass
With sadness not its own;
Legends of anguish, sorrowful tales shall the singer's voice
Temper to that unhappy tune
Till they that listen throb with answering sighs.

Last come the serried huntsmen, knee to knee,
Many as the stars of heaven. For winged hunt
The word is passed; they set the gags between their teeth
And suddenly are dumb
Not yet from arbalest or bow
Is arrow shot; no net is spread.
Over wide streams they wade, through tangled thickets
    stride.
Ere the bird take wind to fly or the beast set foot to roam,
Suddenly, through stroke invisible, blood spirts on haunch
    or claw.
The huntsman's work is ended; the carts are heavy with
    prey.

Such is the Mountain of Kao T'ang.

But should my lord desire to hunt there he must needs practise long abstinence and fasting, and by augury select the day and hour. He must be dressed in black; he must be carried in an unpainted chair. His banner must be woven with clouds; his streamers must be fashioned like the rainbow, his awning, of halcyon feathers.

Then the wind shall rise, the rain shall cease, and for a thousand leagues the clear sky shall be unfurled. And when the last cloud has vanished, he shall go quietly to the place of meeting.

Thereafter shall my lord the King deal kindly for ever with the thousand lands, sorrow for the wrongs of his people, promote the wise and good, and make whole whatever was amiss. No longer shall the apertures of his intelligence be choked; to his soul's scrutiny all hidden things shall be laid bare. His years shall be prolonged, his strength eternally endure.

(ARTHUR WALEY)

The Wind Fu

by Sung Yü

King Hsiang of Ch'u was taking his ease in the Palace of the Orchid Terrace, with his courtiers Sung Yü and Ching Ch'a attending him, when a sudden gust of wind came sweeping in. The king, opening wide the collar of his robe and facing into it, said, "How delightful this wind is! And I and the common people may share it together, may we not?"

But Sung Yü replied, "This wind is for Your Majesty alone. How could the common people have a share in it?"

"The wind," said the king, "is the breath of heaven and earth. Into every corner it unfolds and reaches; without choosing between high or low, exalted or humble, it touches everywhere. What do you mean when you say that this wind is for me alone?"

Sung Yü replied, "I have heard my teacher say that the twisted branches of the lemon tree invite the birds to nest, and hollows and cracks summon the wind. But the breath of the wind differs with the place which it seeks out."

"Tell me," said the king. "Where does the wind come from?" Sung Yü answered:

"The wind is born from the land
And springs up in the tips of the green duckweed.
It insinuates itself into the valleys
And rages in the canyon mouth,
Skirts the corners of Mount T'ai
And dances beneath the pines and cedars.
Swiftly it flies, whistling and wailing;
Fiercely it splutters its anger.
It crashes with a voice like thunder,
Whirls and tumbles in confusion,
Shaking rocks, striking trees,
Blasting the tangled forest.
Then, when its force is almost spent,
It wavers and disperses,
Thrusting into crevices and rattling door latches.
Clean and clear,
It scatters and rolls away.
Thus it is that this cool, fresh hero wind,
Leaping and bounding up and down,
Climbs over the high wall
And enters deep into palace halls.

With a puff of breath it shakes the leaves and flowers,
Wanders among the cassia and pepper trees,
Or soars over the swift waters.
It buffets the mallow flower,
Sweeps the angelica, touches the spikenard,
Glides over the sweet lichens and lights on willow shoots,
Rambling over the hills
And their scattered host of fragrant flowers.
After this, it wanders into the courtyard,
Ascends the jade hall in the north,
Clambers over gauze curtains,
Passes through the inner apartments,
And so becomes Your Majesty's wind.
When this wind blows on a man,
At once he feels a chill run through him,
And he sighs at its cool freshness.
Clear and gentle,
It cures sickness, dispels drunkenness,
Sharpens the eyes and ears,
Relaxes the body and brings benefit to men.
This is what is called the hero wind of Your Majesty."

"How well you have described it!" exclaimed the king.
"But now may I hear about the wind of the common people?"
And Sung Yü replied:

"The wind of the common people
Comes whirling from the lanes and alleys,
Poking in the rubbish, stirring up the dust,
Fretting and worrying its way along.
It creeps into holes and knocks on doors,
Scatters sand, blows ashes about,
Muddles in dirt and tosses up bits of filth.

It sidles through hovel windows
And slips into cottage rooms.
When this wind blows on a man,
At once he feels confused and downcast.
Pounded by heat, smothered in dampness,
His heart grows sick and heavy,
And he falls ill and breaks out in a fever.
Where it brushes his lips, sores appear;
It strikes his eyes with blindness.
He stammers and cries out,
Not knowing if he is dead or alive.
This is what is called the lowly wind of the common people."

(WATSON)

The Owl Fu

by *Chia I* (200–168 B.C.)

In the year tan-o,
Fourth month, first month of summer
The day kuei-tzu, when the sun was low in the west,
An owl came to my lodge
And perched on the corner of my mat,
Phlegmatic and fearless.
Secretly wondering the reason
The strange thing had come to roost,
I took out a book to divine it
And the oracle told me its secret:
"Wild bird enters the hall;
The master will soon depart."
I asked and importuned the owl,
"Where is it I must go?

Do you bring good luck? Then tell me!
Misfortune? Relate what disaster!
Must I depart so swiftly?
Then speak to me of the hour!"
The owl breathed a sigh,
Raised its head and beat its wings.
Its beak could utter no word,
But let me tell you what it sought to say:
All things alter and change;
Never a moment of ceasing.
Revolving, whirling, and rolling away;
Driven far off and returning again;
Form and breath passing onward,
Like the mutations of a cicada.
Profound, subtle, and illimitable,
Who can finish describing it?
Good luck must be followed by bad;
Bad in turn bow to good.
Sorrow and joy throng the gate;
Weal and woe in the same land.
Wu was powerful and great;
Under Fu-ch'a it sank in defeat.
Yüeh was crushed at K'uai-chi,
But Kou-chien made it an overlord.
Li Ssu, who went forth to greatness, at last
Suffered the five mutilations.
Fu Yüeh was sent into bondage,
Yet Wu Ting made him his aide.
Thus forture and disaster
Entwine like the strands of a rope.
Fate cannot be told of,
For who shall know its ending?
Water, troubled, runs wild;
The arrow, quick-sped, flies far.

All things, whirling and driving,
Compelling and pushing each other, roll on.
The clouds rise up, the rains come down,
In confusion inextricably joined.
The Great Potter fashions all creatures,
Infinite, boundless, limit unknown.
There is no reckoning Heaven,
Nor divining beforehand the Tao.
The span of life is fated;
Man cannot guess its ending.
Heaven and Earth are the furnace,
The workman, the Creator;
His coal is the yin and the yang,
His copper, all things of creation.
Joining, scattering, ebbing and flowing,
Where is there persistence or rule?
A thousand, a myriad mutations,
Lacking an end's beginning.
Suddenly they form a man:
How is this worth taking thought of?
They are transformed again in death:
Should this perplex you?
The witless takes pride in his being,
Scorning others, a lover of self.
The man of wisdom sees vastly
And knows that all things will do.
The covetous run after riches,
The impassioned pursue a fair name;
The proud die struggling for power,
While the people long only to live.
Each drawn and driven onward,
They hurry east and west.
The great man is without bent;
A million changes are as one to him.

The stupid man chained by custom
Suffers like a prisoner bound.
The sage abandons things
And joins himself to the Tao alone,
While the multitudes in delusion
With desire and hate load their hearts.
Limpid and still, the true man
Finds his peace in the Tao alone,
Transcendent, destroying self.
Vast and empty, swift and wild,
He soars on wings of the Tao.
Borne on the flood he sails forth;
He rests on the river islets.
Freeing his body to Fate,
Unpartaking of self,
His life is a floating,
His death a rest.
In stillness like the stillness of deep springs,
Like an unmoored boat drifting aimlessly,
Valuing not the breath of life,
He embraces and drifts with Nothing.
Comprehending Fate and free of sorrow,
The man of virtue heeds no bonds.
Petty matters, weeds and thorns—
What are they to me?

(WATSON)

The Upper Grove Fu

by Ssu-ma Hsiang-ju (d. 118 B.C.)

". . . What do the states of Ch'i and Ch'u possess, that
they are worth speaking about? You gentlemen perhaps have

never laid eyes upon true splendor. Have you not heard of the Shang-lin Park of the Son of Heaven?

To the east of it lies Ts'ang-wu,
To the west, the land of Hsi-chi;
On its south runs the Cinnabar River,
On the north, the Purple Deeps.
Within the park spring the Pa and Ch'an rivers,
And through it flow the Ching and Wei,
The Feng, the Hao, the Lao, and the Chüeh,
Twisting and turning their way
Through the reaches of the park;
Eight rivers, coursing onward,
Spreading in different directions, each with its own form.
North, south, east, and west
They race and tumble,
Pouring through the chasms of Pepper Hill,
Skirting the banks of the river islets,
Winding through the cinnamon forests
And across the broad meadows.
In wild confusion they swirl
Along the bases of the tall hills
And through the mouths of the narrow gorges;
Dashed upon boulders, maddened by winding escarpments,
They writhe in anger,
Leaping and curling upwards,
Jostling and eddying in great swells
That surge and batter against each other;
Darting and twisting,
Foaming and tossing
In a thundering chaos;
Arching into hills, billowing like clouds,
They dash to left and right,
Plunging and breaking in waves

That chatter over the shallows;
Crashing against the cliffs, pounding the embankments,
The waters pile up and reel back again,
Skipping across the rises, swooping into the hollows,
Rumbling and murmuring onward;
Deep and powerful,
Fierce and clamorous,
They froth and churn
Like the boiling waters of a cauldron,
Casting spray from their crests, until,
After their wild race through the gorges,
Their distant journey from afar,
They subside into silence,
Rolling on in peace to their long destination,
Boundless and without end,
Gliding in soundless and solemn procession,
Shimmering and shining in the sun,
To flow through giant lakes of the east
Or spill into the ponds along their banks.
Here horned dragons and red hornless dragons,
Sturgeon and salamanders,
Carp, bream, gudgeon, and dace,
Cowfish, flounder, and sheatfish
Arch their backs and twitch their tails,
Spread their scales and flap their fins,
Diving among the deep crevices;
The waters are loud with fish and turtles,
A multitude of living things.
Here moon-bright pearls
Gleam on the river slopes,
While quartz, chrysoberyl,
And clear crystal in jumbled heaps
Glitter and sparkle,

Catching and throwing back a hundred colors
Where they lie tumbled on the river bottom.
Wild geese and swans, graylags, bustards,
Cranes and mallards,
Loons and spoonbills,
Teals and gadwalls,
Grebes, night herons, and cormorants
Flock and settle upon the waters,
Drifting lightly over the surface,
Buffeted by the wind,
Bobbing and dipping with the waves,
Sporting among the weedy banks,
Gobbling the reeds and duckweed,
Pecking at water chestnuts and lotuses.
Behind them rise the tall mountains,
Lofty crests lifted to the sky;
Clothed in dense forests of giant trees,
Jagged with peaks and crags;
The steep summits of the Nine Pikes,
The towering heights of the Southern Mountains,
Soar dizzily like a stack of cooking pots,
Precipitous and sheer.
Their sides are furrowed with ravines and valleys,
Narrow-mouthed clefts and open glens,
Through which rivulets dart and wind.
About their base, hills and islands
Raise their tall heads;
Ragged knolls and hillocks
Rise and fall,
Twisting and twining
Like the coiled bodies of reptiles;
While from their folds the mountain streams leap and
    tumble,

Spilling out upon the level plains.
There they flow a thousand miles along smooth beds,
Their banks lined with dikes
Blanketed with green orchis
And hidden beneath selinea,
Mingled with snakemouth
And magnolias;
Planted with yucca,
Sedge of purple dye,
Bittersweet, gentians, and orchis,
Blue flag and crow-fans,
Ginger and turmeric,
Monkshood, wolfbane,
Nightshade, basil,
Mint, ramie, and blue artemisia,
Spreading across the wide swamps,
Rambling over the broad plains,
A vast and unbroken mass of flowers,
Nodding before the wind;
Breathing their fragrance,
Pungent and sweet,
A hundred perfumes
Wafted abroad
Upon the scented air.
Gazing about the expanse of the park
At the abundance and variety of its creatures,
One's eyes are dizzied and enraptured
By the boundless horizons,
The borderless vistas.
The sun rises from the eastern ponds
And sets among the slopes of the west;
In the southern part of the park,
Where grasses grow in the dead of winter
And the waters leap, unbound by ice,

Live zebras, yaks, tapirs, and black oxen,
Water buffalo, elk, and antelope,
'Red-crowns' and 'round-heads,'
Aurochs, elephants, and rhinoceroses.
In the north, where in the midst of summer
The ground is cracked and blotched with ice
And one may walk the frozen streams or wade the rivulets,
Roam unicorns and boars,
Wild asses and camels,
Onagers and mares,
Swift stallions, donkeys, and mules.
Here the country palaces and imperial retreats
Cover the hills and span the valleys,
Verandahs surrounding their four sides;
With storied chambers and winding porticos,
Painted rafters and jade-studded corbels,
Interlacing paths for the royal palanquin,
And arcaded walks stretching such distances
That their length cannot be traversed in a single day.
Here the peaks have been leveled for mountain halls,
Terraces raised, story upon story,
And chambers built in the deep grottoes.
Peering down into the caves, one cannot spy their end;
Gazing up at the rafters, one seems to see them brush the
    heavens;
So lofty are the palaces that comets stream through their
    portals
And rainbows twine about their balustrades.
Green dragons slither from the eastern pavilion;
Elephant-carved carriages prance from the pure hall of the
    West,
Bringing immortals to dine in the peaceful towers
And bands of fairies to sun themselves beneath the southern
    eaves.

Here sweet fountains bubble from clear chambers,
Racing in rivulets through the gardens,
Great stones lining their courses;
Plunging through caves and grottoes,
Past steep and ragged pinnacles,
Horned and pitted as though carved by hand,
Where garnets, green jade,
And pearls abound;
Agate and marble,
Dappled and lined;
Rose quartz of variegated hue,
Spotted among the cliffs;
Rock crystal, opals,
And finest jade.
Here grow citrons with their ripe fruit in summer,
Tangerines, bitter oranges and limes,
Loquats, persimmons,
Wild pears, tamarinds,
Jujubes, arbutus,
Peaches and grapes,
Almonds, damsons,
Mountain plums and litchis,
Shading the quarters of the palace ladies,
Ranged in the northern gardens,
Stretching over the slopes and hillocks
And down into the flat plains;
Lifting their leaves of kingfisher hue,
Their purple stems swaying;
Opening their crimson flowers,
Clusters of vermilion blossoms,
A wilderness of trembling flames
Lighting up the broad meadow.
Here the crab apple, chestnut and willow,
Birch, maple, sycamore and boxwood,

Pomegranate, date palm,
Betel nut and palmetto,
Sandalwood, magnolia,
Cedar and cypress
Rise a thousand feet,
Their trunks several arm-lengths around,
Stretching forth flowers and branches,
Rich fruit and luxuriant leaves,
Clustered in dense copses,
Their limbs entwined,
Their foliage a thick curtain
Over stiff and bending trunks,
Their branches sweeping to the ground
Amidst a shower of falling petals.
They tremble and sigh
As they sway with the wind;
Creaking and moaning in the breeze
Like the tinkle of chimes
Or the wail of flageolets.
High and low they grow,
Screening the quarters of the palace ladies;
A mass of sylvan darkness,
Blanketing the mountains and edging the valleys,
Ascending the slopes and dipping into the hollows,
Overspreading the horizon,
Outdistancing the eye.
Here black apes and white she-apes,
Drills, baboons, and flying squirrels,
Lemurs and langurs,
Macaques and gibbons,
Dwell among the trees,
Uttering long wails and doleful cries
As they leap nimbly to and fro,
Sporting among the limbs

And clambering haughtily to the treetops.
Off they chase across bridgeless streams
And spring into the depths of a new grove,
Clutching the low-swinging branches,
Hurtling across the open spaces,
Racking and tumbling pell-mell,
Until they scatter from sight in the distance.
Such are the scenes of the imperial park,
A hundred, a thousand settings
To visit in the pursuit of pleasure;
Palaces, inns, villas, and lodges,
Each with its kitchens and pantries,
Its chambers of beautiful women
And staffs of officials.
Here, in late fall and early winter,
The Son of Heaven stakes his palisades and holds his hunts,
Mounted in a carriage of carved ivory
Drawn by six jade-spangled horses, sleek as dragons.
Rainbow pennants stream before him;
Cloud banners trail in the wind.
In the vanguard ride the hide-covered carriages;
Behind, the carriages of his attendants.
A coachman as clever as Sun Shu grasps the reins;
A driver as skillful as the Duke of Wei stands beside him.
His attendants fan out on all sides
As they move into the palisade.
They sound the somber drums
And send the hunters to their posts;
They corner the quarry among the rivers
And spy them from the high hills.
Then the carriages and horsemen thunder forth,
Startling the heavens, shaking the earth;
Vanguard and rear dash in different directions,

Scattering after the prey.
On they race in droves,
Rounding the hills, streaming across the lowlands,
Like enveloping clouds or drenching rain.
Leopards and panthers they take alive;
They strike down jackals and wolves.
With their hands they seize the black and tawny bears,
And with their feet they down the wild sheep.
Wearing pheasant-tailed caps
And breeches of white tiger skin
Under patterned tunics,
They sit astride their wild horses;
They clamber up the steep slopes of the Three Pikes
And descend again to the river shoals,
Galloping over the hillsides and the narrow passes,
Through the valleys and across the rivers.
They fell the 'dragon-sparrows'
And sport with the *chieh-ch'ih;*
Strike the *hsia-ko*
And with short spears stab the little bears,
Snare the fabulous *yao-niao* horses
And shoot down the great boars.
No arrow strikes the prey
Without piercing a neck or shattering a skull;
No bow is discharged in vain,
But to the sound of each twang some beast must fall.
Then the imperial carriage signals to slacken pace
While the emperor wheels this way and that,
Gazing afar at the progress of the hunting bands,
Noting the disposition of their leaders.
At a sign, the Son of Heaven and his men resume their
    pace,
Swooping off again across the distant plains.

They bear down upon the soaring birds;
Their carriage wheels crush the wily beasts.
Their axles strike the white deer;
Deftly they snatch the fleeting hares;
Swifter than a flash
Of scarlet lightning,
They pursue strange creatures
Beyond the borders of heaven.
To bows like the famous Fan-jo
They fit their white-feathered arrows,
To shoot the fleeing goblin-birds
And strike down the griffins.
For their mark they choose the fattest game
And name their prey before they shoot.
No sooner has an arrow left the string
Than the quarry topples to the ground.
Again the signal is raised and they soar aloft,
Sweeping upward upon the gale,
Rising with the whirlwind,
Borne upon the void,
The companions of gods,
To trample upon the black crane
And scatter the flocks of giant pheasants,
Swoop down upon the peacocks
And the golden roc,
Drive aside the five-colored *i* bird
And down the phoenixes,
Snatch the storks of heaven
And the birds of darkness,
Until, exhausting the paths of the sky,
They wheel their carriages and return.
Roaming as the spirit moves them,
Descending to the earth in a far corner of the north,
Swift and straight is their course

As they hasten home again.
Then the emperor ascends the Stone Gate
And visits the Great Peak Tower,
Stops at the Magpie Turret
And gazes afar from the Dew Cold Observatory;
Descends to the Wild Plum Palace
And takes his ease in the Palace of Righteous Spring;
To the west he hastens to the Hsüan-ch'ü Palace
And poles in a pelican boat over Ox Head Lake.
He climbs the Dragon Terrace
And rests in the Tower of the Lithe Willows,
Weighing the effort and skill his attendants have displayed
And calculating the catch made by his huntsmen.
He examines the beasts struck down by the carriages,
Those trampled beneath the feet of the horsemen
And trod upon by the beaters;
Those which, from sheer exhaustion
Or the pangs of overwhelming terror
Fell dead without a single wound,
Where they lie, heaped in confusion,
Tumbled in the gullies and filling the hollows,
Covering the plains and strewn about the swamps.
Then, wearied of the chase,
He orders wine brought forth on the Terrace of Azure
    Heaven
And music for the still and spacious halls.
His courtiers, sounding the massive bells
That swing from the giant bell rack,
Raising the pennants of kingfisher feathers
And setting up the drum of sacred lizard skin,
Present for his pleasure the dances of Yao
And the songs of the ancient Emperor Ko;
A thousand voices intone,
Ten thousand join in harmony,

And the mountains and hills rock with echoes
And the valley waters quiver to the sound.
The dances of Pa-yü, of Sung and Ts'ai,
The Yü-che song of Huai-nan,
The airs of Tien and Wen-ch'eng,
One after another in groups they perform,
Sounding in succession the gongs and drums
Whose shrill clash and dull booming
Pierce the heart and startle the ear.
The tunes Ching, Wu, Cheng, and Wei,
The Shao, Huo, Wu, and Hsiang music,
And amorous and carefree ditties
Mingle with the songs of Yen and Ying,
'Onward Ch'u!' and 'The Gripping Wind.'
Then come actors, musicians and trained dwarfs,
And singing girls from the land of Ti-ti,
To delight the ear and eye
And bring mirth to the mind;
On all sides a torrent of gorgeous sounds,
A pageant of enchanting color.
Here are maidens to match
The goddesses Blue Lute and Princess Fu;
Creatures of matchless beauty,
Seductive and fair,
With painted faces and carved hairpins,
Fragile and full of grace,
Lithe and supple,
Of delicate feature and form,
Trailing cloaks of sheerest silk
And long robes that seem as though carved and painted,
Swirling and fluttering about them
Like magic garments;
With them wafts a cloud of scent,

A delicious perfume;
White teeth sparkle
In engaging smiles,
Eyebrows arch delicately,
Eyes cast darting glances,
Until their beauty has seized the soul of the beholder
And his heart in joy hastens to their side." . . .

(WATSON)

The Poverty Fu

by Yang Hsiung (53 B.C.–A.D. 18)

I, Yang Tzu, hid from life
Fled from the common world to a lonely place,
Where to the right a great wilderness touched me,
And on the left my neighbour was the Hill of Sung.
Beggars whose tenements
Lie wall to wall, though they be tattered and poor,
Rough-used, despised and scorned, are yet in companies
And sociable clans conjoined. But I, for solitude
Too sorrowful, faltered at heart and cried aloud,
"O Poverty, come hither and talk with me!
For should I be flung
To the utmost frontiers of space,
To the tenantless margins of the world,
Yet wouldst thou be with me;
Thy henchman am I, O Poverty,
And thy harsh penalties, my pay.
Not in childhood only, in infancy
When laughing I would build
Castles of soil or sand, wast thou
My more than neighbour, for thy roof

Touched mine, and our two homes were one;
But in manhood also weighed I with the great,
Lighter, because of thee,
Than fluff or feather; more frail my fortunes
Than gossamer, who to the State submitting
Great worth, found small employ;
Withdrawing, heard no blame.''

Then many years I wandered as a stranger
With these thoughts in my heart:
"Others wear broidered coats; my homespun is not
    whole.
Others eat millet and rice, I boil the fennel-leaf.
No toy nor treasure is mine,
Nor aught to make me glad.
The swallows by my father's house
Play on; but I abroad the world
Sell my day-labour, pawn my coat for bread.
Servant of many masters,
Hand-chafed I dig, heel-blistered hoe,
Bare-backed to the wind and rain.
And that all this befell me,
That friends and favourites forsook me,
That up the hill of State so laboured was my climb,
Who should bear blame? Who but thou, O Poverty,
Was cause of all my woe?

"I fled thee high and far, but thou across the hills of
    heaven
Like a hawk didst follow me.
I fled thee among the rocks, in caverns of stone I hid;
But thou up those huge steeps
Didst follow me.

I fled thee to the ocean, sailed that cypress ship
Across the storm, but thou,
Whether on wave-crest or in the hollows of the sea,
Didst ever follow me.
And if I move, you too are stirring;
If I lie down, you are at rest.
Have you no other friend in the world?
What would you seek of me?
Go, Poverty! and pester me no more."

Then said Poverty: "So be it, my master;
For 'tis plain that should I stay
You will not cease to slander and defame me.
But listen, I too have a heart that is full
And a tale that must be told.

"My father's father long, long ago
Was illustrious in the land; of virtue so excellent
That by the King's throne in council he stood,
Admonishing the rulers how to make statutes and laws.
Of earth were the stairs, roofed over with thatch,
Not carved nor hung.
But when the world in latter days
Was given over to folly, fell about in darkness,
Then gluttons gathered together,
Sought wealth and found it,
Despised my grand-dad, they were so insolent and proud;
Built arbours of onyx, terraces of jade,
And huge halls to dwell in; lapped lakes of wine.
On a broth of swans they fed,
And held no Audience at their court.
Thrice daily would they look into their souls and cry,
'Our hearts are free from sin.'

And they that dwelt in the Palace of the King
Had great substance, and their guerdon was gold
Stacked high as the hills.

"Your small woes you remember;
But my blest deeds you have forgot.
Did I not teach you
By gradual usage, indifferent to endure
Summer's heat and winter's cold?
(And that which neither heat nor cold can touch—
Is it not eternal as the Gods?)

"I, Poverty,
Turned from you the envy of the covetous, taught you to
    fear
Neither Chieh the Tyrant nor the Robber Chih.
Others, my master,
Quake behind bolt and bar, while you alone
Live open to the world.
Others by care
And pitiful apprehension are cast down,
While you are gay and free."
Thus spoke Poverty, and when her speech was ended,
Stern of countenance and with dilated eye,
She gathered up the folds of her garment and rose from
    where she sat,
Passed down the stairway and left my house.

"Farewell," said Poverty, "for now I leave you.
To that hill I take my way
Where sheltering, the Lord of Kuchu's sons
Have learnt to ply my trade."
Then I, Yang Tzu, left the mat where I lay

And cried: "O Poverty, let my crooked words
Be as unspoken; forget that I have wronged thee.
I have heard truth, O Poverty, and received it.
Live with me always, for of your company
I shall not weary till I die."
Then Poverty came back and dwelt with me,
Nor since has left my side.

(WALEY)

Some Further Readings

Hughes, E. R. *Two Chinese Poets*. Princeton, N.J.: Princeton University Press, 1960.

Waley, Arthur, trans. *The Temple and Other Poems*. New York: Alfred A. Knopf, 1923.

Watson, Burton, trans. *Chinese Rhyme Prose: Poems in the Fu Form from the Han and Six Dynasties Period*. New York: Columbia University Press, 1971.

8

COUNTRY MUSIC

China—really an empire, not a nation—has been unified at various times in its history as Europe never was. The imperial government had to keep in touch with the people's temper and spirit, even in the remoter provinces of the empire. How did the government thus "keep in touch?" It collected folk songs and used them to read the people's moods and feelings; it is because of this practice that the Chinese today have a great store of folk songs from the earliest periods.

During the Han Dynasty (206 B.C.–A.D. 220), the emperor set up a governmental bureau to collect, to edit, to interpret, and to preserve these songs. The new bureau was called *Yueh Fu* or "Music Bureau," and the name *yueh fu* has come to designate the folk songs which were preserved. We shall read in this section a number of these *yueh fu* pieces, which may appropriately be called "country music."

The term "folk song" may be a little misleading. These *yueh fu* pieces sometimes contain attitudes and expressions which are very sophisticated indeed. The best way to describe *yueh fu* pieces probably is to say that they were written by people who were not members of the scholar class. Some *yueh fu* pieces, no doubt, were by the peasantry or by "simple" folk. But others—like the nineteen poems by the wineshop girl Tzu Yeh which have been included in this chapter—show that they were written by more urbane and sophisticated individuals. The wineshop girls, like today's *maiko* and *geisha* in Japan, were professional entertainers who received careful and serious training. The ability to write a good verse was not the least prized of their skills.

—THEY FOUGHT SOUTH OF THE CITY—

(first century A.D.)

We fought in the south
Died in the north
Field-slain, unburied, crows devour us.
For us, tell the crows:
"For you we stay.
"Field-slain, we'll be unburied.
"Shall rotten flesh get away?"
. . .
God, my God—
What good south;
North, what good?

Corn, wheat unreaped—the lord's food.
We would be true men if we could.

Envoi:
Learn: You were good men.
Good men surely shall learn:
Dawn, go out to battle;
Dusk, you shall not return.

(MCNAUGHTON)

—A BALLAD OF THE MULBERRY ROAD—

The sun rises in south east corner of things
To look on the tall house of the Shin
For they have a daughter named Rafu,
      (pretty girl)

She made the name for herself: "Gauze Veil,"
For she feeds mulberries to silkworms.
She gets them by the south wall of the town.
With green strings she makes the warp of her basket,
She makes the shoulder-straps of her basket
      from the boughs of Katsura,
And she piles her hair up on the left side of her head-
    piece.
Her earrings are made of pearl,
Her underskirt is of green pattern-silk,
Her overskirt is the same silk dyed in purple,
And when men going by look on Rafu
      They set down their burdens,
They stand and twirl their moustaches.

(POUND)

Northern Folk Songs

—SONG OF BREAKING THE WILLOW BRANCH—

Inside of me
    my grief will not be lightened.
I turn and wield
    the horse-whips of Lang.
I go, I come
    wearing the arm of Lang,
I dance, I sit
    beside the knees of Lang:

Far off, I look
    at the Mengford River:
Willows and sallows,
    lovely, curve and weave;
I even I
    come from barbarian home
And don't understand
    the songs of those of Han.

He who is strong
    needs a hard-running horse.
A hard-running horse
    needs him who is strong.
Gallop, gallop
    under the yellow dust—
Then you shall know
    who belongs to the bold.

(MCNAUGHTON)

—THE SONG OF THE LANGYA KING—

The five-foot sword I have just bought
Is hanging from the middle beam.
I fondle it time and again daily
With more devotion than I would a
      maiden of fifteen.

(CH'EN SHOU-YI)

Tzu Yeh Songs (fourth century A.D.)

(1)

A hundred hundred songs and chants
Yet Tzu Yeh most may move me.
Feelingly the clear sounds flower
Brilliantly the turns fall free.

(2)

Guitars and flutes
      echo each phrase
Clear sounds
      rest on steady drums
This singer
      has no studied style
From her heart
      most moving music comes.

(3)

Spring flowers
      seductive thoughts
Spring birds
      sad thoughts

Spring winds
        (chaotic thoughts)
Blow open
        my silk net skirt.

(4)

Dawn
Leaving and thinking
        I pass through the front gate
Evening
Returning and thinking
        I ascend the rear slope
Sighing, I ask
        to whom shall I speak?
In my woman's heart
        dark image of you.

(5)

Birds coldly hang in the high tree
Bitter winds scream in the withered wood
Beloved, this total haggard melancholy's
Bound to do my looks great good.

(6)

Grab the pillow
Wait at our window
Sleep, maybe.

When and if
This guy comes
        we really live.

Few pleasures
Fewer excuses
God!

How many times
       can I forgive?

(7)

In thin silk dress
       red sleeves a-flutter
In crescent earrings
       hairpin of jade
In restless melting mood
In steps across the dews of spring
I stroll.

A sensuous search
       for a bold someone
With a heart like mine.

(8)

From the moment
       my love left
What day's moment
       thought I not of love?

I fear the showering petals of spring
That never gain again
       the branch above.

(9)

Moon bright
       in the high star sky

Spring night
>   and the cool wind rises
Orchid house
>   and they quarrel
>   as they pretty and prepare
Behind lace curtains
Someone waiting
>   once again to be
>   love-stirred.

(10)

Spring's wind makes a Spring heart.
Idle eyes linger on the hills and trees.
Hills and trees bedazzle with their brilliancies
And mating birds erupt in raucous song.

(11)

The hours of the night are gone.
What time will find us here again?
The empty chessboard in the candle flame
Still waits,
>   for the chess game.

(12)

Calling night birds
>   cry in the bamboo wood.
Falling plum flowers
>   fill the moonlit paths.
A pleasing lady
>   strolls in the Spring night,
Gauze hem dragging
>   in the scented grass.

(13)

Shining winds flow over
        an edge of moon.
Budding trees unroll
        bright brocade flowers.
Tender people play
        in Spring's night,
Trailing slender hands
        from silk sleeves.

(14)

Back and forth he goes
        on bamboo flowers
As yet unable to unlatch
        the outside screens,
A bold lord
        caught inside this place
Until I've put on clothes
        and fixed my face.

(15)

Newly yellow
        grow the garden flowers
Southern pools
        are just now turning green.
Someone begins
        to fill the cups with wine
And tuned lutes
        start the last twist.

(16)

I'm too young
to play these games—

False starts,
subterfuge, lies

But you are like
unanchored duckweed

Changing every
shift of Spring's wind.

(17)

Stripped branches
        wind-bend to the light.
White covering dew
        makes crystal frost.
The wish-weary traveler
        climbs to see
High-flying geese
        that cut the heart.

(18)

Snow still stays
        on the dark ridge.
Red-bud shines
        in the sunny wood.
Who need sound
        guitar or flute
When hills themselves
        are reed and lute?

(19)

Autumn moon's
        at the open shutter

The lights put out
           sheer robes gone wide.
Within silk curtains
           someone smiles
The lifted orchids come untied.

           (MAYHEW AND MCNAUGHTON)

Western Twists (Ch'ü)

(1)

Near the third month
           in warm bright spring
Grass and stream
           match yellow
On the road
I walk to meet
           a handsome tender fellow.

A hateful thing
           if just at first
I found I didn't know him
After four years
Or almost five
           of waiting waiting for him.

Today my feelings all are ripe
My soul is vexed and ready.
I want to find
           a private place
And there turn bodies
           and embrace.

(2)
—BY THE STONE WALL—

More than a hundred sails
Curve and recurve at the river ford
Raising my hand to shade my eyes
I watch.
Tears fall.
What day shall I watch
The return of my beloved?

(3)

I saw you leave, beloved
At Plank-Bridge bay.

On top of Three Mountains
I wait today.

A thousand sails
Drift far away,

Following winds
They drift and flow

I know these winds
That always go
        these drifting boats that follow.

Dark on Three Mountains
The boats still go
I long for you
        and the love we know.

A thousand *li* journey
I'd be taking
For love-making.

Dark on Three Mountains
The boats still go
I long for you
          and the love we know.
          (MAYHEW AND MCNAUGHTON)

(4)
—HSIANG YANG TUNE—

Morning, set out
from the Hsiang
Yang wall.

Evening, arrive
at Ta
T'i to lodge

At Ta T'i,
numbers
of women and girls,

Flowerlike in beauty,
bedazzle
the traveler's eyes.

          (MCNAUGHTON)

Some Further Readings

Frodsham, J. D., trans. *An Anthology of Chinese Verse*. With the collaboration of Ch'eng Hsi. London and New York: Oxford University Press, 1967. (Also contains material relevant to Chapters 9, 10, and 11.)

Mayhew, Lenore, and McNaughton, William, trans. *A Gold Orchid: The Love Poems of Tzu Yeh*. Rutland, Vt., and Tokyo: Charles E. Tuttle Co., 1972.

9

THE POETRY OF EXILE

Men of letters, throughout Chinese history, have held such an exalted position, and have been so important to the administration and maintenance of the imperial government, that the poet's or man of letter's situation in political crises was a dangerous one. One poet who wrote the line "What is more red than red?" was beheaded by an emperor because the emperor supposed he was suggesting that another man was fitter to be emperor than he.

During the period in history that followed the Han Dynasty's decay and collapse (A.D. 220), aspirant after aspirant struggled, fought, and died to sit on the "dragon throne" of China's emperor. And when an aspirant failed, it often followed that most of his partisans died with him, or soon afterward.

Many men of letters in this period, seeing what was happening to colleagues who got caught up in factions, cliques, and conspiracies, withdrew completely from politics. Men of letters organized a *ch'ing-t'an* movement.

Ch'ing-t'an is usually translated as "unsullied discourse" or "*pure* conversations"; the participants agreed to exclude from their conversation all topical and political issues. It was self-defense. Naturally they had to eschew the Confucian ideals of social reform and of "trying harder." So they moved to the other pole of Chinese philosophy, and the themes of Taoism run like warp through the poetry of this period.

Some poets chose exile. In China this meant to move from civilization and out into the wild mountainous regions (see also, in Chapter 10, "Rivers and Mountains Poetry"): the theme of the *sennin*—a recluse or hermit, often "bohemian" and eccentric—emerged. Kuo P'u (A.D. 276–324) wrote a sequence called "Poems of the Wandering Sennin." Although this retreat into the mountains was, perhaps, not exile beyond the geographical borders of China, it was exile from the society.

Other poets, remaining in the civilized world, chose an "inner exile." For some of these, "inner exile" meant that their poetry, like the conversation of the *ch'ing-t'an,* was devoted to philosophical speculation and to poems about "the Great Void"; for others, it meant an affected simplemindedness, irresponsibility, or devotion to wine: the famous literary group "The Seven Sages of the Bamboo Grove" includes some of the most famous drunks in Chinese history. These two features—wine and philosophical speculations about "the Great Void"—led Ezra Pound to characterize the age:

> and there were three kingdoms
> and booze in the bamboo grove

>   where they sang: emptiness is the
>   beginning of all things (Canto LIV)

Juan Chi (A.D. 210–263), one of the most famous of the "Seven Sages of the Bamboo Grove," was approached by representatives of the powerful Ssu-ma Chao to form a marriage alliance between their two clans. Juan Chi was too drunk to work out details with the envoys, so they returned the next day, and Juan was drunk again; again they returned, and Juan again was drunk. This scenario was repeated for sixty days in a row, until Ssu-ma Chao had to give up the project, and Juan Chi and his clan got out uncommitted and unentangled.

—THE RUINS OF LO–YANG—

by Ts'ao Chih (192–232)

I climb to the ridge of the Pei-mang Hills
And look down on the city of Lo-yang
In Lo-yang how still it is!
Palaces and houses all burnt to ashes.
Walls and fences all broken and gaping,
Thorns and brambles shooting up to the sky.
I do not see the old old-men;
I only see the new young men.
I turn aside, for the straight road is lost;
The fields are overgrown and will never be ploughed
    again.

I have been away such a long time
That I do not know which path is which.
How sad and ugly the empty moors are!
A thousand miles without the smoke of a chimney.
I think of our life together all those years;
My heart is tied with sorrow and I cannot speak.

(WALEY)

—TAOIST SONG—

by Hsi K'ang (223–262)

I will cast out Wisdom and reject Learning;
My thoughts shall wander in the silent Void.
Always repenting of wrongs done
Will never bring my heart to rest.
I cast my hook in a single stream;

But my joy is as though I possessed a Kingdom.
I loose my hair and go singing;
To the four frontiers men join in my refrain.
This is the purport of my song:
'My thoughts shall wander in the Silent Void.'

(WALEY)

—POEMS OF MY HEART—

by Juan Chi (210–263)

(1)

Twelve o'clock.
          Unable to sleep,
I get up and sit,
          I play and sing to the ch'in.

The fragile cloths
          mirror a brilliant moon;
Metallic wind
          agitates my sleeve.

One single crane
          cries past the farthest fields;
Another bird
          sings in the northward grove
Go back, go forth.
          What shall any of us find?
Sorrowful thoughts.
          Solitude. Shaken nerve.

(2)

Cranes, each
          following other, fly
Fly, fly
          going to the wilderness' end.
Double feathers
          reach to the long wind.
Instantly,
          they travel a thousand *li*.

Mornings, they eat
          fruit of the white coral-tree;
Evenings, they stop
          at Cinnabar Mountain's edge.

They lift their bodies
          into the blue clouds.
With net and snare,
          who can bring them in?

How should one, with
          a small-town guy,
Shake hands,
          together swear an oath?

(MCNAUGHTON)

(3)

Weird dances are performed in the north
          street
And near the river decadent songs are heard.
These flighty, leisured youths,
Enslaved by fads and fashions,
Always take a short cut
To sensual pleasure.
I see no one racing against the sun
Or turning his staff into a forest.
The recipe for a long life
Alone calms my heart.

(4)

His influence—
          the scorching sun or a torrential river—
Extends a myriad miles.
His bow hangs in the tree
          on which the sun rests.
His sword leans
          against the place where the sky ends.
Mountains are his whetstones;
And the Yellow River is long enough to be his belt.
But in the eyes of a wise recluse,
Size is of the least importance.
For a giant corpse
Only feeds more vultures.

Perhaps it is only for this
That heroes and aspirants achieve fame and merit.

(JEROME CH'EN AND MICHAEL BULLOCK)

—THE TEDIOUS WAYS—

by Pao Chao (fifth century A.D.)

(1)

Do you not see, master, the hibiscus?
Its beauty seldom lasts a day.
The young in their gaudy splendour
Will soon follow the same path,
From which there is no return.
For a thousand autumns
Nothing will be heard of them.
Their lonely spirits will walk to and fro
     on empty paths or round their tombs.
They will perhaps hear birds chanting in the wind,
But be quite unable to recall bygone days.
Let us be each other's comfort
And think of them no more.

(2)

Do you not see the young men
Going to the frontiers?
     Probably they will never return.
Day and night
     they will long for a letter.
But the rivers and mountain passes
     will always dash their hopes.
The desert wind chases away scraps of white cloud
And barbarian strings accuse and embitter the cold.

Their saddening notes spiral up the hills
    to look south.
O, the youthful faces,
    have they changed?
Will barbarian horses trample them to death
Will they escape to be reunited with their families?
Life is unending tedium
    about which I have nothing else to say,
But to stand up and draw a deep breath.

(3)
Do you not see the Platform of the Cypress Beam?
Now it is only rubble and weeds.
Do you not see the old palaces
Taken over by quails and mists?
Where are the singers and dancers?
On the slopes there lie so many graves.
Their long sleeves were once deadly rivals
When worn by precious mistresses.
Did they drink and make merry when they were
    alive?
Now, underground, do they grieve?

                      (CH'EN AND BULLOCK)

Some Further Reading

Ch'en, Jerome, and Bullock, Michael, trans. *Poems of Solitude*. London: Abelard-Schuman, 1960. (Also available in an edition published by Charles E. Tuttle Co.)

10

NATURE POETRY

The Chinese have been much praised, by foreigners, for their "nature poetry." To be sure, images of a beautiful and overwhelming landscape pass through Chinese poetry: the Chinese landscape probably is not inferior to any in the world. But the Chinese themselves do not even speak of "nature poetry." They recognize instead two other kinds of poetry, both of which would go into the Western category "nature poetry." These two kinds of poetry are "farm and garden poetry" and "rivers and mountains" poetry.

FARM AND GARDEN POETRY

"Farm and garden poetry" was written in China—or at least was being preserved by anthologists—long before "rivers and mountains" poetry. I have put into our anthology at this point some typical "farm and garden" poems. You will find a bit later in this chapter a section of "rivers and mountains" poems. The way to learn the difference between the two types is to read examples of each type.

"Farm and garden" poems deal with simple, rustic scenes and subjects. Some people argue that "farm and garden" poems express the Taoist viewpoint. They may make you think of the "Taoist Utopia" about which you read earlier (see Chapter 4). The greatest of "farm and garden" poets is T'ao Ch'ien (A.D. 356–427), one of China's most famous and most beloved poets. He quit his civil service post—because he couldn't stand "to crook my knee (to superiors) for a few pecks of rice a day"—and retired to his farm.

Along with several poems, one short prose work by T'ao Ch'ien—"Peach Blossom Spring"—is included in this section on "farm and garden poetry." "Peach Blossom Spring" always has seemed to me to approach the imaginary boundary between prose and poetry, and the Chinese have loved it as much as even their best poems.

—THE VALLEY WIND—

by Lu Yün (fourth century A.D.)

Living in retirement beyond the World,
Silently enjoying isolation,
I pull the rope of my door tighter
And bind firmly this cracked jar.

My spirit is tuned to the Spring-season;
At the fall of the year there is autumn in my heart
Thus imitating cosmic changes
My cottage becomes a Universe.

(WALEY)

T'ao Ch'ien (T'ao Yuan-ming) Poems

(1)

When I was small
  I never was like-minded with the others
But had from birth
  a temperament attaching to the hills
And yet by chance
  I fell into the dust net of this world
Where in an instant
  passed some thirty years.

A trapped bird
  will hanker after his old woods
A pooled fish
  will think of his old deeps
Now that they reclaim
  the southern moors
I, holding to my stupidity,
  reclaim a farm and garden for myself.

With private house
  encircled by its land
Of grass without
  within some nine large rooms in all
Elm and willow
  shade the eaves in back

And peach and plum
                        are planted in straight rows
                                            before the hall.

Distant villages
                     are indistinct
Their thin light smoke
                     ten *li* away.
Dogs bark
                     down the long alleys
Chickens cackle
                     atop the mulberries
But the dust of my walled courtyard
                     is never scattered.

In my empty rooms are time and space.
I was a bird
                     confined within a wicker cage
But now I may return
                     to be myself
Unfretted and unfettered
                     in this self-like place.
                               (MAYHEW AND MCNAUGHTON)

(2)

Shady, shady the wood in front of the Hall;
At midsummer full of calm shadows.
The south wind follows summer's train;
With its eddying puffs it blows open my coat.
I am free from ties and can live a life of retirement
When I rise from sleep, I play with books and lute.
The lettuce in the garden still grows moist;
Of last year's grain there is always plenty left.

Self-support should maintain its strict limits;
More than enough is not what I want.
I grind millet and make good wine;
When the wine is heated, I pour it out for myself.
My little children are playing at my side,
Learning to talk, they babble unformed sounds.
These things have made me happy again
And I forget my lost cap of office.
Distant, distant I gaze at the white clouds;
With a deep yearning I think of the Sages of Antiquity.

(WALEY)

(3)

I built my hut in a zone of human habitation,
Yet near me there sounds no noise of horse or coach.
Would you know how that is possible?
A heart that is distant creates a wilderness round it.
I pluck chrysanthemums under the eastern hedge,
Then gaze long at the distant hills.
The mountain air is fresh at the dusk of day;
The flying birds two by two return.
In these things there lies a deep meaning;
Yet when we would express it, words suddenly fail us.

(WALEY)

(4)

—MOVING HOUSE—

My old desire to live in the Southern Village
Was not because I had taken a fancy to the house.
But I heard it was place of simple-minded men
With whom it were a joy to spend the mornings and
      evenings.

Many years I had longed to settle here;
Now at last I have managed to move house.
I do not mind if my cottage is rather small
So long as there's room enough for bed and mat.
Often and often the neighbours come to see me
And with brave words discuss the things of old.
Rare writings we read together and praise;
Doubtful meanings we examine together and settle.

(WALEY)

(5)

—THE UNMOVING CLOUD—

I

The clouds have gathered, and gathered,
              and the rain falls and falls,
The eight ply of the heavens
              are all folded into one darkness,
And the wide, flat road stretches out.
I stop in my room toward the East, quiet, quiet,
I pat my new cask of wine.
My friends are estranged, or far distant,
I bow my head and stand still.

II

Rain, rain, and the clouds have gathered,
The eight ply of the heavens are darkness,
The flat land is turned into river.
              'Wine, wine, here is wine!'
I drink by my eastern window.
I think of talking and man,
And no boat, no carriage, approaches.

III

The trees in my east-looking garden
          are bursting out with new twigs,
They try to stir new affection,
And men say the sun and moon keep on moving
          because they can't find a soft seat.

IV

The birds flutter to rest in my tree,
          and I think I have heard them saying,
'It is not that there are no other men
But we like this fellow the best,
But however we long to speak
He can not know of our sorrow.'

(POUND)

Peach Blossom Spring

During the reign-period T'ai yuan [A.D. 326–97] of the Chin dynasty there lived in Wu-ling a certain fisherman. One day, as he followed the course of a stream, he became unconscious of the distance he had travelled. All at once he came upon a grove of blossoming peach trees which lined either bank for hundreds of paces. No tree of any other kind stood amongst them, but there were fragrant flowers, delicate and lovely to the eye, and the air was filled with drifting peachbloom.

The fisherman, marvelling, passed on to discover where the grove would end. It ended at a spring; and then there came a hill. In the side of the hill was a small opening which seemed to promise a gleam of light. The fisherman left his boat and entered the opening. It was almost too cramped at first to afford him passage; but when he had taken a few dozen steps he emerged into the open light of day. He faced a spread of level land. Imposing buildings stood among rich fields and pleasant ponds all set with mulberry and willow. Linking paths led everywhere, and the fowls and dogs of one farm could be heard from the next. People were coming and going and working in the fields. Both the men and the women dressed in exactly the same manner as people outside; white-haired elders and tufted children alike were cheerful and contented.

Some, noticing the fisherman, started in great surprise and asked where he had come from. He told them his story. They then invited him to their home, where they set out wine and killed chickens for a feast. When news of his coming spread through the village everyone came in to question him. For their part they told how their forefathers, fleeing from the troubles of the age of Ch'in, had come with their wives and neighbours to this isolated place, never to leave it. From that time on they had been cut off from the outside world. They asked what age was this: they had never even heard of the Han, let alone its successors the Wei and the Chin. The fisherman answered each of their questions in full, and they sighed and wondered at what he had to tell. The rest all invited him to their homes in turn, and in each house food and wine were set before him. It was only after a stay of several days that he took his leave.

"Do not speak of us to the people outside," they said. But when he had regained his boat and was retracing his original route, he marked it at point after point; and on reaching the prefecture he sought audience of the prefect and told him of all these things. The prefect immediately despatched officers to go back with the fisherman. He hunted for the marks he had made, but grew confused and never found the way again.

The learned and virtuous hermit Liu Tzu-chi heard the story and went off elated to find the place. But he had no success, and died at length of a sickness. Since that time there have been no further "seekers of the ford."

(CYRIL BIRCH)

*　　*　　*

MOUNTAINS AND RIVERS POETRY

The "farm and garden" poet finds his soul most at home in the simple, rustic sort of setting about which you have just read. The "mountains and rivers" poet finds congenial to his nature another sort of scenery—a scenery that is wilder, even less populated, even more distant from human affairs. The term "mountains and rivers" for this kind of poetry is apt and descriptive.

Some scholarly effort has been spent to show that "mountains and rivers" poetry was not written in China until after Buddhist ideas, coming from India, began to work on the Chinese imagination. But such effort has mostly been spent in vain. The native Chinese Taoist philosophy has in it plenty of excuse for a "thing" about mountains and rivers. Chinese men with a certain type of Taoist sensibility sought seclusion and isolation in mountains long before the Chinese felt any Buddhist influences. We read a poem from *The Book of Songs* about such a man:

> Lean-to on torrent's brink, laughter in idleness

(see p. 66). The Chinese term for this type of recluse is *hsien-jen* or *sennin*. The Chinese character with which this word is written has in it a man 人 beside a mountain 山 : 仙. Sun Ch'o (later eighth century) shows the basis for this affection when he writes:

> When the Tao dissolves, it becomes rivers;
> When it coagulates, it becomes mountains.

Later on, when Buddhism did come into China, the

sennin type of sensibility felt some affinities for the religion. No wonder: many Buddhist monasteries were set remotely up in the mountains. Two of the finest poets to write "mountains and rivers" poems have been identified as Buddhists: Hsieh Ling-yun (A.D. 385–433) and Wang Wei (A.D. 699–759).

—SENNIN POEM—

by Kuo P'u (276–324)

The red and green kingfishers
        flash between the orchids and clover,
One bird casts its gleam on another.

Green vines hang through the high forest,
They weave a whole roof to the mountain,
The lone man sits with shut speech,
He purrs and pats the clear strings.
He throws his heart up through the sky,
He bites through the flower pistil
        and brings up a fine fountain.
The red-pine-tree god looks at him and wonders.

He rides through the purple smoke to visit the sennin,
He takes 'Floating Hill' by the sleeve,
He claps his hand on the back of the great water sennin.

But you, you dam'd crowd of gnats,
Can you even tell the age of a turtle?

(POUND)

—POEM—

by T'ao Hung-ching (452–536)

Here, beautiful hills and streams
Echoed together since ancient times.
High peaks press into clouds
And clear currents reveal river bottoms.
From two high-rising banks of stone
Criss-crossing shine the five colors.
Dark woods of Emerald Bamboo
Are perpetually green.
When moving mists disperse,
Apes and birds call in cacaphony,
And when the evening sun goes down,
Deeply swimming fish nudge tails and frisk about.
This place lives beyond desire,
Its spirit's difficult to catch.
Who since the Taoist K'ang
Has had a *ch'i* to match?

(MAYHEW AND MCNAUGHTON)

—POEM—

by Wu Chün (469–519)

The wind and mist
              shine together.
The sky and hills
              color each other.

Onflowing streams
        whirl and fall,
Without plan,
          to east or west.
From Fu-yang
         to T'ung-lu,
It's one hundred
        li, and more.
Wild mountains,
         weird streams
Break up
        the earth's face.

Through the streams'
        green glitter,
You see bottom
        a thousand feet down.
The fish zig-zag,
        the stones are bright.
Nothing blocks
        the eye's gaze.

Streams leap out
        like arrows in flight,
Waves press on
        like barbarian hordes.
On river-banks,
        on the mountains' face,
Winter trees
        grow everywhere.

Up-piled mass
        struggles above

Up-piled mass—
                they rise on high.
Mountain-tops
                match mountain-tops
In a hundred thousand
                leaping peaks.

Springs and streams
                burst from the rocks.
"*Ling!*" they sound
                and echo "*ling!*"
Brilliant birds
                sing each to each
"*Ying!*" they cry
                and answer "*Ying!*"

Cicadas invent
                a thousand tunes
                        without wearing out,
Ape mocks ape
                cry on cry
                        without growing tired.

Hawks that fly up
                into the sky
Gaze at the peaks
                and rest their hearts.
Men that would win
                the world's glory
Look at the clefts
                and forget "return."

Above, the branches
          cross and cast shade
So that mid-day
          is like mid-night.
A-level, the branches
          spread and shine,
And now and then
          you see the sun.

(MCNAUGHTON)

Some Further Readings

Chang, Lily Pao-hu, trans. *The Poems of T'ao Ch'ien*. Honolulu: University of Hawaii Press, 1953.

Frodsham, John David. *The Murmuring Stream: The Life and Works of the Chinese Nature Poet Hsieh Ling-yun, Duke of K'ang-Lo*. London and New York: Oxford University Press, 1967.

Hightower, James Robert, trans. *Poetry of T'ao Ch'ien*. London and New York: Oxford University Press, 1970.

11

EROTIC POETRY

The Chinese from of old have had a fanciful and extravagant terminology to refer to the body's sexual and erotic parts. We use "cute" terms with our children, and with our associates (at least until very recently) we use Latin words—words which often seemed as coarse to a Roman as the Anglo-Saxon words we eschew in favor of the Latin word seem to us. The Chinese speak allusively of the Green Dragon, of the White Tiger's Grotto, of the Double Lotus Peak, of the Fabulous Pagoda, of the Jasper Stalk, and so on. The Jade Terrace refers to the *mons veneris*. When the Chinese in the mid-sixth century made their great collection of erotic poetry—the Chinese counterpart of the Greek Anthology's *epigrammata erotica*—somebody stuck on it the name *New Chants of the Jade Terrace*. Erotic poetry in China ever since then has been called "jade terrace poetry." The man who gave the anthology its title was showing a typical sense of humor. A fine teashop (with hostesses) of recent date is named "The Teashop of Green Dragons."

JADE TERRACE POETRY

The men of later ages habitually call *New Chants of the Jade Terrace* simply *The Jade Terrace Anthology*. *The Jade Terrace Anthology* was put together at an emperor's behest. The Chien-wen ("Peruser of Literature") Emperor (A.D. 503–551) of the Liang Dynasty, when he was still the heir apparent, liked to write erotic poems. Later on, he wished to revise his work, and he ordered his minister of state, Hsü Ling, to make him an anthology of erotic poetry. He intended to use it to study style. The poems which Hsü collected date from the Han period (206 B.C.–A.D. 220) to the Liang (then contemporary) period. The poems which you read in this section come from Hsü's collection, *The Jade Terrace Anthology*.

The Chinese also have an extravagant and fanciful terminology to refer to the various styles or "positions" in which love can be made. The Chinese "masters of love" recognize thirty classical positions. These positions are as elaborate and as imaginative as any in the "how to do it" books which you will see advertised in *The New York Times* Sunday book review. The translator or reader of poetry sometimes has trouble because of allusive terminology, and you easily can misunderstand a jade terrace poem if you do not know, for example, that the Chinese call one of these classic positions "Silk-reeling," another "The Pair-eyed Fish," and another "The Winding Dragon." I have taken this opportunity to warn you so that the poems will not be hopelessly obscure. To go into detail would be beyond the scope of this book.

Unless otherwise noted, poems in this chapter have been translated by the editor.

—SONG OF THE BEAUTY—

by Li Yen-nien (second–first centuries B.C.)

In the North
       there is a beautiful girl
In all the world
       she shall stand alone.
Here she looks
       and topples a city-wall;
There she looks
       and topples a people's state
Who doesn't know—
       topple a city-wall
          topple a people's state
The beautiful girl
       were hard again to get.

—POEM—

by Han Wu Ti (156–87 B.C)

The rustling of the silk is discontinued,
Dust drifts over the court-yard,

There is no sound of foot-fall, and the leaves
Scurry into heaps and lie still,
And she the rejoicer of the heart is beneath them:

A wet leaf that clings to the threshold.

(POUND)

—FAN-PIECE, FOR HER IMPERIAL LORD—

by *Pan Chieh-yü* (first century B.C.)

O fan of white silk,
     Clear as frost on the grass-blade,
You also are laid aside.

(POUND)

—OLD POEM—

(first or second century A.D.)

Blue, blue
is the grass
along the river,

Heavy, heavy
the willows
in the yard.

Too much, too much
is the woman
in the tower.

Splendid, splendid
she faces
the lattice-window.

Rare, fair,
she wears
powder and rouge;

Slender, slender
she extends
a white hand.

She used to be
an enter–
taining-girl,

And now she is
some playboy
husband's own.

Playboys
go out
and don't come home

And empty beds
are hard
to hold, alone.

—THE CROW NIGHT-CALLS—

(A Western Twist)

Young, in
      summer singing and dancing,
they are light-
      footed, and leave no prints,

Pitiable!
      as wild flags—
And have names
      strange to our ears.
                (MAYHEW AND MCNAUGHTON)

—AUTUMN THOUGHTS—

by T'ang Hui-hsiu

Autumn cold
      is heavy, heavy.
           Winds on the river pass,
Frost things white,
      Siao! Siao!
           and pierce the wall in waves.
I think of you
      Still non-forms,
           forms quickly fade.
Blink, blink
      and stare in grief.
           What are images?

—POEM—

by Ts'ao P'i (187–225)

Autumn is
      bitter, chill.
           Heaven's breath is cool.
Grass shakes
      trees shed
           dew turns to frost.
Flocked sparrows
      gabble, depart.
           Wild geese fly south.
"He travels
      strange roads,"
           I think, thinking many things.

—TUNG-YANG VALLEY—

by Hsieh Ling-yun (385–433)

1

This I regret—
a woman
I do not know

washes her white
feet
in the dark water.

The bright moon
shines
in the clouds

so far, far away
no one
shall reach it.

II
This I regret—
a man
I do not know

rides a white
boat
on the dark water.

Just as I
would ask
what he is

Up to, the moon
sinks
into the clouds.

—SEPARATION—

by Fan Yun (451–503)

To the East, to the West
of the walls
of Lo–yang,

Often, we have said
goodbye
to each other.

Before, when I left,
the snow
seemed to be flowers;

Today, I come back
and the flowers
seem to be snow.

—POEM—

by Wang Huan

Even yet, what
was said
when we left each other

Whenever I remember it,
I weep to myself
of parting, of distance.

For no reason,
a crane
from the North

flies alone
toward
the Yellow River.

—VAIN THINGS—

by Liu Hung

This I regret.
She should
have escaped the mass.

Such clarity is
clearer
than clearest light.

She's pretty and skillful:
she opens
her perfect eyes

And makes the sound
Of speech, as
scattered on wind.

—MOON ON THE TOWER—

by Wang T'ai-hsiang

Without interest, watch
the moon
on the high tower

For five years,
for three,
no one has come.

Why do you bother
shedding
light on the bed?

She sleeps there—she
always
does—alone.

—DYING LIGHT—

by Chi Shao-yü

The lamp dies
down, yet it
won't go out

guttering, it
casts the
light still higher.

When only one
or two
flames are left

then, then we can
untie
our gauze gowns.

—AUTUMN NIGHT—

by Wang Yuan-chang

The autumn night
draws on
and still draws on

The night draws on
and the music
does not cease

Dancing sleeves
leap
in the candle's flame,

Song and sound
go round
on the Bridge of Phoenixes.

—PICKING LING—

by Chiang Hung

The wind starts up
and the green
leaves gather

The breakers move
and the purple
stalks lie wide.

Hold in your mouth the flower,
then hold
in your mouth the fruit

Now, as you wait
for the beautiful
one to come.

—A REPLY: WIFE TO NEIGHBOR—

by Hsü Yao

The old time seems
shadows
joined to shades

The present seems
access
joined to excess

I don't know
if he travels
far off, or near by

have forgot the day
he left,
the month, the year.

—SPRING PARTING—

by Hsiang Tung-wang

By the gate,
      willows, sallows
            tangle like threads.

Beautiful,
      just put down,
            she won't wait for long.

Fits her words
      Makes a new
            shantung-tearing tune.

Wake up, you!
      set to it
            your silk-reeling song.

—COOL DUSK—

by Wang Shu-ying's wife

Plum-flowers
open
with the heat.

A hundred tongues
greet
Spring too soon.

The colder it gets
the thinner
they wear their clothes.

Unwilling, as yet,
to hug
hip and thigh.

—POEM—

by Liu Hsiao-yi

Gold threads
Flash,
flicker, shine

Fine-woven folds
flop,
flutter, gape

I'm thin, not to ape
the slender
ladies of Ch'u—

My belt gets looser
the longer
I think of you.

—A WALK IN THE GARDEN—

by Hsiao Tzu-hsien

In the third month,
the heart
of Spring trembles.

Stroll, stare:
peach
flowers open.

She turns away,
hides
in a sunlit fan.

But her sleeves, as she
walks, move
in the wind's velleities.

—BEDTIME—

by Tai Hao

She smooths the pillow.
She perfumes
the red cloth.

She sets down the brazier
and then
undoes her robe.

Stander by, you
know that
the night is long.

Go in. Do you
need an
engraved invitation?

—THINKING OF SOMEONE—

by Hsieh T'iao (464–499)

The beauty waits
and waits
and no one comes

She hopes and still
hopes, drops
the singing wheel,

Walks back, walks forth
eastward,
on the raised road.

The moon comes out.
People, now
and then, go by.

—MEETING AT GOLD VALLEY—

by Hsieh T'iao

The beautiful one
sends him off
with crockery cups

An exalted guest
would have
called for jade bowls.

Once the carriage
and horse
go east or west,

She won't think
of this
night again.

—AUTUMN WIND—

by Chiang Hung

At the northward lattice,
the wind
drives on the trees.

By the southward bamboos
in cold,
the crickets cry.

Inside the yard,
in the moon's
unlimited light,

The woman thinks,
and works
at the washing-stone.

—SPRING DAY, FINE WHITE LINEN—

(A Twist)

Orchid leaves
are ragged, jagged.
The peach-trees
have turned half-red.

Scattering scent,
they dance in silk gauze
and play
in Spring winds.

The kingfishers
unite and fly,
fly
without rest.

They would stay
amid the clouds
stretching
the double wings.

—IN THE SOUTHERN GARDEN, I WATCH
THE PASSERS-BY—

by Pao Ch'üan

There's a small
garden
in Lo-yang.

Cars, horses
fill the
roads, and pass—

Green gutters,
racing
going blinds,

Willow-trees,
turning
singing shells,

Double towers,
fading
pendant-sounds

Their hose are
thin, lace
that half-hides.

Floating clouds
have no
place to rest,

How will you
turn cross-
ways
the waves?

*   *   *

THE SERAGLIO POETS

At the same time as certain poets were bringing "mountains and rivers" poetry to a peak in its development, poets with another sort of sensibility were working jade terrace poetry to a high point of perfection. The so-called seraglio school is interesting because the poetry of its members shows jade terrace poetry at this high point, and because the poets belonging to the seraglio school wrote in a difficult metrical and prosodic style. Literary critics call this difficult style the seraglio style. It foreshadowed the formal T'ang Dynasty poetry.

The most famous member of the seraglio school was the Chien-wen ("Peruser of Literature") Emperor for whose sake *The Jade Terrace Anthology* was collected. The group's technician and theorist seems to have been Shen Yueh (A.D. 441–513). Shen Yueh "discovered" the "four tones" of the Chinese language. Besides being a brilliant linguist, he contributed to literary criticism the extremely influential "Doctrine of Eight Flaws"—an early version of "Some Don'ts."

Seraglio poetry, according to a very important present-day Chinese critic, has for content the emotional description of female faces, female dress, female attitudes, female sensibility, and even such things as what females do in bed after drinking wine. He notes that the seraglio poets, looking you straight in the eye, do write of physical love.

All translations in this section are by the editor.

—AN INTERRUPTED EMBOSOMING—

by Shen Yueh

Shadows, carried
on the slanting
moon, fall by.

Perfumes, set on
by the distant
wind, move near.

She says, "It is"
and sees
at once, it is not.

She almost laughs
but the laugh
comes out as tears.

—A BRONZE-WHITE HORSE—

by Shen Yueh

We part. You head,
in the peach
woods, down the bank.

Goodbye! You go off
to the top
of the steep slope.

As if you would
send down
your thought, you stop

And the Han's waters
flow on
toward the East.

—AT NIGHT, A NEGLECTED WIFE STILL FOLLOWS THE BOAT—

by the Chien-wen Emperor

Brocade curtains
are raised,
by the boat's lights.

The orchid-oars
stroke the
waves, then they drift.

Receding lights
make patterns
on the water,

And trailing perfumes
even yet
fill up our raft.

—THE TRAVELER—

by the Chien-wen Emperor

Move on, play on
in the garden
of long willows,

Led by the hand
to the tower
among the clouds.

Delight, desire
wearing
on, wear out

And at dawn, you
go down
the westward slope.

—SPRING-RIVER TWIST—

by the Chien-wen Emperor

The traveler, his mind
only on
the road, moves on.

Together they go
passing
the river's mouth.

Who should know
that someone
standing on the dike

Brushing tears,
for nothing
waves her hand?

—THE GUITAR-PLAYER—

by the Chien-wen Emperor

Somebody's playing
a guitar
at the north window.

The echoes of night
sound clearly
of bitter things

—they draw on and rise,
and the strings
seem about to break—

The heart is hurt,
and we wait
in vain for the close.

—SPRING WIND—

by Ho Sun (d. 527)

You may hear its
tone, but not
see its form;

can wear it in
layers, you'll
still wear it sheer.

In front of the mirror,
it scatters
and blows the rouge;

on the lute-strings,
it sounds,
sings, and resounds.

PART THREE:

T'ANG, FIVE DYNASTIES,
AND SUNG

12

STRANGE LEGENDS OF T'ANG

So far as we know, the first "artistic fiction" to be produced in China was written during the T'ang Dynasty. A lot of this fiction has been preserved and has come down to us as *ch'uan ch'i* or "strange legends." By artistic fiction, I mean fiction written by known individuals, published (or at least preserved) over the individuals' names, and distinguished by conscious artistry and literary style.

We should not be surprised to find literary style and grace in the *ch'uan ch'i*, for the *ch'uan ch'i* that we have are in the literary language ("classical Chinese") which was known to scholars and not known to the uneducated. Some *ch'uan ch'i* authors also had reputations as poets. They wrote these stories to amuse themselves and other members of their educated class. Among the stories, later scholars have identified four major categories: (1) love, (2) heroes, (3) satire, and (4) history.

We can find several sources, or at least antecedents,

for their work. But none of these antecedents really qualifies as artistic fiction. *Mr. Left's History*, for example, may read to us like fiction, but it is written, after all, as if it were annals, and it appears that the author intended, according to the lights of his age, to write and to record objectively. Besides history, we have in China the age-old institution of public storytelling and of various dramatic arts: shadow plays, drum-songs, puppet-shows, and so on. It is impossible to say what influence these may have had on the *ch'uan ch'i*, or even precisely to say which of them flourished in China prior to the T'ang, although we can suppose that the men who wrote them had, as children, listened to the public storyteller in their town or market square. Furthermore, a number of collections of anecdotes and jokes were published before the T'ang—for example, *Sayings of the World* and *Forest of Smiles*. But these do not qualify as artistic fiction, and none of them has in it anything which we would consider a short story.

During the T'ang, it was customary for candidates at the imperial examinations to get powerful older men to patronize and back them. If you were a candidate seeking such patronage, it was a routine ploy to "send in" to the great man some literary compositions. If he felt you had the literary skills which were needed to pass the examinations—and literary skills were all-important— he could do a lot to increase your chances and to advance your career. If you lived up to his expectations, of course, you owed him allegiance and favors, and he came thereby to share in your power. Ambitious candidates discovered tha vivid, or sordid, fiction was more likely to engage an old man's interest than essays on Confucius. And so the "strange legends" were written, and Chinese fiction was born. Or so at least one legend, strange itself, has it.

§ STORIES OF LOVE

The Story of Ying Ying

by Yuan Chen

During the reign-period of Cheng Yuan (A.D. 785-804), there was a man named Chang. Chang had a gentle nature and a handsome face. He also had a strong character, so that he was not easily led into vice by others. If he happened to be among lively men, he would neither condemn nor commend their behavior. And when his companions hurled themselves into pleasures as if there were no tomorrow, Chang maintained his dignity and decorum. So that at twenty-three, he was still a virgin.

Somebody asked him why he was not affected by woman's beauty. "Persons like the famous Teng T'u," Chang replied, "do not really love beauty. What they love is flesh. But I am a lover of true beauty. I have never met a woman that is really beautiful, and so I seem unresponsive to woman's beauty. How do I know this is true? Why, I am very sensitive to beauty in general. My mind will rest in a beautiful thing that I happen to see. So how could I be considered a totally unemotional person?" And when Chang said this, the questioner sneered.

Not long after this, Chang had to go to Puchou. He took a room in the Pu Chiu Temple, which lies about three miles east of the city. At this same time, the widow of a man named Tsui was going back to Chang-an. The widow was going through Puchou, and she lodged at the Pu Chiu Temple, too. Tsui's widow had the maiden name Cheng. Now Chang's mother had been a Cheng. So the two of them figured out the relationship and discovered that the widow was an "aunt" to Chang.

Hun Chen died at Puchou this year. A lieutenant of Chen's, Ting Wenya, had been mistreating the troops, and when Chen died, the troops mutinied and began to terrorize the district. Well, the Tsui family was very wealthy. The widow had many servants with her, and a lot of valuables. She found herself in this crisis away from home, and she did not know what to do for help. Chang, however, had a friend who was officer of the garrison, and Chang got him to send a guard for the temple. So the temple was not raided by the rebellious soldiery, and in ten days the emperor sent General Tu Ch'ueh to take over the troops. The general returned the district to law and order.

The widow was quite grateful to Chang, and she ordered a banquet for him in the central hall. As they dined, the widow said to Chang, "I am a miserable widow. How could I have saved myself and my children in this situation? My young son and my daughter owe their lives to you. You have done for them an extraordinary thing, and I should like them to meet you and to recognize you as an elder brother. How else can they express their gratitude?"

So the widow called in her son, Huanlang. Huanlang was ten or so, and he was a delicate and a handsome boy. The widow then called to her daughter Ying Ying, "Come out and meet your elder brother. He has saved your life!"

For a long time the girl refused to come. She finally sent out word that she was sick. The widow lost her temper at this. She said, "Your brother Chang saved your life! Without him, you would be a prisoner now. Are you going to allow the ordinary considerations of propriety to keep you from thanking him? It is impossible!"

After a long while, the girl came in. She was dressed in her everyday clothes. She had not put on any jewels for the occasion. She wore no makeup save that her eyebrows were joined with a little black, and she wore a little rouge on her cheeks. But her features and her complexion were extraordinary, and she shone with a remarkable beauty. Chang was astounded.

Greetings were exchanged. The girl sat down by her mother. The girl wore an expression of injury, as if she had been forced to do an unpleasant thing. She stared at the floor and looked as if she couldn't stand to be there.

Chang asked how old she was. The mother answered. "She was born in the year *chia-tzu* of the present cycle, the seventh month. It is now the *keng-ch'en* year, so she is. . . seventeen."

Chang tried to get the girl to take part in the conversation. She would not speak to him. So the banquet drew to its end, and Chang took his leave. Chang was obsessed with the girl from then on.

Chang wanted somehow to tell her that he loved her, but he could find no way to do it. But the girl had a maid who was called Hungniang. Chang ran into this maid now and again. One day, he told her flat out that he was in love with her mistress. Hungniang looked for a minute as if she could not believe it, and then she ran away. Chang was sorry he had not kept his mouth shut.

On the following day, Chang saw the maid again. "Look," he said, "I'm sorry about what happened yesterday." He did not speak of what was in his mind.

The maid said to him: "I would be afraid to tell my mistress what you said, I would be afraid even to hint. But you have many acquaintances in the Tsui clan. Why don't you formally propose to marry her? You have just done a big favor for the family, and I'd think you stand a good chance of success."

"I have been," said Chang, "a gentleman from my early childhood. I have met women since my youth, but I have never looked hard at any of them. *Hwo*! I didn't think that now my fate suddenly would come down on me. I scarcely could sit still at the banquet the other day. And during the last few days, I don't know whether I am coming or going. I don't even notice what the food tastes like. How can I go on for long like this? Suppose I send a matchmaker to arrange a marriage between us —it will take months! By then you'd as well look for me in the dried-fish shop. Is that the best suggestion you have?"

"My mistress," said the maid, "is virginal and proud. Even her elders do not dare talk improperly when she's around. Dare a servant like me?

"But wait," continued the maid. "She writes pretty good verse. Sometimes she recites favorite lines to herself, and then she loses herself in melancholy and admiration. Write her a love poem, see what she does. I can't think of a better idea."

Chang thought this was a pretty good idea. He wrote two poems right away and gave them to Hungniang. In the evening, Hungniang came back. She gave Chang a sheet of decorated paper. "This is from my mistress," she said.

The paper had on it a poem. The poem was entitled "The Bright Moon of the Three-Times-Five Night." Here is what the poem said:

> In the western chamber, I wait for the moon;
> The door's half-open, and I greet the wind.
> The flower-shadows stir against the wall
> And I think that my lover has come.

Chang got the point. It was now the second month, the fourth day after the first ten-day cycle. There was an apricot tree east of the wall of the Tsui compound. He could climb that tree and get over the wall.

On the night of the full moon, Chang climbed up the tree and went over the wall. He went on to the western chamber. The door was half-open. Hungniang lay inside asleep on the bed. Chang woke her up.

"What are you doing here?" she said.

"Your mistress," replied Chang, "told me in her message to come." He was not exactly lying, either.

Chang then said, "Tell her I have come."

Eventually, Hungniang came back.

"She's coming, she's coming!" Hungniang said.

Chang was a little surprised and very, very happy. He told himself that his success was in hand. And then the girl came in. She was completely dressed. Her face was rather severe.

She said, "You saved our lives. You did our family a great service. Nice! So my mother trusts you with her young son and her daughter. And you get this bad maid to bring me dirty poems. Oh, yes, noble to protect us from danger! And taking advantage of it make advances to me? You put one wrong in in place of another. Are you any different from the rebellious soldiers?

"I should simply have ignored your poems. But then I would be implicit in the evil. I could have told my mother, but I *am* obligated to you, and it didn't seem right to tell. I might have asked Hungniang to tell you off, but I was afraid she wouldn't do a very good job of it. So I sent you that silly and suggestive poem. I knew that it would bring you here. O, I was ashamed to do it like this. But I knew that we could keep our feelings under control, and that we could avoid exceeding the limits of propriety."

So she said and left the room. Chang stood for a long time,

stunned. Then he climbed back over the wall, went to his room, and gave up his hope of success.

Several days passed. Then one night, as Chang lay asleep, he suddenly was awakened by someone in his room. He sat up and saw Hungniang. She had come with bedding under her arm and a pillow in her hand. Hungniang put out her hand and caressed Chang.

"She's here," the maid said. "She is here! Are you going to sleep through such a moment?"

Hungniang put the pillow next to his pillow, and she laid the bedding on his bedding. Chang rubbed his eyes and rubbed them again. He thought he was dreaming. But he remained upright, waiting.

In time Hungniang came back. Her mistress came with her, leaning on the maid's arm. Ying Ying turned her face away. Chang had the strange feeling that he could see her blush, but it was too dark really to see. She walked as if she could scarcely stand up. Chang remembered her correct and severe bearing during their last interview. It was gone now.

That night was the eighth night of the second ten-day period. The moonlight slanted in, crystalline and bright. It lay across the bed with the irregular shadows which it cast. Chang felt high and light, as if he had been carried up by the Immortals. It seemed unreal to him that this visitor should come from the human world. But Hungniang let go of her mistress and went out of the room.

After some time had passed, the temple bell sounded. Dawn began to rise in the sky. Hungniang came back and helped and hurried Ying Ying to leave. But Ying Ying was not ready to leave, and she held on to Chang for a long while and made soft, inarticulate sounds. Then she finally got up and left as she had come, leaning on the maid's arm. While the night was passing, she had spoken to Chang not a single word, and she left without speaking.

In the first full light of day, Chang got out of bed. He wondered to himself if he had been dreaming. As the brightness grew in his room, he noticed on his arm a red spot of rouge. He noticed that Ying Ying's perfume was still caught in the bedding. And he saw her tears shining still on the mattress.

Ten days went by. Chang heard nothing from Ying Ying. He began to write a poem in thirty rhyming distichs. He called the poem "Meeting a Fairy." He was working on the poem one day when Hungniang came. He had not finished the poem, but he gave it to Hungniang to take to her mistress. And then for almost a month, Ying Ying let Chang come to her in her western chamber. Chang crept out at dawn and climbed in at dusk. Chang once asked Ying Ying what her mother thought of him, and Ying Ying said: "She thinks that you may have something on your conscience. But she realizes that nothing can be done about it, and so she will probably say nothing and simply hope that our relationship will be affirmed formally, by marriage."

A little while after this conversation, Chang had to go to Chang-an. Chang told Ying Ying so. She responded with suitable humility and did not reproach him. But her face was full of regret and anxiety. The night before Chang had to leave for the west, he was not able to see Ying Ying.

Chang returned to Puchou a few months later, and for several months after that, he spent a lot of time with Ying Ying. Ying Ying wrote with a beautiful hand, and she could turn out a fine poem. Chang often asked her to show him her compositions, but she never showed her work to him. Chang tried to elicit a response by showing her his own work, but she did not show any great interest in it. Ying Ying in fact acted as though she knew nothing about the civilized arts, but she excelled in every one of them. She was never inert in real conversation, but she did not much like to make small talk. She was very much in love with Chang, but she did not talk to him about it. Very often she went into a melancholy withdrawal, and yet she pretended that she was never depressed. One very seldom caught her in an outward show of pleasure or anger. She sometimes played the *ch'in* at night. Her music generally was filled with a gentle melancholy, and she showed herself to be capable of deep feeling. Chang often stood outside the wall and listened to her play. He now and then asked her to play for him, but she always declined. And all of these things made Chang love her more.

Chang's affairs moved on to the point where it was necessary for him to leave Puchou and take his examinations. The evening before he was to leave again for the west, he sat down by Ying Ying and tried to tell her how he felt about the imminent separation. He could not find any right word, and so he only sighed. Ying Ying said that she felt this would be their last meeting. She felt that this was fate and there was no point to struggle against it.

"If you abandon me," she said in a low voice, "after you have enjoyed me this way. . . I am not going to complain. Men have always been like this. But if you want our story to have a happy ending, I can only feel that your kindness is very great. Then when we swore to be faithful till death, we shall not have sworn in vain. It will happen as it will happen, and the separation which we face now cannot alter it much. Then why should we cry because you are going away? But you are unhappy about it, so may I do what I can to cheer you up? You have said that I play the *ch'in* well. But I have been diffident to play for you. Now that you are going away, let me play as I can."

She had the maid bring her *ch'in*. She began to play the prelude to "Rainbow Skirts and Feather Jackets." She played the first few notes and then broke into a wild and disturbed improvisation. Chang could hardly recognize the tune. Those who were in the room began to cry.

Ying Ying stopped suddenly. She pushed back the *ch'in* and went weeping to her mother's rooms. She did not come back to Chang that night, and he undertook his journey early the next day.

Chang took his exams the following year and had no success. He stayed in the capital to stand for the exams when they should next be given. And he wrote to Ying Ying to explain this to her.

Ying Ying wrote back to him. She said: "I have read your letter. My heart is filled with joy and with sorrow that you love me so. You sent me a box of ornaments and five sticks of make-up, so that I can brighten my hair and wet my lips. I am grateful that you are so kind. But for whom shall I make up and adorn myself now? These things will only remind me of you, and I shall be the more sorry. You write that you stay in Chang-an to continue your studies. So it is that a man may get ahead. I complain only that this may make permanent what was to be a temporary separation. Well, it is fate. Why should we talk about it?

"Since last autumn, I feel as though I have lost something, I do not know what. I may have laughed or talked during the day's business, but when I am alone at night, I can only cry. I dream of parting's sorrow and wake up crying. I sometimes dream that you come to me as you used to come and make me happy with love and tenderness. But before we have any satisfaction in our secret meeting, my dream-soul is startled by something and returns to life and reality. And when I wake up, the bed seems half-warm with your body's warmth. But I know that you are far away.

"Since we said goodbye, the old year has gone. It seems like yesterday. A person can find pleasure easily in Chang-an, and there are many ways to be distracted. I am lucky that you have not forgotten me, who am insignificant and shut in. You have even said that your interest continues! An uncultivated person like me is quite unworthy of your notice. But I at least can give you unshaken faith in the love we swore.

"We met as cousins at the banquet. And then I was tempted by a maid to meet you in private. A woman's heart is not always strong in its virtue. And so you 'tried me with the sounds of your *ch'in*,' and I was of too weak a character to 'throw the shuttle.' We shared mat and pillow and grew together with a deep faith. I believed in my simple heart that I had found the support for my life. I scarcely imagined that I should meet my Prince and it should fail to conclude in marriage. I did not think that I should give myself to you and yet not win the privilege of attending you publicly with your cap and your kerchief. I shall regret this to the end of my life. And to whom may I speak of my grief? I must cry for it in secret.

"Your kind heart is truly great. If you should decide to fulfill the secret hope of this minuscule speck of life, I shall never die what death may come. But maybe you will decide to be a 'man of the world.' You may decide to still the heart's voice and to throw away things which, as it seems to you, are trivial, so as to gain what is really important to you. Maybe you will decide that your former love is really just a partner in your fault. Maybe you will think it best lightly to break a promise which was made most seriously. Well, even then I shall continue to love you as cinnabar continues in fire. If my bones are consumed and my body is scattered, I shall follow your carriage with the wind and the dew. I have no other thing to say, if living, if dead. I weep as I write. How can I tell you what my heart feels? Ten thousand times, take care of yourself; take care of yourself ten thousand times!

"I send you a jade ring. I have had this ring since I was a child. I hope you will wear it on your belt: jade stands for hardness and constancy; a ring means 'beginning without end.' I also send you a skein of unraveled silk and a tea-grinder made of mottled bamboo. None of these things is valuable. I send them and hope that they will remind you to be true as jade, and that they will tell you my love is unending like the ring. When you see the mottled spots on the bamboo, think of my tears. When you look at the tangles of silk, think that I am as hopeless in my sorrow. I send them to tell you what is in my heart, and to say to you, 'I love you forever.' My body is far from you, but my heart is near to you. How do we know when we next shall meet? If the desire is strong, the soul will look for its mate over a thousand *li*.

"Ten thousand times take care of yourself. The winds of spring are often evil. Eat well against its malice. Do not overdo anything, and please be careful of yourself. Do not worry much about your uncultivated servant, Ying Ying."

Chang showed this letter to his friends. The story became known to many people at the time. One of Chang's friends, Yang Chü-yuan, wrote a quatrain about it. After I read Chang's "Meeting a Fairy," I myself wrote a thirty-distich poem on the affair. Whoever among Chang's friends heard the story was moved.

Chang eventually decided to break with Ying Ying. I was very close to Chang at the time, and I asked him why he made this decision. He said to me, "Haven't you ever noticed? Heaven so reacts to a woman of exceptional beauty that she ruins either herself or those around her. Suppose this Miss Tsui should meet a man with money and rank. She'd bring him utterly under her spell. She'd change into cloud or rain, into scaly dragon or horned dragon, into. . .well, into who knows what else? In the old day, the Yin Dynasty's Hsin and the Chou Dynasty's Yu ruled kingdoms of ten thousand chariots. They held the greatest power. But a woman ruined both of them. Their armies were broken, and they died violent deaths. Men laugh at them for it to this day. My virtue, I know, is not strong enough to withstand the evils which Heaven sends to such unnatural creatures. And so I have put down my passion." Everyone who was there and heard Chang say this, sighed.

A year or so went by. Ying Ying married another man. Chang himself took a wife.

Later on, Chang's affairs took him by Ying Ying's house. Chang sent a message in to her husband. He said that he was Ying Ying's cousin and asked if he could see her. The husband took the request to Ying Ying, and she refused to see Chang. When her response was communicated to Chang, he could not keep his disappointment off his face.

The message-bearer told about his look of such great disappointment, and the story found its way to Ying Ying. She wrote a poem about it and sent the poem to Chang, secretly. It said:

> I have given up my joy and lost my beauty
> And now toss and turn and keep to my bed.
> I don't care who sees me faded like this
> Save him alone who brought it to pass.

She still did not agree to see him.

Chang was getting ready a few days later to move on. Ying Ying sent him another poem to say a last goodbye:

> Let us speak no more of cruel forsaking;
> Let each of us love and honour his spouse.
> We can give the love we had for each other
> To the person whom Fate has given us each.

After that, they never heard of each other again.

Those who heard the story at the time gave praise to Chang. They said he was a man ready to correct his mistakes. I myself often speak of the relation between Chang and Ying Ying, so that they who hear will not make the same mistake, and so that they who already have fallen into error may emulate Chang and pull themselves out of the evil into which they have fallen.

During the ninth month of the Cheng Yuan reign-period, Li Kung-ch'i visited my house on Chingan street. I told him the story. He was much impressed and wrote "The Song of Ying Ying" about it. He called the song this because it was the girl's milk name.

(MCNAUGHTON)

Story of a Singsong Girl

by Pai Hsing-chien

In the Tien Pao period [A.D. 742–756] the Lord of Yingyang, whose name and surname I will omit, was Governor of Changchou. He was highly respected and extremely rich. When our story starts he was fifty and had a son of nearly twenty—an intelligent lad of outstanding literary ability, the admiration of all his contemporaries. His father loved him dearly and had high hopes of him. "This," he would say, "is the 'thousand-league colt' of our family." When the time came for the lad to take the provincial examination, this father gave him fine clothes and equipage for the journey, and money for his expenses in the capital. "With your gifts you should succeed at the first attempt," he said. "But I am giving you an allowance for two years, and a generous one at that, to enable you to work without worrying." The young man was quite confident too, and saw himself passing the examination as clearly as he saw the palm of his own hand.

Setting out from Changchou he reached the capital in little

more than a month and took a house in the Pucheng quarter. One day on his way back from the East Market, he entered the eastern gate of the Pingkang quarter to visit a friend who lived in the southwest part. When he reached Mingko Lane, he saw a house with a rather narrow gate and courtyard. The house itself, however, was a grand one, and from the gate you could see many buildings stretching back. One half of the double door was open and at it stood a girl, attended by her young maid. She was of an exquisite, bewitching beauty, such as the world had seldom seen.

When he saw her, the young man unconsciously reined in his horse and hesitated, unable to tear himself away. He deliberately dropped his whip and waited for his servant to pick it up, all the time staring at the girl. She, for her part, returned his gaze with a look of answering admiration. But in the end he went away without daring to speak to her.

After that he was like a man distracted, and secretly begged a friend who knew the capital well to find out who she was.

"The house belongs to a courtesan named Li," his friend told him.

"Is it possible to get her?" he asked.

"She is very well off," said his friend, "because her previous dealings have been with rich and aristocratic families, who paid her lavishly. Unless you spend a million cash, she will have nothing to do with you."

"All I want is to win her," answered the young man. "I don't mind if she costs a million."

Some days later he put on his best clothes and set out, with a train of attendants behind him, for her house. When he knocked at the door, a young maid opened it.

"Can you tell me whose house this is?" the young man asked.

The maid did not answer, but ran back into the house calling out at the top of her voice: "Here's the gentleman who dropped his whip the other day!"

The girl replied with evident pleasure: "Ask him in. I'll come as soon as I've changed my clothes and tidied myself."

The young man hearing this was inwardly overjoyed as he followed the maid into the house. He saw the girl's mother—a grey-haired woman with a bent back—and bowing low said to her: "I hear that you have a vacant courtyard which you might be willing to let. Is that true?"

"I am afraid it is too shabby and small for a gentleman like you," she said. "You may take it if you like, but I wouldn't dare ask for any rent." She then took him into the reception room, which was a very splendid one, and asked him to be seated, saying: "I have a daughter who is very young and has few accomplishments, but who enjoys the company of visitors. I should like you to meet her."

With that she called for her daughter. The girl had sparkling eyes and dazzling white arms, and moved with such consummate grace that the young man could only leap to his feet in confusion and did not dare raise his eyes. When they had greeted each other, he made a few remarks about the weather, conscious as he did so that her beauty was such as he had never seen before.

They sat down again. Tea was made and wine poured out. The vessels used were spotlessly clean. He stayed on until it was late and the curfew drum could be heard all around, when the old lady asked if he lived far away.

He answered untruthfully: "Several miles beyond Yenping Gate," hoping that they would ask him to stay.

"The drum has sounded," she said. "You will have to leave at once, if you don't want to break the law."

"I was enjoying myself so much," said the young man, "that I didn't notice how late it was. My house is a long way off, and I have no relations in the city. What am I to do?"

"If you don't think our house too shabby," put in the girl, "what harm would there be in your spending the night here?"

He glanced several times at the old lady, who assented.

Calling his servants, he ordered them to bring two bolts of silk which he offered for the expenses of a feast. But the girl stopped him and protested laughingly: "No, you are our guest. We would like to entertain you tonight with our humble household's rough and ready fare. You can treat us another time." He tried to refuse, but in the end she had her way, and they all moved to the western hall. The curtains, screens, blinds and couches were of dazzling splendour, the toilet-boxes, coverlets and pillows the height of luxury. Candles were lighted and an excellent meal was served.

After supper, when the old lady had retired, the young man and girl began to talk intimately, laughing and joking completely at their ease.

"I passed your house the other day," said the young man, "and you happened to be standing at the door. After that, I couldn't get you out of my head. Lying down to rest or sitting down to eat, I couldn't stop thinking of you."

"It was just the same with me," she answered.

"You know, I didn't come today simply to look for lodgings," he said. "I came hoping you would grant the wish of my life. But I wasn't sure what my fate would be. . . ."

As he was speaking the old woman came back and asked what they were saying. Upon being told, she laughed and said: " 'There is a natural attraction between the sexes.' When lovers are agreed, not even their parents can control them. But my daughter is of humble birth—are you sure she is fit to share your bed?"

The young man immediately came down from the dais and, bowing low, said: "Please accept me as your servant!" After that the old lady regarded him as her son-in-law; they drank heavily together and finally parted. Next morning he had all his baggage brought round to their house and made it his home.

Henceforward he shut himself up there, and his friends heard no more of him. He mixed only with actors, dancers and people of that kind, passing the time in wild sports and aimless feasting. When his money was spent he sold his horses and men-servants. In little over a year all his money, property, attendants and horses were gone.

The old lady had begun to treat him coldly, but the girl seemed more devoted to him than ever. One day she said to him: "We have been together a year, but I am still not with child. They say that the spirit of the Bamboo Grove answers prayers as surely as an echo. Shall we go to his temple and offer a libation?"

Not suspecting any plot, the young man was delighted. And having pawned his coat to buy wine and sacrificial meat, he went with her to the temple and prayed to the spirit. They spent two nights there and started back the third day, the young man riding a donkey behind the girl's carriage. When they reached the north gate of the Hsuanyang quarter, she turned to him and said: "My aunt's house is in a lane to the east near here. Suppose we rest there for a little?"

He fell in with her wishes, and they had not gone more than a hundred paces when he saw a wide drive and their servant stopped the carriage, saying: "We have arrived." The young man got down and was met by a man-servant who came out to ask who they were. When told that it was Mistress Li, he went back and announced her. Presently a woman of about forty came out.

She greeted our hero and asked: "Has my niece arrived?" The girl alighted from the carriage and her aunt welcomed her, saying: "Why haven't you been here for so long?" They exchanged glances and laughed. Then the girl introduced him to her aunt, after which they all went into a side garden near the western gate. There was a pavilion set in a profusion of bamboos and trees amid quiet pools and summer-houses.

"Does this garden belong to your aunt?" the young man asked.

The girl laughed, but instead of answering she spoke of something else.

Delicious tea and cakes were served. But almost at once a man galloped up on a Fergana horse which was all in a lather. "The old lady has been taken very ill," he gasped. "She is beginning to be delirious. You had better hurry back."

"I am so worried," said the girl to her aunt. "Let me take the horse and ride on ahead. Then I will send it back, and you and my husband can come along later." The young man was anxious to go with her, but the aunt whispered to her maid to stop him at the gate.

"My sister must be dead by now," she said. "You and I ought to discuss the funeral together. What good can you do by running after her in an emergency like this?" So he stayed, to discuss the funeral and mourning rites.

It grew late, but still the horse had not come back. "I wonder what can have happened?" said the aunt. "You had better hurry over to see. I will come on later."

The young man set out. When he reached the house he found the gate firmly locked and sealed. Astounded, he questioned the neighbours. "Mistress Li only rented this house," they told him. "When her lease was up, the landlord took it back, and she moved away. She left two days ago." But when he asked her new address, they did not know it.

He thought of hurrying back to the Hsuanyang quarter to question the aunt, but it was already too late. So he pawned some of his clothes to procure himself supper and a bed. He was too angry to sleep, however, and did not close his eyes from dusk till dawn. Early in the morning he rode on his donkey to the aunt's house, but although he knocked on the door for the time it takes for a meal, no one answered. At last his loud shouts brought a footman slowly to the door. The young man immediately asked for the aunt.

"She doesn't live here," answered the footman.

"But she was here yesterday evening," the young man protested. "Are you trying to fool me?" He enquired whose house it was.

"This is the residence of His Excellency Master Tsui. Yesterday somebody hired his courtyard to entertain a cousin coming from a distance, but they were gone before nightfall."

Bewildered and nearly distracted, the young man did not know what to do. He went back to his old lodgings in the Pucheng quarter. The landlord was sorry for him and offered to feed him; but in his despair he could eat nothing, and after three days he fell seriously ill. In another fortnight he was so weak that the landlord feared he could not live, and carried him to the undertakers. As he lay there at the point of death, all the undertakers in the market pitied him and nursed him, until he was well enough to walk with a stick.

The undertakers then hired him by the day to hold up the mourning curtains, and in this way he earned just enough to support himself. In a few months he grew quite strong again, but the mourners' chants always made him regret that he could not change places with the dead, and he would burst out sobbing and weeping, unable to restrain his tears. When he went home he would imitate their chants. Being a man of intelligence, he very soon mastered the art and became the most expert mourner in the whole capital.

It happened that the undertakers in the East and West Markets at this time were rivals. The undertakers in the East Market turned out magnificent hearses and biers—in this respect they were unrivalled—but the mourners they provided were rather poor. Hearing of our hero's skill, the chief undertaker offered him twenty thousand cash for his services; and the experts of the East Market secretly taught the young man all the fresh tunes they knew, singing in harmony with him. This went on in secret for several weeks. Then the two chief undertakers agreed to give an exhibition in Tienmen Street to see which was the better. The loser would forfeit fifty thousand cash to cover the cost of the refreshments provided. An agreement to this effect was drawn up and duly witnessed.

Tens of thousands of people gathered to watch the contest. The chief of the quarter got wind of the proceedings and told the chief of police. The chief of police told the city magistrate. Very soon all the citizens of the capital were hurrying to the spot and every house in the city was empty.

The exhibition started at dawn. Coaches, hearses, and all kinds of funeral trappings had been displayed for a whole morning, but still the undertakers from the West Market could establish no superiority, and their chief was filled with shame. He built a platform in the south corner of the square, and a man with a long beard came forward, holding a hand-bell and attended by several assistants. He wagged his beard, raised his eyebrows, he sang the White Horse dirge. Proud of his skill, he looked to right and to left as if he knew himself unrivalled. Shouts of approval were heard on every side, and he was convinced that he must be the best dirge singer of his time who could not possibly be surpassed.

Presently the chief undertaker of the East Market built a platform in the north corner of the square, and a young man in a black cap came forward, accompanied by five or six assistants and carrying a bunch of hearse-plumes in his hand. This was our hero.

He adjusted his clothes, looked slowly up and down, then cleared his throat and began to sing with an air of diffidence. He sang the dirge Dew on the Garlic, and his voice rose so shrill and clear that its echoes shook the forest trees. Before he had finished the first verse, all who heard were sobbing and hiding their tears. They started jeering at the chief undertaker of the West Market until, overcome by shame, he stealthily put down the money he had forfeited and fled, to the amazement of the crowd.

Now the emperor had recently ordered the governors of outlying provinces to confer with him at the capital once a year. This was called the "Yearly Reckoning." Thus our hero's father happened to be at the capital too, and he and some of his colleagues, discarding their official robes and insignia, had slipped out to watch the contest. With them was an old servant, the husband of the young man's foster-nurse. Recognizing our hero's accent and gait, he wanted to accost him but dared not and wept. Surprised, the Lord of Yingyang asked him why he was crying.

"Sir, " replied the servant, "the young man who is singing reminds me of your lost son."

"My son was murdered by robbers because I gave him too much money," said the Lord of Yingyang. "This cannot be he." So saying, he began to weep too and went back to his lodging.

The old servant then went again to ask some of the undertakers: "Who was that singer? Where did he learn such skill?" They told him it was the son of such a one, and when he asked the young man's own name, that too was unfamiliar. The old servant was so much puzzled that he determined to put the matter to the test for himself. But when the young man saw him he gave a start, and tried to hide in the crowd. The servant caught hold of his sleeve, and said: "Surely it is you!" Then they embraced and wept, and presently went back together.

But when the young man came to his father's lodging, the Lord of Yingyang was angry with him and said: "Your conduct has disgraced the family. How dare you show your face again?" So saying he took him out of the house and led him to the ground between Chuchiang and Hsingyuan. Here he stripped him naked and gave him several hundred strokes with his horse-whip, till the young man succumbed to the pain and collapsed. Then his father left, thinking he was dead.

However, the young man's singing-master had asked some of his friends to keep a secret watch on him, and now they came back and told the others what had happened. They were all greatly upset, and two men were dispatched with a reed mat to bury him. When they got there they found his heart still warm, and when they had held him up for some time he started breathing again. So they carried him home and gave him liquid food through a reed pipe. The next morning he recovered consciousness, but for a whole month he was unable to move his hands and feet. Moreover, the sores left by his thrashing festered and gave out such a stench that his friends could not stand it, and one night they abandoned him by the roadside.

The passers-by, however, took pity on him and threw him scraps of food, so that he did not starve. After three months he was well enough to hobble about with a stick. Clad in a linen coat—which was knotted together in a hundred places, so that it looked as tattered as a quail's tail—and carrying a broken saucer in his hand, he started to beg his way through the various quarters of the city. Autumn had now turned to winter. He spent his nights in lavatories and caves and his days haunting the markets and booths.

One day when it was snowing hard, hunger and cold had driven him into the streets. His bitter cry pierced all who heard it to the heart. But the snow was so heavy that hardly a house had its outer door open.

When he reached the eastern gate of the Anyi quarter, he went north along the wall until he came to the seventh or eighth house which he found had the left half of its double door open. This was the house where the girl Li was then living, although the young man did not know it.

He stood at the door wailing persistently. And hunger and cold had made his cry so pitiful that you could scarcely bear to hear it.

The girl heard it from her room, and said to her maid: "That is my lover. I know his voice." She flew to the door and found him there, so emaciated and covered with sores that he seemed scarcely human.

"Can it be you?" she exclaimed, deeply moved. The young man simply nodded, too overcome by anger and excitement to speak.

She threw her arms round his neck, then wrapped him in her own embroidered jacket, led him to the western chamber and said in a choked voice: "It is all my fault that this has happened to you." And with these words she swooned.

The old woman came hurrying over in great alarm, crying: "What is it?" When the girl told her who had come, she immediately raised objections. "Send him packing!" she cried. "What did you bring him in here for?"

But the girl looked grave and protested: "No! This is the son of a noble house. Once he rode in grand carriages and wore fine clothes. But within a year of coming to our house he lost all he had. And then we got rid of him by a contemptible trick. We have ruined his career and made him despised by his fellow men. The love of father and son is implanted by Heaven; yet because of us his father hardened his heart and tried to kill him, then abandoned him so that he was reduced to this state.

"Everyone in the land knows that it was I who brought him to this. The court is full of his relatives. Once the authorities come to investigate this business, we shall be ruined. And since we have deceived Heaven and injured men, no spirits will take our part. Do we want to offend the gods and bring such misfortune on ourselves?

"I have lived as your daughter for twenty years, and my earnings amount to nearly a thousand pieces of gold. You are over sixty now, and I would like to give you enough to cover your expenses for another twenty years to buy my freedom, so that I can live somewhere else with this young man. We will not go far away. I shall see to it that we are near enough to pay our respects to you both morning and evening.''

The old woman saw that the girl's mind was made up, so she gave her consent. When she had paid her ransom, the girl had several hundred pieces of gold left, and with them she hired a few rooms, five doors to the north. Here she gave the young man a bath, changed his clothes, fed him first with hot gruel, which was easy to digest, and later on with cheese and milk.

In a few weeks she was giving him all the choicest delicacies of land and sea. She clothed him, too, in the finest caps, shoes and stockings she could buy. In a few months he began to put on weight, and by the end of the year his health was as good as ever.

One day the girl said to him: ''Now you are strong again and have got back your nerve. Try to think how much you re-member of your old literary studies.''

After a moment's thought he answered: ''About a quarter.''

Then she ordered her carriage to be got ready, and the young man followed her on horseback. When they reached the classical bookshop at the side-gate south of the Flag Tower, she made him choose all the books he wanted, to the tune of a hundred pieces of gold. With these packed in the carriage, she drove home. She now bade him set aside all other cares, to give his whole mind to his studies. Every evening he pored over his books, with the girl at his side, and would not sleep before midnight. If she saw that he was tired, she would advise him to write a poem or ode by way of relaxation.

In two years he had thoroughly mastered his subjects, having read all the books in the kingdom. ''Now I can go in for the examinations,'' he said.

But she answered, "No, you had better revise thoroughly, to be ready for all contingencies."

After another year, she said, "Now you may go."

He passed the examination with high distinction at the first attempt, and his reputation spread through the Ministry of Ceremony. Even older men, when they read his compositions, felt the greatest respect for him and wanted to become his friends.

But the girl said: "Wait a little! Nowadays when a bachelor of arts has passed his examination, he thinks he deserves to become a high official and enjoy fame throughout the empire. But your shady past puts you at a disadvantage beside your fellow scholars. You must sharpen your weapons, to win a second victory. Then you can rival the best scholars."

Then the young man worked harder than ever, and his reputation grew. That year there was a special examination to select scholars of outstanding talent from all parts of the empire. The young man took the paper on criticism of the government and advice to the emperor, and came out top. He was appointed Army Inspector at Chengtu. Many high government officials were now his friends.

When he was about to take up his post, the girl said to him: "Now that you have regained your proper status, I no longer feel I have injured you. Let me go back and look after the old lady till she dies. You must marry a girl from some great family, who is fit to sacrifice to your ancestors. Don't injure yourself by an imprudent match. Take care of yourself! I must leave you."

The young man burst into tears and said: "If you leave me, I shall cut my throat."

But still she insisted that they must part.

He pleaded with her even more passionately, until she said: "Very well. I will go with you across the river as far as Chien-men. Then you must send me back."

To that he consented.

In a few weeks they reached Chienmen. Before they left a proclamation had been issued announcing that the young man's father, who had been Governor of Changchou, had been summoned to the capital and appointed Governor of Chengtu and Inspector of Chienmen. Twelve days later, the governor of Chengtu reached Chienmen, and the young man sent in his card to the posting-station where he was staying. The Lord of Yingyang could not believe that this was his son, yet the card bore the names of the young man's father and grandfather, with their ranks and titles. He was astounded. He sent for his son and, when he arrived, fell on his neck and wept bitterly.

"Now you are my son again," he said, and asked him to tell his story. When he had heard it, the Lord of Yingyang was amazed and enquired where the girl was.

"She came this far with me," answered the young man. "But now she is going back again."

"That won't do," said his father.

The next day he took his son in his carriage to Chengtu but kept the girl at Chienmen, finding suitable lodgings for her. The following day he ordered a go-between to arrange the wedding and prepare the six ceremonies to welcome the bride. Thus they were duly married. In the years that followed the girl proved herself a devoted wife and competent house-keeper, who was loved by all her relations.

Some years later both the young man's parents died, and he showed such filial piety in his mourning that a divine fungus appeared on the roof of his mourning-hut and the grain in that district grew three ears on each stalk. The local authorities reported this to the emperor, and informed him too that several dozen white swallows had nested in the rafters of our hero's roof. The emperor was so impressed that he immediately raised the young man's rank.

When the three years of mourning were over, he was successively promoted to various important posts. Within ten years he was governor of several provinces, while his wife was given the title Lady of Chienkuo. They had four sons, all of whom became high officials, the least successful of them becoming Governor of Taiyuan. All four sons married into great families, so that all their relations were powerful and prosperous and their good fortune was unequalled.

How amazing that a singsong girl should have shown a degree of constancy rarely surpassed by the heroines of old! It really takes one's breath away.

My great-uncle was Governor of Chinchou, an official in the Ministry of Finance, and later Inspector of Roads and Waterways. The hero of this story was his predecessor in these three posts, so that my great-uncle knew all the details of his adventures. One day during the Chen Yuan period [A.D. 785–805], Li Kung-tso of Lunghsi and I happened to be talking of wives who had distinguished themselves by their integrity, and I told him the story of the Lady of Chienkuo. He listened with rapt attention, and asked me to write it down. So I took up my brush, dipped it into the ink, and jotted down this rough outline of the tale to preserve it. It was written in the eighth month of the year Yi Hai [A.D. 795].

(YANG HSIEN-YI AND GLADYS YANG)

§ STORIES OF HEROES

The Kun Lun Slave

Anonymous

During the Ta Li period [A.D. 766–779] there was a young man called Tsui, a palace guard of the Thousand Bulls Order, whose father was a high official and a close friend of a minister. One day his father told him to call on the minister to ask after his health. Now Tsui was a handsome young man, rather bashful and quiet but with a very good manner. The minister ordered his maidservants to raise the curtains and ask him in. And as Tsui bowed and delivered his father's message, the minister took a fancy to him; accordingly he made him sit down and talk.

There were three ravishingly beautiful maids there, who peeled red peaches into golden bowls, then poured sweetened cream over the peaches and presented them. The minister ordered one maid who was dressed in red to take a bowl to Tsui; but the young man was too shy in the presence of girls to eat. Then the minister ordered the girl in red to feed him with a spoon, and Tsui was forced to eat a peach while the girl smiled teasingly.

When the youth rose to go, the minister said, "Come again when you have time. Don't stand on ceremony." He told the girl in red to see him out. Tsui looked back at her as he left the courtyard, and she raised three fingers, turned up the palm of one hand three times, then pointed to the little mirror she wore on her breast and said, "Remember!"

When Tsui had given his father an account of his visit, he went back to his study lost in thought. He became silent and low-spirited, and rapt in sad thoughts would eat nothing. All he did was to chant a poem:

> Led by chance to a fairy mountain,
> I gazed into star-bright eyes.
> Through a red door the moon is shining,
> There forlorn a white beauty lies.

None of his servants knew what was on his mind. But there was a Kun Lun slave in his family called Melek who watched him for a time, then asked,

"What is troubling you that you look so sad all the time? Why not tell your old slave?"

"What do fellows like you understand?" retorted Tsui. "Why pry into my private affairs?"

"Just tell me," urged Melek, "and I promise to get you what you want, be it far or near."

Impressed by his confident tone, Tsui told him the whole story. "That's simple," said Melek. "Why didn't you tell me earlier, instead of moping like that?"

When Tsui told him what signs the girl had made, Melek said, "That's easy to understand. When she raised three fingers, she meant that there are ten rooms in the minister's house where the maids live, and she lives in the third room. When she turned up one palm three times, she was showing fifteen fingers, for the fifteenth of the month. And the little mirror on her breast stood for the full moon on the night of the fifteenth. That is when she wants you to go to her."

Tsui was overjoyed. "Is there any way for me to satisfy my longing?" he asked.

Melek smiled and said, "Tomorrow night is the fifteenth. Give me two lengths of dark blue silk to make two tightly fitting suits. The minister keeps a fierce dog to guard the girls' quarters and kill any stranger who attempts to break in. It is one of the famous Haichou breed, swift as lightning and fierce as a tiger. I am the only man in the world who can kill this hound. Tonight I shall beat it to death for you."

Tsui gave him meat and wine and next evening he left, carrying an iron hammer with chains attached to it. After the time it takes for a meal he came back, saying, "The dog is dead. Now there is nothing to stop us."

Just before midnight, the slave helped Tsui to put on his dark blue suit, and with the young man on his back vaulted over about a dozen walls until they came to the girls' quarters. They stopped at the third room. The carved door was not locked, and the bronze lamp inside shed a faint light. They heard the girl sigh as she sat there expectantly. She was putting on emerald ear-rings and her face was newly rouged, but there was sadness in her face as she chanted:

> Oh, the oriole cries as she longs for her love,
> Who beneath the bright buds stole her jewel away;
> Now the blue sky is cold and no message has come,
> So she plays her jade flute every sorrowful day.

The guards were asleep and all was quiet. Tsui lifted the curtain and entered. For a moment the girl was speechless; then she jumped off the couch and grasping Tsui's hand said, "I knew a clever man like you would understand the signs I made with my fingers. But by what magic art did you come here?"

Tsui told her all the planning had been done by Melek, and that the Kun Lun slave had carried him there.

"Where is Melek?" asked the girl.

"Outside the curtain," he answered.

Then she asked Melek in, and offered him wine in a golden bowl.

"I come from the northern borderland and my family used to be rich," the girl told Tsui. "But my present master was commander of the army there and forced me to be his concubine. I am ashamed that I could not kill myself and had to live on in disgrace. Though I powder and rouge my face, my heart is always sad. We have fine food in jade utensils and incense in golden censers; we wear the softest silk and sleep under embroidered coverlets, and we have mother-of-pearl screens and jewels. Yet these things cannot make me happy, when all the time I feel I am a prisoner. Since your servant has this strange skill, why not rescue me from my jail? If I were free again, I could die content. But I would like to be your slave, and have the honour of serving you. What do you say, sir?"

Tsui changed colour and said nothing, but Melek answered, "If your mind is made up, it is quite simple."

The girl was overjoyed.

Melek asked first to be allowed to take out her baggage. After he had made three trips, he said, "I fear it will soon be dawn." Then with Tsui and the girl on his back he vaulted over about a dozen high walls, just as when they had come in. And all the time the minister's guards heard nothing. Finally they returned to Tsui's quarters, and hid the girl there.

The next morning, when the minister's household discovered that the girl was gone and the dog was dead, the minister was appalled. "My house is always well guarded and locked," he said, "yet now someone seems to have flown in and out leaving no trace. This must be the work of no common adventurer. Don't let word of this get out, for fear harm should come of it."

The girl remained hidden in Tsui's house for two years. Then, one spring day when she rode in a small carriage to Chuchiang to see the flowers, she was recognized by one of the minister's household. When the minister learned of her whereabouts, he was amazed and summoned Tsui to question him. In fear and trembling, the young man dared not conceal the truth, but told the minister the whole story and how he had been carried there by his slave.

"It was very wrong of the girl," said the minister. "But since she has served you so long, it is too late to demand justice. However I feel in duty bound to get rid of your Kun Lun slave: that man is a public menace."

Then he ordered fifty guards, armed to the teeth, to surround Tsui's house and capture the Kun Lun slave. But Melek, a dagger in his hand, vaulted over the wall as swiftly as if he had wings, like some huge bird of prey. Though arrows rained down, they all fell short, and in a flash he made good his escape.

Tsui's family was thrown into a panic. The minister too regretted what he had done, and was afraid. Every night for a whole year he had himself guarded by servants armed with swords and halberds.

Over ten years later, one of Tsui's household saw Melek selling medicine in the market at Lo-yang. He looked as vigorous as ever.

(YANG AND YANG)

The Man with the Curly Beard

by Tu Kuang-ting

When Emperor Yang of the Sui Dynasty [A.D. 605–618] visited Yangchow, Councillor Yang Su was ordered to guard the West Capital. Now Yang Su, that proud noble, plumed himself on the fact that in those unsettled times no one in the empire had greater power or prestige than he. Giving free rein to his love of luxury and pride, he ceased to behave like a subject. He received both officials and guests seated on a couch, and went about supported by beautiful maids, in his behavior usurping the emperor's prerogatives. He became worse, too, in his old age when, forgetting his duty to his sovereign, he made no attempt to save the realm from utter ruin.

One day Li Ching, later to become the Duke of Wei but then a private citizen, asked for an interview in order to offer advice on government policy. Yang Su, as usual, received him sitting. Li approached and said with a bow, "The empire is in a turmoil and the bold are contending for power. As chief councillor to the imperial house, Your Highness should be thinking of how to rally good men, and should not receive visitors sitting."

Yang Su was impressed and stood up to apologize. After talking with Li he was very pleased with him and accepted his memorandum.

Now while Li had been discoursing brilliantly, one of Yang's maids—a very beautiful girl who was standing in front of them holding a red whisk—had watched him intently. When he was leaving, she said to the officer at the door, "Ask him his name and where he lives." Li told the officer. The girl nodded and withdrew, and Li went back to his hostel.

That night, just before dawn, there was a soft knocking at Li's door, and when he got up he found a stranger there in a cap and a purple gown, who was carrying a stick and a bag. Asked who he was, the stranger said, "I am the maid with the red whisk in Councillor Yang's house." Then Li quickly let her in. When she took off her outer gown and cap, he saw she was a beautiful girl of about nineteen with a fair complexion, dressed in bright clothes. She bowed to him, and he returned the bow.

"I have served Yang Su for a long time," said the girl, "and seen many visitors. But there has never been any one like you. The vine cannot grow by itself, but needs a tree to cling to. So I have come to you."

"But Councillor Yang has great power in the capital; how can it be done?" said Li.

"Never mind him—he's an old imbecile," she replied. "Many maids have left, knowing that he will fall; and he makes very little effort to get them back. I have thought it over carefully. Don't worry." Asked her name, she told Li it was Chang, and that she was the eldest in her family. He found her an angel in complexion, manner, speech and character. Both happy and alarmed at this unexpected conquest, he had not a moment's peace of mind. Inquisitive people kept peeping through his door, and for a few days a half-hearted search was made for her. Then Li and the girl dressed in fine clothes and fled on horseback from the capital to Taiyuan.

On the way they stopped at a hostel in Lingshih. The bed was made, meat was boiling in the pot, Chang was combing her long hair in front of the bed and Li was currying the horses at the door, when suddenly a man of medium height with a curly red beard rode up on a sorry-looking donkey. He threw down his leather bag before the fire, took a pillow and lay on the bed to watch the girl combing her hair. Furious but uncertain what course to take, Li went on grooming the horses. The girl looked intently at the stranger's face, holding her hair in one hand while with the other she signed to Li behind her back to prevent his flaring up. Then, quickly pinning up her hair, she curtseyed to the stranger and asked his name. Still lying on the bed, he answered that it was Chang.

"My name is Chang too," she said. "We may be cousins." With a bow she asked his position in the family, and he told her he was the third child. When she informed him that she was the eldest in her family, the stranger laughed and replied,

"Then you are the eldest of my younger cousins."

"Come and meet my cousin," she called to Li, who bowed to him and sat down with them by the fire.

"What are you boiling?" asked the stranger.

"Mutton. It should be cooked by now."

"I am famished," said the man with the curly beard. While Li went out to buy bread, he took a dagger from his waist and cut up the mutton. They ate together, and after they had finished the stranger sliced up what was left and gave it to the donkey. He was very quick in all his movements.

"You seem a poor fellow," the stranger remarked to Li. "How did you get hold of such a marvellous girl?"

"I may be poor but I am no fool," said Li. "I wouldn't tell anyone else, but I won't hide anything from you." And he described how it had come about.

"Where are you going now?" asked the other.

"To Taiyuan," said Li.

"By the way, I have come uninvited: have you any wine?"

Li told him that west of the hostel was a wineshop, and fetched him a pint of wine. As they ate together, he said to

Li: "Judging by your looks and behaviour, you are a stout fellow. Do you know anybody remarkable in Taiyuan?"

"I used to know a man whom I thought truly great," replied Li. "My other friends are only fit to be generals and captains."

"What is his name?"

"His name is Li too."

"How old is he?"

"Only twenty."

"What is he now?"

"He is the son of a provincial general."

"He sounds like the man I am looking for," said the stranger. "But I will have to see him to make sure. Can you arrange a meeting?"

"I have a friend named Liu Wen-ching who knows him well," said Li. "We can arrange an interview through Liu. But why do you want to see him?"

"An astrologer told me there had been a strange portent at Taiyuan, and I should look into it. You are leaving tomorrow—when will you arrive?"

Li calculated how long it would take, and the stranger said, "Meet me at daybreak the day after you arrive at Fenyang Bridge." Then he got on his donkey and made off so swiftly that he was at once lost to sight.

Li and the girl were both amazed and delighted. "Such a brave fellow will not deceive us," they said. "We need not worry." After some time they whipped up their horses and left.

On the appointed day they entered the city of Taiyuan, and were very pleased to meet the stranger again. They went to find Liu, and told him, "A good fortune-teller wants to meet Li Shih-min. Will you send for him?" Liu thought highly of Li, so he immediately sent a messenger to him asking him to come. Presently Li Shih-min arrived, wearing neither coat nor shoes, but with a fur coat thrown over him. He was overflowing with good spirits, and his appearance was very striking.

The curly-bearded man, sitting silently at the end of the table, was struck from the moment of his entry. After drinking a few cups with him he called Li aside and said, "This is undoubtedly the future emperor." When Li told Liu this, the latter was overjoyed and highly pleased with himself too.

After Li Shih-min had left, the man with the curly beard declared, "I am eighty percent certain, but my friend the Taoist priest must see him too. You two go back to the capital, but meet me one afternoon at the wineshop east of Mahang. If you see this donkey and another lean one, that means my priestly friend and I are there, and you can go straight up." Then he left, and again they did as they were told.

On the appointed day they went to the wineshop and saw the two donkeys. Lifting up the skirts of their robes they went upstairs, and found the curly-bearded man and a priest drinking there. They were pleased to see Li, asked him to sit down and drank about a dozen cups together.

"Downstairs in the cupboard," said the man with the curly beard, "you will find a hundred thousand cash. Get a quiet place to lodge your wife, and meet me again another day at Fenyang Bridge."

When Li went to the bridge, he found the priest and the curly-bearded man already there, and they went together to see Liu. They discovered him playing chess, and after greeting him they started chatting. Liu sent a note to invite Li Shih-min to watch the game. The priest played with Liu, while the curly-bearded man and Li watched.

When Li Shih-min arrived, his appearance struck awe into them all. He bowed and sat down, looking so serene and talking so well that the atmosphere seemed to freshen and splendour to be shed all around. At the sight of him the priest had turned pale, and as he made his next move he said, "It's all up with me. I have lost the game, and there's no help for it. What more is there to say?" He stopped playing and took his leave. Once outside he said to the curly-bearded man, "There is no place for you in this country. You had better try your luck elsewhere. Don't give up or lose hope." They decided to leave for the capital.

To Li the curly-bearded man said, "The day after you arrive, come with your wife to my humble lodgings. I know you have no property. I want to introduce my wife to you and talk things over. Be sure not to fail me." Then he sighed and left.

Li rode back to his lodgings. Later he went with his wife to the capital to call on the curly-bearded man. The latter's house had a small, plain wooden door. When they knocked, a man opened the door, bowed to them and said, "The master has been looking forward to your arrival for a long time." They were led through inner doors, each more magnificent than the last. Forty girl attendants stood in court, and twenty slaves led the way to the east hall where they found a great display of rare and precious objects. There were so many fine caskets, cupboards, head-dresses, mirrors and trinkets that they felt they had left the world of men. After they had washed they changed into rich and strange garments, and then their host was announced. He came in wearing a gauze cap, with a fur coat thrown over him, his whole appearance magnificent and kingly. When they had greeted each other cordially, he called his wife to come out, and they discovered that she was a beauty too. They were invited into the central hall, where there was a fine feast spread—richer than the banquets given by princes— and while they feasted twenty women musicians played music which sounded as if made in paradise. When they had eaten their fill, wine was served. Then servants carried out from the east hall twenty couches covered with embroidered silk. They removed the covers, and Li saw that the couches were laden with account books and keys.

"This is all the treasure I possess," said the man with the

300 • *T'ang, Five Dynasties, and Sung*

curly beard. "I turn it all over to you. I meant to make my mark in the world, and fight with brave men for ten years or more to carve out a kingdom. But now that the true sovereign has been found, why should I stay here? Your friend Li Shih-min of Taiyuan will be a truly great ruler, who will restore peace to the empire after three or four years. With your out-standing gifts, if you do your best under his serene guidance, you will certainly reach the top rank of councillors. And your wife with her great beauty and discernment will win fame and honour through her illustrious husband. Only a woman like her could recognize your talent, and only a man like you could bring her glory. An able minister is bound to find a wise monarch. It is no accident that when the tiger roars the wind blows, and when the dragon bellows the clouds gather. You can use my gifts to help the true monarch and achieve great deeds. Go to it! Ten years from now, several hundred miles southeast of China, strange happenings will take place—that will be when I realize my ambition. When that time comes, will you both drink towards the southeast to congratulate me?" He bid his servants pay their respects to Li and his wife, saying, "From now on they are your master and mistress." Then the curly-bearded man and his wife put on military uniform and rode off, attended by one slave only. Soon they were out of sight.

Taking over the curly-bearded man's house, Li became wealthy and used his fortune to help Li Shih-min to conquer the whole empire.

During the Chen Kuan period [A.D. 627–649], while Li was left minister and acting prime minister, the southern tribesmen reported that a thousand big ships and one hundred thousand armed troops had entered the kingdom of Fuyu, killed the king and occupied the land. By now all was peaceful there again. Li realized that the curly-bearded man had succeeded. On his return from court he told his wife, and they put on ceremonial dress and drank to the southeast to congratulate their old friend.

From this we see that imperial power is not won by any great man who aspires to it, let alone any man who is not great. Any subject who vainly attempts to rebel is like a praying mantis dashing itself against the wheel of a chariot, for Heaven has willed that our empire should prosper for a myriad generations.

It has been suggested that much of Li's military strategy was taught him by the man with the curly beard.

(YANG AND YANG)

§ STORIES OF SATIRE

The White Monkey

Anonymous

In the year A.D. 545, during the Liang Dynasty, the emperor sent General Lan Ching on an expedition to the south. He went as far as Kweilin, and wiped out the rebel forces of Li Shih-ku and Chen Cheh. At the same time his lieutenant Ouyang Hei fought his way as far as Changlo, conquering all the cave-dwellers there and leading his army deep into difficult terrain.

Now Ouyang's wife had a white skin and was very beautiful and delicate.

"You should not have brought such a beautiful wife here," his men told him. "There is a god in these parts who carries off young women, especially good-looking ones. You had better guard her carefully."

Ouyang took fright. That night he set guards around the house, and hid his wife in a closely guarded inner chamber with a dozen maidservants on watch. During the night a high wind sprang up and the sky turned dark, but nothing untoward happened and shortly before dawn the exhausted guards dozed off.

Suddenly, however, they were startled from their sleep to find that Ouyang's wife had disappeared. The door was still locked, and no one knew how she had left. They started looking outside on the steep hillside, but a thick fog blotted out everything at one yard's distance, making it impossible to continue the search. Then dawn came, but still they could find no trace of her.

In great anger and grief Ouyang swore that he would not return alone. On pretext of sickness he stationed his troops there, and sent them out daily in all directions to search the valleys and heights for his wife. A month later, on a bush some thirty miles away, they found one of her embroidered shoes, soaked by rain but still recognizable. Overcome with grief, Ouyang intensified the search, taking thirty picked armed men with rations to scour the hills. After another ten days, they reached a place about seventy miles from their camp from where they could see a green, tree-clad mountain to the south which towered above the other hills. When they came to the foot of this mountain, they found it surrounded by a deep stream, which they had to build a little bridge to cross. Between the precipices and emerald bamboos they caught glimpses of coloured dresses and heard the sound of women talking and laughing. When they pulled themselves up the cliffs by vines and ropes, they found green trees planted in avenues with rare flowers between them, and a verdant meadow fresh and soft as a carpet. It was a quiet, secluded, unearthly retreat. There was a gate to the east, hewn in the rock, through which several dozen women in bright new dresses and shawls could be seen passing—singing and laughing as they went. When they saw the strangers, they stopped to stare. And when the men went up to them, the women asked what had brought them there.

After Ouyang had told them, the women looked at each other and sighed. "Your wife has been here over a month," they said.

"Just now she is ill in bed. You may go and see her." Passing through a wooden door in the stone gate, Ouyang saw three spacious enclosures where couches strewn with silk cushions had been placed by the walls. His wife was lying on a bed spread with matting and rugs, with rich food placed before her. At Ouyang's approach she turned and saw him, but signed to him to leave.

"Some of us have been here for ten years already," the other women told him, "while your wife has only just arrived. This is where the monster lives. He is a man-killer, a match for even a hundred warriors. You had better slip away before he comes back. If you will let us have forty gallons of potent wine, ten dogs for him to eat, and several dozen catties of hemp, we shall be able to kill him. Come at noon, not earlier, ten days from now." They urged him to leave quickly, and Ouyang did so.

He was back again on the appointed day bringing with him the strong liquor, hemp and dogs. "The monster is a great drinker," the women told him, "and likes to drink himself silly. When he is drunk he always wants to test his strength, and tells us to fasten his arms and legs with silken ropes as he lies on the couch. Then he frees himself with one leap. But once we twisted three ropes together; he couldn't break them. Now if we twist hemp inside the silk, we are sure he will never be able to snap it. His whole body is like iron, but he invariably protects those few inches under his navel; this must be his vulnerable spot." Then, pointing to a nearby precipice, they said, "That is where he stores his food. You can conceal yourselves there. Keep quiet and wait. Put the wine by the flowers and the dogs in the forest. If our plan works we shall call you."

Ouyang and his men did as they were told, and waited with bated breath. Late in the afternoon, something like a streamer of white silk flew down from the top of a distant hill straight into the cave, and in a little while a six-foot man with a fine beard came out. Dressed in white, with a stick in his hand, he was attended by the women. He gave a start at the sight of the dogs, then leaped at them, seized them and tore them limb from limb, eating greedily until he was sated. The women offered him drinks in jade cups, and together they joked and laughed gaily. After he had drunk several pints of wine, the women helped him in, and sounds of fun and merriment could be heard.

After a long time, the women came out to summon the men, who went in carrying their weapons. They saw a huge white monkey fastened by its four paws on the couch. At the sight of the men it recoiled and struggled in vain to release itself, and its furious eyes flickered like lightning. Ouyang and his men fell on it, only to find its body like iron or stone. But when they stabbed at its belly under the navel, their swords sank in and red blood spurted out. The white monkey gave a long sigh and said to Ouyang, "This must be the will of heaven—for otherwise you would not have been able to kill me. Your wife has conceived. Don't kill the child born to her, for he will grow up to serve a great monarch and your family will prosper." With these words he died.

They searched through his possessions, and found stores of precious things as well as an abundance of rare food on the tables. Every treasure known to man was there, including several gallons of rare scents and a pair of finely wrought swords. The thirty-odd women were all exquistite beauties, some of whom had been there for ten years. They said that when women grew old they were taken away, to what fate no one knew. The white monkey was the only one to enjoy these women, for he had no followers.

Every morning the monkey would wash and put on a hat, a white collar and a white silk dress, wearing the same in winter and summer alike. He had white fur several inches long. When he stayed at home he would read wooden tablets inscribed with hieroglyphics which no one else could decipher; and after he had finished reading he would put the tablets under a stone step. On a clear day he might practise sword play, and then the two swords would encircle him like flashes of lightning making a moon-like halo round him. He ate all manner of things, particularly nuts, and was also very partial to dogs, whose blood he loved to drink. At noon he would fly off to travel thousands of miles in half a day, coming back at night. Such was his custom.

Whenever something caught his fancy, he would not rest till it was his. At night he forwent sleep to gambol through all the beds, enjoying the women in turn. He could chatter away and discourse eloquently too, despite his simian form.

One early autumn day that year when leaves were beginning to fall, the white monkey had seemed in low spirits and said, "I have been accused by the mountain deities and condemned to death. But if I solicit the aid of other spirits, perhaps I shall escape." Just after the full moon, a fire sprang up under the stone step and burned his tablets. "I have lived a thousand years but never had a child; it means my death is near." Running his eyes over the women, he wept for a while. "This mountain is secluded and steep, and no man has set foot here before," he went on. "Looking down from the peaks I have seen packs of wolves with tigers and other wild beasts at the foot of the mountain, while not even a woodcutter has appeared on the heights. If it were not the will of heaven, how could men have come here?"

Ouyang then went back taking the jade, precious stones and beautiful treasures as well as all the women, some of whom were able to find their own homes. In a year's time Ouyang's wife gave birth to a son, and the child took after the monkey. Later Ouyang was condemned to death by Emperor Wu of the Chen

Dynasty. But an old friend of his, Chiang Tsung, was partial to Ouyang's son on account of his outstanding intelligence and took him into his house. Thus the boy escaped death. He grew up to become a good writer and calligrapher and a well-known figure in his time.

(YANG AND YANG)

Some Further Readings

Bauer, Wolfgang. *The Golden Casket: Chinese Novellas of Two Millennia.* Translated by Christopher Levenson from Wolfgang Bauer and Herbert Franke's German version of the original Chinese. New York: Harcourt, Brace and World, 1964. (Also contains material relevant to Chapters 6, 15, and 18.)

Edwards, E. D. *Chinese Prose Literature of the T'ang Period.* 2 vols. London: Probsthain, 1937–38. (Volume 2 contains fiction.)

Lin Yutang, ed. and trans. *Famous Chinese Short Stories.* New York: John Day, 1952. (Also contains material relevant to Chapters 15 and 18.)

Wang Chi-chen. *Traditional Chinese Tales.* New York: Greenwood Press, 1968. (Also contains material relevant to Chapters 15 and 18.)

Yang Hsien-yi and Yang, Gladys, trans. *The Dragon King's Daughter: Ten T'ang Dynasty Stories.* Rev. ed. Peking: Foreign Languages Press, 1962.

13

THE GOLDEN POETS

Wang Wei, Li Po, and Tu Fu

Chinese power may have run to further borders in the Han, but the Chinese genius surely was never more insolent than in the T'ang: poetry and prose flowed from the brushes of a thousand talented men, and the West knows of only the smallest fraction of their work. Yet this is the period on which Western scholars and translators have worked most diligently: Li Po, Tu Fu, Wang Wei, and Po Chü-i all have been translated at some length. We have selections below from Wang Wei, Li Po, and Tu Fu, and from a few minor poets.

Li Po, under his Japanese name of Rihaku, was introduced in translation to London in 1913. Since then we have seen hundreds of translations, and our knowledge of T'ang poetry has increased slightly since the day Ford Madox Ford wrote: "Let us once more quote Li Po, not because he was the greatest of the Chinese poets of the era, that glory being accorded by the Chinese themselves to Rihaku."

Wang Wei was famous as a painter as well as as a

poet; the Sung poet Su Shih said to praise him, "In his poems are paintings, and in his paintings, poems." We probably find in Wang Wei at its finest development the poetic effect for which the Chinese are so famous, the casting of an image on the visual imagination.

Li Po and Tu Fu knew each other and wrote poems for each other, but the two men were rather different in their sensibilities. No friendship of Chinese poets is more famous, and each of the two men represents a Chinese personal archetype: Li Po is a perfect Taoist, and Tu Fu is a splendid Confucian. The Chinese themselves say that "Li Po is the peoples' poet, Tu Fu is the poets' poet."

Tu Fu probably has written more perfect *lü-shih* than any other man; in any case, he is held up as the classical model for work in this rigorous and difficult form. *Lü-shih* may be called the sonnets of China, for they are the formal showpiece of Chinese poetry. The form works out as follows:

Main form: A *lü-shih* has eight lines. Each line has in it the same number of syllables as every other line in the poem. Some *lü-shih* are written in five-syllable lines, and some are written in seven-syllable lines.

Rhyme: The second, fourth, sixth, and eighth lines all end on the same rhyme. The first line sometimes does, and sometimes does not, join in this rhyme scheme.

Tonal balance: The Chinese very carefully control the verbal music of their *lü-shih* lines by playing on the Chinese language's "phonemic tone." Since English does not have this phonemic tone, we can get no real sense of tonal balance unless we hear some Chinese. The practice of balancing tones began with the seraglio poets, and the T'ang poets brought it to its finest development. What the poet is up to, basically, is this: the Chinese vowels are sorted into two categories, depending on whether the tone is "level" or is "unlevel." If we let "a" stand for either of these categories and let "ā" ("non-a") stand for the other, we can summarize as follows the way in which the tones were arranged in seven-syllable verse:

1. Two sequences were permitted:

     1.1.   a–a–ā–ā–ā–a–a
     1.2.   a–a–ā–ā–a–a–ā

2. No two consecutive lines could be exactly alike. A deviation from these patterns was admitted often enough in the first or third syllable of the line. The patterns for five-syllable verse were the same as above, subtracting the first two syllables in each line. The poet, further, was governed by the tone on his rhyme-words; it was usual to rhyme on words that belonged to the "level"-tone category.

Parallel structure: If it is very difficult for us to appreciate or even to understand what the Chinese poets did with tonal balance, because tonal balance is phonological and prosodic, it is not so difficult to understand the "parallel structure" they used in *lü-shih*. For parallel structure is a visual (imagistic) or logical effect.

First let us say what parallel structure is, and then let us see how the poets use it in *lü-shih*. The basic principle is that in a verse-line, the first syllable should "be parallel" to the first syllable of the preceding line, the second syllable should be parallel to the second syllable of the preceding line, and so on through the five or seven syllables. The syllable is parallel to the other syllable if it belongs to the same logical, rational, or notional category. The Chinese can get away with this, of course, because the Chinese single syllable is, in almost every case, also a word. The categories which later scholars have discovered in the poets' work are as follows: (1) heavenly phenomena, (2) times and seasons, (3) landscape features, (4) architectural structures, (5) artifacts, (6) clothing and ornaments, (7) foods and beverages, (8) cultural implements, (9) literary forms and productions, (10) flora, (11) fauna, (12) bodily parts, (13) human affairs, (14) familial relationships, social ranks, professions, and trades, (15) pronouns, (16) locations, (17) numbers, (18) colors, (19) "cyclical signs," (20) personal names, (21) place names, (22) "consecutive synonyms," (23) "consecutive antonyms," (24) clichés, (25) iterations, (26) adverbs, (27) connectives, and (28) expletives.

Here are a couple of examples of parallel distichs. The first example is from Li Po:

> Sea-clouds cover the post road.
> River moon enshadows the rustic tower.

And here is an example from Tu Fu:

> North, wind chases the active air;
> South, the Dipper avoids the patterned stars.

You will be able to find a number of these in the poems which you will read below.

In order to be a *lü-shih,* the poem must include parallel structure in lines five and six. Usually, the "inner distichs"—the second and third distichs—are formed with parallel structure. That is, line three is parallel to line four, and line five is parallel to line six. The reader can see this in Wang Wei's poem "I Watch the Hunt" (below). But the parallel structure may occur in various other ways to make a *lü-shih,* all the way from a single parallel distich (the third) to four parallel distichs (a completely parallel poem). But a parallel structure in the last two lines is extremely rare. In fact, the poets liked to write a final distich in which the language was as natural—as inartificial—as possible, so that the reader would leave the poem with a human voice sounding in his ear.

The *lü-shih* and the *chüeh-chü* are the most stylized of T'ang poetic forms. The *chüeh-chü* is of itself so important, and is so interesting as a poetic form, that a separate chapter on it appears later. But the T'ang poets truly showed themselves to be heirs of earlier ages, and they wrote poems in many other forms and styles—including *yueh-fu* ballads and folksongs and, especially in Li Po's case, poems which are very like the Han *fu* or the work of Ssu-ma Hsiang-ju. Their work has lasted so long, not because they could master a difficult and complicated form, but because they could and did, as musicians put it, "blow soul."

§ POEMS BY WANG WEI
(A.D. 701–761)

—GREEN RIVER—

When we go to Yellow Flower Spring,
We usually follow the winding path which wriggles
Along Green River and through the hills in ten thousand
    turns.

As the crow flies, less than thirty miles.

The bubbling boisterous water roars among scattered
    rocks,
There is the colour of tranquillity in these deep green
    pines.
Water chestnuts and gipsy weeds float idly on the water
Reflecting the slashing knives of reeds and rushes. .

My heart is pure white as silk—at rest
Like this still and placid stream.
I'm going to stay on this large flat rock
And fish! That's all I desire.

            (CHANG YIN-NAN AND LEWIS WALMSLEY)

—ON A SUMMER DAY, I PASS THE MONASTERY
OF THE GREEN DRAGON, AND CALL ON
THE ZEN MASTER—

    I'm old enough
        to be "an old fool."
    I walk slowly
        to visit the Zen Hall

I shall ask
    is it good? the heart is good?
We learn in the end
    it's null: suffering is null.
Mountains and rivers
    exist in the heavenly eye.
Dominions and powers
    are in our ethereal form.
Be not amazed
    melting flames and heat
Are able to shape
    the great earth and air.

(MCNAUGHTON)

—I WATCH THE HUNT—

The wind is stiff.
    The bow of horn sings.
The General
    hunts in Wei Ch'eng.
The grass is withered.
    The eagle's eye is sharp.
Snow melts.
    The horse's hooves are light.
Quickly, they pass
    Hsin-feng, Market
And wheeling, return
    to Hsi-liu Camp
Look back:
    place of an arrowed vulture;
For a thousand *li,*
    the evening clouds lie flat.

(MCNAUGHTON)

—I SEE OFF THE SENIOR OFFICIAL CH'I CHOU-
YUAN AS HE GOES HOME—

Shake hands.
    One sees the other off.
Heart's grief,
        how shall one speak of it?
Autumn wind
    arranges the Southernwood cords.
The traveler leaves
    the Meng-ch'ang Gate.
"The government post
    runs through Locust Village.
Stop for awhile,
    and go down to Hibiscus Plain,
Follow westward
    the old banner-marks,
And from here,
    head for Ho Yuan."

(MCNAUGHTON)

§ POEMS BY LI PO
(*ca.* 701– *ca.* 762)

—THE RIVER-MERCHANT'S WIFE—
A LETTER

While my hair was still cut straight across my forehead
I played about the front gate, pulling flowers.
You came by on bamboo stilts, playing horse,
You walked about my seat, playing with blue plums.

And we went on living in the village of Chokan:
Two small people, without dislike or suspicion.

At fourteen I married My Lord you.
I never laughed, being bashful.
Lowering my head, I looked at the wall.
Called to, a thousand times, I never looked back.

At fifteen I stopped scowling,
I desired my dust to be mingled with yours
Forever and forever and forever.
Why should I climb the look out?

At sixteen you departed,
You went into far Ku-to-yen, by the river of swirling
    eddies,
And you have been gone five months.
The monkeys make sorrowful noise overhead.

You dragged your feet when you went out.
By the gate now, the moss is grown, the different
    mosses,
Too deep to clear them away!
The leaves fall early this autumn, in wind.
The paired butterflies are already yellow with August
Over the grass in the West garden;
They hurt me. I grow older.
If you are coming down through the narrows of the
    river Kiang,
Please let me know beforehand,
And I will come out to meet you
                  As far as Cho-fu-Sa.

                        (POUND)

—POEM BY THE BRIDGE AT TEN-SHIN—

March has come to the bridge head,
Peach boughs and apricot boughs hang over a
    thousand gates,
At morning there are flowers to cut the heart,
And evening drives them on the eastward-flowing
    waters.
Petals are on the gone waters and on the going,
        And on the back-swirling eddies,
But to-day's men are not the men of the old days,
Though they hang in the same way over the bridge-rail.
The sea's colour moves at the dawn
And the princes still stand in rows, about the throne,
And the moon falls over the portals of Sei-go-yo,
And clings to the walls and the gate-top.
With head gear glittering against the cloud and sun,
The lords go forth from the court, and into far
    borders.
They ride upon dragon-like horses,
Upon horses with head-trappings of yellow metal,
And the streets make way for their passage.
        Haughty their passing,
Haughty their steps as they go in to great banquets,
To high halls and curious food,
To the perfumed air and girls dancing,
To clear flutes and clear singing;
To the dance of the seventy couples;
To the mad chase through the gardens.
Night and day are given over to pleasure
And they think it will last a thousand autumns,
        Unwearying autumns.
For them the yellow dogs howl portents in vain,

And what are they compared to the lady Riokushu,
   That was cause of hate!
Who among them is a man like Han-rei
    Who departed alone with his mistress,
 With her hair unbound, and he his own skiffsman!

           (POUND)

—LAMENT OF THE FRONTIER GUARD—

By the North Gate, the wind blows full of sand,
Lonely from the beginning of time until now!
Trees fall, the grass goes yellow with autumn.
I climb the towers and towers
  to watch out the barbarous land:
Desolate castle, the sky, the wide desert.
There is no wall left to this village.
Bones white with a thousand frosts,
High heaps, covered with trees and grass;
Who brought this to pass?
Who has brought the flaming imperial anger?
Who has brought the army with drums and with
  kettle-drums?
Barbarous kings.
A gracious spring, turned to blood-ravenous autumn,
A turmoil of wars-men, spread over the middle kingdom,
Three hundred and sixty thousand,
And sorrow, sorrow like rain.
Sorrow to go, and sorrow, sorrow returning.
Desolate, desolate fields,
And no children of warfare upon them,
   No longer the men for offence and defence.

Ah, how shall you know the dreary sorrow at the
        North Gate,
With Rihaku's name forgotten,
And we guardsmen fed to the tigers.

                                        (POUND)

—EXILE'S LETTER—

To So-Kin of Rakuyo, ancient friend, Chancellor of Gen.
Now I remember that you built me a special tavern
By the south side of the bridge at Ten-Shin.
With yellow gold and white jewels, we paid for songs
        and laughter
And we were drunk for month on month, forgetting the
        kings and princes.
Intelligent men came drifting in from the sea and from
        the west border,
And with them, and with you especially
There was nothing at cross purpose,
And they made nothing of sea-crossing or of mountain-
        crossing,
If only they could be of that fellowship,
And we all spoke out our hearts and minds, and
        without regret.
And then I was sent off to South Wei,
        smothered in laurel groves,
And you to the north of Raku-hoku,
Till we had nothing but thoughts and memories in
        common.

And then, when separation had come to its worst,
We met, and travelled into Sen-Go,

Through all the thirty-six folds of the turning and
    twisting waters,
Into a valley of the thousand bright flowers,
That was the first valley;
And into ten thousand valleys full of voices and pine-
    winds.
And with silver harness and reins of gold,
Out came the East of Kan foreman and his company.
And there came also the "True man" of Shi-yo to
    meet me,
Playing on a jewelled mouth-organ.
In the storied houses of San-Ko they gave us more
    Sennin music,
Many instruments, like the sound of young phoenix
    broods.
The foreman of Kan Chu, drunk, danced
    because his long sleeves wouldn't keep still
With that music playing,
And I, wrapped in brocade, went to sleep with my
    head on his lap,
And my spirit so high it was all over the heavens,
And before the end of the day we were scattered like
    stars, or rain.
I had to be off to So, far away over the waters,
You back to your river-bridge.

And your father, who was brave as a leopard,
Was governor in Hei Shu, and put down the barbarian
    rabble.
And one May he had you send for me,
        despite the long distance.
And what with broken wheels and so on, I won't say
    it wasn't hard going,
Over roads twisted like sheep's guts.

And I was still going, late in the year,
           in the cutting wind from the North,
And thinking how little you cared for the cost,
           and you caring enough to pay it.
And what a reception:
Red jade cups, food well set on a blue jewelled table,
And I was drunk, and had no thought of returning.
And you would walk out with me to the western corner of
    the castle,
To the dynastic temple, with water about it clear as blue
    jade,
With boats floating, and the sound of mouth-organs and
    drums,
With ripples like dragon-scales, going grass green on the
    water,
Pleasure lasting, with courtezans, going and coming
    without hindrance,
With the willow flakes falling like snow,
And vermilioned girls getting drunk about sunset,
And the water, a hundred feet deep, reflecting green
    eyebrows
—Eyebrows painted green are a fine sight in young moon-
    light,
Gracefully painted—
And the girls singing back at each other,
Dancing in transparent brocade,
And the wind lifting the song, and interrupting it,
Tossing it up under the clouds.
              And all this comes to an end.
              And is not again to be met with.
I went up to the court for examination,
Tried Layu's luck, offered the Choyo song,
And got no promotion,

And went back to the East Mountains
White-headed.

And once again, later, we met at the South bridgehead.
And then the crowd broke up, you went north to San
    palace,
And if you ask how I regret that parting:
It is like the flowers falling at Spring's end
        Confused, whirled in a tangle.
What is the use of talking, and there is no end of
      talking,
There is no end of things in the heart.
I call in the boy,
Have him sit on his knees here
     To seal this,
And send it a thousand miles, thinking.

                       (POUND)

—SPRING THOUGHTS—

O Grass of Yen
         like green silk flowing
Green boughs low
        on mulberries of Ch'in
All that time!
       you've been thinking of home
and all that time!
       my heart breaking
In my silk bedcurtain
      spring wind

It does not know me
Why does it come
slipping in?

(C.H. KWOCK AND VINCENT MCHUGH)

—NIGHT MOORING AT COW'S CREEK:
I THINK OF THE OLD MAN—

At Cow's Creek
on Western River
the night
Sky still blue
not a rag of cloud
I go on deck
to look at the bright moon
thinking of
the great General Hsieh of old
I myself
can chant a poem
but that man
cannot hear me
In the morning
we make sail and go
The maple leaves
fall as they will.

(KWOCK AND MCHUGH)

—IN RIVERS AND MOUNTAINS, WAITING FOR THE MOON, I GROW SAD—

I wait for the moon.
   The moon is not yet out.
I gaze at the river.
   The river flows on itself.
Suddenly, startlingly,
   west of the wall, in the suburbs
In the dark sky:
   a hanging hook of jade.
The white flowers,
   although a man might pick them,
In the clear scene
   cannot move on with one.
It's brighter bright
   within the waves of gold,
And I vainly look
   at the "Pavilion of Daw and Jay."
       (MCNAUGHTON)

—WITH THE RECLUSE CHIA AT THE LUNG-HSING MONASTERY I TRIM THE FALLEN WU-T'UNG BRANCHES AND GAZE AT YUNG-HU—

We trim the fallen
   Wu-t'ung branches.
Seated, we can
   watch Yung-hu.

Rain pours.
          The autumn mountains are clean.
The forest shines.
          The quiet jade stirs.

Stream-enclosed,
          the bright mirror turns;
Cloud-encoiled,
          the painted screen moves.
A thousand old
          wind-blown things,
Famous sage,
          gather in this hour.

(MCNAUGHTON)

—"THEY FOUGHT IN THE SOUTH"—

Last year, we attacked
          at Mulberry Flats and its springs;
This year, we attack
          on the Onion River roads.
At the T'iao-chih sea,
          we wash our swords in the surf;
At Heaven's Hills,
          we pasture our horses to snow and grass.

Three thousand miles—
          hang on, march and attack.
Three armies—everyone
          cut up or grown old.
Barbarian gangs
          take slaughter and carnage
                    as plowing and craft.

From of old, they have only sown
        white bones on their yellow sand-fields.

The house of Ch'in hammered up walls
        to hold off the hordes—and there
The House of Han still keeps
        flickering beacon-fires.
Flickering beacon-fires never cease:
March, attack—
        it's always the season for wars.

On the field:
        Attack! Grapple! Struggle! Die!
Knocked-down horses shriek, whine
        and cry to the sky.
Crows, kites peck human bowels;
Carrying them, they fly
        and lay them on dead tree and branch.

Lieutenants, privates
        stain the grass and weeds.
Generals! Secretaries!
        what good does this do?
So we know:
        these so-called "arms"
                are really murderer's tools.
Benevolent men
        seek for them
                neither use nor excuse.

                          (MCNAUGHTON)

§ POEMS BY TU FU

(A.D. 712–770)

—PAINTING OF A FALCON—

Wind and frost seem to rise
From the white silk of this
Grand painting of a falcon!
The bird stares as if to pounce
On a scurrying hare, and do
I see in its eye something
Of a fierce monkey?
Chain and ring seem to invite one
to put out a hand and free it
From the perch that seems so close;
I wish I could ask it attack
Those tiny singing birds, scattering
Their blood and feathers over
The grasslands around.

(REWI ALLEY)

—BALLAD OF THE WAR CHARIOTS—

The jingle of war chariots,
Horses neighing, men marching,
Bows and arrows slung over hips;
Beside them stumbling, running
The mass of parents, wives and children
Clogging up the road, their rising dust
Obscuring the great bridge at Hsienyang;

Stamping their feet, weeping
In utter desperation with cries
That seem to reach the clouds;

Ask a soldier: Why do you go?
Would simply bring the answer:
Today men are conscripted often;
Fifteen-year-olds sent up the Yellow River
To fight; men of forty marched away
To colonize the western frontier;
Village elders take young boys,
Do up their hair like adults
To get them off; if they return
It will be white with age, but even then
They may be sent off to the frontier again;

Frontiers on which enough blood has flowed
To make a sea, yet our Emperor still would
Expand his authority! Have you not heard
How east of Huashan many counties
Are desolate with weeds and thorns?
The strongest women till the fields,
Yet crops come not as well as before;

Lads from around here are well known
For their bravery, but hate to be driven
Like dogs or chickens; only because
You kindly ask me do I dare give vent
To grievances; now for instance
With the men from the western frontier
Still not returned, the government
Demands immediate payment of taxes,
But how can we pay when so little
Has been produced?

Now, we peasants have learnt one thing:
To have a son is not so good as having
A daughter who can marry a neighbour
And still be near us, while a son
Will be taken away to die in some
Wild place, his bones joining those
That lie bleached white on the shores
Of Lake Kokonor, where voices of new spirits
Join with the old, heard sadly through
The murmur of falling rain.

(ALLEY)

—NIGHT IN THE PAVILION BY THE RIVER—

Evening haze creeps up hill paths,
I lie in the pavilion overlooking
The river; light clouds envelop
Cliff sides, and the moon's reflection
Is twisted by the waters;
Cranes and storks rest after
Their flight; wild beasts howl
As they seek their prey; sleep
Does not come to me, for still
I worry about war, knowing I have
No way to set the world aright.

(ALLEY)

—A BOAT RIDE—

South in Cheng-tu
for years a stranger,
I tilled South land.

Gazing north
bitter-souled
I sat at the north window.
Today I take
my old wife,
we loose a small skiff;
Sun-lit, our
younger child
bathes in the clear water.

Together flying,
butterflies
follow one another;
On one stem
two lotuses
each the other's pair.
Tea to drink,
cane-syrup—
we bring what there is.
And our crockery
is not exactly
jade-fashioned ware.

(MCNAUGHTON)

—AT THE TURNING RIVER, DRINKING WINE—

Outside the gardens
at the water's edge
I sit, forgetting to go.
Crystalline,
palace and hall
roll in the fine haze.

Peach blossoms,
 delicately following
  pear blossoms, fall;
A yellow bird,
 sometimes joining
  white birds, flies.

I drink a lot.
 For some time, I haven't
  cared, that I have no friends.
I'm tired of audiences—
 O yes, I'm
  out of step with the mobs.
As official, I feel
 no, know
  Ts'ang-chou is far away.*
I get older
 and my only regret
  I can't shake off these robes.

        (MCNAUGHTON)

—I WEEP AT THE RIVER'S BANK—

I, from Shao-ling,
 an old farmer,
  swallow my voice and weep.
On a Spring day
 I follow alone
  the Turning River's turn.

---

 * Ts'ang-chou is an insular land, a terrestrial paradise. It often is
said that "the mysterious ones live there."

By the river's edge
    in palace and hall
        they've locked the thousand doors.
The delicate willows
    and new sedge,
        for whom will they be green?

I remember, of old
    the banners like rainbows
        came into the South Garden.
Garden-wide,
    nature's multitude
        sprang up in color and shade.
From the Palace
    of Shao-yang,
        she the first lady
In the same chair
    went on with the Emperor
        and stood at the Emperor's side.

Before the chair
    like second concubines,
        they carried bows and arrows.
White horses
    champed and craunched
        yellow-golden bits.
Turning their bodies
    heaven-ward,
        they aimed and shot the clouds.
A single arrow
    bull's-eye! downs
        two birds in flight.

Where are
> her bright eyes
>> and white teeth now?

Blood has stained
> the displaced soul.
>> It shall not go home.

The clear Wei
> flows east,
>> he flees to the Sword Pavilion.

Gone and remaining
> one and another,
>> news will never come.

If we are human,
> alive, have feelings,
>> tears must wet our breast.

Will the river's waters,
> river's flowers,
>> ever not come forth?

Night-fall:
> Tatars ride
>> dust fills the city.

Ready to go
> south from the city,
>> I watch to the south, the north.

(MCNAUGHTON)

Note: Emperor Ming Huang ruled over perhaps China's greatest poetic age, during the T'ang. He also figured in China's most famous "imperial romance." His partner was Yang Kuei-fei: "Kuei-fei" being the title "Precious Concubine" and not the lady's name. She hanged herself during the An Lushan rebellion when loyalist troops refused to fight for the Emperor unless she was slain. In the poem, Tu Fu is preparing to leave before the advance rebels (Tatars) arrive.

—THE IMPERIAL FORCE RECAPTURES HONAN AND HOPEI—

Past Ssu-ch'uan
    sudden news:
        HOPEI AND NORTH REGAINED.
As soon as I hear
    I cry, and weep
        my shirt and jacket wet.
I shall see
    wife and children.
        Where is sorrow now?
I heedlessly roll up
    poems and books.
        Joy! I shall go mad.

In broad day
    break into song
        stone sober, too.
Green Spring
    come along
        a fair home-traveling.
Soon I cross
    Pa Pass
        through Wu Pass
Then go down
    to Hsiang, and south
        and toward Loh, and south.

                (MCNAUGHTON)

——I WRITE OF THE PAVILION IN THE MONASTERY
OF FIRST BEGINNING——

From the one pavilion
     you see as one the country:
Meandering waters
     and then meandering hills.
We cannot fully
     by day's end, admire;
Much less, love
     in our little leisure hour.

We sing at table
     and go from the Gate of Wu.
It cries in the grove—
     the tu-yu comes once more.
His eminence the priest,
     for him there is no desire.
On the westward scene,
     he shuts the temple door.

(MCNAUGHTON)

——I HEAR THAT THE OFFICIAL, HU-SSU,
HAS NOT COME BACK YET——

Old friend,
     to Chiang-ling you are gone
Gone to tie up
     some old "epitaph bills."

You have sold your talent
       before, to make a living
And all the same,
       your house is hung by the heels.

The bramble door
       is deep in creeping grass.
The earthenware dishes
       are cold, and rarely smoke.
You are old and tired
       and should get off the road.
Come on home
       and sleep less often drunk.

(MCNAUGHTON)

—THE AUTUMN FLUTE—

Clear, in shang,
       it will forever play.
Play bitterly.
       Tears stain my gown.
Another day
       it cuts the heart utterly:
The white bones
       of Imperial Troops come home.

They pass each other.
       Afraid lest there be outrage
It so plays
       that the blown sounds decay.

Imperceptibly,
    the autumn clouds move.
In grieving wind
    little by little, they fly.*

(MCNAUGHTON)

§ MISCELLANEOUS POETS

—SONG OF THE BEAUTIFUL GIRL—
by Liang Huang

On road and well,
    flowers of peach emerge.
Pair by pair,
    swallows join and fly.
A beautiful girl
    in her exquisite grace:
Spring's colors
    rise in her gauze robe.

Herself loving,
    she's quick to take out the mirror.
Sometimes, shy,
    she shuts the thatched door

---

* Tu Fu was in office in Ch'in-chou and had Tibetans as neighbors, so that he sometimes heard the "Ch'iang Flute" or "Barbarian Flute." "Shang" is a musical mode.

And not knowing why,
    the traveler going the road
Far-off, is excited
    by five perfumes to return.

          (MCNAUGHTON)

—(ANOTHER POEM)—

by Liang Huang

The apricot bridge
    begins to shine with day.
Green jade,
    behind the hall, unfolds.
Remembering things,
    they copy make-up, and laugh.
Spring's beauties
    fill the Mirror Pavilion.

Their mouths sing out
    and songs, from the door, arise.
They turn to their shadows,
    they dance. The waist is bent.
Elsewhere, there is
    an excellent place to meet.
To the dark tower,
    travelers come at night.

          (MCNAUGHTON)

—ON A SPRING DAY, THE EMPEROR IS
EXPECTED AT THE SPRING PALACE—
(Written to Imperial Request)

by Su T'ing (670–720)

Eastward they look
    look for Spring.
        Spring is pitiful.
Still, whenever
    the day is fine
        willows swallow the haze.
Within the palace,
    they look down
        on South Mountain's peak;
From the city-wall
    near the plain
        the Big Dipper Hangs.
To fine grass
    everywhere, has gone
        the returning *nien*'s place.
Light flowers
    softly fall
        before the up-raised cup.
The Emperor travels
    this way!
        Joy without end!
Bird-song's
    sounding sound
        enters the pipe and string.

(MCNAUGHTON)

—"I LISTEN TO THE CH'IN ON AN AUTUMN NIGHT . . ."—

by Ch'ang Chien

To the *ch'in*
     in the autumn night, I listen.
Yes, there is
     someone in the grottoes.
A single finger
     fingers the answering mode
A single-sound
     sounds "good health and spirits!"
Cold insects
     by the stone step stir;
In clear wind,
     the smoky candle leaps.
Who needs
     Chung Chi's ear?
One can one's self
     be near to mountains and clefts.

(MCNAUGHTON)

—BY NIGHT I ARRIVE AT THE LOH'S MOUTH AND GO INTO THE YELLOW RIVER—

by Ch'u Kuang-hsi (707–ca. 759)

By river and stream,
     there is much dark grass.
Morning, evening
     it's greater, the traveler's grief.

Traveler's grief,
    it's pitiful, morning, evening.
At the twisting banks
    for a while they stop the boat.
At midnight
    the great stream is still.
They untie the cables
    and follow the homeward current.
The river-banks
    are utterly clear and distant.
We follow the backwaters
    where there are no obstructions.
I climb the prow
    and gaze at the setting moon.
They bend the oars.
    Grief renews regret.
Supposing that
    riding a raft I go,
I always talk of
    this trip in the River of Stars.

(MCNAUGHTON)

Some Further Readings

Alley, Rewi, trans. *Selected Poems of Tu Fu*. Peking: Foreign Languages Press, 1962.

Bynner, Witter, trans. *The Jade Mountain: A Chinese Anthology, Being Three Hundred Poems of the T'ang Dynasty*. Translated from the texts of Kiang Kang-hu. New York: Alfred A. Knopf, 1929. (Also available as a Doubleday Anchor paperback.)

Chang Yin-nin and Walmsley, Lewis, trans. *Poems by Wang Wei*. Rutland, Vt., and Tokyo: Charles E. Tuttle Co., 1958.

Davis, A. R. *Tu Fu*. New York: Twayne, n.d.

Frodsham, J. D. *The Poems of Li Ho*. New York: Oxford University Press, 1970.

Graham, Angus Charles, ed. and trans. *Poems of the Late T'ang*. Baltimore: Penguin Books, 1965.

Hawkes, David. *A Little Primer of Tu Fu*. Oxford: The Clarendon Press, 1967.

Hung, William. *Tu Fu: China's Greatest Poet*. Cambridge, Mass.: Harvard University Press, 1952.

Kwock, C. H., and McHugh, Vincent. *Have Pity on the Grass*. San Francisco: The Tao Press, 1971. (Also contains material relevant to Chapter 16.)

————. *Why I Live on the Mountain*. San Francisco: Golden Mountain Press, 1958 (distributed by City Lights Books, San Francisco). (Also contains material relevant to Chapters 2, 14, and 16.)

Liu, James J. *Poetry of Li Shang-yin, Ninth-Century Baroque Chinese Poet*. Chicago: University of Chicago Press, 1969.

Obata, Shigeyoshi, trans. *The Works of Li Po*. New York: Paragon Reprint Corp., 1965 (originally published 1922).

Pound, Ezra. "Cathay." In *Personae*. New York: New Directions, 1949. (Also contains material relevant to Chapters 2, 8, 9, 10, 11, 13, and 14.)

Rexroth, Kenneth. *Love and the Turning Year: 100 More Chinese Poems*. New York: New Directions, 1970. (Also contains material relevant to Chapter 16.)

————. *One Hundred Poems from the Chinese*. New York: New Directions, n.d. (Also contains material relevant to Chapter 16.)

Snyder, Gary. *Riprap and Cold Mountain Poems*. San Francisco: Four Seasons Foundation, 1965.

Waley, Arthur. *The Life and Times of Po Chü-i*. New York: Hillary, 1951.

————. *The Poetry and Career of Li Po*. London: Allen & Unwin, Ltd., 1951.

Watson, Burton, trans. *Cold Mountain: One Hundred Poems by the T'ang Poet Han Shan*. New York: Grove Press, 1962.

Young, David, trans. *Six Poems from Wang Wei*. Oberlin, Ohio: Triskelion Press, 1969.

14

THE BROKEN SENTENCE:
Chüeh-Chü

The "broken-sentence" poetic form, in Chinese called *chüeh-chü,* deserves special attention for several reasons. One Chinese critic, who I suppose has counted, says, "When men in the T'ang wrote verse, they usually wrote *chüeh-chü.*" The *chüeh-chü* is the shortest verse form in the Chinese repertoire, and yet, like the Japanese *haiku* or like some Greek or Roman epigrams, it has become one of the most effective and popular forms in the literature. The Chinese particularly prize the *chüeh-chü* because in it they can do surpassingly well what they so often try to do when writing verse—catch some small moment of experience and stop its passing fo an instant.

The *chüeh-chü* is a four-line poetic form. The Chinese had written four-line poems before the T'ang: all the Tzu Yeh poems you have read, and many of the jade terrace poems, are four-line poems. The *chüeh-chü* line has in it either five or seven syllables, with every line of any one poem having in it the same number of syllables.

The poem rhymes a-b-c-b or a-a-b-a. Often enough line one is parallel to line two. Line three is not parallel to line four.

This studied use of parallelism was a feature which the pre-T'ang four-line poems did not have, although you can find parallelism occasionally even in earlier poems. But the main difference in T'ang *chüeh-chü*, compared with earlier *chüeh-chü*, is a rather subtle stylistic device which might be used as the defining charactertistic of the *chüeh-chü*. Line one and line two of the poem, as is usual in Chinese poetry, are complete sentences. But line three is an incomplete grammatical unit, so that the poem's second distich—lines three and four—is a single sentence, "broken" over the two verse-lines. It is extremely rare in Chinese poetry for the sentence and the verse-line thus not to coincide. This stylistic device, then, may have given the form its name: the broken sentence.

As one reads aloud a *chüeh-chü*, his voice will fall, in "sentence-final" intonations, at the ends of line one and line two. But at the end of line three his voice will rise in "non-final" intonation. The "grammatical drama," as well as the poetic drama, thus hang just at maximum tension for a moment, during the pause between line three and line four. So poets use the grammar and the form to suggest a resistance against "time's irreversible passing"; it makes the form all the more effective and all the more suitable for writing up "the impression of a briefest instant."

All translations in this chapter, unless otherwise noted, are by Mayhew and McNaughton.

—EGRET DYKE—

by *Wang Wei*

Swoop! The egret dives into the red lotus blossoms.
Splash! He breaks the clear water into waves.
How handsome he looks in his new-born feathered silk
Proudly balanced on the old raft, a fish in his beak . . .

(CHANG AND WALMSLEY)

—DUCKWEED POND—

by *Wang Wei*

Broad and deep lies the pond in spring.
I wait to meet the light skiff returning;
Green duckweed closes in the wake of the boat—
Then the weeping willow brushes it wide apart
    once more.

(CHANG AND WALMSLEY)

—A POEM OF DEPARTURE—

by *Wang Wei*

Light rain is on the light dust
The willows of the inn-yard
Will be going green and greener,
But you, Sir, had better take wine ere your departure,
For you will have no friends about you
When you come to the gates of Go.

(POUND)

—GOODBYE—

by *Wang Wei*

Amid these mountains
         we have said our last good-byes.
At sunset
         I must latch the wicker door.
In Spring
         the grass will rise up green again,
But will I see my Wang Sun anymore?

—POEM—

by *Wang Wei*

From the old village
         you lately come.
The news from home
         you likely know.
Just before silk lace curtains
         (on the day you left)
Was the winter plum in blossom
         Yes, or no?

—LI CH'AI—

by *Wang Wei*

In empty mountains no one can be seen.
But here might echoing voices cross.
Reflecting rays
         entering the deep wood
Glitter again
         on the dark green moss.

—WE SET OUT EARLY FROM POTI—

by Li Po

Among the highly colored clouds
    at dawn we left Po Ti,
Coming back to Chiang Ling
    in one day's journey of a thousand *li*.
Between the double banks
    how brief are monkey's cries
As past ten thousand folded hills
    the light boat flies.

—THE JEWEL STAIRS' GRIEVANCE—

by Li Po

The white dew
grows on
the jewel stairs.

Night wears on.
It soaks
her lace hose.

Now she lets down
the curtain
of crystal beads.

In rising light,
she waits for
the autumn moon.

(MCNAUGHTON)

—ON THE MOUNTAIN:
QUESTION AND ANSWER—
by Li Po

You ask me:
                    Why do I live
on this green mountain
        I smile
        No answer
                    My heart serene
On flowing water
                    peachblow
                    quietly going
                    far away
                another earth
This is
                another sky
No likeness
                    to that human world below.
                                (KWOCK AND MCHUGH)

—I SEE OFF MENG HAO-JAN AT GOLD CRANE INN—
by Li Po

            You traveled west
            from Gold Crane Inn

            Down Yang Chou
            where flowers are like mist

And I see
     a sail's far shadow fly
          against green air,

Then only the stretching
river, and the empty sky.

—TOO YOUNG—

by Tu Fu

Who is, I wonder mildly,
This little pretty
Whipper-snapper; jumping
From his horse
So cockily, sitting down
Uninvited; too sure
Of himself to say
Who he is; haughtily
Pointing to the silver
Jug, demanding I pour
Wine for him?

                    (ALLEY)

—I "NOODLE"—

by Tu Fu

It seems to me
    a traveler's grief's
        griefs without end.

Recklessly,
    Spring and its colors
        reach the river-pavilion.
Here it sets
    flowers to open
        in mobbed and wild confusions
There it teaches
    the oriole to cry,
        and re-utter its admonitions.

                (MCNAUGHTON)

—PEACH BLOSSOM VALLEY—

    by Chang Hsü (early eighth century)

In the damp darkness
    the hanging bridge
        divides the mist on the plain.
Over stepping stones
    and up the western bank I go
        to ask a fishing boat.
"In what place
    bordering clear waters
        may I find the cove?
For all day
    I have followed streams
        where peach flowers float."

—I SEE OFF THE MONK "SPIRITUAL CLARITY"—

by Liu Chang-ch'ing (fl. 733)

The Chu-lin
Temple
turns a bluer blue.

The night bells
sound
mile after mile.

As he walks
alone
down the dark hill,

his bamboo
hat
carries the setting sun.

—LIANG-CHOU SONG—

by Wang Han (fl. *ca.* 735)

Let us have strong wine at night
in bright cups
beautiful drinks
Drinks in hand
let us gallop about on horses
and twang the *p'i-p'a*.
Drunk, we can snore
in the sand hills
Don't laugh, friend.

There are always marchers-to-war
But how many men come home
                              at war's end?

—PALACE SONG—

by Ku K'uang (fl. 757)

It's midnight.
You can hear
flutes
sounding in the towers.

Girls' voices
and girls' laughter
are blown
together in the wind.

Wide roofs
cast shadows
in the moon,
clocks drip,

and beaded
blinds become
another
sea of stars.

—SWALLOWS' ALLEY—

by Liu Yü-hsi (772–842)

Field grasses
flower
at the Chu Ch'iao Bridge.

Slanted sunlight
comes
to Swallow's Alley.

There, birds that used
to live
with Wangs and Hsiehs

Fly in
and out
of common people's eaves.

—I ASK LIU, THE 19TH—

by Po Chü-i (772–846)

Dark dregs float
in the thick new wine.
Red ash burns
in the small stove pot.
The sky since evening
has looked like snow—
Can we drink one cup
or not?

—RIVER-SNOW—

by Liu Tsung-yuan (773–819)

On the thousand
mountains,
birds cease to fly.

On ten thousand
paths, foot–
prints disappear.

In a lone boat, in rain–
cloak and
hat, an old man

Alone, fishes
the cold
river, in snow.

(MCNAUGHTON)

—AT NIGHT, ON SHOU-CHIANG WALL,
I HEAR THE FLUTE—

by Li Yi (d. 827)

Before the
Hui-lo Ridge,
the sand
is like snow.

Beyond the
Shou-chiang Wall,
the moon
is like frost.

Somewhere out
there, someone
plays on
Tatar reeds

And through the night,
soldiers turn
their eyes
toward home.

—LOOKING FOR THE RECLUSE, I MISS HIM—

by Chia Tao (788–843)

I stopped to ask a young boy
                    just below the pines.
He said "My master must have gone
                    to pick wild vines."
But deeply settled clouds
                    lie on the mountain's face,
And when he looks for herbs
                    he might be anyplace.

—SPRING GRIEF—

by Liu Fang-p'ing (eighth–ninth centuries)

Past window-gauze
    the sun sets.
        Light turns yellow.
In the inner rooms
    could anyone
        seem sorry now?
In the empty garden
    late Spring
        hesitates
And the piled
    pear-flowers
        stop the swinging gates.

—SOLDIERS' GRIEF—

by Liu Chung-yung (eighth–ninth centuries)

    Year by year,
    Gold River
    reflects
    the Jade Gates.

    Morning by
    morning, sword-
    rings hold
    the horse whips.

In late March,
in snow, as
I go
to Dark Mound,

miles of Yel-
low River
circle
the black peaks.

—I GO UP "RAMBLE OF DELIGHT" PLATEAU—

by Li Shang-yin (813–858)

Towards evening
        in a restless mood
I take the carriage at a gallop
        up the old plateau.
There, evening's sun
        is how illimitably beautiful and bright
Yet to the Yellow Springs
        must go.

—AT NIGHT, IN RAIN, I WRITE NORTH—

by Li Shang-yin

You ask when I'll
    be home. So far,
        there's no "when."

On Pa-shan tonight,
    rain fills up
        autumn ponds.
When, wearing out
    the west window lamp,
        will we two
talk of Pa-shan,
    and this hour
        of night rains?

(MCNAUGHTON)

—CHANG-O—
by Li Shang-yin

On the mother-of-pearl
wind screen,
the candle shadow is tall.

The Long River
spins away,
and the morning stars go down.

Chang-o
must regret
she stole the magic drug,

the jade sea
the dark sky
and the heart of night.

—I CROSS THE HAN—

by Li P'in (fl.854)

From beyond the hills,
    the letters stopped coming
Winter passed
    and we came to spring.
More and more anxious
    I enter my country—
But dare not ask oncomers anything.

—SPRING GRIEF—

by Chin Ch'ang-hsü (tenth century)

Beat the stick and banish
    the yellow orioles!
This singing on the branches
    can not be.
This daily music practice
    can disturb the lady's dream:
How then
    shall she reach
        Liao Hsi?

15

SHORT STORIES OF SUNG

Sung short stories are altogether different from the T'ang "strange legends." In the first place, they are not really short stories at all. The Chinese term for them is *hua-pen*, which means "prompt-book." We already have spoken of the public storyteller who, in China, amused and terrified the young on Saturday mornings in the marketplace. He spoke from a set of notes called a *hua-pen*. As the storytelling industry grew and prospered, as the number of literate nonscholars increased, and as the scholars themselves began to take interest in fiction, a market was made for printed versions of the story-tellers' stories, and many prompt-books got reproduced and published. Naturally, the prompt-book—unlike the T'ang "strange legends"—used the spoken, everyday language that the storyteller used to attract and to reach his audience in the square.

The storyteller, as a practical problem, had to attract and to keep a live audience, and he had to get his story over to a group of listeners in a busy marketplace: these necessities produced a very definite, and rather unusual, form, which can be seen in all the *hua-pen*. Every *hua-pen* had an introduction, so the storyteller could attract his audience and could allow latecomers to shove in without ruining the performance. The introduction might be another story, prefiguring the main story in plot or in moral implications but shorter than the main story. Or the introduction could be a disquisition, with quotations, on various poems. Or it might be a speech or lecture on the moral to be found in the story. One assumes that the storyteller abbreviated or expanded these introductions as his audience grew more or less quickly to profitable size and arranged itself comfortably. Occasionally, the introductions to *hua-pen* are very short and consist only of an exemplary or moral verse, or of such a verse with a brief prose recapitulation.

We can see from the "storyteller phrases" that the storyteller was always conscious of his audience, and he used a number of "platform tricks" to keep them awake and conscious of him. The storyteller often spoke directly to his audience. He might, to introduce an important statement, say, "Now keep your ears clean." He might lead up to a description saying, "Now, how would you say he was dressed?" And so on. The storyteller also usually was very careful to warn his audience when he led them into, and out of, digressions. He might, for example, say, "Let us put down one strand." And then, later on, he might say, "But let us leave off these complications, and return."

The *hua-pen* have verses intermixed with the straightforward narrative and dramatic prose, and this interspersed verse is a "formal characteristic" of the *hua-pen*. The verse may be either *shih* (formal poems) or *tz'u* (brothel or art songs), and the storyteller often used work by well-known poets. The verses served to make the performance more lively and exciting, and the storyteller probably chanted or sang (as appropriate) the verses which occurred. The interposed poem might serve to dilate on a moral issue, to reinforce a description, or to delay a climax, and the storytellers showed real artistic ingenuity and genius in the way they used these poems.

We c n find in the *hua-pen* at least the following major types: (1) *kung-an* or "law-court" stories; (2) supernatural stories, (3) love stories; and (4) historical tales. Of these, the *kung-an* or law-court story is worth mentioning here, because it is different from what we have seen before, and law-court *hua-pen* are probably the world's first detective stories. They have been as popular in China as detective stories have in the West, and they have been around for a much longer time. The basic story is the same, East or West: the hero outsmarts a clever or lucky criminal, solves a baffling crime, and sees to it that justice prevails. But in the *kung-an* story, the hero is not a hardboiled, Sam Spade-type detective; he is rather a scholar and a civil servant, who solves the case because it comes before him as part of his administrative and judicial work.

§ LAW-COURT, OR *KUNG-AN*, STORIES

The Judicial Murder of Tsui Ning

Anonymous
(twelfth–thirteenth centuries)

> Cleverness and cunning are gifts of Heaven,
> Ignorance and stupidity may be feigned.
> Jealousy arises often from a narrow heart,
> Disputes are set off by thoughtless jokes.
> For the heart is more dangerous than the
>   River with its nine bends
> And there are evil faces that ten coats of
>   mail cannot conceal.
> Wine and women have often caused the
>   downfall of states
> But who has ever seen good men spoiled
>   by books?

This poem tells about the difficulties that beset men. The road of life is a tortuous one and the heart of man is hard to fathom. The great Way has receded farther and farther from the world and the ways of men have become more and more multifarious. Everyone bustles about for the sake of gain but in their ignorance they often reap nothing but calamities. One should ponder on these thoughts well if one wants to maintain one's life and protect one's family. It is because of this that the ancients used to say:

> There is a season for frowning,
> There is a season for laughing.
> One must consider most carefully
> Before frowning or laughing.

This time I shall tell you about a man who brought death upon himself and several others and ruin to his family because of something he said in jest under the influence of wine. But first let me tell you another story as an introduction.

In the Yuan Feng period [A.D. 1078–1085] of our dynasty there was a young graduate by the name of Wei Peng-chu, with the derived name Chung-hsiao. He was just eighteen years old and had a wife as pretty "as flower and jade." He had been married for barely a month when "the spring tests approached and the examination halls were thrown open," and Wei had to take leave of his wife, pack his baggage, and set off for the capital to attend the examinations. Said the wife to her husband: "Come back home as soon as you can, whether or not you pass your examinations. Do not leave me all alone."

"Have no fear," replied Wei. "I am going only because I have to think of my career."

Then he set off on his journey and soon reached the capital. There indeed he passed the examinations, the ninth place in the first group. He was appointed to a post in the capital which he assumed with a great deal of pomp and ceremony. Of course he wrote a letter to his wife and sent it by a trusted servant. Besides the usual inquiries after her health and the news of his success, he wrote also the following at the end of the letter: "Since I have no one to look after me in the capital, I have taken a concubine. I look forward to your coming soon, so that we can enjoy our good fortune together."

The servant took the letter and went directly to Wei's home. He congratulated his mistress and presented the letter. After tearing open the letter and reading what it had to say about this and that, she said to the servant: "What a faithless man your master is! Here he has just received his appointment, and yet he has already gotten himself a concubine!"

Whereupon the servant said: "It must be one of the master's jokes, for no such thing had happened when I left the capital.

Please do not worry about it. Madame can see for herself when she arrives at the capital.''

"I'll give the matter no more thought, then, if that is the case,'' Madame Wei said, and, as she was not able to secure boats for the journey right away, she wrote a letter to her husband and sent it by someone who happened to be going to the capital. In the meantime she packed and got herself ready for the journey.

When the messenger reached the capital he inquired his way to Wei's house and delivered the letter. Needless to say, he was given food and wine for his trouble.

Now when Wei opened the letter and read it, he found only this: "As you have taken yourself a 'little wife,' I have also taken myself a 'little husband.' We shall set out for the capital together at the first opportunity." This did not disturb Wei at all, for he knew that his wife was only joking.

But it happened that before he had a chance to put the letter away, one of his fellow graduates came to call on him, and as he was one of his intimate friends and knew that Wei did not have his family with him, he went straight to his inner chamber. After a few minutes of conversation, Wei had to excuse himself and leave his friend alone in the room. While the latter was looking at the papers on Wei's desk, he came upon the wife's letter and was so amused by it that he began to read it aloud. Just then Wei came back into the room. He blushed and said, "It is a very stupid thing. She is only joking because I have joked with her." His fellow graduate guffawed and said, "It is hardly a matter to joke about." Then he went away.

Now this fellow was also young and "liked to talk and loved to gossip," and as a result what was said in the letter was soon all over the capital. What was worse was that some of the officials, jealous of Wei's youthful success, took the matter up and impeached Wei in a memorial to the throne, charging him with impropriety and branding him as unfit for the important post which he occupied. Wei was as a consequence demoted and banished to a provincial post. Regret was then useless. Wei's future was completely ruined and he never rose high in official position.

This is a case of a man who lost his opportunity for official advancement because of a joke. Now I shall tell you about another man who, because of a jest uttered under the influence of wine, threw away his own life and caused several people to lose theirs. How did this happen?

> The paths of this world are tortuous and sad
> And the jeering mouths of men open and shut without cause.
> The white clouds have no desire to darken the sky
> But the wild wind blows them hither without pause.

Now in the time of Kao Tsung, Hangchou, being the capital, was not inferior in wealth and glory to Kaifeng, the old capital. There lived at that time to the left of the Arrow Bridge a man by the name of Liu Kuei, with the derived name of Chun-chien. He came from an old and solid family but its fortunes had declined during his time. He studied for the examinations at first, but later on he found it impossible to continue his scholarly pursuits and had to change his profession and take up business. He was like a man who enters the priesthood after middle life. He knew nothing of business and as a consequence he lost his capital. He had to give up his large house for a small one and ended up by renting only a few rooms. He had a wife by the name of Wang-shih and a concubine whom he took because Wang-shih did not bear him any children. The latter's name was Chen, the daughter of Chen the pastry peddler, and she was called Erh Chieh. He took her before he became quite destitute. The three of them lived together, without anyone else in the family.

Liu Chun-chien was a very good-natured man and was beloved by his neighbors, who used to assure him that his poverty was due to his bad luck and not to any fault of his own and that better days would come when his luck turned. This was what his neighbors said, but his fortune did not grow any better and he lived at home depressed and helpless.

One day as he was sitting home doing nothing, his father-in-law's servant Lao Wang, about seventy years old, came to him and said: "It is the master's birthday and I have been commanded to come and escort the young mistress home for the occasion."

"How stupid of me to forget the Great Mountain's birthday," Liu said. He and his wife gathered together a few articles of clothing that they needed, tied them up in a bundle, and gave it to Lao Wang to carry. Liu instructed Erh Chieh to take care of the house, saying that they would not be able to come back that day, as it was getting late, but that they would surely be back the following evening, and then set out for his father-in-law's house, which was about twenty *li* from the city.

Arriving there, he greeted his father-in-law but did not have a chance to tell the latter about his troubles as there were many guests present. After the guests went away he was put up in the guest room for the night. It was not until the next morning that his father-in-law came to talk to him, saying: "Brother-in-law, you can't go on like this. Remember the saying: 'He who does nothing will eat a mountain clean and the earth bare,' and the one to the effect that a man's gully is as bottomless as the sea and the days pass like the shuttle. You must look ahead. My daughter married you in the hope that you could provide her with food and clothing. Don't tell me that you want to go on like this!"

Liu sighed and said: "You are quite right, Great Mountain. But 'It is easier to go up the mountain and catch a tiger than to open your mouth to ask for help.' At a time like this there is nothing for me to do but sit and wait. To ask people for help is simply to court failure for one's pain. There are not many people who have my welfare at heart as you do, Great Mountain."

"I do not blame you for feeling the way you do," his father-in-law said. "However, I cannot stand by without doing some-something for you two. How would you like me to advance you some money for opening a provisions store?"

"That would be excellent," Liu said. "I shall always be grateful for your kindness."

After lunch, the father-in-law took out fifteen strings of cash and gave them to Liu, saying, "Take this money for outfitting the store. I shall give you another ten *kuan* when you are ready to open up. As to your wife, I should like to keep her here for the present. On the day of the opening I shall take her to you myself and at the same time wish you luck. What do you think of it?"

Liu thanked his father-in-law again and again and went away carrying the money on his shoulder. It was getting late when he entered the city. As he passed by the house of an acquaintance who was also a tradesman he decided to call on him and seek his advice. So he knocked at the man's gate. The man came out and greeted him, and asked him what had brought him. When Liu told him about his plans, the man said: "I have nothing to do at present and shall be glad to come and help you whenever you need me." "That would be fine," Liu said.

And so they talked about business conditions over a few cups of wine. Liu's capacity for wine was not very large and he soon began to feel the effects of the liquor. He got up and took leave of his host, saying, "Thank you for your hospitality. Please come over to my house tomorrow and talk things over." The man escorted Liu to the head of the street and then went home.

Now if I, the story teller, and Liu "had been born in the same year and brought up side by side," and if I "could have put my arms around his waist and dragged him back by the hand," Liu would not have suffered the calamity that he did. But because I wasn't there to prevent him, Liu died a more grievous death than Li Ts'un-hsiao of the Story of the Five Dynasties and P'eng Yueh of the Book of Han.

Now when Liu reached his house and knocked at the gate it was already lamplight time. As Erh Chieh was dozing under the lamp, after waiting for him all day, it was some time before she woke up and said, "I am coming," and then went and opened the gate. Liu went into the room and his concubine relieved him of the load of money and put it on the table, saying: "Where have you got this money from? What is it for?" Now Liu was still under the influence of wine and then too he was annoyed because his concubine had been so slow in answering the gate. He thought he would try to scare her. So he said: "I am afraid you won't like it when I tell you, but you'll have to know sooner or later. I have mortgaged you to a merchant because I am in great need of money. I shall redeem you when things are better with me. That's why I have not mortgaged you for more. But if things should not get any better, I am afraid that I shall have to give you up entirely."

The concubine did not know whether to believe him or not, for she found it difficult not to believe it because of the money right in front of her and she found it difficult to believe that her husband would have the heart to dispose of her thus because both he and his wife had always been so kind to her. The only remark she could make was, "You should have told my parents about it."

Liu said, "Your parents would never have consented if I had told them. After you have gone to that man's house, I shall send someone to break the news to your parents. Perhaps they won't blame me under the circumstances."

The concubine again asked: "Where did you get your wine?" "I drank with the man to bind the contract," Liu answered. "Why hasn't Ta Chieh come back with you?" the concubine asked. "Because she cannot bear to say goodby to you," Liu answered. "She will come back after you have left tomorrow. Please understand that I can't help it and that there is no backing out of it."

After saying this, Liu went to bed without undressing, hardly able to hide his amusement. He was soon sound asleep.

But the concubine could not fall asleep. "What sort of man has he sold me to?" she wondered to herself. "I must go to my parents' house and tell them about it. If he did sell me and the man comes for me tomorrow he can look for me at my parents."

After thus turning the matter in her mind, she piled the money at his feet and taking advantage of his drunken sleep she gathered a few things together and slipped out of the house, pulling the door shut behind her. She went to the house of a neighbor by the name of Chu San and asked Chu's wife to let her stay with them for the night, saying, "My husband has sold me for no good reason at all. I want to let my parents know about it. Please tell him to come to my parents' house if he wants me."

"That's the right thing to do," her neighbors said. "You can go on tomorrow and we shall let your husband know." The next day the concubine took leave of her host and went away.

> A fish that once frees itself from the hook
> Will swim away never to return.

Now to return to Liu Kuei. When he woke up at the third watch the lamp was still burning but there was no sight of his concubine. Thinking that she might be in the kitchen he called to her and asked her to bring him some tea. There was no answer and he fell asleep again after a half-hearted attempt to get up.

Now it happened that a bad man was out that night to steal,

having lost at gambling that same day, and he came to Liu's house. He tried the door and it yielded readily as the concubine had only pulled it to after her. He tiptoed into Liu's room and soon discovered the pile of money by Liu's feet. He began to help himself to it but in doing so he woke up Liu, who got up and shouted: "You can't do that! I have borrowed the money in order to go into business to feed myself. What am I to do if you steal it from me?"

The robber did not answer but struck at Liu's face with his fist. The latter dodged and struck back. After battling thus for a while the robber, seeing that he could not get the better of Liu, retreated to the kitchen and there picked up an axe that happened to be handy and struck Liu in the face just as he was about to raise the alarm. As Liu fell, the robber struck him again and alas! Liu became as dead as can be and quite ready to receive the sacrificial offerings of his heirs.

"I had to make a thorough job of it once I began," the robber said, half to himself and half to the corpse before him. "I did not mean to kill you, really; it was you that forced me to it." So saying he turned back to Liu's room and took the rest of the money, wrapped it up securely and went off, pulling the door to after him.

The following morning when the neighbors found that Liu's door was still shut at a late hour, they shouted to him and receiving no answer, they went inside and there they found his body and his concubine gone. They raised the alarm.

Then Chu San, the neighbor at whose house Erh Chieh had stopped for the night, came forward and told the neighbors assembled that the concubine had stopped at his house and had gone early that morning to her parents' house. "We must send someone to find her and at the same time notify Liu's wife," he said, and his suggestion was carried out accordingly.

Now to return to the concubine. She had hardly gone a *li* or two after she left Chu San's house that morning when her feet began to hurt so that she could not go on but had to sit down by the road and rest herself. Presently a young man carrying a shoulder bag full of money appeared on the scene and stopped to look at her. She was not beautiful but her eyebrows were nicely arched and her teeth bright, and she was undeniably attractive.

> Wild flowers are especially pleasing to the eye
> And country wine goes more to the head.

The young man bowed to her and asked her where she was traveling alone by herself. She returned the bow and told him that she was going to her parents and had stopped to rest. "And where have you come from and where are you going?" she asked. The man, keeping a proper distance, answered: "I have just come from the city where I had gone to sell some silk and I am bound for Chuchiatang." "My parents do not live far from there," the concubine said. "May I go with you?" "Certainly," the man answered. "I shall be honored to escort you there."

The two went on together thus for about two or three *li* when they noticed two men running after them, running so fast that their feet hardly touched the ground, and they were sweating and panting and their coats were open at the front.

They shouted, "Will the young lady please stop for a moment for we want to have a word with you?"

The concubine and the young man stopped and when the two pursuers caught up with them, each laid his hand on one, saying "Come along with us, you two!"

The concubine was astonished. The men were her neighbors, one of them being Chu San who had given her shelter for the night. She said, "I told you last night where I was going. Why are you pursuing me?" Chu San said, "There has been a murder in your house; you have to come back with us."

"I don't believe you," the concubine said. "I left my husband home last night safe and sound. I must go on to my parents. I cannot come with you." "It is not for you to say whether you'll come or not," Chu San said, and thereupon began to shout for help.

When the young man saw the gravity of the situation he said to Erh Chieh, "You had better go with them since things are as they say. I'll go on myself." "But you can't go," the two neighbors cried, "for since you are found in company with her you will have to explain yourself." "Why can't I?" the young man said. "I have only chanced to meet her on the road; it is not as if we had met by design. The road is a free thoroughfare."

But it was useless for Erh Chieh and the young man to explain themselves. By this time they were surrounded by spectators and they all said that the young man could not go away, especially since:

> He that has done nothing unlawful during the day
> Need have no fear of knocks at his door at night.

"If you don't come with us willingly," the two pursuers said, "it means that you have a guilty conscience and we shall have to force you."

There was nothing for the young man and Erh Chieh to do but go with the two neighbors. When the four of them arrived at Liu Kuei's house there was a curious crowd at the door. Erh Chieh went inside and there found Liu Kuei lying dead on the ground and the fifteen strings of money gone from the bed where she had left them. Her mouth dropped open and her tongue stuck out and thus she remained for a long time. The young man too was frightened, saying, "Oh luckless me! That I should be involved in such a calamity just because I walked a distance with the young lady!" The crowd talked excitedly among themselves.

Then Liu Kuei's wife and her father, old Mr. Wang, came running and stumbling on the scene and burst out crying at the sight of the body.

"Why have you killed your husband," Mr. Wang said to Erh Chieh, "and run away with the money? What have you to say for yourself now that by the justice of Heaven you have been caught?"

The concubine told them what had happened and that she knew nothing of her husband's death, but Liu Kuei's wife said, "It couldn't be! Why should he say that he got the fifteen *kuan* from selling you when my father had given it to him to start a business? It is evident that you have been unfaithful and have plotted the murder with your lover and run away with the money. Your stay at the neighbors' was only a ruse. There is no use denying it, for how can you explain that man found in your company?" Then turning to the young man she made a similar accusation.

"My name is Tsui Ning," the young man explained. "I had never seen the young lady before until I chanced to meet her on the road this morning. I asked her where she was going and we have traveled together only because we were going in the same direction. This is the truth; I know nothing of what happened before that."

But the crowd did not believe what he said. They searched his shoulder bag and found in it exactly fifteen *kuan* of cash.

"'The net of Heaven catches everything though its mesh is wide,'" they cried. "You must have had a part in the murder. If you had made good your escape we would have had to answer for your crime."

Thereupon Liu Kuei's wife caught hold of Erh Chieh and Mr. Wang caught hold of Tsui Ning and they dragged the suspects to the prefect's *yamen*, with the neighbors following them for witnesses. When the prefect heard that a murder case had come up, he immediately entered the trial hall and summoned all the parties concerned and commanded them each to tell his story.

First old Mr. Wang told the circumstances of the case as he knew them and ended by appealing for justice against the culprits. The prefect then summoned the concubine and commanded her to confess. But Erh Chieh said, "Though I am only Liu Kuei's concubine, he has always been good to me and the mistress too has always been kind and considerate. So why should I want to do this terrible thing?" Then she went on and told exactly what happened after Liu Kuei's return the evening before.

The prefect was inclined to see things as the neighbors did and was eager to have the case closed, so he brushed aside the prisoners' protestations of innocence and had them mercilessly tortured until they confessed to the crime that they did not commit. The confession was duly signed, witnessed by the neighbors, and Erh Chieh and Tsui Ning were put into heavy cangues and shut up in the death prison. The documents of the case were presented to the throne through the usual channels, and in due course the concubine and Tsui Ning were both sentenced to death, the first by quartering and the second by decapitation. The sentences were duly carried out. Even if the two had had mouths all over their bodies they could not have explained away the evidence against them.

> He who is dumb cannot tell of his distress
> Though the gentian root tastes bitter in his mouth.

Now reflect on the circumstances of the case, reader. If Erh Chieh and the young man Tsui Ning had been really guilty of the murder, would they not have fled the scene during the night? Why should the concubine have gone to the neighbors to stay for the night and thus allow herself to be caught the next morning? If the trial official had thought about the matter carefully he would have seen the falsity of the accusation. But, in his eagerness to close the case, he did not think at all. What confession can you not force if you rely on torture alone? But one's deeds are marked in the book of another judge and one is bound to be punished in due time, punished oneself if the judgment is swift or punished through one's descendants if it is slow. The ghosts of these two who have been unjustly put to death will not rest until they have been revenged, of that you may be sure. For this reason alone—to say nothing of the fact that the dead cannot be called back to life, and that which has been broken cannot be mended—those in official positions should not try cases carelessly and resort to torture but should try to establish justice by every means possible.

But to return to our story. After the trial, Liu Kuei's wife returned home, and set up a spirit tablet to her husband to observe the period of mourning. When her father suggested that she remarry, she said, "I must at least observe one year of mourning if not the required three." At the end of the year her father sent his old servant Lao Wang to fetch her, saying, "Tell the young mistress to get her things together and come back here. She can remarry now after her year of mourning." As there wasn't much else for her to do, Liu Kuei's wife decided to follow her father's suggestion. She tied her things up in a bundle and gave it to Lao Wang to carry. Then saying goodby to the neighbors, she set out for her father's house. On the way she was caught in the rain and went into the wood to seek shelter, and thereby she:

Drew nearer to death step by step,
Like sheep and hogs that wander into a butcher's house.

In the wood they suddenly heard a voice shouting: "I am the King Pacifier of the Mountains. Halt, wayfarers, and pay me toll for the use of the road!" Then a man wielding a huge sword jumped out from behind the trees.

Well, Lao Wang's time must have been up, for instead of handing over what he was carrying to the robber, he rushed at him shouting defiance. The robber dodged and Lao Wang fell to the ground by the force of his own headlong rush. "How dare you defy me, little calf," the robber cried with anger, and brought down his sword on the prostrate figure. Blood squirted out and Lao Wang lived no more.

Realizing that it would be useless to try to run away from the robber, Liu Kuei's wife decided to resort to a ruse. She clapped her hands and said, "Well done, well done!" The man stared at her and said, "Who are you?" She answered, "I am an unfortunate woman who has recently lost her husband and was mated to this old man by a deceitful matchmaker. He was no good at all except to eat and eat. You have relieved me of a burden with your sword."

Pleased with her words and seeing that she was not bad looking, the robber said, "Would you be the mistress of my mountain domain?" Since there wasn't much else she could do, she said, "I shall most willingly serve you, great king."

On hearing this the man's anger changed to joy; he threw Lao Wang's body into a swamp, picked up his sword and led Liu Kuei's wife to an isolated house. He picked up a clump of earth and threw it on the roof, whereupon a man opened the door. Inside the robber ordered a sheep killed and wine brought and performed the wedding ceremony with Liu Kuei's wife.

> One knows well that it is not a proper match,
> But it is better than to lose one's life.

After the robber took Liu Kuei's wife, he made several good hauls in succession and became quite rich after about half a year's time. Being a sensible woman, she tried to persuade him to mend his ways. Thus she used to exhort him day and night: "It is said that the water jug will, sooner or later, break over the well platform and that a solider will die on the battle ground. Just so you will come to a bad end if you keep on doing things against the laws of Heaven. Since we have now accumulated more than enough for the rest of our lives, why don't you give up your present profession and take up some kind of lawful business?''

Finally the robber gave way to her exhortations. He rented a house in the city and opened up a general store. When he could spare the time he would go to the temples to make offerings to atone for his crimes.

One day he said to Liu Kuei's wife: "Though I was a highwayman once, I know well the maxim that each act of injustice must be atoned for, just as a debt must be paid. In my career of evil in the past I have done nothing worse than thieving and robbing except in two cases. In each case I was responsible for killing a man and in one of them I was indirectly responsible for two other lives. These lives have weighed on my mind and I shall not be able to rest in peace until I have hired some priests to pray for their souls."

"How were you responsible for destroying two lives?" Liu Kuei's wife asked.

"One is, as you know, your husband, whom I killed in the forest when he rushed at me. He was an old man and had done nothing against me. His soul must be crying for revenge, especially since I have taken his wife."

"What is done cannot be undone," Liu Kuei's wife said. "Moreover, if you had not killed him we would not have become man and wife. Let us say no more about that. But who was the other man that you killed?"

"It was even a greater crime," the robber said, "for it caused two innocent persons to be put to death." Then he went on and told her about the murder of Liu Kuei, for he was in fact the man who stole into Liu Kuei's house on that fatal night and murdered him in order to make his escape. "These are the worst crimes in my life as a highwayman," he concluded. "I must do something for their souls."

"So this is the man who killed my husband and caused the unjust deaths of Erh Chieh and that young man," Liu Kuei's wife wailed to herself. "Since I was partly responsible for their deaths by my false testimony, their spirits must also hold me responsible." However, she said nothing of her thoughts to the robber but watched her opportunity. When it came she went to the prefect's *yamen* and shouted for justice.

There was then a new prefect for Linanfu, who had been in his post only half a month. Liu Kuei's wife was brought to him in the trial hall and there weeping and wailing she told her story. The robber was seized and under the prodding of instruments of torture, confessed everything. He was sentenced to death and the case was sent up to the throne for review. An edict was issued after the usual period of sixty days ordering the immediate execution of the robber. The original trial official was demoted for miscarriage of justice, and the authorities were charged to seek out the nearest kin of the concubine and Tsui Ning and to compensate them for the injustice done. Since Liu Kuei's wife had marrried the robber under duress and since she was instrumental in avenging her husband's death, she was given half of the robber's property, the other half being confiscated.

After watching the execution, Liu Kuei's wife took the robber's head and made offerings at the tomb of her husband and those of the concubine and Tsui Ning. She gave her share of the robber's estate to the temples and devoted the rest of her long life to praying for the dead.

> Good and evil both end up in the grave
> But a jest may bring about untimely death.
> So pray remember always to tell the truth
> For the tongue is ever at the bottom of calamity.

(WANG CHI–CHEN)

§ THE SUPERNATURAL

The Foxes' Revenge

All living creatures share a common nature,
Whether they are mammals or hatched out
    from eggs;
If you are good to them they won't forget it—
Just think of the bird who repaid its protector with
    rings!

This verse refers to a scholar of the Han Dynasty named Yang Pao, a native of Huahsi, who was a learned and brilliant youth at twenty. During the festival of the Double Ninth one year he went for a walk outside the city, sitting down in a wood to rest when he was tired. Luxuriant trees cast a cool shade and the birds were singing, but suddenly amid all this loveliness a bird fell with a thud at his feet. Cheeping pitifully it tried to fly, but could only flutter helplessly about the ground.

"How odd!" thought Yang Pao. "What can have happened to this bird?"

Upon picking it up he saw that it was a golden oriole somebody had injured, which was crying piteously.

"I'll take you home and look after you till you can fly again," said Yang Pao, pitying the little creature with all his heart.

Just then a young man with a catapult came up from behind him.

"I brought that oriole down, sir," he said. "May I have it?"

"I can easily give it to you," replied Yang Pao, "but though a bird is not like a man, life is equally precious to it. Why should you kill it? If you kill a hundred, you still won't have enough for one meal; and if you sell ten thousand, you still won't make a fortune. Why don't you make your living some other way? I would like to buy this bird from you to save its life."

He took some money from his pocket.

"I don't catch birds for food or money, but for the fun of it," said the young man. "If you want this oriole, sir, you can have it."

"Why should you have fun at the expense of innocent creatures?" asked Yang Pao.

"It was wrong of me," admitted the other, throwing away his catapult as he left.

Yang Pao took the golden oriole home and kept it in a hat box, feeding it on yellow petals until its wing healed. After a hundred days it could fly again. It would fly off, then fly back, and Yang Pao became most attached to it. One day, however, it did not return. Yang Pao was worrying over its disappearance when a lad in a yellow jacket with delicate eyebrows and fine eyes came in and kowtowed to him. Yang Pao hastily helped him to his feet, and the lad produced a pair of jade rings which he gave to him.

"You saved my life, sir," he said, "but I have only these trifles to show my gratitude. With these rings your descendants will become great ministers."

"I have never met you before," replied Yang Pao. "When did I save your life?"

"Don't you know me?" asked the lad with a smile. "After I was shot down in the wood, you fed me with yellow petals in your hat box."

This said, he changed into a golden oriole and flew off. And later Yang Pao's descendants did indeed distinguish themselves in each successive generation.

"Why, storyteller," I hear someone protest, "everybody knows that story about the oriole and the jade rings. Why waste time repeating it?"

Well, readers, it is because I am going to tell you now about another youth who wounded wild animals. But this man did not repent like the fellow who hurt the oriole, and so he lost nearly all he had and became the talk of the town. I used the story about the golden oriole as an introduction; and I advise you all to do good deeds like Yang Pao and not to ask for trouble like the other young man.

> You'd better keep your mouth shut when required,
> You'd better give things up when so desired;
> If you will do these things, free from strife,
> You will enjoy a long and peaceful life.

During the reign of Emperor Hsuan Tsung [A.D. 712–756] of the Tang Dynasty, there lived a young man named Wang Chen, who was a native of Changan. He had a smattering of classical knowledge, could write passable compositions, and enjoyed drinking and fencing. What he liked best of all, however, was riding and shooting with the catapult. Having lost his father when a child, he lived with his mother and wife, a daughter of the Yu clan, and his unmarried brother Wang Tsai, who had great physical strength, excelled in the military arts, and served in the imperial guard. Their family was wealthy, with many servants; and they were living happily together when An Lu-shan revolted, stormed the Tung Pass and made the emperor fly westwards. Wang Tsai left with the imperial train. And Wang Chen, afraid to remain in the capital, packed up his valuables and left home too, taking his mother, wife and whole household to the Yangtse Valley for safety. They bought some land and property in Little Bay near Hangchow, and settled down there.

When news came that the capital had been retaken and the roads were safe once more, Wang Chen decided to return to Changan to look up old friends and relatives and set his estates there in order before moving his family back. Having told his mother of his plan, he lost no time in packing his baggage; then taking only one servant—Wang Fu—with him, he said goodbye to his mother and wife and went by boat to Yangchow. This was a most prosperous city. An important centre in the Yangtse and Huai River area, through which travellers from both north and south had to pass, its harbour was filled with junks, its shore was thronged with people, and its markets were crowded with merchants and customers. Leaving the boat here, Wang Chen dressed himself as an army officer and hired a man to carry his baggage, then proceeded on horseback, enjoying the mountain and river scenery as he travelled. In a few days he reached a place called Fanchuan, not far from the capital; but as there had been fighting in this area all the villagers had fled, the houses along the road were deserted, and few travellers passed this way.

> With mountains all around, and cool, dim woods,
> And lofty peaks that towered to the sky,
> The waterfalls made bright cascades of silver,
> And creepers hung like a thousand silken streamers.
> Few climbed the winding paths through these misty
>   mountains,
> Few lived in the lonely depths of these shadowy
>   forests;
> But lovely mountain flowers laughed in the breeze,
> And nameless birds poured out their songs together.

Feasting his eyes on the mountain scenery, Wang Chen rode slowly along. It was late afternoon when he heard voices in the forest, and drawing nearer saw not men but two foxes! Leaning against an old tree, one of them holding a book in its paws, they were laughing and chatting as they pointed at the pages as if they understood what was written there.

"What are those silly beasts up to?" wondered Wang. "I'd

like to know what they're reading. I'll give them a taste of my catapult."

Reining in his horse he took his polished horn bow, reached into his pocket for some shot and took aim.

"There!"

The bow arched like a full moon, and the missile flew like a shooting star.

Little did the foxes enjoying themselves there suspect that they had been seen. As the bow-string twanged they looked up, and the shot flew straight into the left eye of the fox holding the book. Dropping the volume, it howled in pain and made quickly off; and as the other fox bent to pick up the book Wang Chen shot again, hitting the beast on the left cheek so that it too fled with a howl of pain. When Wang Chen led his horse forward and bid Wang Fu pick up the book for him, he found it filled with strange hieroglyphs not one of which could he understand.

"What language can this be?" he wondered. "I must ask some antiquarian later."

Putting the book in his sleeve he rode out of the forest and down the highway towards the capital. At that time a strict watch was kept at the city gates, and everyone going in or out was questioned; moreover the gates were closed as soon as it grew dark. By the time Wang Chen reached the city dusk had fallen, and finding the gate shut he decided to spend the night in an inn outside the city wall. He alighted at the door, and when the innkeeper saw that he carried sword and bow and was dressed like an army officer, he hurried forward respectfully.

"Please take a seat, sir," he said, and told a pot-boy to fetch a cup of tea.

Meanwhile Wang Fu had unstrapped the baggage and carried it inside.

"If you have good rooms, landlord," said Wang Chen, "please give me one."

"I have plenty of rooms," replied the innkeeper. "Just take your pick, sir."

He lit a lamp to show him round, and when Wang Chen had chosen a clean room the innkeeper moved his baggage in, then stabled his horse for him. This done, the pot-boy came in.

"Will you have a drink, sir?" he asked.

"If you have good wine, bring me two measures with a plateful of beef," said Wang Chen. "And give my man the same."

When the pot-boy had gone Wang Chen went out too, closing his door behind him. Presently the pot-boy returned with the wine and the meat.

"Will you drink in your room or here in the hall, sir?" he asked.

"Out here," replied Wang Chen.

Then the pot-boy set the wine on a table and Wang Chen sat down. Wang Fu poured out the wine for him, and when he had drunk a few cups the innkeeper came over.

"May I ask where you come from, sir?" he inquired.

"From the Yangtse Valley."

"You don't talk like a southerner, sir."

"As a matter of fact, I used to live in the capital. But after An Lu-shan revolted and the emperor went to Szechuan I took my family south to avoid trouble. When I heard that the rebels had been beaten and His Imperial Majesty had returned to the capital, I decided to come back to set my affairs here in order before bringing my family home. Because the road was said to be unsafe, I dressed as an army officer."

"So we are from the same district!" exclaimed the innkeeper. "I hid in the country too, and came back less than a year ago."

As fellow-provincials, they immediately became very friendly and started exchanging reminiscences about the hardships of exile.

The landscape is as lovely as before,
But half the citizens are here no more.

They were in the middle of an animated conversation when
someone called out from behind them: "Have you an empty
room, innkeeper?"

"I have rooms all right," replied the landlord. "How many
of you are there?"

"Just myself."

He was indeed alone, with no baggage.

"In that case, I'm sorry, but I can't take you," said the innkeeper.

"Why not?" demanded the newcomer angrily. "Are you
afraid I won't pay you?"

"Certainly not, sir. But Lord Kuo, the Garrison Commander,
has forbidden all innkeepers to take in strangers. Anyone who
does so on the sly is liable to be severely punished. You have no
baggage, sir, and we don't know you, how can I keep you?"

"So you don't know me, eh? I am Hu Erh, Lord Kuo's
steward. I have been to Fanchuan on business and come back
too late to get into the city: that's why I want to spend the night
in your inn and why I have no baggage. If you don't believe me,
come with me tomorrow morning to the city gate to ask the
guards there. They all know me."

Impressed by the stranger's connection with Lord Kuo, the
innkeeper believed him.

"No offence meant, sir," he said. "I didn't recognize you
at first. Please step inside and rest."

"Later," replied the other. "I am hungry. Bring me some
wine and food. I am fasting," he added, "so don't bring me
any meat."

He walked over to Wang Chen's table and sat down opposite
him, while the pot-boy went for wine and food. Wang Chen

observed that he hid his left eye with his sleeve as if it were hurting him.

"I had bad luck today, landlord," said the stranger. "I met two wild beasts and hurt my eye through a fall."

"What beasts did you meet?"

"On my way back from Fanchuan I saw two foxes rolling on the ground and howling with pain in the forest. When I tried to catch them, though, I slipped and fell. So the foxes got away, while I nearly blinded myself in one eye."

"No wonder you are keeping it covered," said the innkeeper.

"Today I came past Fanchuan too," put in Wang Chen. "I also met two foxes."

"Did you catch them?" asked the stranger eagerly.

"They were reading a book in the forest," replied Wang Chen. "With my catapult I shot the fox holding the book in the left eye, so that it dropped the book and fled. And when the other fox tried to pick up the book I hit it on the left cheek, making it run for dear life too. I got the book but not the foxes."

"Foxes reading a book!" exclaimed the stranger and the innkeeper. "How extraordinary!"

"I'd like to know what's written in that book," said the stranger. "May I have a look at it?"

"It's full of strange hieroglyphs," said Wang Chen. "I can't make out a single word."

Putting down his wine cup, he prepared to take the book from his sleeve. Before he had time to do so, however, the innkeeper's five-year-old grandson came into the yard and saw that one of the guests was a fox, although he did not know what such an animal should be called.

"Grandpa!" he cried, running forward and pointing at the fox. "Why is this big cat sitting here? Why don't you chase it away?"

At once Wang Chen realized that this was the fox whose eye

he had injured, and hastily drawing his sword he struck at its head. The fox dodged backwards, revealing its true from as it rolled on the ground, then dashed out. Sword in hand Wang Chen chased it past several doors until it leapt over a wall; and then, unable to find the gate, he had to turn back. He was met by the innkeeper, carrying a lighted lamp, and Wang Fu.

"You had better let it go," said the innkeeper.

"If your grandson hadn't seen it," replied Wang Chen, "it would have got away with the book."

"Foxes are tricky beasts," said the innkeeper. "It may come back later."

"The next time a stranger mentions those beasts to me, I'll know it's the fox again," replied Wang Chen. "I shall have my sword ready."

While speaking they had reached the inn where the other lodgers, who had heard this story with amazement, gathered round to question Wang Chen. After talking till his mouth was dry he supped and retired to his room for the night. Since the fox had tried to recover the book by a trick in spite of its pain, Wang was sure that the volume must be valuable and prized it more highly than ever.

At midnight there came a knocking at the gate.

"Hurry up and return us that book!" shouted the foxes. "If you do, we shall repay you well! If you don't, you will be sorry for it."

When Wang heard this he was very angry. Throwing on his clothes and seizing his sword, he left his room on tiptoe for fear of waking the others. But when he reached the gate, he found the innkeeper had locked it.

"By the time I call the landlord to open the gate the foxes will have disappeared and I shan't be able to get at them," he thought. "I shall only be disturbing people for nothing. I had better let it go till the morning."

So he went back to bed. But the foxes shouted at the gate

for a long time, waking everybody in the inn; and the next morning the other guests reasoned with Wang Chen.

"Since you can't make out what's in the book, what's the use of keeping it?" they asked. "You had better return it. Otherwise the foxes may really cause trouble, and you'll be sorry when it's too late."

Now if Wang had been sensible enough to take their advice, all would have been well. But since he was too obstinate to listen to them, later the foxes practically ruined him.

> For a man who neglects the advice of a friend
> Will repent and shed tears of regret in the end.

When Wang had breakfasted and settled his bill he packed up and rode into the city, seeing houses in ruins, streets half deserted, and far fewer passersby than in the good old days. He was cut to the quick to find his old home nothing but a heap of rubble; and since he could not stay here he found a lodging where he could leave his baggage, then went to look for his relatives, not many of whom were left. They told each other all that had befallen since last they met, and at the saddest parts of their stories shed tears of grief.

"Many, many families were separated during the rebellion," said his relatives, "to be captured, killed or suffer endless hardships. We ourselves barely escaped with our lives. You should count yourself very lucky that all your family are safe and sound and you have lost only your house. Besides, we have looked after your landed property, so that none of your estates have been seized; and you will still be a wealthy family when you come back."

Wang Chen thanked them, then bought a house, furnished it with all that was needful, and got his farms back into good working order. He had been occupied in this way for two months when one day, as he left his house, a man in mourning with a bundle on his back approached rapidly from the east.

Wang Chen saw with a shock that this was none other than his servant Liu-erh.

"Where have you come from, Liu-erh?" he called. "Why are you dressed like that?"

"So this is where you live, master," said Liu-erh. "I have had a hard time finding you."

"Tell me," repeated Wang, "why are you dressed in mourning?"

"Here is a letter, master. You will see from this."

He carried his bundle into the house and took from it a letter which he handed to his master. Wang saw that it was in his mother's handwriting.

"Son," he read, "after you left us we heard that there was more trouble in the north, and I worried day and night till I fell ill. All drugs have proved useless, and I shall soon be dead; but since I am over sixty I am not dying before my time. I regret only that there have been all these disturbances during my last years, and that I am dying far from home with neither of my sons at my side: this does distress me. As I come from the northwest, I do not want to be buried in a strange land; but the rebels are still strong and as long as the capital may fall into their hands again you should not stay there. After careful thought I believe your best course will be to dispose of all the property in the capital and use the money for my funeral; then, when you have buried me, come back here to the Yangtse Valley, where the soil is rich and the people good. Of course, an estate is not built up easily, so you must not dispose of our Yangtse Valley property carelessly. When the war is over, you can make plans to go back to the north. If you disobey me and are killed by the rebels, so that there is no one to continue our family sacrifices, I shall not recognize you as my son even when you join me in the nether regions. Mark well what I have said!"

When Wang had read this letter he fell weeping to the ground.

"I came to set my estates here in order so that we might come home," he said. "I never dreamed that anxiety for me would cause my mother's death. Had I known, I would not have come. But it is no use regretting that now."

After weeping for some time he asked, "Did my mother say anything else before she died?"

"No," replied Liu-erh, "only that your houses and farms in the north must be ruined, and that even if you recovered and restored them you shouldn't stay here, because there may be another revolt in the capital any time. She wanted you to make arrangements for the funeral as quickly as possible and to settle down safely in Hangchow after bringing her coffin north. She said that if you didn't carry out her wishes, she would not rest easy in her grave."

"Of course I cannot disobey my mother's last wishes," said Wang Chen. "And there is reason in her proposal that we could live in the south, because the fighting is not over here yet. Hence there is much to be said for leaving."

He made haste to procure mourning clothes and set up a shrine, then sent men to prepare the ancestral graveyard, at the same time begging friends to to help him sell his property.

"You will need a month at least to build the sepulchre, master," said Liu-erh two days later, "and the family will be worrying. Shall I go back first to tell them that all is well?"

"That is a good idea," replied Wang.

He wrote a letter to his wife and gave the servant travelling money to go back first.

"I'm going on ahead, master," said Liu-erh when he was leaving. "I hope you will settle things here and come on as quickly as you can."

"You don't have to remind me of that," retorted Wang Chen. "I only wish I could fly home this moment."

Then Liu-erh left the house with a well satisfied air.

When Wang Chen's relatives heard what had happened, they came to offer condolences and advised him not to give up his northern estates. However, since this was his mother's last wish, Wang Chen would not listen to them. In his haste he sold his good land for half its value; and in little over twenty days, when a grave had been dug in the ancestral graveyard and all things made ready, he packed up and left the capital with Wang Fu, to travel post-haste to Hangchow to fetch his mother's coffin.

We will go back now to Wang's family. When his mother and wife heard that rebellion had broken out again in the north, they worried day and night about Wang Chen, regretting that they had ever let him go. So two or three months later, when the gateman announced that the master's servant, Wang Fu, had arrived with a letter from the capital, they ordered him to be admitted immediately. Wang Fu kowtowed to his mistresses, then presented the letter; and although they noticed that his left eye was badly hurt, in their haste to read the letter they did not stop to question him. The letter ran as follows:

"After leaving you, mother, I travelled safely to the capital, where I found all our property safe and have now carried out all the necessary repairs. I was lucky to meet my old friend Secretary Hu here, for he introduced me to the prime minister, who has graciously given me an official post in the northeast. Since I have already received my credentials and must shortly leave, I am sending Wang Fu to invite you to accompany me to my new post. As soon as you receive this letter you should sell all our property in the south and come to the capital as fast as you can. Sell at a loss rather than delay. As we shall soon meet, I will say no more now. Your dutiful son, Chen."

When Wang Chen's mother and wife read this letter, they could hardly contain themselves for joy.

"How did you hurt your eye, Wang Fu?" they asked.

"I'm ashamed to tell you!" replied Wang Fu. "I dozed off in the saddle and fell off my horse, nearly knocking out this eye."

"Has the capital changed much? Are all our relatives still there?"

"The whole city was more than half destroyed," he told them. "It is quite different from the old days. Most of our relatives were killed or captured or else fled. There are only a few families left now, and they all had their property stolen, their houses burnt down or their land seized. Ours is the only family not to have lost a single house or field."

When the women heard this they were even more overjoyed.

"Our property is safe and he has been given an official post!" they cried. "We must thank Heaven and our ancestral spirits which have protected us. When we are ready to leave, let us sacrifice to them and pray for a bright future and continued prosperity."

Then they asked: "Who is this Secretary Hu?"

"An old friend of our master," replied Wang Fu.

"I have never heard him speak of a friend named Hu who is an official," said the old lady.

"Perhaps this is a new friend," suggested his wife.

"That's right," assented Wang Fu. "He only met this man recently."

"Wang Fu, you've had a hard journey," said the old lady after further questions. "Go and have some wine and food now, then rest."

The following day Wang Fu said: "It will take you several days to prepare for the journey, ma'am, and there is no one to look after our master in the capital. Hadn't I better go back first to give him your reply and get everything ready, so that as soon as you arrive we can start for his new post?"

To this the old lady agreed. She gave Wang Fu a letter and some travelling money; and after he had left she sold all their land, houses, furniture and utensils, keeping only some clothes and valuables. Because she was anxious to lose no time she did not bargain about the price, and much of the property was practically given away. Finally she called in monks to perform sacrifices, hired a junk, and chose an auspicious day to start the journey. Some friendly neighbours' wives came to see them off, and so they set sail, travelling from Hangchow to Soochow, then went up the Yangtse River and made for Yangchow. Because their master had received an official post, the servants were in the highest spirits and could hardly keep still for excitement.

After leaving the capital, Wang Chen travelled as fast as he could until he reached Yangchow. There he set down his baggage in an inn by the harbour and disposed of his horse, after which he had a meal and ordered Wang Fu to hire a boat while he sat outside the inn keeping an eye on his baggage and watching the passing vessels. Presently he noticed a large junk coming upstream, and four or five men laughing and singing in the prow. As the boat drew nearer he saw to his surprise that these were his own retainers.

"Why are they not at home?" he wondered. "What are they doing on this boat?"

Then it occurred to him: "Perhaps after my mother's death they have gone to work in another family."

He was speculating in this way when the cabin curtain was lifted, and he recognized the girl who looked out as one of their maidservants.

"How extraordinary!" he exclaimed to himself.

He was about to hail the junk when the servants saw him.

"What brings you here, sir?" they cried. "Why are you in mourning?"

They immediately ordered the boatmen to bring the boat to the shore.

Meanwhile, roused by this commotion, Wang Chen's mother

and wife lifted the cabin curtain to look out; and when Wang Chen saw that his mother was not dead he hastily took off his mourning, unpacked his baggage and changed into ordinary dress. By this time the servants had come ashore to meet him; and, ordering them to pick up his baggage, he boarded the junk to greet his mother. When he saw Liu-erh at the prow, however, he seized him and started beating him.

"He hasn't done anything wrong," declared the old lady, coming out of the cabin. "Why are you beating him?"

When Wang Chen saw his mother, he let go of Liu-erh and bowed.

"By bringing your letter to the capital and raising a false alarm," he said, "this dog has made me act in an unfilial way!"

"But he has been at home all this time," they exclaimed in surprise. "He never took any letter to the capital."

"Only a month ago he brought me my mother's letter," protested Wang Chen. "And I sent him back after two days to reassure the family. Then I sold our property and started back myself post-haste. How can you say he never went to the capital?"

"What can have happened?" they demanded incredulously. "Does Liu-erh have a double?"

Even Liu-erh laughed.

"I never went to the capital, not even in a dream," he declared.

"Show me the letter," said Wang Chen's mother. "Let me see whether it is in my writing."

"If it hadn't looked like your writing," replied Wang, "I would never have believed it."

But when he undid his baggage and took out the letter, he found a sheet of white paper without a word on it. Gaping in consternation, he turned this over and over in his hands.

"Where is the letter?" demanded his mother. "Show it to me."

"This is amazing," muttered Wang Chen. "How could all that writing have disappeared?"

"I can't believe it!" said his mother. "The only letters we've exchanged since you left are the one you wrote when you sent Wang Fu to fetch me, and the reply I sent you by him. How could there be a false Liu-erh to deceive you with a false letter? And now you say it has changed into a blank sheet—I never heard such nonsense in my life!"

When Wang Chen heard that Wang Fu had been home, it was his turn to be astounded.

"Wang Fu has been with me all the time in the capital," he assured them. "He has come here with me now. I never sent him with any letter to you."

"That makes even less sense," objected his mother and wife. "A month ago Wang Fu brought us a letter from you, saying that all our property in the capital was safe and that Secretary Hu had introduced you to the prime minister, who gave you an official post. You told us to sell all our houses and land in the south and come straight to the capital to accompany you to your new post. So we disposed of all our property and hired this boat for the journey. How can you say Wang Fu never came back?"

"This is becoming more and more fantastic!" exclaimed Wang Chen. "No Secretary Hu ever introduced me to the prime minister or got me a job. And I never wrote to invite you to the capital."

"Can Wang Fu be an impostor too?" demanded the old lady. "Fetch him here at once."

"He went to hire a boat," replied Wang Chen. "He will be back presently."

The servants gathered at the prow to keep a lookout, and soon saw Wang Fu in the distance running towards the wharf. He was dressed in mourning too. They waved to him frantically, and Wang Fu recognized them.

"What are they doing here?" he wondered.

When he drew near they saw that he had changed. When he brought the letter, he had been blind in his left eye; but now both his eyes were as round and bright as brass bells.

"Wang Fu!" they called. "When you came home the other day you were blind in the left eye. How is it that you're all right again now?"

Wang Fu spat at them.

"You're the ones who are blind," he retorted. "When did I go home? And why accuse me of being blind?"

"This is an odd business!" they laughed. "Our mistress wants to see you in the cabin. Take off that mourning and go in."

Wang Fu looked flabbergasted.

"Is the old lady still alive?" he demanded.

"Of course she is," they replied.

Wang Fu did not believe them, though, so without removing his mourning he dashed straight into the cabin.

"Fool!" shouted Wang Chen. "Your mistress is here. Go and change your clothes at once."

Then Wang Fu hurried out, removed his mourning and went back to the cabin to kowtow to the old lady, who rubbed her eyes as she stared at him.

"Well, I never!" she declared again and again. "When he came the other day his left eye was blind, but today it is perfectly all right. I suppose it couldn't have been him after all."

She hastily took out her son's letter to have a look at it, only to find that it was a sheet of blank paper too, without an ink mark on it.

The whole family was staggered. They were at a loss to understand who could have masqueraded as Liu-erh and Wang Fu, or why anyone should trick Wang Chen in Changan and his mother in Hangchow in order to ruin the family. Fearing worse might follow, they were filled with doubts and forebodings.

But after thinking hard, Wang Chen recollected that the false Wang Fu had been blind in the left eye, and then he saw light.

"I have it!" he cried. "This is the work of those accursed beasts!"

His mother immediately asked what he meant, and he told her how he had shot the foxes at Fanchuan and taken their book, how one of them had masqueraded as a man in the inn to recover the book, and how they had hammered on the inn gate all night.

"I thought they changed into men simply to get the book," he said. "Little did I dream they had such cunning."

The others shook their heads and shot out their tongues in amazement.

"These fox fairies are fearfully cunning," they declared. "In two places so far apart they were able to fool us by imitating men's handwriting and appearance so well. If you had known this, you should have returned them the book."

"A plague on these wicked beasts!" swore Wang Chen. "I shall certainly not return the book. If they trouble me again, I'll burn the accursed thing."

"We had better keep to the point and discuss our main problem," said Wang Chen's wife. "Here we are—neither north nor south—what shall we do?"

"All the property in the capital has been sold," said Wang Chen. "If we go there, we shall have nowhere to stay. Besides, it's a long way to travel. We had better go back south."

"But we have nothing left in the south either," objected his mother. "Where shall we live?"

"We shall have to rent a place for the time being," said Wang, "and make plans later."

As they headed the boat back south, the servants who had been all fire and spirit before were as cold and dull as puppets whose strings have been snapped—silent and limp. They had set off exultantly, but returned in despair. Upon reaching

Hangchow, Wang Chen and the servants went ashore first to rent a house in the quarter where they had lived before and buy the necessary furniture and utensils. Then they carried over their baggage and fetched Wang Chen's mother and wife. When they reckoned how much money they had left, it was less than half their original capital; so between anger and despair they stayed at home fuming, unwilling to go out. The neighbours who had seen Wang Chen's mother leave and then return came to inquire, and when Wang told them his story they marvelled and spread the tale till half Hangchow knew it.

One day Wang Chen was watching his servants clean the hall when a dignified, well-dressed stranger walked in.

> He had a black gauze cap and green silk gown,
> A jasper ring on his cap and a purple belt;
> His socks were white as snow,
> His shoes like rosy clouds;
> He'd a lordly look and natural dignity.
> A man like that, if not a god,
> Must at least be a high official or ruler of men.

Wang Chen saw that this stranger was no other than his brother, Wang Tsai, who came up to him and bowed.

"How have you been, brother," he asked, "since we parted?"

Wang Chen returned his bow.

"To think of your finding us here!" he exclaimed.

"When I went to the capital and looked for our old home," said Wang Tsai, "I found it had been razed to the ground; and the thought of all you must have suffered in the war made me very sad. Then I was relieved to learn from our relatives that the family had taken refuge in the south. They told me too that you had been to the capital to set our property to rights, but left again after hearing of our mother's death. I came here post-haste and found the house where you used to live; but when the neighbours told me that you had moved and that our mother was well, I went back to the boat to take off my mourning before coming here. Where is our mother now? And why have you moved to such a shabby place?"

"It is a long story," replied Wang Chen. "I will tell you after you've seen mother."

He led Wang Tsai inside, and servants announced his arrival to the old lady. The knowledge that her second son had come home made her very happy, and she hurried out to meet them as they were going in. Then Wang Tsai kowtowed to her.

"Son!" she cried. "I have been thinking of you day and night. Have you been well?"

"Yes, thank you, mother. When I have greeted my sister-in-law, I'll tell you all I've been doing."

After Wang Chen's wife and the maids and servants had greeted him, Wang Tsai took his brother by the sleeve and led him to the hall. Their mother came with them, and they sat down together.

"You start first, brother," said Wang Tsai. "How did you get into this state?"

Wang Chen told him in detail how he had shot the foxes at Fanchuan and how the foxes had tricked him and his mother into selling all their property.

"So that's the reason!" exclaimed Wang Tsai. "Well, it's your own fault; you can't blame the foxes. They were just reading in the forest, while you were passing by on the public highway. They hadn't interfered with you, so why did you have to shoot them and take their book? If one of them went to the inn in spite of its pain to recover the book, that shows they must have needed it desperately. Yet you not only refused to return it, but chased them angrily with drawn sword; and that night when they begged you to let them have it, you refused again. You can't read the book yourself, so it is useless to you. Why should you keep it? You've only yourself to blame for the plight you're in now."

"That's just what I say," agreed their mother. "What's the use of keeping the book? It's only asking for trouble."

Wang Chen made no reply, but this lecture left him thoroughly irritated.

"How big is the book?" inquired Wang Tsai. "What is the writing like?"

"It's a slender volume," replied Wang Chen, "I don't know what language it is, because I can't decipher a word."

"Let me have a look at it," said Wang Tsai.

"That's right," put in the old lady. "Show it to your brother. He may be able to read it."

"I don't suppose I shall," said Wang Tsai. "I'm curious to see it though."

Wang Chen fetched the book and gave it to his brother, who turned the pages from beginning to end.

"This is certainly strange writing," he said.

Then he stood up and walked to the middle of the hall.

"I was Liu-erh the other day," he announced. "Now that you've returned our magic book, I won't worry you any more. You can set your mind at rest."

This said, he rushed outside.

Wang Chen chased furiously after him.

"How dare you, detestable beast!" he cried. "You shan't get away!"

Seizing the fox by its garments, he pulled so hard that the silk gown was torn. Then the fox shook itself, slipped out of its clothes, reverted to its true form and streaked out as swiftly as the wind. Wang Chen and his servants hurried to the street, but though they hunted in all directions not a trace of the beast could they find. Because the foxes had ruined his family, chided him and now taken the book, Wang Chen was gnashing his teeth in rage. As he was gazing round, he saw a blind priest standing under the eaves of the house opposite.

"Have you seen a fox pass by?" asked Wang Chen.

The blind priest pointed eastward.

"It went that way," he said.

Wang Chen and his men started racing down the street, but when they had passed five or six houses they heard a shout behind them.

"Wang Chen!" called the blind priest. "I was Wang Fu the other day. Your brother is here too!"

They wheeled round to see the two foxes gambolling mischievously with the book between their paws. But when they rushed forward to catch them, the beasts made off like wind. As Wang Chen was racing past his own door, his mother called out to stop him.

"I'm glad that source of trouble has gone!" she cried. "Why should you chase them? Come home now."

Though nearly bursting with anger, in deference to his mother Wang Chen had to call his men back. When they picked up the clothes the fox had worn to look at them, the garments changed in their hands.

> The silk gown changed to banana leaves,
> The black gauze cap to a lotus leaf,
> The jasper ring was a willow twig,
> The purple belt a creeper;
> The socks were two sheets of white paper,
> And the red shoes pine tree bark.

At this sight they were all amazed.

"What magic arts those foxes have!" declared the servants.

"Where can our second master be now? Fancy the fox imitating him so well!"

The more Wang Chen brooded over this, the angrier he grew. Finally he had to take to his bed, and his mother called in doctors to attend him.

A few days later some of the servants were in the hall when Wang Tsai walked in again, in the same gauze cap and silk robe. They naturally thought this must be the fox disguised as before.

"That fox is back again!" they shouted.

After running for clubs and sticks, they rushed forward to beat him.

"You fools!" shouted Wang Tsai. "How dare you? Go and tell your mistress I am here."

They paid no attention, however, but went on belabouring Wang Tsai until he lost his temper, seized one of their sticks and laid so lustily about him that they dared not come near, but hid in adjoining rooms.

"You cursed beast!" they swore, pointing at him. "Now that you've got the book, what have you come back for?"

Bewildered but angry, Wang Tsai forced his way in. And as the servants bolted towards the back quarters, the old lady heard the noise and came out to ask what this confusion meant.

"That fox has changed into our second master again," they told her. "He is forcing his way in."

While she was uttering cries of dismay, Wang Tsai entered her presence. At the sight of his mother he put down his stick and stepped forward to kowtow.

"Mother," he asked, "why did those fools call me a fox and beat me?"

"Are you really my son?" she demanded.

"You bore me," he replied. "Of course I am your son."

While they were talking seven or eight men came in carrying Wang Tsai's baggage. Then the servants knew that this was indeed their master and kowtowed to him in apology. And when he asked the reason for what had happened, his mother told him all about the foxes.

"Your brother was so angry that he fell ill," she said. "He is not well yet."

Wang Tsai was aghast.

"In that case," he said, "I suppose that letter Wang Fu brought me in Szechuan was false too?"

"What did the letter say?"

"I went in the imperial train to Szechuan, where I was assigned work under Governor Yen Wu of Chiennan and later promoted to be a lieutenant. That is why when His Imperial Majesty returned to the capital I did not follow him. Two months ago Wang Fu brought me a letter from my brother saying that he had moved to the Yangtse Valley during the revolt, and that you had just died, so that I must come at once to help take your coffin north to our ancestral graveyard. Wang Fu said he had to go to the capital to prepare the graveyard, and left the next day. Then I resigned from my post, disposed of all my property and travelled here as fast as I could. When I reached your old house the neighbours directed me here; and learning that you were alive and well I went back to the boat to change my clothes, meaning to ask my brother what made him send me such false news. Who could imagine an extraordinary thing like this?"

When he took the letter from his baggage and they found it had changed into a blank sheet of paper too, they did not know whether to laugh or swear.

After Wang Tsai went in with his mother to greet his brother and sister-in-law and tell them his story, Wang Chen nearly had an apoplectic fit.

"Though these foxes caused us so much trouble," said the old lady, "they *did* go to Szechuan to fetch Tsai back, and it's thanks to them that we are united again. Let's count this to their credit and stop complaining."

After two months Wang Chen recovered, and they settled down permanently in Hangchow.

And even to this day, readers, in the Yangtse River Valley, an impostor is called a fox.

(YANG AND YANG)

§ LOVE

The Oil Peddler and the Queen of Flowers

Anonymous

(*ca.* fourteenth century A.D.)

Young men like to speak of "breeze and moonlight"
And of their victories over waves and storms.
Money without beauty will not promote genuine feeling,
Beauty without money will also end in failure.
And even if you have both money and beauty,
You must above all practice solicitude,
For he who can read his fair lady's thoughts
Only he is without peer in the arena of love.

This poem is written to the tune known as "Moon over the West River" and expresses a most profound truth in matters concerning "breeze and moonlight." "The courtesan loves a handsome face, but Madame loves gold," goes the saying, and accordingly he who has the beauty of P'an An and the wealth of Teng T'ung will find no trouble in making himself generally welcome and in being lord in the castle of fair bandits. However, this is only true to a certain extent, for even more important than money and beauty is the lesson contained in the words *pang ch'en*. As a compound the expression simply means "to assist," but the root meanings of the individual words are more suggestive, for *pang* means the upper part of the shoe, and *ch'en* means the lining of a garment, both indispensable parts that make up two harmonious wholes. With proper "assistance" a lady with one part loveliness will appear like one with ten, while by the same token proper "assistance" will conceal what defects she may have. That is what is meant by *pang ch'en*, that and such little things as maintaining an attitude of humility toward the fair one, fanning her in summer and shielding her from cold in winter, and generally doing things that please her and avoiding things that do not. He who knows how to practice the art of *pang ch'en* is most likely to succeed · · the arena of love. It endows the homely with beauty and the poor with wealth.

Cheng Yuanho of the T'ang Dynasty was, for instance, empty of purse and sore-ridden in appearance when Li Yahsien encountered him cold and starved in the snow, yet she took compassion upon him and took him home with her, wrapped him up in silken covers and fed him with fine delicacies. It could not have been because she coveted his money, of which he had none, or because she admired his appearance, for he was emaciated and covered with sores. It was, rather, because Chang Yuanho was attentive and knew well how to practice the art of *pang ch'en* when he had money to spend that Yahsien could not now bear to abandon him. If you but recall the incident in which Cheng Yuanho killed his favorite horse in order to gratify Yahsien's wish for horse-tripe soup, you'll understand why she rescued him from his poverty. Later on Cheng Yuanho's luck turned; he became *optimus* in the imperial examinations, and Li Yahsien was given the title of Lady of Chienkuo. Truly it is as the couplet says:

> When luck flees even gold loses its luster;
> When luck returns even iron shines bright.

Now during the reigns of the first seven emperors of the Sung Dynasty [A.D. 960–1280] the country enjoyed peace and prosperity. The warlike arts were neglected, while literature flourished. But when Hui Tsung ascended the throne as the eighth emperor he fell under the evil influence of such infamous ministers as Ts'ai Ching and Kao Ch'iu, and by his indulgence in wanton pleasures and ruinous extravagances he brought the empire to a very low state and caused disaffection among the people. The Kin Tartars took advantage of the situation and invaded the northern provinces. The once prosperous and happy land was thrown into great turmoil, and the Emperors Hui Tsung and Ch'in Tsung (to whom the former had abdicated) were captured by the invaders. It was not until the miraculous escape of the Prince K'ang on a horse of clay and his ascension to the throne at Hangchow (which was renamed Linan or Temporary Security) and the division of the empire into the North and South dynasties that a measure of peace was restored. During the years of war and confusion, the people suffered untold hardships.

Among these unfortunate victims of war there was a man by the name of Hsin Shan who lived in a village outside the capital Pienliang. He had a provisions store and was well off in a modest way. His wife Juanshih bore him an only daughter named Yaochin, a very beautiful and clever girl. Her parents sent her to the village school when she was seven, and by the time she was ten she was able to read poems and compose verses. At the age of twelve she was accomplished in playing the harp and at chess and also in painting and calligraphy. As for her skill with the needle, it was even more to be marveled at. Because he had no son of his own, Hsin Shan wished to get himself a son-in-law who would live with him and comfort him in his old age, but as his daughter was much sought after because of her beauty and accomplishments, he was not able to make up his mind which suitor to choose.

It was then that the Kin Tartars invaded the land and laid siege to Pienliang. There were many armies in various parts of the empire that were ready to rally to the protection of the Emperor, but as the prime minister was for treating with the invaders, they were not allowed to oppose the barbarians. As a result, the Tartar hordes became more insatiable than ever in their lust for conquest; they invested the capital and kidnapped Hui Tsung and Ch'in Tsung. The people in the region all abandoned their homes and fled in terror before the barbarian hordes. Among them were Hsin Shan and his wife Juanshih and their daughter Yaochin. They dodged in and out of the road like homeless dogs and scuttled hither and yon like fish escaped from the nets; they knew not whither they were going, their only thought being to escape the Tartars. Well says the proverb:

> Rather be a dog in time of peace
> Than a man in an age of war and separation.

The refugees did not encounter any Tartars but they did meet with a band of defeated imperial troops. When the demoralized soldiers saw the helpless refugees and the worldly possessions that they were carrying with them, they raised a false cry, "There come the Tartars!" and then proceeded to rob the refugees as they scattered in confusion. Those who refused to yield up their possessions were murdered. Indeed, it was confusion heaped upon confusion and bitterness added to bitterness.

Yaochin was knocked down in the confusion. When she got back to her feet, she had lost sight of her parents. Not daring to shout for help, she hid among the tombs by the road and there spent the night. When day came she found herself quite alone, with nothing in sight except dust in the sky and corpses lying about the road. She trudged on in the southerly direction that she had been following, weeping and crying as she went. After having gone about two *li* she began to feel tired and hungry. She was heartened by the sight of a hut in the distance, thinking that she might find there food and drink, but when she came to it she found it abandoned. She sat leaning against the wall and cried bitterly.

"There can be no story without coincidence," goes the ancient saying. Now it happened that one of her neighbors went by just at this moment. This man was named Pu Chiao, an idler and a worthless fellow who lived by his wits. He too had been separated from the group of refugees by the imperial troops and was traveling by himself. At the sight of a neighbor Yaochin felt as if she had encountered one of her own kin. She stopped crying and asked, "Uncle Pu, have you seen my parents?"

"What luck!" Pu Chiao said to himself. "I have been robbed of everything by the soldiers but now Heaven has sent me this nice article for my use." But aloud he lied to Yaochin thus: "Yes, indeed. They are now a distance ahead. They asked me to take you to them if I should find you."

Though Yaochin was a clever girl, she suspected nothing in her joy at seeing someone that she knew. Gladly she went with him.

Pu Chiao gave her some of the food that he carried with him and said to her, "Your parents did not stop during the night and it may be that we shall not catch up with them until we reach Chienkang on the other side of Yangtze. Let me call you daughter and you call me father, for otherwise we might arouse suspicion."

Yaochin consented and thereafter they traveled together by land and river under the guise of father and daughter. At Chienkang they heard that Prince Wuchu of the Kin Tartars was about to cross the Yangtze to attack that city, so they continued their journey southward and headed for Hangchou, where Prince K'ang had assumed the throne as Emperor Kao Tsung.

By the time they reached Hangchou, which was now known as Linan, Pu Chiao had spent what little money he had, and it became necessary for him to dispose of Yaochin. He made inquiries among the brothel keepers on West Lake and found that a certain Wang Chiu-ma was looking for a girl. He took the woman to the inn to look at Yaochin so that they could agree on a price. Chiu-ma was impressed with Yaochin's beauty and agreed to pay fifty ounces of silver for her. After the silver had changed hands, Pu Chiao took Yaochin to Chiu-ma's house.

Pu Chiao was a clever man. Before Chiu-ma he represented himself as Yaochin's real father and to cover up his deception he solicitously enjoined Chiu-ma to take good care of Yaochin and to be patient with her. To Yaochin he said that Chiu-ma was a close relation of his and that he would come back for her as soon as he had found her parents. The unfortunate girl was completely taken in and went gladly to Chiu-ma's house.

Chiu-ma gave Yaochin a complete change of clothes and housed her in the best room in her establishment. She served her the best of food and drink and comforted her with kind words. When after a few days Yaochin heard nothing from Pu Chiao, she said to Chiu-ma with tears in her eyes, "Why is it that Uncle Pu has not come to see me?" "What Uncle Pu?" Chiu-ma asked. "The man who brought me here," Yaochin said. "But he said that he was your father," Chiu-ma said. Then Yaochin told her how she had become separated from her parents, how Pu Chiao had found her and traveled with her to Linan. "I might as well tell you the truth," Chiu-ma said after she heard Yaochin's story. "That man Pu sold you to me for fifty taels of silver. As you are more beautiful than any of the girls that I have, I shall treat you as my own daughter and see that you have the best of food and clothing the rest of your life."

Yaochin cried bitterly on learning that she had been deceived by Pu Chiao, and it was a long time before Chiu-ma was able to quiet her. After this Chiu-ma changed her name to Meiniang and taught her singing and dancing until she excelled in those arts. By the time she was fourteen she had become a maiden of extraordinary beauty, much sought after by the rich and noble gallants of Linan. They came with generous offerings, some seeking to enjoy her beauty, others to get scraps of her accomplished verses and calligraphy. Soon she became one of the most famous courtesans of the empire, and was nicknamed the "Queen of Flowers."

Because of her fame she began to receive offers "to comb her hair," though she was but fourteen. She was, naturally, unwilling to have her chastity violated and Chiu-ma did not dare to force her because she brought in so much gold.

Another year went by and Meiniang became fifteen. Now among people of Chiu-ma's calling there were certain well-established conventions governing the "combing of the hair." When it was done at the age of thirteen, it was known as "testing the flower," a very unsatisfactory proceeding because of the extreme youth of the girl. It is seldom resorted to except by avaricious keepers who care nothing for the welfare of their charges. When it is done at the age of fourteen it is known as "emblossoming the flower." This is considered the best time, since it marks the beginning of reciprocity. At the age of fifteen, it is known as "plucking the flower" and is considered rather overdue, though in ordinary families fifteen is considered an immature age. When at the age of fifteen Meiniang's hair was not yet combed, the gallants who frequented the West Lake houses began to make jibes about a certain wood quince that was beautiful to look at but quite unfit to eat.

Chiu-ma was distressed by these jibes and tried to persuade her to receive patrons, but Meiniang refused, saying that she would never do so unless her own parents were there to command her. Although Chiu-ma was displeased with her scruples, she did not have the heart to discipline her. Then one day a certain rich man by the name of Chin came and offered Chiu-ma three hundred *taels* for the coveted privilege. Unable to resist the princely sum, Chiu-ma entered into a plot with Chin. They made Meiniang drunk and then forced the unwelcome ceremony upon her. . . .

When she woke up and realized what had happened, Meiniang rose from the bed of her undoing, got dressed, and then laid herself down on a bamboo couch, turned her face toward the wall and began to weep silently. Chin went to her and tried to comfort her, but he only got scratched in the face for his pains. He was naturally much put out and left the house precipitately at dawn.

Now it was the usual custom for a client who had just "combed the hair" of his favorite courtesan to stay a month or two or at least ten or twenty days in her establishment. Chin's behavior was unprecedented. Chiu-ma went up to Meiniang's room and found her lying on her couch weeping. She tried to console her but Meiniang only wept and said nothing.

After that Meiniang refused to leave her own room and would not receive any visitors at all. Chiu-ma became impatient but she did not dare to discipline her for fear of driving her to more desperate action. Yet she could not let things go on as they were; Meiniang was her money tree only so long as she received patrons. One day Chiu-ma suddenly thought of Liu Ssu-ma, one of her sworn sisters, a woman with a very clever tongue and Meiniang's confidante. "Why don't I get her to come and see what she could do to persuade Meiniang?" she said to herself. She sent Pao-erh, one of the servants, for Ssu-ma and when she came told her everything.

"I am a female Sui Ho and a woman Lu Chia," Ssu-ma said. "I can make a Lohan fall in love and persuade the Goddess of the Moon to consider marriage. You can depend on me."

"I shall kowtow to you in gratitude," Chiu-ma said. "But have some tea so that you won't find yourself handicapped by a dry throat."

"Don't worry," Ssu-ma said, "I can talk till tomorrow morning without the need of moistening my throat."

Meiniang's door was shut but she opened it when she recognized Ssu-ma's voice. On her desk was spread out a piece of silk on which she had sketched the outline of a woman's figure but had not yet filled in the colors. "What a fine picture!" Ssu-ma said, "and how clever you are! Indeed, Sister Chiu is lucky to have such a clever girl as you, so beautiful and accomplished in so many things. She couldn't find another one like you even if she searched the length and breadth of Linan with a cartload of gold."

"Don't make fun of me," Meiniang said. "What wind has brought you here, aunt?"

"I have been wanting to come to see you, but have not had the time," Ssu-ma said. "I heard about your 'hair combing' and have come to congratulate you and Sister Chiu."

Meiniang blushed at the mention of her shame. Ssu-ma drew her chair closer to her and taking Meiniang's hands in hers said, "My child, a courtesan cannot afford to be as tender skinned as a soft-shelled egg. You'll never accumulate any great amount of silver by being so shy."

"What need do I have of silver?" Meiniang said.

"But, my child," said Ssu-ma, "your mother expects you to bring in silver for her even if you don't care about it yourself. Remember the saying that he who lives near the mountain eats by the mountain and he who lives near the water eats by the water. Of the powdered faces that Sister Chiu has, is there one who can touch you? In her orchard you are the only melon that she can depend upon to supply her with seeds. You are an intelligent child and should know why it is that she has treated you better than anyone else in the house. I have been told that you have refused to receive any client since your 'hair-combing.' What does this mean? If everyone behaved the way you do how would your mother buy mulberry leaves to feed her hungry silkworms? Since she has been so kind to you, you should try to deserve her kindness. Otherwise the rest of the girls, always jealous, will criticize you."

"Let them criticize me!" Meiniang said. "I am not afraid of them."

"But that is nothing compared to what might happen to you if you persist in your stubbornness," Ssu-ma said. "We who are in the business depend upon our 'daughters' for everything. If by luck we get a promising girl, it is just as if a rich family had acquired a piece of fertile land. We nourish her and care for her till she is ready for her 'hair-combing,' which is to us as the harvest is to the farmers. After that we expect to get returns for our investment, we expect her to receive new clients at the front door after she has sent away the old from the back door, with Mr. Chang bringing rice and Mr. Li sending firewood."

"I can't bring myself to do that," Meiniang said.

"You talk as if you were your own mistress," Ssu-ma said, laughing. "It is for your mother to command. If you do not obey she can whip you until you are neither dead nor alive. Sister Chiu has never subjected you to such humiliation only because you are clever and beautiful. She has just complained to me about your behavior, saying that you are very obstinate and that you do not seem to appreciate such obvious things as the fact that a goose feather is lighter than a millstone, and she asked me to persuade you to change your ways. If you persist in your stubbornness, you may provoke her beyond endurance and make her scold you or even beat you. What would you do then? And once she gets started there will be no end to it; in the end you will have to yield to her wishes. Your reputation will be ruined and your position lowered in the eyes of your sister courtesans. In my opinion the best thing for you to do is to throw yourself in your mother's bosom and enjoy her favors while you can."

"I am from a self-respecting family," Meiniang said, "and have fallen into this life of shame through the treachery of someone else. If you, aunt, should make it possible for me to abandon this life and 'follow the path of virtue' you would be doing a greater good deed than building a nine-storied pagoda; but if it is your intention to make me submit to this life of shame, I would rather die than do what you say."

"It is a worthy ambition to 'follow the path of virtue,' " Ssu-ma said, "but even if such is your wish, you have to begin by receiving patrons. In the first place, your mother will never let you go until she has made a thousand *taels* or more through you. Then surely you will want to marry some one worthy of your beauty and accomplishments, not any common, vulgar fellow that comes along. But how are you to know whom to marry if you see no one? If you persist in your refusal, your mother will probably sell you as a concubine to anyone willing to pay the price. You'll be committed for life then, whether the man be old or ugly or as ignorant as an ox. I think you should do what your mother wishes. With your beauty and talents you don't have to entertain any except noble and rich patrons. Thus you will be able to enjoy yourself while you are still young, enable your mother to make a fortune and save some money for yourself. After five or six years your mother will be willing to let you go. When the right man does come along, then I shall myself be your matchmaker."

Meiniang said nothing after hearing this, but by the smile on her face, Ssu-ma knew that she was beginning to weaken in her resolution. "Everything I have said is for your good," she said, getting up. "You will be grateful to me one of these days for the advice."

Meiniang escorted her to the door and there she saw Chiu-ma, who had been listening outside. She blushed and withdrew, while Chiu-ma and Ssu-ma went to the front hall.

"Niece was as stubborn as iron," Ssu-ma said, "but I talked and talked to her until she melted completely and is now ready to receive guests."

Chiu-ma thanked her and asked her to stay for dinner, and did not let her go until she had eaten and drunk to repletion.

Meiniang's fame grew after she began to receive visitors again; the door of Chiu-ma's house became like a market place. Even at a fee of ten *taels* a visit people fought for her favors. Chiu-ma rejoiced at the money that she made, but Meiniang only looked forward to the time when she might meet someone to whom she could give herself in marriage; as the saying goes:

> It is easier to acquire a priceless treasure
> Than to find the man you love.

Now we must take up a different thread in the story. There was inside the Clear Wave Gate of Linan an oil shop belonging to a man by the name of Chu Shih-lao. A few years back he had adopted a refugee boy from Pienliang by the name of Chin Chung. The boy's mother died in his infancy and he was thirteen when his father sold him and entered the Upper Tien Chu Temple as a lay attendant. Since Chu Shih-lao was recently widowed and without children, he looked upon Chin Chung as his own son. He changed the boy's name to Chu Chung and taught him his own business. Father and son managed very well until Shih-lao was forced by the infirmities of age to hire an assistant named Hsing Chuan.

"Time passes like an arrow." Soon Chu Chung grew up into a handsome young man of seventeen. Now Shih-lao had a bond-maid by the name of Orchid. She was already past twenty. She became interested in Chu Chung and time and again "set out hooks to catch him." But Chu Chung was a good and honest youth. Moreover, he found the maid distasteful because she was homely and untidy. And so "though the fallen flower was full of pity for itself, the flowing stream speeds it on without regret."

Failing to catch the younger Chu Chung, Orchid turned to Hsing Chuan. As he was a man over forty and unmarried, she succeeded without any difficulty. Then she and Hsing Chuan plotted to get rid of Chu Chung for fear that he might surprise them in their secret meetings. Orchid went to Shih-lao and accused Chu Chung of having made advances to her. As she had been more than a bondmaid to Shih-lao, the charge made the old man jealous. Then Hsing Chuan trumped up a false charge of his own against the young man, saying that he had been gambling and losing money and that he had stolen from the shop to pay his debts. At first Shih-lao did not believe them, but their repeated accusations finally swayed him. He called Chu Chung to him and gave him a severe scolding.

Though Chu Chang was innocent, he was wise enough not to try to expose the bondmaid and her lover, for his foster father might not believe him and the guilty couple would hate him the more for it in any case. He said to Shih-lao as a plan came to his mind, "Business has been light and there is no need for two men in the shop. Master Hsing can take care of the shop while I go out and peddle oil in the streets. That would increase the volume of our business."

Shih-lao was about to give his consent to this arrangement, but again he was misled by Hsing Chuan, who said to him, "That is only a pretext on his part. He has accumulated some money and wants to get married and set up a house of his own."

Thereupon Shih-lao said with a sigh, "I have treated him like a son but he has paid me ill. Well, there is nothing to do but let him go. He is after all, not my own flesh and blood." So he sent Chu Chung away, giving him only three *taels* and permitting him to take only his clothes and bedding with him.

After leaving Shih-lao's house, Chu Chung found a room, deposited his belongings in it, and then set out to inquire for his father, who had not, it might be added, told his son where he was going. Chu Chung's search was fruitless and after a few days he had to give it up. As he had been scrupulously honest during the four years with Shih-lao, the three taels that he received as a parting present was the only money he had. It was hardly enough to start a business with. So after thinking things over he decided to become an oil peddler, since he knew something of the business and was acquainted with the mill-owners. He bought himself the necessary outfit and deposited the rest of his money with one of the mills.

Now the mill-owner knew Chu Chung to be an honest man and he knew the circumstances that had led to his disgrace. He was sympathetic and decided to do what he could to help the young peddler. He gave him the best quality oil at the lowest price and measured it out in a manner to give him the advantage. This in turn made it possible for Chu Chung to treat his customers in like manner, so that he had no difficulty in disposing of his load with a nice profit at the end of the day. As he lived frugally and practiced thrift in everything, he was able to save something and buy himself some clothes and necessary household articles. The only thing that preoccupied his mind was that he had not been able to find his father. "I must change my name back to Chin Chung," he said to himself, "so as to make it possible for my father to find me."

Now when a man of position wants to resume his original name, he has to present a petition to the Board of Rites and other appropriate authorities so that his action becomes a matter of public record. How was a humble oil peddler to let the world know that he had changed his name? Well, Chu Chung solved this problem in a very simple manner. He simply wrote on one side of his oil barrel the word "Chin" and on the other side the word "Pienliang," so that people would know at a glance who he was. And indeed the fact that he had resumed his own name soon became known over Linan and people began to refer to him as Chin the oil peddler.

It was the second month, when the weather was neither too cold nor too warm at Hangchou. Hearing that the monks at the Chao Ching Temple were about to hold a nine-day service and concluding that they must need more oil than usual, Chin Chung went thither with his barrels. The monks had heard of him as a peddler whose price was reasonable and whose oil was of the finest quality; they all patronized him and for those nine days he carried on his business at the temple.

> Sharp trade does not always bring profits;
> Honesty may not necessarily cause loss of capital.

On the ninth day Chin Chung left the temple after having sold all his oil. "The day was clear and bright, and pleasure seekers were out like ants." Carrying his empty barrels on a pole over his shoulder, Chin Chung walked along the bank of the lake and took in all the sights of that famous resort. When he began to feel a little tired, he went back to an open space to the right of the temple and sat down on a rock to rest. Presently he noticed several gentlemen in fine clothes emerging from a house not far from him, followed by a young lady. At the door she stopped and bade them goodby and then went back into the house.

In the meantime Chin Chung had been feasting his eyes on the young woman, for in beauty of feature and gracefulness of carriage he had never seen her equal. He became quite intoxicated with her beauty. However, he was an innocent youth and did not know what to make of what he had seen. As he was thus wondering to himself a middle-aged woman came out of the house with a young maid. When the woman saw Chin Chung's oil barrels she said to the maid, "We were just about to send out for oil. Since there is a peddler here, let us get it from him." The maid went inside and returned with a jug. But all this time Chin Chung was thinking about the young beauty he had just seen so that he did not come to himself until the maid approached him and called, "Peddler." Then he answered, "I have no more oil today, but I shall come back tomorrow if you want it."

The maid could read a little and, noting the characters written on the barrels, she said to the older woman, "The peddler's name is Chin." Now the woman had also heard about the reliability of Chin the oil peddler. So she said to him, "We need oil every day. If you are willing to call here I shall be glad to patronize you."

"Thank you, madam," Chin Chung said. "I shall come every day without fail." Then he said to himself as the woman and the maid went in, "What is she to the young lady I have just seen? If I come to deliver oil to her every day I shall at least see the young lady, whether or not I make any money."

Just as he was about to pick up his load and go on, he saw two carriers stop at the house with a sedan, accompanied by two young servants. The latter went into the house. Presently two maids came out, one carrying a red cushion and another a woven bamboo box, which they gave to the carriers to put under the chair. Then the young lady whom he had seen came out followed by the two servants carrying a lute case, some scrolls, and a flute. She got into the sedan and went off, followed by the maids and servants on foot.

This made Chin Chung wonder even more than before. As he went slowly on his way, he passed a tavern by the lake. As a rule he was not given to extravagances, but on this occasion he decided to celebrate. He put down his load, went into the tavern and sat down at a small table.

"Are you expecting friends, sir, or are you going to drink alone?" the waiter asked.

"Alone," Chin Chung said. "Bring me your best wine and some plain relishes without meat." When the waiter poured his wine, Chin Chung asked, pointing to the house where he had seen the beautiful lady, "Who lives in that house over there?"

"It is Chi Ya-nei's villa," the waiter answered, "but it is now occupied by a woman called Wang Chiu-ma."

"Who was the young lady that went off in a sedan chair a little while back?"

"She is the famous courtesan Wang Meiniang, known as the Queen of Flowers. She is a native of Pienliang and was stranded here as a refugee. She is not only skilled in singing and dancing and playing several instruments but is also accomplished in the game of chess and in painting and calligraphy. All her clients are rich men and pay ten *taels* of the bright metal for passing the night with her. She used to live outside the Yungchin Gate, but Chi Ya-nei, one of her intimates, lent this house to her."

When Chin Chung learned that the girl was a native of Pienliang, he felt even more drawn towards her. After finishing his wine, he paid the waiter and left the tavern, and as he walked on he thought thus to himself; "What a pity that such a beautiful girl should fall into a prostitute's house." Then he laughed to himself, saying, "But how could I, a poor peddler, have caught a glimpse of her if she had not fallen into such a house?" Then his thoughts grew bolder. " 'A man has but one life to live and a plant sees but one autumn.' If I could have a beautiful woman like her in my arms for one night, I should die without regret." Then laughing at himself, he said, "I make but a few cash a day in selling oil. How could I think of such impossible things. Like the toad that longs after the flesh of the swan, I shall never have my wish. She would not receive me even if I had the money, since she is accustomed to dealing only with rich and noble people." But another thought occurred to him: "I have been told that brothel keepers care only for money and are ready to receive a beggar if he can pay the price. So she ought to be willing to receive me who carry on a respectable trade. Surely I need not fear that she would reject me if I had the fee. But where would I get so much silver?" And so he thought to himself as he wended his way home.

There was never such a silly man as he, a man who had only three *taels* of silver for his capital and yet entertained the idea of paying ten *taels* for a night with a famous courtesan. But "he who has the will will accomplish his purpose" and in the end he figured out a way. "From tomorrow on," he said to himself, "I shall put something aside toward making up my capital and save the rest for fulfilling my desire. If I save one *fen* a day I shall have three *taels* and six *chien* a year. In three years I shall have accumulated enough money. If I save two *fen* a day, it will only take a year and a half and if I can save more than that it will take only about one year." As he thus thought to himself he reached his room before he realized it. He unlocked the door, and went inside. Everything in the room was much as before, but because of the thoughts that had occupied his mind on his way home, he found it lonely and desolate. So without even eating his supper, he climbed into bed and there he tossed all night, thinking about the beautiful lady he had met.

The next morning he got up at dawn, prepared and ate his breakfast, filled his oil barrels, and set out straight for Wang Chiu-ma's house. "You are indeed a man of your word," Chiu-ma said when she saw him. She bought a jug full of oil weighing about five pounds, and being pleased with the price, she said to him: "This will suffice us for only two days. If you will come every other day I shall buy from you entirely and patronize no one else." The peddler promised that he would and went away. He only regretted that he did not get a glimpse of the Queen of Flowers, but he was a patient man and told himself that if he kept on coming he would see her sooner or later. There was one thing, however, to overcome: Chiu-ma's house was out of his way and it would not be profitable for him to come so far just to sell a jug of oil to her. "I must see," he said to himself, "what I can do at the Chao Ching Temple. The services are over now, but the monks probably need oil on ordinary days, too. If I can obtain their trade, I shall be able to sell all the oil along this route."

It was as Chin Chung had expected when he inquired at the temple. He made arrangements with the monks to come on even-numbered days, which coincided with his call at Chiu-ma's. So thereafter he covered the Chientang Gate section on even-numbered days and the rest of the city on odd-numbered days. On his calls at Chiu-ma's house he sometimes caught a glimpse of the Queen of Flowers and sometimes he did not. If he did not, he was unhappy and dejected; but when he did see her it only increased his longing and desire.

> Heaven and earth may one day come to an end,
> But this love and passion will never cease.

Time flashed by, and soon more than a year had passed. In the meantime not a day went by but Chin Chung put aside some small pieces of silver, sometimes as much as three *fen,* and sometimes two, but never less than one, so that now he had quite a large package of it, not knowing himself exactly how much. So on the first rainy day that happened to be odd-numbered he decided to take it to the silversmith and have his hoard weighed. He took an umbrella of oiled cloth and went to the silversmith's shop opposite him and told the man that he would like to have the use of the scales. "How much silver can an oil peddler have that he wants to use the scales," thought the silversmith, and so instead of uncovering his scales, he brought out a small steel-yard with a maximum capacity of five ounces, thinking that even with that he probably would not have to use the first knot. When Chin Chung opened his package, however, the silversmith was impressed with the pile of small silver that it contained—for it is a fact that the same amount of silver looks more in smaller pieces than when it comes in one lump—and being addicted to fawning upon those who have money, as silversmiths are apt to be, he smiled ingratiatingly now and made haste to uncover his scales, saying to himself, "Indeed, 'a man cannot be judged by his appearance, just as the sea cannot be measured with bushel barrels.' "

Chin Chung's silver came to exactly sixteen ounces, more than enough to pay for the favors of the Queen of Flowers even after deducting his capital of three *taels*. Then it occurred to him that it would not look very well to pay in small pieces of silver and that he should, since he was in the silversmith's shop, have them melted into larger pieces. Therefore he had the silversmith make for him one ten-*tael* piece and another piece of one and eight-tenth *taels*. From the remaining pieces he took some to pay the silversmith and bought for himself a new hat and new shoes and stockings. Then he returned home and laundered and starched his clothes and perfumed them with incense. On the first fine day, he dressed himself up, put his silver in his sleeve, locked his door and went directly to Wang Chiu-ma's house in high spirits.

But arriving at the courtesan's door, he began to grow diffident. "I have always come with my oil barrels," he said to himself. "How am I to broach the subject now that I come as a patron?" Just then Chiu-ma happened to come out and seeing him neatly dressed and without his peddler's outfit she said, "Master Chin, why aren't you carrying on your trade today? What is the occasion for your dressing up like this?"

It was now too late to retreat. Chin Chung steeled himself and said, bowing to Chiu-ma, "I have only come to pay my respects to you." Being an experienced woman, Madame immediately guessed Chin Chung's intention. "He must have taken a fancy to one of the girls," thought she, "and has come to pay a visit or even spend one night. Though he is not the kind of patron that I am used to receive, yet his silver is just as good as the next man's." Then she smiled and said, "Thank you, Master Chin, but I suppose there must be something that you want to see me about?" "Indeed there is," Chin Chung answered, "but I am too embarrassed to know how to begin." "Have no fear," Chiu-ma said. "Come inside and let us talk it over at leisure."

Though Chin Chung had been to Chiu-ma's house well over a hundred times, it was not until now that he had the honor of being invited into her reception hall. Presently a maid brought tea but when she saw who the visitor was she could not help feeling a little puzzled and she giggled under her breath. "What's so funny?" Chiu-ma reprimanded her. "How dare you be so impolite before a guest?" Then after the maid had left the room she again asked Chin Chung, "What is it that you wish to speak to me about, Master Chin?" "I should like to invite one of the girls in the house to a drink of wine," Chin Chung answered. "Surely not just to drink," Chiu-ma said. "You have always been such a steady young man, Master Chin. Since when have you become such a gallant?" "I have entertained this wish for a long time," Chin Chung said truthfully. "You know all my girls," Chiu-ma said. "Which of them have you taken a fancy to?" "I care for no one else," Chin Chung said. "I wish to spend a night with the Queen of Flowers."

Chiu-ma's countenance changed upon hearing this. "What are you saying?" she said testily. "Are you trying to make fun of me?" "I am a straightforward man," Chin Chung said, "and have only spoken the truth." "But even a manure barrel has two ears: have you not heard of the fee that I charge for my Meiniang? It is more than you could pay for half a night even if you sold your entire business. I would advise you to pick some one else." "I never imagined that the fee would be so enormous," Chin Chung said with a grimace of mock terror. "May I ask how many thousand *taels* it is?"

This remark convinced Chiu-ma that Chin Chung was only jesting, so her face softened as she said, "Not anywhere near that much. Her price is only ten *taels,* with wine and other incidentals extra." "If that is all," Chin Chung said, "it is not beyond my resources." Thereupon he took out his ingots and passed them to Chiu-ma saying, "The large piece is exactly ten *taels*. The small piece is about two *taels* which I hope will suffice for wine and other incidentals. I shall be forever grateful if you will be kind enough to help me accomplish my desire."

Chiu-ma was overwhelmed at the sight of the fine *sycee* and could not bear to see them leave her hand, but being afraid that Chin Chung might have his regrets later on when he needed his silver to carry on his trade, she said, in an attempt to clear her own conscience, "It is not an easy thing for a man in your position to accumulate so much silver. You should not be rash but should reflect well what it means to you." "Thank you for your thoughtfulness," Chin Chung said, "but I have made up my mind." "There is yet another difficulty," Chiu-ma said. "Our Meiniang is accustomed to associate only with the best of society and may therefore be unwilling to receive you who are only a humble tradesman." "Surely you must have a way to bring her around," Chin Chung pleaded. "I shall never forget your kindness if you would help me to accomplish my purpose."

Seeing that he was quite determined, Chiu-ma said with a smile, "In truth I have a scheme to help you but it depends on your destiny whether you succeed or not. Meiniang is not home now; she is helping to entertain at a lake party which Huang Ya-nei is giving today; tomorrow she is assisting at a versifying party given by Chang Shan-jen; day after tomorrow the son of President Han is giving a party here, having made arrangements several days ago. So you will have to come and try your luck the day after that. Now another thing: get yourself a silk robe and wear it instead of your cotton garment so that you will not look too out of place here and will thus make it easier for me to pass you off as someone else."

Chin Chung promised to do everything that Chiu-ma suggested. For three days he did not go out to sell, but dressed in a half-new silk gown which he bought in a pawn shop, he strolled along the streets of Linan trying to feel and act like a fine gentleman. On the fourth day he went to Chiu-ma's house bright and early, but found her gate still closed. He left there for a stroll, avoiding the Chao Ching Temple for fear that the monks might see him and laugh at him. On his return to Chiu-ma's house, the gate was open with a sedan chair and horses in front of it and several servants sitting just inside. He discreetly asked one of the grooms and on learning that they were from the Han mansion, he concluded that the young gallant had not yet departed. He betook himself to a restaurant, lingered as long as he could over his food and again returned to Chiu-ma's house. There he found that the young Mr. Han had gone but when he went in, Chiu-ma thus apologized to him: "I am sorry that Meiniang won't be free today, for the young Mr. Han has taken her to his villa to look at the plums in bloom. He is a steady patron and I could not say no. Then Chi Ya-nei has been asking for an appointment two or three times, and I cannot refuse him either since he has loaned us this house. He is apt to stay here four or five days at a time, sometimes even longer. So if you want to see Meiniang you will have to wait, but if you don't want to wait, I still have your generous present untouched and shall return it to you." "My only worry is that you may not want to help me," Chin Chung said. "As long as there is hope, I am willing to wait even though it be for ten thousand years."

"If that is the case, I am sure that I shall be able to help you."

As Chin Chung was about to take his leave, Chiu-ma said, "There is another thing I want to tell you, Master Chin. When you come again, do come so early, but come at twilight. By that time I shall know for certain whether she will be free or not that evening and can tell you accordingly. Do what I say and depend on me."

Thereafter Chin Chung went to Chiu-ma's house every day after his day's selling was over but for more than a month he had no luck.

Then on the fifteenth of the twelfth month his luck came. It had snowed and it was cold as the west wind began to blow. The ground was happily dry because of the cold. After spending the greater part of the day in carrying on his trade, Chin Chung dressed himself up as usual and went to Chiu-ma's house. She met him with a smile on her face, saying, "Luck is with you today, you are ninety-nine parts toward success." "What is the part that is lacking?" Chin Chung asked. "It is that Mei-niang is not yet home. But she ought to be back soon. She is at a snow party given by Yu Tai-wei. He is a man over seventy and no longer interested in matters pertaining to 'breeze and moonlight.' He said he would send Meiniang back before dusk. So go to the bridal chamber and drink a cup of wine against the cold while you wait for her to return."

With Chiu-ma leading the way, Chin Chung passed through several courts and made many turns before he came to Mei-niang's quarters. It was only a one-story structure, but very bright and airy. To the left was a room for maids while to the right was Meiniang's own room, locked from the outside. There were also two side chambers attached to the main building. In the center was the reception room. A large painting by a well-known artist hung on the wall, and all manner of curios were on the tables. There were also many poems pasted on the walls.

These Chin Chung passed over hurriedly, regretting that he could not lay claim to being a scholar. He marveled at the elegance displayed in the room and wondered to himself how much more elegant and luxurious Meiniang's own room must be and decided it was well worth spending ten *taels* to enjoy such luxury and elegance for one night.

Soon a table was spread with all kinds of unfamiliar delicacies and aromatic wine, and Chin Chung was urged to eat and drink while he waited for Meiniang's return. Chiu-ma kept him company, apologizing for the fact that all her girls were engaged.

It is said that waiting makes for an impatient heart. So it was with Chin Chung. He drank and ate but little and allowed Chiu-ma to monopolize the conversation, his mind being all the time on the object of his love. Thus time dragged on until after the second watch when a bustle of footsteps and voices in the front quarter told them that Meiniang had finally returned, and they both rose to meet her. The Queen of Flowers was in a state of great intoxication and was leaning upon a maid. When she saw her room lighted and the remains of a feast on the table, she stopped and asked who it was that was being entertained there. "It is the Mr. Chin that I have been telling you about," Chiu-ma said. "He has been an admirer of yours for a long time and has been waiting for a chance to see you for over a month." "I have never heard anyone speak of a Mr. Chin," Meiniang said. "I don't want to see him." So saying she turned to go away, but Chiu-ma stopped her, saying, "He is an honest and trustworthy man. I am telling you the truth." There was nothing for the courtesan to do but turn back. When she came into the room and saw Chin Chung she was sure that she had seen him before but could not for the moment recall his name. "Mother," she said, "I think I know him. He is no one of any consequence. I shall ruin my reputation if I receive him." Chiu-ma said, "He has a silk shop inside the Yungchin Gate where we used to live. You must have seen him then. I could not refuse him because of his sincere admiration for you, and since I have promised him you must help me to keep my promise. Please entertain him for the night; I shall apologize to you and promise not to make engagements for you without consulting you." As she spoke, she pushed Meiniang gently toward Chin Chung and thus the girl could do nothing but go into the room and meet him.

Chin Chung heard every word that was said but pretended to have heard nothing. Meiniang kept looking at him and the more she looked the more she wondered where she had seen him. She had hot wine brought and poured out a large cup, which she drank herself at a gulp, instead of offering it to Chin Chung as Chiu-ma had expected. "Don't drink so much, my child," Chiu-ma warned. "You are drunk already." But Meiniang kept on drinking cup after cup, protesting that she was not drunk, until, unable to stand on her feet any longer, she had her room unlocked and slumped into bed.

"She is very spoiled," said Chiu-ma apologetically to Chin Chung. "She must have something on her mind, for I know it is not anything that you have done that makes her behave like this. Please forgive her." Then taking him into Meiniang's room, she whispered to him to make allowances for Meiniang's state and be gentle with her. She tried to wake up Meiniang and make her undress for bed, but in vain. She left, followed by the maids after they had cleared the table and brought a pot of hot tea at Chin Chung's request.

When Chin Chung turned to look at Meiniang, she was sound asleep with her face toward the wall and lying on top of her brocaded quilt. Afraid that she might be cold and loath to disturb her, he took another quilt folded across the bed rail and put it gently over her and then lay down by her side, nursing the pot of tea with his left hand and gently enfolding Meiniang with his right. He did not once close his eyes for fear that she might wake and want something.

> Though he has not flown with the cloud or danced with
>   the rain,
> Yet he did inhale fragrance and fondle jade.

After midnight Meiniang woke up feeling sick and miserable. She sat up in bed with her head between her hands and kept on retching. Chin Chung sat up too and tried to ease her by stroking her back. Presently nausea overcame her and as there was no time to lose Chin Chung held his sleeve up to her so that she would not soil her bed. Then she demanded tea and Chin Chung poured for her the tea that he had so thoughtfully kept warm. After drinking two cups she felt better but she was still tired and weak and fell back and went to sleep again.

Meiniang did not wake up again until daybreak. When she saw Chin Chung lying beside her, she asked him who he was and on being told began to recall vaguely the previous evening. "I must have been very drunk," she said. "No, not very," Chin Chung answered. "Did I vomit?" she asked. "No, you didn't," Chin Chung answered. "That's better," Meiniang said with relief, but after a while she said, "But I remember having vomited and drinking some tea. Could I have dreamed it?" Only then did Chin Chung tell her the truth. "What a thoughtful man!" Meiniang said to herself. She began to feel kindly toward Chin Chung.

Then as she looked at him more attentively, she suddenly was reminded of the peddler and asked him who in truth he was. Thereupon Chin Chung told her who he was, how he had admired her ever since he first laid eyes on her, how he had saved for a whole year in order to have his supreme pleasure, and how happy he was for having had a chance to be near her that night. Meiniang was more moved than ever after hearing this recital. "But don't you regret," she said, "that I wasn't able to entertain you last night and that you have spent your hard-earned money for nothing?" "How could that be possible?" said Chin Chung. "You are a goddess in exile and I consider myself fortunate that you do not take me to task for not having served you better." "You should have saved your money for supporting your family instead of squandering it here," Meiniang said, to which Chin Chung answered that he had no wife and children. "Are you going to come again?" Meiniang asked after a brief silence, to which Chin Chung answered, "The happiness I had last night will sustain me the rest of my life. How dare I hope for more?"

"Where can one find such a good man?" Meiniang thought to herself. "So honest and straightforward, and above all so thoughtful. You can't find one like him in ten thousand. It is a pity that he is a mere peddler, otherwise I should not hesitate to marry myself to him."

As she was thus thinking to herself, a maid brought in water for their morning toilet and two bowls of ginger water. Chin Chung washed his face, took a few sips of the ginger water and then begged leave to go. "Stay a while longer," Meiniang said. "I have a few words to say to you." "Nothing would make me happier to stay as long as I can," Chin Chung said, "but one must know one's place. It was enough impudence on my part to come here last night, for it will surely detract from your reputation when it is known that you have entertained a visitor such as I. It is best that I go as soon as possible."

Meiniang nodded and then sending the maid out, she opened a box and took out twenty taels of silver and gave it to Chin Chung, saying, "Please take this for all your trouble last night, but do not tell any one." Chin Chung refused the gift at first but Meiniang thrust it in his sleeve and pushed him away.

Now let us leave Chin Chung and Meiniang for a while and return to Chu Shih-lao's household, where the maid Orchid and the shop assistant Hsing Chuan had been carrying on their affair openly since Shih-lao was lying sick and helpless in bed. After a few reprimands from Shih-lao they decided to flee together and did so one night, taking with them all the money that was in the shop. Shih-lao then realized that he had been deceived by Hsing Chuan and wished to take Chin Chung back. He sent one of his neighbors to Chin Chung, begging him to remember only the good and forget the unpleasant things of the past. In response Chin Chung went immediately to Shih-lao, who turned over everything to him and put him in charge of the shop. Chin Chung also added his twenty *taels* to the capital, and changed his name to Chu again since he was again living with Shih-lao.

A month or so afterwards, Shih-lao's illness took a turn for the worse and soon, alas and alack! he died. Chu Chung mourned for him as if he were his real father and buried him with appropriate rites, so that all the people in the neighborhood praised him for his faithfulness. After the funeral he reopened his shop and soon restored it to the prosperity that it had enjoyed before Hsing Chuan ruined it with his dishonesty and sharp practices. It became necessary to hire an assistant and one day the middleman brought him a man over fifty years of age who was looking for a situation. He was no other than Hsin Shan, the father of Meiniang, who had recently come to Linan in the hope of finding his daughter and had been stranded there without means of subsistence. When Chu Chung heard that he was a fellow countryman from Pienliang, he was moved and said, "Since you have no friends to turn to, please come and live with me. I shall treat you as a relative." He gave Hsin Shan money to pay for his lodgings. The latter brought his wife and thenceforward they lived with Chu Chung and assisted him faithfully in tending the shop.

"Time passes like an arrow," and soon more than a year had gone by. As Chu Chung's business prospered and his reputation for honesty grew, he was approached from all quarters with proposals of marriage, but the beauty of the Queen of Flowers had spoiled him for plain, ordinary faces and made him unwilling to accept such offers.

You cannot talk of water to him who has seen the sea,
Nor of clouds to him who has viewed the mist over
Mount Wu.

In the meantime Meiniang's reputation grew also, and her calendar was full from morning till night. Truly her mouth was satiated with meat and sweets and her body tired of silk and brocade. But her lot was not always an easy one; sometimes a drunken patron would give her annoyance, or a jealous one would make unreasonable demands; sometimes waking up in the middle of the night feeling sick and dejected, she found no one to comfort her. On these occasions she could not help thinking of the peddler and his thoughtfulness, and long for another chance to meet him. Then at the end of about a year, her luck turned and a misfortune befell her.

Now there was at the time a certain young Mr. Wu, the son of the governor of Foochow. He had recently returned from Foochow with a great deal of gold and silver and had been squandering it in gay pursuit of pleasure. He had heard of Meiniang but had not had a chance to see her, for the latter had heard of his ill temper and had refused to receive him. One day during the Clear Bright Festival when every family made offerings at their ancestral tombs and all went out to the countryside to enjoy the spring, Meiniang locked herself in her own room. She was tired from numerous outings and had some painting and calligraphy debts to pay. She lighted some fine incense and got ready the four treasures of the study, but just as she was about to lift her brush she suddenly heard a commotion outside. It was young Mr. Wu with half a dozen insolent servants. He had come to get Meiniang for a boat party, and when Chiuma made excuses for Meiniang, he had become angry and proceeded to vent his displeasure by breaking up furniture and household utensils. He was not deceived when he saw Meiniang's room locked from the outside, for being experienced in such matters he knew that it was only a trick to fool innocent customers. He had his servants break the padlock and then kicking the door open, burst into the room. Before Meiniang had time to hide she was seized by two of the servants and forcibly dragged out and through the streets to Mr. Wu's boat. Never before had Meiniang suffered such humiliation and rough handling; she refused to take part in the entertainment and sat in a corner and cried. Her tormentor berated her for her slight and threatened to have her beaten if she did not stop crying. But Meiniang had no fear; she only cried louder and attempted to throw herself into the lake. Finally in exasperation, the young tyrant took her to a deserted spot outside the Clear Wave Gate and there put her ashore after stripping her of her shoes and footbindings, saying to her, "Cheap whore, since you don't want to stay with us, you can go on home yourself."

Helpless in her barefooted condition, Meiniang sat on the ground and abandoned herself to weeping and lamentations over her cruel fate. Then by coincidence Chu Chung, returning home from Shih-lao's tomb, passed that way and immediately recognized the Queen of Flowers though her hair was disheveled and her face distorted with grief. "What has happened?" he said in astonishment. Meiniang poured out her heart to him and told him everything. Chu Chung's heart ached for her and his eyes were filled with tears. He took out a silk handkerchief and splitting it in two bound up her feet with the strips. Then he wiped her tears for her and did up her black silken tresses, and telling her to wait there, he went and hired a sedan and escorted her back to Chiu-ma's place.

In the meantime Chiu-ma was in a state of great agitation because she did not know what had become of Meiniang, so that when Chu Chung brought the girl back her joy was exactly as if she had recovered a priceless pearl. Moreover, she had heard about Chu Chung's inheritance of Chu Shih-lao's shop and was inclined to receive him with a new deference even if he had not done her such a great favor. She overwhelmed Chu Chung with her gratitude and had a feast prepared for him. After a few cups of wine Chu Chung rose to take his leave, but of course Meiniang would not let him go. "I have been thinking of you," she said, "but have not had the opportunity of seeing you. Since destiny has brought us together, you must stay tonight." Chiu-ma, too, added the weight of her invitation.

That evening Meiniang sang and danced for Chu Chung as she had never sung and danced before in her life, and on his part Chu Chung was as happy as a man being entertained by a fairy goddess. Needless to say, his happiness was even more ineffable when, after feasting far into the night, they both retired to their conjugal bed hand in hand. . . .

Afterwards, Meiniang said to Chu Chung: "I have a request to make of you which you must not refuse." Chu Chung answered, "If there is anything I can do for you, I should not hesitate to go through fire and boiling water. So how can I refuse you anything?" Meiniang said, "I want you to marry me." Chu Chung said, smiling, "Do not jest with me, my lady, for even if you were to marry ten thousand men, it would never come to my turn." "I speak from the heart," Meiniang said. "For ever since I was tricked into losing my chastity at the age of fourteen I have wanted to follow the virtuous path but have not been able to carry out this wish because I have not met the right man. Though I have met many men in my time, they are all of them seekers of pleasure who have not the slightest consideration for my welfare. Among all I have seen, you are the only sincere one. Moreover, I understand that you are not yet married. If you do not despise me because of my past, I shall be most happy to marry you and serve you until death. If you refuse, I shall take three feet of plain silk and strangle myself before your eyes to prove to you the earnestness of my heart. It would be better than to perish in the hands of some vulgar men as I almost did yesterday.'' She began to cry after she finished speaking.

"Do not grieve," Chu Chung said. "The undeserved honor that you have conferred upon me is something I had not dared to dream of, to say nothing of refusing it. But my lady, you are a person of great fame, while I am poor and without influence. How could I then manage this thing, however willing I am myself?" "Your lack of means need not be an obstacle," Meiniang answered, "for I started long ago to put valuables aside for this very purpose." Then Chu Chung said, "Even if you are in a position to buy your freedom, I am afraid that you, who have been accustomed to luxuries, will find life in my poor house unendurable." "I am ready to wear cotton and eat coarse food without ever regretting it," Meiniang assured him. Chu Chung said, "But Chiu-ma will probably not consent to it." "I shall be able to take care of her," Meiniang said and then outlined to him her plan. Thus the two talked on until day-break.

Meiniang had, in fact, stored away many boxes and trunks of jewels and other valuables with her clients. Now on the pretext that she needed them she gradually took them back to her own place and then had Chu Chung take them to his house. When she had everything safely put away, she went to Liu Ssu-ma and told her about her plan to follow the virtuous path. "We have discussed this matter before in some detail," Ssu-ma said. "But you are yet young and I don't know whom you have in mind to marry." "Do not mind who it is," Meiniang said. "Be assured that I have heeded your advice and that it is someone well qualified according to your specifications. I am sure that Mama will not object if Auntie is willing to speak for me. I have little to offer to Auntie to express my regard, but here is ten ounces of gold for Auntie to make some jewelry with." When Ssu-ma saw the gold, she smiled until her eyes were entirely closed. "It is a praiseworthy thing that you propose to do," she said. "I should not be taking this gold from you. However, I'll keep it for you and you may leave everything to me. But since your mother looks upon you as her money tree, she will not let you go unless she has an offer of a thousand *taels*. Is your party ready to put up this sum? Why don't you let me meet him and talk the things over with him?" "Please do not mind who it is," Meiniang said. "Just consider it that I am buying my own freedom." "Does your mother know that you have come to see me?" "No," Meiniang answered. "Then stay here and have something to refresh yourself," Ssu-ma said. "I shall go to speak to your mother and let you know the outcome."

Ssu-ma then hired a sedan and went to Chiu-ma's house. She asked the latter about Meiniang's recent misfortune and then said, "For us who are engaged in the business it is better to have girls of ordinary beauty, for they will be able to make money for us and cause us no trouble. But because Meiniang is over-famous she is like a piece of fish that has been dropped on the ground which even ants will not leave alone. This may appear like good business but actually it has its disadvantages. Even the vaunted fee of ten *taels* is only an empty name, for you have to entertain the guests and servants that the clients bring so that they will not make trouble for you or deliberately ruin your furniture or porcelain. Moreover, there are the poor painters and calligraphers and the poetry clubs and chess societies that are continually making demands on you and whom you must wait upon free several times in a month. Then finally, your rich clients are always fighting over Meiniang, and if you promise her to Li you have to refuse Chang, thus pleasing one but offending the other. This incident of Mr. Wu is but a sample of what might happen in the future. You were lucky that nothing worse happened, bad as it was, for you might have lost Meiniang and your capital investment. You know you can't sue those people. I have heard that Mr. Wu is not yet satisfied but is hatching a new plot against you. As long as Meiniang is as particular as she is, you will always be open to trouble."

"She has given me enough worries," Chiu-ma agreed. "Take Mr. Wu, for instance. He is by no means a nobody but a person of some consequence. Yet the girl simply would have nothing to do with him and thus brought this incident upon herself. She used to listen to me a little, but since she became famous, she has been acting terribly spoiled and insists on having her own way. When a guest calls she will receive him if it so pleases her, but if she is unwilling you can't budge her with a team of nine oxen."

"Girls are all like that the minute they enjoy a reputation," Ssu-ma said.

"I wish you would keep your ears open," Chiu-ma said. "If you hear of some one willing to pay a good price, let me know. It is better that I sell her and put an end to my worries."

"That's an excellent idea," Ssu-ma said. "With what you get for her you can buy five or six girls. With luck you might get ten or more. One would be a fool not to seize such a bargain."

"I have thought the matter over well," Chiu-ma said. "As a rule those who have power and influence always try to take advantage of their position and are not willing to pay a fair price. When some one willing to pay something turns up, Meiniang always finds fault with him. Please take care of this matter for me. If the girl should refuse after you have found a suitable match, you will have to talk to her, she listens to you more than she does to me."

"I have, to tell the truth, come expressly to propose a match for Meiniang," Ssu-ma said, laughing. "How much silver must you have before you let her go?"

"You know how things are, sister," Chiu-ma said. "We in the business always try to buy cheap and sell high. Moreover, Meiniang is renowned all over Linan as the Queen of Flowers. We can't let her go for a mere matter of three of four hundred *taels*. I must have a thousand for her."

"I'll go and find out," Ssu-ma said. "If the party is willing to pay your price, I'll come back to report. If not, I'll not bother to come back." Then she asked as she was taking her leave, "Where is Meiniang today?"

"She has rarely been home since the Wu incident," Chiu-ma said. "She has been going the rounds of the houses of her clients, complaining to them of her grievance. She went to the Chis day before yesterday; yesterday she went to the Huangs. I don't know where she is today."

Ssu-ma said, "As long as you have made up your mind, Meiniang will have to give in. But in case she should refuse, you can depend on me to bring her around. But there is one thing: you must not change your mind and raise objections yourself."

"I have given my word," Chiu-ma said.

Liu Ssu-ma then went home and told Meiniang of what had passed between her and Chiu-ma. "She has given her consent," she concluded. "As soon as the silver passes hands the matter will be concluded." "The silver is ready," Meiniang said. "Please come to our house tomorrow and supervise the conclusion of this matter. Do not let the matter get cold so that we have to start all over again." "I shall come," Ssu-ma promised. Then Meiniang took her leave and returned to her house, without saying a word to Chiu-ma about her part in the matter.

The next day around noon, Liu Ssu-ma came to Chiu-ma's house as agreed. "How did it go?" Chiu-ma asked. "It's complete nine parts out of ten," Ssu-ma said; "We have now to talk to Meiniang." Thereupon she went to Meiniang's room and greetings over, she asked, "Have you seen your party? Where is the silver?" "It is there in those leather trunks," Meiniang said, pointing to the end of the bed. Then she opened the trunks one by one and took out thirteen or fourteen packages of silver of fifty *taels* each and enough jewels and precious stones to make up the remainder of the agreed amount. Liu Ssu-ma was so surprised at this display of wealth that her eyes "gave out sparks and her mouth watered." For a long while she was speechless but wondered and marveled to herself how a young girl like Meiniang could have so much foresight and how she could manage to save up so much. Thinking that her silence meant that she was not satisfied with what she had given her, Meiniang brought out four bolts of fine silk and some jewels and put them on the table, saying, "Please accept these things for the trouble you have taken on my account." Ssu-ma was overjoyed and went to Chiu-ma and said, "It is Meiniang herself who wants to buy her own freedom. It is even better than if some man had wanted her, for she will pay the entire sum agreed upon and there will be no need to go to the expense of feasting the idlers who would no doubt claim credit for the transaction."

Chiu-ma's countenance reflected displeasure when she heard of Meiniang's riches, for one must remember that there is no one in the world to surpass Madame Bustard in greediness and that she is never content unless she gets into her own hands everything that her girls acquire. If a courtesan accumulates a few things of her own, Madame never fails to ransack her room at the first opportunity and appropriate everything of value for herself. But Chiu-ma had not dared to do this to Meiniang because she was such a money maker for her and had many influential clients ready to defend her rights, and so she had no idea that Meiniang had managed to accumulate so much wealth.

Noting the change of color in Chiu-ma's face, Ssu-ma guessed what was in her mind and hastened to say: "Sister Chiu, be not 'of three hearts and two minds.' Niece has saved these things from her own proper share. If she had been inclined toward spending, she would have spent everything or even given it to her poorer lovers without your knowing. Moreover, if she had nothing of her own, you would have to buy her some new clothes and jewels; you know you could not send her away naked. Now, since Meiniang has money of her own, it means that you'll have to lay out nothing but can keep every ounce of the thousand *taels* for yourself."

This little speech made Chiu-ma feel better and she agreed to carry out the bargain she had struck. Ssu-ma then went to Meiniang's room and brought out the packages of silver and handed them to Chiu-ma, together with the jewels, which she appraised piece by piece, saying that if Chiu-ma sold them she was sure to get more money. The turtle—that is, Chiu-ma's husband—was summoned and he wrote a certificate of release and handed it to Meiniang.

"Since Auntie is here," Meiniang said, "I should like to take leave of 'father and mother' now and stay with Auntie until the wedding day. Would you let me do that, Auntie?" To this Ssu-ma readily consented, for since she had received so many valuable presents from Meiniang she was eager to get Meiniang out of Chiu-ma's house so that there would be no possibility for her to withdraw from the bargain.

Thereupon Meiniang packed her own things and took leave of her master and mistress and the other girls in the establishment. Ssu-ma put her in a nice, quiet room, and soon an auspicious day was selected and in due time the wedding took place. Boundless was the happiness of the conjugal chamber, for though theirs was an old love, the joys of marital consummation were not thereby diminished.

The day following the wedding, Hsin Shan and his wife—who, it will be remembered, were helping Chu Chung with the shop —asked to see the bride, and thereupon followed the recognition and reunion of daughter and parents. To celebrate this double happiness, Chu Chung feasted his friends and neighbors, and Meiniang sent presents to all her former friends who had helped her.

After the "Full Month" had passed, Meiniang opened up all her trunks and boxes and exhibited gold and silver and fine silks to a total worth of over three thousand *taels*. She turned the keys over to her husband, who made prudent and gradual use of the wealth in acquiring land and houses and in enlarging his business. In less than a year's time his house became quite impressive with fine furnishings and many servants. To show his gratitude to the gods for his blessings, Chu Chung made a vow to make offerings of candles and incense at all the temples in the region, together with a three-month supply of oil for the "eternal lights" of each. In the course of these pilgrimages he came to the Upper Tien Chu Temple where his father was serving as an incense lighter. Although his father did not recognize him (for both the years and his good fortune had tended to alter Chu Chung's mien), the writing on the oil barrels (for they were the same barrels on which he had written his name and his native city) attracted his father's attention, and a series of questions soon established their true relationship. His father did not wish, however, to return to the mundane world, so Chu Chung built him a neat little apartment on the grounds of the Upper Tien Chu and took care of all his wants. Every ten days he would go there to visit his father and four times a year he would be accompanied by his wife on these visits. The old man Chin lived to be over eighty before he passed away without illness.

As for Chin Chung (for our hero had again assumed his

original name after his reunion with his father) and his wife, they both lived to old age. They had two sons, who both studied and passed the examinations. To this day a man expert in the art of *pang ch'en* is nicknamed "Little Master Chin" or "the oil peddler" by those wise in matters concerning breeze and moonlight.

(WANG CHI-CHEN)

Some Further Readings

Birch, Cyril, trans. *Stories from a Ming Collection*. Bloomington: Indiana University Press, 1958. (Also contains material relevant to Chapter 18.)

Yang Hsien-yi and Yang, Gladys, trans. *The Courtesan's Jewel Box*. Peking: Foreign Languages Press, 1957. (Also contains material relevant to Chapter 18.)

16

BROTHEL SONGS AND
ART SONGS

The linguistic insights and investigations of the seraglio poets led to the formal and rigorous T'ang poetry—to the *chüeh-chü* and the *lü-shih*. Rigorous and formal poetry, or *shih*, was officially to remain the most admired poetry for centuries, and the scholars still worked diligently in its forms. But when a man had something to get off his chest, when a Chinese after the T'ang was moved "to look in his heart and write," he turned more and more to a poetic form called the *tz'u*. It is just this private emotion in the *tz'u* which made the form a little less than respectable, and which leads us today mostly to prefer later *tz'u* to later *shih*.

As to the precise nature of the form, you can get a better idea of this if you know that the Chinese do not say "write a *tz'u*"; they say "fill in a *tz'u*." You saw an earlier poem which says:

> Young, in
>   summer singing and dancing,

```
    they are light-
            footed, and leave no prints,
    Pitiable!
            as wild flags—
    And have names
            strange to our ears.
```

We can infer from this, and we know from contemporary records, that the Chinese brought girls to China from Central Asia and perhaps even from the Middle East—girls who entertained, worked, and sang in the wine-shops of the capital and perhaps of other cities. They sang songs they had learned in their homelands, and the musical basis and the tunes were different from the traditional Chinese music. Late in the T'ang, Chinese poets who had heard the alien tunes began to write Chinese poetry to fit the tunes. So a major revolution in Chinese versification was begun, and the *tz'u* as a poetic form was created. Later poets imitated the earlier poets, and eventually there were compendia of *tz'u* patterns, each pattern identified by a title or line of verse from an earlier poem; the *tz'u* writer could "fill in" his *tz'u* to match the lyrics of his model. The *tz'u* are different from *shih* in that *tz'u* occur in such a variety of patterns. The *tz'u* often has lines of unequal length, and sometimes more than one rhyme is woven through a *tz'u* pattern.

Chao Ts'ung-tsu put together the first great collection of *tz'u,* and he called it *Collection Among the Flowers.* Much of China's greatest poetic talent after this found its expression in the *tz'u* form.

The poems in this chapter are divided into those written during the Five Dynasties period (A.D. 907–959) and those written during the Sung and Southern Sung Dynasties (A.D. 960–1279).

§ FIVE DYNASTIES POEMS

—CLEPSYDRA SONG (I)*—

by Wen T'ing-yun (later ninth century)

Jade burner smokes,
Red wax weeps:
Each lights the painted hall, and autumn thoughts.

Brows are arched
    and thin,
Hair is cloudy
    and pale:
Night is long, the pillow and cover are cool.

Wu-t'ung trees,
Midnight rains—
Don't say 'Parting's taste is like pain's.'

---

*A clepsydra is a water clock; it measures time by marking the flow of water through a small opening.

Singly,
> leaf
>> leaf

Singly
> sound
>> sound

On empty steps, they fall till day.

(MCNAUGHTON)

—CLEPSYDRA SONG (II)—

by Wen T'ing-yun

Willows are silky, long.
Spring rain is delicate.
Past flowers, the clepsydra-sound is remote.

It scares the border goose
Scatters the wall crows
And the painted screen's golden quails.

Fragrant mist, thin,
Seeps through the fine screen.
I think of the House of Hsieh's ponds, pavilions.

Behind the red candle
Brocade blinds are low.
Dreams are long. Lord, you do not know.

(MCNAUGHTON)

—LOTUS-LEAF CUP—

by Ku Hsiung

Spring's at its end.
Flowers fill
the small yard.

One figure moves

And leans on
the railing.
The eyes are in shade.

Be sick
with bitter things,
with thinking
what is dead,

with nerve's uncertainties,
Uncertainty's
                    certitude.

(MCNAUGHTON)

—TO THE TUNE OF NÜ KUAN-TZU—

by Wei Chuang (836–910)

Last night
                    at midnight
on the pillow
                    I saw her!
                    clear in dream
We talked
                    a long time

Face the same
                    like peach blossom
                        Willow-
                            leaf
                            eyes
                    often lowered

Half shy she is
half joyful
When we were
                    leaving each other
                        she
                        clung again
Waking
                    I knew—
                        a dream
and the sadness
                    like a pouring flood!
                            (KWOCK AND MCHUGH)

—(NO TITLE)—

by Wei Chuang

The rain is pouring incessantly on the river,
The grass is growing thickly on the banks.
The Six Dynasties have vanished like a dream;

The birds' cries sound hollow.
The most heartless are the willows along the wall:
They still sway carelessly in the midst of smoke and mist.
                            (JOHN C. H. WU)

—ONE LEAF HAS FALLEN—

by Li Ts'un-hsü (885–936)

One leaf has fallen.
The crimson screen is drawn
A scene is unfolding, withered and sere.
On the pavilion the moon shines cold,
And the west wind blows on the silken curtain.
It blows on the silken curtain,
Recalling to mind what is bygone.

(CH'EN SHOU-YI)

—TO THE TUNE OF YI HSIN TZU—

by Li Ts'un-hsü

Feasted once
           in deep peach glades
one song
      phoinix to phoinix
      danced and sang
I recall
      —how long!
           saying goodbye to her
Tears mingled together
         hand on arm to the door
      like a dream
      like a dream
faded moon
fallen blossoms
      thick mist
        over all.

(KWOCK AND MCHUGH)

—TO THE TUNE OF WANG CHIANG-NAN—

by Li Yü (937–978)

So many sorrows!
and last night

in my dream

as if
the old days were back

inspecting
the Imperial Park

Chariots
like a running stream

so many

The horses

curveting dragons

Moon of flowers

in spring wind!

(KWOCK AND MCHUGH)

—TUNE: "MEETING'S PLEASURE"—

by Li Yü

Without words, alone
I climb the West Tower.
The moon is like a hook.
The Wutung trees are lonely. The deep garden
Locks in the clear Autumn.

Scissored and unsevered
Settled, yet dishevelled
Is parting's sorrow
"Separate" a sort of odd taste
On the heart's edge.

(MCNAUGHTON)

—THE SENNIN BY THE RIVER—

by Li Yü

The cherry blossoms fall away
            and Spring is gone.
Darting butterflies
            with gold-dust wings
                    take flight in pairs.
Goat-suckers chirp
            and the moon lights the small tower
                    in the west.
The screens are painted, the doors, pearl.

Weary with wishing,
            I wind the useless and elaborate beads.
The gated lane is grey and empty.
                    After she left,
I watched grass patterns in the mist
                    and grew confused.

(MAYHEW)

—CLEPSYDRA SONG—

by Li Yü

Gold sparrows held your hair
and for a moment
       among flowers
your face colored
       under its powder.

I knew my mind
I guessed your heart
       but love must answer Heaven.

The incense cones its ash
the candle piles its tears
as tears and ash, our thought.

The mountains on my pillow shine,
my worked silk quilt is cold,
and time's fragmented by the water-clock.

(MAYHEW)

—AT NIGHT, THE CROW CALLS—

by Li Yü

Last night
       the winds came
          with the rain;
Now, Autumn
       bangs and shuffles
          in the window shades,

the candle's dead
                        and the clepsydra, silent.
I twist and turn my pillow,
                        try sitting up,
but nothing
                        keeps me calm.

The world's affairs spread out like water.
As in a dream,
                        I see my floating life:
A drunk on a country road
                        swaying quietly, without accident;
But now, I am afraid of going on.

                                        (MAYHEW)

—TO THE TUNE OF TSUI KUNG-TZU—

(Anonymous woman poet)

Outside my door
                        the dog barking
I know what it is
                        My lover's here
Off with my stockings
                        down
                        perfumed stairs
My good-for-nothing lover
                        is drunk tonight

I help him into
                        my silk-curtained bed
Will he take off the silk gown?
                        O! O! not he

Milord is drunk
            and drunk let him be
Better that
            than sleeping alone.
                        (KWOCK AND MCHUGH)

§ SUNG DYNASTY AND SOUTHERN SUNG DYNASTY POEMS

—THERE IS NO SORROW TO UNTIE—

by Su Shih (1035–1101)

A hundred fleeting years
And people called it a life span.
Having tasted sorrow,
I wonder where sorrow comes from?
And what there is to dispel?
Things are always like wind passing by my ear,
What need is there to take things to heart?
You say, "Cheer up and you will be an optimist."
I fear I can't agree.
This thing is really hard to talk about.
How can we say loafing is just as good as success?
To say it may be all wrong;
Not to say it is not necessarily right.
Neither you nor I really exist here;
What then could we mean by arising above the world of
        material things?
If you say we need drunkenness to dispel sorrow,
How can we be drunk without wine?

                        (CH'EN SHOU-YI)

—FICKLE YOUTH—

by Ch'in Kuan (1040–1100)

With the mountains touched up with traces of clouds,
And the horizons bordered with withered grass,
The painted bugles murmured intermittently from the
    watchtower.
I stop my journey here for a while
And drink my parting wine.

Endless memories of old fairyland
Are now recalled
Faint and fleeting like haze;
Beyond the setting sun,
A few specks of cold crows,
A stream flowing around a lone hamlet.

Soul-stirring recollections:
Especially the moment
Her sachet was detached
And her sash loosened!
All I've won is
The long-lasting name of the "fickle one";
Once departed when will I see her again?
My sleeves and lapel are still tinted with her tears.
Steeped in sadness,
The tall city, now barely visible,
Already glows with its dim yellow lamplights.

                          (CH'EN SHOU-YI)

—TO THE TUNE: "GOOD GIRL"—

by Huang T'ing-chien (1045–1105)

Where is Spring gone?
It was so quiet, no footprints were left.
If anyone knows where Spring is now,
Call it back to reside here.

Who would know since Spring left no traces here,
Unless we ask the Oriole?
Its warblings that no one understands
Are borne by the breeze to the roses.

(CH'EN SHOU-YI)

—(NO TITLE)—

by Chou Pang-yen (1056–1121)

The slanting sun shines below the leaves at the water,
Rolling up light ripples that seem to stretch for a
    thousand li.
The sour wind on the bridge shoots at my eyeballs.
I stand there long
Looking at the dusk
And the lighted market place.

Beneath a cool window of an aged house
While listening to the falling paulownia leaves
I leave my light coverlet to get up again and again—
But who knows
It is to her
I am filling a page?

(CH'EN SHOU-YI)

—TO THE TUNE "CATCHING FISH," WRITTEN
IN 1179 ON MY TRANSFER FROM HUPEH
TO HUNAN—

by Hsin Ch'i-chi (1140–1207)

How many more
storms can we stand?
We already are losing Spring.

Spring-lovers hate
to see early flowers,
How much more, fallen petals of red?

Spring, stay with me.
I've heard the lush grass
overgrows your homeward path.

Spring does not answer.
Cobwebs under the painted eaves
All day till evening, catch the catkins.

Another 'long doors'
affair, another meeting
missed—they always envy arched eyebrows.

Suppose I spent gold
bar on bar for the poet's
fu, could he tell these feelings pulse 'or pulse?

Lord, don't dance:
Beauties of Han
and T'ang end in common dust.

Shut-in grief's
Grief's bitter end:
Don't go lean on the tower railing,

The setting sun
is there
with mist and willows, a bitter place.

(MCNAUGHTON)

—LING: "AS THOUGH DREAMING" (I)—

bv Li Ch'ing-chao (ca. 1084–after 1141)

The kiosk on the creek at sunset: I recall
Being deep drunk at evening's end, unable
To find my way or guide my homeward boat,
Edged into the tangled roots of water-mallows,
Angled, struggled,
Struggled, angled,
And frightened up egrets and terns and seagulls.

(MAYHEW)

—LING: "AS THOUGH DREAMING" (II)—

by Li Ch'ing-chao

Last night, light rains and violent winds
Could not disturb the sleep of heavy wine.
I ask the girl who rolls the curtain up
Tell me,

are they as they were,

the wild crab

—as bright
As last night?
And she says, "They're green enough,
            but not so red."

(MAYHEW)

—WASHING CREEK SAND (I)—

by Li Ch'ing-chao

Scanty sunlight shines
            for this Spring's No-fire Day.
From the aloes in the jade lü

                        steam wisps rise.
Waking from dreams,
            I find the silver head-piece
                        in porcelain pillows.
Sea-swallows are still away,

                        the people gather grass,
River plums have lost their flowers
            and willows wear their floss.
Yellow dusk
            comes dragging rain
                        that wets the garden swing.

(MAYHEW)

—WASHING CREEK SAND (II)—

by Li Ch'ing-chao

Listless with Spring,
she combs again
already-ordered hair.

The evening wind
begins a fall
of plum-flowers in the yard.

Under a high
and distant moon,
patchy cloud-puffs drift.

There, in
the jade-duck burner,
the idle incense rests

And on the scarlet
cherry-covered curtains,
tired tassels hang.

Does the T'ang king's
armored beast
still warm his room, or not?

(MAYHEW)

—LATE SPRING—

(Written to the tune of Wu-ling Ch'un)

by Li Ch'ing-chao

Wind stopped
       earth
       smelling of fallen blossoms
Day almost over
       Too weary to comb my hair

His belongings here
        He here no longer
                Everything useless
Before I can say a word
              tears flow first
At Twin Stream
        they say
                the spring still beautiful
I too
     would like to go rowing in a light boat
but I'm afraid
            that little boat on Twin Stream
Would not carry
        so much sorrow!

                       (KWOCK AND MCHUGH)

—TUNE: SOUND ON SOUND—

by Li Ch'ing-chao

Search, search, seek, seek
Chill, chill, clear, clear
Grieved, grieved, sorry, sorry *ai! ai!*

In false Spring, in still cold air
I can hardly rest.
Three cups, two bowls of weak wine
Can hold off,
Evenings, the impetuous wind?

Geese go over,
Cut my heart,
Them too I used to know.

Everywhere, yellowing flowers pile the ground.
Now who will pick them off?
They cake the windows.
Alone, how should one wait for night?
Wutung trees fade, still; a fine rain
Till dark
Drop, drop, drips, drips.
And in this,
What should one
Hurt word become?

(MCNAUGHTON)

—HAIRPIN PHOENIX—

by Lu Yu (1125–1210)

"All things seem a dream.
How should we meet together?
Pitiful! Alone, like a hairpin phoenix."
    —"I Gather the Fragrance."

Pink, thin hand.
Gold-tied wine.
City-wide, Spring
        colors willow and wall.

East winds moan
And the thought's undone.
One moment, we embraced: grief-enspun,
Years apart
        have now
                unspun—
        Wrong, wrong, wrong!

Spring is as before.
We suffer. What for?
Tears and rouge stain gossamer:
Peach-bloom drifts down
On terrace and pond.
Though the seas still run
Silk letters,
                who shall carry
                              them?
No one, no one, no one.

                                        (MCNAUGHTON)

—THE LIGHT YELLOW WILLOW—

by Chiang K'uei (1155–1235)

In the empty city,
the dawn horn
sounds down streets of hanging willows.

On horseback,
in thin clothes,
the cold is fierce, fierce.

I look everywhere
at pale yellows, delicate greens—
all as I used to know it, south of the River.

The whole is too much.
Tomorrow morning,
it is again "Cold Food Day."

I must take wine
at the "Little Bridge Hut."

I'm afraid the pear-blossoms
will fall finally
and turn Autumn-colors.

Swallows, swallows come flying.
Ask: where is Spring?
Only the ponds, pools are jade-green.

(MCNAUGHTON)

—(NO TITLE)—

by Wang Yi-sun (ca. 1240–1290)

The fragrant woods now drenched clean by last night's
    wind and rain—
I have hastily bid farewell to Spring.
Having barely seen Spring off,
I need to see you leave at the southern bank!
Please hear my plea:
I think by now Spring must be on the roads of Wu as it is
    homeward bound.
When you get there,
Make haste to break a thousand willow twigs,
And with them fasten Spring secure.

Even if Spring could be stayed,
No need to seek out singers of Spring tide,
The fallen petals have turned to dust.

Far away in the mist and ripples around Kusu Terrace,
Convey my greeting to our lady the West Lake.
Will you call out to her?
I fear Spring will leave no trace of its arrival!
Pray invoke your magic powers,
And for my benefit,
Weave Spring with its flowers and willow leaves
Into verdant poetry.

(CH'EN SHOU-YI)

Some Further Readings

Ayling, Alan, and Mackintosh, Duncan, trans. *A Collection of Chinese Lyrics.* Nashville, Tenn.: Vanderbilt University Press, 1965.

————. *Further Collection of Chinese Lyrics.* Nashville, Tenn.: Vanderbilt University Press, 1970.

Clark, Cyril Drummond Le Gros, ed. and trans. *The Prose-Poetry of Sung Tung-p'o.* 2nd ed. New York: Paragon, 1964.

Hu Pin-ching. *Li Ch'ing-chao.* New York: Twayne, 1966.

Lo, Irving. *Hsin Ch'i-chi.* New York: Twayne, n.d.

Watson, Burton, trans. *Su Tung-p'o: Selections from a Sung Dynasty Poet.* New York: Columbia University Press, 1965.

Yoshikawa, Kojiro. *An Introduction to Sung Poetry.* Translated by Burton Watson. Cambridge, Mass.: Harvard University Press, 1967.

PART FOUR:

PLAYS AND SHORT STORIES:
YÜAN AND MING

17

YUAN DRAMA

Chinese literature has passed through only one period in which dramatic works—that is, works for the stage—were produced tha were both sufficient in number to be preserved and sufficient in literary merit to command our attention. That period was the Yüan Period, when Kublai Khan conquered China and his Mongol heirs ruled her. Only one official examination was held under the Yüan, and then the rulers abolished the system. So men of letters turned their talent in other directions, and some of the best of them wrote plays with dialogue and song: the Yüan drama.

China, as you know, long before the Yüan had many quasi-dramatic arts: puppet-shows, shadow-plays, and storytellers' works, some of which you have read. Other Chinese entertainment, popular before the Yüan, were the "song and dance plays" and the so-called *ta chü*. The song and dance plays, transplanted to Japan, became the Kabuki. The *ta ch'ü* were long sequences of songs all in the same key. We can speculate that they told a story, but no texts have been preserved.

The native and traditional dramatic arts continued to flourish in southern China, but the plays—now called "Yüan drama"—written and produced in northern China were something quite new. Perhaps we can best bring out the nature of this northern, or Yüan, drama if we draw up a table to contrast it with the southern drama.

	No. of Singers	Prologue	Main Part	Each Act	Each Song
NORTH	1	Integral	4 (or 5) acts	Same rime for all songs	One rime
SOUTH	Many	Non-integral, moralistic, synoptic	50 or more acts	No rule	No rule

Chinese theatre has conventions which, at first, might strike a Western audience as odd. Of these conventions, at least three probably go back to the Yüan drama and even beyond, to the shadow-play and puppet-play. In the first place, the characters walk on and simply explain to the audience who (in the play) they are, and they may tell the audience a sentence or two about the situation so as to get the action started. In the second place, a good deal of the acting depends on stylized gestures and gaits. These gaits and gestures also fall into certain classes, depending on whether the actor portrays a hero, villain, or other type of character. In the third place, the makeup is conventionalized and mask-like, and the character's temperament—as well as, in some cases, his particular identity—can be inferred from the makeup.

THE BUTTERFLY DREAM

Kuan Han-ch'ing (A.D. 1220?–1307?) probably is the greatest of the Yüan dramatists. You will read below his play *The Butterfly Dream*. He wrote a lot of "twists," or songs, of the sort found in these plays, and he wrote sixty-five plays. Fourteen of them are extant. The major role in each of his is, oddly or not, a woman's role. The form, style, and content of Kuan's *The Butterfly Dream* are typical, and you can get from the play a good idea of what Yüan drama was like.

THE WEST CHAMBER

I have also included, after *The Butterfly Dream,* excerpts from *The West Chamber. The West Chamber* is a Yüan play that is more unique than typical—it is about three times as long as the usual Yüan play. I felt able to include it because *The West Chamber* probably is China's most famous and most popular play—something like *Romeo and Juliet* in the Occident (although *The West Chamber* ends happily). You will read the play as the Chinese very often see it—that is, only in a few of the most famous scenes. And you should have no trouble following the story, for the play is based on the T'ang Dynasty tale *The Story of Ying Ying* (see Chapter 12). The play very closely follows the story up till the end, but public taste or the playwright's sensibility demanded that the story end with the lovers united, not separated as in the earlier version.

The West Chamber was written by Wang Shih-fu and Kuan Han-ch'ing. Wang wrote the first four-fifths of the play, and Kuan finished it. We know very little about Wang Shih-fu save that he may have been born in A.D. 1250. Only two of Wang's plays have been preserved, and his reputation rests on *The West Chamber*.

§ THE BUTTERFLY DREAM

CHARACTERS

WANG

WANG'S WIFE

BIG WANG, *Wang's eldest son*

MIDDLE WANG, *Wang's second son*

LITTLE WANG, *Wang's third son*

KEH PIAO, *a local bully*

BAILIFF

RUNNERS

PAO CHENG, *Prefect of Kaifeng*

CHANG CHIEN, *his sergeant*

LI WAN, *another sergeant*

DONKEY CHAO, *a horse thief*

ACT I

(*Enter Wang, his wife and their three sons.*)

WANG:

Comes the middle of the month, and the moon grows dim:
Comes middle age, and a man is good for nothing.

My name is Wang. I am a native of Chungmou County in the prefecture of Kaifeng. There are five in my family. This is my wife, and we have three sons. They will not work on the land because they prefer to study. When will you show your worth, boys, and become famous?

BIG WANG: What good is farming, father? When I have studied hard for ten years I shall become an official and make you all happy.

WANG and WIFE: Good lad, good lad!

MIDDLE WANG: I may study for ten years by the window without receiving any recognition, father, but when I pass the examination and win fame, then the whole world will know me.

WANG and WIFE: Good lad, good lad!

LITTLE WANG: Father above and mother underneath. . .

WANG: What's that? Why "mother underneath"?

LITTLE WANG: When I was small I saw you in bed together, with mother underneath father.

WANG: You rascal!

LITTLE WANG: Father and mother, all I mean is that scholarship leads to a good career.

WANG: Good lad, good lad!

WIFE: Still, husband, you must find some way to set our boys up for life.

Don't tell me scholarship leads to a good career—
We are short of money now.
What use is your hard study by the frosty window?

In this world rogues do better than honest men,
The clothes—not the men—are respected.
I always speak my mind:
What guarantee is there that our three sons
Will pass their test next spring?
How can they enter the dragon gate of officialdom?

(*Exeunt.*)

(*Enter* WANG.)

WANG: I have come to the main street to buy paper and pens for the boys. Walking has tired me. Let me rest here.

(*Enter* KEH PIAO.)

KEH: Generals and ministers come from common stock:
Men should carve out their own career.

I am Keh Piao. Mine is a powerful family. When I kill men I do not have to pay with my life, but at most go to gaol for it. Today I am free, so I may as well take a ride. (*He knocks into* WANG.) Who is this old fellow who dares get in my horse's way? Beat the old ass! (*He beats and kills* WANG.) The old man is shamming dead in order to blackmail me. I'll let my horse kick and trample him. (*Exit.*)

(*Enter* BAILIFF)

BAILIFF: Big Wang, Middle Wang, Little Wang! Are you there?

(*Enter the three sons.*)

SONS: What do you want?

BAILIFF: I am the bailiff. Somebody has killed your father in the street.

SONS: What! Mother, a fearful thing has happened!

(*They weep.*)

LITTLE WANG: Someone has killed our father! Mother, come here!

WIFE: What are you shouting about?

LITTLE WANG: Someone has killed our father.

WIFE: What! Never!

I puzzle my head over this terrible news,

> Running till I am out of breath
> And my voice is just a croak.
> I wish I had wings!
> What wrong had my husband done?
> When I catch his murderer
> I shall demand an answer.
> He never plotted with the enemy,
> Never harmed any man or the state.
> If my poor husband is really dead,
> I shall sue that wicked scoundrel.
> I run through the streets and market,
> Wiping my tears.

(She sees the corpse.)

> Look at those angry wounds!
> Here he lies, black and blue.
> So devoted a husband and father—
> Who could have thought you would die like this?
> None knows what will happen from one day to the next.
> Covered with blood,
> You lie here cold and limp,
> Your face like yellow paper.
> For an hour I call your name,
> But to my horror you will not wake;
> And you know how it is at home—
> How can we afford a sacrifice
> When we bury you tomorrow?
> All I have left is these three boys;
> It is true that a poor family has good sons.

SONS: Mother, they all say it was Keh Piao who killed our father. We are going to find him and take him to court, to make him pay with his life.

(Exeunt.)

WIFE: Keh Piao is a scholar of the Imperial College,
> Why should he strike a man dead?

Now I must take the corpse home.
He is an official and we are poor,
Yet still I mean to sue him.

(*Enter* KEH PIAO.)

KEH: I am Keh Piao. I have had a few cups of wine. Now there's nothing to do, I may as well go home.

(*Enter* WANG'S *three sons*.)

SONS: There is the murderer! Catch him! (*They seize* KEH.) You beat our father to death!

KEH: What if I did? I am not afraid of you.

WIFE: I shall charge you in the court!
          What does it matter if you are a noble,
          Related to the imperial house?
          Even the emperor's own sons and grandsons
          Must go to court for murder!

(*The three sons set on* KEH PIAO *and kill him*.)

SONS: This murderer is shamming drunk and won't get up.

WIFE: Let me speak to him. (*To* KEH.) See here, what harm did my husband do you that you should beat him to death? And why should you sham drunk on the ground and refuse to get up? You can't escape like that! Get up, get up! Ah! Have you three killed him?

LITTLE WANG: Lucky I didn't hit him!

WIFE: Now what shall we do?
          You should have been more careful;
          What was the use of beating him like that?
          Although you did not pick a quarrel for nothing,
          And it was not wrong to kill him,
          You will have to go to court.
          Your careers are ruined.

(*She points to* KEH'S *corpse*.)

          You did not stop to think either
          That force would be met by force.

> Heaven is just and impartial,
> You acted the bully in the street
> And now you too lie here a bloody corpse.
> A general can be pierced by an arrow too,
> Though he likes to shoot at others.

SONS: We have no money. How can we go to court?

WIFE: Each day one ladle of soup, one single dish—
> How many spare chopsticks have we?
> We need money to go to court,
> But all we have to pawn is a few old books.
> And they will not bring us much.
> It must be your fate to die;
> But though you have killed a man
> You are good sons.

(Enter the RUNNERS.*)*

RUNNERS: Don't let them get away! Catch those murderers!

WIFE: Bitterness in my heart, tears in my eyes!
> Ruin has come down from Heaven!
> We are dragged away and cannot even protest.
> There lies my husband dead,
> And here before my eyes my sons are ruined;
> Good fortune never repeats itself,
> But troubles come thick and fast.

RUNNERS: Murder is no small offence. Come to the court!

WIFE *(weeping)*: Surely Heaven will not tolerate injustice.
> Evil must be repaid,
> And all men long for revenge
> But alas! that the three of you should be involved,
> Three scholars about to pass the dragon gate
> And pluck the cassia bough.
> Because you took revenge
> On your murdered father,
> You will be arrested and tried,

Tortured with rack and thumbscrews;
I never knew that we were so ill-starred,
Never knew that you would kill him.
It was right to avenge your father;
Though you are executed
And go to the nether regions,
Your names will be remembered as filial sons.

RUNNERS: Come to the court!

WIFE: Now you have done this, boys, what shall we do?

SONS: Ah, mother, what can we do?

WIFE: I made you study the classics and history,
As the mother of Mencius taught her son;
But your names will never appear on the golden list,
Instead they will be in the list of felons!
Yet this was no premeditated murder,
And if punishment is decreed
At most only one of you should pay with his life—
How can all my sons be killed?
This will not be the end of our family.

(Exeunt.)

ACT II

(Enter CHANG CHIEN *with* RUNNERS.*)*

CHANG: All is ready to open court.

(Enter PAO CHENG.*)*

PAO: The court drums thunder,
The runners are ranged on two sides;
This is the judgment seat of the King of Hell,
To which all spirits are summoned.

I am Pao Cheng, a native of Laoerh Village in Luchow. I hold the posts of Academician of Lungtu Pavilion and Prefect of Kaifeng. I am now going to preside over the morning ses-

sion in my court. Chang Chien, bring me whatever documents
await my signature.

CHANG: Secretaries and clerks! Have you any documents for
His Honour to sign?

(*There is an answer off.*)

Chang: Why didn't you report this before? Your Honour,
Suantsao County has sent us a horse thief, Donkey Chao.

PAO: Bring him in.

(*The* RUNNERS *bring in* DONKEY CHAO, *who kneels before
the prefect.*)

PAO: Remove the cangue. You there, are you Donkey Chao
and did you steal horses?

DONKEY CHAO: Yes, Your Honour, I did.

PAO: Chang Chien, fasten the cangue on him and have him
sent to the condemned cell.

(DONKEY CHAO *is led away.*)

PAO: I feel a little tired, Chang Chien. Tell the secretaries to
make no noise. I want to take a nap.

CHANG: Now, gentlemen, no noise! His Honour is resting.

(*The prefect dozes off at the table.*)

PAO (*talking in his sleep*): Worried by affairs of state, how can
I sleep? I have strolled to the back of the hall and found a
small gate. Let me open it and have a look. What a beautiful
garden! All the flowers are blooming in the warm spring
weather. Set among the flowers is a pavilion, with a spider's
web on it. A butterfly fluttering from the flowers is caught
in the web. The sight makes me sad. Man may die at any
hour, and even insects are exposed to danger. Ah, even
insects have intelligence! A big butterfly has come to rescue
the smaller. Ah, another butterfly has been caught in the
web. No doubt the big butterfly will save it again. . . . .
How strange! The big butterfly is simply fluttering around
the flowers. Instead of saving the smaller one, it has flown off.

Well, as the sage said, all men have a sense of pity. Since it will not save the butterfly, let me do so. *(He makes a gesture as if releasing the butterfly.)*

CHANG: Your Honour, it is noon.

PAO *(waking)*: In my dream a butterfly's life
　　　　　　Was hanging in the balance,
　　　　　　When I woke to hear Chang Chien
　　　　　　Announcing that it is noon.

Well, Chang Chien, are there any culprits awaiting trial? Send them in.

CHANG: Secretaries, are there any culprits awaiting trial? Send them in.

(There is a shout off.)

CHANG: Your Honour, some felons have been sent from Chungmou County. They are three brothers who beat the noble Keh Piao to death.

PAO: How dare men of a small county kill a noble? Are they here?

CHANG: They are.

PAO: Bring them into court, beating them.

(A RUNNER brings in the three sons and their mother.)

WIFE: We are brought to this cruel yamen in Kaifeng,
　　　　Where the emperor's justice is administered.
　　　　Three scholars, who have not yet made their name,
　　　　Dragged here and tried as criminals.
　　　　Trembling and fearful,
　　　　Knowing our guilt,
　　　　We shall have to confess our crime.
　　　　This is not the county court;
　　　　Here in Kaifeng they are strict,
　　　　With none of our easy-going country ways.
　　　　The drum thunders beneath the steps;
　　　　Awe-struck and terrified,
　　　　I have lost my head and am utterly exhausted.

This is no light offence but a serious crime.
There my old man lies dead on the ground,
And here mother and sons are arrested.
My eyes shall see my own children executed.
I peep fearfully at this court
Which I never entered before.
Today our fate will be decided here,
The prefect will decide between right and wrong.

(She and her sons kneel before the prefect.)

CHANG: The felons are here, Your Honour.

PAO: Remove their cangues, Chang Chien, and dismiss the runner.

(The cangues are removed.)

LITTLE WANG: Let's go home now, mother.

PAO: Where do you think you are going? This is not your county office. Chang Chien, I take it these three young men are the murderers, but who is the old woman? Is she a witness or some relation? Speak up, woman. Are these two young men related to you?

WIFE: They are my sons.

PAO: And the boy?

WIFE: He is my youngest.

PAO: So this is the way you taught your sons! In ancient time the mother of Mencius moved house in order to find good neighbours for her son. The mother of Tao made him cut his hair before seeing guests, and the mother of Chen taught her son until he wore the official purple and golden belt. But you, a village woman, have taught your sons to kill a noble. Confess the truth now!

WIFE: I am wretched to think my sons have broken the law,
But that scoundrel's crime was more than they could bear,
And they should be forgiven for killing him.
We are poor, humble folk,

Your Honour must protect us!
These three lads are all diligent students,
Whose conduct has always been guided by the
classics—
How could they have plotted to kill him?
Tortured and beaten, they cannot put their case,
But how could three of them have made this plot?

PAO: You will not confess without a beating. Chang Chien, give them a good beating.

WIFE *(weeping)*: My sons have broken the law:
Was it for this they studied the Confucian classics?
The poor lads are beaten black and blue,
Their flesh is torn, their bones splintered—
Much worse than self-inflicted pain during study.
Brought up by loving parents,
They never knew such agony before.

PAO: One of these three youths must be the ringleader. Which of you was responsible for that man's death?

BIG WANG: My mother and brothers had nothing to do with this. I killed him.

MIDDLE WANG: Your Honour, my mother and brothers had nothing to do with this. I killed him.

LITTLE WANG: Your Honour, my mother and brothers had nothing to do with this, and neither had I.

WIFE: My three sons had nothing to do with this. When that noble, Keh Piao, beat my husband to death, I could not choke back my anger. So I fought with him and killed him. It was my doing.

PAO: Nonsense! You all admit to murder—this is a plot. We must find the true murderer to make him pay with his life. Chang Chien, give them another beating.

WIFE: No one will speak up to save them;
      I have to look on, helpless.
      Make a clean breast of things, sons!
      I will plead again with the prefect.
      That bully murdered my husband,
      Yet Your Honour had me arrested
      By runners as fierce as tigers and wolves.
      Do not be angry, Your Honour!
      You have instruments of torture, hammer and screws,
      And you question these lads again and again,
      Beating them till the blood streams from their wounds.
      My eldest boy cries out at this injustice,
      But Your Honour turns a deaf ear;
      My second is suffering the torments of hell—
      How can he bear such torture?
      My third is beaten even more cruelly,
      And the sight makes my heart bleed.
      We gaze at each other, weeping.
      You are killing them, Your Honour!
      Their father thought his sons would do well;
      Now we cannot put our case, we can only sigh;
      My heart is broken, my tears stream down like rain.

PAO: Let me read the charge. (*He looks at it.*) What a fool the magistrate of Chungmou County must be! This charge says that Big Wang, Middle Wang and Little Wang beat to death the noble Keh Piao. Hasn't he got a proper secretary? These three lads must have names, or at least nicknames. What is your eldest son's name, woman?

WIFE: Gold.

PAO: And your second son's?

WIFE: Iron.

PAO: And the third?

WIFE: Stone.

LITTLE WANG: Broke.

PAO: What do you mean, broke?

LITTLE WANG: Stone Broke.

PAO: Stop cracking jokes. This is a murder case. Why should common citizens choose such unusual names? Did Gold Wang kill this man?

WIFE: Gold is not hard to refine.

PAO: Did Stone Wang kill this man?

WIFE: Stone is strong and true.

PAO: Did Iron Wang kill this man?

WIFE: Even iron would melt in the furnace of the law.

PAO: Have these stubborn scoundrels beaten!

WIFE: They are not being stubborn:
    They are unjustly accused!

PAO: You know the proverb: A murderer must pay with his life, a debtor must pay his debt. Have the eldest taken out and executed, Chang Chien.

WIFE: I look on and cannot save him—
    He is being dragged down the steps!
    I am at my wit's end!
  What a fool this prefect is!

PAO: What did that woman say just now when I ordered her eldest son to be executed?

CHANG: She clutched the cangue and called Your Honour a fool.

PAO: So she called me a fool, did she? Bring her over here. *(She kneels before the prefect.)*

PAO: I decreed that your eldest son should pay with his life. Why did you call me a fool?

WIFE: How dare I call Your Honour such a name? But this boy is a good son. If you kill him, who will support me?

PAO: Since his mother says the eldest is a good son, and the neighbours will vouch for him, I must be wrong. Let the

eldest live to support her. Chang Chien, take the second son
to be executed.

WIFE: I cannot bear to give up Gold,

   Yet Iron's death would also break my heart.

   If we must pay with a life,

   Let my boys be spared

   And let me die in their place.

   This cruel prefect will not listen to reason,

   So I cling to the cangue and cry that injustice is done!

 What a fool this prefect is!

PAO: What did that woman call out this time?

CHANG: Your Honour, she called you a fool again.

PAO: Bring her over here.

(She kneels before the prefect.)

PAO: See here, woman, I have just sentenced your second son
instead. Why did you call me a fool again?

WIFE: How dare I call Your Honour such a name? But my
second son has a good head for business. If you kill him, who
will support me?

PAO: When I sentence your eldest to death, you say he is a
good son. When I sentence your second to death, you say
he has a good head for business. Who is to pay for the crime
then?

(LITTLE WANG puts on cangue himself.)

PAO: What is that boy doing?

LITTLE WANG: Since my eldest brother is not to die, nor my
second brother either, it looks as if it will be me. So I may
as well make a noble gesture.

PAO: All right. Chang Chien, take the youngest to be executed.

(LITTLE WANG is pushed away.)

PAO: Well, woman, do you agree to let your youngest pay for
the crime?

WIFE: Yes. The proverb says: When there are three partners,

the youngest shoulders the hardships. He is the one who should pay.

PAO: Am I a fool or not?

WIFE: Your Honour is not.

PAO: Wait! Chang Chien, bring him back. I was nearly taken in by this woman. I see now that this is a case of different treatment for one's own children and those adopted. These two older lads must be your own sons, while the youngest is adopted. As you have no fondness for him, you want him to pay for the crime. Speak up, woman. If you tell the truth, I shall take steps accordingly. If you lie, I shall not spare you.

WIFE: All three are my sons. What do you want me to confess?

PAO: Since she won't tell the truth, Chang Chien, beat them!

WIFE: Sons, I shall have to tell the truth. Don't hold it against me.

PAO: Is the eldest boy your own?

WIFE: He is not my son, but I nursed him.

PAO: How about the second?

WIFE: I tended him as a child.

PAO: And the youngest?

WIFE (*weeping*): He is my own. The others are adopted.

PAO: Now look here, woman, aren't you making a mistake? Wouldn't it be better to let one of the adopted sons pay for this crime, and keep your own child to support you?

WIFE: That would not be right, Your Honour. If I let the first wife's son die, it would look as if I were a heartless stepmother. If I took advantage of these boys, I should blush to remember those virtuous mothers of old.

PAO: Well, woman, to be fair to them, you must tell the truth. Who killed that man?

WIFE: How can I make reply?
     I will not answer this question.
     Their flesh is in shreds,
     They stream with blood,

This is a living hell!
All my three boys may be killed,
For officials are all related,
And the prefect takes the side of the dead noble.
(She weeps.)

Now if my eldest son dies for this crime,
My second forfeits his life as well,
And my third becomes a shade too,
I shall be left alone, a poor old woman.
Gold is good to his mother,
Iron, if set free, will support the family:
So say no more, Stony,
It is right you should pay with your life;
The third of three partners is always the one to suffer,
And now the runners are shouting again.

PAO: Hearing this woman, I realize the truth of the saying: A clever merchant will appear to have no goods, and a worthy gentleman will look like a fool. I see what fine people this mother and her sons are—they stand comparison with the men of old. As I was dozing just now, I dreamed that a butterfly caught in a spider's web was rescued by a big butterfly. When this had happened twice, another small butterfly was caught, but instead of saving it the large one flew away. As my heart was touched, I saved the little creature myself. In fact, Heaven was forewarning me of this case so that I might save the boy's life.

I weighed the case according to the law,
But this suit is most involved.
The murder of a noble cannot be pardoned,
Nor the culprit go unpunished.
First I sentenced the eldest lad to death,
But she said he was a good son;
When I sentenced the second,
She said he must support her;

When I sentenced the third,
She was pleased and let him go.
She showed most kindness to the adopted sons,
And hardened her heart against her own flesh and blood.
Such virtuous conduct is most praiseworthy,
Such a good mother deserves to be rewarded.
This flashed into my mind
Because Heaven had given me warning
Through the dream of three butterflies caught in a web.
That was precisely the case of this mother and sons:
Three times she spoke, and abandoned her own child,
Exactly as I saw in my dream at noon.

Chang Chien, take all three of them to the condemned cell.

WIFE (*trying desperately to stop them*):

They are dragging and pushing them off;
I seize the cangue and cry out against such injustice!
They are going, never to return.
I am distracted. What if I die with them?
Yes, best to share their death;
Let me catch hold of their clothes.

(CHANG CHIEN *pushes her away and takes the three sons off.*)

WIFE: This prefect has a reputation for justice,
But today he passed wrong judgment.
He sits in the court with his insignia of office,
And draws a high salary—but all for what?
My sons are unjustly condemned and thrown into
gaol.
I am desperate—I must act.
Shall I appeal to the provincial governor,
Beat the court drum in the capital,
Or call aloud before the imperial carriage?
No, who would pay any heed to a foolish woman?
To die would be better than to live on alone

> With no one to support me,
>> Weeping and wretched to the end of my days. (*Exit*.)

PAO: Come here, Chang Chien! What do you think of all this?

CHANG: Are you sure you are right, Your Honour?

PAO: Do you question my orders, you rascal?

> Well I serve my sagacious sovereign,
> My fame will endure through the ages;
> Unless I pass just sentence on this case,
> How can I be the prefect of Kaifeng?

(*Exeunt*.)

ACT III

(*Enter* CHANG CHIEN.)

CHANG:

> A pitiless club in my hands,
> Tear-stained money in my pockets;
> A tiger or wolf by day,
> At night I sleep beside corpses.

I am Chang Chien. Now the three Wang brothers are in the condemned cell. Let me have them in.

(*Enter* BIG *and* MIDDLE WANG.)

BOTH: Have pity on us, brother!

CHANG: Turn those cangues round, and let me give you three strokes apiece. (*He beats them*.) Where is the third?

(*Enter* LITTLE WANG.)

LITTLE WANG: Here I am.

(*Enter* LI WAN.)

CHANG: Li Wan, bring that bed over and pass me the rope. Let's truss them up tight. (*He pulls the rope and the boys groan*.) Now, Li Wan, go and have your meal while I look after them. I hope the gaoler doesn't turn up.

(*Exit* LI WAN. *Enter* WANG'S WIFE.)

WIFE: All my three sons are in the condemned cell. I have been begging and got some scraps of food for them.

Coming from the alms-house to the prison,
Not daring to lose a second,
I have begged from door to door
And got some left-overs—noodles and dumplings.
My sons were going to pass the examination,
Sit in courtrooms and draw high pay;
But instead they got into this trouble!
They have done nothing wrong,
We skimped and scraped,
And slept on the bare ground—
No one ever put up with such poverty.
As the proverb says: Good sons
Are better than riches and rank.
For this I put up with much.

(*She reaches the gaol gate.*) Here I am. I'll pull the bell.

CHANG: I'm afraid the gaoler is here. Let me open the gate and see who it is.

WIFE: It is me.

CHANG (*striking her*): Is this your home, old crone? What are you doing here?

WIFE: I've brought some food for my three sons.

CHANG: They have paid me nothing for the lamp oil and this thankless job. I have to live on these gaolbirds, so give me what money you have.

WIFE: Have a heart, brother! My old man was beaten to death and my three sons are here in gaol. I can barely keep going myself, and have simply begged some scraps for my hungry children. Don't be hard on us!

Beggars' scraps heated up again,
Rags I have mended;
Take this tattered coat, brother,
And this old sleeve as a tip.

CHANG: I don't want them.

WIFE: Please keep an eye on these wretches;

    Have pity on them, brother.

CHANG: Sentence has already been passed. I can't help them now.

WIFE: We are one loving family,

    My heart bleeds for these boys,

    My tears rain down.

    It is unjust to accuse them of a crime;

    I call on Heaven, and beg you to have pity.

    There they lie, rolling their eyes,

    Trembling in every limb.

    I have cried myself hoarse to save them,

    And despair has bent me double.

CHANG: All right. Come in. Let me close the gate.

WIFE (*entering the gaol*): My poor children!

  (*The three boys weep.*)

BIG WANG: Mother, what are you doing here?

WIFE: I've brought you food. (*She turns to* CHANG.) Could you set them free, brother, to eat?

CHANG: Haven't you got hands, woman? Feed them yourself.

WIFE (*feeding her two elder sons*):

    I stumble forward to feed my boys.

    Spoon after spoon I satisfy their hunger,

    Drop after drop I quench their thirst.

LITTLE WANG: Give me a little, mother.

WIFE: Here's a mouthful for you, boy.

  (*She puts the food on the ground.*)

  Here is some bread for you, Gold. Don't let Stony see it.

  Here is some bread for you, Iron. Don't let Stony see it.

    Beggars' leavings, no rich fare,

    No scholars' feast in the imperial hall.

    You were hauled here from the county court in cangues,

    Not walking as candidates to the golden palace.

Ah, this will be the death of me!

But it is useless to murmur against the gaol.

I am going, Gold. Have you anything to say?

BIG WANG: There is a volume of the Four Books at home, mother. Sell it to buy paper money for father's sacrifice.

WIFE: Have you anything to say, Iron?

MIDDLE WANG: I have a volume of Mencius, mother. Sell it to pay for father's sacrifice.

LITTLE WANG (*weeping*): I have nothing. Let me stroke your head a moment.

(*Their mother goes out.*)

CHANG: Hey, woman! Do you want some good news?

WIFE: Indeed I do.

CHANG (*entering the gaol*): Where is the eldest son?

BIG WANG: Here.

CHANG: You can go. (BIG WANG *leaves the gaol.*) Hey, woman, since this eldest boy is a good son, you can take him back to look after you. Are you glad to see him?

WIFE: Indeed I am!

CHANG: I'll give you some more good news. (*He enters the gaol again.*) Where is the second son?

MIDDLE WANG: Here.

CHANG: Get up, you can go too. (*He lets* MIDDLE WANG *out.*) Hey, woman! As your second boy has a good head for business, you can take him back to support you.

WIFE: How about my youngest?

CHANG: He will be hanged till he is dead, to pay for the death of Keh Piao. Come first thing tomorrow to pick up his corpse outside the wall.

WIFE: The two elder boys are free,

But the third is a prisoner still.

After all that I went through,

Carrying and nursing him!

But if I let his elder brothers be killed,
They will call me a heartless stepmother.
This is unjust—you are bearing the brunt for others;
Still, a life must pay for a life,
So die content!

(*She looks back at* LITTLE WANG.)

If I keep turning back again and again,
They will say I am faint-hearted.

BIG and MIDDLE WANG: Mother, how can we leave our brother to die?

WIFE: Come home with me, children. Don't grieve for him.
Your unhappy younger brother will be killed
And go to the nether regions.

(*She gazes at* LITTLE WANG *and weeps.*)

I turn back and shed tears.

(*The two brothers weep.*)

All right, let us go.

He will die content.
Poor child, so young in years,
We shall never meet again.
I cannot let the sons of others be killed,
Or later generations will reproach me.
I stamp my foot in despair three dozen times.
Tomorrow he will lie dead in the market-place;
I shall never see Stony again.
Before I have burned the paper money for my husband,
My child is found guilty too.
When will son and father meet?
In dreams alone
Shall I see my son again.

(*She goes out, followed by* BIG WANG *and* MIDDLE WANG.)

LITTLE WANG: Where are my brothers?

CHANG: By His Honour's orders, your two brothers have been

pardoned and sent home to support your mother. You alone will pay for Keh Piao's death.

LITTLE WANG: So my two brothers are spared, and I must pay with my life. Put the two other cangues on me then. Though I alone am to die, the three of us are one. How shall I die tomorrow, brother?

CHANG: You will be hanged till you are dead, then thrown over this thirty-foot wall.

LITTLE WANG: Be careful when you throw me, brother. I have a boil on my belly.

CHANG: You'll be dead by then.

LITTLE WANG: A bellyfull of learning. . . .

CHANG: So you still want to sing, eh?

LITTLE WANG: Yes, my last song.

> . . . is no use to me at all.
> I studied the Book of Rites, the Book of
>   Change,
> But death has caught up with me.
> My ambition was to be a high official,
> But now all fame and wealth have passed me
>   by.
> This prefect is an irresponsible judge,
> My father was a fool to make me study,
> And I am no brilliant scholar after all,
> To get myself beaten with a bastinado.
> The prefect is a foolish bureaucrat,
> The clerks pretend to know nothing,
> And the runners ranged in the court
> Are a worthless bunch of fellows.
> By being thrown over the wall
> I shall win renown throughout the empire,
> And a curse on you, Chang Chien:

(*He goes out, followed by* CHANG CHIEN.)

ACT IV

(LITTLE WANG *carries in* DONKEY CHAO'S *corpse, and crouches on the ground. Enter* BIG WANG *and* MIDDLE WANG.)

BIG *and* MIDDLE WANG: We have come with our mother to look for Stony's body. This way, mother!

(*Enter* WANG'S WIFE.)

WIFE: We hear that Little Wang has been hanged, so his two brothers have gone to fetch the corpse. I have begged some cash to buy sacrificial paper money. I have also brought some firewood to burn and bury his body.

> Before dawn I slipped out of the city,
> Fearful lest folk should find out
> And make trouble for me.
> I have bought some paper with money I begged,
> And picked up a few sticks of firewood.
> To think that my son should die like this—
> Without a mat to cover him or a coffin.

(*She weeps.*)

> Ah, my son, unjustly killed,
> You will meet your father at the dividing line,
> Where you must work together
> To push the wicked murderer down to hell!
> The dark sky is turning white,
> All is quiet in this lonely stretch of country,
> At a distance some men are approaching,
> And watching their shadowy forms, I tremble with fear.

(BIG WANG *and* MIDDLE WANG *approach, carrying a corpse.*)

BOTH: Where are you, mother? Here is our brother's body.

WIFE (*glancing at it and weeping*):

> I look hastily at the body,
> A corpse bespattered with blood!

With haste I undo the rope
And swiftly loosen the straps.
Come quickly and help me!
Take his head, holding the chin,
While from high ground I call back his spirit.
Ah, my child!
In your haste you have lost your shoes;
I call, but you do not answer.
I weep and mourn in vain.
Ah, Stony, my son!
I call you with all the strength in my old body,
Calling your pet name clearly—
Where is my good son Stony?
Why have you left your mother?
In vain I beat the ground,
In vain I sob and stamp;
I cannot call back your spirit;
This will drive me out of my mind.
Stony, child!

LITTLE WANG *(standing up)*: Here I am!

WIFE: What is that answering voice?
Where could it come from?
Can it be some mountain goblin?

LITTLE WANG: I am here, mother.

WIFE: A ghost! A ghost!

LITTLE WANG: Don't be afraid, mother. I am your son Stony.

WIFE: He follows me as I run,
I am at my wit's end in terror.
Trembling, I bow before my dead son—
I shall make good sacrifice to you.

LITTLE WANG: Mother, I am flesh and blood.

WIFE: If you are not a ghost,
Tell me quickly
How you escaped.

LITTLE WANG: His Honour hanged that horse thief, Donkey
Chao, and told me to carry his corpse out. Me he spared.

WIFE: So all our troubles are over!

> My sorrow ended, I laugh.
> I thought you were gone
> Like a pebble in the ocean.

But my elder sons deserve a scolding.

> What were you about?
> Don't grumble if I blame you.

How could you be so offhand as to carry another's corpse
here?

> You should have kept your eyes open,
> Instead of bringing me a stranger's corpse.
> Yet what happiness this is,
> What a miracle wrought by fairies!
> You, the youngest, were sentenced to death—
> How was it you were spared?

LITTLE WANG: I knew I should be all right.

WIFE: So it is true that honesty prevails!

> Let us bury this corpse
> Which was carried here by mistake.

(Enter the prefect.)

PAO: What! Are you committing another murder?

(WANG'S WIFE *and her sons are frightened.*)

PAO: Don't be alarmed. That is the corpse of the horse thief,
Donkey Chao. He has paid in your place for the death of Keh
Piao. Now listen to His Majesty's orders:

> You are the sovereign's good subjects,
> Worthy to serve the state as officers.
> The eldest son shall have a post at court,
> The second son shall be a high official,
> The third shall be Magistrate of Chungmou County,
> And their mother shall be a lady;
> For the court sets store by virtuous wives and mothers,

And values those who are good sons to their parents.
So our sage emperor rewards you all.
Face the capital and thank His Majesty!

ALL: Long live the emperor!

WIFE: An amnesty has come down from highest Heaven,
And we no longer complain about the verdict,
But face the capital and bow our thanks,
Hoping our emperor will live for ever.
Like a withered tree which blooms again,
After beating and imprisonment
Our sadness has turned to joy,
Our debt of sorrow is paid,
We have left the castle of darkness.
May Your Honour rise to be chief minister,
With fresh promotion each day.
Now the mother has a lady's rank,
And her son is made Magistrate of Chungmou.
So mother and son will live together in peace,
Free from all calamities, great and small.
May our gracious sovereign reign on his throne for ever!

(YANG AND YANG)

§ ROMANCE OF THE WEST CHAMBER

ACT THREE

YING YING: My mother has instructed Hung Niang to ask the abbot to fix upon a suitable day for the religious services. I have waited long, but I do not see her coming with the reply.

HUNG NIANG *(enters)*: I have gone and delivered the reply to Madame. Now I go to give it to my young mistress.

YING YING: You were told to ask the abbot what time would be convenient for the service.

HUNG NIANG: I have just given the answer to Madame, and even now I am on my way to tell you, little miss. The fifteenth day of the second month is the day decided upon for the sacrifice to the Buddha. He invites your mother and yourself to light the incense. *(Laughing)*

Ying Ying, I must tell you something laughable that happened. The young bachelor whom we saw for a minute in the courtyard the day before yesterday, in front of our pavilion, was sitting inside the monastery. He came out before his gate to await me, Hung Niang. Bowing deeply, he said: "Young girl, are not you the attendant of Ying Ying, and are you not named Hung Niang?" Then he added: "This young student's name is Ch'ang, his childhood name is Chün Jui, his native place is Hsi Lo, his years are just twenty-two, he was born on the seventeenth day of the first month, he has not yet taken a wife."

YING YING: Who told you to ask him questions?

HUNG NIANG: Who asked him? Furthermore he pronounced your name, and asked if you often went walking. But he was roundly scolded by me, Hung Niang.

YING YING: You should not have scolded him.

HUNG NIANG: Little lady, I do not know what he is thinking of. Are there really such kinds of fools in the world? Should I not have scolded him?

YING YING: Did you tell my mother of this or not?

HUNG NIANG: I did not tell your mother anything.

YING YING: Don't tell my mother about it hereafter, either. The shadows of evening are in the sky. Go quietly and bring incense for us to burn in the flower garden. Indeed, this spring is hateful, the way it stirs my heart with vague emotions. I have nothing to do, so I shall léan against the wicker railing and watch the moonlight. (*Exeunt* YING YING *and* HUNG NIANG.)

CH'ANG (*entering, speaks*): I have moved my personal effects inside the temple, and I am settled in the west chamber. I have made inquiries of the monk, and I have learned that each night the maiden burns incense in the flower garden. Luckily the flower garden is on the other side of this wall. When she comes I shall go ahead of her to the T'ai Hu stone, and wait for her at the corner of the marble wall. If I could but once fill myself with the sight of her, how wonderful it would be! Luckily it is late at night, and people have gone to rest. The moon is resplendent, the wind is gentle. How wonderful the weather is! Meanwhile I have a bit of time, so I shall seek out the abbot and sit with him. As wrapped in melancholy I look out upon the west chamber, I shall compose a song about the moon.

(*Sings*): The sky is of jade, without a wisp of cloud.
    The River of Heaven casts its long shadows.
    The brilliant moon lights up the sky from east to
     west.
    The shadows of the flowers fill the court.
    My sleeves of thinnest silk are growing cold.
    My heart is palpitating with excitement.
    I shall incline my ear and listen most intently.
    I shall walk on tiptoe,
    And silent, hidden in the shadows,
    I shall wait for Ying Ying, so noble,
    So delightful, so charming, and so sweet.
    The first watch has now run its course.
    All sounds are hushed.
    I am going straight to the winding porch
    Of Ying Ying's pavilion.

If I meet her by chance (hateful one!)
I shall of a surety seize her
And hold her tightly in my arms.
I shall tell her of our meetings, all too few,
And of our separations, all too many,
There is shadow, alas, but no reality.
Ah, suddenly I hear a sound—the creaking of the
    corner gate.
The wind, as it brushes past her garments,
Brings their sweet perfume to me.
Standing on tiptoe, I stare at her.
Her countenance is more beautiful
Than when I saw her indistinctly
The first time that we met.
This night I can really get a good look
At this wondrous maiden.
If Ch'ang O came down from the moon,
    She would not be such a perfect creature as Ying
    Ying.

(Speaks): I could easily imagine that this wonderful miracle
of spring, wearied of being confined, has waited for an
opportunity to fly out of the Kuang Han Palace. I can see part
of her face. Her body is half in view. She adjusts her flowing
sleeves in silence, and her long skirt ripples noiselessly as
she approaches. She is like the imperial consort Hsiang
Ling, who bowed before the red portals of the Temple of
Shun. She is like the goddess of the River Lo, of whom Ch'ên
Wang has sung in verse. What a wonderful woman she is!

(Sings): With a timid and a hesitant step
    She follows the flowery path.
    It seems as though her feet are so tiny
    That it is difficult for her to walk.
    As she appears before me

> A hundred more evidences of her loveliness
> Pass before my greedy eyes.
> How can her charm fail
> To enthrall the soul of man?

YING YING: Bring the incense.

CH'ANG: I shall listen and learn for what reason the maiden offers up her prayers.

YING YING *(prays, lighting the incense as she does so)*: As I light the incense, may my father, who has passed away, soon be born again in the world above.

As I light this incense *(lighting a second stick)*, I pray that my mother in her inner apartment be granted a hundred years of life.

As I light this incense *(lighting a third stick, she remains silent for some time)*—

HUNG NIANG: Little miss, why this stick of incense? Every night you stand thus silent. Shall Hung Niang make a wish for you? I wish that my lady may win a husband above all other men in the world in talent and in learning, one with the rank of *chuang yüan,* a man of handsome figure, with lofty ideals and a gentle character but at the same time austere, and that he may live in happy union with my little mistress until they shall have accomplished a full hundred years.

YING YING *(adding another stick of incense, and praying)*: The boundless yearnings which fill my heart are all expressed in this one act of adoration. *(She bows low, heaving a long, audible sigh.)*

CH'ANG *(aside)*: Little lady, what are you hiding within your heart, that you sigh thus, leaning against the long railing?

(Sings): In the deep night
> Clouds of incense fill the empty court.
> The screens are no longer stirred
> By the gentle eastern wind.

She has offered up her prayers,
And now leans against the balustrade.
She has sighed audibly twice or thrice.
The smooth disk of the moon is brilliant
As a bright round mirror.
I do not even glimpse
The slightest cloud or wisp of vapor.
There is no movement save
The ascending incense-smoke
And the soft breathing
Of the two young maidens.
They are enshrouded in the vapors.
I can no longer see them clearly.

(Speaks): I am sure that if the young girl sighs thus there must be cause for sorrow in her heart. Though I am not Ssu Ma Hsiang Ju, may you not be another Wên Chün? I shall try and sing a verse aloud, to hear what she will say.

(Recites): Tonight the moon shines in all its glory.
The shadows of the flowers of spring are calm and peaceful.
As I look upon the brilliant surface of the moon,
Can I not see the goddess who has her home therein?

YING YING: There is someone at the corner of the wall, reciting verses.

HUNG NIANG: The voice is that of that young twenty-two-year-old idiot who has not yet got himself a wife.

YING YING: His poetry is clear and refreshing. Hung Niang, I am going to compose a verse in answer.

HUNG NIANG: If you compose a verse in answer, Hung Niang will listen.

YING YING *(recites):*
Behind my maidenly screen are solitude and silence.

There is no way for me to enjoy the fragrant spring.
Why does not he who sings so loudly
Take pity on my long-drawn sighs?

CH'ANG (*startled and rejoicing*): She has answered me, cleverly and with no delay.

(*Sings*):　First I noticed only the rouge and powder
On her smooth cheek,
But deep within her heart there dwells a radiant spirit.
She took my verse and answered it
Cleverly and in tune.
Her emotion is expressed
In each syllable she utters.
Her sentences are full of grace,
The tones and rimes are pure.
That they gave you for your child name "Oriole"
Was no mistake.
If you really love me
I would exchange verses with you
From my side of the wall
Until the bright day dawns.
Then it would certainly come about
That we two people of great talent
Should be united in our love.

(*Speaks*): Shall I come over to see you? How about it?

(*Sings*):　If I come, lifting my gauze robe as I walk,
Will she receive me with a smiling face?
Ungrateful Hung Niang, be not so unkind.
You should say "Do as you wish."
Suddenly I hear a sound. It startles me.

HUNG NIANG: Little mistress, let us go home. I am afraid my mistress will scold us.

(*Exeunt* YING YING *and* HUNG NIANG, *closing the corner gate.*)

CH'ANG *(sings)*:

> At the sound the birds sleeping on the bough
> Have flown away.
> The blossom-laden branches quiver
> Nodding at their shadows.
> Countless red flowers fall and fill the paths.
> On the green moss the cold dew glistens.
> Through the blossoms the moon's eye peers down.
> The whole day long I have been sick at heart,
> My thoughts of her alone.
> This day have I joined my love with hers.
> Her screen is lowered, her door is tightly closed.
> If I try to speak to you, softly,
> You should straightaway answer.
> The moon is bright. The breeze is gentle,
> And the second watch has come.
> Alas! You are ill-destined,
> And good fortune does not favor me.
> I have looked about me and retraced my steps.
> I stand waiting in the empty courtyard.
> The spreading bamboo sways gently in the wind.
> The Great Bear shines through the clouds.
> Ah! This night the cold has swept down
> From the four corners of the world upon me.
> If she will not care for me,
> What shall I do?
> How can I convey my affection by my eyes alone?
> Even though you do not speak,
> I shall surely grasp your meaning.

(Speaks): On this night of nights, how can the spirit of dreams take possession of my eyes?

(Sings):

> The light of my lamp on its low stand dies down.
> My shabby screen does not keep off the bitter cold.

My lamp is dim, my dream has not yet gained its
    object.
A chill wind creeps through my windowpane,
And the paper which covers it rustles and crackles.
My pillow is lonely,
And beneath my cover all is silence.
Even though I were a man of stone or iron,
I would be moved.
I cannot sit, I cannot sleep.
Oh, if one day the willow would cast its shade,
If the flowers would bloom, and the mists cover up
    my screen!
Then, when the world was quiet
And all men asleep,
Would I call upon the sea and the high hills
To bear witness to our everlasting love.
Our future would be as bright as gleaming silk,
And our life in our great love would be all-perfect.
If we were both in the painted bridal room,
How spring itself would be prolonged for us!
In one day I would have won the supreme joy of
    my life;
The two stanzas of verse are a shining proof.
I do not wish to meet her by her green door
In my dreams.
I long to go out and wait for her
Under the blossoms of the green peach trees.

ACT THIRTEEN

YING YING: I gave instructions to Hung Niang to deliver a
letter, in which I made an appointment to meet my beloved
tonight. I am awaiting her return, to decide what I shall
really do.

HUNG NIANG *(enters)*: My little mistress bade me deliver a letter to Ch'ang, making an appointment with him for tonight. I am afraid that she will change her mind again and ruin his life. This is no laughing matter. I shall go to my little mistress and hear what she has to say.

YING YING: Hung Niang, arrange my bedroom. I wish to sleep.

HUNG HIANG: If you go to sleep now, what will happen to that young man?

YING YING: What man?

HUNG NIANG: Little miss, there you go again! You are going to ruin a man's life, and that's no laughing matter. If you break your promise this time, I shall go and tell your mother that I carried a letter for you making an appointment to meet Ch'ang.

YING YING: You're a nasty little thing.

HUNG NIANG: I'm not nasty. But really, little miss, you should not act like this.

YING YING: You make me blush with shame.

HUNG NIANG: Who will see you go? No one except Hung Niang. There is no third person. *(Urging her.)* Go, go. (YING YING *stands silent.* HUNG NIANG, *still urging her.*) Little miss, how can you refuse? Go, go. (YING YING *reflects in silence.*) Little miss, let us go. Come on. (YING YING *remains silent, takes a step, then stops.*) Little miss, why do you stop? Go on, go on. (YING YING *remains silent, then starts to walk.*) Little miss, even though you won't talk, at least you have started and are on your way.

(Sings): My little mistress, with a heart as pure as jade,
　　　　　And like a flower in her loveliness,
　　　　　Could not decide the whole day through,
　　　　　Though she reflected long.
　　　　　Tonight, at last, her heart has made decision,
　　　　　And she has ceased her efforts to deceive.
　　　　　Now she leaves her painted room

And walks to the west chamber
Where her anxious lover waits.
She has left the cave of Tso, and travels to Kao T'ang.
Now she will learn how men steal jade
And the fragrance of the flowers.
She is the goddess of Wu Shan,
And her lord, the king of Hsiang Wang, awaits her
On the terrace of Yang T'ai.

(*Exeunt* HUNG NIANG *and* YING YING.)

CH'ANG: My lady sent me a letter by the hand of Hung Niang, and she has arranged to meet me here this night. The first watch has passed by; why does she not come? All the world's asleep, and the night is calm and silent. Will my divine lady come or not?

(*Sings*): In the dead of night I wait silent on the threshold.
Soft clouds of incense float to me
From the far-off golden land.
Alone, a wandering scholar in my study,
Grief and melancholy have seized upon my heart.
Where are the clouds of many hues?
The moon, brilliant as transparent water,
Now shines brightly on the tower.
The monks sleep soundly in their silent cells;
The crows call hoarsely from the courtyard trees;
The wind whispers in the bamboo grove near by.
I thought I heard the tinkle of her golden girdle.
I saw the shadow of the flowers move gently in the
    moonlight
And thought it was my jade-like lady
Drawing near.
I am on tiptoe with excitement;
My eyes are strained, my soul is strangely stirred.
My body and my heart find no repose.

Like a foolish child I stand, and lean against the door.
Though I wait, the blue bird brings no news,
And even the yellow dog is silent and asleep.
My mind is weary, and only with an effort
Will my aching eyes stay open.
I rest my head a moment on my pillow.
Ah, many a time my soul in dreams
Has wandered
And has entered the gates of the Yang T'ai tower
    of Tso.
If I had known that neither night nor day
Would I be free of grief because of her,
Then from the first I would have thought it wise
Never to have met this maid,
Whose beauty is enough to destroy a town.
If a man commit a fault,
He should accuse himself and then correct his
    course.
But though I praise wisdom, turn from passion,
And guard well my heart,
How can I keep her image
From possessing my whole soul?
I stand in the doorway and rest my cheek upon my
    hand,
I cannot know whether she will come or not.
It may not be too easy
To elude her watchful mother.
My eyes burn from watching and long to close
    their lids.
My poor heart aches from waiting,
And I blame my self alone
That I learned so quickly, all too quickly,
To love and long for her!

(Speaks): She's not coming tonight! I wonder if she has lied to
me again!

(Sings): If she is really coming
She has left her room by now.
And when she comes she will bring with her
Springtime to this cold cell.
If she comes not it will be
As though I had cast a stone
In the depths of the great ocean
To stir it up—in vain.
I count her footsteps as she approaches,
And lean on my window sill.
I must speak again with you.
Have you forgotten, my beloved,
The words we had together, you and I?
I rejoice to see that you have changed again,
And that your love for me has all returned.
Promise me to come at dusk,
And to remain until the dawn.
It seems a full half-year
That I have waited for this night,
And all this time my lot has been
An irksome one to bear.
I was patient in my illness, though sick nigh unto
death.
I think of those long days
When nothing passed my lips save tea and broth,
And all because of you, my best beloved.
I strengthened my sad heart, endured in silence,
And only by severest self-control
Did I hold my body and spirit as they were.
If I called in a geomancer he would say
That half a year of such utter sadness

Would need full ten years of peace and calm
To restore again the chariot of my lacerated soul.

HUNG NIANG *(enters)*: Little miss, I shall walk on ahead. You wait here. *(Knocks at the door.)*

CH'ANG: My little lady has come!

HUNG NIANG: She is here. Arrange your coverlet and pillow.

CH'ANG *(bowing)*: Hung Niang, at this moment it is not possible to tell you all I feel. Heaven only can judge!

HUNG NIANG: Be calm. Don't frighten her. Wait here. I'll bring her to you.

(Re-enters, leading YING YING.)

Little miss, come in. I shall await you outside the window. *(Exit HUNG NIANG.)*

(CH'ANG, seeing YING YING, kneels and embraces her.)

CH'ANG: Oh, how fortunate I am this day! I pray you, condescend to enter.

(Sings):   But one glance, O incomparable lady,
And my ills are nine-tenths cured.
When last we met, and you abused me roundly,
Who would believe that today you could be so changed?
When you show this proof of your affection,
I could bow low in humble adoration.
Though I have not the grace of Sung Yü,
Nor the beauty of P'an An,
Nor yet the brilliant talent of Tzu Chien,
Have pity, little lady, on this wanderer.

(YING YING does not speak. CH'ANG embraces her and leads her to a seat.)

CH'ANG *(sings)*:
Her tiny silken shoe
Is but an inch or two in length,
And my open hand can span her willow waist.

She blushes in confusion, and will not lift her head,
As she reclines upon the fine embroidered pillow.
Her cloud-like hair is unbound,
And her pins of gold have fallen.
The disorder of her headdress but enhances her
  every charm.
Now I loosen her silken garments, and remove her
  slender girdle
And sweet scent of musk and orris
Now perfume my lonely room.
She still seems to wish to try me,
Will she not turn her face to mine?

(CH'ANG *again embraces* YING YING, *who does not speak.*)
CH'ANG *(sings):*

I press close to my body her fragrant breast of jade.
At last have Liu and Yüan arrived in great Tien T'ai!
Spring has come again to man,
And the flowers burgeon forth in all their beauty.
Her willow-slim form stirs gently.
The flower is half-awakened
And the pearly drops of dew
Have caused the peony to open wide its petals.
One draught, and my limbs are all atremble,
And I am happy as a fish
Disporting in the stream,
Or as a butterfly who sips
The evanescent fragrance of the flowers.
You the while seem half-reluctant, yet half-willing.
Filled with love and wonderment
I gently kiss your perfumed cheeks
And then your crimson mouth.
I hold you as my heart and my possession,
And your spotless purity is mine forevermore.
I had forgotten food and thought of sleep;

My heart longed but to die.
If my will had not been firm and steadfast,
How could I have endured life until this hour
When I fulfill my wildest dreams of joy?
For this night I have drained the cup
Of desire, love, and passion,
And now my soul soars upward
To the ninth heaven of delight.
Alas, that I was forced to wait until today, beloved!
See my body, thin with grief,
And my bones as weak as threshed and beaten
    straw.
But I dare not even think
Of the joys of this wondrous night of love.
The dew now dampens the fragrant earth,
And the wind no longer stirs on the silent stair.
The moon still lights my chamber,
And the clouds veil the tower of Yang T'ai.
My soul is illumined with a bright white light,
And I look at you more closely,
To make sure that you are real
And not a vision that will fade and vanish soon.

(CH'ANG *arises, then kneels to thank* YING YING.)

CH'ANG: I have become your slave this night, my lady. Henceforth I am but your dog and horse.

(YING YING *remains silent.*)

HUNG NIANG (*pleading from outside the window*):
Little miss, let us go back. I am afraid your mother will discover where we are.

(YING YING, *without speaking, arises to leave.*)

CH'ANG (*taking her hand and again looking into her eyes, sings*):
    I bid farewell to sorrow.
    What passion, and what fire!
    When first I saw you my heart at once was moved.

When next my eyes beheld you I fell hopelessly in
love.
Now, after your stay with me this night,
I worship and adore you.
When this night I lay with you beneath the blue
silk quilt,
I already began to wonder
When next I might unbind
Your perfumed silken girdle
In this room!

HUANG NIANG *(leading* YING YING *away)*: Little miss, let us
go back quickly. I am afraid your mother will discover where
we are.

(YING YING *does not speak, but goes silently down the stairs.* CH'ANG
takes YING YING'S *hand in both of his, then looks at her again.*)

CH'ANG *(sings)*:

Spring is astir in her milk-white breast,
And the beauty of the springtime gleams upon her
broad fair brow.
She scorns the jades and riches that other men may
give.
Her face as lovely as the blossom of the apricot
And her cheeks so like the flower of the peach
Are illumined by the brilliant moon above,
Making even more resplendent
The crimson and pure white of her fair skin.
She descends the fragrant stair
And walks daintily upon the bright-green moss
With slippers tiny as the phoenix-head.
Ah, how I regret my own unworthiness,
And how I thank you, my beloved one,
For this, the supreme gift of love that you have
brought.

If you can, come back,
Come back early to me, again, this very night!

ACT FOURTEEN

MADAME *(enters, followed by* HUAN LANG*)*: I have been watching
Ying Ying for some days. She talks as though moving in a
daze. Her spirit seems pensive and dreamy. Her form and face
are not what they were. I have an idea in my mind, but I
cannot quite decide about it.

HUAN LANG: The night before last, when you were asleep, I
saw my sister go with Hung Niang into the flower garden to
burn incense. I waited half the night, but they did not come
back.

MADAME: Call Hung Niang, and tell her to come here at once.
(HUAN LANG *summons* HUNG NIANG.)

HUNG NIANG: For what are you calling me, little brother?

HUAN LANG: Madame knows that you went into the flower
garden with my sister. Now she wants to question you about
it.

HUNG NIANG *(terrified)*: Ah, little miss, now you've gotten me
into trouble. Little brother, go on ahead, and I shall follow.
The waters of the golden pool are covered with sleeping
mandarin ducks. The wind has blown open the embroidered
curtain. The parrot has noticed it.

(Sings): When you left your apartments it was night,
And it was daybreak when you finally returned.
Time seemed boundless as the heavens,
And as widespread as the earth,
When you plunged into the joys
And reveled in the delirium of youthful clouds and
rain.
Then indeed was my heart ever in my mouth.

You should have sought more innocent pleasures
In the brilliance of the moon and the gleaming of
the stars.
Who gave you leave to dwell together
Each night among the clouds?
Your mother's heart has much experience,
And her mind is ever full of shrewd suspicion.
She will try to use clever and most persuasive words
To make the false appear to be the true.
She will suspect that the poor student
Has become her son-in-law.
She will suspect that my little mistress
Has become his charming wife.
She will suspect that I, poor Hung Niang,
Have been the go-between.
Moreover, you, my little lady,
Appear as melancholy
As are the high bare mountains in the spring.
Your eyes that were like
Unto the pools of autumn
Have lost their glowing fire.
You should have indeed drawn tighter the girdle
of your robe
And gathered your silken garments much closer to
your form.
If the slimness that was yours
Be compared to your plumpness of today,
It will be seen
That your vigor and your spirit
Have returned,
And that all your old-time charms
Have once more been renewed.
(Speaks): I imagine that when I go to Madame, she will cer-

tainly ask me questions. "Vile creature," she will call me.
(*Sings, imitating* MADAME):

"I ordered you to guard her well,
To follow her footsteps closely and to sit beside her
    ever.
Who taught you to lead her astray,
Through foolish paths?"
If she thus cross-question me,
How shall I reply to her,
And justify myself?

(*Speaks*): I shall say to her: "Noble lady, since her childhood,
Hung Niang has never dared to deceive you."

(*Sings*): And if she really knows the truth,
To what end have I played the game?
Alas, how badly have I acted!
When they met each other
They embraced at once,
And in a hundred different ways
They played as do the phoenix and his mate.
I remained alone outside the window
And dared to do no more
Than cough from time to time.
All the while I stood upon the bright-green moss
My feet in their embroidered slippers
Grew ever colder, until they were no more than
    ice.
And now today upon my tender skin
I already feel the rain of painful blows.
Is this, then, the reward of my devotion?

(*Speaks*): Ah, little miss, I am going. If by dint of speaking
I can save you, do not rejoice too much; but if I do not succeed,
do not be angry. Stay here and listen to what is said.

(HUNG NIANG *sees* MADAME.)

MADAME: Vile creature! Why do you not fall upon your knees? Do you not perceive what a crime you have committed?

HUNG NIANG: Hung Niang has no crime to confess.

MADAME: You deny this with your own lips? If you tell the truth, I shall spare you. If you lie to me, I shall have you beaten until you die. Vile creature! Did you not go out into the flower garden at midnight with your little mistress?

HUNG NIANG: I did not go. Who saw me go?

MADAME: Huan Lang saw you go. And still you persist in denying it?

(*She strikes* HUNG NIANG.)

HUNG NIANG: Madame, control your noble hand. I pray you, calm your anger, and listen to Hung Niang as she tells her tale.

(*Sings*): At night I sat, when I had finished my embroidery,
And talked with my little mistress about this and that.
I told her about her elder brother's illness;
Then we both (without your knowledge, noble lady)
Went to his lodging, to see him where he lay.

MADAME: Tell me at once, what did he say?

HUNG NIANG (*sings*):
He said: "A while ago Madame made of the service I had rendered
A cause for friendship.
Then she stopped me midway in my great happiness,
And changed it into grief."
He said: "Hung Niang, you walk ahead a bit."
And: "Little lady, stop awhile with me."

MADAME: Ai ya! Loathsome creature! She was a young unmarried woman. Why did he ask her to remain?

HUNG NIANG (*sings*):
Of a certainty it was,
That she might try with the sacred needle
And the never-failing burning cone
To heal him.

Surely you could not bring yourself to think
That they planned to do as do the sparrow and the
    oriole
With their mates!
This past month the two have spent each night
    together.
Why do you ask that I give more details?
They have no worries, nor are they melancholy.
Their two hearts beat as one,
And their souls are firm united.
Act wisely in this thing, my noble lady,
That all may come to its proper end.
Why discuss it further?
It would cause useless bitterness,
And deep and vain regrets.

MADAME: Vile creature, you, you are the cause of this.

HUNG NIANG: Not Ch'ang, not my little mistress, and not I, Hung Niang, is to blame for this. You have brought it on yourself, Madame.

MADAME: Low thing, to cast the blame on me! How was it any fault of mine?

HUNG NIANG: Good faith, my lady, is the foundation of all human relations. If one does not keep his word, then that person has no worth. When a short while ago the band of soldiers laid siege to P'u Ch'iu Temple, you promised your daughter in marriage to the man who would succeed in driving away the band. If Ch'ang had not fallen in love with the charm and beauty of my little mistress he would not have worked out the stratagem that saved us, would he? But once they had been driven off and you restored to safety, you forthwith broke the solemn promise you had made. Was not this breaking faith? You would not give your consent to the marriage, but offered money as a reward instead, that he might depart and betake himself to some far-off land. You did not wish him to remain longer in the library, with the girl and him separated but a few paces from each other. The eager young girl and the man deeply in love forthwith watched each other, until—Well, then, this was the cause and the beginning of the affair. If you, Madame, do not maintain the greatest secrecy about it all, in the first place, the Prime Minister's family will appear shameless; and, in the second place, Ch'ang, who after all has been your savior, will be humiliated. In the third place, if you drag this business into court, you will be found guilty of not watching over your household with the proper care. If you will take the advice that I, your humble servant, give you, you will pardon this slight trespass, and bring the affair to a satisfactory conclusion, with advantage and profit to everyone concerned.

(Sings): It has been often said:

"When a maiden reaches adult age,
It is not wise to keep her very long at home."
One of the two is a genius in literature,
The other a very queen among all women.
One is a master of the Nine Schools and Three
    Teachings,
The other sews and paints and does fine needle-
    work.
If you find such cleverness in this wide world of ours,
You should not try to prevent the union of the two.
How has the man who saved your life become your
    enemy?
He wrote to his friend,
And the General on the White Horse came
And slew Fei Hu the bandit.
You have refused to look into his horoscope
And thus to learn his future.
All this would in truth bring shame
And dishonor to Ts'ui the Minister's house.

And for this have I been made to suffer
In my poor skin and in my tender flesh.
Madame, be advised by me,
And do not go too far.

MADAME: This little good-for-nothing reasons well. I am unhappy that I have raised such a daughter, unworthy of her
family. But if I bring this matter into court there will certainly
be no honor within our gates. Ah, well! In my family there
has never been a man who broke the laws nor a woman who
has married twice. Well, then, let us marry her to that beast!
Hung Niang, bring that miserable child of mine to me.

HUNG NIANG (*calls to* YING YING):

Little miss, it is only the stick which has been lustily laid
on my back that has made me speak. And now your mother
wants you to come to her.

YING YING: I blush for shame. How can I face my mother?

HUNG NIANG: Ai ya, little miss! There you go again! Why are
you afraid to go to your mother? Why do you blush? If you
did anything for which you have need to blush, why did you
do it in the first place?

(*Sings*):   When the bright moon rose high above the willows,
And the yellow dusk had faded into night,
When you went to meet your lover in the garden,
Then I was the one to blush and turn away.
I bit hard as I could on my silken sleeve,
And kept my eyes only on your tiny feet.
He gave full play to his passion without ceasing,
While you made no move at all but only sighed.
At that moment you did not blush
Or show your shame.

MADAME: (*enters*) My little daughter! (MADAME, YING YING,
and HUNG NIANG *all weep together*.) My little girl! If this day
you have been ruined by that student, if you have indeed done
this vile thing, all, all is my fault. Whom can I accuse? If

I brought this matter into court, your father's name would be dragged in the dust. This sort of thing should never have happened in the family of a Prime Minister.

(YING YING *bursts into loud weeping*.)

MADAME: Hung Niang, go to the assistance of your young mistress. Alas, alas, this has all come about because I have not had the wisdom to raise my daughter properly. You, go to the library and summon that low creature here.

(HUNG NIANG *calls to* CH'ANG.)

CH'ANG: Who is calling me?

HUNG NIANG: Your secret is out. Madame has sent for you.

CH'ANG: Hung Niang, how can I escape seeing her? I pray you, help me defend myself. I do not know who could have gone to Madame with the tale. I am terrified. What shall I do?

HUNG NIANG: Don't lose courage. Put on a brave front and go quickly.

(Sings): The secret has been discovered. What could I do?
  I was the first to confess. But today
  Her mother offers wine and tea to you.
  Now, when she plans to give her blessing,
  You are gloomy.
  What need is there any longer to seek a go-between,
    or fix the wedding day?
  If I have failed to watch her closely,
  The entire fault was mine.
  Come now! You are like a grain stalk without a
    flower.
  Pull yourself together.
  Indeed you are but a waxen candle,
  And not a silver lamp.

(CH'ANG *sees* MADAME.)

MADAME: A fine sort of scholar you are! Were you not taught:

"Do nothing that is not in accord with the virtues of your ancestors?" If I had you hailed before a magistrate, I would fear to bring dishonor on my house. There is no way out. So take Ying Ying as your wife. But never, in three generations, has our house given its daughters to penniless, white-clothed sons-in-law. However, I insist that tomorrow you proceed to the capital to take your examinations. I shall take upon myself the care of your wife. When you have won an official position, return to see me. If you fail, never let me set eyes on you again.

(CH'ANG, *without speaking, kneels and raises his hands in respectful salute.*)

HUNG NIANG: Offer up your thanks to Heaven, to earth, and to my mistress.

(Sings):   All record of your affair is blotted out,
>   So relax the frown that until now has knit your brow.
>   True love at last has found its own reward.
>   Who could have believed that things would happen thus?
>   Now hasten to enjoy the charms of your young wife.

MADAME: Hung Niang, see that his baggage is packed. Have wine and fruit and other food prepared. Tomorrow we shall accompany him as far as the Ten Li Inn and there speed him on his way with a farewell feast. Send a message to the willows on the West River dyke to receive him in peace and see him safely on his way. (*Exit* MADAME *with* YING YING.)

HUNG NIANG: Ch'ang, are you happy now, or are you melancholy?

(Sings):   When you return again to us
>   There will be music in the painted bridal chamber,
>   Flutes and drums, and songs of spring.
>   Then indeed will you two be

A pair of happy phoenixes.
For the moment do not offer me
The gifts due me as your go-between,
Nor ask me to take from your hand
The wine of recompense.

(HENRY HART)

Some Further Reading

Hart, Henry H., trans. *The West Chamber*. Stanford, Calif.: Stanford University Press, 1936.

Hsiung, S. I., trans. *The Romance of the Western Chamber*. New York: Columbia University Press, 1968.

Scott, A. C., trans. *Traditional Chinese Plays*. 2 vols. Madison: University of Wisconsin Press, 1967 and 1969.

Wells, Henry W. *The Classical Drama of the Orient*. New York: Asia Publishing House, 1965.

Yang Hsien-yi and Yang, Gladys, trans. *Selected Plays of Kuan Han-ching*. Peking: Foreign Languages Press, 1958.

18

MING SHORT STORIES

Under the Mongol rule, while men of letters could not advance under any examination system and were writing plays instead, the more popular native arts and entertainments continued. Comedians told their jokes, puppeteers put on their plays, and storytellers told their tales. The next native dynasty, the Ming, was established in A.D. 1368. Under the Ming, the great literary development was the novel. We shall see in the next chapters how men began to bring together shorter related stories to form coherent, novel-length wholes. But in the present chapter, we shall read two stories which are written in the *hua-pen* style quite as the style existed in the Sung Dynasty. You can see from these stories, which were written or were written down in the Ming Dynasty, that the form remained constant through several dynasties.

The two stories below serve as an effective transition to the section on novels, although they are included here neither to show the stories in *hua-pen* style nor to effect the transition, but simply because they are good stories.

Cultistic Taoists—as distinct from philosophical ones—had pursued chemistry, or alchemy, for centuries, longing for secrets of long life, of immortality. That ordinary men, as in the first story below, should be conned by frauds is no wonder, when sometimes even the emperor was. One emperor received a wizard who claimed to have the elixir of life. It was mercury, and the emperor ate it and died.

The Alchemist and His Concubine

Author unknown

> Though their clothes are too tattered to keep out the cold,
> They assure you they change all base metals to gold.
> Then why don't they make gold for their own uses, pray?
> Why just carry the burden for others all day?

This verse was written by Tang Yin, a Ming Dynasty scholar, to expose the many alchemists who trick and deceive the greedy and gullible, claiming that they can make a philosophers' stone out of herbs, to transmute lead into gold or mercury into silver. They call this the hermetic art. They ask for silver to work with, then seize a chance to run off with it, which they call "absconding with the pot." Once a priest offered to practise this art for Tang Yin.

"You have a saintly air, sir," he said. "For you I can do this."

"I notice you are in rags," countered Tang Yin. "If you have mastered the hermetic art, why don't you transmute gold for your own use? Why just do it for others?"

"Because I have this gift, Nature is against me," replied the priest. "I can do this only when I have found some beneficiary favoured by fortune. I myself have not the luck. Having observed that you were born under a lucky star, I am asking you to be my partner."

"Let me make a proposal," said Tang Yin. "I will not interfere with you while you practise your art, but simply help you with my luck; then when you have obtained the philosophers' stone we can divide the gold equally between us."

When the priest realized that the scholar was making fun of him, he knew that this was no patron for him and quickly made off. Then Tang Yin wrote his poem exposing such impostors. But there are still men of first-rate intelligence who fall into such traps.

Let me tell you about a rich native of Sungchiang named Pan, who was a scholar of the Imperial College. He was widely read, eloquent, and a thoroughly likable fellow; but he had a passion for alchemy. Since birds of a feather flock together, alchemists swarmed around him and in due course fleeced him of a great deal of silver. Yet even after being deceived time and again, he had no regrets, but simply said he had not been lucky enough to meet a genuine alchemist; for an ancient art like this must finally be crowned with success, and then all his former failures would seem as nothing. So his obsession grew. News of this spread until all the alchemists had heard of him, and charlatans from all around conspired to cheat him.

One autumn, when Pan rented rooms in Hangchow, his attention was attracted by a stranger in the next house who had also come to see the West Lake. This man had plenty of servants and baggage; and Pan learned that the woman with him, who was very beautiful, was his concubine. Every day this stranger would hire the biggest boat in Hangchow, order a feast and engage singsong girls to play music, then drink, sing and make merry with his concubine on the lake. He had many finely chased drinking vessels of gold and silver and every evening when he returned to his lodging, escorted by dozens of lanterns, he would distribute largesse on a princely scale. Pan, watching from next door, was tremendously impressed.

"My family is considered wealthy," he thought, "but I can't spend money like that. This man must be fabulously rich."

He soon persuaded an intermediary to convey his respects, after which he and the stranger met and exchanged greetings. As soon as an opening occurred, Pan remarked:

"Your wealth surpasses anything I have ever seen, sir."

"Oh, this is nothing," protested the other politely.

"Indeed," insisted Pan, "you must have mountains of gold and silver. Otherwise, living as you do, you would soon reach the end of your fortune."

"Mountains of gold are easy to spend," replied the stranger. "What's needed is an inexhaustible supply."

Pan's curiosity was aroused.

"What do you mean by an inexhaustible supply?" he asked.

"I cannot speak of such things when we have only just met."

"I must beg you to enlighten me."

"Even if I tell you, you may not understand or believe me."

When these mysterious insinuations only made Pan plead more earnestly to be told, the stranger dismissed his servants.

"I have the philosophers' stone which can transmute lead into gold," he whispered. "Gold is like earth to me."

At this reference to alchemy, which was his passion, Pan was transported with joy.

"So you are an expert in the hermetic art!" he cried. "I am devoted to alchemy, but have never been fortunate enough to meet a real master. I will gladly spend all I have if you will teach me your skill."

"This cannot be taught in a casual way," said the stranger. "But there is no harm in carrying out a few experiments by way of diversion."

He called a servant-boy to light the stove, and melted a few ounces of lead in a cauldron; then took from his pocket a package of powder and flicked some of it into the molten metal. And presently, when he emptied out the contents of the cauldron, all the lead had changed into fine glittering silver! Now, reader, there is no powder in the world that can transmute lead into silver. This was what is called the essence of silver, which this man had distilled by a chemical process from one ounce of silver; and when he melted it in the cauldron, the lead dross absorbed the essence of silver and took on a silvery colour. But there was no more silver than he had put in himself—not a speck more. Alchemists often take people in with this trick.

Pan was quite overcome with joy.

"No wonder he can spend money like water and give all his time to pleasure," he thought. "Apparently it is easy to make silver. I always lost money when I tried before; but this time I am lucky to have met a real adept. I must beg him to help me."

So he asked the stranger: "How do you make the philosophers' stone, sir?"

"This process is called the conception of the mother silver," replied the stranger. "Take any amount of silver as your base, treat it with chemicals and heat it in the cauldron. After you have heated it nine times and brought it to the right temperature, it will citronize, then become silver potate. When you open the cauldron, all you have to do is extract the philosophers' stone, a single particle of which will transform base metals into gold or silver, while the mother silver remains unchanged."

"How much silver is needed?" asked Pan.

"The more silver, the more potent the philosophers' stone,"

was the reply. "With half a casket of it, you will be as wealthy as an emperor."

"Though I am not rich," said Pan, "I can raise a couple of thousand *taels*. If you are willing to teach me and will be my guest while you make a little of this philosophers' stone, the wish of my life will come true."

"I seldom teach my art to others," replied the stranger. "Nor do I usually show others my experiments. But I was struck by your sincerity and air of saintliness, and the fact that we are neighbours here proves that our meeting was predestined. I shall do what I can for you. Let me know where your home is, and I shall call on you."

"I live in Sungchiang, only two or three days journey from here. If you will condescend to come, why not pack up and accompany me now to my humble home? If we part here, something may happen to deprive me of this privilege."

"My home is in Honan Province, where I have left my mother," answered the stranger. "I brought my concubine here to enjoy the celebrated Hangchow scenery, and the time passed so pleasantly that I kept postponing my return; for though I came empty-handed I defrayed all my expenses by means of my cauldron. But now that I have found a kindred spirit, I shall not keep my secret to myself. After I have taken my concubine home and paid my respects to my mother, I shall come to you. That won't be too late, will it?"

"I have a country house where your lady can stay," proposed Pan. "Wouldn't you prefer to bring her with you to keep you company while you work? Though we cannot entertain you well, we shall do our best to please you and make your lady comfortable. I shall be more grateful than words can express if you will come."

The stranger nodded.

"Since you are so much in earnest," he said, "I shall speak to my concubine, then prepare to leave."

Pan was delighted. He immediately wrote a card to invite the alchemist to feast with him the following day on the lake; and the next day escorted the stranger very respectfully to a boat, where each made a parade of his scholarship. They talked on and on, regretted that they had not met earlier, and parted well pleased with each other. Pan had also sent food and wine next door for the concubine. The day after that the alchemist invited him in return to an even more magnificent feast at which, it goes without saying, all the plate was of gold and silver. Since Pan could think of nothing now but alchemy and had lost all interest in the sights, he soon completed his arrangements to travel with the alchemist to Sungchiang. They hired two large junks at the harbour, moved their luggage aboard, and set sail together. The young lady in the alchemist's cabin often peeped out from behind her curtain; and Pan, stealing glances at her, saw that she was ravishingly beautiful. But, alas!

> A bridgeless chasm kept them far apart;
> He could not utter all that filled his heart.

Pan regretted that he had no means of sending her a message.

To cut a long story short, however, the two boats soon reached Sungchiang, where Pan invited the alchemist ashore and escorted him to his house.

"This is where my family lives," he said, offering his guest tea. "But there are too many people here; so I would like to invite you and your lady to my country house which is quite near, and where I can stay too in the study in the front courtyard. We shall not be disturbed there. And it is so secluded that no one will know when you light your furnace. What do you think?"

"I must not be exposed to vulgar curiosity and noise when I practise my art," agreed the alchemist. "And since my concubine is here, there is all the more reason for living in seclusion. It will be most convenient if we can stay in your country residence.''

Pan thereupon ordered the boatmen to take them to his country house; and he and the alchemist walked happily together up to its gate, which bore the inscription ''Garden of Pleasure.''

''This quiet, elegant spot is just right for alchemy,'' declared the alchemist after looking round. ''It is a good place for my concubine too; so I can work with an easy mind. You are a fortunate man.''

Then Pan sent maids to escort the young lady from the boat. Splendidly dressed and accompanied by her two maids, Spring Cloud and Autumn Moon, she swayed gracefully into the garden. Pan stood up to leave as she approached, but the alchemist stopped him.

''We are close friends,'' he said. ''Let me introduce her to you.''

And when Pan looked into her face he saw that she was of more than earthly loveliness. All rich men crave for money and beautiful women; so now he felt himself melting away like a snow man near fire, and forgot even alchemy for the time being.

''There are plenty of inner chambers in this house,'' he told the alchemist. ''Your lady can take her pick of them. And if she has not enough maids, I can send for a few girls to serve her.''

While the alchemist and his concubine looked over the house, Pan hurried home to fetch a pair of gold hairpins and gold earrings, which he gave to the alchemist.

''May I offer these trifles to your lady?'' he asked. ''Please don't be offended by the poorness of the gifts.''

When the alchemist saw that the trinkets were of gold, however, he refused.

"You do me too much honour," he replied. "I can easily make gold, but it costs you a great deal of money; so I cannot accept these gifts."

"I know you are not interested in such trifles," said Pan, rather abashed. "But please accept them as a token of my sincere respect for your lady."

"Since you are so good to us, it would be unfriendly to refuse," replied the alchemist. "Let me accept them then. When I have made the philosophers' stone I shall repay your kindness."

He left the room with a smile to order a maid to take these gifts to his concubine and bid her come out to thank their host, while Pan reflected that to see her once more was well worth the cost of the trinkets.

"This man has not only mastered alchemy but possesses this marvellous beauty," he mused. "What more could one ask of life? Luckily he has agreed to perfect the philosophers' stone for me, and I should be able to transmute gold myself before long. I wonder if I can reach an understanding with this beauty now that she is here? To succeed there too would be wonderful. I mustn't spoil everything though by being too hasty. I had better attend to the alchemy first."

So he asked the alchemist: "When will it be agreeable for you to start?"

"We can start as soon as you provide the silver."

"How much is needed?"

"The more the better. For the more silver, the more philosophers' stone; and if you have enough you need not repeat the process."

"In that case," said Pan, "I shall provide two thousand *taels* of silver for the cauldron. I shall go home today to fetch it, and move over here tomorrow to work with you."

That evening he entertained the alchemist to a feast, and

they were happy in each other's company. That he also sent wine and dainties to the inner chamber goes without saying.

The following day Pan brought two thousand *taels* of silver to his country house, besides all the apparatus: retorts, stills, pelicans, bolt-heads and so forth which he had in his home. With his long experience of alchemy he knew all that was required, and soon had the necessary lead, amalgam and other ingredients ready.

"I appreciate the pains you are taking," said the alchemist. "But you will find my method different from those you are used to."

"That is just what I beg you to teach me."

"This philosophers' stone of mine is the *lapis novenarius*. Nine days complete one cycle, and when nine times nine days have passed the cauldron can be opened and the philosophers' stone will be perfected. On that day you will come into a great fortune."

"I cannot tell you how grateful I am!" cried Pan.

Then the alchemist ordered his page to light the furnace and place the silver in the cauldron little by little. This done, he showed Pan his formula, poured some strange chemicals on the metal so that fumes of different colours arose, and sealed the cauldron with a hermetic seal. Last of all, he dismissed his servants.

"I shall be staying here for about three months," he told them. "Go home and inform my mother."

Accordingly they all left except the furnace boy.

Every day after that the alchemist inspected the furnace to see the colour of the flame, but never opened the cauldron. In his spare time he chatted, drank or played chess with Pan, until they became the best of friends. Pan also sent many little gifts to the concubine to win her favour, and she would send back some trifles with her greetings. More than twenty days had passed like this when a man in hempen mourning garments dashed, sweating, into the country house. It was one of the servants who had been sent home, who now kowtowed to the alchemist.

"The old lady is dead!" he cried. "Please go home at once, sir, to attend to the funeral."

The alchemist looked aghast, then fell weeping to the ground.

"Since your mother had reached the end of her natural span of life, you need not grieve too much," said Pan, much dismayed. "Please do not distress yourself so."

"There is no one in charge at home, sir," said the servant to the alchemist. "You had better lose no time."

Then the alchemist dried his tears and turned to Pan.

"I meant to do you a good turn to show my gratitude; but now this great misfortune has befallen me, which I shall never cease to lament. The philosophers' stone is not perfected yet, and the process must not be interrupted; so I am in a quandary. Although my concubine is only a woman, she has been with me long enough to know the right temperature for the fire; so she could remain here to watch the furnace. But since she is young and has no one to look after her, I do not like to leave her here alone."

"What scruples can you have when we are such close friends?" demanded Pan. "By all means leave your lady here. No prying busybodies will come near the laboratory, and I can send some respectable women over to keep her company. Or, if you prefer it, she can sleep with my wife while I remain here. In this way we can watch over the cauldron until you come back. What objection can there be to that?"

The alchemist hesitated for a few moments.

"The news of my mother's death has confused me," he said at last. "I know that the men of old sometimes entrusted their wives and children to friends; and since you are so kind I agree to leave her here to watch the furnace while I go to attend to my mother's funeral. I shall come back soon to open the cauldron, and in this way I shall have discharged my duty to both sides."

When Pan heard that the concubine would stay behind to watch the furnace, he was ready to agree to anything in his joy.

"If you will do that," he answered, beaming, "we can see it to a successful conclusion."

The alchemist went inside to explain matters to his concubine, then brought her out to see Pan.

"Your task is simply to watch the cauldron," he charged her. "You must on no account open it. If you do anything wrong, you will be sorry for it later."

"What if you cannot return till after the eighty-one days are up?" asked Pan.

"After the silver has been exposed to sufficient heat, a few days more in the cauldron will only produce more of the philosophers' stone," replied the alchemist. "A little delay is of no consequence."

After some words in private with his concubine, he took his leave.

Since the alchemist had left his concubine behind, Pan was not troubled by fears that he might not come back for a long time or that the philosophers' stone might not be perfected. His one thought was that now he had a splendid opportunity to seduce the young woman, which he must not let slip. He was wondering distractedly how to set about this, when Spring Cloud came in.

"My mistress would like you to have a look at the furnace in the laboratory, sir," she said.

Pan hastily spruced himself up and hurried to the young lady's door.

"Your maid told me I might escort you to the furnace, madam," he called.

"Please lead the way," she answered sweetly. "I shall follow you."

Then she emerged from her room, swaying prettily, to greet him.

"You are my guest, madam," protested Pan. "How can I precede you?"

"I am only a woman," she replied. "How dare I presume?"

Thanks to this exchange of courtesies, though neither touched the other they remained face to face for several minutes. Finally Pan prevailed on her to go first with her two maids, and the sight of her tiny feet, like golden lotuses, fired his blood as he followed her. When she reached the laboratory, she turned to her maids.

"Unauthorized persons are not allowed in here," she told them. "Wait for us outside."

Pan hurried after her into the laboratory to inspect the cauldron, but the truth is he had eyes only for the young lady, whom he wished he could swallow alive. He had lost all interest in alchemy! Unfortunately the boy who tended the fire was there; so Pan could only cast admiring glances at the beauty without paying her any compliments. Only as they were leaving did he summon up courage to say:

"Thank you for accompanying me, madam. You must be lonely in your room without your husband."

The young lady said nothing, but smiled to herself and walked off without deferring to him. By now Pan was afire with passion.

"If there were nobody else there, I might succeed with her," he thought. "What a nuisance that boy is, who stays in the laboratory! If I can get him out of the way tomorrow before I ask her to visit the furnace, I should be able to have my way."

He ordered a servant: "Prepare some food and wine tomorrow for the boy who stokes the fire, and tell him that I am treating him because he has been working so hard. Be sure to get him dead drunk."

That evening he drank disconsolately alone, thinking of the beautiful concubine in the inner chamber and of all that had passed that day. Then pacing restlessly up and down he chanted:

> "They transplant a magnificent, beautiful bloom
> In my poor cottage garden today;
> But I sigh by my plain lowly terrace in vain,
> For the spring is fast hasting away."

He walked to the hall and chanted this loudly several times in the hope that the young woman would hear him; and presently Autumn Moon came out with a cup of fragrant tea for him.

"My mistress heard you reciting poetry, sir," she said. "And thinking you may be thirsty she invites you to drink some tea."

Beaming with joy, Pan thanked her profusely. And scarcely had the maid left when he heard chanting from the inner room too.

> "Will no one pity the blossom,
> The sport of the rough spring wind?
> If only you will love her,
> She will not prove unkind."

Then Pan knew that the beauty was favourably disposed towards him; but he dared not break into her room, and as soon as he heard her door shut he went to bed to wait for the dawn. The next morning, his servant invited the boy who stoked the furnace to a meal; and tired of staying every day by the fire, the lad was only too eager to accept; he did not set down his wine cup until he was completely fuddled, then fell fast asleep. As soon as Pan knew that the boy was out of the laboratory, he went to the concubine's door to ask her to accompany him to inspect the cauldron; and she came out as she had on the previous day and walked ahead of him to the door of the laboratory, where she told her maids to wait for her. Pan alone followed her inside. When they reached the furnace and found the boy missing, she feigned surprise.

"How is it there is no one here?" she asked. "Why did you let the fire go out?"

"Because I am afire," replied Pan with a laugh, "I told him to leave his fire for awhile."

"You shouldn't have let the furnace go out," she protested, pretending not to have understood him.

"Let us heat it with our own fire," said Pan.

The young woman looked grave.

"How can anyone studying alchemy speak and think of such things?" she asked.

"Your husband shared a bed with you here," countered Pan. "Isn't that the same thing?"

The concubine had no good answer to make.

"That was right and proper," she murmured. "But you are suggesting something wrong."

"We were destined to love," declared Pan. "This is right and proper too."

And clasping her in his arms he knelt before her.

"What would my husband say?" she asked, helping him to rise. "I dare not do anything wrong. But you have been so good to me, I find it hard to refuse you. I will meet you tonight."

"Why not now?" begged Pan. "The evening is too far away."

"But someone may come in, and that would never do."

"I have taken care to keep the boy away, and nobody else will come. This laboratory is so secluded that no one will know."

"But the furnace is here," she protested. "If we spoil the work, you will be sorry. This really won't do."

By this time, however, Pan had lost all interest in the philosophers' stone. He took her in his arms.

"I don't care if it costs me my life," he swore.

He waited no longer for her consent, but felt he was in paradise.

"Our bliss was too short," he said presently. "You must grant me a night."

He went down on his knees to her again, and she hastily raised him once more.

"I promised to receive you tonight, but you would not listen," she reproached him. "How could you act like this beside the furnace?"

"I dared not let slip such an opportunity," replied Pan. "I couldn't help it."

"Shall I come to your room tonight, or will you come to mine?"

"Just as you wish."

"I have two maids sleeping with me, so my room is not convenient. Tonight I shall slip over to you; and tomorrow I shall tell my maids about you, so that you can come to me."

That night after everyone was asleep, she came to the hall where Pan was waiting for her, and he took her to his room. From then on they enjoyed themselves without restraint in his room or hers. Pan had never had such a wonderful adventure. He did not mind if the alchemist never came back and the philosophers' stone was never perfected. They had taken pleasure in this way for more than ten nights, when one day the gateman announced that the alchemist had returned; and, much taken aback, Pan had to welcome him. Presently the alchemist went in to see his concubine, and after talking to her for some time returned to his host.

"My concubine says that the seal has remained unbroken and the cycle of time has been completed," he said. "Today I have only just arrived. Let us open the cauldron tomorrow after we have sacrificed to the gods."

Though deprived of his usual night's pleasure, Pan found some consolation in the fact that the alchemist was back and would shortly present him with the philosophers' stone. The next day, after purchasing paper charms and offering sacrifice, they walked into the laboratory. Once over the threshold, however, the alchemist's face fell.

"What has caused this strange atmosphere?" he muttered to himself.

He opened the cauldron and looked inside, then stamped his foot.

"All lost! All lost!" he exclaimed. "The philosophers' stone has vanished in smoke, and even the silver base has turned to dross! Someone has ruined this by indulging in vice and lust here."

Pan turned pale and could not reply, for he knew this was the truth. The alchemist, meantime, was grinding his teeth with rage.

"Who else has been here?" he demanded of the boy.

"Only Mr. Pan and the mistress, who came here every day. No one else dared come in."

"How was the philosophers' stone spoilt then?" shouted the alchemist. "Fetch your mistress here at once to answer me that."

The boy hastily brought her.

"What did you do here while you inspected the furnace?" demanded the alchemist fiercely. "How does the philosophers' stone come to be spoilt?"

"I came here once a day with Mr. Pan to look at the cauldron,'' she replied. "The hermetic seal was never tampered with. I don't know how it can have been spoilt.''

"I never said the seal had been tampered with,'' retorted the alchemist. "You're the one who must have been tampered with!''

He asked the boy: "Did you ever leave this place when Mr. Pan and your mistress were here?''

"Only once,'' replied the boy. "One day, when Mr. Pan treated me to a meal because I'd worked so hard, I had a few cups too many and fell asleep outside. That's the only time they were alone here.''

"So that's it,'' sneered the alchemist.

He ran to his baggage roll and pulled out a whip.

"I'll teach you a lesson, you bitch!'' he roared.

"I said it wouldn't do!'' she cried, dodging the blows. "Mr. Pan is to blame for this.''

Pan, quite dumbfounded, longed to sink through the ground.

"What did you say when I entrusted her to you?'' demanded the alchemist with an angry glare. "Yet in the few days that I've been away you've done this vile thing. You are worse than a beast! How could a rogue like you hope to perfect the philosophers' stone? I have been too blind. Well, I had better beat her to death; it is no use keeping such a shameless bawd!''

He charged forward to beat his concubine, who fled in terror to her chamber while her two maids, who begged him to forgive her, received a stroke apiece for their pains. Seeing what a rage the alchemist was in, Pan had to kneel to him.

"I have behaved quite inexcusably,'' he said. "I am willing to say nothing of my loss if you will pardon me.''

"You have only yourself to blame,'' retorted the alchemist. "It was your wickedness that caused the philosophers' stone to disappear in smoke. But why should I give you my favourite concubine, you lecherous dog? How are you going to make amends for what you did to her? I have a good mind to kill her and make you pay for it with your life!"

"Let me atone for my sin," pleaded Pan.

He hastily ordered a servant to fetch two large ingots of silver worth one hundred *taels,* then begged on his knees to be forgiven. But the alchemist did not even deign to look at him.

"I can make silver easily," he scoffed. "Why should I want yours?"

Pan kowtowed again and added another two hundred *taels*.

"With this you can buy another concubine," he said. "It was very wrong of me. Please forgive her for old time's sake."

"I don't want your silver," growled the alchemist. "But if a scoundrel like you doesn't lose money, you will never mend your ways. I'll take this to give to some charity."

He packed the three hundred *taels* of silver in his case, summoned his concubine and servants, and made them move all their baggage to the boat on which he had arrived the previous day.

"I've never been so insulted in my life!" he swore as he left. "Insolent slave!"

He swore all the way to the boat, which set sail as soon as they were aboard.

Pan had been so terrified that the alchemist might kill his concubine, that now, in spite of all the money he had lost, he considered he had got off lightly. He honestly believed that it was his fault that the silver in the cauldron had gone up in smoke.

"I was too impatient," he reflected. "If I had waited till the philosophers' stone was ready and then kept her here a little longer, or if we had kept clear of the laboratory, it would probably have been all right. It was my hastiness that made me lose my silver. What a pity to meet a genuine alchemist yet fail to get the philosophers' stone! Still, it was a marvellous adventure while it lasted!"

He had no idea how thoroughly he had been tricked.

The fact is that when this swindler heard that Pan was coming to Hangchow, he had posed as an alchemist to cheat him. He stayed with him for some time to inspire him with confidence; and when a servant announced that his mother had died and he hurried away, taking the two thousand *taels* of silver with him, he left the young woman there to allay Pan's suspicions. The seduction was planned too, in order that all the blame might be put on Pan, who would have to apologize and could not demand any compensation. The wretched man fell into this trap, convinced that this rich stranger must have the philosophers' stone. Little did he know that what he took to be gold and silver utensils were plated copper and lead; but, of course, no one drinking in the lamplight would think of testing the metal. So he was cleverly taken in.

Even after being deceived like this, however, Pan did not lose hope. He simply blamed himself for missing a golden opportunity, and became more addicted to alchemy than ever. One day he met another alchemist who discussed the hermetic art with him, and Pan found this stranger so congenial that he invited him home.

"The other day," said Pan, "I came across a man who could really transmute base metals into gold and showed me how he did so, then started making the philosophers' stone for me. But unfortunately I offended him, so that he left without completing it."

"I can do that too," declared the stranger.

He proceeded to give the same demonstration, adding a pinch of powder to lead to turn it to silver.

"Good!" exclaimed Pan. "Last time I failed, but this time I shall surely succeed!"

He raised another thousand *taels* of silver for this alchemist, who called in two or three of his men to assist him. After seeing him make silver so easily, Pan trusted him implicitly and did not watch him carefully; so one night the stranger made off with the contents of the cauldron, and the following day was nowhere to be found. These two frauds left Pan quite bankrupt, and angry and ashamed into the bargain.

"To think of all the time and effort I've wasted over this business!" he lamented. "Last time I was to blame for what happened; but this time, when I thought everything was going smoothly, they cheated me! I'll see if I can track them down, because they must be up to the same tricks somewhere else. Or I may meet a genuine alchemist who will show me how to make the philosophers' stone."

So he packed up some clothes and began to roam the country.

One day, in a crowd by the West Gate of Soochow, he came across the same gang. But just as he was about to denounce them they greeted him cheerfully as if he were an old friend, invited him to a clean table in a big tavern, and ordered wine and food.

"The other day we took advantage of your kindness," they apologized. "But this is our way, so please don't take offence. Now we would like to discuss how to pay back what we owe you and settle the matter."

"What do you have in mind?" he asked.

"We spent your silver as soon as we got it, so we can't return it to you. But there is a rich man in Shantung who has also asked us to make the philosophers' stone for him. We have reached an agreement with him, and as soon as our master arrives he will give us the silver. However, our master is on a long journey and will not be back for some time. If you will take his place, as soon as this rich man hands us the silver we will repay you. It is very simple. But if you refuse, we can't pay you however much you may insist. What do you say to this?"

"What sort of man is your master?"

"He is a monk; so we will have to ask you to cut off some of your hair. Then we will travel with you as your disciples to Shantung."

Eager to get his silver back, Pan agreed and cut his hair. Then they treated him with respect and took him to Shantung, where they introduced him as their master to the rich man. The latter invited him most deferentially to sit in the hall and discuss alchemy; and since Pan knew a good deal about this subject and was an educated man, he discoursed learnedly and at length till his host was much impressed. That same night the rich man produced two thousand *taels* of silver, and arranged for the work to start the following day. Then he invited Pan to drink, and had him carried when he was drunk to an inner chamber to sleep. At dawn the tricksters discussed how to set up the furnace; and as Pan knew some of the routine he joined in their discussion and gave them certain instructions. Then the silver was put in the cauldron to be melted; and the men who were pretending to be Pan's pupils watched the furnace while their host took Pan aside to consult him and offer him drinks, so that he could not get away. These rogues thereupon seized the opportunity to abscond with the silver, leaving their master behind. The rich man had no misgivings, because the monk was still there; but when he discovered the next morning that the whole gang had disappeared, he seized Pan and threatened to hale him before the magistrate in order to apprehend the others.

"I am a native of Sungchiang," protested Pan tearfully, "I don't belong to their gang. But I am interested in alchemy and not long ago they cheated me of some money. I met them later on the road, and they promised to pay me back after they had made the philosophers' stone for you if I would cut my hair and pretend to be their master. I came here expecting to get back my money, little thinking they would cheat you too and leave me in the lurch."

He wept long and loud. The rich man questioned him carefully and, after discovering that Pan was indeed a wealthy citizen of Sungchiang who had formerly had dealings with his family and had been tricked into this, he decided not to prosecute him, and let him go. Then Pan, who had no money for the journey and was dressed like a monk, had to start begging his way home as a mendicant friar.

When he reached Lingching Harbour he noticed a beautiful woman peeping out from behind the curtain on a big boat. Her face was familiar, and looking more closely Pan realized that she resembled the alchemist's concubine who had been his mistress.

"Could it be she?" he wondered.

When he approached the boat and made inquiries, he learned that she was a famous courtesan, who had been engaged by a young Honanese scholar on his way to the capital for the palace examination.

"Can he really have sold his concubine?" marvelled Pan "It may be no more than a striking resemblance."

He wandered up and down near the boat watching the woman, until a maid came out from the cabin.

"Our mistress asks whether you are a native of Sungchiang?" she inquired.

"I am," said Pan.

"Is your name Pan?"

"Yes. How did you know?"

Then the woman in the cabin called out: "Ask him to come over here."

Pan walked towards the cabin, and the woman addressed him from behind the curtain.

"I am the woman that alchemist called his concubine," she

told him. "Actually I am a courtesan from Honan; but he told me what to do, and I had to carry out his instructions and help him to trick you. I'm afraid I did you a bad turn. But how did you get into a state like this?"

Pan told her sadly how he had been deceived again and was now trying to beg his way home.

"I can't help feeling sorry for you," said the woman. "I'll give you some money for the road, and you had better go home as fast as you can. If you come across any more alchemists don't let them take you in. After being their accomplice, I know their tricks well; and if you will take my advice I shall feel I've repaid you for those nights of love."

She told her maid to give him a packet containing three *taels* of silver, which Pan accepted thankfully. Although she had turned out to be a courtesan, he was so grateful to her for helping him to reach home that he took her advice and never trusted alchemists again. However, his hair had been cropped and he had been covered with shame; so all his friends who heard of his misadventures had a good laugh at his expense. I hope this will be a lesson to all those who are obsessed by alchemy.

(YANG AND YANG)

A Prefectship Bought and Lost

Author unknown

Who can foretell if fortune will endure?
When you have wealth, why should you
    strive for more?
Clouds change their shape each second in
    the sky,
And even oceans may at last run dry.

Human pomp and glory are nothing but vanity, and must not be considered true or enduring. Yet nowadays when men have a run of luck they think it will last forever, and onlookers think the same; whereas actually it may vanish in a twinkling like smoke or ashes, for all too often the gold mountain becomes a mountain of ice.

The proverb says: Better to start poor but end rich than to start rich and end poor. How a poor man must savour the sweet after the bitter when he suddenly finds himself rich and respected! But if the once rich and mighty fall on evil days, their followers scatter like monkeys when their tree crashes down. Such a downfall is hard to bear. Yet while they prosper the wealthy and powerful behave exactly as they please, without any qualms of conscience and without caring whether they come to a good end or a bad.

This story is about a native of Chiangling named Kuo Chilang, who also lived during the reign of Emperor Hsi Tsung. Kuo's father was a rich merchant in Central China, and Kuo often accompanied him on his journeys by boat. After his father's death, Kuo became the head of the family and the master of a great fortune and thousands of acres of land. His estates were so huge that no crow could fly across them, and his gold and silver so abundant that no thief could steal all his wealth. The richest man of the Upper Yangtse River Valley, Kuo lent money to all the merchants there and mixed solely with wealthy men.

Kuo had one weakness which was only natural: when accepting payment he weighted his scales, when lending money he used sub-standard weights; moreover, he considered his silver as the best quality and that of others as the worst. So all merchants who borrowed from him lost by the transaction. They had to put up with this unfair treatment, though, for he had the capital. While the merchants suffered all the hardships of travel, Kuo could tamper with the accounts in any way he pleased; but they could make their profit only by using his capital. If they offended him and he demanded repayment of his loan, then they were out of the game; so they put up with his squeeze because it was worth their while. Thus Kuo's fortune grew from day to day, for money breeds money.

A very rich merchant, who had borrowed many thousand *taels* of silver from Kuo to do business in the capital, had remained away for several years and sent no message back. At the beginning of the Chien Fu period [B.C. 874–879], Kuo remembered that this debt was not yet paid; and though his debtor was such a prosperous merchant that nothing was likely to go wrong, he wished he could send someone to the capital to collect payment.

"I hear the capital is a marvellous place where a man can have a wonderful time with singsong girls," thought Kuo. "I may as well take this opportunity to make a trip there. First, I shall collect the debt; secondly, I shall have some fun with singsong girls; and thirdly, I may have a chance to get an official post which will set me up for life." So he made up his mind to go.

Kuo was not married but had an old mother, younger brother and sister at home, as well as many servants and retainers. He told his brother and sister to look after their mother well, appointed a chief steward to manage his household, and left the others to their various tasks; then, taking with him a few servants who were used to travelling long distances on business for him, he set out for the capital. Since boyhood Kuo had been accustomed to sailing on merchant junks and was a good hand at punting and rowing, so he did not find the journey hard, and before long he reached his destination.

The rich merchant to whom Kuo had lent money was Chang Chuan, otherwise known as Moneybags Chang. He owned several pawnshops and silk shops in the capital, and lent money to officials and bigwigs. He was a good negotiator too; and if he agreed to act as middleman or buy anyone an official rank or title, he was always as good as his word. Since all the citizens of the capital knew this merchant, Kuo found him at once upon asking for him.

When his creditor arrived, Chang remembered that it was Kuo's money that had enabled him to come to the capital, set up in business and prosper; so he welcomed him heartily. After the usual exchange of compliments, Chang ordered a feast and sent sedan-chairs to fetch a few famous singsong girls to keep Kuo company. Both guest and host had a good time; and after the feast Chang kept a beautiful girl named Wang Sai-erh to sleep with Kuo in the library. Since this was a rich man entertaining another rich man, it goes without saying that the room and the furnishings were of the finest.

The next morning, before Kuo had got up or had time to mention the purpose of his visit, Chang reckoned up his debt and found that principal and interest mounted to several hundred thousand *taels*. This sum he gave to Kuo.

"I have been too busy to leave the capital," he said. "Besides, it would hardly be safe to travel with so much money, and I could not very well entrust it to anyone else; so I am a few years behind with the payment. I am very glad that you have come now yourself, so that we can settle this matter."

Kuo was pleased by Chang's good faith.

"I have never been here before and I have no place to stay," he remarked. "You have been good enough to pay me back my principal with interest; I wonder if I may trouble you now to find me lodgings?"

"I have many empty rooms," replied Chang, "and I often invite friends to stay. How can an old friend like you think of going elsewhere? I must insist on your being my guest. Whenever you want to leave, you can arrange your journey from here. I assure you it will be no trouble."

Kuo was delighted, and moved into a large guest-house next to Chang's own residence. That same day he gave Sai-erh ten *taels* of silver for her services the previous night; and in the evening he invited Chang to a feast at which he asked the girl to accompany them. Chang did not want his guest put to any expense, so he gave Sai-erh ten *taels* of silver, bidding her return the other ten. Kuo, however, would not agree to this. They pushed the money back and forth and, when neither would take it, the girl was lucky enough to pocket both shares, to the satisfaction of both men.

That evening the two merchants played drinking games with the girl and had a gay time, enjoying each other's company so much that they did not part till they were tipsy. Sai-erh was a noted courtesan. When she saw how rich Kuo was, she used all her wiles to charm him; and after two nights with her Kuo was completely bewitched. He would not suffer her to leave his side or go back to her quarters; but from time to time she invited other singsong girls from her establishment to drink with Kuo and amuse him, and he gave them innumerable presents. On top of that, the procuress devised all manner of excuses to ask for money: birthdays that had to be celebrated, purchases that had to be made, debts that had to be paid, and so forth.

Since Kuo was open-handed and spent money like water, a band of parasites swarmed round him and persuaded him to visit other courtesans. These spendthrifts from rich families are never constant in their love, but drift from flower to flower and court each fresh beauty they meet; so, apart from Sai-erh, Kuo saw a great deal of other girls as well. And wherever he went he scattered money recklessly. Then his worthless companions introduced him to some young nobles who were fond of gambling, who cheated him so that he almost invariably lost, and most of his silver found its way into their pockets.

But though Kuo was fond of pleasure, he was after all a man of property with an eye to the main chance. At first he spent lavishly because he had received so much interest in addition to his principal; but after two or three years he felt he had squandered enough and found, upon reckoning, that he had run through more than half his money. Then he thought of his home, and decided to go back. He broached the subject to Chang.

"Now that Wang Hsien-chih has revolted in the provinces," said Chang, "the roads are cut. You must not think of travelling with so much money: you would never reach home. I advise you to stay here a little longer until things quiet down."

So Kuo stayed a few days more. Then a vagabond friend of his named Pao Ta happened to mention that, because of the military emergency and lack of funds, the government was selling official posts, the rank depending on the amount paid. Kuo's mouth watered when he heard this.

"For a few million cash, what sort of post could I get?" he asked.

"The government is utterly corrupt," said Pao. "If you paid in the regular way, you would get a minor post only; but if you give a few million cash secretly to the officer in charge, you should get a prefectship at the very least."

Kuo was shocked.

"Do you mean to say one can buy a prefectship?" he demanded.

"What honesty can you find in the world today?" retorted Pao. "With money you can buy anything. Haven't you heard how Tsui Lieh bought the post of Minister of Civil Affairs for five million? A commander's title is worth only the price of a drink; and a prefectship is not difficult to get either. Provided you go through the right channels, I guarantee you will have no trouble."

As they were talking, Chang came in, and Kuo jubilantly told him what they had been discussing.

"Yes, it can be done," said Chang. "In fact, I have done it for quite a few people. But I wouldn't advise you to do this."

"Why not?" demanded Kuo.

"It's hard to be an official nowadays," explained Chang. "To do well you have to have backers and supporters, kinsmen at court and followers on all sides. Only then can you strike roots, make money, climb higher and higher and squeeze the people as shamelessly as you like. With backing and connections you can get away with anything. But you are all on your own. Suppose you do get a good post, if you have no one to stand by you when you arrive there, things may not turn out too well. Even if you do manage all right remember that the government is out for all it can get. Since the authorities know that you bought your post, they will wait till you've been there one or two months and are doing well, then swoop down on you and smear you with mud. You'll find you've spent all that money for nothing. If it were good to be an official, I would have become one long ago."

"That's not the way to look at it," countered Kuo. "I have plenty of money at home, but no official rank; and since it wouldn't be easy to take back the sum I have with me, why not spend some of it here? If I can get a gold belt and purple gown, I shan't have lived in vain. Even if I don't make anything out of it, what does it matter? I don't need the extra money anyway. I don't care if I don't do well; I shall have been an official. And even if my term of office is short, I shall still have the glory. I've made up my mind to this, friend. Don't try to dissuade me!"

"Well, if you are determined," answered Chang, "I shall help you."

Then and there he and Pao Ta discussed what steps to take. Pao Ta had plenty of experience in such work, and Chang was a substantial citizen who was used to big deals: between them they could arrange the matter easily.

In the Tang Dynasty people used copper cash, and a thousand cash made one string. Even when silver was used, sums were reckoned in terms of cash, one string of cash being equivalent to one *tael* of silver. Now Chang and Pao Ta privately sent five thousand strings to the officer in charge of ranks—the treasurer to the eunuch, Tien Ling-tse, and as able a man as you could find. As luck would have it, a man named Kuo Han, who was about to be notified of his appointment to the prefectship of Hengchow in Kwangsi, had just fallen ill and died; and his letters of credence were still in the office. When the officer in charge received the five thousand strings of cash, he changed the place of domicile on the papers and gave them to Kuo, who thus became Kuo Han.

The prefectship of Hengchow once secured, Chang and Pao came with great joy to congratulate Kuo, who felt quite lightheaded and drunk with greatness. Then Pao Ta hired a company of actors and Chang gave a feast. Kuo changed into official dress, and all his hangers-on hearing he had become a prefect came to congratulate him too. With trumpets and drums they feasted for a whole month.

As the proverb says: Flies gather on filth, and ants on grease, while pigeons fly to the homes of the rich. Since Kuo had been known for his prodigal ways in the capital, now that he was a prefect many begged him to be their patron, and these followers became fiercer than their master. As stewards and runners they heralded Kuo's approach wherever he went, bullied local officers, and cheated traders and country folk. Then Kuo felt he was walking on air and, anxious to parade his splendour at home, he chose a date for his departure. Chang gave him a farewell feast, and his good-for-nothing friends came with the singsong girls to say goodbye too. Kuo by now was very high and mighty. While he haughtily distributed gifts as if these people were far beneath him, they fawned on him because he was a prefect, and put up meekly with all his insolence. If he but glanced at one of them or mentioned his name, the man felt overwhelmed with honour.

When this had gone on for several days, preparations were

made for the journey and Kuo set off in great style, looking every inch a high official. On his way he was thinking: "Now I have not only a large property at home, but am also prefect of an important prefecture. In future, there is no knowing how far I may go!"

With the prefect so pleased that he could not resist making a parade, the servants who had accompanied him to the capital boasting to the new followers of Kuo's wealth, and the new men exulting to think what a wonderful master they had found, needless to say they gave themselves airs all the way to Chiang-ling, whether travelling by horse or by boat.

But when Kuo reached his native place, he was shocked at what he saw. For—

No smoke was there, no sign of human life,
The whole deserted countryside was dead,
With charred and gutted ruins underfoot,
And withered, dying branches overhead.
White walls were stained with blood of those cut down,
Red beams were blackened with the flames of war;
The corpses lay unburied where they fell,
For ants to tear, for crows to peck and claw.
Upon the hens and dogs left homeless now
The savage wolves and kites were free to prey.
A man of stone or iron who saw this sight
Must shed a tear before he went his way!

This region had been laid waste by rebels, and barely one out of every hundred inhabitants was left. If not for the river which formed a landmark, nobody could have recognized the locality. When Kuo saw this desolation, his heart began pounding; and when he reached his home and gazed around, he could not help giving a cry of despair. For the whole place was in ruins, his great mansion had been razed to the ground, and he did not know what had become of his mother, brother and sister, or all his household.

In fear and bewilderment he searched for several days until he found a former neighbour and learned that, when the place was plundered by the rebels, his brother had been killed and his sister carried off—to what fate none could tell! His mother was living with two maids in a tiny thatched hut near an old temple; but since all the other family retainers had fled and the money was gone too, she had nothing to live on but what she and her maids earned by their sewing. When Kuo heard this he was cut to the heart. He quickly led his followers to where she was, and mother and son clasped each other and wept.

"Who could foresee the disaster that happened after you left!" sobbed his mother. "Now your brother and sister are lost, and we are penniless."

Presently Kuo wiped his tears.

"It is no use lamenting," he said. "Luckily I have an official post, so there will be wealth and splendour coming to us. You mustn't worry, mother."

"What official post have you got?" she asked.

"Not a bad one," he replied. "The prefectship of Heng-chow."

"How could you get such an important post?"

"Now the eunuchs are in power, you don't have to pass the examinations to become an official. When I went to collect the debt from Chang, he paid me back with interest; so I had plenty of money there, and I paid a few million for this post. I came home in style to see the family; and now I must travel post-haste to Hengchow."

Then he ordered his servants to fetch his official cap and belt, and having donned his official robes he asked his mother to sit down while he kowtowed to her. After this he told his old servants and the new servants from the capital to kowtow to the old lady too. His mother felt a little comforted; but still she sighed.

"While you were doing so well outside, son," she said, "you didn't know that the family was broken up and every cent we had was stolen. If you hadn't bought this post, you could have brought more money home."

"You are talking like a woman, mother," protested Kuo. "Won't I have money now that I'm a prefect? All officials nowadays make millions by squeezing the people. Since we have no property left, we had better leave here and go to my post. After a year or two, we shall easily be able to restore our family fortunes. I still have two or three thousand strings of cash with me, quite enough for our present needs; so don't worry."

Then his mother's grief turned to joy.

"How lucky that you have managed so well, son," she said, beaming. "Heaven be praised! If you hadn't come back, I wouldn't have lived much longer. Now, when can we leave?"

"I was thinking of finding a good wife to share my splendour before going to my post. I'd like you to come aboard my boat to rest today, mother. As there is nothing to keep us here, tomorrow I shall hire a big boat, choose an auspicious day and start. The earlier we get there the better."

That evening Kuo escorted his mother to the boat, leaving all her broken pots and pans in the thatched hut. He then ordered his men to hire a large vessel to take them all the way to Kwangsi, had his baggage carried over the following day to the new junk, burnt sacrificial papers for luck, and set sail amid sounding trumpets and drums.

Both Kuo and his mother looked cheerful, prosperous and haughty now. Kuo had suffered no hardships but lived well all along; so although he looked proud and complacent, this was nothing new. His mother, however, had gone through such difficulties that she now seemed like one transported from hell to heaven. She felt puffed up to twice her normal size!

They travelled past Changsha down the Hsiang River to Yung-chow. North of the river was a Buddhist Monastery called Tushita Monastery, and here the boatmen moored for the night; for on the bank was a huge banyan tree, so large that it took several men to encircle the trunk, and they made fast the mooring rope to this tree, then pegged it to the ground.

Kuo went ashore with his mother to visit the monastery, accompanied by attendants carrying official umbrellas. When the monks saw that this was an official, they came out to welcome him and served tea; and upon learning after discreet inquiries that this was the new prefect of Hengchow, they became even more respectful and showed Kuo and his mother round the whole monastery, stopping before each image of Buddha so that the old lady could bow in gratitude for his protection. When dusk fell they returned to their junk.

That night a high wind lashed the trees, heaven and earth turned dark, and a great storm raged.

Then the wind and the rain made display of their might,
Like ten thousand swift horseman that gallop by night;
While the booming of waves was like drum beats in war,
And the banks fell away at the thunderbolts' roar.
Then the howling of tigers affrighted the air,
And the dragons shrank back in their watery lair;
Though the boat was made fast to a tree's mighty trunk,
Yet the tree was uptorn, and the vessel was sunk!

When this gale sprang up the boatmen were alarmed, but they thought their junk was fastened to such a large and deeply-rooted tree that it should be safe no matter how fierce the wind. While they were sleeping, however, there came a mighty crash. For the banyan tree was old and its roots had loosened the bank which was washed day and night by the river waves: thus it was by no means firmly rooted. Then the tree was big and bore the full brunt of the wind; and, on top of this, here was this heavy boat fastened to its trunk. When the wind beat against the junk, the vessel wrenched at the banyan which was already shaken by the force of the storm; and when the roots could no longer keep their hold on the loosened rocks, the tree fell with a crash on the boat. The tree was heavy and the vessel light, so water rushed in and the junk sank, its broken cabin planks floating away, while the servants who had been sleeping were washed overboard.

In less time than it takes to tell, the panic-stricken boatmen raised a cry and Kuo awoke. Since he had learned to sail a boat when young, he helped the boatmen tug the rope until they got the prow of the junk ashore; then he hastily assisted his mother on to the bank. But though his mother's life was saved, the men in the back cabin had been swallowed up with all Kuo's baggage by several great waves; and when the boat broke up they were drowned.

It was then pitch dark and the monastery gates were firmly bolted, so their cries for help went unheeded in the noise of the storm. Huddled there in their wet clothes, they could only beat their breasts and stamp their feet as they lamented their fate. They waited till dawn, when at last the monastery gate opened and they hurried inside to ask for the abbot whom they had met the previous day.

"Have you been robbed?" demanded the abbot, when he saw the state Kuo was in.

Kuo told him how the tree had fallen and sunk their boat. Quickly going to the bank, the monks were shocked to find the battered junk half under water, with the banyan tree lying across it. They ordered the monastery attendants to help the boatmen salvage what they could from the wreckage; but, alas, everything had been washed away by the waves. Nothing was left, not even the prefect's credentials. When the abbot had given Kuo a quiet room where his mother could rest, Kuo decided to report this accident to the Prefect of Lingling, requesting the authorities to issue a written statement of his loss in the storm so that he could proceed to his post. Having made this decision, he asked the abbot to send to the yamen; and the abbot, who was friendly with the prefect, sent a messenger with a report of the matter.

As everyone knows, however, troubles never come singly. Kuo's mother, who had only just recovered from the shock of losing her younger son and daughter in the revolt, could not stand this second shock. Now that all their servants and money were lost, her face turned waxen for grief; she would take neither food nor drink but lay weeping sadly in bed, refusing to get up. Seriously alarmed, Kuo tried to console her.

"As long as the forest is left, we need fear no lack of fuel," he said. "Although we have been so unfortunate, I still have my post. Once we reach Hengchow, all will be well."

"Son," replied his mother, sobbing, "my heart is broken. I shall never get over this fright. You needn't try to comfort me. Even if you become an official, I shan't live to see it."

Kuo still hoped that his mother would recover, and that the local authorities would give him a written statement so that he could go to his prefectship in Hengchow and live well there. But the shock had indeed been too much for the old lady, for her illness proved mortal and within two days she was dead. Kuo lamented bitterly, but there was nothing he could do. After consulting with the abbot, he called himself at the yamen to beg for help. The Prefect of Lingling had read the report of the accident a few days earlier, and knew that it was true; moreover since Kuo was the prefect of another district, he, as a fellow official, was bound to help him. He could not wash his hands of the matter. So he sent men to have the old lady buried, gave Kuo a generous sum for his journey, and saw him out politely.

Thanks to the Prefect of Lingling, Kuo's mother had received a respectable funeral; but because Kuo had to observe mourning for three years, he could not proceed to his post; and when the monks saw that he had no power, they gradually grew insolent and tried to get rid of him. Having no home to turn to, Kuo was reduced to staying in the house of a Yungchow dock-master whom his father had met during his travels. He had no money beyond what the prefect had given him, and this sum dwindled daily until soon it was exhausted. But what compassion do hucksters have? The dockers began to complain, and became less and less willing to supply him with tea, food and utensils. Kuo, for his part, was well aware of their resentment.

"As head of a prefecture I am equal in rank to a baron," he protested. "Though I am in mourning, my day will come. How can you treat me so badly?"

"What's a prefecture?" retorted his host. "Even an emperor who loses power will starve or fare ill. You have not gone to your post yet, and even if you had, we don't live in Hengchow—why should we look after you? Fellows like us have to work for a living. We can't afford to support idlers."

Kuo had no answer to this. Tears welled up in his eyes, but he had to swallow his humiliation. A couple of days later, his host deliberately picked a quarrel with him, and his situation became even more intolerable.

"My friend," said Kuo to the dock-master, "I am all alone in a strange place with no one to turn to. I know it is wrong to have put you to so much trouble, but I have no choice. If you know of any way by which I can make a living, please tell me."

"People like you with high rank and low ability are not fit for anything," replied his host. "If you want to find a job, you must lay aside your official airs and work like an ordinary labourer. That's the only way out for you. But are you willing to do that?"

The suggestion that he should work for hire made Kuo angry.

"I am still a local official," he said indignantly. "How can I stoop so low?"

Then he thought: "The prefect here treated me quite handsomely. If I tell him of my difficulty, he is sure to find me a way out. How can he allow a prefect to starve in his district?"

He wrote a card, but since he had no attendants he had to take it to the yamen himself; and when the runners saw how shabby he looked, they took him for some shameless fellow come to beg for money, and would not accept his card. Only after he had pleaded with them, told them his whole story and described how liberally the prefect had treated him and attended to his mother's funeral—which the runners knew to be true—did they consent to take his card in. But when the prefect saw Kuo's card he was annoyed.

"How can he be such a fool?" he exclaimed. "When I heard that he had this accident in my district and knew that he was a high official, I treated him very well. Why should he come and trouble me again? Quite likely the tale he told me before was false, and he is a rogue who cheats people of their money. Even if his story was true, he must be a barefaced scoundrel who will never be satisfied. I acted out of kindness, but I seem to have laid myself open to trouble. Well, I won't arrest the fellow, but I'll pay no attention to him from now on.

He ordered his attendants to return Kuo's card and tell him that the prefect would not see him.

After losing face like this, Kuo was unwilling to leave. He sat down in front of the yamen and waited for the prefect to emerge, then called out for all the street to hear.

"Who is making so much noise?" demanded the prefect from his sedan-chair.

"Prefect Kuo of Hengchow!" shouted Kuo.

"What proof have you?"

"I had credentials, but they were lost in a great storm which capsized my boat."

"Since you can produce no proof," replied the prefect, "how do I know that you are telling the truth? And even if your tale is true, I have already given you money for the road. Why do you go on making trouble here? You are obviously a rogue. If you don't clear off quickly I shall have you beaten."

When the attendants saw that the prefect was angry, they started beating Kuo with their rods, and he had to take to his heels. He returned despondently to his lodgings, where his host already knew what had happened at the yamen.

"How did the prefect treat you?" inquired the dock-master sarcastically.

Thoroughly ashamed, Kuo sighed but dared not say a word.

"Didn't I tell you to lay aside your official airs?" went on his host. "But you wouldn't listen to me, so you got snubbed. Nowadays even the title of prime minister is not worth anything. You must stop dreaming and work for your living."

"What would you advise me to do?" asked Kuo.

"Just think: what are you fit for?"

"The only thing I understand is rowing or steering a boat," said Kuo. "I learned that when I was travelling with my father as a boy."

"Fine!" replied his host, delighted. "Plenty of vessels put in at this dock, and they often need boatmen. If I introduce you, you'll be able to make enough money to feed yourself."

Kuo had perforce to agree. Thereafter he worked on the boats which passed there, and as time went by saved up a few strings of cash. When the traders in the market came to know him and learned his story, they nicknamed him Prefect Kuo the Boatman; and when he was wanted on a boat, they asked for Prefect Kuo.

This song was also sung about him in the market:

What kept you, Sir Prefect, from going to Hengchow?
    'Twas Fate that willed it so.
Your post was a bought one, your office a short one,
    For soon Fate brought you low!
Your rudder is now all your placard of office,
    Your yamens are afloat;
And this is the end of a lordly official,
    For now you row a boat!

After working for two years as a boatman, Kuo's period of mourning expired. But with no credentials he could not take up his post; and to obtain fresh credentials in the capital, he would again have had to spend a few thousand strings of cash. How could he raise so much money? So he resigned himself to his life as a waterman. It is undeniable that a man's way of life sets its mark on his appearance; for when Kuo was a prefect he looked like an official, but now that he had worked several years on boats he looked and behaved like a boatman. It is amusing, is it not, to think of a prefect ending in this fashion? And since it seems that human wealth and splendour count as nothing, I warn you, good people all, not to set too much store by power and profit.

The poor should not bewail their fate,
Nor the rich make proud display;
It is the end of life that counts,
And not the present day!

(YANG AND YANG)

PART FIVE:

THE NOVELS OF MING
AND CH'ING

19

A TALE OF THREE KINGDOMS

China's novel began in the mid-fourteenth century
A.D. A vagabond and poet (his nickname was "Wanderer
on Seas and Lakes"), Lo Kuan-chung, pulled together a
large amount of material—authentic material from the
histories and parahistorical material from the story-
tellers—to make a long novel about the "Three Kingdoms" period [A.D. 221–265]. He called it (or later
generations called it) *A Tale of Three Kingdoms*. The
Chinese reader, in talking of novels, is likely to refer to
"the four miraculous works." Of these, *A Tale of Three
Kingdoms* is the first. The other three are *A Saga of the
Marshes, The Way West,* and *The Golden Lotus*. Lo Kuan-
chung also composed or revised *A Saga of the Marshes*.

Before the fourteenth century, a whole string of
stories had grown up about the fascinating and romantic
"Three Kingdoms" period. China was divided during
this period, and region fought region to determine who
would sit on the "dragon throne" and rule all China.
Official history had recorded the kings, ministers, and

strategists of this epoch and their vicissitudes, defeats, and victories. The Chinese had talked about them, told stories about them, ever since.

Lo Kuan-chung worked at a period when the story-tellers already had begun to gather up individual *hua-pen* to make longer entertainments—entertainments perhaps like our old Saturday morning movie serials. These new, longer entertainments were still divided into discrete and coherent sections and were called *chang-hui,* or "chapter-divided" stories. Lo took such a storyteller's work on the "three kingdoms," deleted some parts of it, added incidents and events from the official histories, and took from the histories actual poems and memoranda by the main characters. His main improvement, from an artistic point of view, was to enliven the characterizations.

A Tale of Three Kingdoms and *A Saga of The Marshes* both devote a lot of time and space to battlefield action. A good part of the military lore of China, in fact, is said to repose in these two novels, and Mao Tse-tung learned much of it because he loved and enjoyed the novels. The master strategist of *A Tale of Three Kingdoms* is Chuko Liang, and the master strategist in *A Saga of the Marshes* is Wu Yung. Wu Yung is an ex-village school-teacher and Chuko Liang is a scholar, not a militarist, by training and background. Both men, in their characters, conform with the idea! described by Confucius in one of his very few disquisitions on warfare:

> Tzu-lu said, "Suppose you had charge of the Three Armies? Whom would you take along to help you?"

Confucius said, "A man who is ready to beard a tiger or to charge a river, indifferent whether he lives or dies—such a man I would not take. I would take somebody who comes up on difficulties with caution and who preferred to succeed by strategy."

But behind the thought of both Chuko Liang and Wu Yung lies Sun Tzu, China's most important military thinker and the author of her greatest military classic, *The Art of War*. The heroes in the novels refer frequently to *The Art of War* and show time and again that they know it well.

Sun Tzu's doctrine can be summarized in five "fundamental factors." Sun Tzu himself discovers and defines these five factors:

1. *Moral influence:* that which brings the people into harmony with their leaders. The commentator Chiang Yu says, "When one treats the people with benevolence, justice, and equity, and places confidence in them, the army will be united in mind and will be happy to serve the leaders."
2. *Weather.*
3. *Terrain.*
4. *Command:* the general's qualities of wisdom, sincerity, humanity, courage, and strictness.
5. *Doctrine:* *i.e.,* organization, control, assignment of appropriate ranks to officers, regulation of supply routes, and the provision of principal items used by the army.

In the pages that follow are two chapters from C.H.

Brewitt-Taylor's translation of *A Tale of Three Kingdoms*.
Note that the novel's hero, Chuko Liang, is also sometimes called by another name, K'ung-ming, in this version.

Chapter 90: *Wild beasts as warriors; K'ung-Ming's
sixth victory; Burning of the Rattan Army;
Seventh capture of the king.*

All the prisoners were released; and Yang Fêng and his sons
were rewarded with ranks, and his men were given presents.
They expressed their gratitude and returned to their own,
while Mênghuo and his hastened home to Silver-pit Ravine.

Outside this ravine were three rivers, the Lu, the Kannan
Shui, or Sweet South Water, and the Hsich'êng Shui, or West
Water. These three streams united to form one river which
was called the Sanchiang, or Three Rivers. Close to the ravine
on the north was a wide and fruitful plain; on the west were
salt wells. The Lu River flowed about two hundred li to the
south-west, and due south was a valley called the Liangtu
Ravine. There were hills in, as well as surrounding, the ravine,
and in these they found silver; whence the name "Silver Pit."

A palace had been built in the ravine, which the Man kings
had made their stronghold, and there was an ancestral temple,
which they called Chia-kuei, or Family Devil, where they
solemnised sacrifices of bulls and horses at the four seasons.
They called these sacrifices "Enquiring of the Demons." Human
sacrifices were offered also, men of Shu or men of their own

people belonging to other villages. Sick persons swallowed no drugs, but prayed to a chief sorcerer, called Drug Demon. There was no legal code, the only punishment for every transgression being death.

When girls are grown and become women they bathe in a stream. Men and women are kept separate, and they marry whom they will, the parents having no control in that particular. They call this *hsüeh-i* (Learning the Trade). In good seasons the country produces grain, but if the harvest fails they make soup out of serpents and eat boiled elephant flesh. All over the country the head of the family of greatest local consideration is termed "Lord of the Ravine," and the next in importance is called a "Notable." A market is held in the city of Sanchiang, or Three Rivers, on the first day of every moon, and another on the fifteenth; goods are brought in and bartered.

In his own ravine Mênghuo gathered his family and clan to the number of a thousand or more and addressed them: "I have been put to shame by the men of Shu many times, and I have sworn to take revenge for the insults. Has anyone any proposal to make?"

Thereupon a certain one replied, saying, "I can produce a man able to defeat Chuko Liang."

The assembly turned to the speaker, who was a brother of Mênghuo's wife. He was the head of eight tribes of barbarians, and was named Tailai. He was a chief.

"Who is the man?" asked Mênghuo.

Chief Tailai replied, "He is Mulu, Prince and Lord of the Pana Ravine. He is a master of witchcraft who can call up the wind and invoke the rain. He rides upon an elephant and is attended by tigers, leopards, wolves, venomous snakes and scorpions. Beside, he has under his hand three legions of superhuman soldiers. He is very bold. O King, write him a letter and send him presents, which I will deliver. If he will consent to lend his aid, what fear have we of Shu?"

Mênghuo was pleased with the scheme and ordered the "State Uncle" to draft a letter. Then he ordered Tossu to defend Sanchiang and make the first line of defence.

K'ung-ming led his men near Sanchiang. Taking a survey of the country, he noted that the city could be reached by a bank on one face, so he sent Wei Yen and Chao Yün to march along the road and attack. But when they reached the rampart they found it well defended by bows and crossbows.

The men of the city were adepts in the use of the bow, and they had one sort which discharged ten arrows at once. Furthermore, the arrows were poisoned, and a wound meant certain death. The two captains saw that they could not succeed, and so retired.

When K'ung-ming heard of the poisoned arrows, he mounted his light chariot and went to see for himself. Having regarded the defences, he returned to his camp and ordered a retirement of ten li. This move delighted the Mans, who congratulated each other on their success in driving off the besiegers, who, as they concluded, had been frightened away. So they gave themselves up to rejoicing and kept no watch. Nor did they even send out scouts.

The army of Shu made a strong camp in their new halting place and closed the gates for defence. For five days they gave no sign. One evening, just at sunset, a slight breeze began to blow. Then K'ung-ming issued an order that every man should provide himself with a coat by the first watch. If any one lacked he would be put to death. None of the captains knew what was in the wind, but the order was obeyed. Next, each man was ordered to fill his coat with earth. This order appeared equally strange, but it was carried out. When all were ready, the men were told to carry the earth to the foot of the city wall, and the first arrivals would be rewarded. So they ran with all speed with the dry earth and reached the wall. Then with the earth they were ordered to make a raised way, and the first man on the wall was promised a reward.

The whole of the ten legions of Shu, and their native allies, having thrown their burdens of earth near the wall, then quickly rushed up the incline, and with one great shout were on the wall. The archers on the wall were seized and dragged down; those who got clear ran away into the city. Tossu was slain in the melee that followed on this attack. The men of Shu moved through the city slaying all they met. Thus was the city captured and with it great booty of jewels, which were made over to the army as a reward for their prowess.

The few soldiers who escaped went away and told the king what had happened. He was much distressed. Before he had recovered they told him that the men of Shu had come over and were encamped at the mouth of his own ravine.

Just as he was in the very depths of distress, a laugh came from behind the screen, and a woman appeared, saying, "Though you are brave, how stupid you are! I am only a woman, but I want to go out and fight."

The woman was his wife, Chujung. Her family had lived long among the Mans, but she was a descendant of the Chujung family. She was expert in the use of the flying sword and never missed her aim.

Mênghuo rose and bowed to her. The woman thereupon mounted a horse and forthwith marched out at the head of many captains, leading five legions of men of the ravines, and set out to drive off the men of Shu.

Just as the host got clear of the ravine it was stopped by a cohort led by Chang I. At once the Mans deployed, and the woman leader armed herself with five swords such as she used. In one hand she held an eighteen-foot signal staff, and she sat a curly-haired, reddish horse.

Chang I was secretly troubled at the sight before him, but he engaged the amazon. After a few passes the lady turned her steed and bolted. Chang I went after her, but a sword came flying through the air directly at him. He tried to fend off with one hand, but it wounded his arm, and he fell to the ground. The Mans gave a loud shout; some of them pounced on the unlucky leader and made him prisoner.

Then Ma Chung, hearing his comrade had been taken, rushed out to rescue, but only to be surrounded. He saw the amazon holding up her staff and made a dash forward, but just then his steed went down under him, and he was also a prisoner.

Both captains were taken into the ravine and led before the king. He gave a banquet in honour of his wife's success, and during the feast the lady bade the victors put the two prisoners to death. They hustled the two captains in and were just going to carry out their orders when Mênghuo checked them.

"No; five times has Chuko Liang set me at liberty. It would be unjust to put these to death. Confine them till we have taken their chief; then we may execute them."

His wife was merry with wine and did not object. So their lives were spared.

The defeated soldiers returned to their camp. K'ung-ming took steps to retrieve the mishap by sending for Ma Tai, Chao Yün and Wei Yen, to each of whom he gave special and private orders.

Next day the Man soldiers reported to the king that Chao Yün was offering a challenge. The amazon forthwith mounted and rode out to battle. She engaged Chao Yün, who soon fled. The lady was too prudent to risk pursuit, and rode home. Then Wei Yen repeated the challenge; he also fled as if defeated. But again the lady declined to pursue. Next day Chao Yün repeated his challenge and ran away as before. The amazon signalled no pursuit. But at this Wei Yen rode up and opened a volley of abuse and obloquy. This proved too much, and she gave the signal to go after him and led the way. Wei Yen increased his pace, and the amazon doubled hers, and she and her followers pressed into a narrow road along a valley. Suddenly behind her was heard a noise, and Wei Yen, turning his head, saw the lady tumble out of her saddle.

She had rushed into an ambush prepared by Ma Tai; her horse had been tripped up by ropes. She was captured, bound and carried off to the Shu camp. Some of her people endeavoured to rescue her, but they were driven off.

K'ung-ming seated himself in his tent to see his prisoner, and the amazon was led up. He bade them remove her bonds, and she was conducted to another tent, where wine was laid before her. Then a message was sent to Mênghuo to say that she would be exchanged for the two captive leaders. The king agreed, and they were set free. As soon as they arrived, the lady was escorted by K'ung-ming himself to the mouth of the ravine, where Mênghuo welcomed her half gladly, half angrily.

Then they told Mênghuo of the coming of the Lord of the Pana Ravine, and he went out to meet him. He rode up on his white elephant, dressed in silks, and with many gold and pearl ornaments. He wore a double sword at his belt, and he was followed by the motley pack of fighting animals that he fed, gambolling and dancing about him.

Mênghuo made him a lowly obeisance and then poured out his tale of woes. Mulu promised to avenge his wrongs and was led off to a banquet which had been prepared.

Next day the deliverer went out to battle, with his pack of wild creatures in his train. Chao Yün and his colleague quickly made their array of footmen and then took their station in front side by side and studied their opponents. The Man banners and weapons were all extraordinary. Most of the men wore no armour and none wore any clothing. Their faces were ugly. They carried four sharp pointed knives in their belts. Signals were not given by drum or trumpet, but by a gong.

King Mulu had two swords in his belt and carried a hand bell.

He urged his white elephant forward and emerged from between his flags.

"We have spent all our life in the army, but we have never
seen the like of that before," said Chao Yün.

As they talked to one another they noticed that the opposing
leader was mumbling something that might be a spell or a curse,
and from time to time he rang his bell. Then suddenly the wind
got up, stones began to roll and sand to fly, and there was a
sound as of a heavy shower of rain. Next a horn rang out, and
thereupon the tigers and the leopards, and the wolves and the
serpents, and all the other wild beasts came down on the wind
snapping and clawing. How could the men stand such a thing
as that? So they retreated, and the Mans came after them
fiercely, chasing their enemies as far as the city.

Chao and Wei mustered their defeated men and went to
their leader to confess their failure. The chief, however, was
neither angry nor dejected.

"The fault is not yours," he said. "Long ago, when I was
still in my forest hut, I knew the Mans possessed certain powers
over beasts, and I provided against this adventure before we
left Shu. You will find a score of small sealed carts in the baggage train. We will use half of them now."

He bade his staff bring forward ten of the red box-carts.
They all wondered what would happen. Then the carts were
opened, and they turned out to be carved and coloured models
of huge wild beasts, with coats of worsted, teeth and claws of
steel; each could accommodate half a score of men. Choosing
a sufficient number of seasoned warriors, he told off ten companies and bade each company stuff the mouths of the beasts
full of inflammables.

Next day the army of Shu marched out to the attack and
were arrayed at the entrance to the ravine. The Man soldiers
went into the ravine and told their lord. Mulu, thinking himself perfectly invincible, did not hesitate, but marched out,

taking Mênghuo with him. K'ung-ming, dressed in the simple robe of a Taoist, went out in his light chariot. In his hand he held a feather fan. Mênghuo, who recognised his enemy, pointed him out to Mulu.

"That is Chuko Liang in that small chariot. If we can only capture him, our task is done."

Then Mulu began to mutter his spells and to ring his bell. As before, the wind got up and blew with violence, and the wild beasts came on.

But at a wave of the simple feather fan, lo! the wind turned and blew the other way. Then from out of the host of Shu there burst the wonderful wild beasts. The real wild beasts of the Mans saw rushing down upon them huge creatures, whose mouths vomited flames and whose nostrils breathed out black smoke. They came along with jingling bells, snapping and clawing, and the real beasts turned tail and fled in among the men of their own side, trampling them down as they sped. K'ung-ming gave the signal for a general onset, and his men rushed forward with beating drums and blaring trumpets. Mulu was killed. Mênghuo's whole clan fled in panic and tore up among the hills out of the way. And thus the Silver Pit Ravine was taken.

Next day, as K'ung-ming was telling off parties to search for and capture the king, it was announced that the brother-in-law of Mênghuo and Chief Tailai, having vainly tried to persuade the king to yield, had made prisoners of him and his wife and all his clan and were bringing them to K'ung-ming.

Hearing this, Chang I and Ma Chung were called and received certain orders, upon which they hid themselves in the wings of the tent with a large body of sturdy warriors. This done, K'ung-ming ordered the keepers to open the gates, and in came Chief Tailai with Mênghuo and his people in custody. As he bowed at the entrance of the hall, K'ung-ming called out, "Let my strong captors appear!" At once out came the hidden men, and every two of them laid hands upon a prisoner and bound him.

"Did you think your paltry ruse would deceive me?" said K'ung-ming. "Here you are a second time captured by your own people and brought before me that you might surrender. I will not hurt you, but I firmly believe this surrender is part of a plot to kill me."

Then he called out to his men to search the prisoners. They did so, and on every man they found a sharp knife.

"Did you not say that if your family were taken prisoners you would yield? How now?" said K'ung-ming.

"We have come of our own will and at the risk of our lives; the credit is not yours. Still I refuse to yield," replied Mênghuo.

"This is the sixth time I have captured you, and yet you are obstinate; what do you expect?"

"If you take me a seventh time, then I will turn to you and never rebel again."

"Well, your stronghold is now destroyed. What have I to fear?" said K'ung-ming.

He ordered the bonds to be loosed, saying, "If you are caught again and lie to me once more I shall certainly not be inclined to let you off."

Mênghuo and his people put their hands over their heads and ran off like rats.

The defeated Mans who had fled were many, and most of them were wounded. They fell in with their king, who restored what order was possible and felt glad that he had still some men left. Then he and the Chief Tailai took counsel together.

"Whither can we go?" said Mênghuo. "Our stronghold is in the hands of the enemy."

Tailai replied, "There is but one country that can overcome these men; that is the Wuko country. It lies seven hundred li to the southeast. The king of that state is named Wut'uku. He is a giant. He does not eat grain, but lives on serpents and venomous beasts. He wears scaly armour, which is impenetrable to swords and arrows. His men wear rattan armour. This rattan grows in gullies, climbing over rocks and walls. The inhabitants cut the rattans and steep them in oil for half a year. Then they are dried in the sun. When dry they are steeped again, and so on many times. Then they are plaited into helmets and armour. Clad in this the men float across rivers, and it does not get wet. No weapon can penetrate it. The soldiers are called the Rattan Army. You may seek aid from this king, and with his help you can take Chuko Liang as easily as a sharp knife cleaves a bamboo.''

Mênghuo went to the Wuko country and saw the king. The people of this country do not live in houses, but dwell in caves. Mênghuo told the story of his woes and obtained a promise of help, for which he expressed great gratitude. Wut'uku called up two decurions named T'uan and Hsini and gave them three legions of the rattan-armoured soldiers and bade them march north-east.

They came to a river called the Peach-flower Water (T'ao-hua Shui), on both banks of which grow many peach trees. Year after year the leaves of these trees fall into the river and render it poisonous to all but the natives. But to the natives it is a stimulant which doubles their vigour. They camped on the bank of this river to await the coming of the army of Shu.

Now K'ung-ming was informed of the journey of Mênghuo and its results, and he knew when the rattan-clad army camped at the ford. He also knew that Mênghuo had collected all the men of his own that he could to help. He at once marched to the ford. Really, the Man soldiers did not seem human; they were so hideous. He questioned the natives, and they told him that the peach leaves were falling and the water of the river was undrinkable. So he retired five li and camped.

Next day the Wuko men crossed the stream, and, with a rolling of drums, Wei Yen went out to meet them. The Wuko men approached bent double. The men of Shu shot at them, but neither arrows nor bolts penetrated their armour; they rolled off harmless. Nor could swords cut or spears enter. The enemy, thus protected and armed with swords and prongs, were too much for the men of Shu, who had to run away. However, they were not pursued. When, on the retreat, they came to Peach-flower Water ford they saw the Mans crossing. Some of them were tired, so they took off their rattan breast-plates, sat upon them and floated to the other side.

When K'ung-ming heard the report of his captain he summoned Lu K'ai and called in some natives. Lu K'ai said he had heard of the Wuko country as perfectly barbarous, the people having no notion of human relations as they were understood in the Central Land. He had heard of this rattan armour and the harmful Peach-flower Waters. He wound up by saying that these people were really untameable and advised retreat.

"No, no," said K'ung-ming merrily; "we have had too much difficulty in getting here to go back so easily. I shall have a counter-plan for these people tomorrow."

Having provided for the defence of his camp and given strict orders to his captains not to go out to fight, K'ung-ming went to reconnoitre. He rode in his light chariot with a few natives as guides. He came to the ford, and from a secluded spot in the mountains on the north bank he looked about him.

The whole country was mountainous and difficult, impassable for any carriage. So he got out and went afoot. Presently, from a hill he saw a long winding valley, like a huge serpent. The sides were very precipitous and bare. However, a road ran through the middle.

"What is the name of the valley?" asked K'ung-ming.

"It is called 'Coiled Serpent Valley,' " said the guides. "At the other end you come into the high road to Sanchiang. The valley was formerly called 'T'alangtien.' "

"The very thing," cried K'ung-ming. "Surely this is providence. I shall score a great success here."

Having seen enough, he retraced his steps, found his chariot and returned to camp. Arrived at the camp, Ma Tai was called and put in charge of the preparations. He was to take the ten black painted carts and get a thousand long bamboo poles. What the carts contained and what was to be done with the contents K'ung-ming told his captain in confidence. Then he was to keep the two ends of the valley. Half a month was allowed to carry out his task, which was to be performed with the most perfect secrecy under pain of severe punishment.

Next Chao Yün was sent to a point on the Sanchiang road; Wei Yen to camp at the ford. If the Mans came over the river he was to abandon the camp and march toward a certain white flag he would see. Further, he was warned that in half a month he would have to acknowledge defeat some fifteen times and abandon seven camps. On no account was he to come to interview K'ung-ming even after fourteen defeats.

Wei Yen went off, not a little hipped at the prospect, but prepared to obey. Next, Chang I was sent to make a stockade at a certain indicated point, and others were given other tasks.

Mênghuo had begun to have a real terror of K'ung-ming, and he warned the king of the Wuko, saying, "This Chuko is exceedingly crafty. Ambush is one of his favourite ruses, so you should warn your soldiers that on no account should they enter a valley where the trees are thick."

"Great King, you speak with reason," said Wut'uku. "I have always heard that the men of the Central State are full of wiles, and I will see that your advice is followed. I will go in front to fight, and you may remain in the rear to give orders."

Presently the scouts told them of the arrival of the men of Shu on the bank of the Peach-flower Water. Wut'uku sent his two captains to cross the river and engage them. The two sides met, but Wei Yen soon left the field. The Mans were afraid to pursue as they dreaded an ambush.

In the meantime, Wei laid out another camp. The Mans crossed the river in greater force. Wei came out to meet them but again fled after a very short fight. This time the Mans pursued, but having lost their hold of the enemy and coming then to the late camp of the men of Shu, which seemed quite safe, they occupied it.

Next day the two captains asked their King Wut'uku to come to the camp, and they reported what had happened. He decided to make a general advance to drive the men of Shu before him. They fled, even casting aside their breastplates and throwing away their arms, they were in such haste to flee. And they went toward a white flag that appeared in the distance. They found a camp already made, which they occupied.

Soon, however, King Wut'uku came near, and as he pressed forward Wei Yen abandoned this camp and fled. When the Mans reached the camp they took up quarters therein.

Soon after they set out to renew the pursuit, but Wei Yen turned back and checked them. This was only a temporary check, for he fled after three encounters, going toward a white flag in the distance.

To avoid wearisome iteration it may be said that this sort of thing continued daily until the men of Shu had been defeated and driven out of the field fifteen times and had abandoned their camp on seven different occasions.

The Mans were now warm in pursuit and pressed on with all their might, the King Wut'uku being in the forefront of the pursuers. But then they came to a thick umbrageous wood; and he halted, for he saw flags moving about behind the sheltering trees.

"Just as you foretold," said Wut'uku to Mênghuo.

"Yes; Chuko Liang is going to be worsted this time. We have beaten off his men now daily for half a month and won fifteen successive victories. His men simply run when they hear the wind. The fact is he has exhausted all his craft and has tried every ruse. Now our task is nearly done.''

Wut'uku was greatly cheered and began to feel contempt for his enemy.

The sixteenth day of the long fight found Wei Yen leading his oft-defeated men once more against the rattan-protected foe. King Wut'uku on his white elephant was well in the forefront. He had on a cap with symbols of the sun and moon and streamers of wolf's beard, a fringed garment studded with gems, which allowed the plates or scales of his cuirass to appear, and his eyes seemed to flash fire. He pointed the finger of scorn at Wei Yen and began to revile him.

Wei whipped up his steed and fled. The Mans pressed after him. Wei made for the Coiled Serpent Valley, for he saw a white flag calling him thither. Wut'uku followed in hot haste, and as he saw only bare hills without a sign of vegetation, he felt quite confident that no ambush was laid.

So he followed into the valley. There he saw some score of black painted carts in the road. The soldiers said to each other that they must be the commissariat wagons of the enemy, abandoned in their hasty flight. This only urged the king to greater speed, and he went on toward the other mouth of the valley, for the men of Shu had disappeared. However, he saw baulks of timber being tumbled down across the track and great boulders rolled down the hill side into the road.

The pursuers cleared away the obstacles. When they had done so and advanced a little they saw certain wheeled vehicles in the road, some large, some small, laden with wood and straw, which was burning. The king was suddenly frightened and ordered a retreat. But he heard much shouting in the rear, and they told him that the wood-laden carts on being broken open had been found to contain gunpowder, and they were all on fire. However, seeing that the valley was barren and devoid of grass and wood, Wut'uku was not in the least alarmed and merely bade his men search for a way round.

Then he saw torches being hurled down the mountain side. These torches rolled till they came to a certain spot, where they ignited the fuses leading to the powder. Then the ground suddenly heaved with the explosion of bombs beneath. The whole valley was soon full of flames, darting and playing in all directions, and wherever they met with rattan armour the rattan caught fire, and thus the whole army, huddled and crowded together burned in the midst of the valley.

K'ung-ming looked on from the heights above and saw the Mans burning. Many of the dead had been mangled and torn by the explosions of the mines. The air was full of suffocating vapour.

K'ung-ming's tears fell fast as he saw the slaughter, and he sighed, saying, "Though I am rendering great service to my country yet I have sacrificed many lives."

Those who were with him were also deeply affected.

King Mênghuo was in his camp awaiting news of success when he saw a crowd of his men come along, and they bowed before him and told him that King Wuko was fighting a great battle and was about to surround Chuko Liang in the Valley of the Coiled Serpent. But he needed help. They said they themselves had had no alternative when they had yielded to Shu, but now they had returned to their allegiance and were come to help him.

So Mênghuo placed himself at the head of his clansmen and those who had just come to him, and lost no time in marching out. He bade them lead him to the spot. But when he reached the valley and saw the destruction, he knew he had been made a victim again. As he made to retire there appeared a body of his enemies on each side, and they began to attack. He was making what stand he could when a great shouting arose. The

Mans were nearly all disguised men of Shu, and they quickly surrounded him and his clansmen to make them prisoners.

Mênghuo galloped clear and got into the hills. Presently he fell upon a small chariot, with a few men about it, and therein sat K'ung-ming, simply dressed and holding a fan.

"What now, rebel Mênghuo?" cried he.

But Mênghuo had galloped away. He was soon stopped by Ma Tai and lay a helpless prisoner bound hand and foot. His wife, Chujung, and the other members of his family were also taken.

K'ung-ming returned to camp and seated himself in the high place in his own tent. He was still sad at the thought of the sacrifice of life, and he said to his officers, "There was no help for it; I had to use that plan. But it has sadly injured my inner virtue and destroyed my self-satisfaction. Guessing that the enemy would suspect an ambush in every thicket, I sent persons to walk about in wooded places with flags. Really there was no ambush. I bade Wei lose battle after battle just to lead the enemy on and harden their hearts. When I saw the Valley of the Coiled Serpent, with its bare sides of smooth rock and the road in its depths, I recognised what could be done and sent Ma Tai to arrange the contents of the black carts, the mines, which I had prepared long ago for this purpose. In every bomb were nine others, and they were buried thirty paces apart. They were connected by fuses laid in hollow bamboos that they might explode in succession, and the force was enormous. Chao Yün prepared those carts laden with straw and rolled down the baulks of timber and boulders that blocked the mouth. Wei Yen led the king on and on till he had enticed him into the valley, when he took up a position to escape. Then the burning began. They say that what is good for water is not much good for fire, and the oil-soaked rattan, excellent as a protection against swords and arrows, was most inflammable, catching

fire at sight. The Mans were so stubborn that the only way was
to use fire, or we should never have scored a victory. But I
much regret that the destruction of the men of Wuko has been
so complete."

The officers praised his ability and flattered his craftiness;
that need not be said.

Then Mênghuo was summoned. He appeared and fell upon
his knees. His limbs were freed from the bonds, and he was
sent into a side tent for refreshment. But the officers told off
to entertain him received certain secret orders.

The chief prisoners were Mênghuo, his wife, brother and
the Chief Tailai. There were many of his clan as well. As they
were eating and drinking a messenger appeared in the door of
the tent and addressed the king, "The Minister is ashamed and
does not wish to see you again, Sir. He has sent me to release
you. You may enlist another army if you can and once more
try a decisive battle. Now you may go."

But instead of going Mênghuo began to weep.

"Seven times a captive and seven times released!" said the
king. "Surely there was never anything like it in the whole
world. I know I am not entirely devoid of a sense of propriety
and rectitude. Does he think that I feel no shame?"

Thereupon he and all his fell upon their knees and crawled
to the tent of the Commander-in-chief and begged pardon,
saying, "O Minister, you are the majesty of Heaven. We men
of the south will offer no more opposition."

"Then you yield?" said K'ung-ming.

"I and my sons and grandsons are deeply affected by your
all-pervading and life-giving mercy. Now how can we not
yield?"

K'ung-ming asked Mênghuo to come up into the tent and be
seated, and he prepared a banquet of felicitation. Also he con-
firmed him in his headship and restored all the places that had

been captured. Everyone was overwhelmed with K'ung-ming's generosity, and they all went away rejoicing.

A poem has praised K'ung-ming's action:—

> He rode in his chariot green,
> In his hand just a feather fan,
> Seven times he released a king
> As part of his conquering plan.
> Having chosen a beautiful spot
> Where the valleys debouch on the plain
> Lest his kindness should e'er be forgot,
> The vanquished erected a fane.

Chang Shih and Fei Wei ventured to remonstrate with K'ung-ming on his policy. They said, "You, O Minister, have led the army this long journey into the wilds and have reduced the Man country, and have brought about the submission of the king; why not appoint officials to share in the administration and hold the land?"

K'ung-ming replied, "There are three difficulties. To leave foreigners implies leaving a guard for them; there is the difficulty of feeding a guard. The Mans have lost many of their relatives. To leave foreigners without a guard will invite a calamity; this is the second difficulty. Among the Mans dethronements and murders are frequent, and there will be enmities and suspicions. Foreigners and they will be mutually distrustful; this is the third difficulty. If I do not leave men I shall not have to send supplies, which makes for peace and freedom from trouble."

They had to agree that the policy was wise.

The kindness of the conqueror was rewarded by the gratitude of these southern people, and they even erected a shrine in his honour, where they sacrificed at the four seasons. They called him their "Gracious Father" and they sent gifts of jewels, cinnabar, lacquer, medicines, ploughing cattle and chargers for the use of the army. And they pledged themselves not to rebel.

When the feastings to the soldiers were finished, the army marched homeward to Shu. Wei Yen was in command of the advanced column. He marched to the Lu waters. But on his arrival the clouds gathered and a gale blew over the face of the waters. Because of the force of the gale the army could not advance. Wei Yen then returned and reported the matter to his chief. K'ung-ming called in Mênghuo to ask what this might mean:

> The Mans beyond the border have yielded now at last,
> The water demons raging mad won't let our men go past.

The next chapter will contain Mênghuo's explanation.

Chapter 95: *Ma Su's wrangling loses Chieht'ing;*
K'ung-Ming's lute repulses Ssuma.

Beside sending Chang Ho as van-leader, Ts'ao Jui appointed two other captains, Hsin P'i and Sun Li, to assist Ts'ao Chen. Each led five legions. Ssuma's army was twenty legions strong. They marched out through the pass and made a camp.

When encamped, the Commander-in-chief summoned the leader of the van to his tent and admonished him, saying, "A characteristic of Chuko Liang is his most diligent carefulness; he is never hasty. If I were in his place I should advance through the Tzuwu Valley to capture Ch'angan and so save much time. It is not that he is unskilful, but he fears lest that plan might miscarry, and he will not sport with risk. Therefore he will certainly come through the Hsieh Valley, taking Meich'êng on the way. That place captured, he will divide his force into two, one part to take Chi Valley. I have sent orders to guard Meich'êng strictly and on no account to let its garrison go out to battle. The captains Sun Li and Hsin P'i are to command the Chi Valley entrance, and should the enemy come they are to make a sudden attack."

"By what road will you advance?" asked Chang.

"I know a road west of Ts'inling valley called Chieht'ing, on which stands the city Liehliuch'êng. These two places are the throat of Hanchung. Chuko Liang will take advantage of the unpreparedness of Ts'ao Chên and will certainly come in by this way. I and you will go to Chieht'ing, whence it is a short distance to Yenp'ing Pass, and when K'ung-ming hears that the road through Chieht'ing is blocked and his supplies cut off, he will know that Shênsi is in danger, and will retire without losing a moment into Hanchung. I shall smite him on the march, and I ought to gain a complete victory. If he should not retire, then I shall block all the smaller roads and so stop his supplies. A month's starvation will kill off the men of Shu, and Chuko will be my prisoner."

Chang Ho took in the scheme and expressed his admiration of the prescience of his chief.

Ssuma continued, "However, it is not to be forgotten that Chuko is quite different from Mêng, and you, as leader of the van, will have to advance with the utmost care. You must impress upon your captains the importance of reconnoitring a long way ahead and only advancing when they are sure there is no ambush. The least remissness will make you the victim of some ruse of the enemy."

Chang Ho, having received his instructions, marched away. Meanwhile a spy had come to K'ung-ming in Ch'ishan with news of the destruction of Mêng Ta and the failure of his conspiracy. Ssuma, having succeeded there, had gone to Ch'angan when he had marched through the pass.

K'ung-ming was distressed. "Mêng's destruction was certain," said he. "Such a scheme could not remain secret. Now Ssuma will try for Chieht'ing and block the one road essential to us."

So Chieht'ing had to be defended, and K'ung-ming asked who would go. Ma Su offered himself instantly. K'ung-ming urged upon him the importance of his task. "The place is small, but of very great importance, for its loss would involve the loss of the whole army. You are deeply read in all the rules of strategy, but the defence of this place is difficult, since it has no wall and no natural defences."

"I have studied the books of war since I was a boy, and I may say I know a little of the art of war," Ma replied. "Why alone is Chieht'ing so difficult to hold?"

"Because Ssuma I is an exceptional man, and also he has a famous second in Chang Ho as leader of the van. I fear you may not be a match for him."

Ma replied, "To say nothing of these two, I would not mind if Ts'ao Jui himself came against me. If I fail, then I beg you to behead my whole family."

"There is no jesting in war," said K'ung-ming.

"I will give a written pledge."

The general agreed, and a written pledge was given and placed on record.

K'ung-ming continued, "I shall give you two legions and a half of veterans and also send an officer of rank to assist you."

Next he summoned Wang P'ing and said to him, "As you are a careful and cautious man I am giving you a very responsible position. You are to hold Chieht'ing with the utmost tenacity. Camp there in the most commanding position so that the enemy cannot steal by. When your arrangements are complete, draw a plan of them and a map of the local topography and let me see it. All my dispositions have been carefully thought out and are not to be changed. If you can hold this successfully it will be of the first service in the capture of Ch'angan. So be very, very careful."

After these two had gone and K'ung-ming had reflected for a long time, it occurred to him that there might be some slip between his two leaders, so he called Kao Hsiang to him and said, "North-east of Chieht'ing is a city named Liehliuch'êng and near it an unfrequented hill path. There you are to camp and make a stockade. I will give you a legion for this task, and if Chieht'ing should be threatened you may go to the rescue."

After Kao Hsiang had left, and as K'ung-ming knew his man was not a match for his opponent Chang Ho, he decided there ought to be additional strength on the west in order to make Chieht'ing safe. So he summoned Wei Yen and bade him lead his troop to the rear of Chieht'ing and camp there.

But Wei Yen thought this rather a slight, and said, "As leader of the van I should go first against the enemy; why am I sent to a place where there is nothing to do?"

"The leadership of the van is really a second-rate task. Now I am sending you to support Chieht'ing and take post on the most dangerous road to Yenp'ing Pass. You are the chief keeper of the throat of Hanchung. It is a very responsible post and not at all an idle one. Do not so regard it and spoil my whole plan. Be particularly careful."

Wei Yen, satisfied now that he was not being slighted, went his way.

K'ung-ming's mind was at rest, and he called up Chao Yün and Têng Chih, to whom he said, "Now that Ssuma I is in command of the army the whole outlook is different. Each of you will lead a force out by Chi Valley and move about so as to mislead the enemy. Whether you meet and engage them or not you will certainly cause them uneasiness. I am going to lead the main army through Hsieh Valley to Meich'êng. If I can capture that, Ch'angan will fall."

For this march Chiang Wei was appointed leader of the van.

When Ma Su and Wang P'ing had reached Chieht'ing and saw what manner of place it was, Ma Su smiled, saying, "Why was the minister so extremely anxious? How would the Wei armies dare to come to such a hilly place as this?"

Wang P'ing replied, "Though they might not dare to come, we should set our camp at this meeting of many roads."

So Wang ordered his men to fell trees and build a strong stockade as for a permanent stay.

But Ma Su had a different idea. "What sort of a place is a road to make a camp in? Here is a hill standing solitary and well wooded. It is a heaven-created point of vantage, and we will camp on it."

"You are wrong, Sir," replied Wang. "If we camp on the road and build a strong wall the enemy cannot possibly get past. If we abandon this for the hill, and the men of Wei come in force, we shall be surrounded, and how then be safe?"

"You look at the thing like a woman," said Ma Su, laughing. "The rules of war say that when one looks down from a superior position one easily overcomes the enemy. If they come I will see to it that not a breastplate ever goes back again."

"I have followed our general in many a campaign, and always he has carefully thought out his orders. Now I have studied this hill carefully, and it is a critical point. If we camp thereon and the enemy cut off our water supply we shall have a mutiny."

"No such thing," said Ma Su. "Sun Wu says that victory lies in desperate positions. If they cut off our water will not our men be desperate and fight to the death? Then every one of them will be worth a hundred. I have studied the books, and the minister has always asked my advice. Why do you presume to oppose me?"

"If you are determined to camp on the hill, then give me part of the force to camp there on the west so that I can support you in case the enemy come."

But Ma Su refused. Just then a lot of the inhabitants of the hills came running along saying that the Wei soldiers had come.

Wang was still bent on going his own way, and so Ma said to him, "Since you will not obey me, I will give you half a legion and you can go and make your own camp, but when I report my success to the minister you shall have no share of the merit."

Wang P'ing marched about ten li from the hill and made his camp. He drew a plan of the place and sent it quickly to K'ung-ming with a report that Ma Su had camped on the hill.

Before Ssuma marched, he sent his younger son to reconnoitre the road and to find out whether Chieht'ing had a garrison. He had returned with the information that there was a garrison.

"Chuko Liang is rather more than human," said his father regretfully when the son gave in his report. "He is too much for me."

"Why are you despondent, father? I think Chieht'ing is not so difficult to take."

"How dare you utter such bold words?"

"Because I have seen. There is no camp on the road, but the enemy are camped on the hill."

This was glad news. "If they are on the hill then Heaven means a victory for me," said his father.

Ssuma changed into another dress, took a small escort and rode out to see for himself. The moon shone brilliantly, and he rode to the hill whereon was the camp and looked all round it, thoroughly reconnoitring the neighborhood. Ma Su saw him, but only laughed.

"If he has any luck he will not try to surround this hill," said Ma.

He issued an order to his captains that in case the enemy came they were to look to the summit for a signal with a red flag, when they should rush down on all sides.

Ssuma I returned to his camp and sent out to enquire who commanded in Chieht'ing. They told him Ma Su, brother of Ma Liang.

"A man of false reputation and very ordinary ability," said Ssuma. "If K'ung-ming uses such as he, he will fail."

Then he asked if there were any other camps near the place, and they told him Wang P'ing was about ten li off. Wherefore Chang Ho was ordered to go and check Wang P'ing.

This done, the hill was surrounded and the road to the water supply was blocked. Lack of water would cause a mutiny, and when that occurred it would be time to attack. Chang Ho marched out and placed himself between Wang P'ing and the hill. Then Ssuma led the main body to attack the hill on all sides.

From the summit of his hill Ma Su could see the banners of his enemy all round, and the country about was full of men. Presently the hemming in was complete, and the men of Shu became dejected. They dared not descend to attack although the red flag signalled for them to move. The captains stood huddled together, no one daring to go first. Ma Su was furious. He cut down two officers, which frightened the others to the point of descending and making one desperate rush. But the men of Wei would not fight with them, and they re-ascended the hill.

Ma Su saw that matters were going ill, so he issued orders to bar the gates and defend till help should come.

When Wang P'ing saw the hill surrounded he started to go to the rescue, but Chang Ho checked him, and after exchanging a half score encounters Wang was compelled to retire whence he had come.

The Wei men kept a close siege. The men in the hill camp,

having no water, were unable to prepare food, and disorder broke out. The shouting was audible at the foot of the hill and went on far into the night. The men on the south face got out of hand, opened the gates and surrendered. The men of Wei went round the hill setting fire to the wood, which led to still greater confusion in the beleaguered garrison. At last Ma Su decided to make a dash for safety toward the west.

Ssuma allowed him to pass, but Chang Ho was sent to pursue and chased him for thirty li. But then there came an unexpected roll of drums. Chang Ho was stopped by Wei Yen while Ma Su got past. Whirling up his sword, Wei Yen dashed toward Chang, who retired within his ranks and fled. Wei followed and drove Chang backward toward Chieht'ing.

The pursuit continued for fifty li, and then Wang found himself in an ambush, Ssuma I on one side and his son on the other. They closed in behind Wei Yen, and he was surrounded. Chang Ho then turned back, and the attack was now on three sides. Wei Yen lost many men, and all his efforts failed to get him clear of the press. Then help appeared in the person of Wang P'ing.

"This is life for me," said Wei Yen as he saw Wang coming up, and the two forces joined in a new attack on the men of Wei. So the men of Wei drew off, while Wei Yen and Wang P'ing made all haste back to their own camps—only to find them in the hands of the enemy.

Shên I and Shên Tan then rushed out and drove Wei and Wang toward Liehliuch'êng. There they were received by Kao Hsiang, who had come out to meet his unfortunate colleagues.

When Kao Hsiang heard their story, he at once proposed a night attack on the Wei camp and the recovery of Chieht'ing. They talked this over on the hillside and arranged their plans, after which they set themselves to wait till it was dark enough to start.

They set out along three roads; and Wei Yen was the first

to reach Chieht'ing. Not a soldier was visible, which looked suspicious. He decided to await the arrival of Kao Hsiang and they both speculated as to the whereabouts of their enemy. They could find no trace, and the third army had not yet come up.

Suddenly a bomb exploded, and a brilliant flash lit up the sky; drums rolled as though the earth was rending, and the enemy appeared. In a trice the armies of Shu found themselves hemmed in. Both leaders pushed here and shoved there, but could find no way out. Then most opportunely from behind a hill rolled out a thunder of drums, and there was Wang P'ing coming to their rescue. Then the three forced their way to Liehliuch'êng. But just as they drew near to the rampart another body of men came up, which, from the writing on their flags, they recognised as Kuo Huai's army.

Now Kuo was here from unworthy motives. He had talked over Ssuma's recall with his colleague Ts'ao Chen, and, fearing lest the recalled general should acquire too great glory, Kuo had set out to anticipate him in the capture of Chieht'ing. Disappointed when he heard of his rival's success there, he had decided to try a similar exploit at Liehliuch'êng. So he had diverted his march thither.

He engaged the three Shu armies at once and slew so many of them that at Wei Yen's suggestion they all left for Yang-p'ing Pass, which might be in danger.

Kuo Huai, pleased with his success, gathered in his army after the victory and said to his officers, "I was disappointed at Chieht'ing, but we have taken this place, and that is merit of high order."

Thereupon he proceeded to the city gates. Just as he arrived, a bomb exploded on the wall, and, looking up, he saw the rampart bedecked with flags. On the largest banner he read the name of the general, Ssuma I. At that moment Ssuma himself lifted a board that hung in front of him and looked over the breast-high rail. He looked down and smiled saying, "How late you are, friend Kuo!"

Kuo was amazed. "He is too much for me," said he. So he resignedly entered the city and went to pay his respects to his successful rival.

Ssuma was gracious, and said, "K'ung-ming must retire now that Chieht'ing is lost. You join forces with Ts'ao Chen and follow up quickly."

Ssuma called to him his van-leader, and said, "Those two thought we should win too great merit, so they tried to get ahead of us here. We are not the only ones who desire to achieve good service and acquire merit, but we had the good fortune to succeed. I thought the enemy would first try to occupy Yang-p'ing Pass, and if I went to take it then Chuko would fall on our rear. It says in the books on war that one should crush a retreating enemy not pursue broken rebels, so you may go along the by-roads and smite those withdrawing down the Chi Valley, while I oppose the Hsieh Valley army. If they flee, do not fight, but just hold them up on the road and capture the baggage train."

Chang marched away with half the force to carry out his part of this plan, while Ssuma gave orders to go to Hsieh Valley by way of Hsich'êng, which, though a small place, was important as a depot of stores for the Shu army, beside commanding the road to the three districts of Nanan, T'ienshui and Anting. If this place could be captured the other three could be re-captured.

Ssuma left Shên Tan and Shên I to guard Liehliuch'êng and marched his army toward the Hsieh Valley.

After K'ung-ming had sent Ma Su to guard Chieht'ing he was undecided what to do next. Then arrived the messenger with the plan prepared by Wang P'ing. K'ung-ming went over to his table and opened the letter. As he read it he smote the table in wrath.

"Ma Su's foolishness has destroyed the army," he cried.

"Why are you so disturbed, O Minister?" asked those near.

"By this plan I see that we have lost command of an important road. The camp has been made on the hill, and if the Wei men come in force our army will be surrounded and their water supply interrupted. In two days the men will be in a state of mutiny, and if Chieht'ing shall be lost how shall we be able to retire?"

Here the *Chang-shih* Yang I said, "I am none too clever I know, but let me go to replace Ma Su."

K'ung-ming explained to him how and where to camp, but before he could start a horseman brought the news of the loss of Chieht'ing and Liehliuch'êng. This made K'ung-ming very sad, and he sighed, saying, "The whole scheme has come to nought, and it is my fault."

He sent for Kuan and Chang, and said, "You two take three companies of good men and go along the road to Wukungshan. If you fall in with the enemy do not fight, but beat drums and raise a hubbub and make them hesitate and be doubtful, so that they may retire. Do not pursue, but when they retire make for Yangp'ing Pass."

He also sent Chang I to put Chienko in order for retreat and issued instructions for making ready to march. Ma Tai and Chiang Wei were told to guard the rear, but they were to go into ambush in the valleys till the army was on the march. Trusty men were sent with the news to T'ienshui, Nanan and Anting that the officers, army and people might go away into Hanchung. He also sent to remove to a place of safety the aged mother of Chiang Wei.

All these arrangements made, K'ung-ming took five companies and set out for Hsich'êng to remove the stores. But messenger after messenger came to say that Ssuma I was advancing rapidly on Hsich'êng with a large army. No leader of rank was left to K'ung-ming; he had only the civil officials and the five companies, and as half this force had started to remove the stores, he had only two and a half companies left.

His officers were all frightened at the news of near approach of the enemy. K'ung-ming himself went up on the rampart to look around. He saw clouds of dust rising into the sky. The Wei armies were nearing Hsich'êng along two roads. Then he ordered all the banners to be removed and concealed, and said if any officer in command of soldiers in the city moved or made any noise he would be instantly put to death. Next he threw open all gates and set a score of soldiers dressed as ordinary people cleaning the streets at each gate. When all these preparations were complete, he donned the simple Taoist dress he affected on occasions and, attended by a couple of lads, sat down on the wall by one of the towers with his lute before him and a stick of incense burning.

Ssuma's scouts came near the city gate and saw all this. They did not enter the city, but went back and reported what they had seen. Ssuma I smiled incredulously. But he halted his army and rode ahead himself. Lo! it was exactly as the scouts had reported; K'ung-ming sat there, his face all smiles. A lad stood on one side of him bearing a sword and on the other a boy with the ordinary symbol of authority, a yak's tail. Just inside the gates a score of persons with their heads down were sweeping as if no one was about.

Ssuma hardly believed his eyes and thought this meant some peculiarly subtle ruse. So he went back to his armies, faced them about and moved toward the hills on the north.

"I am certain there are no soldiers behind this foolery," said his second son. "What do you retire for, father?"

"Chuko is always most careful and runs no risks. Those open gates undoubtedly mean an ambush, and if our men enter the city they will fall victims to his guile. How can you know? No; our course is to retire."

Thus were the two armies turned back from the city, much to the joy of K'ung-ming, who laughed and clapped his hands as he saw them hastening away. The officials gasped with astonishment, and they asked K'ung-ming to explain the phenomenon of a great army marching off at the sight of a single man. So he told them.

"He knows my reputation for carefulness and that I play not with danger. Seeing things as they were made him suspect an ambush, and so he turned away. I do not run risks, but this time there was no help for it. Now he will meet with Kuan and Chang, whom I sent away into the hills to wait for him."

They were still in the grip of fear, but they praised the depth of insight of their chief and his mysterious schemes and unfathomable plans.

"We should simply have run away," said they.

"What could we have done with two companies and a half even if we had run? We should not have gone far before being caught," said K'ung-ming.

> Quite open lay the city to the foe,
> But Chuko's lute of jasper wonders wrought;
> It turned aside the legions' onward march
> For both the leaders guessed the other's thought.

"But if I had been in his place I should not have turned away," said K'ung-ming, smiling and clapping his hands.

He gave orders that the people of the place should follow the army into Hanchung, for Ssuma would assuredly return.

They abandoned Hsich'êng and returned into Hanchung. In

due course the officials and soldiers and people out of the three districts also came in.

It has been said that Ssuma I turned aside from the city. He went to Wukungshan. Presently there came the sounds of an army from behind the hills. The leader turned to his sons, saying, "If we do not retire we shall yet somehow fall victims to this Chuko Liang."

Then appeared a force advancing rapidly, the banners bearing the name of Chang Pao. The men of Wei were seized with sudden panic and ran, flinging off their armour and throwing away their weapons. But before they had fled very far they heard other terrible sounds in the valley and soon saw another force, with banners inscribed "Kuan Hsing." The roar of armed men echoing up and down was terrifying, and as no one could tell how many men there were bearing down on them the panic increased. The Wei army abandoned all the baggage and took to flight. But having orders not to pursue, the two Shu generals let their enemies run in peace, while they gathered up the spoils. Then they returned.

Seeing the valley apparently full of men of Shu, Ssuma dared not leave the main road. He hurried back to Chieht'ing.

At this time Ts'ao Chên, hearing that the army of Shu was retreating, went in pursuit. But at a certain point he encountered a strong force under Ma Tai and Chiang Wei. Valley and hill seemed to swarm with enemies, and Ts'ao became alarmed. Then his van-leader was slain by Ma Tai, and the soldiers were panic-stricken and fled in disorder.

Meanwhile the men of Shu were hastening night and day along the road into Hanchung. Chao Yün and Têng Chi, who had been lying in ambush in Chi Valley, heard that their comrades were retreating. Then said Chao Yün, "The men of Wei will surely come to smite us while we are retreating. Wherefore let me first take up a position in their rear, and then you lead off your men and part of mine, showing my ensigns. I will follow, keeping at the same distance behind you, and thus I shall be able to protect the retreat."

Now Kuo Huai was leading his army through the Chi Valley. He called up his van-leader Su Yung and said to him, "Chao Yün is a warrior whom no one can withstand. You must keep a most careful guard lest you fall into some trap while they are retreating."

Su Yung replied, smiling, "If you will help me, O commander, we shall be able to capture this Chao Yün."

So Su Yung, with three companies, hastened on ahead and entered the valley in the wake of the Shu army. He saw upon a slope in the distance a large red banner bearing the name of Chao Yün. This frightened him, and he retired. But before he had gone far a great uproar arose about him, and a mighty warrior came bounding forth on a swift steed, crying, "Do you recognise Chao Yün?"

Su Yung was terrified. "Whence came you?" he cried. "Is there another Chao Yün here?"

He could make no stand, and soon fell victim to the spear of the veteran. His men scattered, and Chao Yün hurried on after the main body.

But soon another company came in pursuit, this time led by one Wan Chêng. As they came along Chao Yün halted in the middle of the road. By the time Wan had come close the other Shu soldiers had gone about thirty li along the road. However, when Wan drew nearer still and saw who it was standing in his path, he hesitated and finally halted. Presently he turned back and retired altogether, confessing on his return that he had not dared to face the old warrior, who seemed as terrible as ever.

However, Kuo Huai was not content and ordered him to return to the pursuit of the retreating army. This time he had many horsemen with him. Presently they came to a wood, and, as they entered, a loud shout arose in the rear, "Chao Yün is here!"

Terror seized upon the pursuers, and many fell from their horses. The others scattered among the hills. Wan Chêng braced himself for the encounter and went on. Chao shot an arrow which struck the plume on his helmet. Startled, he tumbled into a water-course. Then Chao pointed his spear at him and said, "Be off! I will not kill you. Go and tell your chief to come quickly, if he is coming."

Wan fled for his life, while Chao continued his march as rear-guard, and the retreat into Hanchung steadily continued. There were no other episodes by the way. Ts'ao Chen and Kuo Huai took to themselves all the credit of having recovered the three districts.

Before the cautious Ssuma was ready to pursue the army of Shu it had already reached Hanchung. He took a troop of horses and rode to Hsich'êng and there heard from the few people who had formerly sought refuge in the hills, and now returned, that K'ung-ming really had had no men in the city, with the exception of the two and a half companies, that he had not a single military commander, but only a few civil officers. He also heard that Kuan and Chang had had only a few men whom they led about among the hills making as much noise as they could. Ssuma felt sad at having been tricked. "K'ung-ming is a cleverer man than I am," said he with a sigh of resignation.

He set about restoring order, and presently marched back to Ch'angan. He saw his master Ts'ao Jui, who was pleased with his success and said, "It is by your good service that Shênsi is again mine."

Ssuma replied, "But the army of Shu is in Hanchung undestroyed; wherefore I pray for authority to go against them that you may recover Shu also."

Ts'ao Jui rejoiced and approved, and authorised the raising of an army.

But then one of the courtiers suddenly said, "Your servant can propose a plan by which Shu will be overcome and Wu submit."

> The captains lead their beaten soldiers home,
> The victors plan new deeds for days to come.

Who offered this plan? Succeeding chapters will tell.

(C. H. BREWITT-TAYLOR)

Some Further Readings

Brewitt-Taylor, C. H., trans. *Romance of the Three Kingdoms*, by Lo Kuan-chung. 2 vols. Rutland, Vt., and Tokyo: Charles E. Tuttle Co., 1959.

Hsia Chih-tsing. *The Classical Chinese Novel: A Critical Introduction.* New York: Columbia University Press, 1968. (Also contains material relevant to Chapters 21–23.)

20

A SAGA OF THE MARSHES
(The Bridge-Mountain Gang)

During the Chin (A.D. 1115–1234) Dynasty in the north and the Sung (A.D. 1127–1279) Dynasty in the south, legends were born about Sung Chiang and his bandit gang. From the historical records, we know that such a man and such a gang of outlaws, or rebels, did exist. But Chinese legend-lust altered and embellished the details of the original story, and the storytellers began to put together pieces, anecdotes, and earlier stories to make a "story-cycle." Such cycles were set in various geographical areas, but the most important of these was the "Bridge-Mountain" area which came to be the outlaws' lair. At the turn of the Yuan and Ming dynasties (*ca*. A.D. 1368), the cycles were worked over and transformed for the first time into a novel. Lo Kuan-chung is credited with authorship.

Like those in *A Tale of Three Kingdoms*, the characters in *A Saga of the Marshes* act with unique personalities and speak with individual voices. Chinese readers enjoy trying to identify by style, on the basis of a sentence or two, which of the characters is speaking, and the various characters have become personality types or archetypes in Chinese lore. A Western reader may amuse himself finding similarities between the Bridge Mountain Gang and Robin Hood and his Merry Men. Each legend has had enormous appeal in its own culture, and they must flatter similar human aspirations and ideals.

Chapter 15: *Yang Chi guards the bearers of the gift-treasure. Wu Yung takes the gift-treasure by guile*

IT IS SAID:

As Kung Sun Sheng was in the little corner room talking and as he said to Ch'ao Kai, "This gift to be sent to Peking is an ill-gotten treasure and if we seize it what harm is there?" a man from outside came rushing in, and seizing Kung Sun Sheng he said to him, "How much daring have you? I know all this you have been talking about!"

That man indeed was no other than The Great Intelligence, Wu Yung.

Ch'ao Kai, laughing, said, "Sir, do not play a joke, but pray become acquainted with each other."

The two then had some courteous talk together and Wu Yung said, "The people about the lake for a long time have spread abroad the fame of the Dragon In The Clouds, Kung Sun

Sheng, and they have told your great name. But how could I have thought to meet you this day!"

Ch'ao Kai said, "This honorable gentleman of learned degree is no other than The Great Intelligence and teacher of learning, Wu Yung."

Kung Sun Sheng said, "I have heard the people about the lake and they have all spoken of this teacher of great light and of his famous name. Now we have opportunity to meet here in the village of the lord Ch'ao and this is because the lord Ch'ao is no seeker after money and he is a doer of good works and for this reason the great of all under Heaven come hither to this place."

Ch'ao Kai said, "There are yet a few other friends to be in the plot and so now let us go into a place yet more inner and secret and talk there together."

The three then went inside and there they met Liu T'ang and the three Juans. All said, "Today this meeting is not by chance. We ask our elder brother, the lord Ch'ao, to sit in the highest place in our midst."

Ch'ao Kai said, "This humble one is but a poor host and how do I dare to sit above you?"

Wu Yung said, "Elder Brother, you are older than any of us; let it, therefore, be as I say."

Then Ch'ao Kai could but sit down in the first place; Wu Yung sat in the second place, Kung Sun Sheng sat in the third place, Liu T'ang in the fourth place and Juan The Second in the fifth, Juan The Fifth in the sixth, Juan The Seventh in the seventh. Wine was poured out and the table was once more cleared and rearranged and again wines and meats were set forth. All drank wine and Wu Yung said, "The lord Ch'ao dreamed of the seven stars of the northern constellation. Today we seven men are banded together to carry out a great endeavor. Have we not then fulfilled what was shown forth in the heavens? Now we have but to spit on our hands and seize this piece of good fortune. Day before yesterday we said we would ask Liu T'ang to go and find out by what road they were coming and now it is already evening and therefore let us on the morrow do this."

Kung Sun Sheng said, "But it is no longer necessary to do it. I am but a common Taoist, but I have already heard and I know by what road they come. They are coming on the highway by The Yellow Mud Ridge."

Ch'ao Kai said, "Three miles to the east of that place there is a village called Peaceful Happiness. In it there lives an idle fellow called Rat In The Daylight, Pei Sheng. He also came here to me once in the past, and I gave him some spending money."

Wu Yung said, "The great white light that came from the northern stars—did it not point to this one? Surely we can use him!"

Liu T'ang said, "This place is somewhat far from The Yellow Mud Ridge. Where can we hide nearer?"

Wu Yung said, "Surely in this Pei Sheng's home—there is the place for us to rest. And we must also use Pei Sheng."

Then Ch'ao Kai asked, "Teacher, are we to take the treasure gently by guile or hardly by force?"

Wu Yung laughed and replied, "I have already prepared the trap; we must only see how they come; if with force, then we will use force; if with guile, then we will use guile. I have a plan but I do not know whether or not it is in accord with your wishes. It is like this—it is like this—"

Ch'ao Kai, hearing it, was mightily pleased and stamped his foot, crying out, "Most excellent! Not wrongly have men called you The Great Intelligence. Your plan is better in comparison than that of the ancient Chu Kuo Liang's! Most excellent plan!"

But Wu Yung answered, "Speak no more thus. The old proverb says, 'There are ears in the corners of the wall and are there not people outside the windows?' Only you may know and I.''

Ch'ao Kai then spoke, "Three brothers Juan, I pray you now return to your home and on that day come here and meet us at this village. Teacher Wu, pray you go now and teach your school. Kung Sun Sheng and Liu T'ang, pray live on at my humble village.''

That day they drank wine until night and then each went to the guest hall to sleep and the next day at the fifth watch they arose and prepared and ate their breakfast. Ch'ao Kai chose out thirty ounces of stamped silver and gave it to the three brothers Juan, saying, "Thus poorly do I show forth my heart to you and I beg you will not refuse it.''

But how could the three Juans take it?

At last Wu Yung said, "One must not oppose the wish of a friend.''

And only then would they receive it. They all went outside the village gate and Wu Yung whispered into their ears, "It is like this—like this—when the day comes you must not delay.''

Then they separated and the three Juans went back to the Village Of The Stone Tablet. Ch'ao Kai kept Liu T'ang and Kung Sun Sheng at the village and Wu Yung came continually there to plan further.

It is not necessary to speak in wearisome detail. But let it now be told of Peking's governor Liang who had bought with his own hand ten thousand strings' worth of congratulatory gifts, lacking nothing, and on the appointed day he was to send forth men with it. He then sat a little in the inner halls and there his lady asked, "My lord, when does the gift go forth?''

The governor Liang replied, "The gifts are all completed and by the day after tomorrow they can set forth. There is only one thing now that goes back and forth in my mind unsettled.''

His lady said, "What is this going back and forth unsettled?"

The governor Liang answered, "Last year I spent for nothing ten thousand strings with which I bought gold and gifts to send up to the eastern capital and because I did not have trustworthy bearers half way on the road robbers seized it. And even until today we have not caught them. This year in these before me I do not see one who understands how to manage business and because of this I think back and forth."

His lady pointed out to the terrace and she said, "You are constantly saying, 'That man understands ten parts of everything.' Why do you not appoint him as the chief guard and send him forth? All will then go well."

The governor Liang, looking out on the terrace, saw there the blue-scarred Yang Chi. Now Liang ruminated and he commanded Yang Chi to come and he said, "I truly had forgotten you. If you really will take the birthday gift for me, surely I will raise you up in rank."

Yang Chi clasped his hands, and then he said humbly, "If The Most Gracious commands, how dare I not obey? Only I do not know how to set about it and when I am to start."

The governor Liang said, "Bid the magistrate to send the official carts and from my guards choose forth ten leaders to guard the carts and on each cart place an imperial yellow flag on which is written 'Birthday gifts to be presented to the lord of the eastern capital.' On each cart let there be also a soldier to go with it. In three days you must start forth."

Yang Chi said, "It is not I, humble one, who am unwilling, but indeed we cannot go. Let my lord choose another skillful and careful man to go."

The governor Liang said, "I have the desire to raise you in rank. In the letter which I send to the prime minister I have placed another, recommending you that you may receive an imperial mandate for a position. Why do you refuse and give me talk of other matters? You may not refuse."

Yang Chi said, "Most Gracious One On High, I have heard that last year the gifts were seized by robbers, and even today these robbers have not been captured. This year about the lakes the robbers are more plentiful than ever and from here to the eastern capital there is no water way. One must go by land, by such places as Purple Brightness Mountain, The Mountain Of The Two Dragons, Mountain Of The Peach Blooms, The Umbrella Covered Mountain, The Yellow Mud Ridge, The White Sand Dikes, The Ford Of The Wild Clouds, Red Pine Woods—all these places. All these are hiding places for robbers and even a person with nothing on him does not dare go through. If they knew there were gold and silver and treasures, why should they not come and seize them? It would be to give up my life for nothing. For this reason I cannot go."

The governor Liang said, "If that is so, I will appoint more guards and soldiers to go with you."

But Yang Chi replied, "Most Gracious, if you should appoint ten thousand it would not be enough. These would be gone before they even heard the robbers come."

The governor Liang said, "If it is as you say, then it is not necessary even to send the gift."

Yang Chi again humbly said, "There is one way by which, if you are willing, I will dare to take it."

The governor Liang said, "Since I have put this thing on your person, why should I not be willing to listen to you?"

Yang Chi said, "If indeed it can be as I say, carts are not wanted. Put all the gifts into ten-odd separate loads as though they were merchandise and appoint ten strong soldiers disguised as carriers and only one other to go with me as though we were travelers and we will secretly take the things to the eastern capital. This alone is a good way."

The governor Liang said, "What you have said is true. I will write the letter and will heartily stand guarantor for you in the imperial court."

Yang Chi said, "Deeply do I thank my lord."

On that day Liang commanded Yang Chi on the one hand to tie the goods into burden loads, and on the other hand to choose out soldiers. On the next day he commanded Yang Chi to come and stand in front of the hall to await orders, and Liang came out of the hall and he said, "Yang Chi, when do you start?"

Yang Chi answered respectfully, "I will answer The Most Gracious One. On the morning of tomorrow I shall assuredly set forth. I wait your command."

The governor Liang then said, "My lady has also a load of gifts to give to the ladies in her father's house and this also you are to take. It is feared you will not know for whom each gift is intended and so particularly she has commanded the husband of her nurse, the steward Sie, and two of his guards to accompany you."

Yang Chi then answered, "Most Gracious, I cannot go."

The governor Liang said, "These gifts are all tied up into burden loads. How is it that again you cannot go?"

Yang Chi then said respectfully, "These ten loads of gifts are all on my humble person and these ten soldiers who are with me are all obedient to my will. If I wish to start early, they will start early; if I wish to start late, they will start late; if I bid them stop the night, they will stop the night; if I bid them rest, they will rest; and in everything they will obey my will. If now you command the old steward and his guards to come with us, he is the servant of my lady and is also the husband of a nurse in the old lord's house, and if on the road there arises a situation where he differs with me, how can Yang Chi dare to quarrel with him? If we bungle this important matter, how then can the real trouble be discerned between us?"

The governor Liang said, "This is also easy. I will command the three of them all to listen to your commands."

Yang Chi answered, saying, "If this has been clearly told to them, then I wish to start at once. If in any way the gifts are lost I am willing to take great punishment."

The governor Liang was mightily pleased, and he said, "Nor will I forget to raise you up. Surely you have foresight."

So immediately he called the old steward and the two guards to come out and in the hall he commanded them, saying, "The captain, Yang Chi, is willing to take a paper that is the list of the gifts and protect the eleven loads of gifts and go to the capital and there present it before the old lord. The responsiblity for all is on his person. You three are to go with him. Throughout the whole journey the hour to rise in the morning to start, the hour to stop at night, where to sleep, where to rest—in everything you are to listen to his command. You are forbidden to disobey him. The commands of my lady you can fulfill for yourselves. Be careful and take heed. Start soon and return early. Do not lose anything."

The old steward promised, command by command.

On that same day Yang Chi led them forth. On the next morning at dawn in his quarters he had the loads all put out and the old steward and the guards brought also a small load of treasure. There were in all eleven loads and eleven stout soldiers were called forth and they were all dressed as carriers. Yang Chi wore a big straw hat and wore a long sky-blue cotton robe and he wound about himself a long girdle and on his feet were hempen shoes. A girdle knife hung at his waist, and he carried a sword. The old steward was dressed also as a traveler and the two guards were dressed as retainers. Each person had a sword and each of them took several rattan whips. Liang then gave them the sundry papers and all of them ate themselves full and then said farewell in the hall. The governor Liang saw the carriers take up their burdens and start and Yang Chi and the steward Sie walked behind to watch. Altogether there were fifteen persons who left the palace of Liang and went out of the gate of the northern capital and went on the big road to go toward the eastern capital.

At this time it was just the season of the middle of the fifth moon. The sky was clear and bright but the heat was heavy to bear and it was hard to go. Yang Chi had determined with his whole heart that he would reach his destination in time for the birthday which was the fifteenth of the next month and so he urged them on their way. When they had left the northern capital for five or seven days, without fail he arose each day at dawn to set forth in the coolness and rested in the heat of the noonday sun. After five or seven days the homes of the people became fewer and there were fewer travelers upon the road. And step by step they came into mountains.

Yang Chi now set out about eight o'clock in the morning and marched until four or five in the evening. The burdens of the eleven carriers were heavy and no one's load was lighter than the others. The days were hot and they could not go on and whenever they saw the shade of a tree they fain must go and rest there. Yang Chi was behind them pushing and urging them to go on, and if they stopped he at least cursed them bitterly and at most beat them with the rattan whips to hasten on. The two guards who only carried their own bundles were panting in the rear and complaining that they could not go on. Yang Chi was very angry and he said, "You two are stupid enough! This responsibility is mine. Not only do you not beat these carriers for me to make them go, but you also lag behind me. This road is not a place to play."

The guards then said, "It is not that we two want to walk slowly, but it is so hot we cannot go and for this reason we fall behind. In the days before when we went in the cool of the dawn it was too good and now that we have to hasten in the hottest time of the day it is too evil."

Yang Chi said, "You two who speak thus are simply passing

forth wind. Before when we went it was through good country. Now it is through evil country and we must hasten through it by day. Who would dare to come through in the night?"

The two guards said nothing in their mouths but they thought secretly within themselves, "Is this thing to begin to curse us also?"

Then Yang Chi took up his sword and took up his rattan whip and himself went and urged on the carriers and the two guards sat under the shade of a willow tree and waited until the old steward came. Then the two guards told him, saying, "At his very highest that Yang Chi is nothing but a small captain at the gates of our lord. And look how big he can act!"

The old steward said, "But you know that the lord told us to our faces we must not in any way differ from him and for this reason I have said nothing at all, although these two days I have not been able to endure the sight of him. But now we must bear with him in everything."

The two guards said, "But those words which the lord said were only words of courtesy. You must simply act for yourself."

The old steward again said, "Let us yet be patient with him awhile."

On that day when they had come to the late afternoon they sought for an inn where they might rest and those ten carriers were dripping with sweat as though with rain and their breathing came in gusts, and they said to the old steward, "We have the ill luck to be soldiers. Well we know we are sent forth by an official but on this kind of a day it is as hot as fire and we are bearing a heavy burden as well. These few days we do not travel any more in the cool of morning and whenever he comes near us he beats us with a great whip of rattan. We are all the same flesh and bones from our parents and yet we must suffer like this!"

The old steward said, "You must not bear ill-will but we will struggle on to the eastern capital and there I will reward you."

The soldiers then said, "If we were treated as you would treat us then indeed would we bear no ill-will."

When another night had passed on the next day before the sky had brightened to dawn all arose and wished to take advantage of the coolness. Yang Chi leaped up and shouted out, "Where are you going? Lie down! We will talk later."

All the soldiers said, "You will not go in the early day and we cannot go in the heat of the day and then you beat us."

Then Yang Chi cursed them mightily, and he said, "What do you know of anything?" And he took his rattan to beat them, and the soldiers swallowed their wrath and dared not speak and could only lie down again.

On that day about the fifth watch slowly they heated the stove and cooked the early meal and set forth again and all along the road Yang Chi urged them and beat them and would not let them go into the shade to rest. Those eleven soldier-carriers muttered angrily together. The two guards in the presence of the old steward talked back and forth of the matter of Yang Chi. The old steward heard them and seemed to pay little heed to them, but in his heart he hated Yang Chi.

Let it not be told in tiresome detail. They went on like this for fourteen or fifteen days. Of those fourteen people there was not one who did not hate Yang Chi secretly. That day in the inn about the fifth watch they slowly lit the fire and ate breakfast and set forth. It was exactly the sixth moon and the fourth day and it was not yet at the height of noon. The great red sun was high in the sky and there was not the slightest half dot of a cloud and it was nothing but great heat. The road they went on that day was only a narrow path clinging to cliffs and lonely, without anyone passing. On the north were high and lonely mountains; on the south were ranges of mountains; and Yang Chi watched the eleven soldiers. When they had gone somewhat more than six miles those soldiers thought they would like to go and rest in the shade of the trees and Yang Chi for this beat them with the rattan whip and he shouted, saying, "Go quickly! I told you to rest earlier at the inn!"

All the soldiers seeing what the time of day was by the sky and that on all four sides there was not so much as a half small cloud felt that most certainly they could not bear the heat. Yang Chi hurried the group of them to go in the lonely mountain path. They saw the sun was exactly in the middle of the sky and the rocks were so hot their feet hurt and they could not go.

The soldiers all said, "Thus hot is the day! Is it not enough to burn a man to death?"

But Yang Chi shouted at the soldiers, saying, "Hasten on! Hasten to that upper ridge and pass over it and then we will think of a way."

Even as they were going the first ones had already reached the ridge and all the fifteen leaped upon the ridge and let down their load poles and those eleven men all went into the pine wood and lay prone.

Yang Chi then said, "Ah, bitterness! What sort of a place is this that you must rest here! Quickly rise and hasten on!"

All the soldiers said, "Even though you took a knife and cut us into pieces, yet could we not go on."

Yang Chi took up his rattan whip and beat them about their heads and as soon as he had beaten this one up, that one was prone again. And what could Yang Chi do to prevent it? But he then saw the old steward and the two guards, panting breathlessly, crawl up over the ridge and they sat under the pine trees to pant. Seeing Yang Chi beating the soldiers the old steward said, "Captain, truly it is too hot and we cannot go on. Do not count it to them for a fault."

Yang Chi said, "Steward, you do not understand that this is the pass where the robbers come to and fro to rob. The name of the place is The Yellow Mud Ridge. Even in times of peace in broad daylight they will come out to rob travelers and how much more in these evil unpeaceful times! Who dares to stay his foot here?"

The two guards having heard Yang Chi say this then said, "We have heard you say this several times and you only bring forth these words to frighten people."

The old steward said, "At least let them all rest a little and let the sun pass a little over the zenith before we go on."

Yang Chi said, "You also understand nothing. How can we do this? From here to the bottom of the ridge there are yet two or three miles without anyone's house. What sort of place is this to stop?"

The old steward said, "I will just sit a little and then go. You hasten on in front with the others."

Yang Chi took up his rattan whip and shouted, "He who does not go on will eat twenty blows from this!"

All the soldiers shouted out together, and from among them one spoke out in protest, "Captain, we are carrying loads of over a hundred catties, and of course we cannot compete with you who walk empty handed. You have never considered men as men. Even the governor Liang when he commands us lets us speak a word or two. How little you can feel either pain or discomfort! You can only talk and scold."

Yang Chi cursed, saying, "You beasts anger me to death! I can do no other than to beat you."

And he took up his rattan whip and beat them on their faces. The old steward cried out, saying, "Captain Yang, cease! Hear me speak! When I was steward in the house of the lord in the eastern capital, in the courts of the lords I saw thousands of soldiers and when I spoke to them at any time they all shouted out, 'Aye! Aye!' It is not that my mouth is free of speech, but you are a soldier who was once near death. Our lord pitied you and raised you to be a captain, but as an officer you are no larger than a mustard seed and yet you are as mightily arrogant as this.

I do not need to mention that I am steward in my lord's house, but were I only an old man in a village, yet you ought to listen to my exhorting. But you do nothing but beat them. What way is this to consider them and to treat them?"

Yang Chi said, "Steward, you are a man from the city and you have grown up in lords' houses and how can you know the great dangers and difficulties of the wild roads?"

The old steward said, "Formerly I also have been in Szechuan and Kuangsi, but never have I seen such arrogance as this of yours."

Yang Chi said, "But these are not peaceful times."

The steward said, "You say this talk and you ought to have your mouth dug out and your tongue cut off! How are the times now not peaceful?"

Yang Chi was just about to retort when he saw in the wood opposite the shadowy figure of a man who was there, peeping this way and that.

Yang Chi said, "What did I say? Here is an evil man come already."

And he threw down his rattan and seized his sword and hastened to the wood and he gave a shout and said, "You fellow, how dare you? How dare you look at my goods?"

And he rushed forward to see and he saw in the wood a row of wheelbarrows and six men there stripped stark naked for coolness, one of whom had on his temple a huge scar. He held a sword, and seeing Yang Chi hastening forward, the seven men all yelled out at once, "Ah yah!" and they all leaped up.

Yang Chi shouted, saying, "Who are all of you?"

Those seven men said, "Who are you?"

Yang Chi asked again, saying, "Are you not evil men?"

Those seven men said, "Who are you?"

Yang Chi asked again, saying, "Are you not evil men?"

Those seven men said, "You are asking the wrong ones. We

are small merchants. How can we have any money to give you?"

Yang Chi said, "You small merchants? Then am I a wealthy one?"

Those seven asked, "Who are you, in truth?"

Yang Chi said, "You tell first from whence you come."

Those seven then said, "We are seven brothers and we are from Hao Chou. We are taking dates to the eastern capital and on our way are passing through here and we have heard many say that here at this Yellow Mud Ridge there are ever robbers to attack travelers. We have on one hand been going on, and on one hand saying to each other, 'We seven have only dates and besides this have no treasure and we can go over the ridge.' But when we came on top of the ridge we could not endure the heat and so we all stayed in the wood to rest and wait until the coolness of night to go on. Then we heard there were people coming up the ridge and we were afraid it was evil men and so we sent this brother out to see."

Yang Chi said, "If indeed it is so, then you are also travelers like us. But just now when I saw you peeping out secretly I held you perhaps to be evil men and for this I hastened here to see."

Those seven then answered, "Sir Traveler, pray take a few dates."

Yang Chi said, "It is not necessary."

And he took up his sword and went again to the loads.

The old steward, seated, said, "If there are indeed robbers here then let us go."

Yang Chi said, "I feared they were evil men, but they are only a few date merchants."

The old steward turned his face aside and said to all the others, "If what you said had been true then all these would have been lifeless."

Yang Chi said, "It is not necessary to think of that. If only no trouble comes it is well enough. Rest then, and wait until coolness comes to go on.''

And all the soldiers laughed. Yang Chi struck his sword into the earth and went alone to a tree and sat down to rest.

Before he had rested so long as a man may take to eat half a bowl of rice, he saw a fellow in the far distance carrying on his shoulder pole two buckets, singing as he came up the ridge, and he sang, saying,

> "The sun burns with a fiery hand,
> The rice is scorched on the dry land.
> The farmer's hearts are hot with grief,
> But idle princes must be fanned.''

That fellow singing thus came up the ridge and in the pine wood he put down his bucket loads and sat down in the shade.

The soldiers, seeing him, then asked him, saying, "What is in your buckets?''

That fellow then answered, "It is white wine.''

The soldiers asked, "Where are you carrying it?''

That fellow said, "I am taking it to the villages to sell it.''

The soldiers asked, "How much is it a bucket?''

That fellow said, "Five thousand real cash.''

The soldiers consulted together, saying, "We are hot and we are thirsty. Why should we not buy and drink? It will drive out the heat from our bodies.''

Just as they were there collecting the money Yang Chi saw it and shouted out, "What are you doing now?''

The soldiers said, "Buying a bowl of wine to drink.''

Yang Chi took up his sword and beat them with the handle and cursed them, saying, "You did not wait until I had given consent but in disorder decided you would buy wine to drink. How great daring!''

The soldiers answered, "When we have done nothing he comes again making trouble! We are collecting our own money to buy wine to drink and what has it to do with you? You come again to beat people!"

Yang Chi said, "You country bumpkins, what are you answering me? You eat and drink anything that comes before you and you do not understand the dangers of traveling and how many goodly fellows have been confused with drugged drinks!"

That wine carrier saw Yang Chi and smiled a cold smile and said, "Such a traveler as you knows nothing at all. It is fortunate I did not sell to you to drink since you can speak such cowardly words as these."

Even as they were quarreling under the pine trees they saw in the pine wood opposite those date merchants all taking up their swords and coming out and asking, "What quarrel are you making?"

That wine carrier said, "I am only carrying this wine to take it over the ridge and sell it in the villages and because it is hot I rested here. These all wanted to buy some of me to drink. But I had not yet sold it to them when this traveler said there was some sort of drug in my wine. Would you not say this was a thing to laugh at?"

As he was saying these words those seven travelers said, "P'ei! We thought it was evil men come out. If it is only like this, it is of no matter. We were just wanting some wine to take away our thirst but because of their doubt of you, then sell a bucket to us to drink."

That wine carrier cried, "I will not sell! I will not sell!"

These seven merchants said, "You accursed fellow, you do not understand anything either. We did not accuse you of anything. You take it right and left into the villages to sell and we will give you the same money. Sell some to us, therefore, and what cursed matter is that? If you sell us the wine you have not the trouble of giving alms and yet you have quenched our heat and thirst."

That wine carrier answered, "It would not matter if I sold a bucket to you, but they would say it was evil; and moreover I have no bowl or dipper to dip it out for you."

Those seven men then said, "You remember too easily a slight. Even if they have said a few words, what cursed matter is it? We have half a cocoanut shell here."

And then they saw two of the date merchants come in front of their wheelbarrow and take out two half cocoanut shells, and the others brought a great double handful of dates out. The seven stood beside the bucket and opened the bucket cover and each in turn dipped and drank the wine and then ate dates to cool their mouths of the wine. Before any time had passed the whole bucket of wine was drunk empty and the seven merchants said, "Truly it is we who have not yet asked you what the price is."

That fellow said, "From the first to the last, I have never bargained price. Full five thousand cash a bucket, ten thousand for the load."

The seven merchants said, "If it is five thousand you want, then we will give you five thousand, but allow us one dipperful extra."

That fellow said, "It cannot be allowed. It is a fixed price."

One merchant gave him the money and one went to lift the lid of the bucket and dipped up a dipperful, and lifted it to drink of it. That fellow went to seize it away, and the merchant with the dipperful in his hand went toward the pine wood and that fellow hastened after him. Then he saw a merchant from the other side of the pine wood walk forth, a half cocoanut shell in his hand, and go to the bucket and dip out a cocoanut of wine. That fellow seeing it, darted forward and seized his arm and threw the wine back into the bucket, covered the bucket lid, dropped the cocoanut to the ground, and from his mouth he said, "Such a merchant as you, how unmannerly you are! You with that head and that goodly face to behave in this outrageous way!"

The soldiers opposite, seeing this, began to itch in their hearts and all wanted to drink too, and among them one looked at the old steward and said, "Old Sir, speak a little for us. Those date merchants have bought a bucket from him and drunk it. Let us just as we can buy this other bucket and drink it and moisten our dry throats. Truly we are hot until we are parched. There is no other way. Here on this ridge there is nowhere that we can go to get water. Sir, be generous."

The old steward hearing what had been said, and his own heart was desirous of drinking, came at last to Yang Chi and said, "Those date merchants have already bought a bucket from him and drunk it. Now there is only this one bucket left. Let us then buy it and drink of it and so dispel our heat. On this ridge there is indeed no water to be had." Yang Chi thought to himself, "From afar I saw all these buying his wine and drinking it. From that bucket also I have seen them in my presence drink half a cocoanut shell full. I think it is good wine. I have beaten them for half a day. I will just let them buy some to drink."

So he said aloud, "Since the old steward thus speaks, let them buy and drink and then we must go on." And he rose.

All the soldiers hearing these words collected together the full five thousand cash and came to buy wine to drink.

That wine seller said, "I will sell no more—I will sell no more. This wine is drugged!"

The soldiers all laughed apologetically, "Elder Brother, how is it you return these words to us?"

That fellow said, "I will not sell. Do not keep me."

Then the date merchants exhorted him, saying, "You accursed fellow! That fellow spoke wrongly and you are too revengeful. You even brought us into your talk, but it has nothing to do with these others. Just let them all buy some to drink."

That fellow said, "Why without reason did he suspect me then?"

These date merchants took that wine-selling fellow, pushed him to one side and did nothing else than to lift up the bucket of wine and take it to the soldiers. Those soldiers lifted up the bucket lid but they had nothing wherewith to dip it. And they said to the travelers, "We pray you lend us your cocoanut shell to use."

The merchants said, "We will also give you these few dates to take after your wine."

The soldiers thanked them, saying, "What is this courtesy?"

The merchant said, "Do not think it needful to thank us. We are all travelers alike. What matters these hundred-odd dates?"

The soldiers thanked them and first dipped two cocoanut shells full and told the old steward to drink one and Captain Yang to drink one. But how was Yang Chi willing to drink? The old steward alone first drank and each of the guards drank one shell and all the soldiers then went forward together and in the space of an instant the wine was gone.

Yang Chi seeing that all had drunk and nothing come of it, and although at first he would not drink, yet because the day was indeed very hot and also because he could scarcely endure the dryness of his mouth, took up the shellful and drank half of it and he took a few dates and ate them.

That wine-selling fellow said, "Out of this bucket that merchant seized a shellful and drank it and so you are short some wine and so now I will ask of you five hundred cash less."

All the soldiers then collected money to pay him. That fellow having taken up the money put the empty buckets on his shoulder pole, and as before, singing his song, went down from the ridge.

Then those seven date merchants stood beneath the pine trees and pointed at the fifteen men and said, "Down they go! Down they go!"

They then watched these fifteen men; their heads were heavy and their feet light and each stared speechless at the other, and all fell feebly to the ground. Those seven merchants came out from the woods, and brought out the seven barrows and took the dates and threw them on the ground, and then took these eleven loads of jewels and gold and put all into the barrows, and covered them up and shouted to the prone figures gaily, "Ah, we have troubled you!" and then they went straight down The Yellow Mud Ridge. Yang Chi, half unconscious, muttered, "Ah, bitter, bitter!" But his body was faint and he could not rise. The fifteen men with distended eyes looked at the seven as they took all the gold and jewels away but they could not rise, could not gather strength, could not even speak. Let me ask here, who were these seven date merchants in very truth? They were no other—they were indeed Ch'ao Kai, Wu Yung, Kung Sun Sheng, Liu T'ang and the three Juans—these seven. That fellow who was carrying the wine was indeed the Rat In The Daylight, Pei Sheng. How did they use this drug? When he first carried the buckets up the ridge in both buckets was good wine. The seven first drank a bucket. Liu T'ang lifted the lid of the bucket and again dipped out half a shell to drink, and did it on purpose for the others to see and so fix their hearts like dead hearts as far as doubt was concerned. Then Wu Yung went into the wood and brought out the drug and shook it into the shell and acted as though he would drink and when he put the shell in, the drug was mixed in the wine and he only pretended to dip to drink and Pei Sheng seized his hand and threw it into the bucket. This was their plot. This was all thought out by Wu Yung. Thus was the birthday treasure taken by guile.

Since Yang Chi had drunk but little wine, he came to himself the more quickly. He crawled up but he was unsteady upon his feet. As he looked at the other fourteen, the saliva running from their mouths and not one able to move, Yang Chi was wild with anger and he said, "It would not have mattered if you had taken my birthday treasure, but how can I go back and face the governor Liang? This paper I can never take back."

And so he tore it up. And he said, "From now on you have made me rootless as lightning so that although I have a home I cannot go to it, although I have a country I cannot take refuge there. Whither shall I go? It is better that I find a place to die here on this ridge"—and he gathered up his robes and prepared to leap down from the ridge. Truly is it

Rains of the third moon, and spring flowers droop and die;
Frosts of the winter moon, and willow leaves fall and lie.

Thus did Yang Chi seek his death on The Yellow Mud Ridge. What then of his life? Pray hear it told in the next chapter.

Chapter 16: *The Tattooed Priest alone conquers The Double Dragon Mountain. With The Blue Faced Beast he captures The Temple Of The Precious Pearl*

IT IS SAID:

Since Yang Chi had lost the birthday gift on The Yellow Mud Ridge how could he go back to the city and see the governor Liang? He determined to seek the road to death there on the ridge. But even as he was about to throw himself over a cliff of a sudden he thought of something and stayed his feet. To himself he thought, "My father and my mother gave me my life and they gave me this fine and useful body of mine, which from childhood has learned the eighteen ways of war. I cannot come to such an end as this. If I seek death today it is still not as good as though I waited until the hour when I am seized and then even at that time it may be I can plan escape again."

He went back and looked at those fourteen men and they stared with distended eyes at Yang Chi but there was not one who could crawl up. Yang Chi pointed at them and cursed, saying, "It is all the fault of you who would not listen to me and so this has come about and thus I am entangled in what you have done."

He took up his sword from the root of a tree and thrust his knife in his girdle and he looked on all sides of him but he saw nothing else to be done. Yang Chi heaved a sigh and went straight down the ridge.

Those fourteen men did not wake until mid-morning and one by one they crawled up and they cried bitterness without ceasing.

The old steward said, "All of you would not listen to Captain Yang's good words and today you have as good as killed me."

But the others said, "Sir, today's work is already finished. Let us now take counsel together."

The others said, "This is indeed our fault. The ancients have these words, 'When the fire burns, each person only thinks of brushing it off.' If a wasp is on a person, he tears off his clothes. If Captain Yang were here, we would not indeed be able to face him. But he has gone himself, we do not know where. Let us go back to our lord, the governor Liang, and why not put it all on to Yang Chi? Let us say that all along the way he oppressed us and beat and cursed us all and persecuted us so that we could not move. He was in league with the robbers and gave us the drug to confuse us and tied our hands and feet and took the gold and precious stones all away."

The old steward said, "These words can be spoken. Let us wait until dawn and then let us go first and announce the business at the local magistrate's court and leave the two guards to carry on the search and catch the robbers. I will go with the rest of you and day and night hasten back to the northern capital and tell our own lord, and ask him to put out a proclamation saying that this has happened and arrange for the capture of these robbers about Chi Chou.''

The next day in early dawn the old steward and the others came to the Chi Chou magistrate's courts and of this there is no more to be said.

Let it be told further of Yang Chi. He took up his sword and his heart was heavy beyond words. He left The Yellow Mud Ridge and went toward the south for half the night and went into the wood to rest, and to himself he thought, ''I have now no more traveling money and if I look up, there is not one whom I know and now what is best?''

Little by little the sky grew clear and now he wanted to take advantage of the dawn to go on, and again he went more than six-odd miles and he went on in great hardship and came at last to the door of a wine shop and there he said to himself, ''If I do not have some wine to drink, how can I endure on?''

So he went into that wine shop and sat down on a stool made of mulberry wood and put his sword beside him, and he saw a woman standing by the earthen oven, who said, ''Sir Guest, shall I not light the fire?''

Yang Chi said, ''First bring me two measures of wine to drink and lend me some of your rice for food. If you have meat, prepare some, and in a little while I will pay you for all together.''

Then he saw that woman first call a young man to come and put down the wine. On the one hand she prepared the rice and on the other she fried the meat and brought it all to Yang Chi to eat, and he ate it. Then Yang Chi stood up, took his sword and went out of the wine shop door. That woman said, ''The money for your wine and rice and meat—all has not been given."

Yang Chi said, "Wait until I come back to give it to you. Let me owe for this once."

So saying he went away. But that young man who had poured out the wine hastened out and laid hold on Yang Chi and was struck down with one blow of Yang Chi's fist. The woman set up a great wailing, but Yang Chi paid no attention to anything but his going and then heard behind his back someone hastening on, shouting and saying, "Ha, you, where do you go?"

Yang Chi, turning his head, saw a half-naked man dragging a staff and leaping forward, and Yang Chi said, "And is this not ill luck for me! He is coming to seek me."

And he stood fast and did not go and looked behind him. Then the young man who had poured out the wine, carrying a fork, hastened forward also and he brought with him two or three villagers each carrying poles, hastening on as though they flew thither. Yang Chi said to himself, "I will kill the first fellow and the others will not dare to pursue me."

So he raised his sword and prepared to fight that fellow. That one then brought forward his staff and rushed forward to meet Yang Chi, and the two fought twenty or thirty rounds, but how could this fellow compete with Yang Chi? He could only feint and parry and defend himself, and so dodge with head and foot.

The last come man and all the villagers were about to come to the attack when they saw this fellow suddenly leap out of the ring and cry out, saying, "Let no one move his hand! Ah, you big fellow who wield the sword, tell me what your name is!"

Yang Chi struck his breast and said, "I, I do not change my name when traveling. When I seat myself, I do not change my surname. I am Yang Chi, The Blue Faced Beast."

That fellow said, "Is it now the officer, Yang Chi, of the eastern capital?"

Yang Chi said, "How did you know it was the officer, Yang Chi?"

That fellow threw down his staff and did obeisance and said, "I, although I have eyes, yet I do not recognize the T'ai Mountain."

Yang Chi raised him up and asked, "What good friend are you?"

This fellow said, "Sir, I was formerly of Kai Feng and I was apprenticed to Ling Ch'ung, who was captain of eight hundred thousand men. My surname is Ch'ao and my name Cheng and from the time of my ancestors, generation by generation, we have been pig butchers. Well enough I, humble one, can kill them, and well I can separate the muscle and scrape the bones, and well I can skin the beasts and cleanse their bellies. I am called The Dagger Devil. A rich man in my city gave me five thousand cash and told me to come here to Shantung to do business, but I had not thought that I might lose my capital and not be able to go back to my place. Here I must be a son-in-law and adopted son in a farmer's house. That woman who was beside the oven, she is my woman. This man carrying a fork is my woman's brother. Even now when I was fighting with my lord I saw the skill of your hand that it was like that of my teacher Ling, and for this reason I could not withstand it."

Yang Chi said, "If you are formerly the Instructor Ling's apprentice, your teacher has been injured by the Commander Kao and he has taken to the wilds and he is now a robber in Liang Shan P'o."

Ch'ao Cheng said, "I have heard people also say this, but I do not know if it is true or not. Pray let the official come to my place and rest."

Yang Chi then went back again with Ch'ao Cheng to the wine shop and Ch'ao Cheng asked Yang Chi to sit inside and he told his woman and the wine waiter all to come and make obeisance to Yang Chi. On the one hand they again prepared wines and meats and while they were in the midst of drinking wine, Ch'ao Cheng then asked, saying, "And why did you come hither?"

Yang Chi then told him from the beginning to the end in detail of his having lost the precious rocks and of again now having lost the birthday treasure.

Ch'ao Cheng said, "If indeed it is so, then pray stay in my humble home for a while and we will take counsel together."

Yang Chi replied, "Now truly do I thank you for your great kindness, but I am only afraid the magistrate will pursue me here and I dare not stay."

Ch'ao Cheng asked, "If you speak so, where do you seek to go?"

Yang Chi replied, "I, if I go to Liang Shan P'o, will seek your teacher, Instructor Ling. When I passed through there before I met him on the way down and we measured swords together. Wang Lün, seeing our skill was equal, would have had us both stay in the mountain lair and thus I know your teacher, Ling Ch'ung. Wang Lün would fain have me stay, but I did not wish to take to robbery. Today since I have a criminal's brand on my face, if I go again to him it will seem too mean a thing, and for this reason I have been thinking back and forth without end. Go forward I cannot, nor can I go back."

Ch'ao Cheng said, "Sir, you see aright. This humble one has also heard me say that the heart of Wang Lun is crooked and narrow and cannot allow those in his presence peace. They said that when my teacher went to the lair he received the fullest of his anger. It is not so good as the place not far from us here. That is at Ch'ing Chou, the mountain that is called The Double Dragon Mountain. There is a temple on the mountain called The Temple Of The Precious Pearl. The mountain has always encircled the temple and there is but one road to ascend to it. The priest who controls it has now renounced his vows and allowed his shaven head to grow hair and the other priests have all followed him in this. There are those who say that the four or five thousand people he has gathered together go in all directions to rob. The chief is called The Gold Eyed Tiger, T'eng Lung. If you have the desire to turn to the wilds, why not go there and there you can find peace.''

Yang Chi said, "If there is this place to go, why should I not go there and seize the place and find rest for my body and save my life?"

From that time he lived for a while in Ch'ao Cheng's home and he borrowed some travel money and he took his sword and bade farewell to Ch'ao Cheng and went forth toward The Double Dragon Mountain. When he had traveled for a day, seeing that dusk fell and that he had long seen in the distance a high mountain, Yang Chi said, "I will go into the wood and rest there for a night and tomorrow I will go up the mountain."

He turned into the wood and he started with fright. There he saw a great fat priest, stripped stark naked, and on his back a tattooed pattern, sitting on a root of a pine tree for the coolness. That priest, seeing Yang Chi, grasped from the root his long staff and leaped up and with a great shout, he said, "Ah, you accursed beast, from whence are you?"

Yang Chi, hearing it thought, "Surely this priest is also from Kuangsi. I am from one country with him. I will ask him a question."

Yang Chi called out, saying, "Whither do you come, holy man?"

That priest did not answer but lifted his staff up in his hands and took thought only to bring it down. Yang Chi said, "This bald-head is without any decorum whatever! I will vent my anger on him," and he lifted his sword that was in his hand and came to fight with the priest.

The two there in the wood rushed backward and forward, up and down, and they struggled against each other. And they fought for forty or fifty rounds and it could not be told which was victor and which vanquished. The priest then feigned to make a mistake and purposely leaped outside the circle of battle and cried a shout, "Let us rest awhile!" And the both of them stayed their hands.

Yang Chi secretly thought, "Good, good! From whence has come such a priest as this? Surely he has great skill and the power of his hand is high. I, with all my ability, can but just hold my own with him."

That priest called out, saying, "Ha, you blue-faced fellow, what man are you?"

Yang Chi said, "I am Yang Chi of the court of the governor in the northern capital."

That priest asked, "Did you not sell a sword in the eastern capital? And are you not he who killed that rascal, Liu The Second?"

Yang Chi replied, "Do you not see this gold brand on my face?"

That priest laughed and said, "To think that after all I should meet you here!"

Yang Chi said, "I do not dare to ask who Brother Priest is and how you know I was selling a knife."

That priest said, "I am no other than an officer in the old general's camp in the city of Yien An. I am Captain Lu, and because I let out my fist and killed with three blows the Pig Butcher Cheng, I escaped to The Five Crested Mountain where I shaved my poll, and people seeing that I had patterns tattooed on my back call me The Tattooed Priest, Lu Chi Shen."

Yang Chi laughed and said, "Then you are from my own countryside! Everywhere, on river and lake, I have heard of my Brother Priest's great name and have heard it said that Brother Priest had hung his girdle in the courts of the temple of the prime minister. How is it that you have come here today?"

Lu Chi Shen answered, "It is hard to say it all in a word. In that temple I governed the vegetable gardens and there I met The Leopard Headed, Ling Ch'ung, who was being pursued to his death by Commander Kao. Seeing an injustice I sent him to Ch'ang Chou and thus saved his life, but I never thought that the two escorting guards would come back and tell that Kao Ch'iu, saying that they would have killed Ling Ch'ung in the wild wood but he was saved by Lu Chi Shen of that temple and that that priest then escorted him to Ch'ang Chou so that he might not be injured. These two incestuous scoundrels hate me enough to kill me and they went and told the abbot at the temple not to let me hang my girdle knife there and also sent men to come and catch me, but fortunately there were some rascals who came early and told me of it, and I did not fall into their hands. With a torch I set fire to the houses in the vegetable gardens and escaped to river and lake, and east and west they could not catch me.

"Thus I came to Meng Chou to The Valley Of The Cross Roads and was in mortal danger, for there was a woman in a wine shop who was nearly the death of me. She gave me a drug and confused me. But fortunately her husband came home early and seeing what manner of man I am, and seeing with a great start my staff and my girdle knife, in great haste he gave me an antidote and saved me thus. Then he asked me my name and bade me stay for several days and adopted me as his brother. Of those two, man and wife, the man was also a well-known fellow among the rivers and lakes and all called him Chang Ch'ing, The Gardener. His wife was nicknamed The Female Savage and her maiden surname was Sheng. They were very hospitable and there I lived for four or five days and then I heard that The Temple Of The Precious Pearl on this Double Dragon Mountain could receive me there to rest. I then came especially to join T'eng Lung, but that hateful thing would not allow me to live on his mountain and he and I had mortal combat. He could not stand against me and he barred fast the three gates and there was no other way to go up. That accursed beast paid no heed to me however I might shout and curse, but he would not come down to combat again. He has surely angered me to a mighty bitterness here, and there is no way out of it. But I did not think Elder Brother would come.''

Yang Chi was mightily pleased and the two bowed low to the ground to wish each other well and there they spent the night. Yang Chi told him of the affair of selling his sword and killing Liu The Second and of the loss of the birthday treasure—all in great detail. And he told him that Ch'ao Cheng had directed him to come here and he said, ''If he closed all the gates fast and we stay here how can we get him to come down? Let us go to Ch'ao Cheng's home and discuss it.''

The two, one after the other, left that wood and came to Ch'ao Cheng's wine shop and Yang Chi led Lu Chi Shen to see his face and Ch'ao Cheng in great haste ordered wine for hospitality and they talked of how to attack The Double Dragon Mountain and Ch'ao Cheng said, ''If they have truly barred the gates, even if you had ten thousand horses and men you could not ascend. It cannot be done by force and it must be done by guile.''

Lu Chi Shen said, ''Curses to that accursed beast! When I went first to him, I could only see him outside the gates and because he would not receive me we fought to mortal combat. But I kicked him in the lower belly so that he fell over and I would have taken away his life, but because his men were many who rescued him, they took him up the mountain and closed the accursed gates and they let me stay below and curse but he will not come down to combat.''

Yang Chi asked, ''If it is a good place to go, why do not you and I go together and fight with all our might?''

Lu Chi Shen replied, ''But there is no pass there by which we can ascend, and there is no way to get there.''

Then Ch'ao Cheng said, "I have a guile, but I do not know if you two Honorable Ones will consider it worth while."

And Yang Chi said, "I would like to hear what this good guile is."

So Ch'ao Cheng said to Yang Chi, "You, sir, must not dress like this but wear a garb such as the villagers about here wear. I, humble one, will take from this teacher his knife and his staff, but I will bid my wife's brother to take several companions and lead you to the foot of that mountain and take a rope and bind you, Sir Priest, but bind you with slip knots. We will go to the foot of the mountain and shout, 'We are villagers from a near-by wine shop. This priest came to my shop to drink wine and drank himself mightily drunk and would not pay his money down and he said he would fight the men on Double Dragon Mountain. Hearing this, we took advantage of his drunkenness and brought him bound hither to present to the great lord!' Those things will surely bid us mount the mountain and take us into their lair and when we see T'eng Lung we will pull the knot of your rope and I will give you your staff and you two good fellows may both rush forward. Then where can those things go? When you have killed the head, the lower ones will not dare not to support you. How is this for guile?"

Lu Chi Shen and Yang Chi together said, "Wonderful! Wonderful!"

That night as they all feasted they prepared food for the road and on the next day at dawn they had all eaten themselves full. Lu Chi Shen left his bundle and baggage at Ch'ao Cheng's home and on that day Yang Chi, Lu Chi Shen and Ch'ao Cheng and his wife's brother and five or six villagers went on the road to The Double Dragon Mountain. Just after noon they went to the pine woods and took off their clothes and bound Lu Chi Shen in slip knots and bade two villagers to grasp the rope firmly in their hands. Yang Chi, wearing a wide straw hat and on his body a torn shirt and in his hand his short knife, and Ch'ao Cheng with his staff, and all with sticks and poles surrounding him, all came to the foot of the mountain.

Seeing the gates they looked above them and saw great bows and arrows and lime bottles and great stones, and the robbers were above the gates. Then, seeing the priest brought there bound, they went as though they flew up the mountain. After a while two small heads appeared above the gates and these men asked, saying, "From whence do you come? Why do you come to our lair? Where did you catch this priest to bring him here?"

Ch'ao Cheng answered, saying, "We, humble ones, are villagers from neighboring villages and we opened a little wine shop. This fat priest ever comes to my shop to drink wine and he drank himself mightily drunk and would not pay money for it. And he said he would go on to Liang Shan P'o and call some hundreds and thousands of men to come and fight this Double Dragon Mountain, and that he would lay low even the neighboring villages. And for this I gave him good wine to drink and got him fast drunk and with a rope bound this thing to present him to the great lord to bear witness that we of the small villages give respect to him, hoping that thus we may avert harm later to our villages."

The two small chieftains, hearing these words, were glad to Heaven and joyous to earth, and they replied, "Good—it is done! Pray wait here just a little while."

Then the two small chieftains went up the hill to tell T'eng Lung and they said, "They have brought that fat priest hither!"

T'eng Lung, hearing it, was full of joy, and he bade them to bring the priest bound and guarded and he said, "I will dig out his heart and liver to eat with my wine and so shall I take the hatred out of my belly that he kicked."

The robbers did what he commanded and came and unbarred the gates in the pass and told them to bring the priest. Yang Chi and Ch'ao Cheng, holding Lu Chi Shen by force, brought him to the lair and looking up they saw the three lofty fortresses and felt that it was a very high fierce place. On both sides were the cliffs of the two high mountains encircling them, enwrapping the temple. The crest of the mountain was boldly shaped and there was but one road in the center by which to approach the fortress. The approach to the three fortresses was heaped with thunder wood and cannon, stones and repeating arrows and mighty bows. Around all was a fence of sharp-pointed bamboos, closely set together. When they had passed the drop gates of the three fortresses, then they came to the front of The Temple Of The Precious Pearl and they saw the three gates of the hall. There was a space as smooth as a mirror and around it all was a fence of wooden posts. Below the gates of the temple stood seven or eight robbers. Seeing Lu Chi Shen come bound, all pointed at him with their fingers and cursed him, saying, "You scabby, bald-headed donkey, you have injured our great king, but today you are taken captive! Wait a little and your flesh will be sliced off your bones!"

Lu Chi Shen did not answer. Then they brought him by force into the hall of the chief god. All the gods had been carried out and in the middle was placed an arm-chair spread with a tiger's skin. The robbers held weapons and staves and stood on both sides. In a short time two robbers were seen helping T'eng Lung out and he sat in the arm-chair. Ch'ao Cheng and Yang Chi held Lu Chi Shen very tightly there before the chieftain.

T'eng Lung said, "You scabby-headed donkey, day before yesterday you kicked me over and you injured my belly and the bruise is still swollen upon it today now when you see me!"

Lu Chi Shen opened his eyes fearsomely wide and gave a great shout, "Accursed beast, do not move!"

The two villagers gave a jerk at the slip knot rope and the slip knot burst and the bond was loosed. Lu Chi Shen seized his staff from Ch'ao Cheng's hand, and like a flying cloud, he made his fighting positions. Yang Chi pulled off his hat and whirled the knife he held in his hand. Ch'ao Cheng held up his long staff and all the villagers fell into threatening postures and gathered their strength together to rush forward. T'eng Lung in great haste rose to escape but he was early felled by a blow on his head, for Lu Chi Shen's staff split T'eng Lung's skull in two and even the chair was split to pieces. Four or five of the robbers were already stabbed by Yang Chi. Ch'ao Cheng shouted, saying, "All come here and give obeisance to me! If you do not follow me I will kill every one of you as though I swept refuse away!"

Altogether, in front and behind, there were four or five thousand robbers and several lesser chieftains, all frightened out of their wits, and all came and knelt to Yang Chi and gave obeisance. Swiftly they took out the dead bodies of T'eng Lung and the others and carried them to the back mountain and burned them up. Then after this they took stock of all the goods and stores there and repaired all the fallen houses, and they went and looked behind the temple to see how many rooms there were and first they had a great feast of meats and wine, and Lu Chi Shen and Yang Chi took the position of lords of the lair and poured wine and distributed meats and gave toasts. The robbers then transferred all their allegiance to these while the lesser chieftains controlled affairs. Ch'ao Cheng bade farewell to the two good fellows and led his villagers and went home again. Of this there is no more to be said.

Let it then be further told. The old steward who guarded the treasure of the birthday gift and the several soldier carriers rose early to travel by dawn and they rested at night and they hastened back to the northern capital and came to the governor Liang's palace and they went straight to the entrance of the great hall and there they all fell on their faces to acknowledge their crime.

The governor Liang said, "And did you suffer much hardship on the journey? I have troubled you all greatly." And he asked again where Captain Yang was.

They answered him, saying, "It can scarcely be told. This man is a greatly daring robber, forgetful of all favors. When he had left here about five or seven days and we had reached The Yellow Mud Ridge the weather was mightily hot and we were all resting in the coolness of the pine wood. We never dreamed that Yang Chi had plotted with seven robbers who pretended to be villagers and date merchants. Yang Chi had covenanted with them, and they appeared on one road, pushing seven barrows; on that Yellow Mud Ridge they waited in the pine wood. They had told a fellow to carry a load of wine and to come and rest on the ridge pass. All of us humble ones should not have bought his wine to drink because we were confused by that thing's sleeping drug and then he took ropes and bound us. Yang Chi and the seven robbers then took the entire treasure and our possessions as well and put them all into the barrows and took them away. Now this matter has already been proclaimed by the magistrate of Chi Chou, and we left two guards there to obey the magistrate and assist in seizing the robbers. We lowly ones by day and night returned to tell The Most Gracious One."

The governor Liang, hearing this, was mightily frightened and he cursed Yang Chi, saying, "Accursed thievish soldier! You were but a criminal and exile and I lifted you up to be a man again! How dared you do this inhuman and ungrateful thing? . . . If I take him I will immediately cut him into ten thousand pieces!"

Immediately he called his scribe to record the whole matter and sent men to go by day and night to Chi Chou, and he also wrote a letter home and he sent others to go by day and night to the eastern capital so that the prime minister might know of it.

It will not be told now concerning the ones who went to Chi Chou, but of those who went to the eastern capital to the presence of the old prime minister Ts'ai. They saw him and they presented the letter to him. The old minister, reading it, was mightily frightened and he said, "Such robbers as these surely have a great daring! Last year they robbed the gifts of my son-in-law and to this day they have not been captured and this year they are too without any virtue. How can the matter end here?"

Immediately he commanded two serving men to get a messenger from the court and to go by day and night to Chi Chou to carry a notification and urge the magistrate there as he stood to catch these robbers and tell him he would have an answer immediately.

Let it be told now of the court officials at Chi Chou. They had received the letter from the governor Liang at the northern capital, but every day they could not accomplish what was wanted. Even as the magistrate was in the depths of his melancholy, he saw the gateman announce, "The lord Ts'ai of the eastern capital has sent his officers to come hither and he has important and urgent business to lay before the magistrate here."

The magistrate, hearing this, was in terror and he said, "It must certainly be about the matter of the birthday treasure."

And in haste he went into his great hall and there met the messengers, and he said, "Of this matter I, but a small official, have received a record from the governor Liang and I have already appointed seven robber catchers to follow after the robbers, but they have not yet found them. Day before yesterday another letter was sent to me. I had appointed my captain of soldiers and the head of the robber catchers to finish this affair within a definite time on pain of punishment by beating, but no robbers have been caught. If we see the slightest clue or movement I will myself go to the palace of the great lord to make announcement."

The messenger said, "I, humble one, am a loyal servant of the lord Ts'ai and one on whom he depends, and now having the command of my lord I am especially appointed to come hither and demand every one of these robbers. At the time I left, the lord himself commanded me to come to this palace and live here and wait until the magistrate have caught these seven date sellers and this one wine seller and that escaped captain named Yang Chi. The robbers must be the very ones themselves and not others appearing for them. Only ten days will be given you to capture every one and you are to appoint persons to guard and compel them to go to the eastern capital. If within ten days this work is not done, I fear that most certainly will my lord magistrate be exiled to some distant island of the sea. And I, if I do not accomplish the command, can scarcely return to my own lord for I do not know how it would be with my own life. If my lord magistrate does not believe it, please see this newly come written order of my lord's."

The magistrate after he had seen it was mightily frightened and immediately he ordered out the robber catchers. Then he saw a man calling out salutation and making obeisance, standing before the curtain. The magistrate asked, "Who are you?"

That one humbly said, "I am Ho T'ao, the head of the robber catchers."

The magistrate asked, "On a past day on The Yellow Mud Ridge, that birthday treasure was robbed. Was this the work to which you were appointed?"

Ho T'ao answered, saying, "Let me now answer my lord. I, Ho T'ao since I undertook to lead this work, have been without rest day and night. I have appointed clearly discerning, swift-handed men to go to The Yellow Mud Ridge to catch the robbers, but although I have beaten and upbraided them continually, we have not even found the footsteps of those robbers. It is not indeed that I have put your commands to one side; it is truly that I have not found a way to obey them."

The magistrate shouted, saying, "You speak like a fool! If those at the top are not severe, those below are lax. Since I came out after getting my fourth degree I have risen step by step, but it has all been hard for me. Today the prime minister at the eastern capital has sent his deputy to come here to me and they have brought the minister's own soldiers and they have given only ten days within which we must seize every robber himself and there cannot be one lacking. If this command is not obeyed I will not only lose my official position, but I shall be exiled to a distant island in the sea. You are a leader of the robber police but you do not use your heart and for this you have brought this curse on me. I shall exile you to so evil a place and so distant a one that the wild geese of the air cannot even fly there."

And so saying he called a tattooer and tattooed on the man's face these words, "This man shall be exiled to—," but the name of the place was left empty. And again he said with anger, "Ho T'ao, if you do not catch these robbers this great crime will surely not be forgiven you."

Ho T'ao received this command and left the hall and came to the place of his business and he met many of his underlings and they all went into a secret place to take counsel together. All the underlings stared at each other and their mouths were like that of a wild goose whose jaws are transfixed by a hunter's arrow, or like a fish in whose jaws a hook is caught, and not one spoke a word.

Ho T'ao said, "In ordinary times you get your wage from this office and now there is this hard thing to be done and no one speaks. You ought all to pity me for these letters on my face."

Then they said, "It is thus, Sir Officer. We are men and not trees or grass, and how is it you think we cannot understand? But in truth these date merchants are surely men from a far city and another province, men from some high mountain or some wild desert, who thus robbed the birthday treasure. Now they are happy in their lair, and how can we get at them? Even if we knew them we could only look at them."

Ho T'ao, hearing this, had before been only five parts distracted, but now when he heard this talk he added five more parts of distraction, and he left that secret room and mounted his horse and went home and led the horse back to the stable and tied his horse and in his home he meditated alone, full of unrest. At last his wife asked him. "Husband, why is it that today you have such a mouth and face as these?"

Ho T'ao said, "You do not know, but the magistrate has given me a written order about a group of robbers on The Yellow Mud Ridge who robbed away the birthday treasure the governor Liang sent to his lady's father, the prime minister. There were eleven loads and truly I do not know what sort of men took them away, for since I have received this order, even until today I have not seen them. Today, having gone to ask for an extension of time, I did not think that the prime minister would again send his deputy here and want me to catch this group of robbers immediately. The magistrate asked me for a report and I answered, saying, 'I have not found them nor have I caught them yet.' The magistrate then commanded that on my face should be tattooed these letters, but I do not know what name is to be added in this space that is left and I do not know afterwards how it will be with my life."

The wife then said, "And what is best to do now? This is the very end of all!"

Even in the midst of saying this, Ho T'ao saw his brother, Ho Ch'ing, come in and Ho T'ao said, "What do you come to do? Why do you not go and gamble? Why are you here?"

But Ho T'ao's wife, who was a sly woman, quickly waved

her hand to him to come and said, "Brother-in-law, come to the kitchen. I have something to say to you."

Ho Ch'ing then at once followed his sister-in-law and went into the kitchen and sat down, and his sister-in-law prepared meats and vegetables and heated several cups of wine and invited Ho Ch'ing to eat.

Then Ho Ch'ing said to his sister-in-law, "My brother and you have both played far too many tricks with me. Although I am worthless enough, yet am I your brother, and although you both are so high and mighty, yet am I your close brother, and now can you not invite me to dine and drink in the same room with you?"

His sister-in-law replied, "Brother-in-law, you do not understand. Your brother's heart can scarcely endure to live."

Ho Ch'ing said, "My brother every day gains money and goods and where is it all gone? Although I am his brother, yet I do not come to beg of him and so what has he to endure that he can endure no longer?"

His sister-in-law said, "You do not know. Because of these date merchants on The Yellow Mud Ridge who robbed the birthday treasure that was to be sent to the prime minister in the eastern capital, the magistrate at Chi Chou has today received a command from the prime minister that within ten days he certainly must capture the robbers. If the very robbers themselves cannot be caught, then he will brand my husband and send him to a wild and distant place. Did you not see that your brother is already branded in all except the name of the place? We only do not know to what place he is to go. If in these few days we do not capture them, assuredly bitterness must be eaten and how has he the heart then to drink wine with you? Therefore, although I have still prepared meats and wines for you to drink, he has already been in despair for a long while and you cannot blame him."

Ho Ch'ing said, "I also have heard flying gossip of this, that robbers took away the birthday treasure. Where truly did it happen?"

His sister-in-law said, "I have only heard them mention The Yellow Mud Ridge."

Ho Ch'ing said, "What sort of men took it?"

His sister-in-law said, "Brother-in-law, you are not drunk, are you? Did not I just say it was date merchants who took it?"

Ho Ch'ing gave a great ha-ha of laughter.

"If it was really thus—if they were really the date merchants—then why does he despond? Why does he not send clever and careful persons to catch them?"

His sister-in-law said, "What you say sounds very well, but we have no place to go and catch them."

Ho Ch'ing laughed and said, "Sister-in-law, and why should you be sad? Brother has some wine-drinking, meat-eating friends who are here continually, but the one whom he never heeds is his own brother. Today now that there is trouble and all these others say, 'There is no place to find them'—if my brother but told me even carelessly to come and drink a few cups of wine on the side—even today there would have been a chance to discuss something about these small robbers."

His sister-in-law said, "Brother-in-law, you have a clue!"

Ho Ch'ing laughed and said, "Just wait until my brother gets into extremity and then I'll see if I have a way to save him or not."

Saying this he arose to go, but his sister-in-law urged him to stay and drink a couple more bowls, for this woman, hearing this talk, wondered much at it and hastily she went and told it in detail to her husband. Ho T'ao in great haste told his brother to come into his presence, and then he made a smiling face and said, "Brother, do you really know whither the robbers are gone, and if you do why do you not save me?"

Ho Ch'ing said, "I do not know from whence these robbers

came. I was only joking with my sister-in-law. How can I, a younger brother, save my elder brother?''

Ho T'ao said, ''Good Younger Brother, do not stand aside and see me suffer heat and cold. Only remember the good with which I have treated you in the past and not the evil. Save this life of mine!''

Ho Ch'ing said, ''Elder Brother, do you not have under the control of your hand some two hundred clear-eyed, swift-handed men? Why do these not spend some breath and strength for you? How can such a younger brother as I save you?''

Ho T'ao said, ''Brother, do not speak of them. There is something hidden in your words. Do not let only others be good fellows. Give me a clue of the robbers. Surely I shall reward your kindness—surely will my heart be easier!''

Ho Ch'ing asked, ''What clue is there? I do not know!''

Ho T'ao said, ''Do not tease me—only remember that we are born of one mother!''

Ho Ch'ing answered, ''Do not be in haste. Wait until extremity; then I will bring forth my breath and strength and catch this group of small robbers.''

His sister-in-law then said, ''Brother-in-law, do you only somehow save your brother. Remember the tie of brotherhood! But the command of the prime minister demands these robbers instantly, and the matter is as big as Heaven and yet you speak of small robbers!''

Ho Ch'ing said, ''Sister-in-law, you must know that because of my gambling I have suffered how many times my brother's curses and beatings. I fear my elder brother, and I do not dare to contend and quarrel with him. Usually when he has food and wine he only makes himself happy with other people. But of a sudden it seems even I have a use!''

Ho T'ao, seeing that in his words was some hidden purpose, hastily brought out a ten-ounce piece of silver and put it on the table and he said, "Brother, pray take first this small piece of silver, and afterward when the robbers are captured gold and silver, satin and silk, and all such rewards will I guarantee to give to you myself."

Ho Ch'ing laughed and said, "Brother, you are like a man who in despair pulls at the feet of the god, although before he has not even burned incense. If I take this silver now, it is as though I blackmailed my own brother. Quickly put the silver away and do not bring it out to bribe me. If you do thus, surely I will not say a word. If my elder brother and his wife, the two of you, speak these insulting words to me, I will tell you not to take the silver out to frighten me."

Ho T'ao said, "The silver and gold is a reward from the magistrate and so how can there not be three hundred or five hundred thousand strings of money! Brother, you must not refuse me. I ask you, where are these robbers? There must be some clues."

Ho Ch'ing slapped his thigh and said, "These robbers, I have already got them in my pocket!"

Ho T'ao in great fright said, "Brother, how can you say these robbers are in your pocket?"

Ho Ch'ing said, "Do not ask me how I can say it, Elder Brother. It is enough that they are every one here. Elder Brother, put the silver away and do not bring it forth to bribe me. Only do you be always mindful of our relationship."

Ho Ch'ing without haste and without hurry said all this out, and so from this in Yün Ch'en county there arose a hero mighty to help others. In Liang Shan P'o there gathered together goodly fellows great enough to smite the heavens.

Of whom in truth did Ho Ch'ing speak? Pray hear it told in the next chapter.

(PEARL BUCK)

Some Further Reading

Buck, Pearl, trans. *All Men Are Brothers*. New York: John Day, 1968.
(This is *A Saga of the Marshes*.) The most recent edition of this
translation was published in 1968.

21

THE WAY WEST

A Tale of Three Kingdoms was born in the official histories, and *A Saga of the Marshes* was born in the oral tradition and in popular legend. *The Way West* also has many antecedents in Chinese literature and lore: the most important of these antecedents might be called "church history." It is a historical fact that the Buddhist monk Hsuan-tsang in the seventh century A.D. was sent by the Chinese emperor to India. He was to bring back for China the Buddhist scriptures, so that the nation might be enlightened or even converted. *The Way West* gives the record of his journey to India, and the title comes from that trip.

Men say that earlier writers collected Buddhist legends and stories to make something like the novel *The Way West*. Wu Cheng-en later revised or rewrote it, and he generally is given the credit of authorship.

The Way West, even apart from its connection with Buddhist lore, most resembles the "supernatural stories" which we have read. On his journey the monk survives eighty-one terrifying crises and adventures, most of which involve the malice of monsters and deities living along the way. *The Way West* is written by a man with clear eyes and a clever brush, and the novel contains much satire of national and universal types. But the supernatural element accounts for most of its wide appeal and great popularity.

The monk survives his encounters and adventures— he himself is very simpleminded and trusts just about everybody—because he is guided and aided by three supernatural assistants: Monkey, Pigsy, and Sandy. Of these three, Monkey is by far the most important, and Arthur Waley not unreasonably retitled his translation of *The Way West* as *Monkey*. The first few chapters of the book take up the monkey, explain how he achieved immortality, and tell how he fell into the role of monk's assistant. The monkey's name is Sun Wu-kung, and the selections below recount some of his early career.

Chapter 6

So the great Sage quietly rested, while the hosts of Heaven encompassed him. Meanwhile the Great Compassionate Bodhisattva Kuan-yin had come at the invitation of the Queen of Heaven to attend the great feast. With her she brought her chief disciple, Hui-yen, and on arriving they were astounded to find the banqueting halls in utter desolation and confusion.

The couches were broken or pushed aside, and although there were a good few Immortals, they had not attempted to take their places, but were standing about in noisy groups, protesting and disputing. After saluting the Bodhisattva they told her the whole story of what had occurred. "If there is no banquet and no drinks are going," she said, "You had better all come with me to see the Jade Emperor." On the way they met the Red-legged Immortal and others, who told them that a heavenly army had been sent to arrest the culprit, but had not yet returned. "I should like to see the Emperor," said Kuan-yin. "I must trouble you to announce my arrival." Lao Tzu was with the Emperor, and the Queen of Heaven in attendance behind the throne. "What about the Peach Banquet?" Kuan-yin asked, after the customary greetings had been exchanged. "It has always been such fun, year after year," said the Emperor. "It is terribly disappointing that this year everything has been upset by that terrible ape. I have sent 100,000 soldiers to pen him in, but the whole day has passed without news, and I don't know whether they have been successful!"

"I think you had better go down quickly to the Mountain of Flowers and Fruit," said the Bodhisattva to her disciple, Hui-yen, "and investigate the military situation. If hostilities are actually in progress, you can give a hand. In any case let us know exactly how things stand."

When he arrived, he found a close cordon many soldiers deep, with sentries on watch at every exit. The mountain was completely surrounded, and escape impossible. Day was just breaking when Hui-yen, who was the second son of Vaiśravana and had been called Prince Moksha before his conversion, was shown into his father's tent. "Where do you come from, my son?" asked Vaiśravana. "I have been sent to see how things are going on," he said. "We camped here yesterday," said Vaiśravana, "and I sent the Nine Planets as challengers, but they were unable to stand up against this rogue's magic and

returned discomfited. Then I led an army myself and he marshalled his followers. We were about 100,000 men, and fought
with him till dusk, when he used some magic method of self-
multiplication, and we had to withdraw. On examining our
booty we found we had captured a certain number of tigers,
wolves, leopards and other animals, but not a single monkey.
To-day the fight has not yet begun.''

While they were speaking a messenger rushed in and announced that the Great Sage and all his host of monkeys were
outside, shouting their battle cries. The kings of the Four
Quarters, Vaiśravana and his son Natha had just agreed to go
out and meet him, when Hui-yen said, ''Father, I was sent by
the Bodhisattva to obtain information. But she said that if
hostilities were in progress I was to lend a hand. I confess I
should like to go and have a look at this Great Sage of yours.''
''My son,'' said Vaiśravana, ''you cannot have studied with the
Bodhisattva for so many years without having learnt some form
of magic. Don't forget to put it into practice.''

Dear prince! Girding up his embroidered cloak and brandish-
ing his iron cudgel with both hands, he rushed out to the camp-
gate, crying in a loud voice, ''Which of you is the Great Sage
Equal to Heaven?'' Monkey held up his wishing staff and
answered, ''I am he. Who are you, that you so rashly dare
enquire for me?'' Hui-yen said, ''I am Vaiśravana's second
son, Moksha. Now I am pupil and defender of the Bodhisattva
Kuan-yin, and stand before her throne. My name in religion is
Hui-yen.'' ''What then are you doing here?'' asked Monkey.
''I was sent,'' said he, ''to get news of the battle. And as they
are having so much trouble with you, I have come myself to
arrest you.'' ''How dare you talk so big?'' said Monkey.
''Stand your ground and taste Old Monkey's cudgel.'' Moksha
was not at all afraid, but advanced flourishing his iron cudgel.
Those two stood face to face at the foot of the mountain, out-
side the gate of the camp. It was a grand fight. They closed

fifty or sixty times, till at last Hui-yen's arms and shoulders were aching, he could resist no more and fled from the battlefield. Monkey too withdrew his monkey troops, and bade them rest outside the cave.

Moksha, still gasping and panting, tottered into his father's camp. "It's only too true," he said. "That Great Sage is indeed the most formidable of magicians! I could do nothing with him and have had to come back leaving him in possession of the field." Vaiśravana was very astonished. He saw nothing for it but to write out an appeal for further help. This he entrusted to the demon-king Mahabali and his son Moksha, who at once passed through the cordon and soared to Heaven. "How are you people down below getting on?" asked Kuan-yin. "My father told me," said Hui-yen, "that in the first day's battle they captured a number of tigers, leopards, wolves and other animals, but not a single monkey. Soon after I arrived, the battle began again, and I closed with the Great Sage some fifty or sixty times, but could not get the better of him and was obliged to retire to the camp. My father then sent the demon-king Mahabali and me to ask for help." The Bodhisattva Kuan-yin bowed her head and reflected.

When the Jade Emperor opened Vaiśravana's missive and saw that it contained an appeal for help, he said laughing, "This is preposterous! Am I to believe that a single monkey-spirit is so powerful that a hundred thousand heavenly troops cannot deal with him? Vaiśravana says that he must have help, but I don't know what troops he expects me to send." Before he had finished speaking, Kuan-yin pressed together the palms of her hands and said, "Your Majesty need not worry. I know of a divinity who can certainly catch this monkey." "Whom do you mean?" asked the Emperor. "Your nephew, the magician Erh-lang," she said. "He lives at the mouth of the River of Libations, and there receives the incense that is burnt in the world below. In old days he once overcame six ogres. He has his brothers with him and one thousand plant-headed deities of very great magical powers. Though he would not come if ordered to, he would listen to an appeal. If you send an appeal to him for troops, with his assistance we could effect a capture.''

The demon-king Mahabali was sent as messenger, and in less than half an hour the cloud he rode on reached Erh-lang's temple. He came out with his brothers, and after burning incense, read the appeal. ''Let the heavenly messenger go back,'' he said, ''and announce that I will help to the utmost of my power.''

So he called together his brothers and said, ''The Jade Emperor has just asked us to go to the Mountain of Flowers and Fruit, and receive the submission of a troublesome monkey. Let's be off!'' The brothers were delighted, and they at once marshalled the divinities in their charge. The whole temple set out, falcon on wrist, or leading their dogs, bow in hand, carried by a wild magic wind. In a trice they had crossed the Eastern Ocean and reached the Mountain of Flowers and Fruit.

Having announced their mission they were led through the cordon and shown into the camp. They asked how matters stood. ''I shall certainly have to try a transformation,'' Erh-lang said. ''Keep the cordon closely drawn, but don't worry about what goes on overhead. If I am getting the worst of it, do not come to my assistance; my brothers will look after me. If I conquer him, do not try to bind him, but leave that to my brothers. All I ask is that Vaiśravana should use an imp-reflecting mirror, standing with it half way up the sky. If he tries to run away and hide, watch his reflection in the mirror, so that we don't lose sight of him.'' The heavenly kings then took up their places, and Erh-lang and his brothers went out to give the challenge, telling their fellows to form a circle, keeping their falcons tethered and their dogs on leash. When he reached the door of the cave, Erh-lang found a host of monkeys drawn up in coiling dragon formation. In their midst was a banner with

"The Great Sage Equal to Heaven" inscribed upon it. "How dare the cursed monster call himself equal to Heaven?" snarled Erh-lang. "Don't worry about that," said the brothers, "but go and challenge him at once."

When the small monkeys at the entrance to the camp saw Erh-lang coming, they scuttled inside and made their report. Monkey seized his metal-bound cudgel, donned his golden breastplate, put on his cloud-treading shoes and golden cap and rushed out to the gate, glaring about him. "What little captain are you and where do you hail from," shouted Monkey, "that you dare come here and challenge me to battle?" "Have you eyes with no eyeballs, that you fail to know me?" shouted Erh-lang. "I am the Jade Emperor's nephew. I have come now by his Majesty's command to arrest you, rebellious groom-ape that you are! Your hour has come!" "I remember," said Monkey, "that some years ago the emperor's sister fell in love with a mortal of the world below, became his consort and had a son by him, who is said to have split the Peach Mountain with his axe. Are you he? I am half minded to give you a bit of my mind, but you are not worth it. I should be sorry to strike you, for one blow of mine would be the end of you. Go back where you came from, little fellow, and tell the four kings of Heaven to come instead." Erh-lang was furious. "Keep a civil tongue in your head," he cried, "and taste my blade." Monkey dodged aside and swiftly raising his cudgel struck in his turn. They closed over three hundred times without reaching a decision. Erh-lang exerted all his magic power, shook himself hard and changed into a giant figure a hundred thousand feet high. His two arms, each holding aloft a magic trident, were like the peaks that crown Mount Hua, his face was blue and his teeth stuck far out, the hair on his head was scarlet and his expression malignant beyond words. This terrible apparition advanced upon Monkey, aiming a blow straight down upon his head. But Monkey, also using his magic powers, changed himself into an exact counterpart of Erh-lang, save that he held above him a single gigantic cudgel, like the solitary pillar that towers above Mount K'un-lun, and with this he fended off Erh-lang's blow. But Monkey's generals were completely discomfited by the giant apparition, and their hands began to tremble so much that they could not wave their banners. His other officers were in panic and could not use their swords. At a word from the brothers the plant-headed divinities rushed in, letting loose their falcons and dogs, and bow in hand all charged into the fray. Alas, Monkey's four generals fled and two or three thousand of the creatures they commanded were captured. The monkeys threw down their weapons and rushed screaming, some up the mountain, some into the cave. It was just as when a cat at night disturbs roosting birds and their panic fills the starry sky.

When Monkey saw his followers scatter, his heart fluttered, he abandoned his giant form and fled as fast as his feet could carry him. Erh-lang strode after him with huge steps, crying, "Where are you off to? Come back this minute, and I will spare your life." But Monkey fled faster than ever to his cave, where he ran straight into the brothers. "Wretched monkey, where are you running to?" they cried. Monkey, trembling in every limb, hastily turned his cudgel into an embroidery needle, and hiding it about his person, changed himself into a fish, and slipped into the stream. Rushing down to the bank, Erh-lang could see nothing of him. "This simian," he said, "has certainly changed himself into a fish and hidden under the water. I must change myself too if I am to catch him." So he changed himself into a cormorant and skimmed hither and thither over the stream. Monkey, looking up out of the water, suddenly saw a bird hovering above. It was like a blue kite, but its plumage was not blue. It was like a heron, but had no tuft on its head. It was like a crane, but its feet were not red. "I'll be bound that's Erh-lang looking for me. . . ." He released a few bubbles and swam swiftly away. "That fish letting bubbles," said Erh-lang to himself, "is like a carp, but its tail is not red; it is like a tench, but there are no patterns on its scales. It is like a black-fish, but there are no stars on its head; it is like a bream, but there are no bristles on its gills. Why did it make off like that when it saw me? I'll be bound it's Monkey, who has changed himself into a fish." And swooping down, he opened his beak and snapped at him. Monkey whisked out of the water, and changed himself into a freckled bustard, standing all alone on the bank. Seeing that he had reached the lowest possible stage in transformation, for the freckled bustard is the lowest and most promiscuous of creatures, mating at hazard with any bird that comes its way, Erh-lang did not deign to close with him, but returned to his true form, and fetching his sling, shot a pellet that sent Monkey rolling. Taking advantage of his opportunity, Monkey rolled and rolled down the mountain side, and when he was out of sight he changed himself into a wayside shrine; his mouth wide open was the door-opening, his teeth he turned into door flaps, his tongue into the guardian Bodhisattva. His two eyes were the two round windows; he didn't quite know what to do with his tail, but sticking up straight behind it looked like a flag-pole. When Erh-lang arrived at the bottom of the slope, he expected to find the bustard that he had toppled over, but instead he only found a small shrine. Examining it closely he noticed the "flag-pole" sticking up behind and laughed, saying, "That's Monkey, that is! He's trying his tricks on me again. I have seen many shrines, but never one with a flag-pole sticking up behind. No doubt about it, this animal is playing one of his games. He hopes to lure me up close to him, and then he will bite me. He won't get me that way. I'll clench my fist and bang in the windows first. Afterwards I'll kick down the doors." When Monkey heard this he was horrified. "That's a bit too much," he said to himself. "The doors are my teeth and the windows are my eyes. If he kicks my teeth and bangs my eyes, that won't be nice." So saying, he made a tiger-spring and disappeared into the sky. Erh-lang was just getting tired of the vain pursuit, when his brothers arrived. "Well, have you caught the Great Sage?" they asked. "He has just been trying to dodge me," said Erh-lang, "by turning into a shrine. I was just going to hit his windows and kick down his doors, when he suddenly disappeared. It's a queer business." They all began peering helplessly about in every direction, but could find nothing. "You stay here and keep a look out," said Erh-lang, "while I go up and search for him." He mounted the clouds, and half way up the sky came across Vaiśravana, who was holding the magic mirror, his son at his side. "Have you seen the Monkey King?" he asked. "He has not been up here," said Vaiśravana. "I can see him in my mirror, you know." When Erh-lang had told him about the capture of the lesser monkeys and the Great Sage's repeated transformations, he added, "Then he changed into a shrine, and when I hit at him he suddenly disappeared." Vaiśravana looked in his mirror and burst out laughing. "Make haste, Erh-lang, make haste," he cried. "That monkey has made himself invisible, decamped and made straight for your River of Libations." When Erh-lang heard this he picked up his magic lance and fled towards the River of Libations as fast as he could.

Now as soon as Monkey reached the river, he changed himself into the exact image of Erh-lang and went straight into Erh-lang's shrine. The guardian demons of the shrine could not tell the difference and bowed low as he came in. He examined the incense-smoke, and was looking at the votive paintings round the walls, when someone came and announced "Another Erh-lang has arrived." The guarding deities rushed out, and could hardly believe their eyes. "Has a creature calling himself the Great Sage Equal to Heaven been here?" the real Erh-lang asked. "We've seen nothing of any Great Sage," they said, "but there's another holy Erh-lang inside, examining the incense-smoke."

He rushed in, and as soon as Monkey saw him he changed into his true form and said, "Erh-lang, I don't mind telling you the surname of that shrine was Sun."

Erh-lang raised his three-pronged, two-bladed magic lance and struck at Monkey's cheek. Monkey dodged, and the two of them, cursing and fighting, edged towards the shrine-gate and out into the mists and clouds, struggling as they went, till at last Monkey was driven to the Mountain of Flowers and Fruit, where the kings of the Four Quarters were keeping strait guard. The brothers came to meet Erh-lang and surrounded Monkey, pressing about him on every side.

Meanwhile, in Heaven everyone was wondering why a whole day had passed without any news from Erh-lang. "Would your Majesty," asked Kuan-yin, "permit me and the Patriarch of Tao to go down in person and see how things are going on?" "Not a bad idea," said the Jade Emperor, and in the end he and the Queen of Heaven as well as Kuan-yin and Lao Tzu all went to the Southern Gate of Heaven and looked out. They saw the great cordon of heavenly troops, and Vaiśravana standing half way up the sky, holding a mirror, while Erh-lang and his brothers pressed round Monkey, tussling fiercely with him. "That Erh-lang, whom I proposed, hasn't done so badly," said Kuan-yin. "He has hemmed the Great Sage in, though he has not yet taken him prisoner. With a little help, I think he could manage it." "What weapon do you propose to use, how are you going to help him?" asked Lao Tzu. "I shall throw my vase and willow spray down on to his head," said Kuan-yin. "That won't kill him; but it will make him lose his balance, and Erh-lang will easily be able to catch him." "Your vase," said Lao Tzu, "is made of porcelain. If it fell in just the right place, it might be all right. But if it misses his head and falls on his iron cudgel, it will get broken. You had better leave him to me." "Have you got a weapon?" asked Kuan-yin. "I certainly have," said Lao

Tzu, and he produced from his sleeve a magic snare. "This," said he, "is called the Diamond Snare. In old days, when I left China, converted the barbarians of the West and became a god, I owed my success entirely to this snare. It comes in handy for keeping off all manner of dangers. Let me throw it down on to him." Standing at the gate of Heaven, he cast his snare, and it went rippling down straight on to Monkey's head. Monkey was busy warring with Erh-lang and his brothers, and did not notice that a weapon was falling upon him out of the sky. It hit him just on the crown of the head, and toppled him over. He scrambled to his feet and fled, pursued by Erh-lang's dogs, who went for his calves, so that he stumbled again. Lying on the ground, he cursed, saying, "That has done for me! Why can't you go and trip up your own master, instead of coming and biting Old Monkey's legs?" He twisted and turned, but could not rise, for the brothers were holding him down. Soon they had bound him tightly with ropes, and severed his lute-bone with a knife, so that he could not transform himself.

Lao Tzu drew in his snare, and begged the Emperor, Kuan-yin, the Queen of Heaven and all the Immortals to go back to the palace. On earth below the kings of the Four Quarters and Vaiśravana, and all the heavenly host sheathed their swords and plucked up their palisades. Then they came up to Erh-lang and congratulated him, saying, "We owe this victory to you." "Not at all," said Erh-lang. "It was entirely due to the Founder of Tao and the gallant performances of the heavenly contingent. I can claim no credit at all." "Elder brother," said the brothers of Erh-lang, "you have said enough. What we must do now is to hoist this fellow up to Heaven and get a ruling from the Jade Emperor as to how he is to be disposed of." "Brothers," said Erh-lang, "you are not on the roll of Immortals, and cannot appear before the Emperor. Heavenly troops must be told to carry him up, and Vaiśravana and I will go up and report. The rest of you had better search the mountain, and when you can report that all is clear, come to the River of Libations and let me know. Meanwhile I will claim the reward due for my services, and then come back to make merry with you." The brothers bowed their assent. Erh-lang mounted the clouds, chanting songs of victory, and made his way to Heaven. Here he sent in a message, saying, "The Great Sage has been captured by the hosts of Heaven, and I have come to receive your instructions." The Jade Emperor accordingly told the demon-king Mahabali and a contingent of heavenly troops to hoist Monkey up and bring him to the executioner's block, where he was to be cut into small pieces.

If you do not know what now became of this Monkey King, listen to what is told in the next chapter.

Chapter 7

Monkey was brought to the place of execution, where heavenly soldiers bound him to a pillar and began to hew him with axes, stab him with spears, slash him with swords. But all this had no effect whatever, and presently the Southern Polestar sent for the spirits of the Fire Stars to come and set him alight; but they were quite unable to burn him. The thunder spirits hurled thunderbolts at him; but this had even less effect. "I don't know where the Great Sage got this trick of inviolability," said Mahabali to the Jade Emperor. "Neither weapons nor thunderbolts have the least effect on him. What are we to do?" "Yes, indeed," said the Jade Emperor, "with a fellow like that, what line can one take?" "It's not surprising," said Lao Tzu. "After all, he ate the peaches of Immortality, drank the wine of Heaven and stole the Elixir of Long Life; five bowls full, some raw, some cooked, are all inside him. No doubt he has worked on them with Samadhi fire and fused them into a solid, that makes his whole body harder than diamond, so that he is very difficult to damage. The best thing would be to bring him to me. I'll put him in my Crucible of the Eight Trigrams and smelt him with alchemic fire. In a little while he will be reduced to ashes, and I shall recover my elixir, which will be left at the bottom of the crucible." So Monkey was handed over to Lao Tzu, and Erh-lang was rewarded with a hundred golden flowers, a hundred jars of heavenly wine, a hundred grains of elixir, along with a great store of jewels, pearls, brocades and embroideries, which he was asked to share with his brothers. He thanked the Emperor, and went back to the River of Libations.

When Lao Tzu got back to the Tushita Palace, he untied Monkey's ropes, removed the blade that was stuck through his lute-bone, pushed him into the crucible, and told his servant to blow up a good fire. Now this crucible was in eight parts, each representing one of the eight trigrams. Monkey wriggled into the part corresponding to the trigram *sun*. Now *sun* is wind, and wind blows out fire; but wind raises smoke, and Monkey's eyes smarted and became red; a condition from which he never recovered, which is why he is sometimes called Fiery Eyes. Time passed, and at last the forty-ninth day came, and Lao Tzu's alchemical processes were complete. When he came to the crucible to take off the lid, Monkey was rubbing his eyes with both hands, so hard that the tears fell. When he heard the lid being moved, he looked quickly up, and the light that came in hurt him so much that he could not bear it and jumped straight out of the crucible, uttering a piercing cry and kicking over the crucible as he jumped. He rushed out of the room pursued by Lao Tzu's servants, all of whom he tripped up, and when Lao Tzu clutched at him, he gave him such a push that he went head over heels. Then he took his cudgel from behind his ear and, armed once more, ran amok in Heaven, frightening the Nine Planets so much that they locked themselves in, and the kings of the Four Quarters vanished from the scene. This time Monkey hit out recklessly, not caring whom he struck or what he smashed. No one could stop him, and he would have broken up the Hall of Magic Mists, had not the divinity Wang Ling-kuan rushed forward with his great metal lash. "Halt, cursed Monkey!" he cried. "See who stands before you, and cease your mad pranks!" Monkey did not deign to parley with him, but raised his cudgel and struck. Ling-kuan faced him with his whip aloft. It was a great fight that the two of them had, in front of the Hall of Magic Mists, but neither gained the advantage. At last the thirty-six thunder deities came to Ling-kuan's aid, and Monkey found himself beset on every side by swords, lances, spears, whips, axes, hooks, sickles. He thought it time to transform himself, and took on a form with three heads and six arms, and wielded six magic cudgels which he whirled like a spinning-wheel, dancing in their midst. The thunder deities dared not approach him.

The noise of the combat reached the Jade Emperor who in great consternation sent two messengers to the Western Region to see if Buddha could not come and help. When they had recounted Monkey's misdeeds and explained their mission, Buddha said to the Bodhisattvas who surrounded him, "You stay quietly here in the Hall of Law, and don't relax your yoga postures. I've got to go and deal with this creature who is making trouble at the Taoist court." But he called on his disciples Ananda and Kaśyapa to follow him. Arriving in Heaven, they heard a fearful din and found Monkey beset by the thirty-six deities. Buddha ordered the deities to lower arms and go back to their camp, and called Monkey to him. Monkey changed into his true form and shouted angrily, "What bonze are you that you ask for me in the middle of a battle?" "I am the Buddha of the Western Paradise. I have heard of the trouble you have been giving in Heaven. Where do you come from, and how long ago did you get your Illumination, that you should dare behave like this?"

Born of sky and earth, Immortal magically fused,
From the Mountain of Flowers and Fruit an old monkey
am I.
In the cave of the Water-curtain I ply my home-trade;
I found a friend and master, who taught me the Great
Secret.
I made myself perfect in many arts of Immortality,
I learned transformations without bound or end.
I tired of the narrow scope afforded by the world of man,
Nothing could content me but to live in the Green Jade
Heaven.
Why should Heaven's halls have always one master?
In earthly dynasties king succeeds king.
The strong to the stronger must yield precedence and
place,
Hero is he alone who vies with powers supreme.

So Monkey recited; at which Buddha burst out laughing. "After all," he said, "you're only a monkey-spirit. How can you delude yourself into supposing that you can seize the Jade Emperor's throne? He has been perfecting himself for 1750 kalpas, and every kalpa is 129,000 years. Just see how long it takes to achieve such wisdom as his! How can you, an animal, who have only in this incarnation received half-human form, dare make such a boast? You exceed yourself, and will surely come to a bad end. Submit at once and talk no more of your nonsense. Otherwise I shall have to deal sharply with you, and there won't be much left of the longevity you crave." "He may have begun young," said Monkey, "but that is no reason why he should keep the throne forever. There is a proverb that says 'This year, the Jade Emperor's turn; next year, mine.' Tell him to clear out and make room for me. That is all I ask. If he won't, I shall go on like this, and they will never have any peace." "What magic have you got," asked Buddha, "that would enable you to seize the blessed realms of Heaven?" "Many," said Monkey. "Apart from my seventy-two transformations, I can somersault through the clouds a hundred and eight thousand leagues at a bound. Aren't I fit to be seated on the throne of Heaven?"

"I'll have a wager with you," said Buddha. "If you are really so clever, jump off the palm of my right hand. If you succeed, I'll tell the Jade Emperor to come and live with me in the Western Paradise, and you shall have his throne without more ado. But if you fail, you shall go back to earth and do penance there for many a kalpa before you come to me again with your talk."

"This Buddha," Monkey thought to himself, "is a perfect fool. I can jump a hundred and eight thousand leagues, while his palm cannot be as much as eight inches across. How could I fail to jump clear of it?" "You're sure you are in a position to do this for me?" he asked. "Of course I am," said Buddha.

He stretched out his right hand, which looked about the size of a lotus leaf. Monkey put his cudgel behind his ear, and leapt with all his might. "That's all right," he said to himself. "I'm right off it now." He was whizzing so fast that he was almost invisible, and Buddha, watching him with the eye of wisdom, saw a mere whirligig shoot along.

Monkey came at last to five pink pillars, sticking up into the air. "This is the end of the World," said Monkey to himself. "All I have got to do is to go back to Buddha and claim my forfeit. The Throne is mine." "Wait a minute," he said presently, "I'd better just leave a record of some kind, in case I have trouble with Buddha." He plucked a hair and blew on it with magic breath, crying "Change!" It changed at once into a writing brush charged with heavy ink, and at the base of the central pillar he wrote, "The Great Sage Equal to Heaven reached this place." Then to mark his disrespect, he relieved nature at the bottom of the first pillar, and somersaulted back to where he had come from. Standing on Buddha's palm, he said, "Well, I've gone and come back. You can go and tell the Jade Emperor to hand over the Palaces of Heaven." "You stinking ape," said Buddha, "you've been on the palm of my hand all the time." "You're quite mistaken," said Monkey. "I got to the end of the World, where I saw five flesh-coloured pillars sticking up into the sky. I wrote something on one of them. I'll take you there and show you, if you like." "No need for that," said Buddha. "Just look down." Monkey peered down with his fiery, steely eyes, and there at the base of the middle finger of Buddha's hand he saw written the words "The Great Sage Equal to Heaven reached this place," and from the fork between the thumb and first finger came a smell of monkey's urine. It took him some time to get over his astonishment. At last he said, "Impossible, impossible! I wrote that on the pillar sticking up into the sky. How did it get on to Buddha's finger? He's practising some magic upon me. Let me go back and look." Dear Monkey! He crouched, and was just making ready to spring again, when Buddha turned his head, and pushed Monkey out at the western gate of Heaven. As he did so, he changed his five fingers into the Five Elements, Metal, Wood, Water, Fire and Earth. They became a five-peaked mountain, named Wu Hsing Shan (Mountain of the Five Elements) which pressed upon him heavily enough to hold him tight. The thunder spirits, Ananda and Kaśyapa all pressed the palms of their hands together and shouted "Bravo!"

Buddha, having thus quelled the baleful monkey, called to Ananda and Kaśyapa to come back with him to the Western Heaven. Just as they were leaving, two messengers arrived from the Hall of Magic Mists saying, "We beseech the Tathagata to wait a minute. Our master is on his way." Buddha turned his head, and a moment later saw a chariot drawn by eight phoenixes, covered by a canopy gleaming with jewels. There was a sound of many instruments and a chanting of innumerable spirit hosts. Flower-petals fell through the air, and the smell of incense belched. "I am profoundly beholden to you for dealing with that monster," said the Jade Emperor, when his equipage drew up, "and if you will consent to stay for a while, I will invite all the Immortals to join us in a feast of thanks." Buddha did not like to refuse. "I could not do otherwise than come at your Majesty's request," he said. "What small success we have had is however not my work, but is entirely due to the Founder of Tao and the other divinities."

The banquet was nearing its end when one of the heavenly detectives arrived saying "The Great Sage is sticking out his head!" "No matter," said Buddha, and he took out of his sleeve a seal on which was engraved OM MANI PADME HUM. He gave it to Ananda and told him to stamp it on the top of the mountain. So Ananda left Heaven, carrying the seal, and when he got to the mountain of the Five Elements, he stamped the seal hard upon a square slab of rock that lay right on the top of the mountain. At once this mountain struck root and joined its seams. There was enough air to breathe, but not a crack through which hand or head could squeeze.

"I have sealed him down," Ananda announced; whereupon Buddha said goodbye to the Jade Emperor and all the spirits, and with his two disciples left the gate of heaven. But in his mercy he appointed a guardian spirit to watch over the mountain. "When he is hungry," he said, "give him an iron pill to eat. When he is thirsty, give him verdigris to drink. When the days of his penance are fulfilled, there will be one who will come to rescue him."

And if you do not know how long afterwards, in what year

and in what month, the time of his penance was fulfilled, you must listen to what is related in the next chapter.

(ARTHUR WALEY)

Some Further Reading

Waley, Arthur, trans. *Monkey*. New York: John Day, 1943. (This is *The Way West*.)

22

THE GOLDEN LOTUS

Golden Lotus is the most original novel which we have considered, for the author took a minor incident from the earlier *Saga of the Marshes* and expanded it into a whole new, and rather long, novel. *Golden Lotus* differs dramatically from the earlier novels in many other ways, too. Hsi-mên Ch'ing is the protagonist, and he is an ordinary businessman. We do not find in his life the heroism of *Three Kingdoms,* nor the romance of *Saga of the Marshes,* nor the supernatural phenomena of *The Way West.* Hsi-mên Ch'ing devotes his attention to the craft of making money, and he spends such artistic energy as he has to elaborate and to refine his sexual pleasure.

Hsi-mên has six wives, but his experience with women is not restricted to so narrow a circle. He accompanies his colleagues to the wineshops and the brothels, and he tampers with his wives' attendants and serving-girls. The novel is not called *Golden Lotus* in Chinese, in fact; it is called *Gold-vase Plum,* which very cleverly refers to the three leading female characters, Golden Lotus (a

673

wife), Lady of the Vase (a wife), and Plum Blossom (a maid). The novel is written with such attention to this darker aspect of the protagonist's soul—the author so accurately and so lavishly describes the pleasures of Hsi-mên's bed—that the novel has been suppressed at various times on Taiwan, and now you cannot buy an unexpurgated version. The really fine English translation by Clement Egerton and Lao She has put these lavish and accurate descriptions into Latin, in order to keep it among scholars.

The author, of course, did not so vividly describe sexual pleasure because he delighted in it. He had a more serious moral purpose, which should lead us to commend and to read him. Wang Shih-cheng was a successful scholar and a renowned Confucian of the sixteenth century A.D. But his father had been impeached and thereafter executed by a Yen, and the son of this Yen was a colleague and contemporary of Shih-cheng's. The son was as evil as the father, and when he heard that Shih-cheng had written a novel, he asked to read it. Shih-cheng went straight home and wrote the *Golden Lotus,* using the Yen as a model for his protagonist and paragon of vice. In these days, the only way conveniently to turn the thin pages of Chinese books was to use a moistened finger, and Shih-cheng flavored the upper corner of each page with a little poison. The Yen read on and on, delighted by the vice, corruption, and luxury described, until he reached the last page. Then the poison took effect, and he dropped dead. Shih-cheng, disguised as a mourner, visited the Yen home while the Yen was lying encoffined before burial. He wailed and wept to pay his respects and then, when the servants were not looking, cut off the dead man's right arm and carried it away in his cloak. So at least says the legend about the composition of *Golden Lotus*.

Chapter 10

Wu Sung was taken by the watch to the city gaol. Meanwhile Hsi-mên Ch'ing, who had jumped out of the wine-shop window, found himself in a courtyard which belonged to old Doctor Hu. One of the maids had just gone to the privy and had lifted her skirts. Suddenly she saw a man crouching at the foot of the wall. As she could not run away, she called, "Thief! thief!" as loudly as she could, and Doctor Hu ran out to see what was the matter. He recognised Hsi-mên Ch'ing, and said:

"My Lord, I must congratulate you on your escape from Wu Sung. He has killed a man, and they have taken him to the lock-up. But you may go home now, Sir, I don't think there is likely to be any more trouble."

Hsi-mên thanked the doctor, and went home with all the assurance in the world. He told Golden Lotus what had happened, and they clapped their hands with delight to think that all their troubles were now over. Golden Lotus advised Hsi-mên to send bribes to all the officials, so that they might make sure that Wu Sung would be sentenced to death, for they by no means desired to set eyes on him again. Hsi-mên Ch'ing called his servant Lai Wang, and told him to take the magistrate a set of gold and silver drinking-cups, with fifty taels of silver, and sums of money for all the other officials, both great and small, and to ask that Wu Sung should be punished with all the rigour of the law. The magistrate accepted the bribe, and the next morning, as soon as he entered the Hall of Audience, had Wu Sung brought before him, with the waiter and the two singing-girls. His manner had now completely changed.

"Wu Sung," he said, "you are a desperate fellow and have brought accusations against perfectly innocent people. I have overlooked this more than once. Now you yourself have killed a man, without the slightest cause. Why don't you obey the laws?"

"My quarrel was really with Hsi-mên Ch'ing," Wu Sung said, "but, as ill luck would have it, I met this man. He refused to tell me where Hsi-mên Ch'ing was, and I lost my temper and killed him. My Lord, I implore you to give me justice, and bring Hsi-mên Ch'ing to answer to the law for my brother's death. As for myself, I am ready to give my life for this dead man's."

"You are talking nonsense," the magistrate cried. "Do you mean to say you did not know he was an officer of this court? You must certainly have had some other reason for killing him. Why do you try to drag Hsi-mên Ch'ing into the matter? I can see that I shall never get the truth out of you without a beating."

He ordered his attendants to punish Wu Sung. Three or four of them pulled him down and gave him twenty strokes of the rod, like drops of rain falling. Wu Sung continued to insist that he was being unjustly dealt with. "I have done much for you," he cried, "and you should deal with me accordingly and not have me beaten so severely."

This only made the magistrate more angry. "You killed a man with your fist," he cried. "Now your boldness seems to have gone into your mouth.'' He ordered the thumbscrews to be put on, and Wu Sung's fingers were pressed and his hands beaten fifty times, after which a cangue was put about his neck and he was returned to prison.

Some of the officers had been Wu Sung's friends and knew that he was a man who had taken upon himself to avenge another's quarrel. They would have liked to clear him, but, as they had accepted Hsi-mên Ch'ing's bribes, their mouths were sealed and they were unable to do anything. As Wu Sung persisted in demanding justice, the magistrate waited a few days and then drew up a dossier without hearing any evidence. All he did was to appoint an officer to go to Lion Street to examine Li's body and fill in the necessary particulars. Then the crime sheet was drawn up as follows:

> The accused Wu Sung called to see Li, and there was a dispute with regard to the division of certain moneys. The parties became drunk and began to fight. The deceased was kicked and beaten and thrown from a high place. Green and red marks were found on his left side, his face, ribs, and groin.

After completing their examination, the officials went back to the office, and a document was drawn up to be sent with Wu Sung to the Prefect of Tung-p'ing, where the matter would have to be further investigated and the final judgment made.

The Prefect of Tung-p'ing, His Excellency Ch'ên Wên-chao, was a native of Ho-nan and an official of exceptional probity. As soon as the documents were brought to him, he began the hearing of the case.

Ch'ên Wên-chao went to his court and ordered everyone to be brought before him. He read through all the documents which had come from Ch'ing Ho and examined the depositions. The indictment said:

Prefecture of Tung-P'ing, District of Ch'ing Ho

An Indictment

The accused Wu Sung is twenty-eight years of age, formerly domiciled in the District of Yang Ku. On account of his splendid physique he was appointed Captain of the Police in this District.

After returning to this District from a tour of duty, the accused visited his brother's tomb. He ascertained that his sister-in-law had not observed the required period of mourning, but had remarried. The same day he inquired from people in the streets concerning the matter, and ultimately proceeded to a wine-shop in Lion Street, where he met Li Wai-ch'uan. Being drunk, he endeavoured to recover the sum of three hundred cash which he alleged Li had previously borrowed from him, but Li refused to pay the money and the two men fought. Li was struck and kicked, and so severely injured that he died shortly afterwards.

In proof whereof the singing-girls Niu and Pao are witnesses.

The watch arrested Wu Sung, and officers deputed for that purpose proceeded to the place where Li's body lay and made a careful examination. We then heard Wu Sung and prepared the accompanying depositions. We trust that upon further investigation you will find the particulars to be correct.

It is our submission that Wu Sung fought with and killed the man, and that he should be executed in accordance with the law for the capital offence, not for fighting or the dispute over money. The waiter Wang, and the two girls Niu and Pao, appear to be guiltless in the matter, and we only await your permission to release them.

Dated this eighth day of the eighth month of the third year of Chêng Ho:

> Li Ta-tien, *Magistrate.*
> Lo Ho-an, *Deputy Magistrate.*
> Hua Ho-lu, *Keeper of the Archives.*
> Hsia Kung-chi, *Prosecutor.*
> Ch'ien Lao, *Chief Gaoler.*

When the Prefect had read this document, he asked Wu Sung how he had come to kill Li Wai-ch'uan. Wu Sung kotowed.

"My Lord of the Blue Heavens," he said, "I trust that, in your court, justice may be done. If you will allow me to speak, I will tell the truth about the matter."

"Say on," the Prefect ordered.

Wu Sung told him the whole story, not omitting a single detail, from Hsi-mên Ch'ing's seduction of Golden Lotus to the rejection of his accusation at the Ch'ing Ho court. He ended by saying: "I wished only to avenge my brother, and it was Hsi-mên Ch'ing of whom I was in search. Unhappily, I did kill this man, but the fault is not mine alone. Hsi-mên Ch'ing is very rich, and the officers did not dare to arrest him. I am not afraid of death. My sole desire is to avenge my murdered brother, whose remains lie in the tomb awaiting vengeance."

"I understand the case," the Prefect said. "That will do for the present." He called forward Ch'ien Lao and ordered him to be given twenty strokes. "Your magistrate does not seem to know how to perform his duties. He should not allow himself to be moved by personal interest and sell justice in this way."

Again he questioned Wu Sung, and amended the indictment which had come from Ch'ing Ho. Finally he said to his officers: "This fellow was anxious to avenge his brother and killed this man more or less accidentally. He seems a good man and he ought not to be treated like a common criminal." He gave orders that the cangue should be removed from Wu Sung's neck and a lighter one put in its place, and that he should be detained in the prison. The rest of the party were sent back to Ch'ing Ho with instructions to the magistrate that Hsi-mên Ch'ing, Golden Lotus, old woman Wang, Yün Ko, and Ho IX should be sent to the prefect to be examined. When all this had been done, the Prefect said, he would send forward the documents to the Imperial Court.

Wu Sung was still in prison, but the officials soon found what a good fellow he was, and sent him wine and food without taking anything in return. The news reached Ch'ing Ho and, when Hsi-mên Ch'ing heard it, he was greatly alarmed. He knew that Ch'ên Wên-chao was incorruptible, and did not dare to try to bribe him, but he decided to send word to his relative Ch'ên and ask for help. He told Lai Wang to go to the Eastern Capital in all haste with a letter to Marshal Yang, the Provincial Commander-in-Chief, begging him to use all his influence with the Imperial Tutor Ts'ai. When Ts'ai heard of the matter he was afraid that the magistrate Li would suffer, so he secretly wrote to the Prefect of Tung-p'ing asking him not to proceed with the examination of Hsi-mên Ch'ing and Golden Lotus. Now Ch'ên Wên-chao had been the chief magistrate of Ta Li Ssu before he had been appointed to the Prefecture of Tung-p'ing. He had been befriended by Ts'ai, and knew that Marshal Yang was in high favour at court. He finally decided that the best thing he could do was to settle the matter without injury to either side.

He reprieved Wu Sung, but ordered him to be given forty strokes, branded, and banished two thousand li. In Wu Ta's case, it was declared that, as the body had been burned, the matter must be considered closed. The others were ordered to be sent home. This was all duly written down, and the documents sent, first to the Provincial Office, then to the Court.

They were returned by the higher authorities with orders that the Prefect's proposals should be put into execution. Ch'ên Wên-chao took Wu Sung from the gaol, read over the papers in the case, gave him forty strokes, and set a cangue upon him. Two columns of characters were branded on his face, and he was ordered to leave for Mêng-chou in charge of two officials, who took the document with them. Then the other parties in the case were dismissed.

That day Wu Sung, in charge of two officers of the court, left the prefecture of Tung-p'ing for Ch'ing Ho. There, he sold all his furniture and gave the money to the officers, and asked one of his neighbours, named Yao, to look after Jasmine. "If His Majesty pardons me," he said, "I will pay you back. I can never forget your kindness."

Wu Sung's neighbours knew well that he was a good man in misfortune, and they gave him, some silver, some a little wine; others offered food, money, and rice. He went once again to his own rooms and got a soldier to bring his personal belongings, and the next day they set off from Ch'ing Ho along the high road for Mêng-chou.

When Hsi-mên Ch'ing heard that Wu Sung had really started for Mêng-chou, he felt secure at last. The canker which had ravaged his heart so long was now removed, and he felt completely at ease. He gave orders to Lai Wang, Lai Po, and Lai Hsing to make preparations in the garden. They set up folding screens and arranged embroidered hangings in the Hibiscus Arbour; a banquet was prepared, and a band of musicians engaged to sing and dance. The Moon Lady and the other ladies enjoyed the repast, and men-servants, serving women, and maids waited upon them.

Incense was burned in precious censers, and flowers set
out in golden vases

Treasures from Hsiang-chou in all their glory.
When the lattice was raised, the shining pearls from Ho
    P'u gleamed.
Flame-like dates and pears from Chiao heaped on crystal
    dishes
Cups of green jade filled with a precious juice, a liquid
    jade.
Of roasted dragon's liver, of fried phoenix giblets, one
    chopstick's load was worth ten thousand pence.
The palms of black bears, the hooves of purple camels
Mingled their sweet savour with the wine's, filling the air.
Then were ground the phoenix balls of tea,
And a small clear wave rose in the white jade cups.
As the precious liquid was outpoured, there came fra-
    grance from the golden jar.
The lord Mêng Ch'ang was now outdone
The wealth of Shih Ch'ung rivalled.

Hsi-mên Ch'ing and the Moon Lady sat in the place of
honour, and the other ladies arranged themselves according
to their position in the household. As they passed the cups from
one to the other, they seemed as full of grace as the flowers of
a posy or the pattern upon a piece of brocade.

They were drinking when Tai An brought in a boy and a
young maid of great beauty, whose hair was dressed in a fringe
upon her brows. She was carrying two boxes.

"Our neighbours the Huas," Tai An said, "have sent some
flowers for the ladies."

The maid came before Hsi-mên and the Moon Lady, kotowed
to them, and said, "My mistress has sent me with this box of
cakes and these flowers for you." The Moon Lady opened the
boxes. One contained pastries, some of which were stuffed with
fruit, and others with peppers. They were like those made in
the Imperial palaces. The other box contained freshly picked

lilies. She was greatly pleased, and told the little girl to thank her mistress. After giving them something to eat, she presented the girl with a handkerchief and the boy with a hundred coppers.

"Tell your Mistress," she said, "that I am most grateful to her." She asked the little girl her name.

"I am called Welcome Spring, and this boy is T'ien Fu." Then they both withdrew.

"Mistress Hua is really very kind," the Moon Lady said to Hsi-mên Ch'ing. "She is always sending her servants with something or other for us, and I have never made her any return."

"Brother Hua married the lady two years ago," Hsi-mên said. "He himself told me what a sweet disposition she has, but that is clearly to be seen from the excellence of her maid."

"I saw her once," the Moon Lady said, "at her father-in-law's funeral. She is moderately tall and has a round face. She has two delicately arched eyebrows and a very clear skin. She certainly seems very gentle, and still quite young, not more than twenty-four or twenty-five, I should think."

"You may not know," Hsi-mên said, "that before she married Hua, she was one of the second ladies of Minister Liang. She brought Hua a very good fortune."

"Well, she has sent us these two boxes," the Moon Lady said, "and we must not be less courteous than she is. I will send her something in return tomorrow."

The family name of Hua Tzu-hsü's wife was Li. She was born on the fifteenth day of the first month, and on that day somebody had sent the family a pair of fish-shaped vases. She was given the name of the Lady of the Vase. She had once been the concubine of Minister Liang of the Prefecture of Ta-ming, a son-in-law of the Imperial Tutor Ts'ai. His wife was a very jealous woman, and had made an end of several maids and concubines, and buried their bodies in the garden. So Lady of the

Vase had to live hidden away in his study, with an old woman to wait on her.

On the fifteenth of the first month in the third year of Chêng Ho, Minister Liang and his wife were in the Green Jade Pavilion, when the whole family except Lady of the Vase and her servant were murdered by Li K'uei. They succeeded in escaping, Lady of the Vase taking with her a hundred large pearls and a pair of jewels as black as a raven's wings. They went to the Eastern Capital in the hope of finding some relatives there. At that time Eunuch Hua, one of the Imperial Chamberlains, had just been appointed to the Governorship of Kuang-nan. His nephew Hua Tzu-hsü was unmarried, so the eunuch secured the services of a go-between and arranged a marriage between his nephew and the woman. The eunuch went to Kuang-nan and they with him, but they had not been there very long before old Hua fell ill, had to resign his appointment, and go home again. His home was in the district of Ch'ing Ho. Then he died, and all his property came to his nephew. Every day this gentleman and his friends frequented the bawdy-houses, and he had become a member of the brotherhood which Hsi-mên Ch'ing had founded.

With Ying Po-chüeh, Hsieh Hsi-ta, and the rest, he amused himself with singing-girls, and they were all most intimate. It was well known that he was a nephew of one of the Imperial Chamberlains and very free with his money, and his friends were always dragging him away to the bawdy-house. Often he did not return for three or four nights at a time.

Hsi-mên Ch'ing and his ladies made merry in the Hibiscus Arbour. They drank till it was late, and then went to their own apartments. Hsi-mên Ch'ing went to Golden Lotus's room. He was already half drunk, and soon wished to enjoy the delights of love with his new lady. Golden Lotus hastily burned incense, and they took off their clothes and went to bed. But Hsi-mên Ch'ing would not allow her to go too fast. He knew that she played the flute exquisitely. He sat down behind the curtains of the bed, and set her before him. Then Golden Lotus daintily pushed back the golden bracelets from her wrists and put Hsi-mên's little spike up to her lips while he leaned forward to enjoy the delight of her movements. She continued for a long time, and all the while his delight grew greater. He called Plum Blossom to bring in some tea. Golden Lotus was afraid that her maid would see her, and hastily pulled down the bed curtains.

"What are you afraid of?" Hsi-mên said. "Our neighbour Hua has two excellent maids. One of them, the younger, brought us those flowers today, but there is another about as old as Plum Blossom. Brother Hua has already taken her virginity. Indeed wherever her mistress is, she is too. She is really very pretty, and of course no one can tell what a man like Brother Hua may do in the privacy of his own home."

Golden Lotus looked at him.

"You are a strange creature, but I will not scold you," she said. "If you wish to have this girl, have her and be done with it. Why go beating about the bush, pointing at a mountain when you really are thinking about something quite different. I know you would like to have somebody else to compare with me, but I am not jealous. She is not actually my maid. Tomorrow, I will go to the garden to rest for a while, and that will give you a chance. You can call her into this room and do what you like with her. Will that satisfy you?"

Hsi-mên Ch'ing was delighted. "You understand me so well!" he said, "How can I help loving you?" So these two agreed, and their delight in each other and in their love could not have been greater. After she had played the flute, they kissed each other, and went to sleep.

The next day Golden Lotus went to the apartments of Tower of Jade, and Hsi-mên Ch'ing called Plum Blossom to his room, and had his pleasure of her.

From that day, Golden Lotus showered favours on this girl. She would not allow her to go and wait at the kitchen, but kept her to attend to her bedroom, and serve her with tea. She chose beautiful clothes and ornaments for her, and bound her feet very tightly.

Chapter 18: *Hsi-mên Ch'ing bribes officers of the court*

Lai Pao and Lai Wang set out to the Eastern Capital to try to put matters right there. They travelled at early dawn when the rising sun threw a purple haze over their path; they travelled in the evening when its setting cast a rosy light upon the dust. At last they came to their destination and entered the city through the Gate of Eternal Life. They found an inn and rested there. The next day they set out to pick up what news they could in the street. They heard people saying that Wang, the Minister for War, had been tried the previous day, and that the Emperor had ordered his execution in the coming autumn. Of Marshal Yang it was said that his case was not yet done with, for his household and his staff had not all been arrested.

Lai Pao and Lai Wang took the treasures they had brought and went in haste to the palace of the Imperial Tutor. They had been there before and knew the way well, but, when they came to the Arch of Dragon Virtue, they waited for a time to see if they could learn anything more of interest. After a while a man wearing black robes came hurriedly from the palace and went eastwards. Lai Pao recognised him as one of the household of Marshal Yang. He would have liked to go and ask a few questions, but his master had told him to keep in the background, and he let the man pass. At last they went up to the palace gate, politely greeted the keeper of the gate, and asked if his Eminence was at home.

"His Eminence is still detained at the Court," the keeper of the gate said. "What is your business?"

"We should like to see Master Chai the Comptroller of the Household," Lai Pao said. "Will you be good enough to ask him to see us?"

"His Lordship is not at home," the keeper of the gate said.

Lai Pao realised that the officer was not telling the truth and that something was expected of him. He took a tael of silver from his sleeve and gave it to the gatekeeper.

"Whom did you say you wished to see?" the man said. "His Eminence or his Excellency the Vice-Chancellor? Chai Ch'ien is the great Comptroller of the Household and matters affecting the Imperial Tutor are referred to him. The lesser Comptroller Kao An deals with the Vice-Chancellor's affairs. Their duties are quite distinct. The Imperial Tutor himself is not at home, but the Vice-Chancellor is. What is the real nature of your business? Shall I ask Master Kao to come and see you? He will serve your purpose just as well."

"We are from Marshal Yang's palace," said Lai Pao, "and shall be very glad to see anyone."

The officer of the gate hastened into the palace, and, after a short delay, Kao An appeared. Lai Pao went forward and made a reverence, at the same time offering ten taels of silver. "I was to have come," he said, "with one of Marshal Yang's household. We hoped to see the Imperial Tutor to find out what is happening. But I had to stay for food, and so was late and missed the officer."

"Marshal Yang's courier has just gone," said Kao An, accepting the present, "but if you will wait a moment or two I will take you to see the Vice-Chancellor." He took Lai Pao through the entrance-hall, and passing through a side door they came to three large rooms on the north. Here was a green screen, with a scroll upon which the Emperor had written in his own hand "The Music Chamber of the Vice-Chancellor."

Ts'ai Yu, the son of Ts'ai Ching, was, like his father, a favourite at court. He was an Imperial Delegate at the Temple of the Great Monad and held high office at the Hsiang Ho Palace and in the Board of Rites.

Lai Pao waited till Kao An, who had gone to announce him, came to summon him. Then he went in and knelt down. Ts'ai Yu was dressed in his ordinary attire with a soft hat. He asked Lai Pao where he had come from.

"I am a servant of Ch'ên Hung's household," said Lai Pao. "He is a kinsman of Marshal Yang. I was to have come with the Marshal's courier in the hope of seeing his Eminence and obtaining some information. Unfortunately, the courier got here before me." He took a paper from his sleeve and offered it to the minister. Ts'ai Yu read on it the words "Five hundred measures of purest rice," and called Lai Pao nearer.

"His Eminence," he said, "has avoided becoming mixed up in this matter in view of the fact that his own name was mentioned to the Emperor in the Censor's report. Li, the Minister of the Right, dealt with the case yesterday. But so far as Marshal Yang is concerned, we heard from the Court that his Majesty is inclined to be merciful and will not deal severely with him, though his underlings, no doubt, will still have to be tried and sentenced. You must go and see Li."

Lai Pao kotowed. "I am quite unknown at Li's palace," he said. "Pray have pity on me for Marshal Yang's sake."

"Go as far as the Bridge of the Heavenly River," said Ts'ai Yu. "North of it you will see a very high building, and there you must ask for Li Pang-yen, Minister of the Right. Everybody knows him. But I will send someone with you."

He called for official paper, set his seal upon it, and instructed Kao An to go with Lai Pao and introduce him. The two men left the hall together. They called to Lai Wang to bring the presents, went down the street of Dragon Virtue, and, passing the Bridge of the Heavenly River, came to the palace of Li Pang-yen.

The minister, who had just returned from the Presence, was still wearing his robes of crimson silk and a girdle around his waist, fastened by a jade clasp. After bidding farewell to some man of rank, he had gone to his hall when the gatekeeper informed him that Vice-Chancellor Ts'ai had sent his Comptroller, Kao An, with a message. Kao An was then summoned, and, after he had exchanged a few words with the minister, Lai Pao and Lai Wang were called forward. They went into the hall and knelt down. Kao An stood beside them and handed Ts'ai Yu's note and the list of presents they had brought to the minister. Pang-yen looked at it.

"You are connected with Marshal Yang," he said, "and Ts'ai has been good enough to send you to me. How can I possibly accept presents from you? Besides, his Majesty is now quite well disposed to Marshal Yang; he will not be troubled further. But I fear the Censor has been so severe upon some of the Marshal's subordinates that they can hardly escape punishment." He called for the memorial which the Censor had laid before the Emperor the previous day.

"Wang Fu's archivist, Tung Shêng; his chamberlain, Wang Lien; Captain Huang Yü; Yang Chien's servant, the scrivener Lu Hu; Yang Shêng, his administrator; Fu Ch'üan, his comptroller; Han Tsung-jên; Chao Hung-tao; Captain Liu Shêng; Ch'en Hung; Hsi-mên Ch'ing; and Hu IV. These are all men of utter unworthiness, scoundrelly fellows who, like foxes, invest themselves with the dignity of a tiger. We pray that justice may be done upon them. Some should be banished to the frontier that there may be an end to their deceits; some should be put to death that the majesty of the law may be vindicated."

When Lai Pao heard this document read, he was greatly excited. Again and again he prostrated himself before the minister. "In truth, your Excellency," he cried, "I am Hsi-mên Ch'ing's servant. I implore you to be generous and spare my master's life." Kao An knelt down and added his prayers to those of Lai Pao. The minister allowed his glance to fall upon the gold and silver. There were, in all, five hundred taels, and it seemed to him that such a present might suffice to purchase the name of a single man. Why should he hesitate? He called for writing materials, took up a brush, and changed the name of Hsi-mên Ch'ing to Chia Lien. Then he accepted the presents and dismissed the men, sending a polite message to the Vice-Chancellor Ts'ai Yu. To each of the three domestics he gave five taels of silver. Lai Pao and Lai Wang took their leave of Kao An, returned to their inn, packed their luggage, paid their reckoning, and made haste back to Ch'ing Ho.

As soon as they reached home, they hurried to Hsi-mên and told him all that had happened in the Eastern Capital. When he realised how narrowly he had escaped, he shivered as though he had been plunged into a bath of ice-cold water.

Chapter 27: *The garden of delights*

Lai Pao returned from the Eastern Capital and made his report to Hsi-mên Ch'ing. "When I reached the Capital," he said, "I went to see the Comptroller of the Household and gave him your letter. Then I was taken to the minister. When his Eminence had looked at the list of presents he accepted them. Then I explained the case. His Eminence said: 'I will send at once to the Governor of Shan-tung and ask him to liberate the salt merchant Wang Ssu-fêng of Yang-chou and the others.' Master Chai sent his greetings to you. He says he would like to have a talk with you and that you ought to go to the Capital for his Eminence's birthday on the fifteenth day of the sixth month."

Hsi-mên Ch'ing was satisfied. He sent Lai Pao to tell Master Ch'iao. While he was speaking, Pên IV and Lai Hsing came in, but seeing their master occupied, they stood aside until Lai Pao had gone. Then Hsi-mên Ch'ing said to Pên IV: "I suppose you have come back from the funeral?" Pên IV hardly dared to speak, but Lai Hsing came forward and whispered: "Sung Jên came to the funeral pyre, and refused to allow the body to be burned. He said it was extremely irregular. He said other things which I should not like to repeat."

Hsi-mên Ch'ing was very angry. "What a detestable, hateful creature!" he cried. He sent a boy at once for Ch'ên Ching-chi, told the young man to write a letter to Magistrate Li, and sent Lai An with it to the Town Hall. The magistrate dispatched two runners who bound Sung Jên and took him to the court. He was charged with blackmail and attempting to use the dead woman as a means of extorting money. He was brought in fetters to the Hall of Audience and there given twenty strokes so severe that the blood flowed down his legs in streams. The magistrate then bound him over never again to be a nuisance to Hsi-mên Ch'ing. At the same time he ordered police and firemen to go with Hsi-mên's servants to the place of burning and burn the body. Sung Jên, his legs all beaten and bleeding, crawled home. He was so exasperated that he took a fever and died, bitterly lamenting his fate.

Now that he had finally disposed of Wistaria, Hsi-mên Ch'ing got ready gold and silver to the value of three hundred taels and sent for Silversmith Ku and several others to make a set of silver figures for the birthday of the Imperial Tutor. They worked beneath the awning at Hsi-mên Ch'ing's house. Each of the figures was over a foot high. They also made a pair of golden flagons with the character Shou engraved upon them.

Hsi-mên had bought two pairs of peach-shaped cups of jade, two sets of crimson robes from Hang-chou, and dragon cloaks embroidered in five colours. He still wanted two rolls of a particular kind of black cloth and some crimson dragon silk, but he could not find it at any price. Then the Lady of the Vase said to him, "I have some sets of dragon robes which have never been made up. They are upstairs in my place. Come and look at them."

Hsi-mên Ch'ing went with her and they picked out four sets, two of crimson silk and two of the special black cloth. They all were edged with gold braid, and embroidered with five-coloured dragons. They were certainly much finer than anything they could have bought. Hsi-mên Ch'ing was delighted. He had them all packed up and Lai Pao and Clerk Fu left again for the Eastern Capital on the twenty-eighth day of the fifth month.

Two days later it was the beginning of the sixth month. The weather was very hot and at noon the fiery sun was like a blazing umbrella in a cloudless sky. Not a particle of cloud was to be seen and it seemed hot enough to scorch the stones or to melt metal.

It was so hot that Hsi-mên Ch'ing did not go out. He stayed at home with his hair undone and his clothes unbuttoned, trying to keep cool. He sat in the bower by the Kingfisher Hall watching the boys watering the flowers. In front of the Kingfisher Hall there was a bowl of sweet-smelling daphne. He told Lai An to take a little watering-can, and watched him sprinkle the flowers.

Golden Lotus and the Lady of the Vase were both dressed in the lightest of silver silk, with skirts of dark red and a fringe of gold thread. The Lady of the Vase was wearing a short crimson cape and Golden Lotus had one of silver and red. Golden Lotus wore nothing on her head but a blue Hang-chou head-dress, through which four braids of hair peeped out. On her brow were three flowers made of kingfisher feathers, which enhanced the beauty of her white face and glossy hair, her red lips and pearly teeth. The two women came smiling, holding each other's hands.

"You here, watering the flowers!" Golden Lotus cried, when she saw Hsi-mên Ch'ing. "Why don't you go and dress your hair?"

"Tell one of the maids to bring me some water," Hsi-mên said, "and I will do my hair here."

"Put down your watering-can," Golden Lotus said to Lai An, "and send a maid with some water and a comb. Be quick about it." Lai An bowed and went to do what he was told. Then Golden Lotus, seeing the sweet-smelling daphne, was going to pick some to put in her hair, but Hsi-mên Ch'ing stopped her. "Don't touch them, little oily mouth. I will give one to each of you." He had already picked a few blossoms and put them into a crackleware vase.

"Ah, my son," Golden Lotus said, "so you've been plucking the flowers, have you? What do you mean by hiding them there instead of offering them to your mother?" She snatched one up and set it in her hair. Hsi-mên Ch'ing gave one to the Lady of the Vase. Then Plum Blossom came with a mirror and comb, and Chrysanthemum brought water. Hsi-mên gave three flowers to Plum Blossom, for the Moon Lady, Picture of Grace and Tower of Jade, and said: "Ask the Third Lady to come and play her guitar for me."

"Plum Blossom can go to the Great Lady and Picture of Grace, and if you want Tower of Jade, I'll go and fetch her," Golden Lotus said. "When I come back, I shall expect another flower, and, if I bring someone to sing for you, still another one."

"Go first," Hsi-mên said, "and we'll see about that when you come back."

"My son," Golden Lotus said, "wherever can you have

been brought up? What a naughty boy to think of trying to cheat me like that! If I go and fetch Tower of Jade, I shall never get one. No, let me have it first, and then I'll go.''

"You wicked little rascal,'' Hsi-mên Ch'ing said, laughing, "even in trifles like this you will have your own way.'' He gave her the flower. Golden Lotus set it in her hair, and went towards the inner court, leaving the Lady of the Vase alone with Hsi-mên Ch'ing.

Through the light silk skirt, Hsi-mên could see her crimson trouser; the sun's rays made them so transparent that he could clearly distinguish the cool flesh beneath them. The sight aroused his passion, and finding that they were alone, he stopped dressing his hair, and carried the Lady of the Vase to a long summer couch. He pulled aside her skirt, took down the crimson trousers, and played with her the game which is called "Carrying fire over the mountains.'' They played for a long time without his bringing matters to a conclusion, and their pleasure was like that of a love bird and his mate.

Golden Lotus did not go to the inner court. She went as far as the corner gate and then decided to give Tower of Jade's flower to Plum Blossom. She went back on tiptoe to the Kingfisher Hall. There, she stood listening outside the window, and, for quite a long time, could hear the lovers amusing themselves.

"My darling,'' she heard Hsi-mên Ch'ing say to the Lady of the Vase, "above all else I love your little white bottom. I shall do my very utmost to give you pleasure to-day.''

After a pause, she heard the Lady of the Vase say softly, "My dearest, you must be gentle with me, for I am really not too well. The other day you were rough with me, and my belly hurt so much that only during the last day or two has it begun to feel better.''

"You are not well?'' Hsi-mên cried. "What do you mean?''

"I will not keep it from you any longer," the Lady of the Vase told him. "For a month now, I have been cherishing a little one within me. Please treat me with some indulgence."

Hsi-mên Ch'ing was delighted beyond all measure. "Why, my precious one," he said, "why didn't you tell me before? If that is how things are, I will bring this game to an end at once." His happiness reached its culmination and his joy was complete. He set both hands upon her legs, and the evidence of his delight was overwhelming. The woman beneath him raised herself to welcome it.

After a while, Golden Lotus could hear Hsi-mên breathing heavily, and his lover's gentle voice, like an oriole's, answering him. No sound escaped her as she stood beneath the window. Tower of Jade came up suddenly from behind. "What are you doing here?" she asked. Golden Lotus signed to her to be silent and they both went into the summer-house. Hsi-mên Ch'ing was a little taken aback and did not quite know what to do.

"What have you been doing all this long time I've been away?" Golden Lotus said. "How is it you haven't washed, or combed your hair?"

"I am waiting for a maid to bring me some jasmine soap," Hsi-mên said.

"I have no patience with you," Golden Lotus cried. "Why must you have that particular kind of soap? Is that why your face is cleaner than some people's bottoms?"

Hsi-mên Ch'ing paid no attention to this remark, but, when he had finished dressing, sat down beside Tower of Jade. "What have you been doing in the inner court?" he said. "Have you brought your guitar?"

"I have been making a pearl flower for the Great Lady to wear at a party. Plum Blossom is bringing the guitar."

Soon Plum Blossom came. She said she had given the flowers to the Great Lady and the Second Lady. Hsi-mên told her to set out wine, and a bowl of ice with plums and melons in it was brought. In the cool summerhouse Hsi-mên Ch'ing enjoyed the society of his ladies.

"Why didn't you tell Plum Blossom to ask the Great Lady to come?" Tower of Jade said. "She does not care for wine," Hsi-mên Ch'ing said, "I thought there was no purpose in troubling her."

Then Hsi-mên took the seat of honour and the three women sat down facing him. The exquisite wine was poured out for them and many delicacies were placed before them. Golden Lotus would not sit on a chair but took a porcelain stool for herself.

"Come and sit on a chair," Tower of Jade cried, "you will find that stool too cold."

"Don't worry," Golden Lotus said, "I am getting old. I've no reason to fear an internal chill or anything of that sort. Why should I?"

The wine was passed round three times and Hsi-mên Ch'ing told Plum Blossom to give Tower of Jade her guitar, and a lute to Golden Lotus. "Play the tune 'The God of Fire rules the world and his glory fills the void.'" Golden Lotus refused. "How well you must have been brought up," she cried, "to ask us to sing while you two sit there and enjoy yourselves. I will not play for you. Tell the Sixth Lady to play something."

"She doesn't know how to play," Hsi-mên said.

"Well, even if she doesn't know how to play, she certainly knows how to count the beats," Golden Lotus said.

Hsi-mên Ch'ing laughed. "You little whore," he cried, "you always try to pick on something"; but he told Plum Blossom to give the Lady of the Vase a pair of red ivory castanets. Then the two women began to play, spreading their exquisite fingers and slowly plucking the silken strings. They sang the song of "The geese flying over the sand," while Hibiscus stood at the side and fanned them. When the song was over, Hsi-mên offered each of them a cup of wine. Golden Lotus went to the table, drank deeply of iced water, and ate some fruit.

"Why are you eating only cold things to-day?" Tower of Jade said.

"Nothing of any particular interest is happening in my distinguished belly," Golden Lotus replied. "Why should I be afraid of cold things?"

The Lady of the Vase was so embarrassed that she became white and red in turns. Hsi-mên Ch'ing glanced sharply at Golden Lotus. "You little villain," he said, "you do nothing but talk nonsense."

"Brother," Golden Lotus said, "old women like me get nothing but dry meat to eat. We have to eat it sinew by sinew."

As they were drinking the clouds began to gather. Far away the thunder rolled and suddenly a storm broke, drenching the flowers in front of the summer-house.

In a few moments the rain stopped again. A rainbow appeared in the sky. The sun came out again and in a twinkling the jasper steps glistened and a cool evening breeze freshened the court-yard. Tiny Jade came from the back court to call Tower of Jade.

"The Great Lady wants me," Tower of Jade said. "I have still some pearl flowers to finish. I must go now or she will be angry."

"I will go with you," the Lady of the Vase said. "I should like to see the flowers."

Hsi-mên Ch'ing said he would go with them too. He took the guitar and asked Tower of Jade to play. He beat time with his hands and they all sang together.

It is evening.
The storm has passed over the southern hall
Red petals are floating on the surface of the pool.
Slowly the gentle thunder rolls away

The rain is over and the clouds disperse
The fragrance of water lilies comes to us over the distance.
The new moon is a crescent
Fresh from the perfumed bath, decked for the evening
Over the darkening courtyard it wanes
Yet will not go to rest.
In the shade of the willow the young cicada bursts into song
Fireflies hover over the ancestral halls.
Listen. Whence comes this song of Ling?
The painted boat is late returning
The jade cords sink lower and lower
The gentlefolk are silent.
A vision of delight.
Let us rise and take each other by the hand
And tire our hair.
The moon lights up the silken curtains.
But there are no sleepers there.
The brave mandarin duck tumbles the lotus leaves
On the gently rippling water
Sprinkling them with drops like pearls.
They give forth fragrance.
A perfumed breeze moves softly over the flower-beds
Beside the summer-house
How can our spirits fail to be refreshed?
Why crave for the islands of the blest, the home of
fairies?
Yet, when the west wind blows again, Autumn will come
with it.
Though we perceive it not, the seasons change.

So singing, they reached the corner gate almost before they
knew it. Tower of Jade gave her guitar to Plum Blossom and
went to the inner court with the Lady of the Vase.

"Wait for me," Golden Lotus cried, "I am coming too." Hsi-mên Ch'ing caught her by the hand and pulled her back.

"So you would run away from me, little oily mouth," he cried. "I shall not let you go." He pulled so hard that she almost fell.

"You funny creature," Golden Lotus cried. "They are both going. Why won't you let me go?"

"We will drink a little wine together," Hsi-mên said, "and play 'Flying Arrows beneath the T'ai Hu rock.' "

"We can play quite well in the summer-house," Golden Lotus said. "Why stay here? And it's no use asking this young scamp Plum Blossom to bring any wine. She won't do it."

Hsi-mên Ch'ing told Plum Blossom to go. She handed the guitar to Golden Lotus and went off with her head in the air. Golden Lotus strummed the guitar for a while. "I have learned a few bars from Tower of Jade," she said. She saw how freshly the pomegranate flowers were blooming after the rain, and laughingly plucked one and set it in her hair. "I am an old lady, wearing on my brow a 'starving-for-three-days' flower."

Hsi-mên seized her tiny feet. "You little villain," he cried, "if I weren't afraid of somebody seeing us, I'd make you die of delight."

"Don't get so excited, you naughty fellow," Golden Lotus said, "Let me put down this guitar." She laid the intrument beside a flower-bed. "My son," she said, "you have only just finished amusing yourself with the Sixth Lady. Why should you come and plague me now?"

"You are still talking nonsense," Hsi-mên said, "I never touched her."

"My boy," Golden Lotus said, "you may try as hard as you like, but you will never succeed in deceiving the God who watches over Hearth and Home. What is the use of trying to hoodwink an experienced old woman like me? When I went to the inner court to take that flower, the pair of you wasted no time."

"Oh, do not talk such rubbish," Hsi-mên cried. He set her down among the flowers, and kissed her lips. She slipped her tongue into his mouth.

"Call me 'darling,' and I'll let you get up," he said. Golden Lotus could not help herself. She called him "darling," but, she added, "It isn't me you really love, so why do you bother me?"

They amused themselves for a while, and then Golden Lotus suggested that they should go and play "Flying Arrows" in the Arbour of the Vines. She took the guitar into her lap and played.

They walked side by side. Soon they had turned by the shaded pool and passed the Hall of the White Rose. Then they went in front of the Kingfisher Hall and came to the Arbour of the Vines. It was a very beautiful place.

They came to the arbour. There were four summer stools there, and near them a vase for the game of "Flying Arrows." Golden Lotus set down the guitar and played the arrow game with Hsi-mên Ch'ing. Then Plum Blossom came with wine, and Chrysanthemum carrying a basket of delicacies, with a bowl of iced fruits.

"You went off in a huff, young woman," Golden Lotus said. "What has made you decide to bring the things?"

"We have looked everywhere for you," Plum Blossom said. "How were we to know that you'd take it into your head to come here?"

Chrysanthemum set out the refreshments and Hsi-mên Ch'ing opened the basket. There were eight rows of exquisite fruits and sweetmeats in it, a little silver jar of grape wine, two small Golden Lotus cups and two pairs of chop-sticks. These they set upon a rustic table. Hsi-mên and Golden Lotus sat down before it but went on with their game. They played "Feathers through the Arch," "The Geese Flying on their Backs," "The Ch'iao Sisters Studying their Books," and "Yang Kuei-fei asleep in the Spring." Then they played "The Dragon entering his Cave" and "Pearls upon the Blind." All together, they had more than ten games. Then the wine went to Golden Lotus's head. The peaches began to bloom upon her cheeks, and her eyes lost their shyness. Hsi-mên thought he would like to drink the love-potion known as the wine of the five fragrances, and told Plum Blossom to go and fetch it.

"Little oily mouth," Golden Lotus said, "you can do something for me too. In my room you will find a summer mat and a pillow. Bring them here. I feel very sleepy and I think I shall lie down."

Plum Blossom professed to raise objections. "Oh dear," she said, "you give so many orders that nobody could possibly carry them all out."

"If you won't go," Hsi-mên said, "send Chrysanthemum. You bring the wine and we'll leave it at that." Plum Blossom went off, tossing her head. After a while Chrysanthemum came back with the mat, the pillow and some coverlets. Golden Lotus ordered her to set them out. "Then fasten the garden gate and go to your room, and don't come back until I call you." Chrysanthemum did as she was told, and went away.

Hsi-mên rose, and took off his jade-coloured light gown. He hung it on the trellis, and went to wash his hands by the peony arbour. When he came back, Golden Lotus had already prepared the mat and its cushions inside the arbour of the vines, and had undressed till not a thread of silk remained upon her body. She lay flat on her back, a pair of crimson shoes still upon her feet, fanning herself with a white silk fan to gain some relief from the heat.

When Hsi-mên Ch'ing saw her, his wanton heart was quickly

stirred, for the wine had not been without its effect upon him. He took off his clothes, and sat down on a stool, letting his toes play around the treasure of this beautiful flower.

Then the signs of desire appeared from her, like the moisture from snails' shells that makes the walks white and slippery. Hsi-mên removed her embroidered and decorated slippers. Taking the ribbons that bound her feet, he tied her feet loosely to the trellis, so that the golden dragon could clearly be seen, from tip to tail. The exquisite flexible door was open, and the protective overlooking ridges, delicately red, lay wide.

Hsi-mên Ch'ing lay down and, taking his weapon in his hands, prepared to storm the breach, resting one hand upon the pillow, and proceeding to the attack as he had played "Feathers through the Arch" when at the Flying Arrow game. He strove with all his strength, till from the scene of combat a mist arose, spiralling, like an eel rising from the mud.

Golden Lotus beneath him never ceased to murmur, "Darling, my darling." Then, as he was just about to reap the fruits of victory, Plum Blossom came suddenly with the wine for which Hsi-mên had asked. But when she saw them she put down the jar of wine, and fled to the top of the artificial mound, and there went into the arbour which was called the Land of Clouds. She rested her elbows on the chess-table, and amused herself setting out the chessmen. Hsi-mên Ch'ing lifted his head and looked at her; then he beckoned her to come down, but she refused. "If you don't come down, I will make you," he cried. He left Golden Lotus and ran up the stone steps to the arbour. Plum Blossom fled down a tiny path to the right, through the grottoes, till she reached a point half-way, where among the hanging foliage and flowers she tried to hide. Hsi-mên Ch'ing caught her there, and took her in his arms. "I've got you at last, little oily mouth," he cried. He then carried her like a feather to the Arbour of the Vines.

"Have a cup of wine," he said, laughing, setting her on his

knee, and they drank together mouth to mouth. Suddenly Plum Blossom saw that her mistress's feet were tied to the trellis.

"I don't know how you could do such a thing," she said. "It is the middle of the day, and if anybody should come in, what would they think of such goings on."

"Isn't the corner gate shut?" Hsi-mên asked.

"Yes," Plum Blossom said, "I shut it when I came in."

"Now," Hsi-mên said, "watch me. I'm going to play Flying Arrows with a living target. The game is called 'Striking the Silver Swan with a Golden Ball.' Watch! If I hit the mark at the first shot, I shall treat myself to a cup of wine." He took a plum from the iced bowl, and cast it at the exquisite flexible door. Some fell, some struck the secret flower. One plum clung. He had not gone on and carried to its conclusion the work that he had begun, so that the woman's heart worked, straining, beat harder and skipped beats. Her starry eyes were half closed, and her body fell back limply upon the mat. "You are indeed a roguish enemy," she murmured. "You will be the death of me." Her voice trembled.

Hsi-mên paid no attention to her, but told Plum Blossom to fan him, while he refreshed himself with wine. Then he lay down in an easy chair, and went to sleep. When Plum Blossom saw that he was asleep, she went softly over and touched him, then ran like a wisp of smoke to the Snow Grotto and so to the other side of the garden. There she heard someone knocking, opened the gate, and saw the Lady of the Vase.

Hsi-mên Ch'ing slept for an hour or so, and when he opened his eyes, Golden Lotus's white legs were still hanging from the trellis. Plum Blossom had gone. Again his passion was aroused.

"Now, you abandoned little creature," he cried, "I'll attend to you." He took out the plum, and gave it her to eat. Then, sitting on the pillow, he took from a pocket in his gown a case of love instruments. First he put on the clasp, and tied a sulphur ring about the root of evil. Showing no desire to go in, he played for a long time around the opening, until Golden Lotus cried wildly, "My love, my sweet, be a man fast or I'll go mad. I see what it is. You are angry with me because of the Lady of the Vase. That is why you tease me like this. But now I have found how cunning you can be, I will never make you angry again."

"Ah," cried Hsi-mên, laughing, "so you have learned your lesson. Well, speak nicely to me."

He looked ready to drive in to the deepest. But pulling back then, he came curve-wise seeking the arena that we call the "room of delight," the magically scented. On the edge, like a frog, he paused. Again he got ready to attack, and at once the warrior appeared tall and splendid, brilliantly glowing and warm, as Hsi-mên started to attack. On the mat, the woman lay, with her eyes half-closed, and whispered "My sweet savage! You can't get that into me. That thing terrifies me. Spare me, I beg." So she spoke without reserve. But Hsi-mên, not pausing, attacked with all his strength, placing his two hands on the mat. Now he pulled out, now he pushed in. He thrust to the deepest a hundred times before he withdrew. The woman covered her aching opening with a kerchief, but in vain; taking off the covering, he went openly to the battle, and the warrior, wrinkled and savage, permitted no pause. "It's time," Hsi-mên cried, "to strike the cymbals and drum." He thrust at once to the innermost castle: for within the exquisite flexible door there lies a castle, like the stem of a flower; and whoever reaches this is, indeed, the victor in love. The woman felt pain and pulled back; but within her, the sulphur ring cracked and broke in two.

She closed her eyes and her breath came faintly; only a faint murmur issued from her lips, the tip of her tongue became icy cold, and her body fell back apparently lifeless upon the mat.

Hsi-mên Ch'ing was alarmed. He hastily untied the ribbons, and removed the sulphur ring. It was broken into two pieces. Then he helped the woman to sit up, and at last her starry eyes began to gleam again, and she showed signs of life once more. In a caressing voice she said, "Darling, why did you treat me so cruelly today? You nearly killed me. You mustn't do this again. It is not simply fun. My head and eyes swim so that I hardly know where I am."

The sun was already setting. Hsi-mên hastily helped her into her clothes, and then called Plum Blossom and Chrysanthemum to come and take away the mat and the pillows. Then they supported her to her room. Plum Blossom came back to the garden to see that Chrysanthemum removed all the empty cups. She was just shutting the garden gate, when suddenly Lai Chao's little son Little Iron Rod jumped out of the summer-house, and asked her to give him some fruits.

"What have you been doing, you young rascal?" Plum Blossom cried. She gave him a few peaches and plums. "Your father has been drinking," she told him, "and you had better run off, for he will certainly beat you if he sees you."

The little monkey took the fruit and disappeared. Plum Blossom fastened the garden gate, returned to her mistress and Hsi-mên Ch'ing and helped them to retire.

Chapter 36: *Hsi-men Ch'ing entertains the laureate*

My heart is oppressed when I think of the distance before
  me
My spirit shrinks with fear before the journey I must
  take.
How can I not dread the hardship of the way?

Yet always I think of my duty to my country.
Chi Pu never forgot his promise
Hou Ying was faithful to his word.
In human hearts devotion always conquers
And men give up the thought of gold.

The next morning, Hsi-mên Ch'ing went with his colleague Hsia to welcome the new governor. He also went to see his new property and distributed gifts to all the workmen to show his appreciation of their labours. It was late when he reached home. As soon as he came to the gate, P'ing An told him that a messenger from Tung-ch'ang Fu had brought a letter for him from Chai, the Comptroller of the Imperial Tutor's household. "I took the letter to my mistress's room," he said. "To-morrow about noon the messenger will call for your answer." Hsi-mên Ch'ing hastened to the upper room, opened the letter, and read it.

To be delivered at the mansion of the most worthy Hsi-mên [it read]. For long I have been hearing of your fame and great renown, but it is long too since I beheld your glorious countenance. I have often benefited by your most gracious kindness and it is almost impossible for me to express my sense of indebtedness.

Some time ago, you were good enough to convey to me your instructions, and I have engraved them upon my heart. In every possible manner, I have done my utmost to serve you with his Eminence. So now, if I may trouble you about a trifle, there is a matter which I have already mentioned to your worthy attendant, and, doubtless, you have done what I desired. I take this opportunity of sending you my humble card together with ten taels of gold. Now I await your convenience. Meanwhile, may I present my best respects and trust that your high-mightiness will condescend to reply. Your kindness shall be ever in my heart.

The new laureate, Ts'ai I-ch'üan, is His Eminence's ward. He has just received the Imperial Command to return to his native place to visit his parents. He will pass by your honourable mansion and I trust you may find it possible to entertain him. He will be grateful for any kindness you may show him.

From my heart, the day after the Autumn Day, your servant Chai Ch'ien at the Capital.

When he had read this letter, Hsi-mên Ch'ing sighed. "Send a boy for a go-between at once," he cried. "However did I come to forget all about this matter?"

"What are you talking about?" the Moon Lady said.

"Comptroller Chai, of the Imperial Tutor's household," Hsi-mên said, "wrote to me the other day. He said he had no son and asked me to find a young girl for him. He does not care whether she is rich or poor, expense is no object with him. He simply wishes to find a good girl who will present him with a son and heir. He said if I told him what I spent on wedding presents he would repay me in full. And he said he would do all he could for me with the Imperial Tutor. But I have been so busy going to the office and attending to one matter and another, that I had forgotten all about it, and Lai Pao has not reminded me, since he is at the shop every day. Now Chai has been put to the trouble of sending someone all this way with a letter, and he asks me what has been done in the matter, and sends a present of ten taels. To-morrow the messenger is coming for an answer. What can I say to him? He will be very angry. Send at once for the go-between and tell her to find a girl without delay. She need not trouble about the girl's family. She must be a good girl and somewhere about sixteen or eighteen years old, that's all. Whatever it costs, I will pay.

Wait! Why shouldn't we send him Hibiscus, the Sixth Lady's maid? She is a pretty girl."

"You lazy-bones!" the Moon Lady said, "what have you been thinking about? He asked you to get him a really fine girl, and you ought to have done so. But you yourself have not left Hibiscus alone; we can't send her. You must treat this business as one of real importance. Sometime in the future Chai may be very useful to you. If you let your boat drift into the rapids, how can you use your oars? It isn't like buying ordinary merchandise, where you go to the market with your money and carry off what you like. When you are buying a girl, you must wait and give the go-between a chance, and see one after another. Some girls are good and some are bad. You don't seem to realise that it is not a simple matter."

"But he wants an answer to-morrow," Hsi-mên Ch'ing said. "What am I to say to him?"

"Have you been a magistrate all this time and can't manage a little affair like this? Tell the boy to be ready for the messenger when he comes; give him plenty of journey-money and a letter saying that you have found the girl, but that her clothes and things are not ready yet, and you will send her as soon as they are. When the messenger has gone, you can get someone to find a girl for you. There will be plenty of time. That's the way out of your difficulty, and you will have done a good day's work."

Hsi-mên Ch'ing smiled. "You are right," he said. He sent for Ch'en Ching-chi to write the letter. Next day when the messenger came, Hsi-mên Ch'ing himself went to see him and questioned him. "When does the Laureate's boat arrive? I must get ready to welcome him."

"When I left the Capital," the man said, "he had just left the court. Master Chai said he feared the Laureate might be short of money for his expenses, and perhaps you would lend him some. Then, perhaps, you will write to Master Chai, and he will repay you."

"Tell Master Chai," Hsi-mên Ch'ing said, "that no matter how much the Laureate needs, I will gladly lend it to him." He told Ch'ên Ching-chi to take the messenger to an anteroom and entertain him. When he was ready to leave, Hsi-mên gave him a letter and five taels of silver for journey-money. The man made a reverence and set out well pleased upon his long journey.

It may be remembered that some time before, An Shên had passed the examination in the highest place, but that the censors had objected that he was the younger brother of An Chun, who had been the first minister in the last reign. As a younger son of an evil party, they declared, he must not be placed at the head of all the scholars. Consequently, Hui Tsung could not do otherwise than put Ts'ai Yün in the position. Ts'ai Yün then went to the palace of the Imperial Tutor to be his ward. Later, he was appointed head of the Office of Secret Archives, and given leave to go and visit his parents.

The Moon Lady sent a boy for the two old women Fêng and Hsüeh, and another marriage-maker. She told them to make a thorough search for a good girl, and to bring her full particulars when they thought they had found one.

One day Hsi-mên Ch'ing instructed Lai Pao to go to the river to see what he could find out about Ts'ai's boat. Ts'ai was travelling on the same boat as An Chun, who had been given the third degree at the same examination as himself. An was so poor that he had not remarried. He seemed to be unlucky in every way. He had left the Court to try to find a wife in his native place, and so the two scholars came to be travelling together on the same boat.

Lai Pao took Hsi-mên Ch'ing's card and went on board. He had a dinner sent from the shore.

Before the Laureate had left the Capital, Chai had told him that at Ch'ing Ho he would meet a certain Captain Hsi-mên, one of the Imperial Tutor's clients. "He is a rich man," Chai had said, "and a very pleasant fellow. It was through his Eminence's influence that he came into his present position. I am sure that he will entertain you most hospitably if you should go there."

The Laureate had not forgotten this and he was delighted when he found that Hsi-mên Ch'ing's servant had come so far to meet him, bringing such a handsome present.

The next day he and An came to call on Hsi-mên Ch'ing who had arranged a feast in their honour. Hsi-mên had seen a number of actors and singers from Su-chou, and now he sent for four of them. Ts'ai offered a present of a silk handkerchief, a number of books, and a pair of shoes. An brought a gift of books and a handkerchief, with four bags of young tea and four Hang-chou fans. Both the scholars wore robes of ceremony and black hats, and sent their cards before them. Hsi-mên Ch'ing, wearing his ceremonial hat, welcomed them and invited them to go to the great hall. There they made reverences to one another; the two young men offered their presents to Hsi-mên Ch'ing, and they all sat down in the proper order of guests and host.

"My friend Chai at the Capital," the Laureate said to Hsi-mên Ch'ing, "has spoken very highly of you. He says your honourable family is the most important in Ch'ing Ho. Consequently, I have been longing to see you for some time, but this is the first opportunity I have had. Now that to-day I have been permitted to enter your hall, I feel that Heaven has indeed been gracious to me."

"You are unduly kind," Hsi-mên said. "I had a letter from master Chai the other day telling me that your worthinesses were about to visit us on your emblossomed boat. I should have been there to welcome you, but, unfortunately, my official duties would not allow me. I must most humbly beg your pardon. May I be allowed the honour of knowing from what enchanted country and glorious family you worthy gentlemen come?"

"The humble student before you," Ts'ai said, "is a native of K'uang-lu in Ch'u-chou, and his poor name is I-ch'üan. I had the good fortune to take the first place in the examination and to receive an appointment as head of the Department of Secret Archives. At the moment, I am on leave, and on my way to visit my parents."

"The humble student before you," An said, in his turn, "is a native of Ch'ien-t'ang of Chê-chiang, and his undistinguished name is Fêng-shan. I have just received the appointment of Inspector of the Board of Works. I, too, am on leave and am returning to marry in my native place. May we know your own honourable second name?"

"I am only a poor military officer of low rank," Hsi-mên Ch'ing said, "how should I dare to allow myself to be called by my second name?" When they pressed him, he said at last: "My poor name is Ssu-ch'üan. I have frequently been favoured by the kindness of his Eminence through the good offices of Master Chai, and, in that way, was granted my present appointment as Captain. I perform certain legal duties but am really quite unfitted for the post."

"Honoured Sir," the Laureate said, "you are not a man of mean ambition, and your reputation for delicacy has long been known. Do not let us stand on ceremony with one another."

Hsi-mên Ch'ing invited them to take off their robes of ceremony in the pavilion in the garden. But the Laureate said: "I am anxious to get home and our boat is at the wharf. Really I ought to go now. Yet, since I have basked in the sunshine of your company, I feel I cannot leave you so soon. What shall I do? What shall I do?"

"If you two noble gentlemen," Hsi-mên Ch'ing said, "do not disdain this snail's abode, pray let the banner of literature rest here a while. Take a little food with me, and let a small repast of celery prove the earnest of my goodwill."

"Since we are offered such exalted hospitality," the Laureate said, "we humble students can do no less than obey your commands." They took off their ceremonial robes and sat down.

The servants brought more tea. Ts'ai looked about him. The garden, the pool, the pavilions and the flowers stretched so far and were so luxuriant that he could not see everything at a single glance. "This is fairyland," he said delightedly. A table was set and they played chess.

After a while, Hsi-mên said: "I have brought a few actors here to-day for your amusement."

"Where are they?" An said. "Why not send for them?"

In a moment the four actors appeared and kotowed.

"Which of you take the part of the hero and heroine?" Ts'ai said. "And what are your names?"

One replied: "I take the hero's part; my name is Kou Tzu-hsiao. This is the heroine and he is called Chou Shun. This one takes the second part: he is called Yüan Tan, and the other, the young man, is Hu Tsao."

An asked them where they came from. Kou Tzu-hsiao said they were from Su-chou. "Good!" said An. "Now go and dress and then play for us."

The four actors went away to dress. Hsi-mên Ch'ing told someone to find women's clothes and ornaments for them. He told Shu T'ung to dress up too. So, three women and two men, they played Hsiang Nang Chi.

At the upper end of the great hall two tables were set. The two scholars sat in the seats of honour, and Hsi-mên Ch'ing in the host's place. While they drank their wine the actors finished one act. An saw Shu T'ung dressed as a girl and asked who he was.

"That is my boy Shu T'ung," Hsi-mên Ch'ing told him.

An called the boy to him and gave him some wine. "This boy excels all the boys I have ever seen," he said. Meanwhile Ts'ai summoned the actors who had taken the parts of girls and gave wine to them. Then he called for the song of Ch'ao Yüan. Kou Tzu-hsiao obeyed, and, clapping his hands, began.

By the willows and the flowers
The spider weaves a glistening web under the eaves.
Beside the mountains and the waters
The east wind is kind to the horse's back.
But I must journey like a wandering spirit
Dreaming about my home, whether I will or not.
The geese are silent, and the fishes deep beneath the water
And my heart is broken with the pain of separation
The day is short. My mother, in the northern hall, wearies
  of her dreams.
When shall I come to the Ninth Palace of Gold?

Then An asked Shu T'ung if he knew the lines beginning: "The mercy of the gods is infinite" from the Yü Huan Chi. "I do," Shu T'ung said, and began.

The mercy of the gods is infinite
I met my father and my mother again
It is a kindness man may seldom hope for.
Fortune has given me a peaceful life, a worthy mate.
I fly as the clouds fly in the wind
My love to me is like a female phoenix to her mate.
True it must be that not in this life marriages are made
And, in my last life, I must have set the jade in Lan-t'ien.

An, who was from Hang-chou, was fond of boys. He was delighted with Shu T'ung's singing, held his hand, and took wine from his mouth.

After a time they had all had wine enough, and Hsi-mên Ch'ing took his guests to look at the gardens. They played chess in the summer-house. Hsi-mên told the boys to bring two boxes filled with every kind of delicacy to eat with their wine.

"This is the first time we have met you," the Laureate said. "We must not place too great a strain upon your hospitality. It is late and we should go."

"Noble Ts'ai," Hsi-mên cried, "how can you think of going yet? Are you really thinking of going back to your boat?"

"I propose to spend the night in the Temple of Eternal Felicity, outside the walls," Ts'ai said.

"It is too late for you to go outside the city now," Hsi-mên Ch'ing said. "Keep one or two of your attendants here and let the rest return to-morrow for you. Then we shall all be content."

"I greatly appreciate your kindness," Ts'ai said, "but I hesitate to give you so much trouble." Nevertheless, he and his companion told their servants to go to the temple and spend the night there, and come again in the morning with their horses. They played two games of chess in the summer-house, and the actors performed till it was late. Then Hsi-mên paid and dismissed them. Shu T'ung alone remained to serve wine and other things.

They drank till it was dark and the lamps were lighted. Then they went to change their clothes. The Laureate took Hsi-mên's hand and said to him:

"I am going home to see my parents and I am a little short of money."

"Please do not let that trouble you," said Hsi-mên, "I shall be only too glad to do what Master Chai suggested."

He asked the scholars to go into the garden with him and led them round the white wall till they came to the Cave of Spring and into the Snow Cavern. There the lamps and candles were lighted. The place was comfortable and warm. A table was set with fruits and wine, and couches were arranged, with books and musical instruments. There they drank wine again and Shu T'ung sang for them.

"Do you know the song about the Fairy Peaches touched with red?" the Laureate asked Shu T'ung.

"Yes, I think I remember it," the boy answered, "it goes to the tune of the Moon in the Hall of Tapestries." He poured wine for them, then clapped his hands and began to sing.

An's feelings were indescribably moved. "The boy is perfectly adorable," he said to Hsi-mên Ch'ing. He emptied his cup.

Shu T'ung was wearing a green gown with a red skirt, a golden ribbon at his waist. He raised the jade cup high in the air to offer wine to them, and then sang another song. They enjoyed themselves until far into the night. At last they were ready to go to bed. Hsi-mên Ch'ing had had silken coverlets prepared for them in the Cave of Spring and the Kingfisher Hall. He told Shu T'ung and Tai An to wait on them. Then he said good-night and went to the inner court.

The next morning the servants came for the two scholars, bringing horses and sedan-chairs. Hsi-mên Ch'ing had food made ready in the great hall, and refreshments for all the attendants. Two boys brought in square boxes of presents. To the Laureate Ts'ai he offered a roll of gold silk, and silk for making collars, perfume and a hundred taels of white gold. He gave to An a roll of coloured satin, one piece of silk for collars, perfume, and thirty taels of white gold. The Laureate at first refused to accept it. "Ten taels will be quite sufficient for my needs," he said. "Why should you give me so much? You are too generous."

"Brother Ts'ai," An said, "do you accept, but I dare not."

Hsi-mên Ch'ing smiled. "These trifling things are nothing more than a token of my regard for you. You are going home and you are about to take a wife. I should like to help you to get a little tea."

The scholars rose and thanked him. "We shall never forget your kindness," they said. Then they bade their servants remove the presents. "We must go," Ts'ai said to Hsi-mên Ch'ing, "and renounce the benefit of your instruction for a while. But before long we shall be returning to the Capital. Then, if a slight measure of advancement should come to us, we shall do something to return your kindness."

"I hope to behold the glory of your dignity again," An said.

"Indeed," Hsi-mên said, "I only hope your honour has not been tarnished by this stay in my snail's nest. I beg your indulgence for all that has been done amiss. I would come to see you on your way, but, unfortunately, my duty calls me and I can only say good-bye."

He took them to the outer gate and watched them mount their horses.

Chapter 41 :   *The baby Kuan Ko is betrothed*

Hsi-mên Ch'ing watched the tailors as they hastily made up the dresses, and the work was finished in two days. On the twelfth, a messenger came from the Ch'iao household to renew the former invitation. That morning Hsi-mên Ch'ing had sent presents. The Moon Lady, Aunt Wu, and the others set off together in six sedan-chairs, leaving Beauty of the Snow behind to look after the house. The nurse, Heart's Delight, took Kuan Ko, and Lai Hsing's wife, Fragrant Blossom, went with them to act as tiring-maid. They too went in sedan-chairs. At home Hsi-mên Ch'ing watched the firework-makers making their fireworks, and superintended the hanging of the lanterns in the great hall. He sent a boy with his card to the house of the princely family of Wang to engage the actors.

In the afternoon he went to Golden Lotus's room. Golden

Lotus was not there, and Plum Blossom gave him something to eat.

"I have invited several ladies to come on the fourteenth," he told her. "You four girls must wear your best clothes when you wait upon them."

Plum Blossom leaned over the table. "You should say that to the other girls. There will be no dressing for me."

"Why?" said Hsi-mên.

"The ladies will all be dressed in their new clothes," Plum Blossom said. "They will be very smart, and we shall look like burned paper. Everybody will laugh at us."

"But you all have dresses and ornaments, and pearls and flowers," Hsi-mên Ch'ing said.

"The ornaments are all right, but we have no clothes," Plum Blossom said. "I have only two old dresses and I am not fit to be seen."

"I see," Hsi-mên said, laughing. "I have had clothes made for the ladies, and you are jealous, little oily mouth. Never mind. I am going to tell the tailor to make three dresses for my daughter, and you four girls shall each have a suit and a short dress of figured satin."

"Don't put me in the same class with the rest," Plum Blossom said. "I want a white silk coat and a scarlet-figured silk wrapper."

"If it were only for you," Hsi-mên said, "it would be all right; but if you have one, my daughter will have to have one."

"Your daughter has one already," Plum Blossom said. "I have not. I don't see how she can object."

Hsi-mên Ch'ing took the keys and went upstairs. He chose enough material for five dresses and two figured satin wrappers, and took a roll of white silk for two double-breasted white cloaks. The wrappers for his daughter and Plum Blossom were scarlet; those for the other three maids were bluish green. There were scarlet satin short coats and light blue skirts for all of them, seventeen pieces of material in all. Hsi-mên told the tailor to make the clothes, and gave him a roll of thin yellow silk for the tops of the skirts, and Hang-chou lining silk for the linings. Plum Blossom was satisfied. She laughed and talked all day with Hsi-mên Ch'ing and served him with wine when he wished for it.

Madam Ch'iao had invited several ladies to her party. There was the wife of Master Shang, Censor Sung's wife, a young woman named Ts'ui who was connected with the family, two nieces, Miss Tuan and Wu Shun-ch'ên's sister-in-law Chêng. She had engaged two singing-girls to play for them. When the Moon Lady, Aunt Wu, and the others arrived, Madam Ch'iao went to the second door to welcome them and took them to the great hall. There they exchanged greetings. She called the Moon Lady "Aunt," and the others "Second Aunt," and "Third Aunt," and so on. Then she introduced the other ladies and all took their places in due order. The maids brought tea, and Master Ch'iao came to ask them to go to the inner room to take off their cloaks. A table was set, tea brought, and they all sat down to drink it. Heart's Delight and Fragrant Blossom looked after the baby and were entertained in another place.

After tea they came back to the great hall, where handsome screens were placed about and cushions embroidered with lotus flowers. Four tables were set and the Moon Lady was asked to take the place of honour. The eleven ladies all sat at one table, except for Miss Tuan and Miss Chêng, who were at a table apart. The two singing-girls sang for them. When soup and rice had been served the cooks served up a crystal goose. The Moon Lady gave them two ch'iens of silver. Then stewed trotters were served, and the Moon Lady gave the cooks another ch'ien. Then came roast duck and again the Moon Lady gave the cooks a ch'ien. After this course Madam Ch'iao rose and offered wine, first to the Moon Lady and then to Master Shang's wife. The

Moon Lady left the table and went to the inner room to change her clothes and powder her face.

Tower of Jade went to Madam Ch'iao's room, where Heart's Delight had the baby Kuan Ko. He was in a small crib placed on the bed, and, lying beside him, was the little girl baby of the Ch'iaos. The two babies were playing together, putting out their hands to touch one another. This delighted the Moon Lady and Tower of Jade. "These two babies," they said, "are like bride and bridegroom." Aunt Wu came in, and they said to her: "Come here, Aunt Wu, and look at this young couple."

"Yes," Aunt Wu said, smiling, "they are stretching out their hands and kicking their little heels, touching one another, just like a young husband and wife."

Madam Ch'iao and the other ladies heard what Aunt Wu said. "How might an inconsiderable family like mine," Madam Ch'iao said, "aspire so high as to ally itself with that of my aunts?"

"You are very kind," the Moon Lady said, "but indeed what manner of lady are you, and Miss Chêng too? I should very much like to enter into an alliance with this household, if only my son will not make your house ashamed. Do not say that."

Tower of Jade pushed forward the Lady of the Vase. "Sister," she said, "what have you to say?" The Lady of the Vase smiled but said nothing.

"If Madam Ch'iao does not agree," Aunt Wu said, "I shall be very disappointed."

Master Shang's wife and the Censor's lady both said together: "For the sake of your kinswoman, Lady Wu, you must not stand too much on ceremony. Your Chang-chieh was born in the eleventh month of last year."

"And our baby," the Moon Lady said, "was born on the twenty-third day of the sixth month. He is just five months older. Their ages could not be more suitable."

The others would allow no further parley. They urged Madam Ch'iao, the Moon Lady and the Lady of the Vase to the great hall. There, pieces were cut from the bosoms of their dresses. The two singing-girls sang for them and Master Ch'iao was told. He brought out fruits, three pieces of red cloth, and offered wine. The Moon Lady told Tai An and Ch'in T'ung to go home and refer the matter to their master. In a short time, two jars of wine, three rolls of silk, red and green thread, flowers of gold wire, and four large boxes of cakes and fruit were brought from Hsi-mên's place, and the two households together hung up red charms and drank wine to celebrate their union.

Tall silver candlesticks blazed with light in the hall. Flower-shaped lamps burned brightly. Incense filled the air with delightful perfume. Smiling serenely, the two singing-girls opened their ruby lips, showed their white teeth and gently plied their jade plectrums. They held their lutes in one hand and sang. The ladies put flowers and red talismans on the heads of the Moon Lady, Madam Ch'iao, and the Lady of the Vase. When wine had been served, the ladies made reverence to one another and began their banquet again. As the first course, the cook brought in a snowflake pie, filled with mincemeat. The word Long-Life was fashioned upon it. There was lotus-seed soup, which looked as delightful as a pool, the seeds floating side by side upon its surface. The Moon Lady sat in the place of honour; she was very happy. She told Tai An to give the cook a roll of silk, and each of the singing-girls a roll of silk also. They all kotowed to thank her.

Madam Ch'iao would not allow the ladies to go away. She took them to the inner court where she had prepared all kinds of delightful refreshments for them. It was not until the first night-watch that the Moon Lady was able to leave.

"My dear relative," she said to Madam Ch'iao, "you must come to our poor house to-morrow."

"You are very kind," Madam Ch'iao said. "My husband has spoken to me of your invitation, but I fear I am no fit person to come to your party just now. Perhaps you will allow me to come some other time."

"There will be no strangers present," the Moon Lady said. "Please do not stand on ceremony." Then she said to Aunt Wu: "There is no reason why you should leave when we do. You will be coming with Madam Ch'iao to-morrow."

"Madam Ch'iao," said Aunt Wu, "if you do not care to go to-morrow, any other day will serve as well, but the fifteenth is your new kinswoman's birthday, and that day you must not fail to go."

"Oh," Madam Ch'iao said, "if it is my relative's birthday, how should I dare not go?"

"If Madam Ch'iao does not come to see me I shall blame you," the Moon Lady said to Aunt Wu. Then, leaving Aunt Wu behind, she said good-bye and got into her chair. Two soldiers carried a large red lantern before the sedan-chair and behind it were two boys with lanterns. The Moon Lady was at the head of the procession, then Picture of Grace, Tower of Jade, Golden Lotus and the Lady of the Vase each in her place. Then came the chairs with Heart's Delight and Fragrant Blossom. The nurse had Kuan Ko closely wrapped in a red silk coverlet, and as still further protection against the cold, she had a brass warming-pan in the chair. Two more boys followed her.

When they came to their gate and got out of their chairs, Hsi-mên was drinking in the Moon Lady's room. The Moon Lady and the others came in and made reverence to him. Then the Moon Lady sat down and all the maids came to kotow to her. She told her husband about the betrothal. He asked what ladies had been present. She told him.

"This marriage," he said, "is all very well, but the families are not of equal rank."

"It was my sister-in-law's doing," the Moon Lady said. "She saw the Ch'iaos' baby lying on the same bed as Kuan Ko, covered with the same bedclothes, so that the children looked like two young lovers, and she called me to look at them. When we were having supper, we could not help talking about it, and it was arranged. I sent the boy to tell you and get you to send the boxes of fruits."

"Now that it has been settled," Hsi-mên Ch'ing said, "it doesn't matter, but there is a certain inequality of position. Ch'iao has some property, but he is only a private citizen, while I am an officer and have duties at the courts. If we have to ask him to a party here, he will wear an ordinary hat, and I don't see how I can invite him to sit with me. It will be most awkward. Only the other day Ching Nan-kang sent one of his people to try to arrange a marriage. His daughter was five months old, the same age as our own child, but I did not care much for the arrangement because the baby's mother is dead. Besides, she was not the daughter of the first wife. So I would make no promises. Now, without my knowing anything about it, you have gone and settled everything yourself."

"If you did not care for that child because she is a second wife's daughter, what are you going to do now?" Golden Lotus said. "The Ch'iao baby is a second wife's daughter too. It seems to me like Hsien Tao-shên and the God of Long Life, one complaining that the other is too tall, and the other objecting that the first is too short."

This made Hsi-mên very angry. "You strumpet," he shouted, "why don't you take yourself off? We are talking, but nobody asked you to put in your word."

Golden Lotus flushed and went out of the room. "Of course," she said, "I have no right to speak in this place, or in any other place, for that matter."

When, at the party, Golden Lotus saw the arrangements

being made between Madam Ch'iao and the Moon Lady, and the Lady of the Vase wearing flowers and red charms upon her hair, it had made her very jealous. Now that Hsi-mên spoke angrily to her, she was still more upset and went to cry in the Moon Lady's inner room.

"Why has Aunt Wu not come back with you?" Hsi-mên asked the Moon Lady.

"Madam Ch'iao said she would not come to-morrow because we have ladies of rank coming, so I left Aunt Wu there, and they will come together."

"I told you there would be difficulties about precedence," Hsi-mên said. "I don't know what you are going to do about it."

Some time later, Tower of Jade went into the inner room and found Golden Lotus in tears. "Why are you so upset?" she said. "Let him say what he likes."

"You heard what I said to him," Golden Lotus cried. "It was nothing wrong. He said that child was not born in proper wedlock, and I said that neither was the Ch'iao baby. There is nothing there to complain about. But that bandit—he will come to a bad end—glared at me and swore without rhyme or reason. What does he mean by saying I had no right to speak? He has changed his tune completely. I'll see he gets paid out for it. There is that baby, a miserable, puny little thing that can do nothing but piddle, and they begin arranging a marriage for him. It is because they have so much money they don't know what to do with it. May he tear his coverlets and have nothing to cover him! May he be like a dog snapping at a bladder and get no joy out of it.

"To-day the prospects of this marriage seem rosy. Let us hope they won't look different in time to come. They are behaving just like a man who puts out the light, blinks his eyes, and wonders what on earth is going to happen next.

They think this is a good house to marry into; we shall see what they think in four or five years' time. This is the only child he has."

"In these days, people are always trying to be clever," Tower of Jade said. "I don't care much for this sort of behavior, myself. It seems to me too early. The baby is so young. They might have dispensed with the cutting of the cloth. But perhaps they only want to be friendly and do this sort of thing for fun."

"If it is meant for fun, well and good," Golden Lotus said, "but why should that rascal curse me?"

"You shouldn't have said what you did say," Tower of Jade said. "He couldn't help himself."

"I find it hard to say all I think about it," Golden Lotus said. "That woman is not a second wife any longer. She is the lady of the house. But even if Ch'iao's baby is the daughter of a second wife, there is no doubt she has old Ch'iao's blood in her veins. Whereas, in our household, people have not always gone straight, and who knows whose blood runs in our baby's veins?"

Tower of Jade said nothing. They talked a while longer, then Golden Lotus went to her own room. The Lady of the Vase waited until Hsi-mên Ch'ing had gone away, then she kotowed most gracefully to the Moon Lady.

"I am grateful to you," she said, "for all that you have done for my child to-day."

The Moon Lady smiled and returned her reverence. "It is you who are to be congratulated."

"You also, Sister," the Lady of the Vase said. She stood up while the Moon Lady and Picture of Grace sat down to talk. Beauty of the Snow and Hsi-mên's daughter came in and kotowed to the Moon Lady, making an equal reverence to the Lady of the Vase. Tiny Jade brought tea. While they were drinking it, Hibiscus came and said the baby needed his mother. Hsi-mên Ch'ing had told her to come.

"It was thoughtless of the nurse to take the child to my room," the Lady of the Vase said. "I ought to have gone with them, for I don't suppose there was a light."

"When they came home," the Moon Lady said, "I told Heart's Delight to take the child to your room. It was so late."

"I saw Heart's Delight with the baby," Tiny Jade said; "Lai An was carrying a lantern for them."

"That is all right, then," the Lady of the Vase said, and went to join her baby. She found Hsi-mên Ch'ing in her room and the baby asleep at his nurse's breast.

"Why didn't you tell me you were going to bring the child here?" she said to the nurse.

Heart's Delight told her that the Moon Lady had seen Lai An with a lantern and told her to bring the baby to his mother's room. "Young Master cried for a while," she said, "but I have got him to sleep now."

"Yes," Hsi-mên Ch'ing said, "the baby wanted you for a while but he has gone to sleep now."

"He has been betrothed to-day," the Lady of the Vase said, "and I must kotow to you." She knelt down. Hsi-mên was very pleased with her and beamed with delight. He quickly raised her to her feet and sat beside her. They told Welcome Spring to set a table, and they drank together.

Golden Lotus went to her room in a most vicious temper. She knew that Hsi-mên Ch'ing was with the Lady of the Vase and, when Chrysanthemum was a moment slow in opening the door for her, she boxed her ears and cursed her loudly.

"You thievish slave," she cried, "why did I have to knock so long before you opened the door? What are you here for? I shall not speak to you again." She went into her room and sat down. Plum Blossom came and gave her some tea.

"What was that thievish slave doing?" Golden Lotus said.

"She was sitting in the courtyard," Plum Blossom said. "I told her to open the door for you but she didn't pay any attention."

"Oh, I know," Golden Lotus cried; "just because he and I have had words, she is like Grand-Marshal Tang eating a tablet. She thinks she will put on airs and annoy me."

Golden Lotus would have liked to give Chrysanthemum a beating but she was afraid Hsi-mên Ch'ing might hear. She said no more for the moment, but she was angry none the less. Then she undressed. Plum Blossom prepared her bed. She got into it and went to sleep.

Next day when Hsi-mên Ch'ing had gone to his office Golden Lotus made Chrysanthemum balance a piece of stone on her head and kneel down in the courtyard. When she had finished dressing her hair she told Plum Blossom to take down Chrysanthemum's trousers and beat her with a thick stick.

"I shall soil my hands if I take down your trousers," Plum Blossom said to her fellow-maid. She went to the front court and called for Hua T'ung. The boy took down the girl's trousers while Golden Lotus stood by and cursed her.

"You thievish slave," she cried, "where did you learn to give yourself such airs? Others might forgive you but I never will. Sister, you know I understand your little ways, and you would do well to restrain yourself. Who are you to put your face forward and show what a great person you are? Sister, don't count on getting help from any other quarter. I shall keep my eyes skinned and watch you." She struck and cursed her and cursed and struck her till Chrysanthemum squealed like a pig being killed.

Meanwhile the Lady of the Vase had got up. The nurse was trying to rock the baby to sleep but he kept on waking. She could hear Golden Lotus cursing Chrysanthemum, and recognised all the references to herself in what was said. But she said nothing, and only covered Kuan Ko's ears with her hand.

"Go and ask the Fifth Lady not to beat Chrysanthemum," she said to Hibiscus. "Tell her the baby has just had his milk and is going to sleep."

Hibiscus gave the message, but Golden Lotus beat Chrysanthemum more severely still. "You thievish slave," she cried, "you shout as loudly as though someone were sticking ten thousand knives into you. But I am a queer person; the louder you cry, the more I shall beat you. I did not expect outsiders to interfere because you were having a beating. Why do you come to have a look? My good sister, you ought to tell our husband to get rid of her."

The Lady of the Vase heard all this, and knew that the curses were aimed at her. She was so angry that her hands were as cold as ice, but she swallowed her anger and did not show any temper. That morning she had no tea. She carried Kuan Ko in her arms and rocked him to sleep.

When Hsi-mên Ch'ing came back from his office he went to see his son. The Sixth Lady's eyes were red with weeping and she was lying on the bed.

"Why have you not dressed your hair?" he asked her. "The one in the upper room wishes to see you. And why are your eyes red?"

Instead of telling him about her trouble with Golden Lotus, the Lady of the Vase said she was not very well. Hsi-mên told her that the Ch'iaos had sent some birthday presents for her, a roll of silk, two jars of southern wine, a plate of longevity peaches, another plate of noodles, and other dishes. "They have sent something for the baby too," he said, and told her all the different things that had come. "We have done nothing for them," he added, "and now they have sent all these things for your feast day. That is why the one in the upper room wishes to talk to you. They sent old woman K'ung and Ch'iao T'ung with the presents. Aunt Wu has come back. She says

Madam Ch'iao cannot come until the day after to-morrow. She has a relative, Lady Ch'iao V, who is related in some way to the royal family. This Lady has heard about the betrothal and is very pleased. She is coming on the fifteenth too, so we must send a card to her."

The Lady of the Vase got up and slowly dressed her hair. Then she went to the inner court to see Aunt Wu and old woman K'ung. They were having tea in the Moon Lady's room. The presents were set out there. She looked at them all. The cases were returned, and old woman K'ung and Ch'iao T'ung were each given two handkerchiefs and five ch'iens of silver. When a card of thanks had been written out they went away.

(CLEMENT EGERTON)*

Some Further Readings

Egerton, Clement, trans. *Golden Lotus*. 4 vols. London: Routledge, 1939.

Marin, Richard, trans. *Jou Pu Tuan* (The Prayer Mat of Flesh), by Li Yu. Translated from a German version by Franz Kuhn. New York: Grove Press, 1963.

*Latin parts of this translation have been rendered into English by McNaughton.

23

DREAM OF THE RED CHAMBER

As far as many specialists and even general readers are concerned, "the great Chinese novel" is *Dream of the Red Chamber*. *Dream of the Red Chamber* tells us about a very wealthy and powerful Chinese family, about their enjoyment of power and wealth, and about their loss of them. Of Chinese novels, *Red Chamber* introduces us to a higher social class than any we have seen before. The author, Ts'ao Hsüeh-chin (A.D. 1719–1763), knew what he was writing about, for his father had held extremely high position, and the family had enjoyed extraordinary luxury and, later on, had suffered extraordinary reverses.

The title has multiple significances. The word usually translated as "chamber" is *lou,* which really means a storied building. Since only the wealthy lived in *lou,* you know from the title that the novel is about wealth. Some students take the "red *lou*" to refer to young ladies' quarters, which fits the novel well enough; other students see in the "red" a Buddhist drift about material glory, and that fits the novel well enough, too.

The central figure of the novel is Pao Yu. Pao Yu, like Ts'ao Hsüeh-chin, is the son of an eminent and wealthy official. But it is not contradictory that a young man should be the "central figure" in a novel whose title alludes to the young ladies' quarters, since that is where Pao Yu spends most of his time. The two other most important characters are Precious Clasp and Black Jade. Pao Yu wants to marry Black Jade, and his elders want him to marry Precious Clasp. One of the author's greatest successes is his drawing of these two female characters, and part of the success comes because the two ladies so nicely contrast with each other.

Everybody lives in one of the great compounds in which powerful Chinese families—including more remote members and branches of the clan—traditionally lived. Besides Pao Yu, Black Jade, and Precious Clasp, the main characters are Pao Yu's father, Pao Yu's grandmother, and Madame Phoenix. The father is after Pao Yu to study for the examinations, and the grandmother protects Pao Yu from his father. Pao Yu doesn't study much; he is too busy enjoying the gardens, writing poetry with Black Jade and Precious Clasp, and licking the lipstick off the serving-girls in his entourage. Madame Phoenix manages many of the household affairs, and she eventually becomes an efficient cause of the family's woe by practicing an art which for ages was the curse of China's populace: usury.

Whether Ts'ao Hsueh-chin himself actually went through all this, we do not know. His father's wealth, it seems, was reduced more by personal visits from the emperor and his party than by mismanagement or crime. But Ts'ao is said to have had many of Pao Yu's weaknesses, and he never passed the examinations. He wrote *Red Chamber* while living in a poorer section in Peking. And according to the prevailing scholarly view, he himself did not even finish the novel; the last third of it was written twenty years or so later by Kao O.

Dream of the Red Chamber is more of a novel, in the modern critical sense, than the other novels we have seen in this anthology: that is, it examines with a more sophisticated eye the difficult spiritual and philosophical questions of life; it makes certain serious assumptions and statements about values. That fact is no doubt responsible, in part, for the high esteem in which its Chinese readers hold it and for the reputation which it seems to be winning as a masterwork of world literature.

Also responsible for its reputation, of course, is the great artistry with which it is plotted, characterized, and written. This artistry is based on the novelist's great familiarity with the scene—the life and people—he describes. In traditional China the most important arena for the individual's life was the clan or "greater family," and no other novelist has presented this arena or the archetypal events in it as brilliantly as Ts'ao Hsüeh-chin. Although they enjoyed reading about them and their adventures, few Chinese could really identify with a pilgrim monk, the members of a bandit gang, or a paragon of vice. On the other hand, almost any Chinese might find part of himself, or of someone he knew well, in the main characters of *Dream of the Red Chamber*. "Over the the past hundred and more years," a modern Chinese literary historian says, "*Dream of the Red Chamber* has had a following in every social class and has been loved by a wide variety of readers. It has especially affected the emotional attitudes of the sons and daughters of intellectuals."*

The novelist has woven together with the events in his characters' lives the main spiritual forces in Chinese society—Buddhism, Taoism, Confucianism. He has done so with such superb objectivity that, as my literary historian says, "Even to recent days, there have been schools of 'Red Chamber fanatics' and 'Red Chamber specialists,' including even some Taoists, who have bored into the book and have found there their own twisty interpretations." Some Confucians say that the novel is a moral treatise to exemplify the opening sentences of the Confucian classic *The Great Learning*:

> The way of *The Great Learning* lies in bringing to light illustrious virtue. It lies in treating the common people like relatives. It lies in being at rest in perfect good.

The novel's German translator says that it "is undeniably Taoist." I would prefer not to take a position among these various disputants. Let the reader find his own truth in the book where he may.

---

* Liu Ta-chieh, *Chung-kuo wen-hsueh fa-chan shih* [Chinese Literature, Its History and Development] (Shanghai: Ku-tien wen-hsueh ch'u-pan-she, 1958), 3 vols., Vol. III, p. 336.

Chapter 6: *Pao Yu tries for the first time the "Play of Cloud and Rain." In the Ningkuo palace he becomes acquainted with his nephew Chin Chung*

Pao Yu lay on the bed for a while longer, quite exhausted and giddy from the experience of his dream. He felt as if he had lost something. Having strengthened himself with a few sips of cinnamon soup, he got up and the maid Pearl helped him to dress. As she was about to fasten his garter her finger chanced to touch his bare thigh and she felt something like cold, sticky sweat. She drew her hand back in alarm.

"What has happened to you?" she whispered. His blush and a light pressure of the hand was the answer. Now, Pearl was quite an intelligent girl and besides she was two years older than he and already knew the facts of life. She understood at once, blushed herself, and did not ask anything more.

When she was helping him to undress again that same night before he went to bed, she happened to be in the room with him alone for a while.

"Look here, dear sister, you will keep it to yourself, won't you?" he begged her, blushing again.

"What did you actually dream, that this happened to you?" she replied, with an understanding smile.

"I cannot tell it all to you in one word." And he began to describe his dream adventure in detail. When he came to the part of his story where the fairy instructed him in the practice of the "Play of Cloud and Rain," Pearl coyly covered her face with her hands and doubled up with laughter. Pao Yu had always been very familiar with Pearl. He liked the friendly, pretty little thing better than all the other maids and servants. Pearl on her part was aware of the special position of confidence with which the Princess Ancestress had honored her. Because of this she permitted herself some liberties in her association with her charge.

In short, she did not hesitate to try out at once with him the "Play of Cloud and Rain," whereby they faithfully followed the instructions imparted to him. Luckily, they were left undisturbed while thus occupied. From that hour he no longer treated her as a servant but as an intimate friend, and she rewarded his confidence with still more ardent devotion.

One day Madame Phoenix was over in the Ningkuo palace visiting Princess Chen and her daughter-in-law Mistress Yung. At his own request she had taken Pao Yu with her. While the three ladies were conversing as usual about household matters the time seemed very long to him. Mistress Yung, who noticed that he was restlessly fidgeting about this way and that way on his seat, said to him:

"My younger brother, for whom you recently asked, happens to be here today. He is probably in the library now. If you like, go and welcome him!"

Pao Yu quickly slid down from the heated divan.

"Why do you not have him come here? I should also like to make his acquaintance," suggested Madame Phoenix. "Or perhaps I should not ask to?"

Mistress Yung tried to dissuade her from her request. The boy was so shy and simple, quite different from the cheeky, lively boys of the Chia clan. She would be disappointed and would only be inclined to laugh at him. But Madame Phoenix stuck to her request, and so to please her Chin Chung, for so the boy was called, was brought in. Madame Phoenix was most agreeably surprised. The boy, who bowed to her and politely inquired her health, compared very well with Pao Yu, who was the same age. He was somewhat slimmer than the latter, but in beauty of face and form, in liveliness of expression, in his whole deportment and his charm of manner, he almost surpassed him, except that he was a little shy and awkward, almost like a girl. Madame Phoenix took him by the hand, drew him down to her side, and began questioning him energetically about his name, age, lessons, and everything possible. Meantime she had hurriedly sent some servants of her retinue back to the Yungkuo palace belatedly to fetch some gifts such as are usually presented by the elder to the younger upon first meeting. Bearing in mind the close friendship between Madame Phoenix and Mistress Yung, they chose some specially valuable presents, namely, a piece of silk for a new coat, and two gold medallions inscribed with the wish that the owner would win first place at examinations. Madame Phoenix considered these gifts too insignificant, so great was her sympathy for her new nephew.

While the ladies then settled down to a game of chess, Pao Yu took the opportunity of leaving the table with his nephew and going to chat with him undisturbed in a side room. The boy had made a deep impression on him. When he first saw him, he thought to himself, quite abashed: Compared to such a person I am no better than a dirty pig or a mangy dog! Who knows, if I, like him, had grown up in the cold poverty of a simple, honorable, middle-class family, I might have made his valuable acquaintance long ago and not dawdled away my time uselessly as I have done up to now. What is the good of riches and rank? This silk finery which I wear only hides the hollow, rotten core of an inferior being. These luxurious meals, on which I feed every day, only conceal the dirty refuse-pit of a corrupt character. The two conceptions, riches and rank, mean nothing but dirt and poison!

The painful reflection of Chin Chung upon seeing Pao Yu for the first time, in all his finery and with his large retinue, was exactly the opposite. Oh, what misfortune, he mused, to come from a poor, even though honorable, civil service family! That is indeed the curse of poverty, that it sets up an insurmountable barrier between people like him and people like me. If it were not for that I should probably long ago have enjoyed the advantage of his company.

Thus, both one and the other of them was moved by confused, foolish reflections. After a few opening questions about books and studies, they became friendly. Pao Yu was so eager to get to know the inner family circumstances of his new companion that he quite forgot about the dainty morsels and fruits which had been sent over to them from the table. He learned that at the moment Chin was without schooling, as his previous tutor had had leave of absence for months past. His father was old, sickly, and overburdened with official duties, and therefore unable to bother much about his education. All he could do at present was to go through his old lessons over and over again, but unfortunately he lacked the company of a good comrade, for one could learn much better in company than alone.

"That is what I think too!" interrupted Pao Yu eagerly. "You know we have a free family school here for those members of the clan who cannot have their own tutor or do not want to keep one. At my father's wish I myself am soon going to attend this school for a time; for my former tutor has also got several months' leave, and my father does not want to have me sitting around idle meantime, forgetting what I have learned. I would have been attending the school long ago if I had not been ill. Besides, Grandmother was against it up to now, because she thinks that in a class with a lot of pupils there would be nothing but disturbance and mad pranks. But my father now insists that there must be an end to my idling. Would you not like to come to our school too? Then we could learn together and help one another. Won't you speak to your father about it?"

"With pleasure! Only recently my father greatly praised the institution of your family school. In fact, he has been intending to apply to my sister's father-in-law, Prince Chen, to accept me. But he has put off doing so again and again because he did not like to bother his illustrious relatives about such a trifle, and did not wish to seem obtrusive. But if my uncle thinks that his nephew would be of any use to him in the school, maybe to stir the India ink or to clean his writing implements, perhaps he would see about the matter himself and put in a word of recommendation? How grand it would be if we could study together! Besides, we could become real friends and give our parents less to worry about. There would be many advantages in it."

"Do not worry! I will speak about it to my grandmother at once. We will also tell your sister Yung and my sister-in-law Feng of our wishes, and you yourself must talk to your father. Then we shall see if the thing can be managed."

Meantime darkness had fallen and the time had come to get their lanterns. The two finished their earnest consultation, joined the company at the table again, and watched the ladies playing chess for a while. Princess Chen and Mistress Yung lost the game to Madame Phoenix and pledged themselves to pay their gambling debt by standing a banquet and theater the evening after next. Then they sat down again for an evening snack, after which the guests started to depart.

"Who is going to take Chin Chung home?" Princess Chen asked her women attendants.

"The majordomo has ordered Chiao Ta to do so," they said. "He is tipsy again and in his usual abusive humor."

"It is just too stupid to choose that old boor as an escort," exclaimed both Princess Chen and Mistress Yung at the same time, with annoyance. "But to cancel the order now would only irritate the old man."

"Is the carriage ready?" asked Madame Phoenix, turning to her attendants.

"It is waiting in front of the great hall," they replied. Madame Phoenix said good-by, took Pao Yu by the hand, and walked through the brightly illuminated hall between a solemn double row of silent servants to the carriage. Among the servants was old Chiao Ta, who was so drunk that he could not be prevented, even before the visitors, from disturbing the stately farewell ceremony by kicking up a horrible row and uttering filthy abuse. His rancor was directed against the majordomo Lai Sheng: "Is that the thing to do, to chase out an old man like me on a cold winter's night?" he howled at him. "When there's an unpleasant job to be done, I'm good enough for it, but for a nice job there are others. Is that justice? And to think that such a clumsy, blind tortoise should be majordomo! But beware that old Chiao Ta does not raise his foot and crush you, you miserable worm!"

During this volley of abuse Chia Yung walked through the hall by the side of Madame Phoenix and escorted her to her carriage. When the old man would not stop reviling, in spite of appeals from the other servants, Chia Yung rebuked him angrily:

"Will you shut up at last? If not, I will have you tied and locked up until you are sober again! And we shall see if you get out this time safe and sound!"

But the angry old man refused to be intimidated. He walked up to him menacingly, shouting: "Little friend, don't play the great gentleman before old Chiao Ta! If your forefathers did not dare to reprimand old Chiao Ta, how dare you, little cock, start cackling! Where would all your greatness be today without old Chiao Ta? Nine times I snatched your grandfather from the jaws of death! It was he who piled up all your riches. Is this treatment the thanks I get for my good services? Instead of rewarding me properly, you blow yourself up like a frog and play the great gentleman! The least I can expect is that you keep your mouth shut. Otherwise, just take care that my sword does not go into your body white and come out red!"

"Why have you not got rid of that dangerous old bandit long

ago?" whispered Madame Phoenix to her nephew from the carriage window, disgusted at the painful scene. "He is endangering the reputation of the whole family and making you a laughingstock before the people."

"You are right," agreed her nephew, nodding; and he ordered the servants to fetter the old man and lock him up in an empty shed near the stable. While they were dragging him away by force, Chiao Ta continued to shout and rage. "I will go to the Temple of the Ancestors and complain to the great old master! He shall learn what a clean-living brood he has left behind! Whoring like rutting dogs and fowls; cousins and brothers-in-law carrying on together 'scratching in the ashes'— that's all the accursed brood is good for! . . ."

In the face of this horrible, grossly obscene speech, which caused the sun to disappear behind the clouds in shame, and made the souls of the listeners almost leave their bodies in horror, the servants who were dragging him away could do nothing but stop his mouth with mud and horse manure.

Madame Phoenix and her nephew Yung, who understood every word of his abusive speech, behaved nevertheless as if they had heard nothing. But Pao Yu, in his innocence, could not refrain from asking Madame Phoenix during the journey in the carriage: "Sister, what did he mean by the expression 'scratching in the ashes'?"

Violently angry, which was quite unusual for her, she rebuked him: "Do not ask stupid questions! You not only listen to the foolish chatter of a drunkard, but have to ask questions about it! Just wait until I tell your grandmother! You will pay for this with a thrashing!"

"Ah, dear big sister, please do not tell on me! I certainly will not ask such a stupid question again," pleaded the frightened Pao Yu. Indeed, he would not have asked if he had known that the expression "to scratch in the ashes" referred to illicit association between a father-in-law and a daughter-in-law.

"Very well, dear child," said Madame Phoenix, quickly appeased. "And when we are home I shall speak to Grandmother and ask her for your sake to help to have your nephew Chin Chung admitted to your school."

Chapter 18: *Pao Yu falls out with two of his cousins at the same time. Two lovers tease one another with quotations from "The Play of the Western Pavilion"*

Chia Lien remained standing.

"Well?"

"The twenty-first will be Cousin Precious Clasp's birthday. How shall we celebrate it?"

"You must surely know that best yourself. You have had sufficient experience in celebrating birthdays."

"Yes, those of grown-up people; there are definite rules about those. But one cannot yet count Cousin Precious Clasp as an adult, and neither is she a child. That is the trouble."

"It's quite simple. We can celebrate her birthday just as Black Jade's was celebrated last year."

"Of course I had already thought of that. But it won't do, for when Grandmother recently inquired the ages of her various grandchildren, we realized that Precious Clasp is now fifteen, so she is marriageable. Grandmother thinks that we should pay special attention to the importance of this day."

"Good. Then we can arrange for the celebration to be somewhat more sumptuous than that for Black Jade's birthday."

"That's what I think too. I only wanted to have your agreement, so that you would not reproach me afterwards and scold me inconsiderately."

"Very well, very well! I am not as petty as all that. You worry yourself with unnecessary scruples. I am quite satisfied if you do not lecture me about my own affairs; I just mind my own business."

And he turned away laughing.

At the wish of the Princess, Precious Clasp, for whom she had a particular affection on account of her even, kindly, and courteous manner, was specially honored on her birthday with a theatrical performance as well as with the usual banquet. The evening before she was permitted to choose the menu and also the theatrical program. Precious Clasp was wise enough to choose certain sweet dishes and sensational and gruesome dramas, which she knew for certain were the Princess Ancestress's favorite dishes and favorite theatrical pieces. The banquet was held in the apartments of the Princess Ancestress. The nice little private stage, on which a troupe of youthful artists from Suchow showed their versatile talents, was set up in the inner courtyard of her residence.

When the performance was about to begin and all the female relatives had assembled, Black Jade was the only one missing. Pao Yu went off to fetch her. He found her lying on the divan in her room poring over books.

"Get up! Get up! It's time for breakfast. And besides, the performance is going to begin at once," he rallied her. "Have you any special wish with regard to the program? If so, I shall have it noted at once."

"No, thank you. If I were to choose, I would choose the whole program. The performance today is not in my honor."

"Have patience a little while! Then your turn will come, and you will be able to choose the whole program. But come now!"

And he laughingly dragged the reluctant Black Jade back with him. The performance lasted from morning until night, and exciting scenes from the adventurous "History of a Journey to the West" were alternated with merry farces such as "Mr. Lu Mislays his Coat" and "The Drunken Lu Brawls on the Wu tai shan," for the Princess Ancestress liked coarse low comedy turns too. After the entertainment she had two of the young artists with whom she was specially pleased brought to her. One of them had played the heroine; the other, the merry buffoon. The whole company gasped with admiring surprise when the two gifted artists declared, when asked, that they were only eleven and nine years old respectively. The Princess Ancestress had them sumptuously entertained and gave each of them a thousand-piece string of money as an extra fee.

"Does not the elder one, in his female attire, resemble a certain person we all know?" remarked Phoenix.

Precious Clasp understood at once whom she meant; she did not mention a name, however, but just nodded her head. Pao Yu followed her example. But Cousin Little Cloud could not refrain from bursting out in her impetuous way: "Why, of course, he is like Sister Black Jade!"

The warning, sidelong glance which Pao Yu shot at her came too late. Everyone noticed now; all scrutinized Black Jade and agreed amid laughter: "Yes, indeed, they are so much alike one could mistake them for one another!"

When Pao Yu was going to bed that night he heard Little Cloud in the next room ordering her maid to pack her things, and saying in reply to the maid's astonished question: "Yes, I am going away early in the morning. I do not wish to stay here any longer. This everlasting criticizing and watching of every word and every look does not suit me."

Pao Yu ran across to her room.

"Dear little sister, you are unjustly angry," he said, trying to placate her. "Black Jade is so terribly sensitive, and that is why I tried to warn you by a look not to mention her name; I was afraid she would take offense at being compared to an actor. I meant it well and you need not be so angry with me on account of it. If it was about anyone else. . ."

"That's enough!" Little Cloud interrupted him indignantly.

"Spare me your flowery words! What am I beside your cousin Black Jade? An ordinary girl beside a high-born lady, isn't that so? Others may make remarks about her, but I dare not. If I open my mouth, it's a crime."

"If I have ever thought of slighting you in the least, may I be turned instantly into the dirt of the road, on which everyone may trample!" protested Pao Yu in dismay.

"Make those flowery speeches to inferior people of your own kind, who, in their insensitiveness, know no better than to ridicule and mock their fellow beings, but spare me your common street jargon and do not provoke me to spit out before you!" replied Little Cloud furiously as she ran out of the room to the apartments of the Princess Ancestress, where she spent the night.

Pao Yu, who had run after her in vain, turned back much dejected. He was longing for Black Jade's company; but scarcely had he set foot in her room than Black Jade pushed him out and shut the door behind him. Pao Yu was perplexed.

"Dearest, best Mei mei!" he called with gentle entreaty through the door to her.

But Black Jade remained silent and invisible. Pao Yu hung his head and sank into sad thoughts. As there was no sound for a long time, Black Jade, thinking he had gone to his room, opened the door. Then she saw him still standing there like a poor sinner. Now she had pity on him and let him in.

"Will you not at least tell me why you are angry?" he began hesitantly.

She gave a short, dry laugh.

"You ask that? I should take it quietly when I am compared with a comedian and made ridiculous before the whole company?"

"But I did not make such a comparison, neither did I laugh at you."

"No, but your secret exchange of glances with Little Cloud

hurt me even more. I know well what you meant by it, that you think more of Little Cloud than of me, that she gives up something and lowers herself when she associates with me. Naturally, she is a high-born lady, a count's daughter, and I am only an ordinary girl of the people! Is not that what you meant? It's a pity that with your good intentions you have found so little reciprocal love from her and have to be reproached by her for going about with an inferior person like me, who, in her insensitiveness, knows no better than to ridicule and mock her fellow beings! I really do not understand your anxious consideration for her. She certainly does not thank you for it."

Pao Yu understood that she had been listening just now to his argument with Little Cloud.

That is what I get for my good intention of trying to play the part of mediator between them! he thought to himself bitterly. Now I have fallen foul of both of them, and have to put up with reproaches from both sides. The wise Chuang Tzu was right when he said "Why so much activity? It only gives one worry. Why trouble about all sorts of things? One is only annoyed by them. How splendid, on the other hand, only to care about one's own modest necessities of life, and so float on the waves free and alone as a boat adrift!" How useless is my striving and trouble! I do not even succeed in bringing about reconciliation and harmony between two girls! Why should I set myself higher aims?

Sunk in thought, he turned away from Black Jade to go back to his room.

"Go away! You need not come back again and you need not speak to me any more," she called after him.

Without taking any more notice of her he slipped back to his room and threw himself on the bed with a sigh. Pearl's voice startled him out of his brooding.

"We shall probably see more theatrical performances in the

next few days, for Miss Precious Clasp is sure to make the best of her opportunity," she remarked, trying to distract him.

"It's all the same to me," he replied, brusquely.

"How is that? In this happy New Year season everyone is merry and in good spirits. Why are you alone out of humor?"

"What is it to me if the others are enjoying themselves?"

"You should get on better with them; then you also would enjoy yourself."

"What have I to do with the others? After all, I am alone, quite alone. No one wants me."

Tears came to his eyes and he gave a loud sob. Then he got up, went to the writing table, took his brush, and worked off his ill-humor by writing a stanza full of the weariness of life and Buddhist renunciation of the world. Having done this, he felt more free and relieved, and lay down peacefully to sleep.

A little later Black Jade slipped into his room full of curiosity, under the pretext of looking for Pearl.

"He's already asleep," Pearl intimated to her quietly. "Here, read this! He has just written it."

Black Jade scanned the page of writing. She was amused at the contents but at the same time felt sorry for the boy.

"It's only a little foolery and means nothing," she said with apparent indifference, but she could not refrain from taking the sheet of paper away with her and giving it to Little Cloud and the next morning to Precious Clasp to read.

> "Do what you want to! Come, go, as you please!
> Weep! Laugh! It's all the same to me.
> What do I care about the world!"

Thus read the stanza, the first part of which was written in the Sutra style.

"Oh, Cousin Pao Yu wants to join the saints and renounce

the world!" the three of them cried, looking at each other with embarrassed smiles. Each of them felt a little bit guilty.

"Come, let us go to him together and bring him to reason!" suggested Black Jade. And the three of them set off together to the Chamber of the Fragrance of Culture. Black Jade drew his attention to the fact that his Buddhist stanza was incomplete, and she added the missing conclusive point; and Precious Clasp mentioned the case of a well-known Buddhist sectarian who had resigned the leadership of his sect in favor of his cook, when the latter put him to shame by the correct criticism of a similarly defective stanza which he had composed. Pao Yu remarked with embarrassed astonishment that his clever cousins knew more than he himself did about a sphere which he had thought quite unknown to them. If they in spite of this did not presume to belong to the "awakened," he concluded that his chance of attaining to even a modest degree of holiness was positively nil. He therefore resigned himself to abandoning all idea of further striving after Buddhist contemplation.

"It was only a jest, the mood of a moment," he explained, smiling. And with this the happy old relationship between the cousins was restored.

When Beginning of Spring, the Emperor's wife, had returned to the Court from her visit to the Park of Delightful Vision, she had expressed the wish that a monument should be erected in the park with an inscription which would commemorate for all time the happy event of her visit. Chia Cheng hastened to fulfill her wish, and entrusted the work to the most skillful stonecutters and engravers he could find.

The Imperial wife reflected, furthermore, that the Park of Delightful Vision, which had been made specially for her visit, would be shut up and sealed by her father after the visit through a sense of dutiful respect, and she said to herself that it would really be a pity if these beautiful places were to be left abandoned and unused in the future. Why should it not be made accessible to her sisters and cousins, who could make rhymes and stanzas so splendidly? Were they not worthy to lift up their minds and hearts amid the beautiful vistas of the park? And should not her brother Pao Yu also share this special privilege? For since his childhood he had been accustomed to the company of girls, and would find himself terribly lonely and neglected if he were suddenly deprived of the accustomed companionship.

Moved by these considerations, the Imperial spouse sent the Chief Eunuch Hsia to the Yungkuo palace with orders to this effect. Mr. Cheng and his wife lost no time in sending people to the park to clean up and furnish comfortably the various places of abode destined for Pao Yu and the young girls.

Pao Yu was very specially pleased with the changes which were to take place. He was just then with his grandmother discussing this and that matter regarding the change-over, when a servant came in to call him to his father. Pao Yu turned pale. His happy mood was swept away immediately. Craving protection, he pressed convulsively against his grandmother's right side as if she were a piece of sugar which was to be crushed to besprinkle a sweet dish. He did not want to go at any price, for he believed it was again to be one of those fatherly reprimands which he feared so much. The Princess Ancestress encouraged him, saying that he had nothing to fear, and that his father probably only wished to give him some instructions on good behavior before he left for the future dwelling. Accompanied by two worthy matrons, who had to act as personal guards, Pao Yu set out on the dreaded journey, but he went so slowly and unwillingly that he hardly progressed three inches every step. At last, very hesitantly, he entered the parental pavilion. How unpleasant were those half-curious, half-mocking glances which met him as he walked through the rows of servants in front of the entrance. A maid named Golden Bangle was actually so impudent as to pluck his sleeve as he passed by and whisper: "Now, what about it? Would you not like to lick the rouge from my lips? It is quite fresh and has a perfume."

Whereupon an older maid named Bright Cloud gave her a push and said reprovingly: "Ill-mannered creature! You see that he is not in a mood for such jests just now! Be off!"

Inside, Pao Yu found his father and mother sitting opposite each other on the divan engaged in conversation. The three Spring girls, and the younger brother Chia Huan, the son of a secondary wife of his father, were sitting at their feet on low stools. The younger relations, Taste of Spring, Grief of Spring, and Chia Huan, stood up as Pao Yu entered. Mr. Cheng scrutinized the newcomer sharply, then his glance wandered over to the other son, and he compared them. How favorably Pao Yu's prepossessing, cultivated appearance compared with the thickset, coarse appearance of the bastard! Mr. Cheng went on to reflect that his hair was already beginning to turn gray, and that he could scarcely hope to have another and better offspring than Pao Yu. Nine-tenths of the aversion which he usually felt towards Pao Yu vanished as a result of this silent reflection, and he sounded more gentle than usual when he said: "Her Imperial Highness has deigned to give orders that you are to continue your studies in future, in the company of your sisters and cousins, in the Park of Delightful Vision. But she desires you to pull yourself together and study seriously instead of loafing around. So now, comply with this order and be on your guard!"

Pao Yu managed to murmur a hurried *shih*—yes; there followed a short conversation between mother and son concerning his health, then a gruff "Why is that creature, that plague of my life, still standing there?" scared him quickly outside the door. Now looking happy, he ran nimbly through the lines of servants in the anteroom, cheekily sticking out his tongue at the maid Golden Bangle as he passed.

Chia Cheng fixed the twenty-second of the month as the most suitable day for the move. Meantime the various buildings which had been assigned as dwellings had been put in habitable order. Pao Yu and Black Jade managed to arrange for their quarters to be quite near one another. They each lived on their own, and besides the maids whom they had had up to now each had two elderly chaperons to supervise them and four maids for the rough work of the house.

Thus, on the twenty-second of the month, life and youth entered the hitherto desolate park, and the colorful flower beds and the willow leaves waving in the zephyr breezes could no longer be sad and complain of loneliness. The change of dwelling seemed to alter Pao Yu's whole personality. His dejection vanished and gave place to merry spirits. From now on he passed his days with the girls, reading and writing, strumming the lute or playing chess, painting or reciting verse, while the girls embroidered their phoenix patterns industriously, plucked flowers and identified plants, amused themselves playing dice and other drawing-room games, and sang songs in their gentle voices. He was completely happy and had never before been in such a good mood for writing poetry. Many of his verses and stanzas, though not perhaps showing extraordinary talent, but replete with feeling and keen observation of nature, as, for instance, his "Songs of the Four Seasons," found their way to the public. For there was no lack of flatterers and spongers eager to win his favor, who felt obliged to noise abroad in the streets and market places the fame of the distinguished fourteen-year-old boy poet of the Yungkuo palace, and to display copies of his poems. It became the fashion among the gay young set to decorate fans and walls of rooms with the latest soulful outpourings from the brush of the celebrated Pao Yu; it was considered intellectual to recite his latest poems at social functions; people competed fiercely to obtain a few lines written by his own hand, whether verse, or maxims, or even just short mottoes. Pao Yu felt very important and had his hands full satisfying all the claims made on him from outside.

Who would have thought that in spite of everything his old restlessness would be stirred up again so soon? One day the splendors of the park, which had charmed him so much in the beginning, began to bore him. He found fault with this and criticized that, and felt annoyed and dissatisfied. Also, the society of his companions did not satisfy him; their merry, boisterous playing, their ingenuous, frivolous, girlish ways left him cold. He longed for new diversions, stronger impressions. The fool!

His valet Ming Yen had been trying in vain for a long time to banish his ill-humor with various suggestions and distractions, but at last he got a new idea which succeeded. One day, after a walk through the booksellers' lane, he took home to his master a whole stack of unknown light literature, all novels and romances both old and modern, obscene love stories and tales of the adventures of famous courtesans and the like.

Pao Yu had never before seen such books. When he peeped into them now he became as if intoxicated, and as happy as if they were a valuable find. And the fact that he might only read these books secretly, as Ming Yen impressed upon him, made them doubly fascinating. He hid them as well as he could in his bed and in other safe places, and from now on he spent his time, whenever he was alone and undisturbed, eagerly delving into them.

One day, about the middle of the third month, he sauntered along after breakfast to the bridge leading to the Weir of Penetrating Perfumes, carrying the Hsi Hsiang Chi, "Play of the Western Pavilion," in his hand, and sat down to read on a rock under blossoming peach trees at the edge of the pond. As he was sitting there and had just come to a place in the book which described "falling red, gathered up in heaps," a sudden gust of wind blew through the branches and caused a heavy rain of petals to ripple down on him and his book. He was covered all over with the reddish petals and had to shake himself to get rid of the delicate burden. So lovely and charming did these petals seem to him that he would have been sorry to tread on them with his feet. Therefore, he gathered up with both hands the rosy piles which lay round about his seat and carried them to the near-by bank, there to shake them over the surface of the water. And each time that he had shaken out two handfuls in this way, he remained for a while on the bank looking after the flower petals thoughtfully, as they danced about on the waves and were gently drawn by the current towards the weir.

Just as he was bending down to gather together another heap of petals, he heard a girl's voice behind him asking: "What are you doing here?"

He turned around. There he saw Black Jade standing in front of him. She was carrying a spade over her shoulder, on the handle of which hung a flower carrier made of light gauze; in her left hand she had a broom.

"It's good that you have come! You can help me to sweep up these flower petals and throw them into the water. I have already thrown in quite a lot," he said.

"You should not do that! Here the water is tolerably clean, but later on when the petals have drifted farther along with the current, and float into other estates, they will come in contact with all kinds of dirt and refuse. It would be a pity for the lovely, pure petals to become soiled. No, it is better if we take them to the petal grave which I have just dug behind that hill. I shall sweep them up. You stuff them into the bag and then we will carry them to the grave together. In the course of time they will turn into good garden soil. Is not that nicer and cleaner than throwing them into the water?"

Pao Yu had to admit that she was right.

"Wait a moment until I put my book away; then we will set to work at once."

"What book have you got?" she asked.

"Nothing special; a commentary on 'The Great Philosophy'"

of Master Confucius," he replied quickly, trying to hide the book from her sight.

"Show it at once, you rogue!"

"For all I care you may see it, Mei mei, but please be so kind as not to say a word about it to other people. Anyway, it is quite a splendid book; the style is wonderful. You will not be able to give a thought to sleeping or eating if you read it. Here."

Black Jade laid down her garden implements and took the book. She sat down on the rock and began to read, and the more she read the more she was fascinated by the book, and she did not stop reading until she had skimmed through all its sixteen chapters in one go. Content and style enchanted her equally, and when she had finished she seemed still to taste in her mouth, as it were, the sweetness she had enjoyed; and, lost in thought, she recited to herself this and that passage which had remained impressed on her memory.

"Well, how did you like it?" he asked, smiling.

"It is really fascinating."

"Yes, isn't it? And does it not apply most remarkably to the two of us? I am the hero full of faults and weaknesses, and you— you are the heroine whose beauty causes the downfall of cities and countries," he quoted jokingly.

His remark made Black Jade flush a sudden deep crimson right up to her ears. She raised her brows and her dilated pupils flashed with anger as she hissed: "What impertinence! I must object to your connecting those common expressions and those improper passages with me! It is an insult. But just wait, I shall tell your parents!"

At the word "insult" fine little red veins became visible around her pupils. Now she turned away quickly and ran off. He ran after her dismayed and held her firmly.

"Dearest Mei mei, I beg your pardon a thousand—ten thousand times!" he pleaded. "I see that I have been talking nonsense, but I did not mean to insult you. If I did, may I be drowned in a deep pond and may a mangy tortoise eat me, and may I myself be turned into a big tortoise, and in some future time when you, the wife of a mandarin of first rank, have died of old age, may I for all time carry the socket of the pillars of your grave on my back!"

Black Jade could not help bursting out laughing on hearing this long, comical oath. She was soon appeased again. Casting a roguish glance at him, she said: "Besides, I could reply to you in the same tone if I wished to, and by way of example speak of a certain someone who resembles the famous lance with the silvered wax point."

"If you say such things I also will go and tell tales on you!" he threatened, jokingly.

"I only wanted to show you that I can read just as quickly as you can, and can remember what I read just as easily as you can. It is nothing to me to read ten lines of writing with one single glance. Or do you doubt that?"

"Oh, indeed I believe it. But now we will be sensible again and bury our poor petals."

They set to work again, and swept up and heaped the fallen petals and carried them to the petal grave behind the hill. Meantime the maid Pearl appeared. She had been sent by the Princess Ancestress to fetch Pao Yu. Prince Shieh was not well and Pao Yu was to go to him straight away and wish him a speedy recovery, as was proper. The Spring girls had already visited the sickbed. Pao Yu therefore bade farewell to Black Jade and left the park accompanied by Pearl.

Deep in thought, Black Jade sauntered slowly back to her house. As she was passing by the wall of the Pear Garden she heard from within the gentle sounds of flute playing and charming singing. The music came from the twelve dancing girls from Suchow, who had their quarters in the Pear Garden and were just now practicing a new theater piece. Black Jade was not paying particular attention to the singing, but two lines of one of the songs caught her ear so distinctly that she was able to understand every word. It was about a wonderfully beautiful purple flower, which blooms gloriously, only to be plucked, to wither, and to end miserably in some refuse pit.

Black Jade was touched to the core by the melancholy expressed in these two lines. Involuntarily she slackened her pace and listened hard in an effort to follow the rest of the text. And she could not but silently agree with the sentiments of the next two lines, which spoke of the transience of exterior splendor and good living when inner happiness was destroyed. And she had to sigh, thinking of the superficiality of human beings, who go to the theater only to be entertained and do not think at all of looking into themselves and applying to their own lives the truths which they hear on the stage. While still sunk in meditation, she heard the words:

> "As a flower in spring, beauty fades,
> As a fleeting wave, youth passes."

She felt deeply moved and frightened. Her head became dizzy, her feet refused to move, she staggered as if she were drunk, and had to sit down on a near-by rock. There she sat, murmuring to herself again and again the words she had just heard:

> "As a flower in spring, beauty fades,
> As a fleeting wave, youth passes."

At the same time it occurred to her that in the past she had read in old stories and also today in the "Play of the Western Pavilion" similar words about falling petals and running waters, passing spring and lasting sorrow. A feeling of infinite anguish and sadness stole upon her, her heart shrank, tears dropped from her eyes. She would have so loved to speak to someone, to let herself be comforted. Suddenly she felt a light tap on her shoulder. She turned around. A young girl was standing before her. You will learn from the next chapter who this girl was.

(FLORENCE AND ISABEL MCHUGH)

Some Further Readings

Lin Tai-yi, ed. and trans. *Flowers in the Mirror,* by Li Ju-chen. Berkeley: University of California Press, 1965.

McHugh, Florence, and McHugh, Isabel, trans. *The Dream of the Red Chamber.* Translated from the German adaptation by Franz Kuhn. New York: Pantheon, 1958.

Shadick, Harold, trans. *The Travels of Lao Ts'an,* by Liu T'ieh-yun. Ithaca, New York: Cornell University Press, 1952.

Wang Chi-chen, trans. *Dream of the Red Chamber.* New York: Twayne, 1958.

Yang Hsien-yi and Yang, Gladys, trans. *The Scholars.* Peking: Foreign Languages Press, 1957.

PART SIX:

THE LITERATURE OF
MODERN CHINA

24

MODERN FICTION AND
MODERN VERSE

The reader who has pursued Chinese literature with me
up to modern times will need very little introduction to
Chinese modern fiction or to Chinese modern verse.
China's fiction and poetry in the twentieth century have
been as much examples of what Goethe foresaw as
Weltliteratur as have the poetry and fiction of any nation.
Chinese poets and story writers made diligent and in-
tensive efforts to educate themselves in Western literature
and to bring to China, and to the resources of their
native literature, the resources and the insights of
European and American literature. The literate Westerner already is prepared to deal with this "new"
element in Chinese literature, and his readings so far
in the anthology should have prepared him to recognize
and to understand the basically Chinese elements.

It is no accident that the modern Chinese man of letters
should show Western influence. Even before the twentieth century, the Chinese nation was sending some of
her brightest students abroad to acquire "Western

learning" and to bring it back so as to modernize China. Chinese students studied in Japan, America, France, Germany. Many of them came back, with new techniques and new ways of writing which they had learned abroad, to attack with the pen China's problems and the vices— or what seemed to them to be the vices—of China's traditional society. They were influenced by Shakespeare, Shelley, Valery Laforgue, Mayakovsky. . . Perhaps the greatest difference between the pioneers of modern Chinese literature and the modern Western writers who so much have been influenced by China—Kenneth Rexroth in *Saturday Review* writes "more by Chinese literature than any other"—is that the Chinese actually went to the countries and actually learned their languages.

Lu Hsun (A.D. 1881–1936) probably is the most important of the fiction writers whose work appears below. Lu had been in Japan to study medicine and saw newsreels of the Russo-Japanese War in which Chinese men and women were drafted by the Japanese for manual labor. Lu decided his countrymen needed their minds and souls tended before their bodies, and he gave up medicine and began to write fiction. His first works were translations from Western fiction, and he did a book of them in collaboration with his brother. It sold about two copies. His later original fiction, especially *True Story of Ah Q* and "Diary of a Madman," was more popular. Lu Hsun also wrote a *Brief History of Chinese Fiction*.

Chinese poetry probably had a greater distance to travel in the twentieth century than did Chinese fiction, and the distance was largely linguistic. For fiction, there already existed in China the *hua-pen* and the novels which were written in colloquial—as opposed to classical—Chinese. The Chinese poet was expected to write in this classical Chinese—it was about as little like the language he spoke as Latin is like English—and, unlike the fiction writer, the poet had no precedent to appeal to, no "practical example" to imitate. The "literary revolution" which eventually brought China's poets to write more or less in the modern colloquial language, and which gained for such poetry both respectability and popularity, was started by Hu Shih (A.D. 1891–1965).

Hu Shih was studying at Columbia University, in New York, when he first saw the possibilities of a poetry in the colloquial language; he began to write poems to exemplify, and articles to promote, this new literature. Like Dante, who wrote *De Vulgari Eloquentia* in Latin to defend the use of Italian for his poetry, so Hu Shih in 1917 wrote in classical Chinese his first defenses of a Chinese literature in the colloquial language. His goal, as he put it, was "literature written in a modern language, and a modern language with literary capabilities." As a nation with twenty-five hundred years of literary tradition, China has seen her modern writers and poets make continual use of traditional literature; but the language which her poets and writers now use, though it owes no small part of its "literary capabilities" to China's traditional literature, is a modern language, and China now has what Hu Shih envisioned for her.

§ MODERN FICTION

A Madman's Diary

by Lu Hsun

Two brothers, whose names I need not mention here, were both good friends of mine in school; but after a separation of many years we lost touch. Some time ago I happened to hear that one of them was seriously ill, and since I was going back to my old home I broke my journey to call on them. I saw only one of them, however, who told me that the invalid was his younger brother.

"I appreciate your coming such a long way to see us," he said, "but he recovered some time ago and has gone elsewhere to take up an official post." Then, laughing, he produced two volumes of his brother's diary, saying that from these the nature of his past illness could be seen, for there was no harm in showing them to a friend. I took the diary away and read it through, and found that he had suffered from a form of persecution complex. The writing was most confused and incoherent, and he had made many wild statements; moreover he had omitted to give any dates, so that only by the colour of the ink and the differences in the writing could one tell that it was not written at one time. Certain sections, however, were not altogether disconnected, and I have copied out a part to serve as a subject for medical research. I have not changed a single word in the diary except for the names, even though the people referred to are all obscure country folk, unknown to the world. As for the title, it was chosen by the diarist himself after his recovery, and I did not change it.

*　　　*　　　*

Tonight the moon is very bright.

I have not seen it for over thirty years, so today when I saw it I felt in unusually high spirits. I begin to realize that during the past thirty odd years I have been in the dark; but now I must be extremely careful. Otherwise why should that dog in the Chao family have looked at me twice?

I have reason for my fear.

Tonight there is no moon at all, I know that is unlucky. This morning when I went out cautiously, Mr. Chao had a strange look in his eyes, as if he were afraid of me, as if he wanted to murder me. There were also seven or eight others, who had their heads together discussing me. And they were afraid of my seeing them. All the people I passed were like that. The fiercest among them bared his teeth in a smile; whereupon I shivered from head to foot, knowing that their preparations were complete.

I was not afraid, however, but continued on my way. A group of children in front were also discussing me, and the look in their eyes was just like that in Mr. Chao's, while their faces too were ghastly pale. I wondered what quarrel I could have with these children, to make them behave like this. I could not help calling out: "Tell me!" But then they ran away.

I wonder what quarrel I can have with Mr. Chao, what quarrel I can have with the people on the road. I can think of nothing except that twenty years ago I trod on Mr. Ku Chiu's account sheets and Mr. Ku was very displeased. Although Mr. Chao does not know him, he must have heard talk of this and decided to avenge him, so he is conspiring with the people on the road against me. But then what of the children? At that time they were not yet born, so why should they have eyed me so strangely today, as if they were afraid of me, as if they wanted to murder me? This really frightens me, it is so bewildering and upsetting.

I know. They must have learnt this from their parents!

I can't sleep at night. Everything requires careful consideration if one is to understand it.

Those people—some of them have been pilloried by the magistrate, some slapped in the face by the local gentry, some have
had their wives taken away by bailiffs, some have had their
parents driven to suicide by creditors; yet they never looked as
frightened and as fierce then as they did yesterday.

The most extraordinary thing was that woman on the street
yesterday who was spanking her son and saying, "Little devil!
I'd like to bite several mouthfuls out of you to work off my
feelings!" Yet all the time she was looking at me. I gave a start,
unable to control myself; then all those pale-faced, long-toothed
people began to laugh derisively. Old Chen hurried forward
and insisted on taking me home.

He took me home. The folk at home all pretended not to
know me; they had the same look in their eyes as all the others.
When I went into the study, they locked the door outside as if
cooping up a chicken or a duck. This incident left me even more
bewildered.

A few days ago a tenant of ours from Wolf Cub Village came
to speak about the crops, and told my elder brother that a no-
torious character in their village had been beaten to death by
everyone there; then some people had taken out his heart, fried
it in oil and eaten it, as a means of increasing their courage.
When I interrupted, the tenant and my brother both stared at
me. Only today have I realized that they had exactly the same
look in their eyes as those people outside.

Just to think of it sets me shivering from the crown of my
head to the soles of my feet.

They eat human beings, so what is to stop them from eating
me?

I see that woman's "bite several mouthfuls out of you,"
the laughter of those pale-faced, long-toothed people and the

tenant's story the other day are obviously secret signs. I realize all the poison in their speech, all the daggers in their laughter. Their teeth are white and glistening, used for eating human beings.

It seems to me, although I am not a bad man, ever since I trod on Mr. Ku's accounts I have been suspected. They seem to have secrets which I cannot guess, and once they are angry they will call anyone a bad character. I remember when my elder brother taught me to write compositions, no matter how good a man was, if I produced arguments to the contrary he would mark that passage to show approval; while if I excused evildoers, he would say: "Good for you, that shows originality." How can I possibly guess their secret thoughts—especially when it comes to the time for eating?

Everything requires careful consideration if one is to understand it. In ancient times, as I recollect, people often ate human beings, but I am rather hazy about it. I tried to look this up, but my history has no chronology, and each page bears the words: "Virtue and Morality." Since I could not sleep anyway, I read carefully half the night, until I began to see words between the lines, the whole book being filled with the two words—"Eat people."

All these words written in the book, all the words spoken by our tenant, gaze at me strangely with an enigmatic smile.

I too am a man, and they want to eat me!

In the morning I sat quietly for some time. Old Chen brought lunch in: one bowl of vegetables, one bowl of steamed fish. The eyes of the fish were white and hard, and its mouth was open just like those people who want to eat human beings. After a few mouthfuls I could not tell whether the slippery morsels were fish or human flesh, so I brought it all up.

I said, "Old Chen, tell my brother that I am feeling quite

suffocated, and want to have a stroll in the courtyard." Old Chen said nothing but went out, and presently he came back and opened the gate.

I did not move, watching to see how they would treat me, knowing that they certainly would not let me go. Sure enough! My elder brother came slowly out, leading an old man. There was a murderous gleam in his eyes, and fearing that I would see it he lowered his head, stealing glances at me from the side of his spectacles.

"You seem to be very well today," said my brother.

"Yes," said I.

"I have invited Mr. Ho here today," said my brother, "to examine you."

"All right," said I. But actually I know quite well that this old man was the executioner in disguise! He was simply using the pretext of feeling my pulse to see how fat I was; for by so doing he would be given a share of my flesh. Still I was not afraid. Although I do not eat men, I am braver than they. I held out my two fists, watching what he would do. The old man sat down, closed his eyes, fumbled for some time and remained still for some time; then he opened his shifty eyes and said, "Don't let your imagination run away with you. Rest quietly for a few days, and you will be all right."

Don't let your imagination run away with you! Rest quietly for a few days! When I have grown fat, naturally they will have more to eat; but what good will it do me, or how can it be "all right"? All these people wanting to eat human flesh and at the same time stealthily trying to keep up appearances, not daring to act promptly, really made me nearly die of laughter. I could not help roaring with laughter, I felt so amused. I knew that in this laughter were courage and integrity. Both the old man and my brother turned pale, awed by my courage and integrity.

But just because I am brave they are the more eager to eat me, in order to acquire some of my courage. The old man went out of the gate, but before he had gone far he said to my brother in a low voice, "To be eaten at once!" And my brother nodded. So you are in it too! This stupendous discovery, although it came as a shock, is yet no more than I had expected: the accomplice in eating me is my elder brother!

The eater of human flesh is my elder brother!

I am the younger brother of an eater of human flesh!

I myself will be eaten by others, but none the less I am the younger brother of an eater of human flesh!

These few days I have been thinking back: suppose that old man were not an executioner in disguise, but a real doctor; he would be none the less an eater of human flesh. In that book on herbs, written by his predecessor Li Shih-chen, it is clearly stated that men's flesh can be fried and eaten; so he can still say that he does not eat men?

As for my elder brother, it is also impossible to exonerate him. When he was teaching me, he said with his own lips, "People exchange their sons to eat." And once, in discussing a bad man, he said that not only did he deserve to be killed, he should "have his flesh eaten and his hide slept on." I was still young then, and my heart beat faster for some time. And the story about eating a man's heart and liver that our tenant from Wolf Cub Village told us the other day, he did not consider at all strange but kept nodding his head. It is evident that his outlook is unchanged. Since it is possible to "exchange sons to eat," then anything can be exchanged, anyone can be eaten. In the past I simply listened to his explanations, and let it go at that; now I know that when he was explaining to me, not only was there human oil at the corner of his lips, but his whole heart was set on eating men.

Pitch black. I don't know whether it is day or night. The Chao family dog has started barking again.

The fierceness of a lion, the timidity of a rabbit, the craftiness of a fox. . . .

I know their way; they are not willing to kill anyone outright, for fear of the consequences. So they have all banded together and set traps, to force me to kill myself. Just look at the behaviour of the men and women in the street a few days ago, and my elder brother's attitude these last few days, it is quite obvious. What they like best is for a man to take off his belt, and hang himself from a rafter; for then they are not blamed for murder, and can enjoy their heart's desire. Naturally that sets them roaring with delighted laughter. On the other hand, if a man is frightened or worried to death, although that makes him rather thin, they are still willing to eat him.

They will only eat dead flesh! I remember reading somewhere of a hideous beast, with an ugly look in its eye, called "hyena" which only eats dead flesh. Even the largest bones it grinds into fragments and swallows: the mere thought of this is enough to terrify one. Hyenas are related to wolves, and wolves belong to the canine species. The other day the dog in the Chao family looked at me several times; obviously it is in the plot too and has become their accomplice. The old man's eyes were cast down, but how could that deceive me!

The most deplorable is my elder brother. He is also a man, so why is he not afraid, why is he plotting with others to eat me? Is it that when there is sufficient historical precedent it is not considered as a crime? Or is it that he has hardened his heart to do something he knows is wrong?

He shall be the first man-eater I condemn, the first I start to dissuade.

Actually, such arguments should have been acknowledged long ago. . . .

Suddenly someone came in. He was only about twenty years old and I did not see his features very clearly. His face was wreathed in smiles, and when he nodded to me his smile did not seem genuine. Then I asked him: "Is it right to eat human beings?"

Still smiling, he replied, "When there is no famine how can one eat human beings?"

I realized at once, he was one of them; but I summoned up courage to repeat my question:

"Is it right?"

"What makes you ask such a thing? You really are. . . fond of a joke. . . . It is very fine today."

"It is fine, and the moon is very bright. But I want to ask you: Is it right?"

He looked disconcerted, and muttered: "No. . . . "

"No? Then why do they still do it?"

"What are you talking about?"

"What am I talking about? They are eating men now in Wolf Cub Village, and you can see it written all over the books, in fresh red ink."

His expression changed, and he grew ghastly pale. "It may be so," he said, staring at me. "It has always been like that . . . . "

"Is it right because it has always been like that?"

"I refuse to discuss these things with you. Anyway you shouldn't talk about it. To talk about it is wrong!"

I leapt up and opened my eyes wide, but the man had vanished. I was soaked with perspiration. He was much younger than my elder brother, but even so he was in it. He must have been taught by his parents. And I am afraid he has already taught his son: that is why even the children look at me so fiercely.

Wanting to eat men, at the same time afraid of being eaten

themselves, they all look at each other with the deepest suspicion. . . .

If they could only get rid of this obsession, they could go to work, walk, eat and sleep free from anxiety, very comfortably. They have only this one step to take. And yet fathers and sons, husbands and wives, brothers, friends, teachers and students, sworn enemies and even strangers, have all joined in this conspiracy, encouraging and implicating each other. And not for anything will they change their stand.

Early this morning I went to look for my elder brother. He was standing outside the hall door looking at the sky, when I walked up behind him, barred the door, and with exceptional poise and politeness said to him:

"Brother, I have something to say to you."

"Well, what is it?" said he, quickly turning towards me and nodding.

"It is very little, but I find it difficult to say. Brother, probably all primitive people ate a little human flesh to begin with. Later, because their outlook changed, some of them stopped, and because they tried to be good they changed into men, changed into real men. But some are still eating. Just like reptiles: some have changed into fish, birds, monkeys and finally men; but some do not try to be good, and remain reptiles still. When those who eat men compare themselves with those who do not eat men, how ashamed they must be. Probably much more ashamed then the reptiles before the monkeys.

"In ancient times a cook boiled his son for a tyrant to eat; that is the old story. But actually since the creation of heaven and earth men have been eating each other, down to the time of that cook, continuing to the time of the Revolution, and from the time of the Revolution to the case of the man caught in Wolf Cub Village. Last year they executed a criminal in the city, and a consumptive soaked a piece of bread in his blood and sucked it.

"They want to eat me, and of course you can do nothing about it singlehanded; but why should you join them? As man-eaters they are capable of anything. If they eat me, they can eat you; members of the same group can still eat each other. But if you will just change your ways immediately, then everyone will have peace. Although this has been going on since time immemorial, today we could be particularly kind to each other. You say it is impossible, brother, but I think it is possible. The other day when the tenant wanted the rent reduced, you said it was impossible."

At first he only smiled cynically, then a murderous gleam came into his eyes, and when I spoke of their secret his face turned pale. Outside the gate stood a group of people, including Mr. Chao and his dog, all craning their necks to peer in. I could not see all their faces, for they seemed to be wrapped up in cloths; some of them looked pale and ghastly still, concealing their laughter. I knew they were one band, all eaters of human flesh. But I also knew that they did not all think alike by any means. Some of them thought that since it had always been so, men should be eaten. Some of them knew that they should not eat men, but still wanted to; and they were afraid people might discover their secret; thus when they heard me they became angry, but they still smiled their cynical, tight-lipped smile.

Suddenly my brother looked furious, and shouted in a loud voice:

"Get out of here, all of you! What is the point of looking at a madman?"

Then I realized part of their cunning. They would never be willing to change their stand, and their plans were all laid; they had prepared the name of madman for me. In future when I was eaten, not only would there be no trouble, but people would probably be grateful to them. When our tenant spoke of the villagers eating a bad character, it was exactly the same device. This is their old trick.

Old Chen came in too, in a great temper, but they could not stop my mouth, I had to speak to those people:

"You should change, change from the bottom of your hearts!" I said. "You must know that in future there will be no place for man-eaters in the world.

"If you don't change, you may be eaten yourselves. Although so many are born, they will be wiped out by the real men, just like wolves killed by the hunters. Just like reptiles!"

Old Chen drove everybody away. My brother had disappeared. Old Chen advised me to go back to my room. The room was pitch black. The beams and rafters shook above my head. After shaking for some time they grew larger. They piled on top of me.

The weight was so great, I could not move. They meant that I should die. I knew that the weight was false, so I struggled out, covered in perspiration. But I had to say:

"You should change at once, change from the bottom of your hearts! You must know that in future there will be no place for man-eaters in the world. . . ."

The sun does not shine, the door is not opened, every day two meals.

I took up my chopsticks, then thought of my elder brother; I know now how my little sister died; it was all through him. My sister was only five at the time, sweet and lovable, I can still see her in my mind's eye. Mother cried and cried, but he begged her not to cry, probably because he had eaten her himself, and so crying made him feel ashamed—that is, if he had any sense of shame.

My sister was eaten by my brother, but I don't know whether Mother realized it or not.

I think Mother must have known, but when she was crying she did not say so outright, probably because she thought it proper. I remember when I was four or five years old, sitting in the cool in front of the hall, my brother told me that if a man's parents were ill he should cut off a piece of his flesh and boil it for them, if he wanted to be considered a good son; and Mother did not contradict him. If one piece could be eaten, obviously so could the whole. And yet just to think of the mourning then still makes my heart bleed; that is the extra-ordinary thing about it!

I can't bear to think of it.

I have only just realized that I have been living all these years in a place where for four thousand years they have been eating human flesh. My brother had just taken over the charge of the house when our sister died, and he may well have used her flesh in our rice and dishes, making us eat it unwittingly.

It is possible that I ate several pieces of my sister's flesh un-wittingly, and now it is my turn. . . .

How can a man like myself, after four thousand years of man-eating history—even though I knew nothing about it at first—ever hope to face real men?

Perhaps there are still children who have not eaten men? Save the children. . . .

(YANG AND YANG)

Kung I-chi

by Lu Hsun

The wine shops in Luchen are not like those in other parts of China. They all have a right-angled counter facing the street, where hot water is kept on tap for warming wine. When men come off work at midday and in the evening they buy a bowl of wine; it cost four cash twenty years ago, but now it costs ten. Standing beside the counter, they drink it warm, and relax. Another cash will buy a plate of salted bamboo shoots or spiced beans, to accompany the wine; while for a dozen cash you can buy a meat dish. But most of these customers belong to the short-coated class, few of whom have much money to spare. Only those in long gowns enter the adjacent room to order wine and dishes, and sit and drink at leisure.

At the age of twelve I started work as a waiter in Hsien Heng Tavern, at the entrance to the town. The tavern keeper said I looked too foolish to serve the long-gowned customers, so I was given work in the outer room. Although the short-coated customers there were more easily pleased, there were quite a few trouble-makers among them too. They would insist on watching with their own eyes as the yellow wine was ladled from the keg, looking to see if there were any water at the bottom of the wine pot, and inspecting for themselves the immersion of the pot in hot water. Under such keen scrutiny, it was very difficult to dilute the wine. So after a few days my employer decided I was not suited for this work. Fortunately, I had been recommended by someone influential, so he could not dismiss me, and I was transferred to the dull work of warming wine.

Thenceforward I stood all day behind the counter, fully engaged with my duties. Although I gave satisfaction at this work, I found it monotonous and futile. Our employer was a fierce-looking individual, and the customers were a morose lot, so that it was impossible to be gay. Only when Kung I-chi came to the tavern was any laughter heard. That is why I still remember him.

Kung was the only long-gowned customer to drink his wine standing. He was a big man, strangely pallid, and scars often showed among the wrinkles of his face. He had a large, unkempt beard, streaked with white. Although he wore a long gown, it was dirty and tattered, and looked as if it had not been washed or mended for over ten years. He used so many archaisms in his speech, it was impossible to understand half he said. Whenever he came into the shop, everyone would look at him and chuckle. And someone would call out:

"Kung I-chi! There are some fresh scars on your face!"

Ignoring this remark, Kung would come to the counter to order two bowls of heated wine and a dish of spiced beans. And he would produce nine cash. Someone else would then call out, in deliberately loud tones:

"You must have been stealing again!"

"Why spoil a man's good name groundlessly?" he would ask opening his eyes wide.

"What good name? Day before yesterday I saw you with my own eyes being hung up and beaten for stealing books from the Ho family!"

Then Kung would flush, the veins on his forehead standing out, as he remonstrated: "Taking a book can't be considered stealing. . . . Taking a book, the affair of a scholar, can't be considered stealing!" Then followed quotations from the classics, like "The perfect man is content with poverty," and a jumble of archaic expressions till everybody was roaring with laughter and the whole tavern was gay.

From gossip I heard, Kung I-chi had studied the classics but had never passed the official examination, and had no way of making a living; so he grew poorer and poorer, until he was practically reduced to beggary. Happily, he was a good calligrapher, and could get enough copying work to support himself. Unfortunately he had failings: he liked drinking and was lazy. So after a few days he would invariably disappear, taking books, paper, brushes and inkstone with him. And after this had happened several times, nobody wanted to employ him as a copyist again. Then there was no help for him but to take to pilfering. In our tavern his behaviour was exemplary. He never failed to pay his debts, although sometimes, when he had no ready money, his name would appear on the board where we listed debtors. However, in less than a month he would always settle, and his name would be wiped off the board again.

After drinking half a bowl of wine, Kung would regain his composure. But then someone would ask:

"Kung I-chi, do you really know how to read?"

When Kung looked as if such a question were beneath contempt, they would continue: "How is it you never passed even the lowest official examination?"

At that Kung would look disconsolate and ill at ease. His face would turn pale and his lips move, but only to utter those unintelligible classical expressions. Then everybody would laugh heartily again, and the whole tavern would be merry.

At such times, I could join in the laughter without being scolded by my master. In fact he put such questions to Kung himself, to evoke laughter. Knowing it was no use talking to them, Kung would chat to us children. Once he asked me:

"Have you had any schooling?"

When I nodded, he said, "Well then, I'll test you. How do you write the character 'hui' in 'hui-hsiang' [a kind of spice] beans?"

I thought, "I'm not going to be tested by a beggar!" So I turned away and ignored him. After waiting for some time, he said very earnestly:

"You can't write it? I'll show you how. Mind you remember! You ought to remember such characters, because later when you have a shop of your own, you'll need to use them."

It seemed to me I was still very far from owning a shop; besides, our employer never entered "hui-hsiang" beans in the account book. Amused yet exasperated, I answered list-lessly: "Who wants you to teach? Isn't it the character 'hui' with the grass radical?"

Kung was delighted, and tapped two long finger-nails on the

counter. "Right, right!" he said, nodding. "Only there are four different ways of writing 'hui.' Do you know them?" My patience exhausted, I scowled and made off. Kung I-chi had dipped his finger in wine, in order to trace the characters on the counter; but when he saw how indifferent I was, he sighed, and a hurt look came into his eyes.

Sometimes children in the neighbourhood, hearing laughter, came to join the fun, and surrounded Kung I-chi. Then he would give them spiced beans, one apiece. After eating the beans, the children would still hang round, their eyes on the dish. Flustered, he would cover the dish with his hand and, bending forward from the waist, would say: "There isn't much. I haven't much as it is." Then straightening up to look at the beans again, he would shake his head. "Not much! Verily, not much, forsooth!" Then the children would scamper off, with shouts of laughter.

So amusing was Kung I-chi. However, without him we got along all right too.

One day, a few days before the Mid-Autumn Festival, the tavern keeper was laboriously making out his accounts. Suddenly, putting down his slate, he said: "Kung I-chi hasn't been in for a long time. He still owes nineteen cash!" That made me realize how long it was since we had seen him.

"How could he come?" one of the customers said. "His legs were broken in that last beating."

"Ah!"

"He was stealing again. This time he was fool enough to steal from Mr. Ting, the provincial scholar! As if anybody could get away with that!"

"What then?"

"What then? First he had to write a confession, then he was beaten. The beating lasted nearly all night, until his legs were broken."

"And then?"

"Well, his legs were broken."

"Yes, but after that?"

"After? . . . Who knows? He may be dead."

The tavern keeper did not pursue his questions, but went on slowly making up his accounts.

After the Mid-Autumn Festival the wind grew colder every day, as winter came on. I spent all my time by the stove, sometimes wearing my padded jacket. One afternoon, when the shop was empty, I was sitting with my eyes closed when I heard a voice:

"Warm a bowl of wine."

At this point my employer leaned over the counter, and said: "Is that Kung I-chi? You still owe nineteen cash!"

"That. . . I'll settle next time," replied Kung, looking up disconsolately. "Here's ready money; the wine must be good."

The tavern keeper, just as in the past, chuckled and said:

"Kung I-chi, you've been stealing again!"

But instead of protesting vigorously, the other simply said:

"You like your joke."

"Joke? If you didn't steal, why did they break your legs?"

"I fell," said Kung in a low voice. "I broke them in a fall." His eyes pleaded with the tavern keeper to let the matter drop. By now several people had gathered round, and they all laughed. I warmed the wine, carried it over, and set it on the threshold. He produced four cash from his ragged coat pocket, and placed them in my hand. As he did so I saw that his hands were covered with mud—he must have crawled here on them. Presently he finished the wine and, amid the laughter and comments of the others, slowly dragged himself off by his hands.

A long time went by after that without our seeing Kung again. At the end of the year, when the tavern keeper took down the board, he said, "Kung I-chi still owes nineteen cash!" At the Dragon Boat Festival the next year, he said the same thing again. But when the Mid-Autumn Festival came, he did not mention it. And another New Year came round without our seeing any more of him.

Nor have I ever seen him since—probably Kung I-chi is really dead.

(YANG AND YANG)

Black Li and White Li

by Lao She (1899–1966)

Love is not the central theme in this story of the two brothers, but it forms a convenient point of departure.

Black Li was the elder brother, White Li the younger, with a difference of five years between them. Both of them had been my schoolmates, though Black Li and I graduated shortly after White Li entered the middle school. Black Li was a good friend of mine and as I was a frequent visitor at his house, I came to know a little about White Li. However, five years make a wide gulf between you when you are young. The brothers were as unlike as their nicknames—Black and White—for Black Li was the epitome of old China just as White Li was of the new. But the two did not quarrel on this account; they just saw things in a different light. Black Li was not really black. He was called Black Li only because he had a mole above his left eyebrow and the young brother was called White Li because he didn't have any mark. Nothing could be more logical to the middle school students who gave them the nicknames. Actually both of them had very light complexions and they looked much alike.

Both of them were pursuing the same girl—pardon me for not revealing her name. She wasn't sure which one she loved and would not say that she loved neither of them. We all expected trouble between the brothers on account of her, for though they were not inclined to quarrel ordinarily, love is a thing that does not recognize friendship or fraternity.

However, Black Li surprised everyone by withdrawing from the contest.

I remember it well. It was an evening in early summer with a light rain falling. I went to see him and found him alone in the room with four fine porcelain teacups decorated with red fish before him. As we never stood on ceremony with each other, I sat down with a cigarette while he went on studying the cups. He turned first this one and then that and went on doing that until he had all the fish exactly facing him. After he had arranged them to his satisfaction he leaned back and looked at them like a painter withdrawing from his canvas in order to get a better perspective of his work. Then he rearranged the cups so that the fish on the other side faced him and again leaned back to look at them. He turned and smiled at me with satisfaction.

He loved these hobbies of his. He was not expert in any of them but liked to play at them all. He never pretended to be a connoisseur; he took them up only as a form of relaxation. He was a very gentle soul and easily pleased. He could while away pleasantly an entire afternoon mending his books.

He turned to me and said with another smile: "I have given her up in favor of Four." White Li was Ssu-yeh, the fourth in his generation when you figure in all his first cousins. "I can't let a girl come between brothers."

"That's why you're not a man of this age," I said jokingly.

"It's not that, but you can't teach an old circus bear new tricks. I can't go in for these triangular affairs. I have told her; I said that I was not going to see her any more whomever she may love. I feel much better for having told her."

"I have never seen anyone in love behave like this."

"You may never have seen anything like it but it has troubled me enough as it is. She can do what she likes. The only thing I am interested in is that nothing should come between Four and myself. Should you and I find ourselves in a similar situation I hope either you would retreat or I withdraw."

"And then peace would reign?"

We both laughed.

Perhaps ten days later Black Li again came to see me. I had learned to read him. Whenever his brows were darkened, it meant that he had something on his mind, and whenever he had something on his mind we always drank a pot of Lotus White together. I got the wine ready, for his brows did not exactly radiate joy that day.

His hand trembled a little as we drank our second cup. He never could keep anything in his heart; he showed everything on his face in spite of his efforts to hide it. He was a most candid man.

"I have just come from her," he said with a wry smile.

I did not prompt him for we were accustomed to each other's long silences and communicated more through them than the actual words themselves. That was one of the reasons why White Li called us hopeless when he saw us drinking together without saying anything.

"Four and I had quite a little row," he went on after a while, "because of her. It was my fault, because I know too little about a woman's psychology. Didn't I tell you that I had given her up in favor of Four? I did that in all sincerity and good faith, but she took it as a deliberate insult. You were right: I am not of this age. I thought that one can do what one thinks is right in this business of love between man and woman as in all other human relationships, but it appears that women like to be pursued by as many men as possible. So she felt insulted and decided to take revenge on me by refusing to see Four. Naturally Four blamed me for it. I had to go to her today and apologize. I had hoped that she would feel better after giving me a scolding and be friends with Four again, but she did not scold me. She only wanted both of us to continue to be her friends. I don't want to do such a thing, though I did not say that to her. That's why I have come to you. If I don't do what she wants, she will refuse to see Four and Four will blame me for it."

"And there is nothing you can do about it," I said it for him. After a while I said, "Should I see Four and explain the situation to him?"

"Yes, you might do that." He contemplated his wine cup for a moment. "It probably won't do any good. But I have made up my mind not to have anything more to do with her. I'll just say nothing when Four kicks up a row with me."

Our conversation drifted to other matters. He told me that he had taken up the study of religion. I knew, however, that it was just another hobby with him and it was not going to make any great difference in his life.

White Li came shortly after Black Li left. White Li had not yet graduated from college but you could easily see that he was a man of more experience and resolve than his elder brother. The minute you saw him, you knew that he was a born leader, a man who was always trying to bring you to his point of view and always ready to send you to the guillotine if need be. He was direct and forthright, quite unlike his brother.

On my part I always tried to avoid politeness and circumspection so as not to incur his contempt.

"I suppose Two has been here?" he asked. Black Li was Erh-yeh, the second of his generation. "And I suppose he must have told you all about it?" I waited for him to go on; the two "supposes" made any answer unnecessary. It was as I thought. He went on: "Did you know that with me it was only a pretext?"

That I did not know.

"Did you think that I really cared about that girl?" He laughed. The way he laughed was like his brother except that there was an undertone of contemptuousness which I never detected in Black Li. "I've been seeing her only to provoke Two; otherwise I would not have wasted my time. Since animal desire is at the bottom of relationship between men and women, why should I insist on her? Two, however, seems to think there is something sacred about it and insists on kowtowing before her. Now after he only got his nose smeared with dirt for all the kowtowing he did, he wants me to do the same thing. I am sorry, but I don't care for that sort of thing." He burst out into a loud guffaw.

I did not laugh and I did not break in, but only watched him and wondered how it was possible for two persons to be so much alike and yet so unlike.

"No, I don't kowtow, but I would kiss her whenever I had the opportunity. She likes it too, it is much more satisfying than being kowtowed at. However, this is not what I have come to see you about. What I want to know is this: do you think that I ought to live with Two always?"

I did not know what to say.

He laughed again, probably calling me a stupid fool in his mind. "I have my own future and my own plans and he has his. Don't you think that the best thing to do is for us to go our separate ways?"

"Yes, but what plans do you have?" I finally hit upon this after an awkward silence.

"I can't tell you that now. I want to divide up our inheritance first. You'll find out what my plans are in time."

"You have quarreled with Two only because you wanted to divide up the inheritance?"

He nodded and smiled but said nothing, as if he knew that I had another question. I did have another question: "Then why don't you speak to him openly instead of kicking up a row over nothing?"

"Because he would not understand. You two can talk with each other but I find it impossible to talk to him. The minute

I mention dividing up he would probably weep and then give me the usual line about what mother said on her deathbed and how she wanted us to live together in harmony always. He is bound to give me that line, as if the dead were to rule the living. Another thing: when he hears that I want to divide up, he probably will offer everything to me. I don't want to take advantage of him. He is always so solicitous about me, his didi, always trying to work on my feelings, always pretending that he knows better about me than I do myself, but in reality he is way behind the times. I belong to this age, and can take care of myself. He doesn't have to worry about me." His face had suddenly become serious as he spoke.

As I watched the change that had come over his face I began to see White Li in a different light. I began to realize that this was not a case of the arrogance of youth but one of deep conviction born of a genuine desire to lead his own life. I began to see too why he had adopted his method of attack, for if he had tried to discuss the matter rationally with Black Li, there was, as he said, bound to be long and fruitless homilies on fraternal love. There was something to be said for making as clean a break as possible instead of dragging on in a relationship that only hindered his free development.

"Do you want me to talk to Two?"

"That's exactly it. I don't want any more rows." He laughed again. "I don't want to make it any more unbearable for Two than I have to. We are brothers, after all." The word "brothers" seemed distasteful to him.

I promised him that I would do what he wished.

"Try to make it as strong as you can. We can't be brothers for the next twenty years." He stopped and essayed a smile. "I have been thinking about Two. The best thing for him is to get married. It will make it easier for him to forget his didi after he gets a nice fat baby. After twenty years I shall be behind the times too and shall be ready, if I am still alive then, to come home and be an uncle. But tell him that to be successful in love he must kiss more and kowtow less, he must chase after her instead of kneeling there and waiting."

So for a while I went to see Black Li every day. We drank Lotus White and talked but never got anywhere. This went on for at least half a month. He saw my point of view and was willing for Four to cultivate self-reliance and independence, but he invariably ended with the sentence: "I can't bear to give up Four."

"Plans? What kind of plans?" He paced back and forth and asked that again and again, his mole almost lost in the furrows of his brow. "What could they be? You ask him. I'll feel better if I know."

"He won't tell what they are," I said for the fiftieth time or more.

"If he won't tell, it can only mean that they are of a dangerous character! He is the only brother I have. Let him have his rows if he must. I don't mind. He didn't use to be like this. It is probably because of that girl after all! So he wants me to get married, eh? But how can I get married when we have rows like this even before I am married? I wonder what his plans are. As to dividing up, it is entirely unnecessary, for he can have whatever he wants."

Thus he rambled on, an hour at a time. He took up more and more hobbies: he tried all kinds of fortune-telling games, but none of them helped him find out what Four's plans were; they only gave him more worries and fears. This didn't mean that he acted worried, for he was as unhurried and phlegmatic as he had always been. His outward behavior never quite caught up with his feelings; no matter how anxious he was inside, he was always outwardly calm and unconcerned as if life itself was to him nothing more than a hobby.

I suggested that by plans Four had in mind the future and not anything immediate and concrete, but he shook his head.

Things went on like this for about another month.

"Four can't have anything immediate in mind," I said in sudden fit of inspiration. "He hasn't tried to hurry me at all during all this time."

Again he shook his head.

As time went on he took up more hobbies. One Sunday morning I caught him entering a church. Thinking that he might have gone to see someone, I waited for him outside. He did not come out, however, and I gave up waiting for him. He had apparently decided to seek refuge in religion.

I found him home that afternoon. For more than a month now Four had been our sole topic of conversation, but on this occasion he deviated from that usual routine. He eyes gleamed and there was a serene smile on his face, as if he had just acquired a rare old edition of some book.

"I saw you," I spoke first.

He nodded and smiled, saying, "It is very interesting."

That was his invariable comment on every new hobby, on anything that people might tell him, including the most impossible ghost stories.

"The same philosophy is behind all religions and all systems of moral instruction," he said. "They all enjoin us to sacrifice ourselves for the sake of others."

"Haven't you sacrificed your own love?" I said, stating a matter of fact.

"That's hardly sacrifice in the real sense of the word. That was only a sort of passive relinquishment and involved no actual sacrifice of anything that was part of myself. I have been reading the Gospels during the past two weeks and I have decided that I ought to share some of Four's burdens instead of only trying to keep him for myself. Just think, if all he wanted was to divide up, why shouldn't he come to me and tell me about it openly?"

"He is afraid that you won't do it," I replied.

"No! that's not it. I have thought the matter over and I am sure that he had definite plans, plans that involve danger. That's why he wants to make a clean break: he is afraid to involve me. You thought it was the impetuosity of youth, didn't you? That's where you and I were wrong, and he has taken advantage of our mistake to fool us. What he has been trying to do is to safeguard me, to place me in a safe position so that he can do his work without worrying about me. It must be that! I cannot disregard him, I must make some sacrifice for him. Before mother died. . ." He did not go on as he knew that I was thoroughly familiar with that line.

I was not alarmed at the time, for I was inclined to think that he was merely indulging in noble generalities under the influence of his newly acquired religion. However, I decided to see White Li to make sure. I did not take Black Li seriously, yet I did not want to take any chances.

But White Li was nowhere to be found. I went to his school and made enquiries in the dormitories, in the library and on the tennis courts and I tried the restaurants around the school, but no one had seen him. That was typical of him. If Black Li had to go away for a few days, he would not only leave word at home but would even notify the more intimate of his friends. In my helplessness I decided to call on "her" and ask her about it.

She hadn't seen White Li either. She appeared to be still annoyed with the Li brothers, especially Black Li. However, when I asked her about White Li, she insisted on talking about Black Li. It dawned upon me that she at least preferred Black Li to White Li if she did not love him. She probably had placed a check mark against Black Li as a standard of comparison: she would scratch him off the list if a better suitor came along but might marry him eventually if she could find no better. It was only a fleeting thought, but it made me feel disinclined to promote Black Li's suit. I was too fond of him to think that any one short of an angel would be worthy of him.

I found myself in a quandary after leaving her. I couldn't tell of White Li's disappearance to Black Li. He was sure to place advertisements in the papers if he knew and to get up in the middle of the night to consult the fortune-telling manuals. Yet I felt it necessary to share the information with someone.

When I got near his window Black Li was intoning something to himself, which he never did except when he was feeling pleased and happy, but instead of such favorites of his as

> In the maiden's chamber
> A piece of pure, flawless jade. . .

I found that he was singing softly some Christian hymn. He had no ear for music and intoned the hymns as he did everything else in his customary singsong voice. But that was neither here nor there; what interested me was that he was singing to himself and that he was therefore pleased with something. What could it be?

He put the hymn book down when I entered the room.

"Good thing you came. I was just going to call on you. Four was here. He asked me for a thousand dollars and said nothing about separating, nothing at all about that!"

Obviously he did not ask his brother what he wanted the thousand dollars for; otherwise he would not have been so happy. All he wanted was that his brother should live with him, as if as long as they lived in the same house nothing else mattered, no danger could touch them.

"Prayer is a great thing," he said seriously. "I have been praying every day and my prayers have been answered already. He said nothing about separating at all. I don't care if he throws all the money away as long as I have him."

I proposed that we drink a bottle of Lotus White on that, but he shook his head, saying, "You go ahead. I'll eat something with you, for I have sworn off alcohol."

I did not drink any either and I did not tell him that I had not been able to find Four. There was no use alarming him since Four had just been to see him. I mentioned my visit to "her," however, but he did not comment.

He told me some Bible stories. As I listened to him I could not help marveling at his attitude toward his brother and her and feeling that it was very odd to say the least. I could not put my finger on just what was wrong with it, but a sense that something was amiss troubled me even after I left him and went back to my own house.

One evening four or five days later, Wang Wu came to see me. He was the ricksha man of the Lis and had been with them more than four years. He was an honest and reliable man, about thirty years old, with a scar on his head from a nip by an ass when he was a child. He had no fault except occasional indulgence in liquor.

He had been drinking that evening, and the scar on his head was red.

"What has brought you, Wang Wu?" We were on friendly terms. He always tried to take me home when I stayed late at the Li house and of course I always tipped him.

"To see how you are," he said, sitting down.

I knew, however, that he had come to tell me something. "There is freshly made tea. Have a cup."

I gave him a cigarette. "What's on your mind?"

"*Heng*, something I shouldn't tell, but I have just drunk two pots of wine and it itches to come out." He took a strong puff at his cigarette.

"If it is something that concerns the Lis, you'll make no mistake in telling me about it."

"That's what I think too," he said but hesitated a while before he went on. "I have been with the Li family for four years and thirty-five days now. I find myself in a difficult position. Erh-yeh is very good to me and Ssu-yeh, why, he is just like a friend. That makes things difficult. Ssu-yeh forbids me to tell Erh-yeh about his affairs and yet I do not feel right to keep things from him. If I tell, I wouldn't be doing right by Ssu-yeh. That's what makes things so difficult. By rights I should stand with Ssu-yeh. Erh-yeh is a good man, true, but he is after all just my employer, and an employer is an employer no matter how good he is to you. He can never be like a friend or brother. Erh-yeh is really very good to me. For example, when I go out with him on these hot days, he is always stopping for little errands. It may be to buy a package of matches or to look at bookstalls. Why? Because he wants to give me a chance to rest and catch my breath. That's what makes him a good master. And because he is good to me, I respect him and am grateful to him. This is what people call to exchange good with good. I understand such things; I have been around."

I offered him another cup of tea, to show him that I appreciated his point of view. After he drank the tea, he pointed to his breast with his cigarette and said:

"Here, but I love Ssu-yeh here. Why? because Ssu-yeh does not look upon me as a ricksha man. Their attitudes—the way they feel here—are different. As I have said, Erh-yeh tries to give me a chance to rest on hot days. Now Ssu-yeh doesn't think about such things. He makes me run for all I am worth no matter how hot it is. But when we get to talking, he would say why should one man pull a ricksha and another man sit in it? You see he feels the injustice for us ricksha men, for all the ricksha men in all the world. Erh-yeh is good to me but never thinks of us ricksha men as a whole. Erh-yeh only thinks of the little things but Ssu-yeh thinks of the big things. Ssu-yeh doesn't care anything about my legs, but he cares about my heart. Erh-yeh is considerate and pities my legs, but he doesn't care anything about here." He pointed to his heart again. I knew that he had more to tell and being afraid that the tea might get the better of the stimulating effects of the wine I urged him on: "Go on, Wang Wu! Tell me everything. I can gossip just as well as any woman, don't you worry!"

He reflected for a moment, stroking his scar, and then pulled up his chair closer and said in a low voice: "You know, the streetcar line will be finished soon. We ricksha men will be driven out of business the minute the cars start running. I am not worried about this myself; I am thinking about all us ricksha men." He looked at me, and I nodded.

"Ssu-yeh understands this, else why should we be friends? Wang Wu, we must think up something, Ssu-yeh says. Ssu-yeh, there is only one thing to do, says I, and that is to wreck the streetcars! That's right, Wang Wu, says Ssu-yeh, we must wreck them. And so a plan was adopted. However, I can't tell you about it. What I want to tell you is this," he spoke even lower, "Ssu-yeh is being followed by the detectives! It may not be because of the streetcar business but it is always bad business to be followed by detectives. This is what makes things so difficult for me: I wouldn't be doing right by Ssu-yeh if I should tell Erh-yeh, and if I don't tell I might get Erh-yeh in trouble too. I don't know what to do."

Black Li had guessed right, I thought to myself after Wang Wu had left. White Li did have immediate plans that involved danger, perhaps even more radical plans than wrecking the streetcars. That's why he wanted to live separately from his brother; he did not want to drag him in. White Li was not afraid to sacrifice himself and he would not hesitate to sacrifice others if necessary, but he did not want to sacrifice his brother when there was no occasion for it.

What was I to do? To warn Black Li would only cause him to worry more about his brother. It was not only useless to try to dissuade White Li from his dangerous undertaking, but it would get Wang Wu into trouble.

The crisis came when the streetcar company announced the date for the opening of operations. I had to forget my scruples and tell Black Li.

He was not home but he had not taken the ricksha.

"Where is Erh-yeh?" I asked Wang Wu.

"He's gone out."

"Why didn't he ride?"

"He has gone out without the ricksha for several days now."

"Wang Wu, have you told him?" I could tell from his manner that he must have.

"I drank a few cups too much and couldn't help it." Wang Wu's scar was purple.

"How did he take it?"

"He almost cried."

"What did he say?"

"He asked me only one question—'What are you going to do, Wang Wu?' I said, 'Wang Wu will follow Ssu-yeh.' 'That's all,' he said. After that he went out without the ricksha."

It was after dark and I had been waiting for fully three hours when he came in.

"How goes everything?" I asked, trying to lump together all the questions I had in mind in those three words.

"All right," he said, smiling.

I did not expect him to answer me like that, but I did not ask him any more questions since he did not want to confide in me. I should have liked some wine, except it was no fun to drink alone. As I got up to go, I said: "How about going away for a few days with me?"

"Let's talk about that after a few days," he said.

I have since realized that one is often coolest in one's outward manner when one is most agitated inside, but I did not expect him to behave that way to me.

The day before the streetcar line opened I went to see him again in the evening. He wasn't home. I waited until midnight, but there was still no sign of him. He was probably trying to evade me.

Wang Wu came back and smiled at me, saying, "Tomorrow!"

"Where is Erh-yeh?"

"I don't know. After you left the other day he burned his mole away with something or other and studied himself a long time in the mirror."

That meant the end of Black Li, for he was exactly like White Li without the mole. I decided to wait for him no longer.

On the threshold Wang Wu stopped me. "If anything happens to me tomorrow," he said, stroking his scar, "I hope you'll take care of my old mother."

Around five o'clock the following day Wang Wu came running into my house, his clothes wet through with sweat. "We— we wrecked everything!" He stopped for want of breath. After recovering his breath, he seized the teapot and drank from the spout. "We wrecked everything in sight and did not disperse until the mounted troops bore down on us. I saw them grab Little Ma Liu. The trouble with us was that we had no arms; you can't do much with just bricks."

"How about Ssu-yeh?"

"I didn't see him," he reflected, biting his lips. "*Heng,* it was a serious business. Ssu-yeh is bound to be among them if further arrests are made. He is the leader, you see. But you can't tell, for Ssu-yeh is pretty smart though he is so young. Little Ma Liu is done for but maybe Ssu-yeh will get away."

"Did you see Erh-yeh?"

"He hasn't been home since he went out yesterday." He thought for a moment and said, "I have to hide here for a few days."

"That's all right."

The riot was reported in the papers the next morning. Li, ringleader of the rioters who wrecked the streetcars, had been arrested on the spot together with a student and five ricksha men.

Wang Wu recognized only the character Li in the headlines, but it was enough to confirm his worst fears. "Ssu-yeh is done for, Ssu-yeh is done for!" Tears fell on the paper as he lowered his head over it, pretending to scratch his scar.

The news was soon all over the city that Li and Little Ma Liu would be paraded through the streets prior to being shot.

The burning sun beat down on the street and made the pebbles so hot that they scorched the feet, but that did not prevent a crowd. Two men sat in an open cart with their hands tied behind their backs. They were guarded by policemen in khaki and soldiers in gray, their bayonets glinting cool in the sun. Tied to the cart and dipping and swaying with its movement were two white cloth banners with the offense of the prisoners written on them. The eyes of the man in front were closed, there were a few drops of sweat on his forehead, and his lips moved as if in prayer. As the cart rattled past close in front of me, I was overcome with grief. He did not once raise his head all the way to the execution ground.

When I went up to claim the body, his mouth was slightly open as if he had prayed to the last.

A few months later I met White Li in Shanghai. He would have passed me without recognition if I had not called to him.

"Lao Ssu!" I called.

"Oh!" he exclaimed, as if taken aback. "It's you! I thought Lao Erh had come back to life."

I suppose I might have sounded like Black Li. I didn't do it intentionally but perhaps Black Li, who still lived in my heart, spoke for me.

White Li looked older and more like his brother than ever. We didn't say much to each other, and he appeared to be disinclined to talk with me. I only remember his saying:

"Lao Erh has probably gone up to Heaven. That's the right place for him. I, however, have to go on trying to break down the gates of Hell."

(WANG CHI-CHEN)

Smile!

by Chang T'ien-yi (b. 1907)

"Look, Chiang-san, what a pretty face Fa-hsin-sao has!"

Chiang-san laughed, sticking up one thumb: "Chiu-yeh has good eyes. You do have good eyes, I say."

"How strange that a country lout should have such a wife. It's like sticking a flower in a pile of dung for Fa-hsin to have such a nice morsel of white flesh in his mouth. Our Fa-hsin-sao is. . . what do you say, Fa-hsin-sao?"

As Chiu-yeh leaned toward Fa-hsin-sao the lamplight struck one side of his red face, showing up clear and distinct his large pores. He grinned and showed a row of irregular teeth, some yellow and some black. Two of them glittered in the light, the color of old brass. Li Tao-shih used to say that they were not real gold but only covered with yellow tin foil which foreigners use to wrap up their candy in.

That was what Li Tao-shih used to say. Now no one dared to say anything disparaging about Chiu-yeh. Even Li Tao-shih changed his tune: "That ring around Chiu-yeh's finger is made of solid gold."

Then he would sigh and comment upon the evil days that had befallen. "These are trying, years of visitation. The bandits have not given us here any trouble only because of Chiu-yeh. If not for him. . . ."

"Chiu-yeh has a few tricks. Formerly he. . ."

But formerly no one thought much of him. In the meantime he had somehow come up in the world: he had quite a few henchmen and had a monopoly of the drug traffic in the district. And he commanded the local militia.

Chiu-yeh was a clever man. Otherwise why should His Honor Ming put so much trust in him? His Honor was the nominal head of the militia but actually Chiu-yeh had charge of everything.

"Leave everything to me," Chiu-yeh would say, thumping his chest. "Don't worry. I'll be responsible for anything that might happen in our district."

He wasn't boasting either. He had no difficulty in dealing with the people in the district, men or women. He had, for instance, dealt swiftly with that insolent egg Yang Fa-hsin, and he had no trouble with Fa-hsin's wife. All he had to do was to send Chiang-san to talk to her and there she was right in front of him.

He fixed his eyes on her and stuck his head closer and closer to her. His eyes were discolored with red threads, his left eye only about half the size of his right.

Fa-hsin-sao did not dare to look at his face; she only stared at the buttons on his coat.

But a hand seized her shoulder, a cold tongue cut at her chin like a chisel.

"Don't . . . don't . . ."

She twisted herself free and retreated to the door.

Chiang-san, who was in the act of conveying the wine cup to his lips, suddenly guffawed and almost dropped it.

Chiu-yeh frowned, his right eye growing larger still. In a shrill voice—"Eh . . !"

To tell the truth, he had not been thus rebuffed for a long time.

The woman said in a trembling voice: "Chiu-yeh, Chiu-yeh, I beg you. . ."

"What, are you backing out?"

"Chiu-yeh, you are. . ."

Chiang-san decided that he had done enough laughing. He took a drink, wiped his thick lips with the back of his hand and stole a glance at Chiu-yeh's face. " 'Tisn't going right, 'tisn't going right," he thought to himself.

He knew Chiu-yeh: Chiu-yeh didn't like to be crossed in anything. If Fa-hsin-sao should refuse to do what was good for her, he, Chiang-san, would be held accountable.

"Hey! Fa-hsin-sao, think it over. I tell you, you had better be nice to Chiu-yeh, so that. . ."

He belched and stole another glance at Chiu-yeh.

"Hm, Hm, Hm."

The noise through Chiu-yeh's nose sounded partly as if he was trying to clear his throat and partly like a sneer.

"It was her own idea in the first place. Do I look as if I couldn't get all the women I want? What do I care whether she. . ."

It was true that Fa-hsin-sao meant little to Chiu-yeh. He had three concubines and several "regulars" in the city brothels, besides occasional purchases. He wanted her only because she was new and because. . .

"And because I want to show Yang Fa-hsin what I, Chiu-yeh, can do to him. How dare he, a country lout, disturb the earth over my head? *Heng,* I'll show him. I'll make him suffer the consequences of the law and make a cuckold of him besides. I'll show him what it means to cross me!"

But just now Fa-hsin-sao had her sweaty hand on the door, ready to run away.

Chiu-yeh sat down, his right eye twitching. His huge shadow darkened the entire room.

The third person in the room first looked at Chiu-yeh and then at Fa-hsin-sao. He belched. Something came up, but he swallowed it down.

"Better think what you're doing, Fa-hsin-sao, think what you're doing. You mustn't. . ."

Suddenly the door opened and Fa-hsin-sao dashed out.

Chiang-san followed immediately and caught hold of her: "You can't run away, you can't run away!"

She struggled against him.

"Hey, hey, hey!" Chiang-san warned her in a low voice. "Do you want your Fa-hsin to live or don't you? Do you or don't you?"

Silence. Fa-hsin-sao stood still, panting.

"You know how Chiu-yeh is." Chiang-san spoke in her ear. He reeked of liquor and his voice made her ear ring though he tried to lower it. "Chiu-yeh has had your Fa-hsin arrested; he has his life in his hands. If you won't. . ."

"But I. . . but I. . ."

"Hey, listen to me, listen."

He looked around as if afraid of being overheard. He suddenly belched, frightening himself. He put his right hand to his mouth for a while.

"Chiu-yeh wants to have Fa-hsin punished as a bandit. Yes, as I have said, he can. . ."

Fa-hsin-sao wailed: "But how could he be a bandit!"

After a brief silence, Chiang-san spoke slowly: "Listen to me. Chiu-yeh has often told His Honor Ming that the peasants are not very law-abiding nowadays and that Fa-hsin is their ring leader. Yes, Chiu-yeh said that to His Honor. Now let me see—yes, the other day Fa-hsin actually dared to talk back to Chiu-yeh, and cursed him and threatened him with physical violence. Of course Chiu-yeh had him arrested. . . Now Fa-hsin is suffering the consequences of the law, as you know. If you will be nice to Chiu-yeh, I assure you that Chiu-yeh will have him released, I assure you. If you. . ."

Chiang-san searched her face.

A ray of light shone through a crack in the door and played on Fa-hsin-sao.

"Think it over," Chiang-san said.

Fa-hsin-sao glanced at the door.

What was Chiu-yeh doing in the room? He might be drinking quietly inside, smiling with unconcern and twitching his right eye. But then it might be that he was being very angry, and thinking up ways of torturing Fa-hsin and then charge him with banditry and have his head cut off.

Then Fa-hsin's head would be hung up on a tree the next day and His Honor Ming would give Chiu-yeh a banquet and slap him on his shoulder—

"You have done it: You have rid the district of a great menace."

Fa-hsin and His Honor Ming have been enemies for a long time.

And then her entire family—her blind and deaf old mother-in-law and her two children and herself—they would all. . .

Chiang-san knew that Fa-hsin-sao understood these things. He belched and swallowed again and urged her repeatedly: "You think it over, think it over. Let me tell you."

He waited for a sign of her yielding so that he could go to Chiu-yeh and report the success of his mission.

But the other only bit her lips and said nothing.

Suddenly there was a crashing sound in the room, making both of them jump. Four eyes stared at the door, wondering whether there might be a sequel.

Silence.

Chiang-san wiped his mouth with the back of his hand and began to talk in a confidential tone to Fa-hsin-sao. After the warning sound from the room he must finish his job as soon as possible. He wanted her to know that Chiu-yeh could be a generous man if she consented.

"Money means nothing to Chiu-yeh."

He asked her if it were not true that she needed money then and again belched as if affirming his own question.

"You are short of money, aren't you? Isn't that right, eh?"

Of course he was right; he knew how it was with Fa-hsin-sao. Her two children were waiting to be fed and were crying themselves hoarse for her; she could see her two-year-old daughter crawling on the ground, sniveling and stuffing dirt into her mouth. Then there was the old mother-in-law, mumbling no one knew what to herself all day long. Her stomach, too, had to be filled. She did not know yet that her son had been arrested and was suffering the consequences of the law.

Fa-hsin-sao needed money, too, at the militia headquarters. A little money stuffed into the proper hands would make Fa-hsin suffer less.

Chiang-san sighed and urged Fa-hsin-sao solicitously to think it over.

"Think well, think well," he imitated the doleful manner in which His Honor Ming had urged the famine refugees to leave the district a few years back, as if he were about to cry any moment. "You are most pitiable. Ai, you are. . ." He shook his head, so sorrowful that he could hardly lift his face. "However, Chiu-yeh is willing to save Fa-hsin, yes, willing to save him, I tell you. If you would consent and be real nice to him, he will give you money and save your Fa-hsin. If you won't do what he wants, then. . ."

Then Chiu-yeh would be hard and everything would be finished.

Fa-hsin-sao shuddered. She glanced around with a scared look and went back into the room.

"Chiu-yeh, Chiu-yeh, Fa-hsin is only. . . please, honored one, let him off. . ."

Chiu-yeh said triumphantly: "Ha, ha. I knew you would come back. I knew. But why such a sad face? You must put on a more pleasant one."

He glanced in the direction of the door where Chiang-san stood. The latter knew that Chiu-yeh meant to commend him for the success of his mission but pretended indifference.

The woman's face was pale, her eyes filled with tears.

"Please raise high your honored hand and let him off. It is his bad temper that made him cross you. He is. . . A peasant is. . ."

"Come, give me a kiss!"

The huge shadow on the wall raised two steam shovels as Chiu-yeh clutched her face.

She did not struggle against him. Her tears streamed down her chin, glistening in the lamplight.

"Hey, hey, hey." Chiu-yeh warned, but not as harshly as he might. "As long as you've come here, you might as well put on a nice face. Did you think that I would spend good money for a sour face? What you want is money and what I want is pleasure. Come now, smile!"

The man at the door watched them, shifting his glance whenever one or the other of the two happened to look in his direction, and scraping his feet against the ground. He did not know whether to approach them or to go away. Finally he said with a sigh: "Ai, Fa-hsin-sao, think well, think over what I told you."

Fa-hsin-sao paid no attention to him but kept her eyes on Chiu-yeh's.

"Chiu-yeh, Chiu-yeh. . ."

"None of that, none of that. Come now, smile for me, smile!"

"Chiu-yeh, you must. . ."

"No, you must smile for me first."

Chiang-san had always had Chiu-yeh's complete confidence; he was a clever man and read Chiu-yeh's thought. Now he thrust out his chest, bracing himself for the important task before him: "Smile now, Fa-hsin-sao. It costs you nothing. Please smile once, please. Think well. . ."

He swallowed and wiped his mouth, and was about to continue when he was interrupted by Chiu-yeh—"Smile! It won't do otherwise!"

After an impasse of about a minute or so, Fa-hsin-sao gritted her teeth and forced a smile, while a large tear rolled down her face.

Chiu-yeh gave her wet face a pinch: "Ah, that's better!"

Chiang-san walked quietly out of the room, his face beaming because he had done a good job of persuasion. He peeped through the door for a while and then went back to his room.

"How much money would Chiu-yeh give her," he asked himself.

In any case country goods couldn't compare with city stuff; she shouldn't cost so much.

Money, however, did not really enter into the picture. What Chiu-yeh really wanted was to humiliate Yang Fa-hsin. The very next morning, he, Chiang-san, would go to Yang Fa-hsin and tell him all about it.

"All right, cross Chiu-yeh if you think you can get away with it. . . Now let me tell you, even your wife has given herself to Chiu-yeh. . . you bandit, you. . ."

He tried to think of something more adequate but could think of none. And a bandit deserved only one fate and that was to have his head cut off. Chiang-san knew all along that Chiu-yeh had no intention of letting Yang Fa-hsin off and that Fa-hsin-sao would not be able to save her husband after being nice to Chiu-yeh.

"You can't leave such a bandit around to terrorize the district, can you?"

Chiang-san crawled up on his bed and blew out the lamp. Suddenly he saw the shadowy figure of Yang Fa-hsin before him. He was covered with red and purple bruises and his legs tottered under him because they had been crushed in the press.

"Don't come to haunt me," Chiang-san said calmly.

The fellow's soul had wandered off his body because he was about to die. But could he blame anyone else?

"A good deed has its reward and an evil one has its proper punishment. . . This is fate, I tell you. Who told you to cross Chiu-yeh? Why must you run afoul of the law?"

Chiang-san recalled how Yang Fa-hsin had refused to pay his share of the assessment for the support of the militia, declaring that he had no money. He had argued with Chiang-san and even now the latter's ribs ached from the blow that he had received.

"Hm, you just wait."

Thus he pulled the covers over his head with a clear conscience.

Somewhere outside a woman was calling for the wandering soul of her child. Her voice was hardly human and made your hair stand on end.

A dog howled as if some disaster was imminent.

What strange days these were: the district was far from being peaceful in spite of the fact that such a clever man as Chiu-yeh was in control. His Honor Ming was always in terror of what might happen.

It was not even very peaceful in the house where he was sleeping. Twice during the night he was awakened by the shrieks and threats that came from Chiu-yeh's room. . .

When Chiang-san got up, Chiu-yeh was just ready to send

Fa-hsin-sao away. Chiu-yeh picked out a silver dollar from his pouch and held it in his hand.

"Give me a smile, Fa-hsin-sao. You must give me a smile before I give you this. Ah, that's right!"

He threw the dollar on the table with a significant glance at Chiang-san.

Fa-hsin-sao seized the dollar with a trembling hand.

"Now thank Chiu-yeh for the money," Chiang-san prompted.

But instead Fa-hsin-sao burst into crying, her whole body shook.

"Now, now," Chiu-yeh's lips were pressed together and his right eyelid twitched. "I don't like to see people cry. You mustn't cry here."

The woman turned and started to go, but Chiu-yeh caught her by the shoulder: "Come, let me. . ."

She ground her teeth and tried to struggle free.

Chiu-yeh jumped up. "That won't do! Remember I have spent a dollar on you! You must understand that you can't cross Chiu-yeh!"

He dragged her to him and pinched her on the thigh.

Fa-hsin-sao shuddered and shrieked. She did not scream a second time, but only shuddered when he pinched her again. Finally he gave her two pinches on her face, leaving two red marks.

"Go away." He gave her a push that sent her stumbling out of the room.

The two men in the room roared with laughter.

"So Chiu-yeh spent one milled-edge. . ."

"It was that dollar which Yu Pa had." Chiu-yeh could not help laughing again as he buttoned himself up, showing his discolored and irregular teeth and twitching violently his right eye. "She'll come back for another one."

Chiu-yeh was right. Fa-hsin-sao went to the tea house that afternoon to look for Chiu-yeh and asked him to give her another dollar.

"Please, honored one, give me another dollar for this one. This is. . ."

Her face was as pale as ash and swollen purple where she had been pinched.

Chiu-yeh first stared at her, then glanced at the faces in the tea house, and finally returned to the original object of his attention, and said in a loud voice: "Why?"

"This dollar is brass. I have shown it to. . ."

"How come that I'd give you a counterfeit dollar?"

Chiu-yeh again glanced all around him.

Fa-hsin-sao swayed. She gritted her teeth and put her hand on the table to steady herself.

"The dollar you gave me this morning. . ."

Chiu-yeh rolled his eyes and smiled.

"How does it happen that I, Chiu-yeh, should have given you a dollar? What kind of debt have I contracted? Tell me in front of every one here and I'll immediately give you another dollar in exchange."

Every one laughed.

"Now, tell us, why should Chiu-yeh give you a dollar all of a sudden?"

"A love debt, a love debt! Chiu-yeh must owe her. . ."

"Ah, there must be some reason for it. Ah, Chiu-yeh. . . ha, ha, ha!"

"So Chiu-yeh has a weakness for country stuff! oh. . ."

"Like husband, like wife," said an old man, looking at the gathering and repeating himself seven times to make sure that he was heard above the noise.

"Her man is that Yang something or other."

"Yang Fa-hsin."

"So? Nowadays even peasants are becoming difficult. He is. . ."

Chiu-yeh interrupted: "He took part in robbing the Wang family."

"What a team, what a team, with the man a bandit and the woman a prostitute."

The sound of voices and laughter became like one; the tea house was never so merry before.

"Tell me, Chiu-yeh: how much does she charge for a night?"

"Hey there! Are you trying to cut in on Chiu-yeh?"

Another thundering burst of laughter.

"I wonder if Yang Fa-hsin would try to cross Chiu-yeh now; even his woman has. . ."

Chiu-yeh took a sip of tea and then raised his hand to command attention: "What is this little widow to do after I am done with Yang Fa-hsin? Such a pretty face. . ."

"Let her come to Chiu-yeh, let her come to Chiu-yeh, that's what I say."

"If she wants to come to me. . ."

Suddenly a teapot flew through the air. Chiu-yeh dodged and the pot crashed to the ground.

All eyes were turned on Fa-hsin-sao. She picked up another pot, but her arm was seized by Chiang-san.

"Hai, what's the world coming to. Even women. . ."

Fa-hsin-sao's legs grew weak and she slumped to the ground. Her face was like quick lime and her mouth foamed like a crab's.

(WANG CHI-CHEN)

"A True Chinese"

by Mao Dun (b. 1896)

Lao-yeh always had his milk with two lumps of sugar in it promptly at seven while he was still in bed; it was brought him on a Fukien lacquer tray by Taitai herself, together with his morning paper.

Taitai always sat by him on the bed while he slowly drank his milk and rather hurriedly turned the pages of his paper. He always looked at the advertisements first, then the local news and then, finally, the national and foreign news. Having finished his paper and milk, he would turn to his wife and smile at her. That done, he would stretch himself with a yawn or rub his temples with his fingers and then fall back on his pillow and close his eyes so that he might review the business that he had to attend to in the course of the day. In the meantime Ah Wo, the maid, would have glided into the room like a shadow in answer to Taitai's ring and cleared the things away, and Taitai would follow her out, closing the door gently after her.

This had been the invariable routine in the household since Lao-yeh decided to adopt a more scientific mode of life two years ago. When Lao-yeh first began "to serve society" he did not insist on this ritual. He had milk in the morning as he did now, but he did not have to have it in bed nor did he have to have his wife bring it and put in the sugar herself and sit by him while he drank it. As a matter of fact, he used to get up first and open the windows and admit the servants while Taitai lay dozing in bed.

But since Lao-yeh's enterprises had prospered and he had graduated from "serving society" to "serving the Nation," he had come to feel that he should take better care of himself for the sake of the people and had decided that he would conserve his energies by taking things in a slower tempo and insure more wholesome food by sending his wife "back to the kitchen." Taitai, however, could only go back to the kitchen in a manner of speaking, for Lao-yeh had lunch home only two or three times a year and his supper about thirty or forty times and it was only in this morning ritual we have just described that Taitai was able to fulfill her duties as a wife.

One day Lao-yeh broke the rigid routine by opening up his paper at the section devoted to national news.

Taitai must have been preoccupied with her own thoughts, for she did not notice the change that had come over Lao-yeh's face until the rustle of the paper as he threw it aside recalled her to the present.

"Eh?" she turned to him enquiringly.

Lao-yeh only grunted but she knew from his tone and the frown on his face that there was something amiss. She felt his forehead with her hand and thought that it was slightly feverish. She was about to give utterance to her concern when Lao-yeh pushed her hand aside and reached for his milk.

"Oh, it's nothing," he said in a tone of irritation after sipping his milk. "Did you put more sugar in the milk than usual?"

"No, I put the usual two lumps in," Taitai said, her eyes fixed on Lao-yeh's face. Then she laughed and said, "You must have something on your mind. The milk is all right but there is probably something wrong in the paper."

Lao-yeh was non-committal. He only smiled dryly and went back to his milk.

Taitai reached for the paper to see what had upset her lord, but Lao-yeh put one hand down on it while he gulped down the rest of his milk in one breath. Then he put down the cup and fell back on his pillow.

"Why distress yourself like this? After all it's the Government's—" But Taitai did not finish as she remembered just in time that her husband had now dedicated his services to the Nation.

"So the rumor I heard last night was true!" Lao-yeh murmured to himself. "All this nonsense about solution by peaceful means! Their mothers'—" He stopped short and glanced apologetically in the direction of his wife, for he had never indulged in this "national oath" before in the presence of such as his wife, though he resorted to it frequently in his office at the factory. Then addressing Taitai, he said: "You don't realize how important it is to maintain law and order. What is a few thousand lives if it is necessary to resort to military measures to put down these Communist bandits? But some of these people insist on peaceful compromise. Even Chien, the big banker, is for peace. It is most maddening."

"Now, now," Taitai said soothingly, for she did not want her husband to get upset so soon after breakfast. "You are right, of course, but what's the use of getting upset about it since they have decided on a peaceful solution? Moreover, our factory makes yarns. It is not as if you were a munitions dealer. Didn't you used to hope for peace during the One-Two-Eight War?"

An impatient grunt from Lao-yeh made Taitai stop. Then diffidently she lifted her hand to feel Lao-yeh's brow, but the latter brushed her hand aside.

"I have no fever," he said. "But Taitai, how can you be so blind as not to see the difference? Let me explain by analogy: we should, of course, be as peaceable as possible with our neighbors, but what can we do except to take stern measures if cook and the servants should get impudent?"

Taitai smiled and nodded her head.

"Moreover," Lao-yeh continued, using Taitai as a foil, " 'One who does not attend the future is bound to have immediate trouble.' Haven't our neighbors [the Japanese] been talking about a united campaign against the Communist bandits? To forestall them we ought to suppress the bandits quickly and ruthlessly. How can we talk of peace at a time like this? What are we going to do if they should seize the excuse to land a few divisions and send over a few hundred airplanes? Can we offer any effective resistance? Do you think we can actually wage war against them? Remember, Taitai, that when that happens not only would our factory be reduced to ashes, but we won't be able to chat in comfort and security as we are doing now!"

Taitai opened her eyes wide, completely acknowledging her mistake.

Lao-yeh did not take much comfort in Taitai's agreement with him, for she was after all only a foil to practice his devastating argument on. On the contrary, he was carried away by the force of his own arguments and became more worried and frightened than ever by the uncertain future. He buried his head deeper in the pillow and closed his eyes in weariness.

Suddenly hearing footsteps outside, Taitai tiptoed to the door and asked who it was.

"It is I," Ah Wo's voice answered. "I thought the bell might have got out of order as it did not ring."

The interruption recalled Taitai to the morning routine.

"It is working all right," she said, subconsciously pressing on the button.

Taitai followed Ah Wo as the latter carried out the tray, and pulled the door shut gently behind her. She forgot the paper, however, and left it on Lao-yeh's bed.

At eight-thirty the children went to school in Lao-yeh's automobile; at nine the car returned and took Lao-yeh to his office, leaving Taitai to guard the house with her youngest daughter.

At four in the afternoon Taitai telephoned Lao-yeh to ask whether to send their own car to get the children back from school or to send a servant for them in a taxi. This was Lao-yeh's rule, to guard against kidnapping.

Taitai was busiest around five, having to supervise the preparation of tea for the children, hear them tell of their activities at school (which she later relayed to Lao-yeh in the evening), and telephone around for Lao-yeh to find out whether he would be home for supper. Otherwise, however, Taitai had little to do the rest of the long day except to gossip with her friends over the telephone.

On this particular day Taitai had an early lunch, having decided to spend the afternoon with her youngest daughter in one of the department stores. Just as she was about ready to leave the house, Lao-yeh returned unexpectedly. He was sitting on the sofa in the living room with a cigar in his hand when Taitai went down. Remembering his bad humor that morning, she made a motion to feel his forehead.

But Lao-yeh intercepted her hand and thrust it aside none too gently, saying: "There is nothing the matter with me and I need none of your feminine doctoring. I was having lunch with some friends at Meijui's when I began to feel a little indisposed. But it's nothing. I'll be all right in a few minutes."

"Should I send for Dr. Huang?" Taitai said hesitatingly, sitting down on a low stool near the sofa.

"It isn't necessary," Lao-yeh said, shaking his head. He closed his eyes for a moment and then said with a grunt, "I can't understand it, Taitai. Even Mr. Lu is for peace. I was all alone at lunch, one mouth against four."

The beginnings of a frown appeared around Taitai's artificially elongated eyebrows, but she replaced it with a smile when Lao-yeh threatened to open his eyes.

"That's not all," Lao-yeh went on. "They told me that the *North China Daily News* had an editorial endorsing the Government's policy. Can you imagine a respectable British paper taking such a view of things?"

The youngest daughter now edged up to Taitai and looked at her, obviously asking her whether she was going to take her to the store. Taitai hesitated and then said to the maid: "Ah Wo, you take the young mistress to the store. Let her get a few playthings but don't let her buy anything to eat."

"Oh, were you thinking of going to the store?" Lao-yeh asked, noticing for the first time that they were dressed to go out. "Please go as you planned. I want to spend the afternoon in writing a letter to the *Daily News*."

"What do you want to write them for? You should not worry yourself since you are not feeling well."

"I'll feel better after I get it off my chest," Lao-yeh said. "So please go as you planned."

Taitai stared at Lao-yeh in surprise, for he had always had a contempt for people who wrote letters to editors. Then it occurred to her that the editor might not publish the letter at all or might publish it with some ironical comment, neither of which was a pleasant thing to contemplate. One could never tell what one of these foreign papers might do. She decided that it was her duty to advise her husband against such a rash step.

"It is best not to bother," she said. "You are a man with a responsible position. It is not worth your while to get mixed up with these writing fellows."

"Never mind!" Lao-yeh said with some impatience. "You go on to the store." Then a little more gently, "Don't worry, Taitai; I am not going to sign my own name."

"What name are you going to use then?"

"I am going to sign myself 'A True Chinese,'" Lao-yeh said, standing up. "But don't you worry. Go on to the store now and remember to bring me back two boxes of cigars."

(WANG CHI-CHEN)

§ MODERN POETRY

—SNOW—

(to the melody *Shen Yuan Chun*)

by Mao Tse-tung (b. 1893)

This is the scene in that northern land:
A hundred leagues are sealed with ice,
A thousand leagues of whirling snow.
On either side of the Great Wall
One vastness is all you see.
From end to end of the great river
The rushing torrent is frozen and lost.
The mountains dance like silver snakes,
The highlands roll like waxen elephants,
As if they sought to vie with heaven in their height;
    And on a sunny day
You will see a red dress thrown over the white,
    Enchantingly lovely!

Such great beauty like this in all our landscape
Has caused unnumbered heroes to bow in homage.
But alas these heroes!—Chin Shih Huang and Han Wu Ti
Were rather lacking in culture;
Rather lacking in literary talent
Were the emperors Tang Tai Tsung and Sung Tai Tsu;
    And Genghis Khan,
Beloved Son of Heaven for a day,
Only knew how to bend his bow at the golden eagle.
    Now they are all past and gone:
To find men truly great and noble-hearted
    We must look here in the present.

(ANDREW BOYD)

—KUNLUN—

(to the melody *Nien Nu Chiao*)

by Mao Tse-tung

Rising straight in the air above this earth,
Great Kunlun, you have witnessed all that was fairest
    in the world of men.
Your three million white jade dragons in their flight
Freeze the sky with penetrating cold;
In summer days your melting torrents
Fill the streams and rivers over the brim,
Changing men into fish and turtles.
What man can pass judgment
On all the good and evil you have done these thousand
    autumns?

But now today I say to you, Kunlun,
You don't need this height, don't need all this snow!
If I could lean on the sky, I would draw my sword
And with it cut you into three pieces.
One I would send to Europe,
One to America,
One we would keep in China here,
So should a great peace reign in the world,
For all the world would share in your warmth and cold.

Author's note: An ancient poet said: "When the three million white jade dragons are fighting, their tattered scales flying fill the air." Thus he described the flying snow. Here I have borrowed the image to describe the snow mountain. In summer, when you climb Minshan, you look out on to a crowd of mountains, sweeping away as if in a dance, and all white. Among the common people there was a saying that years ago, when Monkey King passed by here, these were all

mountains of flaming fire; but Monkey borrowed the palm-leaf fan
and put out the flames, and that was how they froze and turned white.

(BOYD)

—LOUSHAN PASS—

(to the melody *Yi Chin O*)

by Mao Tse-tung

Cold is the west wind;
Far in the frosty air the wild geese call in the morning
        moonlight.
                In the morning moonlight
The clatter of horses' hooves rings sharp,
And the bugle's note is muted.

Do not say that the strong pass is guarded with iron.
This very day in one step we shall pass its summit,
        We shall pass its summit!
There the hills are blue like the sea,
And the dying sun like blood.

(BOYD)

—ON A RIVER 'N LATE AUTUMN—

by Liu Ta-pai (1880–1932)

A homing bird,
Though tired,
Still carries a load of setting sun.

A flip of the wings
Spills the sunset on the river;
The hoary-haired reeds
For a moment appear in a coat of rouge.

(HSÜ KAI-YU)

—THERE IS A GRAVE—

by Chu Hsiang (1904–1933)

There is a grave,
In front of it grow wild thickets,
There is a grave,
The grass under the wind crawls like a snake.

There is a dot of firefly,
Encircled by darkness,
There is a dot of firefly,
Blinking its bean-size glow.

There is a strange bird
Hidden in the shade of a gigantic tree,
There is a strange bird
Mourning in a voice unheard in this world.

There is a hook of pale moon,
Peeping from behind dark clouds,
There is a hook of pale moon,
Suddenly sinking beyond the hill.

(HSÜ KAI-YU)

—THE PAWNSHOP—

by Chu Hsiang

Beauty runs a pawnshop,
Accepting only the hearts of men.
When the time comes for them to redeem their
    belongings,
She has already closed the door.

(HSÜ KAI-YU)

—SOFT VOICE—

by Fang Wei-tah (d. 1935)

I count the stars in the sky,
And I ask: "Which one is it,
That now shines over her home?"
The stars are silent,
Tonight
Dewdrops fall on my cheeks.

I cross a river,
And I ask: "What time was it
When you passed by her home?"
The water gives me no answer,
Tonight
Silence falls on my heart.

(HSÜ KAI-YU)

—A THOUGHT—

by Li Chin-fa (b. ca. 1900)

Like fallen leaves
Splashing blood
On our feet,

Life is but
A smile on the lips
Of death.

Under a half-dead moon,
You drink and sing,
The sound splitting your throat
Disappears in the northern wind.
Ah!
Go and caress your beloved.

Open your doors and windows,
Make her timid, and
Let the dust of the road cover

Her lovely eyes.
Is this the timidity
And anger
Of life?
Like fallen leaves
Splashing blood
On our feet.

Life is but
A smile on the lips
Of death.

(HSÜ KAI-YU)

—THE ALLEY IN THE RAIN—

by *Tai Wang-shu* (1905–1950?)

Carrying an oilpaper umbrella, I alone
Paced the long, long
Lonely alley in the rain,
Hoping to encounter
The lady who carried her melancholy
Like a clove flower.

She had
The color of clove blossoms
And the fragrance of clove blossoms
And the melancholy of clove blossoms
She carried her sorrow in the rain,
And in the rain she sauntered.

She seemed to be, in this rainy alley,
Carrying an oilpaper umbrella
Like me,
And like me she silently
Paced, her steps moving slowly
In loneliness and quiet sorrow.

Silently she came close;
She walked close to me and cast
A glance, like a sigh,
She drifted away—
A dream,
Such a soft and blurred dream.

Like a spray of clove flowers
Drifting by in a dream,

The lady passed by me,
Receding into the distance,
To the toppled hedges and walls,
To the end of the alley under rain.

Her colors
And her fragrance
Vanished in the sorrowful tune of the rain,
And vanished also
Her sighing glance,
And her clove-like melancholy.

Carrying an oilpaper umbrella, I alone
Paced the long, long
Lonely alley in the rain,
Hoping to see drifting by
A lady who carried her melancholy
Like a clove flower.

(HSÜ KAI-YU)

—I GO OUT OF THE CAFE—

by *Wang Tu-ch'ing* (1898–1940)

I go out of the cafe,
from the wine, my legs
are more than
fatigued,
I don't know
which way to walk to find my
furnished room. . . .
O, the chilly streets
the yellow light, the fine rain!

I go out of the cafe,
I am drunk,
speechlessly, I walk
by myself,
and in my heart
I feel a grief that soon I shall lose
my country's beautiful people. . . .
O, the chilly streets
the yellow light, the fine rain!

(MCNAUGHTON)

—SPRING MORNING—

by Chien Hsien-ai

Beyond silk windows,
the settled calm
of morning warms the air.

Lit clouds break
like gold waves,
the wind brings singing voices,

Even the forest-birds
have waked up,
                    startled
by the growing light in their dark dreams.

The singing sounds—fading,
   fading—come
from the court of falling locustflowers.

Bright layers of mist
wrap round
half-broken walls and stiles;

On the trellises,
wistaria flutters
like so many purple butterflies.

The shadow of the moon-
boat's sail
grows paler in the Western sky,

And, lifted at the narrow
lane's end,
I hear the peddler's strident cries.

(MCNAUGHTON AND MAYHEW)

—COME—

by Shao Hsun-mei (b. ca. 1903)

and so
I left you
like this

and so
I left you
like this,
weeping

you are
a dark leaf
with dew

I am
like the earth
flowers are
shaken
down on

the love
under us
that lasts
and lasts

seems like
streaky clouds
hanging
instants
on sky
and sea

oh, come
love, please come
love, come
quick, like
finest rain
like tears
come fly
to me

(McNAUGHTON)

—NINE LINES—

by Chou Meng-tieh (b. 1920)

The shadow
below you's
a bow. You

use self to
pull back self

and pull back
slow, pull slow.

Every day
the sun shakes
and drops from
the East. Kernel

by kernel,
a red-gold
autumn thing
takes shape in

your hands which
the wind dries.

Why don't you
come out with
thousands of
hands, thousands
of eyes? All

at once, there's
autumns and
autumns for
you, and self

on self, that
waits for the
shock, the drop.

(McNAUGHTON)

—IN GREEN GARB—

by Hu P'in-ch'ing (b. 1920)

All hail! Your servant bows low,
Majestic, imperious, untemptable messenger!

I shall sing to you praises
Shall sing to you curses
Shall sing to you paeans

And yet you come
indifferent, in the morning light
leaping the ribbon-like freeways, you come
leaping the hole-covered alleys, you come
carrying the awful soul's burden, you come,
Self-unconscious Ah-ti-las.

Strike the strident gate-bell's scale!
For the elegant wait for you
and the indolent wait for you
and the insolent wait for you

and the embittered wait for you
and the impetuous wait for you
and the impotent wait for you

You may be a messenger of Light
and bring delight and desire

May be a messenger of Dark
and bring disgust and despair

May be a messenger of Nothing
and wipe out one or another man's name

And yet, you're always a messenger of Hope
You put on uncountable tomorrows before our eyes
And out of our hearts, put uncountable dreams.

(MCNAUGHTON)

Some Further Readings

Birch, Cyril, ed. *Chinese Communist Literature*. New York: Praeger, 1963.

Eberhard, Wolfram, ed. *Folktales of China*. Chicago: University of Chicago Press, 1965.

Hsia, C. T. *A History of Modern Chinese Fiction*. New Haven, Conn.: Yale University Press, 1961.

Hsü Kai–yu, ed. and trans. *Twentieth Century Chinese Poetry*. New York: Doubleday, 1963.

King, Evans, trans. *Rickshaw Boy*, by Lau Shaw. New York: Reynal and Hitchcock, 1945.

Jenner, W. J. F., ed. *Modern Chinese Stories*. London and New York: Oxford University Press, 1970.

Lin, Julia C. *Modern Chinese Poetry: An Introduction*. Seattle: University of Washington Press, 1972.

Mao Tse-tung. *Nineteen Poems*. Peking: Foreign Languages Press, 1958.

——. *Poems*. Translated and annotated by Wong Man. Hong Kong: Eastern Horizons Press, 1966.

——. *Ten More Poems*. Translated by Wong Man. Hong Kong: Eastern Horizons Press, 1967.

——. *The Poems of Mao Tse-tung*. Trans. by Willis Barnstone. New York: Harper & Row, 1971.

Shen Yen-ping (Mao Tun). *Midnight*. Peking: Foreign Languages Press, 1957.

Ting Yi. *A Short History of Modern Chinese Literature*. Translated by Chang Hsing-lien et al. Peking: Foreign Languages Press, 1957.

Wang Chi-chen, trans. *Contemporary Chinese Short Stories*. New York: Columbia University Press, 1944.

Yang Hsien-yi and Yang, Gladys, trans. *Selected Works of Lu Hsun*. 4 vols. Peking: Foreign Languages Press, 1956–60.

Yip Wai-lim, ed. and trans. *Modern Chinese Poetry: Twenty Poets from the Republic of China 1955–65*. Iowa City: University of Iowa Press, 1970.

Yuan Chia-hua and Payne, Robert, eds. and trans. *Contemporary Chinese Short Stories*. London and New York: N. Carrington, 1946.

INDEX

This is an index to all the translated material in *Chinese Literature: An Anthology*, listing titles, authors, and translators. Titles of works are printed in italics. Authors' names are in capitals, and translators' names are in ordinary roman type.

The page number after each title entry refers to the page on which the work begins. The page numbers after each author's name refer to the pages on which each of the author's stories, poems, or novels begins. The numbers after each translator's name refer to the inclusive pages on which material translated by him or her appears.

Chinese names are listed in the Chinese style: family name first, individual name second, with no comma dividing the two.

Alchemist and His Concubine, The, 521

All Men Are Brothers; see *A Saga of the Marshes*

Alley in the Rain, The, 819

Alley, Rewi, 326–28, 348

Analects, The, 91

(Another Poem), 337

At Night, a Neglected Wife Still Follows the Boat, 254

At Night, in Rain, I Write North, 356

At Night, on Shou-chiang Wall, I Hear the Flute, 353

At Night, the Crow Calls, 453

At the Turning River, Drinking Wine, 329

Autumn Flute, The, 335

Autumn Night, 243

Autumn Thoughts, 237

Autumn Wind, 249
Axes Broken, 77

Ballad of the Mulberry Road, A, 198
Ballad of the War Chariots, 326
Bedtime, 247
Birch, Cyril, 224–25
Black Li and White Li, 779
Blue Flies, 76
Boat Ride, A, 328
Book of Documents, The, 17
Book of Songs, The, 47
Boyd, Andrew, 813–15
Brewitt-Taylor, C. H., 572–606
Bronze-White Horse, A, 254
Buck, Pearl, 608–51
Bullock, Michael; *see* Jerome Ch'en and Michael Bullock
Butterfly Dream, The, 472
Buzzards Fly, The, 69
By Night I Arrive at the Loh's Mouth and Go Into the Yellow River, 339

Castrato, 75
CH'ANG CHIEN, 339
CHANG HSÜ, 349
Chang-O, 357
CHANG T'IEN-YI, 795
Chang Yin-nan and Walmsley, Lewis, 312, 344
Chan-Kuo Ts'e; see Policies of War
Chariots, Rank on Rank, 65

Ch'en, Jerome, and Bullock, Michael, 215–17
Ch'en Shou-yi, 200, 450, 455–57, 465–66
CHI SHAO-YÜ, 242
CHIA I, 175
CHIA TAO, 354
CHIANG HUNG, 243, 249
CHIANG K'UEI, 464
CHIEN HSIEN-AI, 821
CHIEN-WEN EMPEROR (LIANG CHIEN-WEN-TI), 20, 254, 255, 256
CHIN CH'ANG-HSÜ, 358
CH'IN KUAN, 456
Chin P'ing Mei; see The Golden Lotus
Chiu Ko; see The Nine Songs
CHOU MENG-TIEH, 824
CHOU PANG-YEN, 457
CHU HSIANG, 816, 817
CH'U KUANG-HSI, 339
Ch'u Tz'u; see The Elegies of Ch'u
CH'Ü YUAN, *The Elegies of Ch'u*, 132
CHUANG TZU, *Chuang Tzu's Book*, 115
Chuang Tzu's Book, 115
Clepsydra Song, 446, 447, 453
Come, 822
CONFUCIUS, *The Book of Songs*, 41; *The Analects*, 88
Cool Dusk, 245
Courtyard Torches, The, 58
Crow Night-Calls, The, 237

Crump, James I., Jr., 157–60

Deer Sing, 62
Dip the Flood Water Up, 82
Doctrine of the Mean, The, 106, 108
Dream of the Red Chamber, 733
Duckweed Pond, 344
Dying Light, 242

Eastern Gate, The, 48
Eastern Lord, 140
Egerton, Clement, 675–728
Egret Dyke, 344
Elegies of Ch'u, The, 132
Exile's Letter, 318

FAN YUN, 239
Fan-Piece, 235
FANG WEI-TAH, 817
Fickle Youth, 456
Fish in Ts'ao, 78
Fish to Net, 63
Fleecy Coats, 73
Foxes' Revenge, The, 379

Golden Lotus, The, 675
Goodbye, 345
Goodbye to Hangchow, 18
Great Digest, The; see *The Great Learning*
Great Fate-Master, The, 138
Great Learning, The, 17, 107, 732
Green River, 312
Green Robe, 79

Guitar-player, The, 256

Hairpin Phoenix, 463
HAN WU TI, 234
Hart, Henry, 498–524
He's to the War, 68
Historical Records, 109
Ho Po (The River God), 134
HO SUN, 257
How Cut Haft?, 81
Hsi-Hsiang Chi; see *Romance of the West Chamber*
HSI K'ANG, 213
HSIANG TUNG-WANG, 245
HSIAO TZU-CHIEN, 247
HSIEH LING-YUN, 238
HSIEH T'IAO, 248, 249
HSIN CH'I-CHI, 458
Hsü Kai-yu, 815–20
HSÜ YAO, 244
HU P'IN-CH'ING, 825
HUANG T'ING-CHIEN, 457
Hung Lou Meng; see *Dream of the Red Chamber*
Hut in the Vale, 66

I Ask Liu, the 19th, 352
I Cross the Han, 358
I Go Out of the Café, 820
I Go Up "Ramble of Delight" Plateau, 356
I Hear that the Official, Hu-Ssu, Has Not Come Back Yet, 334
I Listen to the Ch'in on an Autumn Night, 339
I "Noodle," 348

I See Off Meng Hao-jan at Gold Crane Inn, 347
I See Off the Monk "Spiritual Clarity," 350
I See Off the Senior Official Ch'i Chou-yuan, 314
I Watch the Hunt, 313
I Weep at the River's Bank, 330
I Write of the Pavilion in the Monastery of the First Beginning, 334
Imperial Force Recaptures Honan and Hopei, The, 333
In Green Garb, 825
In Rivers and Mountains, Waiting for the Moon, I Grow Sad, 323
In the East, It Is Still Not Light, 57
In the Mirror, 20
In the Southern Garden, I Watch the Passers-by, 251
Intrigues of the Warring States, see Policies of War
Interrupted Embosoming, An, 253

Jay's Nest, 60
Jewel Stairs' Grievance, The, 346
JUAN CHI, 213
Judicial Murder of Ts'ui Ning, The, 362

Kao T'ang Fu, The, 166
KU HSIUNG, 448
KU K'UANG, 351
KUAN HAN-CH'ING, The Butter-fly Dream, 472; Romance of the West Chamber, 498
"Kuan!" Cries the Hawk, 59

Kung I-chi, 773
Kun Lun Slave, The, 289
Kunlun, 814
KUO P'U, 227
Kwock, C. H., and McHugh, Vincent, 321–22, 347, 448–49, 450–51, 454–55, 461–62

Lament of the Frontier Guard, 317
LAO SHE, 779
LAO-TZU, Tao Te Ching, 113
Late Spring, 461
Li Ch'ai, 345
LI CHIN-FA, 818
LI CH'ING-CHAO, 459, 460, 461, 462, 463
LI P'IN, 358
LI PO, 314–25, 346, 347
LI SHANG-YIN, 356, 357
LI TS'UN-HSÜ, 450
LI YEN-NIEN, 234
LI YI, 353
LI YÜ, 451, 452, 453
LIANG CHIEN-WEN-TI; see CHIEN-WEN EMPEROR
Liang-Chou Song, 350
LIANG HUANG, 337
Light Yellow Willow, The, 464
Lily Bud, 72
Ling: As Though Dreaming, 459
Little Stars, The, 50
LIU CHANG-CH'ING, 350
LIU CHUNG-YUNG, 355
LIU FANG-P'ING, 355
LIU HSIAO-YI, 246
LIU HUNG, 241

LIU TA-PAI, 815

LIU TSUNG-YUAN, 353

LIU YÜ-HSI, 352

LO KUAN-CHUNG, *A Tale of Three Kingdoms*, 572; *A Saga of the Marshes*, 607

Looking for the Recluse, I Miss Him, 354

Lord of the Clouds, 133

Lotus-Leaf Cup, 448

Loushan Pass, 815

LU HSUN, 762, 773

LU Yu, 463

LU YUN, 219

Madman's Diary, A, 762

Man With the Curly Beard, The, 294

MAO DUN, 807

Mao Mount, 67

MAO TSE-TUNG, 813, 814, 815

Mayhew, Lenore, 18, 20–21, 452–54, 459–61

Mayhew, Lenore, and Mc-Naughton, William, 200–08, 220–21, 228, 237, 345–58 passim, 821–22

McHugh, Florence, and Mc-Hugh, Isabel, 733–54

McHugh, Vincent; *see* C. H. Kwock and Vincent McHugh

McNaughton, William, 48–80 passim, 91–107 passim, 113–28, 132–42, 197–98, 199, 208, 213–15, 228–31, 234, 235–36, 237–52, 253–57, 263–75, 312–15, 323–25,

328–40, 346, 348–49, 353, 356–57, 446–48, 451–52, 458–59, 462–65, 820–21, 822–26; *see also* Mayhew and McNaughton

Meeting at Gold Valley, 249

Monkey, see *The Way West*

Moon on the Tower, 241

Mountain Spirit, see *Shan Kuei*

Moving House, 222

"MR. LEFT" (TSO SHIH), 146

Mr. Left's History, 146

'Neath East Gate Willows, 57

'Neath Thick Willow, 66

Night in the Pavilion by the River, 328

Night Mooring at Cow's Creek: I Think of the Old Man, 322

Nine Lines, 824

Nine Meshes, 78

Nine Songs, The; see *Elegies of Ch'u*

(No Title), 449, 457, 465

Nothing to Do, 49

Oil Peddler and the Queen of Flowers, The, 404

Old Poem, 235

On a River in Late Autumn, 815

On a Spring Day, the Emperor is Expected at the Spring Palace, 338

On a Summer Day, I Pass the Monastery, 312

On the Mountain: Question and Answer, 347

One Leaf Has Fallen, 450
Over the Hills, 68
Owl Fu, The, 175
Ox-Tail Flag, The, 61

PAI HSING-CHIEN, 275
Painting of a Falcon, 326
Palace Song, 351
PAN CHIEH-YÜ, 235
PAO CHAO, 216
PAO CH'ÜAN, 251
Pawnshop, The, 817
Peach-Blossom Spring, 224
Peach Blossom Valley, 349
Peach-Tree Fair, 60
Pheasant-Cock, 51
Pick a Fern, 70
Picking Ling, 243
Please, Chung, 47
Plucking the Vine Leaves, 53
Plum Time Now, 64
PO CHÜ-I, 18, 352
Poem, 228, 234, 238, 240, 246, 345
Poem by the Bridge at Ten-shin, 316
Poem of Departure, A, 344
Poems of My Heart, 213
Policies of War, 154
Pound, Ezra, 14, 47–87 passim, 89–90, 92–108 passim, 198, 223–24, 227–28, 234–35, 314–21, 344
Poverty Fu, The, 191
Prefectship Bought and Lost, A, 548
Pro Patria Mori, 141

Prowls Fox, 56

Rapids Float No Fagot Here, 52
Rat Too, A, 80
Rats, 74
Reply: Wife to Neighbor, A, 244
River-Merchant's Wife: A Letter, The, 314
River-Snow, 353
Romance of the West Chamber, 498
Ruins of Lo-yang, The, 212

Saga of the Marshes, A, 607
San Kuo Chih-yen-i; see A Tale of Three Kingdoms
Sennin by the River, The, 452
Sennin Poem, 227
Separation, 239
Shan Kuei (The Mountain Spirit), 136
SHAO HSUN-MEI, 822
SHEN YUEH, 253, 254
Shih Ching; see The Book of Songs
Shu Ching; see The Book of Documents
Shui Hu Chuan; see A Saga of the Marshes
Smile!, 795
Snow, 813
So He Won't, 48
Soft Voice, 817
Soldiers' Grief, 355
Song of Breaking the Willow Branch, 199
Song of the Beautiful Girl, 336
Song of the Beauty, 234

Song of the Langya King, 200

Spirit-Tower, The, 86

Spread, 84

Spring Day, Fine White Linen, 250

Spring Grief, 355, 358

Spring Morning, 821

Spring Parting, 245

Spring-River Twist, 256

Spring Thoughts, 321

Spring Water, 52

Spring Wind, 257

Ssu-ma Hsiang-ju, 178

Story of a Singsong Girl, 275

Story of Ying-ying, The, 263

Su Shih, 455

Su T'ing, 338

Su Tung-p'o; *see* Su Shih

Sun's in the East, 56

Sun Up; Work, 14

Sung Yü, 166

Swallows' Alley, 352

Swallows, Swallows, 54

Sweet Peartree, 77

Tai Hao, 247

T'ai 1: Lord of the East, 132

Tai Wang-shu, 819

Tale of Three Kingdoms, A, 572

T'ang Hui-hsiu, 237

T'ao Ch'ien, *Poems*, 220

T'ao Hung-ching, 228

Tao Te Ching, 113

T'ao Yuan-ming, *see* T'ao Ch'ien

Taoist Song, 213

Tedious Ways, The, 216

There Is a Grave, 816

There Is No Sorrow to Untie, 455

"They Fought in the South," 324

They Fought South of the City, 197

Think to Thine Art, 82

Thinking of Someone, 248

Thorn-Elm on Mountain, 64

Thought, A, 818

To the Tune "Catching Fish," Written in 1179 on My Transfer from Hupeh to Hunan, 458

To the Tune: "Good Girl," 457

To the Tune of Nü Kuan-tzu, 448

To the Tune of Tsui Kung-tzu, 454

To the Tune of Wang Chiang-nan, 451

To the Tune of Yi Hsin Tzu, 450

Too Young, 348

Traveler, The, 255

Tribulus Grows on the Wall, The, 79

True Chinese, A, 807

Ts'ao Chih, 212

Ts'ao Hsueh-chin, *Dream of the Red Chamber*, 733

Ts'ao P'i, 238

Tso Chuan; see *Mr. Left's History*

Tso Shih; *see* "Mr. Left"

Tu Fu, 326–36, 348

Tu Kuang-ting, 294

Tune: "Meeting's Pleasure," 451

Tune: Sound on Sound, 462

Tung-Yang Valley, 238

Tzu Yeh, 200

Tzu Yeh Songs, 200–06

Unmoving Cloud, The, 223
Unwobbling Pivot. The; see The
    Doctrine of the Mean
Upper Grove Fu, The, 178

Vain Things, 241
Valley Wind, The, 219

Waley, Arthur, 166–72, 191–
    95, 212–13, 219–20, 221–
    23, 654–72
Walk in the Garden, A, 247
Walmsley, Lewis; see Chang
    Yin-nan
Wang Chi-chen, 362–78, 404–
    43, 779–812
WANG HAN, 350
WANG HUAN, 240
WANG SHIH-CHENG, The Golden
    Lotus, 675
WANG SHIH-FU, Romance of the
    West Chamber, 498
WANG SHU-YING'S WIFE, 245
WANG T'AI-HSIANG, 241
WANG TU-CH'ING, 820
WANG WEI, 312–14, 344, 345
WANG YI-SUN, 465
WANG YUAN-CHANG, 243

Washing Creek Sand, 460
Watson, Burton, 146–57, 172–
    91
Way West, The, 654
We Set Out Early from Po Ti, 346
WEI CHUANG, 448, 449
WEN T'ING-YUN, 446, 447
West Chamber, The; see Romance
    of the West Chamber
Western Twists (Ch'ü), 206
White Monkey, The, 301
Wicker Is Broke, The, 74
Wind Fu, The, 172
With the Recluse Chia at the
    Lung-Hsing Monastery, 323
WU CH'ENG-EN, The Way West,
    654
WU CHÜN, 228
Wu, John C. H., 449

Yaller Bird, 55
Yang Hsien-yi and Yang, Gladys,
    275–306, 379–404, 472–98,
    526–65, 762–79
YANG HSIUNG, 191
Yellow Wings, 83
YUAN CHEN, 263